John Goodison

1861.

OBJECT TEACHING

AND

ORAL LESSONS ON SOCIAL SCIENCE

AND

COMMON THINGS,

WITH VARIOUS ILLUSTRATIONS OF THE

PRINCIPLES AND PRACTICE OF PRIMARY EDUCATION,

AS ADOPTED IN THE

Model and Training Schools of Great Britain.

REPUBLISHED FROM
BARNARD'S AMERICAN JOURNAL OF EDUCATION.

PARTS I., II., III., IV.

NEW YORK:
PUBLISHED BY F. C. BROWNELL,
25 HOWARD STREET.
CHICAGO: GEORGE SHERWOOD
1860.

THE following PAPERS, originally prepared for publication in Barnard's "*American Journal of Education,*" are collected in the present form as a valuable contribution to the history of Elementary Education in England, Scotland and Ireland, and especially of the more advanced views and methods of instruction in the Primary and Popular Schools of Great Britain.

CONTENTS.

PART I.

OBJECT LESSONS AND ORAL INSTRUCTION

PAPERS I.—VII.

I. SCHOOL-HOUSES AND THEIR EQUIPMENT

IN GREAT BRITAIN.

[THE following suggestions and plans for the construction and equipment of school-rooms, and the location and adornment of play-grounds, particularly for Infant and Primary Schools, are selected as an appropriate introduction to the Papers which follow on the Principles and Practice of Early Education in the Model and Training Schools of Great Britain.]

Any scheme of school organization will be imperfect which does not include special arrangements for the systematic training and instruction of very young children, especially in all cities, manufacturing villages, and large neighborhoods. Among the population of such places, many parents are sure to be found, who, for want of intelligence or leisure, of constancy and patience, are unfitted to watch the first blossoming of the souls of their children, and to train them to good physical habits, virtuous impulses, and quick and accurate observations ; to cleanliness, obedience, openness, mutual kindliness, piety, and all the virtues which wise and far-seeing parents desire for their offspring. The general result of the home training of the children of such parents, is the neglect of all moral culture when such culture is most valuable ; and the acquisition of manners, personal habits, and language, which the best school training at a later period of life can with difficulty correct or eradicate.

No one at all acquainted with the history of education in this country, can doubt that the establishment of the Primary School for children under six years of age, in Boston, in 1818, as a distinct grade of schools, with the modifications which it has since received there, and elsewhere, from the principles and methods of the Infant School system, has led to most important improvements in the quality and quantity of instruction in our public schools, and the sooner a Primary School properly organized, furnished and managed, can be established in every large neighborhood, and especially in the "infected districts" of cities and manufacturing villages, the more rapid and more thorough will be the progress of education. Its doors should stand wide open to receive such children as are abandoned by orphanage, or, worse than orphanage, by parental neglect and example, to idle, vicious, and pilfering habits, before the corruptions incident to their situation have struck deep into their moral nature, and before they have fallen under the alluring and training influences and instruction of bad boys who infest such regions, polluting the atmosphere by their profane and vulgar speech, and participating in every street brawl and low-bred riot. From all such influences, the earlier the children of the poor and the ignorant are withdrawn, and placed under the care and instruction of an Infant or Primary School, the better it will be for them and for society. But in every locality the Primary School should be established, and brought as near as possible to the homes of the children, in order to secure their early and regular attendance, and to relieve the anxiety of parents for their safety on their way to and from school. The peculiarities of play-ground, school-room, and teachers required for this class of schools, should be carefully studied, and promptly and liberally provided. The school-room should be light, cheerful, and large enough for the evolutions of large classes,—furnished with appropriate seats, furniture, apparatus, and means of visible illustration, and having a retired, dry, and airy play-ground, with a shelter to resort to in inclement weather, and with flower borders, shrubbery, and shade-trees, which they should be taught to love and respect. The play-ground is as essential as the school-room for a Primary School, and is indeed the uncovered school-room of physical and moral education, and the place where the manners and personal habits of children can be better trained than elsewhere. With them, the hours of play and study, of confinement and recreation, must alternate more frequently than with older pupils.

To teach these schools properly, to regulate the hours of play and study so as to give variety, vivacity, and interest to all of the exercises, without over-exciting the nervous system, or overtasking any faculty of mind or body,—to train boys and girls to mild dispositions, graceful and respectful manners, and unquestioning obedience,—to preserve and quicken a tenderness and sensibility of conscience as the instinctive monitor of the approach of wrong,—to cultivate the senses to habits of quick and accurate observation and discrimination,—to prevent the formation of artificial and sing-song tones,—to teach the use of the voice, and of simple, ready, and correct language, and to begin in this way, and by appropriate exercises in drawing, calculation, and lessons on the properties and classification of objects, the cultivation of the intellectual faculties,—to do all these things and more, require in the teacher a rare union of qualities, seldom found in one in a hundred of the male sex, and to be looked for with the greatest chance of success among females, "in whose own hearts, love, hope, and patience have first kept school," and whose laps seem always full of the blossoms of knowledge, to be showered on the heads and hearts of infancy and childhood. In the right education of early childhood, must we look for a corrective of the evils of society in our large cities and manufacturing villages, and for the beginning of a better and higher civilization than has yet blessed our world. The earlier we can establish, in every populous district, primary schools, under female teachers, whose hearts are made strong by deep religious principle,—who have faith in the power of Christian love steadily exerted to fashion anew the bad manners, and soften the harsh and self-willed perverseness of neglected children,—with patience to begin every morning, with but little, if any, perceptible advance beyond where they began the previous morning,—with prompt and kind sympathies, and ready skill in music, drawing, and oral methods, the better it will be for the cause of education, and for every other good cause.

The following plan of a Play Ground for an Infant or Primary School is copied from "*Wilderspin's Early Education.*"

Play-Ground for an Infant or Primary School

The house should stand in a dry and airy situation, large enough to allow a spacious play ground. No pains should be spared on this principal and paramount department of a proper infant school. The more extensive the ground may be, the better; but the smallest size for 200 children ought to be 100 feet in length, by at least 60 in breadth. It should be walled round, not so much to prevent the children from straying, as to exclude intruders upon them, while at play: for this purpose, a wall or close paling, not lower than six feet high, will be found sufficient. With the exception of a flower border, from four to six feet broad all round, lay the whole ground, after leveling and draining it thoroughly, with small *binding* gravel, which must be always kept in repair, and well swept of loose stones. Watch the gravel, and prevent the children making holes in it to form pools in wet weather; dress the flower border, and keep it always neat; stock it well with flowers and shrubs, and make it as gay and beautiful as possible. Train on the walls cherry and other fruit trees and currant bushes; place some ornaments and tasteful decorations in different parts of the border—as a honeysuckle bower, &c., and separate the dressed ground from the graveled area by a border of strawberry plants, which may be protected from the feet of the children by a skirting of wood on the outside, three inches high, and painted green, all round the ground. Something even approaching to elegance in the dressing and decking of the playground, will afford a lesson which may contribute to refinement and comfort for life. It will lead not only to clean and comfortable dwellings, but to a taste for decoration and beauty, which will tend mainly to expel coarseness, discomfort, dirt, and vice, from the economy of the humbler classes.

For the excellent and safe exercise afforded by the *Rotary Swing*, erect, at the distance of thirty feet from each other, two posts or masts, from sixteen to eighteen feet high above the ground; nine inches diameter at the foot, diminishing to seven and a half at top; of good well-seasoned, hard timber; charred with fire, about three feet under ground, fixed in sleepers, and bound at top with a strong iron hoop. In the middle of the top of the post is sunk perpendicularly a cylindrical hole, ten inches deep, and two inches in diameter, made strong by an iron ring two inches broad within the top, and by a piece of iron an inch thick to fill up the bottom, tightly fixed in. A strong pivot of iron, of diameter to turn easily in the socket described, but with as little lateral play as possible, is placed vertically in the hole, its upper end standing 4 inches above it. On this pivot, as an axle, and close to the top of the post, but so as to turn easily, is fixed a wheel of iron, twenty-four inches diameter, strengthened by four

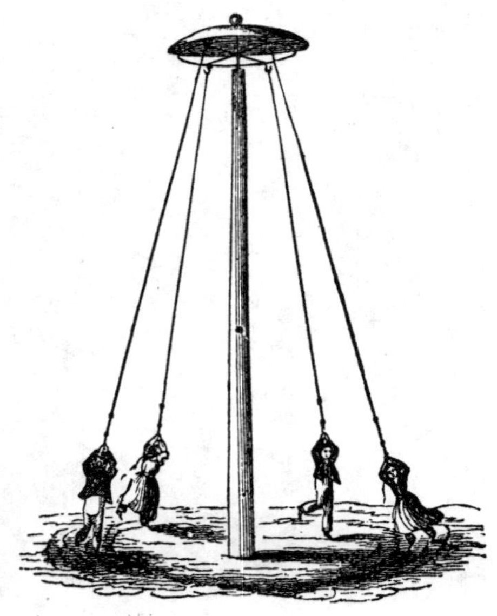

Rotary Swing.

spokes, something like a common roasting-jack wheel, but a little larger. The rim should be flat, two inches broad, and half an inch thick. In this rim are six holes or eyes, in which rivet six strong iron hooks, made *to turn in the holes*, to prevent the rope from twisting. To these hooks are fixed six well-chosen ropes, an inch diameter, and each reaching down to within two feet of the ground, having half-a-dozen knots, or small wooden balls, fixed with nails, a foot from each other, beginning at the lower extremity, and ascending to six feet from the ground. A tin cap, like a lamp cover, is placed on the top of the whole machine, fixed to the prolongation of the pivot, and a little larger than the wheel, to protect it from wet. To this, or to the wheel itself, a few waggoners' bells appended, would have a cheerful effect on the children. The operation of this swing must, from the annexed cut, be obvious. Four, or even six children, lay hold of a rope each, as high as they can reach, and, starting at the same instant, run a few steps in the circle, then suspend themselves by their hands, drop their feet and run again when fresh impulse is wanted ; again swing round, and so on. A child of three or four years old, will often fly several times round the circle without touching the ground. There is not a muscle in the body which is not thus exercised ; and to render the exercise equal to both halves of the body, it is important that, after several rounds in one direction, the party should stop, change the hands, and go round in the opposite direction. To prevent fatigue, and to equalize the exercise among the pupils, the rule should be, that each six pupils should have thirty or forty rounds, and resign the ropes to six more, who have counted the rotations.

Toys being discarded as of no use, or real pleasure, the only *plaything* of the playground consists of bricks for building, made of wood, four inches by two and one and a-half. Some hundreds of these, very equally made, should be kept in a large box in a corner of the ground, as the quieter children delight to build houses and castles with them ; the condition, however, always to be, that they shall correctly and conscientiously replace in the box the full complement or *tale* of bricks they take out ; in which rule, too, there is more than one lesson.

In a corner of the playground, concealed by shrubbery, are two water closets for the children, with six or eight seats in each ; that for the boys is separate from, and entered by, a different passage from that for the girls. Supply the closets well with water, which, from a cistern at the upper end, shall run along with a slope under all the seats, into a sewer, or a pit in the ground. See that the closets are in no way misused, or abused. The eye of the teacher and mistress should often be here, for the sake both of cleanliness and delicacy. Mr. Wilderspin recommends the closets being built adjoining the small class-room, with small apertures for the teacher's eye in the class-room wall, covered with a spring lid, and commanding the range of the place. There is nothing in which children, especially in the humbler ranks, require more training.

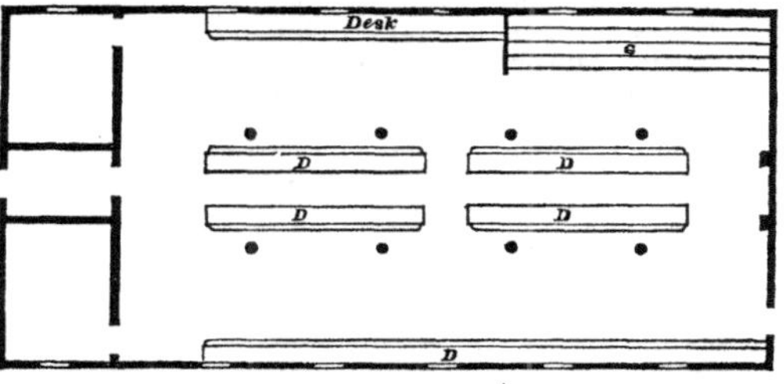

The annexed cut represents an infant school-room, modified in a few unimportant particulars, from the ground plan recommended by Mr. Wilderspin in his "*Early Education*," published in 1840. The original plan embraces a dwelling for the teacher's family, and two school-rooms, one for the boys and the other for the girls, each school having a gallery, class-room, and playground. The school-room is about 60 feet long by 38 wide, and the class-rooms each 13 ft. by 10. D. Desks and Seats. G. Gallery, capable of accommodating 100 children.

The chief requisites in an infant-school play-ground are the following: A Climbing Stand; a Horizontal Bar; Parallel Bars; Wooden Swings; a Double Inclined Plane.

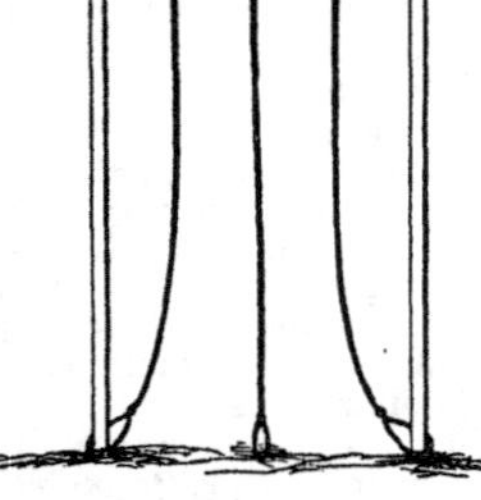

The Climbing Stand consists essentially of a frame-work of poles, which support ropes for climbing. One of the most simple and economical is made of two ordinary scaffold poles, planed smooth and painted, which support a transverse beam having hooks, to which the ropes are attached.

The dimensions may be as follows: Length of perpendicular poles, 15 feet, of which 4 feet are sunk in the ground; circumference of poles at the surface of the ground, 14 inches; length of transverse beam at top, 9 feet. To this beam are attached, by screwing in, two iron hooks, which support the ropes; these are 1½ inches in diameter, to afford a firm grasp to the hand. In order that the ropes may not wear through where attached to the hooks, they are spliced round an iron ring, which is grooved on the outer surface to give a firmer hold to the rope. Both the ropes should be attached to the bottom of the poles so as to hang loosely: if not fastened at the bottom, the children use them as swings while clinging to them, and are apt to injure themselves by falling, or others by coming violently in contact with them.

No apparatus is more advantageous: it is economical in its erection, and not liable to get out of order; it affords exercise to a number of children at the same time, a succession being constantly engaged in climbing and descending the ropes and poles; the muscular exertion is not violent, but decidedly beneficial, expanding the chest, and giving power and freedom of motion to the arms. This exercise is also quite free from danger, the children never advancing higher up the ropes than they feel themselves secure. During the seven years the Home and Colonial Infant-school has been established, 200 children have been the average attendance, but no accidents have occurred from the use of the climbing-stand.

The Horizontal Bar consists of a wooden bar formed of beech, red deal, or some other tough wood not apt to splinter or warp, about three inches in diameter, and usually six feet long, turned or planed round and smooth, in order that the hands may not be blistered by the friction.

Every play-ground should possess two or three of these useful additions; one 6 feet from the ground, another 5 feet, and a third 4 feet high,—each one being supported and fixed firmly by a post at both ends. Or they may be arranged so that four posts will support the three bars. The exercises performed on the horizontal bars consist in the child remaining suspended by the arms and hands; in drawing the body up so as to look over the bar several times in succession; in traversing from one end of the bar to the other (suspended by the hands,) both backwards and forwards; in swinging the body whilst suspended from the bar.

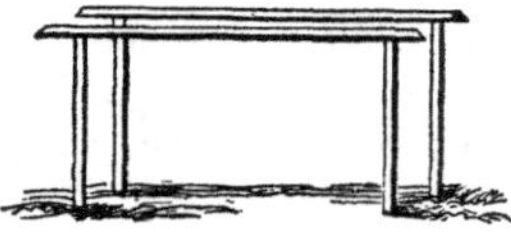

The Parallel Bar consists of two bars placed parallel with one another, each being from 6 to 8 feet long, 4 inches deep by 2 inches wide, with the corners rounded off. The posts that support these bars in their position should be 18 inches apart. The bars should project four inches beyond the post. Two sets of parallel bars are advantageous, one being 2 feet 9 inches high for the younger children, the other 4 feet high for the elder.

The exercises on these bars consist in supporting the body on the arms, one hand resting on each bar, and by moving each hand alternately, proceeding forwards and backwards along the bars; in swinging the body between the arms; and in springing over the bar on each side, both backwards and forwards.

The Wooden Springs afford a kind of exercise extremely popular with the younger children, who are not sufficiently active to take part in the other exercises. Each swing consists of two distinct parts: 1. A piece of 2-inch deal, 1 foot wide and 3 feet long, one end of which is sunk firmly in the ground, the other projecting 18 inches above the surface. At each edge of this piece is screwed on an iron plate, with an eye to receive the iron pivot on which the upper piece works. The upper, or horizontal piece, is made of 2-inch plank, 1 foot wide and 12 feet long. At each end of this piece three handles, formed of 1½-inch deal, are strongly mortised in, 1 foot apart, thus forming seats for three children at each end. Between the handles the plank should be rounded at the edges, so as to form an easy seat. At the under surface of each end a small block of wood is fixed, to prevent the plank wearing by striking the ground.

The above directions should be adhered to. If the support be made lower, the motion of the swing is much lessened; if the plank be made shorter, or the support higher, the swing approaches too nearly to the perpendicular, and serious accidents may ensue from the children being thrown violently from the seats. The whole should be made as stout as recommended, otherwise it is apt to break from the violent action.

The Double Inclined Plane is adapted more especially for the younger children. It consists merely of a support of two-inch deal, 1 foot wide, and projecting 3 feet from the ground. On this is laid the ends of two planks, each 12 feet long, 1 foot wide, and 1½ inch in thickness. On the upper surface of each plank may be nailed, at intervals of eight or ten inches, small cross-pieces, to prevent the feet slipping.

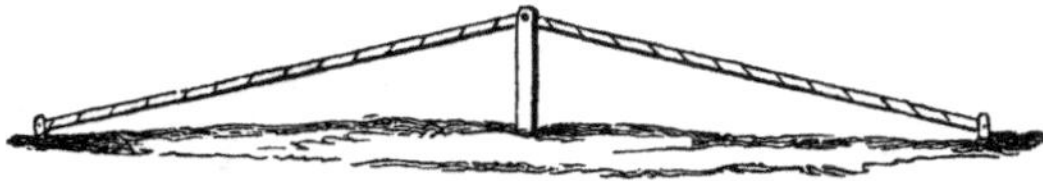

The use of the inclined plane is, that by ascending and descending it, children acquire a facility in balancing themselves. The exercise is beneficial, as it calls into action the muscles of the legs and even of the body. It also furnishes an excellent situation to jump from, as the children can themselves vary the height of the leap at pleasure.

The general use of all these various exercises is, that the different muscles of the body may be strengthened, and the children thus fitted for a future life of labor, and better prepared to escape in case of accidents.

Plan, &c., of School-room and Grounds for an Infant School.

The following plan and explanations are condensed from a valuable manual for teachers in infant and primary schools, entitled "Infant Education," one of Chambers' Educational Course, published at Edinburgh, in 1840. It is nearly similar to the plan recommended by Mr. Wilderspin in his "Infant School System," and his "Education for the Young," and by Mr. Stow, in the "Manual on the Training System for Infant and Juvenile Schools."

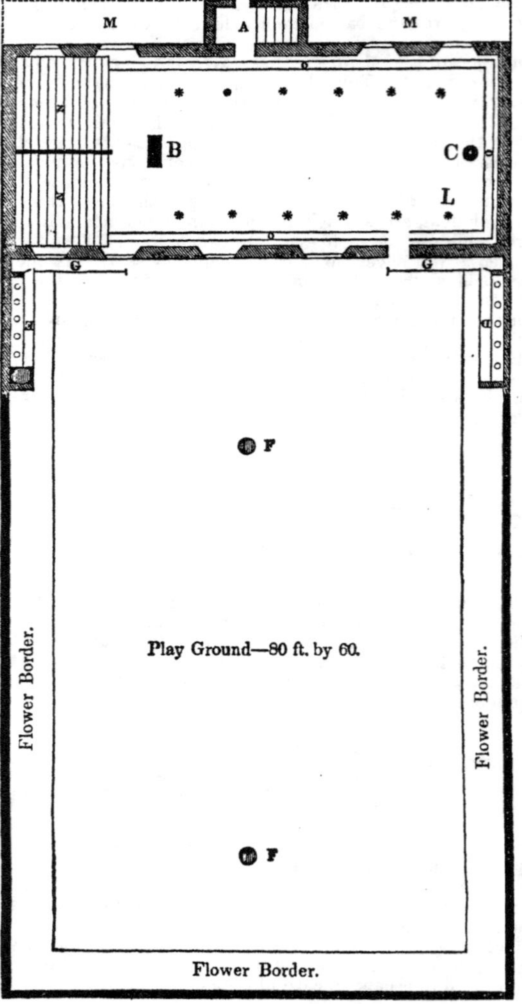

School-room, 60 feet long by 25 wide, and 18 feet high.

A. Porch and lobby, with stairs to the story above, if there should be a second story for a school for older pupils. The infant school should never be higher than the ground story. B. Movable rostrum, or small platform to hold one, two, or three children, when acting as general monitors to the whole school in the gallery. A low rail round it, will prevent them from falling from it. C. Stove, surrounded with a low rail.—(The room should be heated by a furnace.) N. Gallery, consisting of a series of steps the whole width of the room, each eight inches high, and 18 inches wide, divided in the center by a railing, one side for the boys, and the other for the girls. L. Lesson posts, to attach cards, &c. O. Seats round three sides of the room. M. Space for flowers and shrubbery protected by open fence. D. Boys', and C, Girls', water closet, on different sides of the play ground and concealed by a screen and shrubbery, entered by covered way G. F. Gymnastic swing posts

PLANS, &c., FOR SCHOOLS ON THE MONITORIAL OR MUTUAL SYSTEM.

The "Manual of the System of Primary Instruction pursued in the Model Schools of the British and Foreign School Society," published in 1839, contains the following remarks on the arrangement for schools of mutual instruction connected with that Society.

The school-room should be a parallelogram, the length about twice the breadth.

The height of the walls should be proportioned to the length of the room, and may be varied from 11 to 19 feet. It is recommended that the walls be worked fair and lime whitened, in order to give a neat and clean appearance, reflect light, and contribute to the preservation of health. As it is of great importance to admit as much light as possible into the school, there must be a considerable number of windows, each of which should be fixed in a wooden frame, and movable upon pins or pivots in the center, so that by drawing the upper part into the room, the school may be sufficiently ventilated in hot weather—a circumstance of the utmost importance to be attended to, as the health of the pupils in a great measure depends upon it.

The lower parts of the windows should be at least 6 feet from the floor, in order that the light may not be inconvenient, and the walls be at liberty for the reading lessons, &c., which are to be attached to it; if piers are required, they should be on the outside of the building.

There should be holes in the roof, or in the wall near it, to let foul air escape. This may be effected by a sufficient number of tubes so contrived that they can be opened or shut at pleasure, and at the same time fresh air be admitted from the outside of the building by tubes communicating with the lower part of the room.

All projections in the walls, as well as pillars to support the roof, ought to be avoided; for they interfere with the arrangement of the school, and obstruct the view of the master and of visiters. But if pillars are necessary, they should be placed at each end of the desks, but never in the middle of the room.

Roman Cement, cast into flags, and jointed with the same material, forms a good flooring; it is perfectly dry and durable, and emits but little sound.

In order that all the children may be completely seen by the master, it is of great importance that the floor should be an inclined plane, rising one foot in twenty from the master's desk, to the upper end of the room, where the highest or eighth class is situated.

At the lower end is the platform, elevated in proportion to the length of the room from 2 to 3 feet. The length and breadth of the platform must be in proportion to the size of the room.

The center of the platform is the place for the master's desk; and on each side there may be a small desk for the principal monitors.

The entrance door should be on the side of the platform, in order that visiters on entering the school, may have a commanding view of all the children at once.

Whatever be the size of the school-room, it may be sufficiently warmed by means of one or two stoves placed at the extremities of the apartment. But the most uniform and constant temperature is obtained by steam, when conducted along the lower parts of the room through pipes, or by heated air conveyed into the room through tubes communicating with a stove, which is surrounded by a close casing of iron, leaving a sufficient space for a current of fresh air to be brought in through a tube: this, coming in contact with the stove and the outside of the flue or iron chimney which passes through the casing, is heated, and may be discharged into the room by means of iron pipes. This method has been found to answer extremely well.

The middle of the room is occupied by the forms and desk, a passage being left between the ends of the forms and the wall, 5 or 6 feet broad, where the children form semicircles for reading.

The forms and desks must be fixed firmly in the ground; the legs or supports should be 6 inches broad and 2 inches thick, but cast iron legs are preferable, as they support the desk-board with equal firmness, occupy less room, and have a neater appearance; their number of course will be in proportion to the length of the forms. A form 20 feet long will require five, and they must be so placed, that the supports of the forms may not be immediately opposite to those of the desks; the corners of the desks and forms are to be made round, in order that the children may not hurt themselves.

The general rules for fitting up school-rooms are,—1. One foot for the space or passage between a form and the next desk.

2. Three inches for the horizontal space between a desk and its form.

3. Nine inches for the breadth of a desk, and six for the breadth of a form.

4. Twenty-eight inches for the height of a desk, and sixteen for the height of a form.

5. Eighteen inches in length of the desk for every child to occupy while seated upon his form.

6. From five to six feet for the passage between the walls and the ends of the forms and desks.

The semi-circles for the reading classes are formed opposite to the wall, and are marked by an incision in the floor.

Dimensions of school-rooms for 300 children, length, 62½ ft., breadth, 34 feet; for 200 do. 55 by 28; for 150 do. 52½ feet by 25.

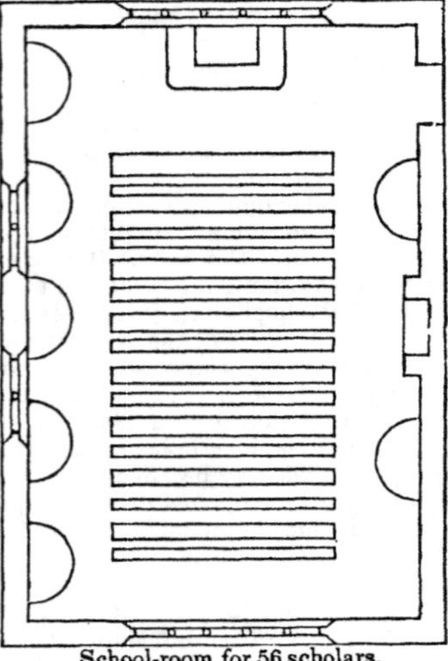

School-room for 56 scholars.

The following suggestions are abridged from the "*General Observations on the construction and arrangements of school-rooms, &c.,*" published by the National Society, London.

The form of the room should be oblong. If the room is built large to accommodate boys and girls together, it may be divided by a frame partition, made to slide upon rollers in an iron groove.

The superficial area should include 7 square feet for each child: hence, 50 children will require 350 ft; 80 do. 560 ft.; 100 do. 700 ft., &c.

The desks are generally attached to the wall, and consist of a horizontal ledge two or three inches wide to receive the inkstand, and an inclined plane ten inches wide, made to let down by hinges and movable brackets. The benches or forms are ten inches wide, and supported by standards of cast iron.

The benches for the classes in recitation, are arranged in the floor without desks. The floor is entirely level.

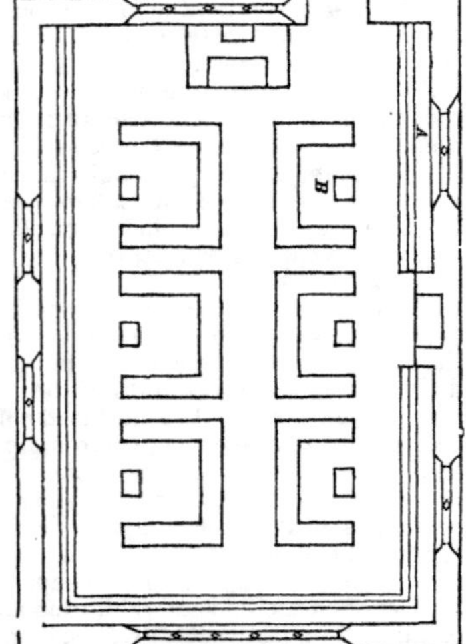

In the "Minutes of the Committee of Council on Education for 1851–52," under the general head of Organization of Schools, the following memorandum and diagrams "respecting the organization of schools in parallel groups of benches and desks," are published to aid committees in determining the internal dimension of school-rooms, and the best modes of fitting them up, in reference to schools organized on the plan recommended by the committee.

Preliminary Remarks.

"Before a school-room is planned,—and the observation applies equally to alterations in the internal fittings of an existing school-room,—the number of children who are likely to occupy it,—the number of classes into which they ought to be grouped,—whether the school should be "mixed," or the boys and the girls should be in different rooms, should be carefully considered, in order that the arrangements of the school may be designed accordingly.

A. Every class, when in operation, requires a separate teacher, be it only a monitor acting for the hour. Without some such provision it is impossible to keep all the children in a school actively employed at the same time.

The apprenticeship of pupil-teachers, therefore, is merely an improved method of meeting what is, under any circumstance, a necessity of the case; and, where such assistants are maintained at the public expense, it becomes of increased importance to furnish them with all the mechanical appliances that have been found by experience to be the best calculated to give effect to their services.

B. The main end to be attained is the concentration of the attention of the teacher upon his own separate class, and of the class upon its teacher, to the exclusion of distracting sounds and objects, and without obstruction to the head master's power of superintending the whole of the classes and their teachers. This concentration would be effected the most completely if each teacher held his class in a separate room; but such an arrangement would be inconsistent with a proper superintendence, and would be open to other objections. The common school-room should, therefore, be fitted to realize, as nearly as may be, the combined advantages of isolation and of superintendence, without destroying its use for such purposes as may require a large apartment. The best shape (*see diagrams annexed*) is an oblong about eighteen feet in width. Groups of desks are arranged along one of the walls. Each group is divided from the adjacent group or groups by an alley, in which a light curtain can be drawn forward or back. Each class, when seated in a group of desks, is thus isolated on its sides from the rest of the school. The head master, seated at his desk placed against the opposite wall, or standing in front of any one of the classes, can easily superintend the school; while the separate teacher of each class stands in front of it, where the vacant floor allows him to place his easel for the suspension of diagrams and the use of the black-board, or to draw out the children occasionly from their desks, and to instruct them standing, for the sake of relief by a change in position. The seats at the desks *and* the vacant floor in front of each group are *both needed*, and should therefore *be allowed for* in calculating the space requisite for *each class.*

C. By drawing back the curtain between two groups of desks, the principal teacher can combine two classes into one for the purpose of a gallery lesson; or a gallery (doubling the depths of rows) may substituted for one of the groups. For simultaneous instruction, such a gallery is better than the combination of two groups by the withdrawal of the intermediate curtain; because the combined width of the two groups is greater than will allow the teacher to command at a glance all the children sitting in the same line. It is advisable therefore always to provide a gallery.

The drawings annexed to the following rules purport simply to show the best internal dimensions of school-rooms, and the best mode of fitting them up, the doors and windows being placed accordingly. The combination of such rooms with others of the same kind, with teachers' residences, and with the remainder of the school premises, as well as the elevations which may thereby be obtained, depending, as they always must, upon local circumstances, are not intended to be here shown.*

The Committe of Council do not recommend that the benches and desks should be immovably fixed to the floor in any schools. They ought to be so coustructed as to admit of being readily removed when necessary, but not so as to be easily pushed out of place by accident, or to be shaken by the movements of the children when seated at them.

The reasons of the following rules will be readily inferred from these preliminary explanations.

1. In planning a school-room, if it be not more than 18 feet in width, about 8 or 9 square feet will be sufficient for each child in actual attendance. If the width be greater, there must be a proportionate increase of area allotted to each child.

2. A school not receiving infants should generally be divided into at least four classes. (*The varying capacities of children between seven and thirteen years old will be found to require at least thus much subdivision.*)

3. Parallel benches and desks, graduated according to the ages of the children, should be provided for all the scholars in actual attendance, (*see* ***Preliminary Remarks***, B.;) and therefore a school-room should contain at least four groups of parallel benches and desks. (*See* ***Rule*** 2.)

4. A group should not contain more than three rows of benches and desks, (*otherwise the distance of the last row is to great for the teacher to see the children's slates, and he must also raise his voice to a pitch which is exhausting to himself and adds inconveniently to the general noise.*)

5. As a general rule, no group of benches and desks should accommodate *more* than twenty-four children, *i. e.* eight children in each of the three rows of the group, (*otherwise the width is too great. See* ***Preliminary Remarks***, C.)

6. The proper lengths are 7 feet 6 inches for five children in a row; 9 feet for six in a row; 10 feet 6 inches for seven in a row; 12 feet for eight in a row; *i. e.* 18 inches for each child.

[The other dimensions and details are shown in the annexed drawings.]

7. Each group of desks must be separated from the contiguous group, either by an alley for the passage of the children, or by a space sufficient for drawing and withdrawing the curtains.

It will be sufficient to provide an alley for the passage of children *at one end only* of each group. At the other end a space of 3 inches will suffice for drawing and withdrawing the curtains.

[Alleys intended for the passage of children must not be less than 18 inches wide in the smallest school, and need not be more than 2 feet wide in any school, unless where a door or fireplace requires a greater interval.]

8. The best width for a school-room, intended to accommodate any number of children between 48 and 144, is 17 or 18 feet. This gives sufficient space for each group of benches and desks to be ranged (with its depth of three rows) along one wall, for the teachers to stand at a proper distance from their classes, and for the classes to be drawn out, when necessary, in front of the desks around the master or pupil-teachers. (*No additional accommodation being gained by greater width in the room, the cost of such an increase in the dimensions is thrown away.*)

9. Where the number of children to be accommodated is too great for them to be arranged in five, or at most, six groups, an additional school-room should be built, and placed under the charge of an additional schoolmaster, who may, however, be subordinate to the head master, or a large school may be built on the plan of diagram No. 6. Where neither of these arrangements can be accomplished, the school-room should not be less than 32 feet wide, and the groups should be arranged along both sides of the room, the children in all cases facing the centre. (*But such an arrangement is very inferior to that of the single row along one wall. The opposite classes see each other, and their several teachers have to stand too close together. See* ***Preliminary Remarks***, B.)

10. A curtain, capable of being readily drawn and withdrawn, should separate

* Specimen of the plans recommended by the committee, combining the foregoing object may be seen on page

the several groups; but not so as, when drawn, to project into the room more than 4 inches in front of the foremost desk.

11. If the school-room be lighted from above, which is the best possible mode, great care should be taken to prevent the skylights from leaking, and to provide channels for the water which the condensation of the children's breath will deposit on the inside of the glass.

12. All sashes, both upper and lower, should be hung; and all windows, whether in the roof or elsewhere, should be made to open.

13. It is better to have a few large and well placed windows than many small ones.

14. It is important to provide that the faces of the children and teachers, and also the blackboards and diagrams, should be placed in full clear light.

15. If the school-room be not lighted from above, there should be windows, if possible, at each end and on one side of the room. The windows should be carried up as high as possible; and those which are placed at the backs of the children, an arrangement which should be avoided as far as possible, should not come down within 5 feet 6 inches, or at least 5 feet, from the floor

16. When the benches and desks are arranged on both sides of the room, it should be lighted from above, or there should be, if possible, windows in *each* of the side walls.

17. Except when a school-room is very broad, there should be no fireplace in the center of an end wall.

[A good place for a fireplace is under a window.]

18. The desks should be either quite flat or *very slightly* inclined. The objections to the inclined desks are, that pencils, pens, &c., are constantly slipping from it, and that it can not be conveniently used as a table. The objection to the flat desk is, that it obliges the children to stoop. A raised ledge in front of a desk interferes with the arm in writing.

19. A large gallery for the simultaneous instruction of two or more classes, without desks, may advantageously be provided in a class-room or at one end of the school-room. Such a gallery may be better placed along than across the end of the school-room, for the reason stated in the Preliminary Remarks, B.

20. No such gallery, nor any gallery in an infant school-room, should be placed in front of a window, unless it be very high up above the heads of the children when they stand on the top row of the gallery.

21. No infant gallery should hold more than eighty or ninety infants.

22. An infant school should (besides a large gallery) have a small group of benches and desks, for the occasional use of the elder infants.

23. The alleys leading to a gallery should be at its sides, not in its center. (*See Rules* 5 *and* 6.)

24. Great care should be taken that the valves which admit the fresh air into the school-room should be placed so as not to create draft where the teachers and children sit.

25. An easel and a blackboard should be provided for each class, and a larger blackboard for the gallery.

26. The dimensions shown in the drawings annexed to this memorandum, are adapted to children of from 11 to 12 years of age. *It is very important that these dimensions should be graduated to suit the sizes of the elder and younger children in a school.*"

Although the following diagrams of the internal arrangements of school-rooms are drawn in reference to schools organized on a peculiar plan, as set forth in the foregoing memorandum, they will suggest valuable hints to a judicious architect or committee. There are some features in them, which we do not approve, and we think will not be found in practice as convenient as several of the more recent plans embodied in this volume.

No. 1. A School for 48 children of one sex, in 4 classes; with a class-room having a gallery capable of containing two of the classes.

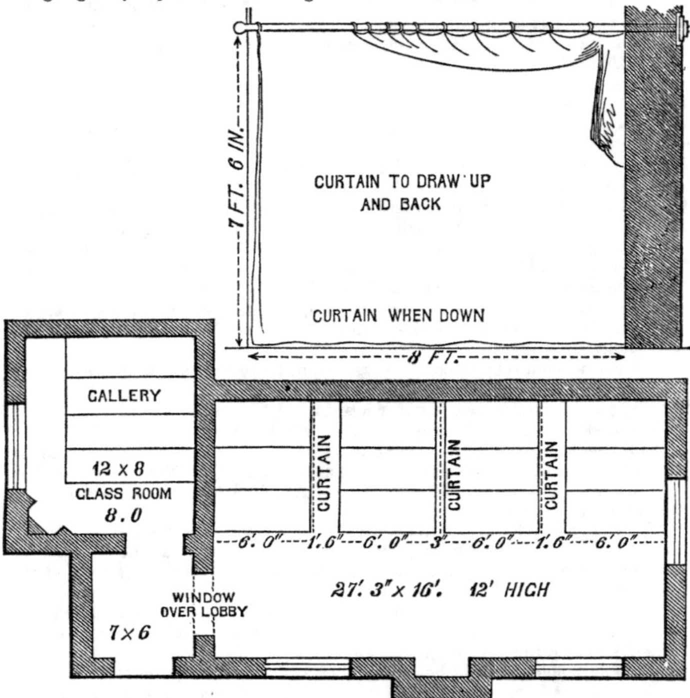

No. 2. A School for 48 boys and girls, in 4 classes; with a class-room having a gallery capable of containing two of the classes.

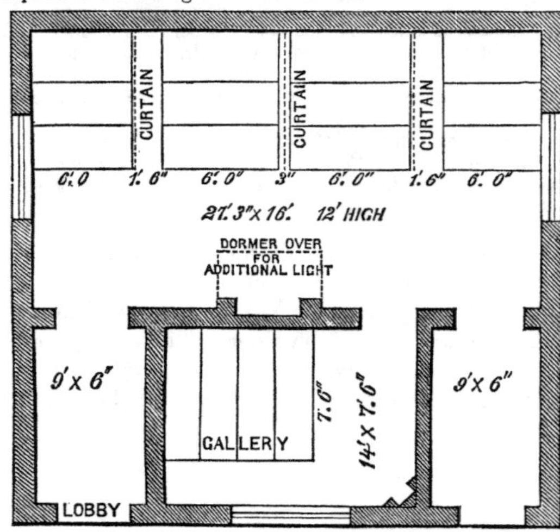

No. 3. A School for 72 children of one sex, in classes; with a class-room having a gallery capable of containing two of the classes.

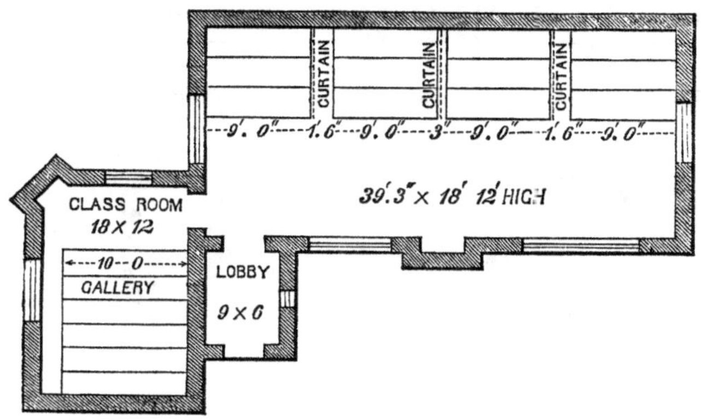

No. 4. A School for 72 boys and girls, in 4 classes; with a class-room having a gallery capable of containing two of the classes.

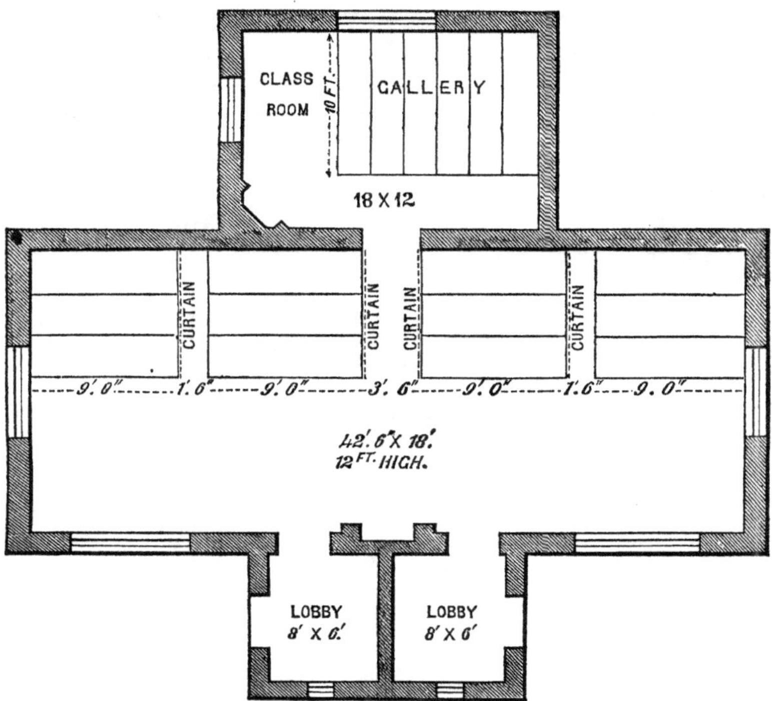

No. 5. A School for 120 children of one sex, in 5 classes; with a class-room having a gallery capable of containing two of the classes.

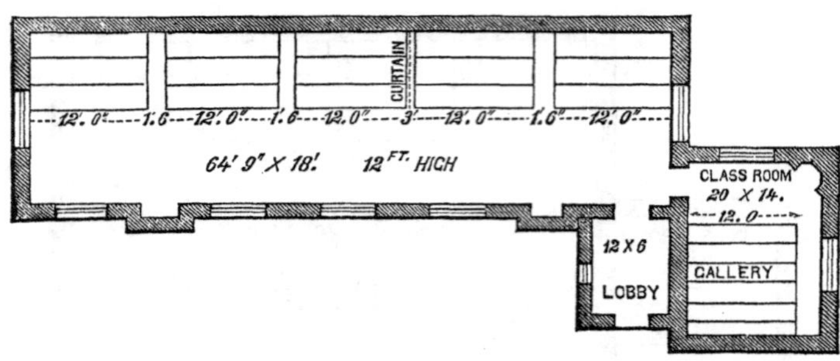

No. 6. A School for 168 children of one sex, in 7 classes, with a gallery; and with a class-room having a gallery capable of containing two of the classes.

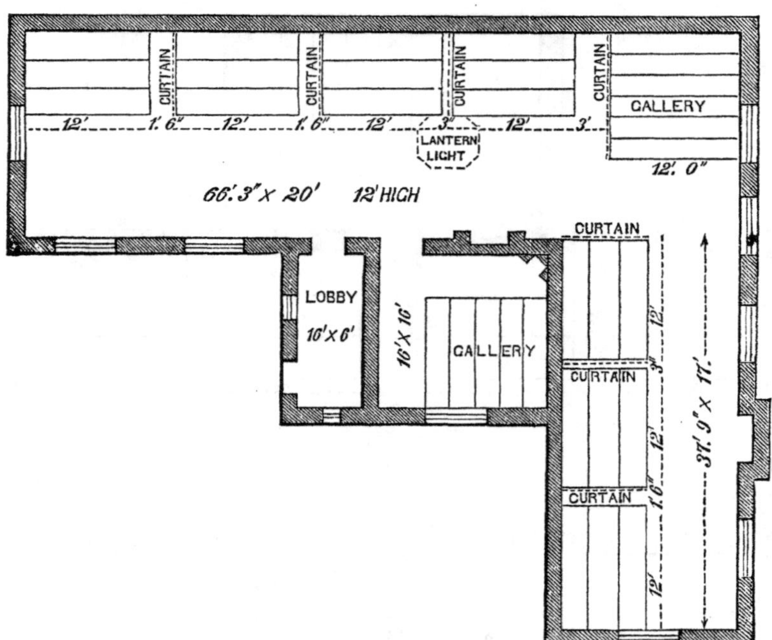

No. 7. A School for 240 children of one sex, in 8 classes, and a gallery; with a class-room having also a gallery capable of containing two of the classes.

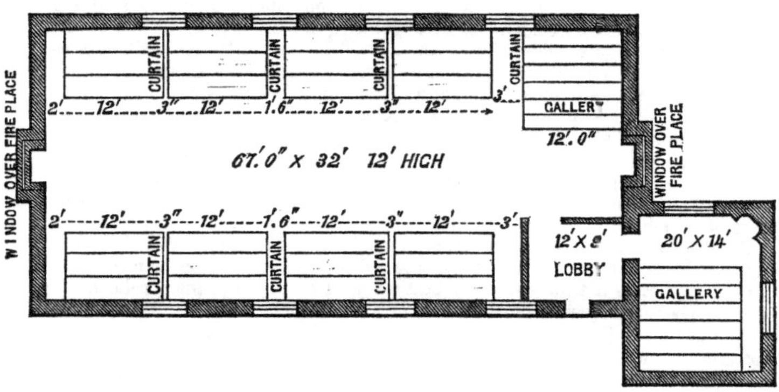

No. 8. Infant Schools for 100 infants, with a gallery capable of accommodating 72 infants, and a group of benches and desks capable of accommodating 15 infants.

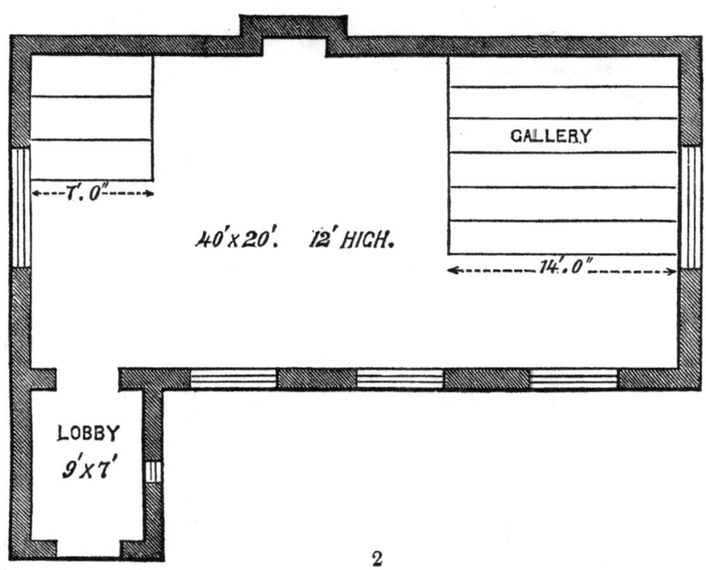

Gallery and Furniture for Infant and Primary Schools.

The gallery, or a succession of seats rising one above the other, on which the children can be gathered at suitable times for simultaneous exercises, such as singing, lessons on real objects, pictures, simple operations of mental arithmetic, &c., has been found an economical arrangement, in respect to space and expense, in schools for a large number of very young children, variously modified; it is used in Great Britain, not only in infant and primary schools, but in national schools of the highest grade as to the age and proficiency of the pupils, for assembling the whole school for lectures, or for the collective teaching of large classes in writing, drawing, singing, and dictation.

The common mode, of constructing benches without backs, and without regard to the size of the pupils, for six or eight young children, or even a larger number, has nothing to recommend it but economy, and not even that, when the waste of the teacher's time, in discipline caused by the children's discomfort, is considered.

But the opposite extreme, of separate chairs for each child, especially if the chairs are set far apart for the purpose of preventing all communication and to secure quiet, is not therefore the best mode of seating a primary school. The social disposition of young children should be regarded, and their seats, whether the old fashioned form with the "new fangled back," or the neat chair with back and arms, should be contiguous, so that two can be seated near each other.

Even the youngest pupils should be provided with a desk, or with some facility for using the slate in drawing and printing. In the absence of a desk for each child, a leaf with slates inserted, or painted black, should be hung low against the wall for the use of primary classes.

Primary School Bench.

A movable bench for more than two pupils is an objectionable article of school furniture; but if introduced at all,

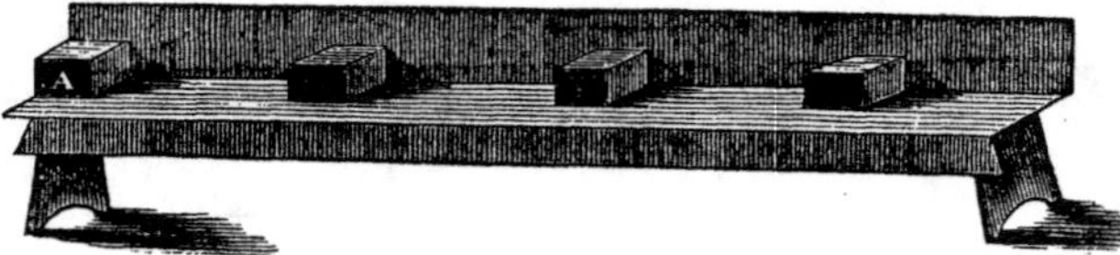

the above cut represents a style of this article which combines economy and convenience. The back is inclined slightly from a perpendicular, and the seat is hollowed. The scholars are separated by a compartment, or box, A, which serves as a rest for the arm, and a place of deposit for books.

Gallery and Sand Desk for Primary and Infant Schools.

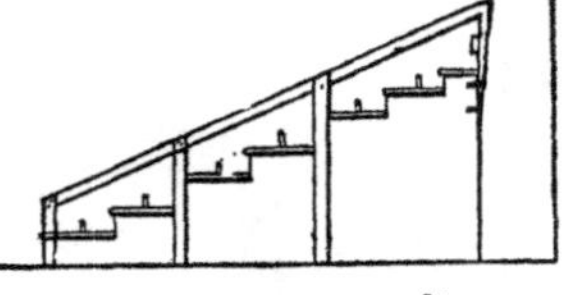

For very small children a *Gallery* consisting of a succession of seats rising above each other, varying in height from seven to nine inches, and provided with a support for the back. This arrangement, in large schools, affords great facility for instruction in music and all simultaneous exercises.

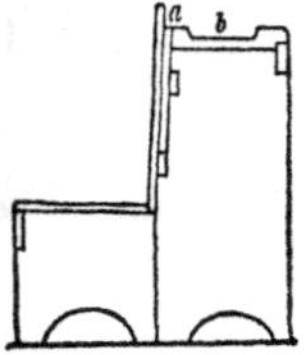

The *Sand Desk* having a trench (*b*) painted black, to contain a thin layer of sand, in which to trace letters and rude attempts at imitating forms, was originally much resorted to with the young classes, in schools educated on the Lancasterian or Mutual system. This style of desk is still used in the primary schools of the New York Public School Society, but very much improved by Mott's *Cast Iron Scroll Stanchions* and *Revolving Pivot Chair.* Every scholar is furnished with a slate, which is deposited in the opening (*a*) in the top of the desk.

The following cut, Fig. 4, represents a section of a gallery recommended in a memorandum of the Committee of Council on Education.

FIG. 4.

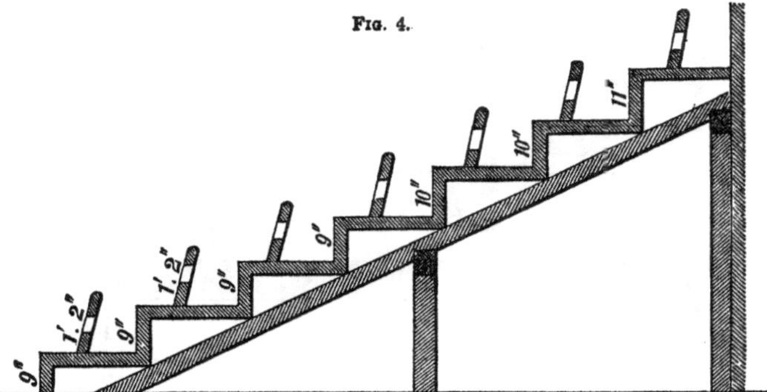

Fig. 5 represents a large gallery in the lecture-room of Borough Road School of the British and Foreign School Society; and Fig. 6, a small gallery in the corner of a class-room in the same school.

FIG. 5. FIG. 6.

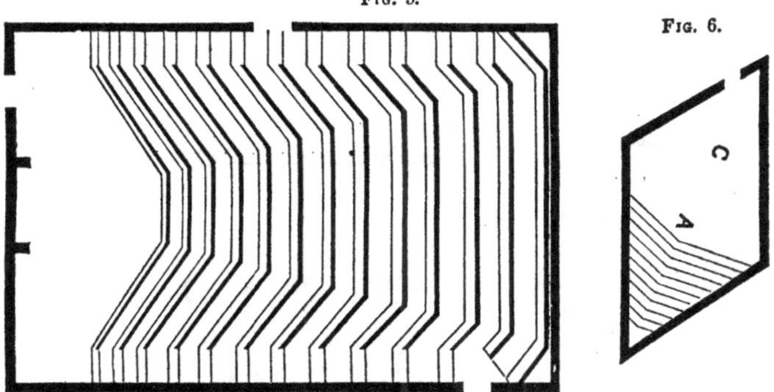

Figure 7 represents a *Closing Gallery*, designed for small rooms. Two steps, *b b*, are fixed, and two, *a a*, are made on rollers, and when out of use are pushed under *b b*. When used, they are kept in their place by a bolt to the floor.

FIG. 7.

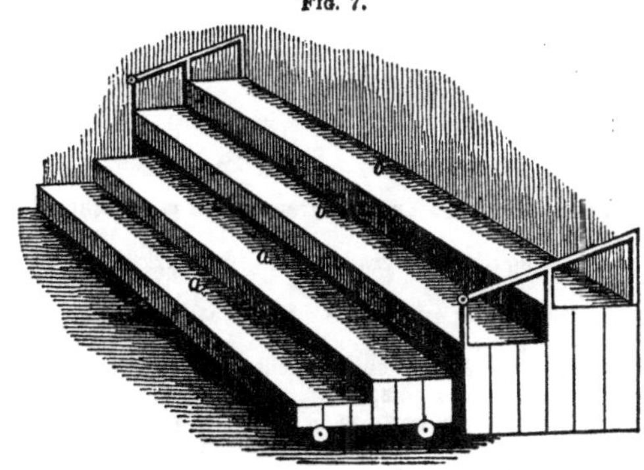

The following cuts represent a front view (Fig. 1,) and end section (Fig. 2,) of the desk, and a front view and section of a drawing board (Fig. 3,) recommended for the use of the drawing schools in connection with the Department of Practical Art in the Board of Trade, England.

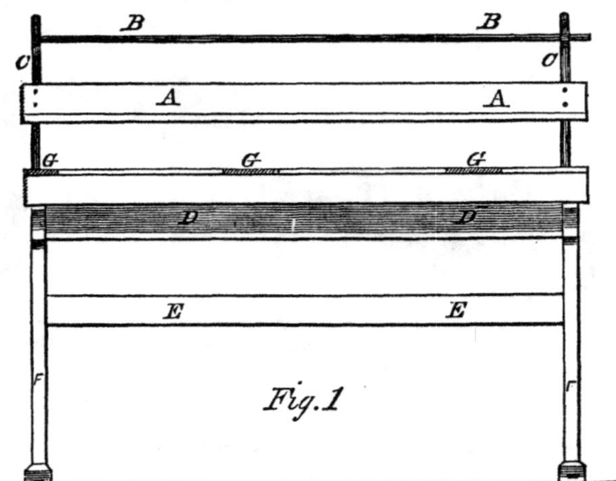

Fig. 1.—Front View of Drawing Desk.

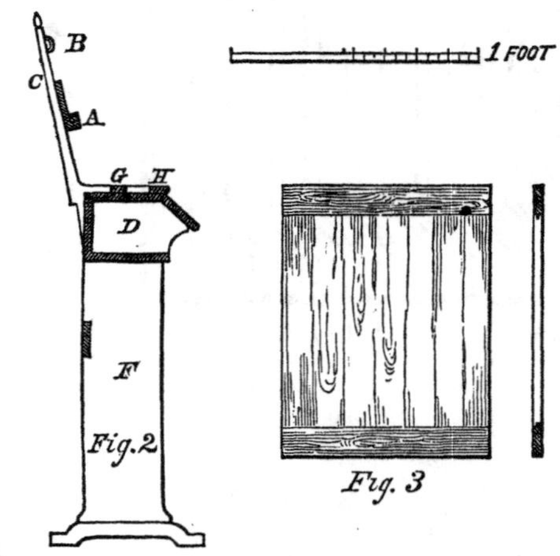

Fig. 2.—Section of Drawing Desk. Fig. 3.—Drawing Board.

A, A, Fig. 1, A, Fig. 2—A wooden rail, screwed to iron uprights C, C, to hold the examples or copy.

B, B, $\frac{5}{8}$ inch rod, passing through eyes in $\frac{5}{8}$ inch iron uprights, C, C, C, to support the examples.

C, C, C, $\frac{5}{8}$ inch iron uprights, screwed to the desk at I, and punched at the upper end to receive the iron rod B.

D, D, hollow space to hold the students' pencils, knives, &c.

E, E, wooden rail to stiffen uprights, F, F, F, which are screwed to the floor.

G, G, (Fig. 1,) short fillets, as shown at G, (Fig. 2,) placed opposite each student, to retain the board, or example more upright if necessary.

H, (Fig. 2,) a fillet running along the desk, to prevent pencils, &c., rolling off.

II. ORAL LESSONS ON COMMON THINGS.

BY THOMAS MORRISON.*

Rector of the Free Church Training College, Glasgow.

1. Oral instruction ought to be employed in dealing with the principles of all the ordinary branches of school education. Text-books are mainly valuable, in that they present a connected and systematic view of any subject, and supply the various definitions and technical terms employed in connection with it. But no text-book can furnish information in principles, so clear and so conclusive as to supersede the necessity of oral instruction on the part of the master. In treating of such branches as arithmetic, geography, or grammar, by far the most valuable part of the information—that, namely, which relates to the fundamental principles on which these sciences are based—to be given successfully, must be given orally by the master. But, in addition to these regularly stereotyped branches of education, much useful and highly important information may and should be communicated to children in school—information which no series of text-books can adequately supply. We refer to incidental oral lessons upon various portions of natural history, natural science, and upon what has been termed in these modern days "common things." The books used in school too generally deal with dry abstract subjects—while the little world in which the child lives, his home—his food—his garments—the air he breathes—the various operations which he sees going on around him—are carefully and most religiously shut out from school.

2. In all these oral lessons, the knowledge acquired should be directed to practical purposes. In this way the child becomes acquainted with the science of common things. The mere knowledge of principles, whether in the region of natural or moral things, does not imply the power of directing that knowledge to practical use. It is quite a possible, nay it is, unfortunately, a too common thing, to find a person whose creed is thoroughly orthodox, and who has a clear intellectual discernment of the relation of the various doctrines which constitute that creed, but whose practice is sadly at variance with his belief. So it is in natural things. Our education is too formal. It is too much shackled with absurd conventionalities. We give our

* Abridged from "*Manual of School Management.*"

pupils much knowledge, but little wisdom. We supply abstract principles, but no directions as to their application. Now it must be borne in mind that we do not speak here of the attempt which some hair-brained visionaries have made, to convert the school into a general workshop, where the boys are taught shoemaking, tailoring, and other trades; and where girls are trained to bake and wash, and to perform such like domestic operations. We have already lifted up our voice in solemn protest against the introduction of such things into the elementary school. Much of our education has been, no doubt, an unreal, a visionary thing; much of it has been concerned with words, and nothing more, and, perhaps, it was natural, when a reaction set in against this state of matters, that many should err in the other extreme, and deny the use of knowledge of any kind which could not be immediately applied to practical purposes. We make no reference here to such attempts as these; but, while we deprecate with all our might such misapplications of the child's school life, we would insist on giving the child as much information as possible upon the application of those principles which we present to him. Thus, in dealing with the atmosphere, while we would give the child a knowledge of those ingredients which compose it, and of the laws which regulate it when in motion, we would also give him information upon the connection which subsists between health and a constant supply of fresh air—of the means whereby a dwelling-house, or other building, may be safely and effectively ventilated—of the cause and the evil results of draughts, &c.; so, when speaking of dwelling-houses, we would not only unfold the nature of the material employed in constructing the edifice, but also the necessity of having a dry foundation—how this might be obtained—the evils consequent upon over crowding, &c. We would not only teach the child the philosophy of the art of swimming, but that it is unsafe to bathe in all states of the body, &c. These illustrations will serve to show what we mean by the science of common things. The advantages arising from such lessons are obvious. The child associates the abstract principles of science with the common affairs of every-day life, and finds illustrations of them in objects the most unlikely. His interest is thus continually kept up, and, when he leaves school and enters on the actual battle of life, instead of performing his work blindly and in virtue merely of imitation, he does it with the intelligence of a man who has learned to trace the relations which subsist between theory and practice. We are satisfied that, were lessons of this kind more common, they would create an intelligence that would result in the greatest benefits to the body politic; and that such things as smoke-nuisances—over-crowding nuisances—and many other foul and loathsome nuisances—would not be tolerated, no not for a day. At present, our laboring classes, more particularly in country districts, do their work mechanically, with little more intelligence than is shown by the dumb animals whose services they employ. Their school education enabled them to read but very imperfectly, and soon after their life of toil began, the little technical learning they had acquired became obsolete through want of practice, and so they settled down into that sad and most melancholy position in which nothing interests them which does not appeal to their senses. We need not wonder at the alarming prevalence of vice among our rural population. The lessons we are now treating of would, to a certain extent, serve to counteract the tendency which uneducated natures have to gravitate to the earthly and sensual. By opening up to them some of the wonders which meet in the most common objects, by training them to reflect on the principles involved in the most simple operations, and by guiding them to make, from a knowledge of principles, improvements in the mode of conducting these operations, we supply them with the means whereby their attention and their curiosity may be kept ever on the alert, and their minds exercised upon what is both usefûl and profitable.

ORAL LESSONS.—FIRST STAGE.

3. It is evident that, if young children are to receive any instruction at all, it must be given orally. For a very considerable time after entering school, they are unable to employ the art of reading in such a way as to derive much benefit from what they read. If their minds, accordingly, are to be exercised at all, if their young faculties are to be trained and developed, something more must be done than merely teach them the arbitrary signs of sounds. To keep a poor child for some months, or, it may be, years, poring over the A, B, C, and its combinations, is the sure and certain way to make him a dunce of the first water. In fact it would appear eminently natural to delay introducing the child to the acqusition of written signs, until he has been some time in school. The method which nature suggests, is to follow out the line of education which the child has instinctively pursued before entering school. He has been exercising his perceptive faculties on the various objects which surround him; he has been examining their properties and qualities, and acquiring a marvelously large stock of ideas, and of language in which to give expression to them. By means of oral lessons the teacher can take him up at the exact point at which he has arrived at the time when

his school life begins, and carry him gradually forward from one degree of knowledge to another. At first, accordingly, the attention of the child should be directed, in such lessons, to those properties of the object which he can discover by his senses. For this purpose the object must not only be described to him in words, but he must also see it, handle it, smell it, taste it, or hear it, as the case may be. Every one has observed how natural it is for children to touch those objects which interest them. So strong is this desire, that in galleries of art, in museums and such-like places, it is found necessary to caution visitors against touching any of the articles. This tendency is the exhibition of Nature's method of communicating information to the young or the unlearned. The teacher should fall in with this instinct of children, and allow them to exercise their senses upon the objects which he selects as the subjects of his early lessons. In this way they will acquire correct conceptions of them.

4. After a time, and when lessons of the kind described in last paragraph have given the master a basis on which to work, he should select, as subjects of lesson, objects which do not come within the sphere of the personal observation of the children. There are many objects in the world of nature which the children can never personally examine, but which ought not on that account to be excluded from their notice. Personal examination is a mighty help to clearness of conception, but, even without this personal examination, children may be trained to form very correct notions of many things of which they may never be able to take any direct sensible cognizance. The actual presence of an object in school is not necessarily of the essence of an oral lesson upon that object. Thus, the children may never have had the opportunity of seeing a lion, tiger, or elephant; and the master will find it rather difficult to obtain actual specimens of these animals, whether alive or dead, to take with him to school. What then? Is he to give no lessons upon such animals? Nay, verily; he may, by the use of proper methods, convey to the pupils a very accurate and, on the whole, distinct conception of the shape, appearance, and habits of these creatures. By means of a good drawing he can convey to the mind the general idea of the appearance of the animals, and, by comparing the unknown animal with one that is known, he may give distinctness to the general conception. Thus, the tiger resembles the cat, but is much larger. It is as high as some known animal—or as this (pointing to some part of the wall,) it is longer than—— about as long as——, &c. Anecdotes, illustrative of his character and strength, will still further serve to give distinctness to their conceptions, and, although the children might not be able, from

the description thus given, to draw an exact likeness of the tiger (supposing them capable of drawing,) they would still have some correct ideas of the animal, and the name would thus be associated with a distinct mental picture. To confine these oral lessons to familiar objects would be to limit most unnecessarily and prejudicially their sphere of usefulness.

5. One important end served by these lessons is that, by means of them, the child is acquiring a command of words, which will be of essential service in his future career. Even before entering school, the child has made considerable progress in the acquisition of words, many of which may not be over pure, although remarkably expressive. In acquiring these words, the child has almost invariably proceeded, unknown to himself, on the principle of obtaining first a knowledge of the thing, and then, as necessity arose for it, of the name. This furnishes to the teacher the true method whereby he ought to teach language in connection with these lessons. If the children have an expression of their own for the idea, it ought to be accepted; but, if the term is local or provincial, this ought to be pointed out, and the correct word given. If, on the other hand, the children require to be taught a new term, this should not be done until the idea, of which the term is a sign, has been clearly and thoroughly pictured out. This simple principle, in practice so often lost sight of, is so consistent with the soundest philosophy, that one is at a loss to conceive how any objection could be taken to it; and yet there are men who characterize it as a piece of humbug. The opposite method—that of giving first (and in too many instances *only*) the sign, is opposed to the very first principles of true education, and, if carried out, can only result in giving the semblance of knowledge without its reality. In all cases let the teacher present first to his pupils a clear picture of the idea, and its name will then acquire a meaning which it would not otherwise have, and when used, will call up a distinct conception in the mind. This linguistic aspect of these oral lessons is one, in our estimation, of great importance, which ought never to be lost sight of. It has been admirably remarked "What we have in the first place to do with, as representative reality, is spoken language. Now, it may be asked, to what is it owing that the same person, in humble life, whose provincial tongue is pregnant with meaning and full of vivacity, when he tries to speak correctly, which he may in some measure be able to do, expresses himself in the most formal and insipid manner? We think it the chief reason, as language possesses little or no intrinsic interest, deriving its suggestiveness from objects connected with it in the mind, that the rich

provincial dialect has been associated in countless repetitions with objects of living and perceived interest; whereas the correct mode of speech is chiefly remembered as having been met with in books, and it is therefore unaccompanied with fancy or lively conception. * * In order to be clearly understood, language must be easily spoken. The mere reading of school lessons will not fully accomplish either. The only successful course will be to associate words of pure English with felt and living realities."*

ORAL LESSONS.—SECOND STAGE.

6. The elementary lessons, briefly described in the last paragraphs, train the children to observe the properties and qualities of objects, and supply them with correct terms for the expression of their ideas. A subsequent series of lessons should have in view the tracing of the relations which subsist among the various parts of an object, or between different objects. This calls for a higher exercise of mind than the foregoing class of lessons, and may be made most valuable as a means of mental discipline, besides communicating a large amount of useful and valuable information. Thus, in an elementary lesson upon the elephant, it might be sufficient to convey to the children a very general idea of his size, appearance, and parts. In this second stage, however, the relation between the various parts of the animal should be pointed out, and attention called to the connection which subsists between his structure and his habits. The animal has got a very large and heavy body; hence we might infer something regarding his legs. They would require to be strong. The children may be told that they are almost perpendicular, like pillars supporting a heavy roof. He has also a heavy head, the weight of which is increased by the tusks. Suppose he had a long tapering neck like the camelopard, what might the consequences be? What kind of neck has he? But he obtains part of his food on the ground. His body being large and his neck very short, how can he accomplish this? Such questions prepare the mind for seeing a beauty and a wisdom in the compensation supplied in the shape of the trunk. We shall give several specimens of such lessons when we come to treat of subjects of oral lessons.

ORAL LESSONS.—THIRD STAGE.

7. A still higher grade of oral lessons should be given, with the view of training the reasoning powers, and of leading the children to infer consequences from premises laid down for them. "By books,

* Prize "*Essay on Education.*"—Rev. D. Smith, p. 8.

the pupil can never be properly exercised in reasoning. As conclusion and premises follow one another, both of them being placed before the reader, he is under great temptation to assume both on equal authority. Hence the means must be used, in the first instance, to induce him to draw inferences which he has not thought of beforehand. Some men, entirely unexercised in reasoning, know just as much as they are told in plain language, or as they can perceive by their senses; but all men of ordinary capacity are able to acquire the power of concluding something involved in what is sensible, and deducing inferences from the information communicated to them. We would set out in lessons of this sort from something which the pupil knows, or which can be made patent and palpable to his senses, and go on from simple processes to more difficult, the complex conceptions thus acquired forming the components of new reasonings."* This series of lessons might embrace various portions of physical science—such lessons as we have specified in the chapter on geography—the more common pieces of machinery—the instruments employed in philosophical pursuits, such as the barometer, thermometer, &c. It is during this stage chiefly that the application of science to the explanation of common things should be dwelt upon. Every lesson should aim at turning the attention of the pupil to an examination of those phenomena that meet him in his daily life. In this way all these lessons become lessons on the science of common things.

8. To conduct these lessons aright, the master must make himself well acquainted with each subject in all its bearings. The ability to talk to children upon a great variety of subjects does not necessarily imply that the master is capable of communicating real information, or of training the minds of his scholars. Something more is necessary than merely the power of speaking. The master must have ideas to communicate, and, in order to this, he must make a point of familiarizing himself most thoroughly with the subject. It is, no doubt, true that a person, whose stock of knowledge is large, may not on that account be the one who is best adapted to teach. But, if we were compelled to make our choice between the man of full mind and exact knowledge, but who may be somewhat defective in the art of communication, and the man of shallow views and vague conceptions regarding a multitude of things, but who may be apt to teach, we would have little hesitation in choosing the former. Where there is a full mind, there will constantly be streaming forth from it suggestions, and hints and thoughts, which will have far more effect in kindling the spark of intellectual life in children than the common-

* Prize "*Essay on Education*."—Rev. D. Smith, p. 23.

place verbiage of him who has a mere smattering of science. The first essential requisite, accordingly, in conducting these lessons, is that the master be at home in regard to each particular subject. Mr. Mosely remarks very justly and pertinently on this point—"That which lies very generally at the root of the failure of such lessons, and makes of what would, under other circumstances, be the most successful expedient and the highest resource of education, in too many cases an impediment to it—is an inadequate knowledge on the part of the teacher of that which he is teaching. He may know many things, and be generally a well-informed man, but if he fails in his lesson, it is commonly because he does not know the particular subject of that lesson. If his knowledge of it had covered a larger surface, he would have selected matter better adapted to the instruction of the children. If he had comprehended it more fully, he would have made it plainer to them. If he had been more familiar with it, he would have spoken more to the point. Wanting this knowledge of the subject, the time allotted to his lesson is filled up with words foreign to the matter in hand, as though it were a time set apart to be covered with a certain amount of talk, and as though a teacher must be assumed, as a matter of course, to be teaching so long as he is talking." Mere surface knowledge will not suffice. Where the knowledge extends no deeper than the surface, the teacher will to a certainty get into the habit of repeating, and of causing the children to repeat, words to which no definite meaning is attached. The knowledge must be deep and searching. The teacher must know the subject in its own nature and in its relations to other things. And, not only must the teacher have thus a thorough knowledge of the subject, but he must also possess skill and judgment to select those materials which are logically connected with the main subject, and to reject those which are connected in appearance but not in reality. All extraneous matter must be cast aside. Each lesson should have some one definite object in view, and while many things may be brought out incidentally in the course of it, they must be of such a nature as to bear upon the central idea of the whole. All the lines of each lesson must converge to one focus, and the lesson is not complete until they have all met, and until each is seen to have had a certain definite share in producing the final result. The skillful teacher will be known as much by what he rejects as by what he admits. We need only further add that, while each lesson is thus complete in itself, it is not necessary that the lessons follow any due order. One day the lesson may be upon some part of pneumatics, the next day on hydrostatics, and so on. But while this is the case, the teacher should carefully keep a memorandum of the lessons given, and of the points brought out, that he may thus know the exact point at which to begin any new lesson. Unless some such memorandum be kept, there will be little likelihood of the successive lessons fitting into each other, and progress will be uncertain and unsatisfactory. To enable the teacher to ascertain where, in any given lesson, he ought to begin, he should preserve carefully the notes and heads of the lessons which he prepares for his own use previous to coming to the class.

9. Having thus selected the materials for his lesson, the teacher's next duty is to arrange them in the order in which he wishes to present them to his scholars. There is no stereotyped method of arrangement; nor can any models be presented which the teacher can, in all cases, implicitly follow. He must have the subject in all its bearings clearly mapped out in his own mind; and must determine on treating it in some given order; but the method of treatment will vary with the varying subjects. To adopt a plan which must be rigidly adhered to throughout, will be productive of as much harm as good. Many suggestions will be made by the pupils, as the lesson proceeds, and it is essential to success that the teacher be able to catch up these suggestions, and work them in to the lesson naturally and without effort. The chief thing to be attended to is that the teacher have some definite end in view in giving the lesson; for, when this is the case, he can intuitively turn to advantage every hint which occurs in the course of it. Where he adheres too rigidly to some one mode of arrangement, he may be able to see straight before him, but will miss many of the beauties which adorn the bye-paths. If, on the other hand, he has no definite end in view, he will be apt to linger altogether upon the various paths which cross the main road, and will thus never arrive at his destination. In all lessons he must commence with what the children know. Where he has to lay a foundation for the lesson, he ought to commence with that which possesses most interest, and makes the deepest impression, and thence proceed to what is less interesting, but, it may be, equally valuable. In giving lessons upon animals, the teacher may commence with the structure, and thence infer the habits and uses; or he may commence with the habits and uses, and thence infer the structure. As the structure of such domestic animals as the cow, the horse, &c., is well known to children, we would commence at this point in lessons on these animals. In lessons, however, on animals of the structure and habits of which the children were equally ignorant, we would prefer beginning with the latter, inasmuch as we could render such instruction very inter-

esting by the introduction of anecdotes, &c. Having thus laid the foundation, the pupils would follow with interest that part of the lesson which bore on the structure. In lessons on science and common things, the analytic or synthetic methods may be adopted, according as the teacher finds the one or the other more suitable. Thus in a lesson on "Smoke," we might commence with the smoke as it is seen issuing from the chimney, and trace its history backwards until we reached its cause. In a lesson on the "Winds," on the other hand, we might commence with the causes, and follow these out to their effects. In many subjects, especially those involving important discoveries and inventions, we might adopt what has been termed the Genetic method—that is, carry back our pupils to the very first steps of the discovery or the invention, and lead them gradually onwards to the present time. These hints, combined with the specimens we shall give, may be of some service to the young teacher in the matter of arrangements.

10. To assist the memory, and to make sure of due preparation, the teacher ought to commit to writing the leading points in each lesson. These "Notes of Lessons," as they are termed, are liable to be much abused; and we must be cautious in our recommendation of them. Sometimes the teacher writes out a series of questions and answers, and comes before his class in the expectation that the answers given by the pupils will correspond to those he has written. This seldom, if ever, happens; and accordingly the master, not receiving the answer he looked for, is thrown off his guard and is apt to become confused. Others again write out the substance of the whole lesson, which is of service in so far as it gives a mastery of the subject which nothing but writing can bestow. This plan, in the case of every lesson, entails an immense amount of labor, and, where the master has many duties to attend to, can not be well adopted. We would advise the teacher first to determine the leading points which he desires to bring before his pupils, and to write these down as the main stays of the lesson. He should next proceed to take up each part in detail—to reflect upon the method he would adopt in illustrating it and making it clear to his pupils, and thereafter commit to writing the leading thoughts under each division. He would thus have an abstract of the lesson in the order in which it was thought out, and a glance at the abstract would bring the whole vividly before him. For convenience in reference, he should next arrange the notes in such a way that, in the margin he would have the leading heads of the lesson, and in the remainder of the page those hints, illustrations and suggestions which presented themselves to his mind in the course of

preparation. Should he desire to write out the notes in full, this could be easily done. In the actual business of teaching the teacher should trust to his notes as little as possible. The heads of the lesson should be amply sufficient to guide him to the whole. The best notes are a full and thorough understanding of the subject, without which, indeed, all the notes in the world are but so much waste paper.

11. In conducting these oral lessons, it must be borne in mind that both master and scholars should bear their respective shares of the work. Any approach to the style of the pure lecture is to be deprecated, inasmuch as it encourages idleness in the pupils, and tends to render the master contented with giving information, without taking any precautions to ascertain if the information has been received. The master's part in the work is to have the particular subject in hand thoroughly got up, to be well acquainted with it in all its bearings and connections, and to have the various parts of it arranged in logical order, so that, when put together, they may form a connected whole. When he has all this ready, he introduces the subject to the notice of his pupils, and by means of questions, ellipses, suggestions and illustrations, he aids them to reason out consequences from the premises which he supplies. Oral instruction thus assumes the form of a conversation, in which the master acts the part of guide, while the minds of the pupils are constantly employed in making what to them amounts almost to new discoveries. This must never be lost sight of, because the tendency to lecture instead of train the scholars is naturally strong. In school, the lecture is comparatively useless. In its own place, and among those whose minds are sufficiently developed to follow a long train of reasoning, it may be turned to high account; but with pupils of the age ordinarily found in our elementary schools, the ability to listen to or comprehend a lengthened discourse has not been acquired. The master, accordingly, must supply his pupils simply with the facts on which he intends his reasoning to be based, and must lead them to draw the inferences from these facts. For this purpose he must make large use of analogy and illustration. Whenever a term is employed with which the pupils are not familiar, it must be clearly explained, and in the case of illustrations, he must always employ a known thing to illustrate an unknown. Unless this be attended to, no real progress can be made. The illustration must, in all cases, be from a familiar subject to one which is not so familiar. Thus, to illustrate the fact that air exerts a pressure, the case of the boy's sucker may be employed. This is a thing with which children are generally well acquainted, and the introduction of such an illustration will give the lesson a vividness and a naturalness, which it

might not otherwise possess. Analogies, in like manner, should be real and not apparent. Thus, in conducting a lesson on the circulation of the blood, recourse may be had for illustration to the mode by which a town is supplied with water. We have, in both cases, the great central reservoir, constantly sending off a fresh supply of the precious fluid ; and in both we have the means of conveying away the fluid when it has served its purpose. The teacher should constantly endeavor to set before his pupils a distinct mental picture of the subject of which he treats; and, for this purpose, should press into his service every possible aid. Illustrations, analogies, pictures, drawings on the blackboard, &c., should be all employed to render the lesson graphic and interesting; for, unless it be made interesting and life-like, it will assuredly be a failure. While, therefore, in conducting any lesson, the teacher must attend to his manner, must modulate aright the tones of his voice, and must use appropriate gestures, he must not forget that all these things are but means to an end; and that, while in these respects the lesson may be faultless, it may still fail in making any impression on the scholars, simply because it was not interesting to them.

12. The remark with which we concluded last paragraph, furnishes one of the test which the teacher should employ in judging of the success with which he has conducted any lesson. In ordinary circumstances the teacher has nothing to guide him in this respect but the effect which the lesson is seen to produce. But the very fact of his isolation renders it incumbent on the conscientious teacher to adopt tests, whereby he may judge of the practical success of his teaching. In oral lessons, the life and interest displayed by the pupils will generally be a sure index to the ability and skill, or the reverse, with which the master conducts the lesson. Whenever, accordingly, he finds the pupils listless, dull, and restless, he may rest assured that he has failed to secure their interest, which is the first requisite in all teaching. After every oral lesson he should ask himself, not what stores of information have I poured out since the lesson began, but how much of that information have the children received? Let him adopt it as a maxim that a lesson has never been thoroughly given until it has been received. In addition to the test of which we have spoken, the master should devote a few minutes at the close of each lesson to the questioning of individuals on the leading points brought out; occasionally, also, the pupils may be required to write out the substance of the lesson, an exercise which will at once show how much of it has been received, and to what extent it has been understood.

13. NOTES OF LESSONS.—FIRST STAGE.

Example I.—The Cow.

Introduce the subject in a simple, natural way—Ask what the children take along with their porridge—*milk.* Whence do we obtain the milk—*from the cow.* Where will the cow generally be seen—*in the fields.* What doing—*eating grass.* What does the cow generally live upon? Notice the different *colors* of the animal; and see that they know what each color is like—some are *white,* some *black,* some *spotted,* and so on. What has the cow, of which this is a picture, got upon her head? *horns.* Have all cows horns? Of what use are the *horns* to the cow? How does the dog defend himself? the horse? the cat? &c. What is the *size* of the cow? Point out some object in the room about the same height, the same length. What do you call the young of the cow—*a calf.* You have said that we obtain milk from the cow. Is the cow of any other use? When the cow is killed, what do we do with her flesh? *eat it.* What do you call the cow's flesh, when she is killed? *beef.* Where do you buy cow's flesh or—*beef? In the flesher's,* or in the—*butcher's?* Is the skin of any use? What do you wear on your feet to keep them warm? *shoes.* Who makes the shoes? *the shoemaker.* What does he make them of? *leather.* Where does he get the leather? What is it made of? Notice in the same way the uses to which the horns, the hair, the milk, &c., are put. Such a lesson as the foregoing exercises simply the observation of the children, and gives them correct terms in which to express their ideas.

Example II.—A fire.

Where do you find fires generally placed? *in the grate.* (In a country district, in which there may be few grates, a different answer would be given.) What is the fire made of? of *coals,* of *sticks,* or *peats,* as the case may be. Did you ever see any one putting on a fire? What did they do first? Were the coals placed exactly at the bottom? What was placed below them? Why were the sticks placed below? Were the sticks placed flat on the grate? How were they placed? *slanting.* Why? After the sticks were laid in, what was next done? Were the coals thrown in or laid in? What would have happened to the sticks if the coals had been thrown in? What kind of coal were placed first upon the sticks? Why small pieces, and not large? Where was the fire applied? What did the sticks then begin to do? *to burn.* And what did this do to the coals? *It kindled them.* What did you see rising from the coals? *Smoke.* And what became of the smoke? *It went up the chimney.* What then is the use of a chimney? *To carry away the smoke.* If there were no chimney, where would the smoke go? *It would fill the room.* And how would you feel when the smoke filled the room? *Sore, uncomfortable, uneasy, unpleasant.* It would not be—*nice,* or—*pleasant,* to sit in a room filled—*with smoke.* Is the fire of any use? *It warms us.* Yes, it warms you, and makes the room—*warm.* What would the fire do, if you went too near it? *It would burn us.* Little children should never meddle with—*the fire;* they should always keep away—*from it.* Various other uses might be pointed out, and other simple lessons drawn. At a somewhat more advanced stage, the most economical way of making or of kindling a fire might be pointed out, and thus even to young children might be taught the science of common things.

Example III.—The Camel.

Exhibit a picture of the animal, and then ask them such questions as the following: What animals do we employ in drawing carts, carriages, and other machines? *The horse—the ass.* You have all seen a horse; what has he got on his feet? *Shoes.* What are they made of? *Of iron.* Why does the horse require shoes? What might happen to your feet, if you went barefooted among stones and such-like things? I saw a boy, when I was coming to school, running very fast along the road, and he had no shoes on. He struck his foot against a stone, and what happened, think you? *The foot was cut.* Yes, he hurt—*his foot*, and it felt—*very sore.* Now the horse has to go on rough stony ground, and what might this do to his hoof—*it would hurt it.* *Please, sir, I saw a horse which had lost his shoe, and he was lame.* Quite so, the horse would soon become lame if he had to work without—*shoes.* Now did you ever see a camel in this country? Do any of you remember where the camel lives? Yes, in—*hot, sandy countries.* Do you think will the sand be as hard as our roads, or streets? No it will be—*soft and yielding.* Do you think then that the camel will have shoes on his feet? Whether would you walk more easily through soft sand, with your shoes off or on? *With our shoes off.* Why? In this way, by noticing the habits of the animal, and by familiar illustrations, the children will be prepared to expect a difference between the camel's foot and that of the horse. In a similar way, by describing to them the long journeys which he is obliged to take through deserts, in which there is no water, they are prepared to appreciate the full value of the remarkable provision whereby this animal deserves the appropriate name of "the ship of the desert." As already remarked, instead of commencing with the habits and uses, the teacher may begin with the structure, and thence proceed to infer the uses. In all these lessons the teacher should never fail to call the attention of the children to the goodness of God in accommodating each animal to the circumstances of its life. We shall divide the following example into two parts, the first being suitable for young children, and the second for those who are more advanced.

Example IV.—The Elephant.

FIRST STAGE.

Introduction. Form and shape. Size. Uses.

Who have seen one? where? are they to be found in our fields, like the cow? no. Where then? in Asia and Africa.

Exhibit a picture of one—note the form—the body very clumsy—rounded, and large—neck very short, with large head—tusks—trunk—eyes small—ears long—feet short and thick.

Exhibit picture of comparative sizes of animals, show its position among other creatures—then by comparison give an idea of his actual size—compared with the horse—is he larger or smaller? Give average absolute height—about 12 or 15 feet—show this height by reference to the height of ceiling—give some idea of his actual bulk by showing what part of the room he would occupy.

Give anecdotes to show his disposition—his uses to man—the mode of his capture and so on.

By means of illustrations, comparisons, and contrast, animals which the children may never have seen can thus be brought somewhat vividly before them. Assuming the foregoing facts to be known, we proceed, in the next stage, to reason, compare, and deduce conclusions from what has been observed.

SECOND STAGE.

Relation between body and legs. Relation between skin and eyes, and mode of life. Relation between head and neck.

Show if there is any connection—use of legs—a bridge for foot passengers, and one for a heavy railway train, would require what kind of pillars? Why the difference? Compare also the support of a heavy building and a light one—the legs of a child and a man. The legs must be made to support the body, their size and strength will depend what on? Now notice the remarkable fact that the legs of the elephant are verticle—like a pillar—each bone resting vertically on the one beneath it—the strongest form that could be devised. Note God's wisdom and goodness.

Either give the facts as to the skin and eyes, by showing how the first is hard and wrinkled, and the latter small and sunk, and from these facts deduce the mode of life; or, which in this case might be better, give his mode of life—living in the thick jungles of tropical forests, requiring to move among the tangled masses of undergrowth, with his huge unwieldy body, and then deduce what kind of skin and eyes would have been most suitable—a soft, easily pierced, or a hard, almost impenetrable skin—large protruding eyes, or small sunken ones. Note again the wisdom of God.

Note the head with tusks of great weight, and show how a long, tapering neck would have suited—and then observe the remarkable compensation supplied in the trunk, and the exquisite construction of this instrument so as to suit the creature's wants.

14. We subjoin a brief list of lessons suitable for the first stage of instruction. They are arranged in no given order, and are intended to indicate to the young teacher the almost inexhaustible supply of subjects of lessons. The great majority are selected from the list of those given in the Initiatory Department of the Practicing Schools of the Glasgow Free Church Training College.

Monkey,	Rose,	Linnet,	Rat,
Seal,	Gooseberry,	Lark,	Sloth,
Bear,	Cabbage,	Hen,	Horse,
Lion,	Barrow,	Swallow,	Reindeer,
Dog,	Window,	Vulture,	Eagle,
Hare,	Table,	Deer,	Thrush,
Mouse,	Bell,	Hog,	Duck,
Camel,	Chimney,	Rabbit,	Cuckoo,
Whale,	Chair,	Squirrel,	Crow,
Owl,	Clock,	Badger,	Worm,
Starling,	Cherry,	Leopard,	Moth,
Turkey,	Apple,	Bat,	Crab,
Goldfinch,	Lobster,	Hedgehog,	Strawberry,
Partridge,	Butterfly,	Cat,	Peas,
Herring,	Frog,	Weasel,	Watch,
Spider,	Elephant,	Wolf,	Sofa,
Grate,	Ass,	Carrot,	Clay,
Door,	Sheep,	Carriage,	Mortar,

Mole,	Hawk,	Stool,	Milk,
Tiger,	Pigeon,	Book,	Cheese,
Ferret,	Sparrow,	Paper,	Sponge,
Fox,	Salmon,	Glass,	Gutta Percha,
Beaver,	Oyster,	Leather,	India Rubber,
Gold,	Pear,	Grass,	Pen,
Silver,	Lead,	Leaves,	Wax,
Hair,	Tin,	Copper,	Coals,
Shilling,	Thimble,	Iron,	Stones,
Sugar,	Pin,	Scissors,	Needle,
Slates,	Honey,	Shoes,	Balloon.

The various trades might also be made the subjects of lessons—the shops in the neighborhood, and the most common domestic operations—thus :—

The making of { Tea, Bread, Butter, Cheese, Candles, Porridge, Jam, Jelly,

The Grocer's, The Baker's, The Butcher's, The Greengrocer's, The Tailor's } Shop.

The Washing of Dishes.
Scouring the Floor.

As examples of lessons of a miscellaneous character, we may subjoin the following :—

Cleanliness and neatness of Person,
Advantages of Punctuality,
Covering of Birds,
Harrowing, Ploughing, &c.,
The principle of Weaving,
Yarn and Thread.

NOTES OF LESSONS.—SECOND STAGE.

15. We have already given one specimen of notes suitable for the second stage under the head "Elephant." We may also give the following :—

Example I.—Winnowing of Corn.

Why necessary. Object of winnowing. Grain and chaff. Separated by wind. Modes of winnowing. a. *Natural. Objections to this mode.* b. *Artificial. The fanners. Construction. Winnowing defined.*

To protect the grain when growing it has a covering—chaff. As the seed of the pea is contained in a pod, and that of the cherry in a pulpy substance, so grain has a covering for its protection. This covering—this chaff—becomes mixed with the grain when it is thrashed, and requires to be separated from it before the grain is fit for use.

The chaff must be separated from the grain. We have a heap of grain and chaff combined. What we require is the grain, not the chaff. What must we therefore do? We must obtain some means of getting rid of the chaff. The chaff is light, the grain is comparatively heavy. The chaff is very easily blown away. When you pull some stalks of growing corn from the field, you rub them in your hand, and then, changing the particles from one hand to the other, you blow upon them. Why do you do so? By blowing you drive away the chaff, and leave the grain. The chaff can thus be separated from the grain by wind. Would such a plan as this suit if there was a large heap? No, it would be too tedious—would take too much time: we must therefore devise some other way.

Suppose we have a barn with two doors opposite each other—a strong wind is blowing, which causes a current of wind to pass through the barn—if we now throw up the corn, what will the current do to the chaff? It will blow it away, and the grain will fall. This plan is adopted, and was once very common; only, instead of throwing up the corn, it was put through a sieve or riddle. (Show how.)

To winnow in this way, we require to have two doors opposite each other—both open. We require also wind, but this we have not always; and even when we have wind, it might happen to be raining, and the rain would be blown in along with the wind; hence this plan is not very convenient.

If I move this book rapidly backwards and forwards before your face, what do you feel? Wind. What causes it? (Show by this, and other simple illustrations, that we can produce currents of wind artificially, and these currents may be as strong as we choose.) It is on this principle that the fanners are constructed. There is a wheel, something like the paddle-wheel of a steamboat. This wheel is turned rapidly round. Its revolution produces a strong current of wind, which is made to play upon the corn, and thus the chaff is separated from the grain.

Winnowing is separating the chaff from the grain; and is commonly effected by means of the wind artificially produced by a machine called the fanners.

Example II.—The Spider's Web.

Food of spider. How obtained. By means of its web. Web where formed. Of what formed. How formed. Spider's citadel. Dryden's description of the spider in her web.

The spider lives on flies and small insects. How do we catch flies? We might do it by the hand. The swallow catches them by its mouth, as it darts swiftly through the air. The spider has no hands, nor has it the rapidity of the swallow. How then does it obtain its food? If we wish to catch mice, what do we do? We set a trap. So the spider, *taught by instinct*, sets a trap to catch the flies on which it lives.

This trap is its web. It cunningly weaves a web with which to entrap the unwary flies, and, having entrapped them, it then feeds on them.

The house spider generally forms its web in the corners of a room or window. Why in the corners? Because it is more convenient to fix the two ends of the main threads on the corners; and on the window, because flies are more numerous there than on any other part of the house. The garden spider, for a like reason, generally forms his web among the bushes, in order to have points on which to hang it.

When we want to make a web we require threads. How does the spider obtain threads? Does it buy them, as we do, from a shop? No. The spider has in its body a gluey substance, from which it forms the web. "Nature has supplied it with a large quantity of glutinous matter within its body, and with five papillæ or teats, for spinning it into thread."

"When a house or common spider is about to form a web, it selects some commodious and secure spot, where insects appear to be in sufficient abundance.

It then distils a small drop of its glutinous liquor, which is exceedingly tenacious; and, creeping up the wall, and joining its thread as it proceeds, darts itself, in a very surprising manner, to the opposite station, where the other end of the web is to be fastened. The first thread thus spun, the spider runs on it to and fro, assiduously employed in doubling and strengthening it, as on its force depends the strength of the whole. The scaffolding being thus complete, the spider draws a number of threads parallel to the first, and then crosses them with others; the adhesive substance of which they are formed serving to bind them together when newly spun." When we make a web, we first lay thread lengthwise, then we insert others crosswise; so the spider. Having thus made the web, it covers it over with the gluey substance, that the feet of the fly may stick to it. It then spins a small house for itself, which is connected with the web, where it lurks until an unwary fly becomes entangled in its web, when it sallies forth and instantly destroys the unhappy intruder.

The treacherous spider, when her nets are spread,
  Deep ambushed in her silent den does lie,
And feels, far off, the trembling of her thread,
  Whose filmy cord should bind the struggling fly.
Then, if at last she find him fast beset,
  She issues forth and runs along her loom;
She joys to touch the captive in her net,
  And drags the little wretch in triumph home.

Example III.—The common Bat.

Description of. Belongs to the class mammalia. Its habits and mode of living. Why it exists. Adaptation to its mode of life. Senses of hearing and touch acute. Flies lightly. Can live on a small amount of food. In winter becomes torpid.

About the size of a mouse, and somewhat similar in appearance—has long ears, small eyes, four feet, and a covering of soft, darkish-colored hair, tipped with red. Feet five toed. Each of the fore feet has the inner toe loose from the others, and furnished with a hooked claw; the other four are enveloped in a thin, loose membrane, extending over all the body except the head, which, when the toes are spread, form the animal's wings. Toes of hind feet have hooked claws—mouth provided with teeth.

For a long time it was reckoned a bird; but it must be ranked among the mammalia, as it brings forth its young alive, suckles them, and has lungs like those of quadrupeds.

It makes its abode in holes of trees, caves, old ruins, etc.—is seen only during fine, calm evenings of summer and early autumn. Why? Its food consists of small nocturnal insects. It can not support itself on the wing for more than an hour at a time. Why? Owing to the delicacy of its wings. It builds no nest. Why? It can not easily raise itself when resting on its feet. It hangs by its hooked claws to the side of its hole, and in that position suckles its young. It passes the most of its time asleep. On the approach of cold weather, becomes torpid, and remains hanging to the side of its hole.

During the day many birds are clearing the air of noxious insects, but as evening comes on, they retire to rest. Many noxious insects fly only during evening and night; these are preyed on by the bat.

Most nocturnal animals are provided with large eyes. Train out why? The bat has small eyes; therefore must be adapted for finding its food in the dusk by some other means. What are these? It senses of hearing and touch are very acute. Train out how the delicacy of these senses enables the bat to find its food. Noise made by the insects, and the vibration of the air.

To prevent the insects being scared by the flight of the bat, it flies very lightly, and without noise.

But the delicacy of its wings renders it unfit to fly long at a time; it must therefore be enabled to live on a small amount of food. It is so—and how?

It sleeps most of its time; and in winter and spring, when there is no food for it, it is torpid. GOD'S WISDOM AND GOODNESS.

Example IV.—Reaping of Corn.

Corn when ripe is cut by the hook or scythe. Mode of cutting. Effect of wind. Effect of rain. When cut it is put in stooks. Why? The stack yard.

When reaped—why not in summer, when the corn is green? It must be allowed to ripen to render the grain of any use. No fruit or grain is of much service until it is ripe—an apple—the potato—wheat, &c. Grain is ripe in autumn. How does the farmer know when it is ripe?—by its color and by the firmness of the grain, &c. When ripe he cuts it. Why not pluck it?—it would be difficult—it would cause much earth to mingle with it, which would be difficult to remove again. Sand is not very nice in bread or porridge; and the farmer keeps as much of the sand out as he can. Does he cut it with a knife, as you would a stick?—no. Why not?—it would take him too long time. What then does he use?—he uses either a hook or a scythe. Show how they are shaped, and why. If he uses a hook, does he work it as he would a scythe? no. Show how the reaper uses the hook—catches a handful of corn in his left hand, and cuts with the right. When using the scythe, does the farmer catch the corn with one of his hands?—why not?—what enables the scythe to cut through?—why does he cut it close to the ground?

If wind was blowing, would the farmer cut with or against the wind? What wind most favorable? Why would not the farmer cut in a very high wind?—why not in a wet, rainy day? What effect would the rain have on the cut corn?—hence what day most suitable for harvest operations?—a dry day, with a moderate wind blowing.

When the corn is cut, does the farmer leave it lying on the ground? What does he do?—he binds it into sheaves, and puts it into stooks—the shape of the stooks. What is the object of so putting it in stooks? Bring out that when uncut, even though ripe, the stalks had sap in them, and that if they were tied up in sheaves, and built in the stack-yard, they might rot. Why? Hence the grain is left in the field until it is quite dry.

What is then done with it?—it is built into stacks—their shape—why sometimes raised from the ground, and hollow inside.

Example V.—Why do we Water our Streets in Summer?

State of streets in hot weather. Water cools the streets. Water cools the air. Effects of watering our streets.

In summer, if the weather is hot, what happens to our streets?—they become parched, filled with dust, and very disagreeable. The dust, moreover, is injurious to our clothes, and to goods in shops, where the doors require to be open. Show how penetrating is the dust. How may we allay it?—by sprinkling water on the streets, just as a servant sprinkles tea leaves on the carpet before beginning to sweep it. The sprinkling of water thus keeps down the dust.

It does more. On a hot summer day, when the sun is shining, how do you feel if walking along the street?—very warm. Which side of the street do you walk on?—on the side sheltered from the sun. Why?—it is cooler and more pleasant. How do the stones feel?—hot—and they radiate that heat to the atmosphere, which also becomes hot, parched, and disagreeable. Sprinkling water on the streets not only keeps down the dust, it cools the streets.

It does more. What becomes of the water thus sprinkled?—it evaporates—passes off in the form of vapor. What causes it so to do?—heat. Heat is the cause of evaporation; but whence does the water obtain this heat? If you place your hand on a piece of iron or brass, how does your hand feel?—cold. Why?—the iron or brass abstracts the heat from the hand—the heat passes from your hand into the iron, which is in contact with it. So here, the warm, heated air is every where around the water—the heat passes from it into the water, and so causes it to evaporate. But will the air, having thus parted with a portion of its heat, be warmer or colder than before?—colder. It will be cooled.

The watering of our streets not only keeps down the dust, but it also cools the streets and the air, and makes it more pleasant for people to move about.

Example VI.—The Duck.

Form and shape. Its mode of life determines the kind of covering, the supply of oil, the position of legs and kind of feet, and the bill. Uses.

The Duck is about the size of a hen—about 23 inches in length—35 in girth—and weighs about 2½ lbs. Exhibit picture of—has two legs, placed pretty far back—effect of this—too much weight in front—hence when walking how does it appear? *Clumsy.* Covered with feathers—bill—eyes, &c.

Aquatic—picture out the term—lives partly on water, partly on land. Feeds on insects, grubs, and grain. Trace the connection that subsists between its living in water and its covering—what might the water do—make it cold—hence what? A thick downy covering—where? On those parts which are most exposed to the water, *i. e.* on breast and belly—note the wisdom in this—specific provision for a specific want.

Again what does water do to the feathers—ruffles them—now what may you observe ducks doing on a rainy day?—picking and dressing their feathers. Note the oil—compare it in this respect with a *droukit* hen—again a specific provision for a specific want.

Compare legs with those of the hen—what difference?—shorter. Why? Long legs would interfere with its motion when swimming. Compare feet with those of the hen—they are webbed—why? Show how it uses them. Bring out at this point the reason why the legs are placed far back—illustration—in driving a boat are the oars exactly in the middle—why? Again a greater weight in front enables the animal to plunge its head more easily beneath the water.

Compare its bill with that of hen—what difference do you observe—the duck's is shaped like a spoon—why? Show the nature of its nostrils, which act like a sieve in separating the food from the mud—the tongue also is very broad.

Eggs—Feathers—Flesh.

Example VII.—The Nests of Birds.

HEADS.—1. The use of the nest.
2. When formed.

3. What determines the situation.
4. What determines the material.
5. What determines the size.
6. Particular examples.
   a. The thrush.
   b. The lark.
   c. The eagle.

Example VIII.—The making of Grain into Meal.

HEADS.—1. Why grain requires to be ground.
2. The process.
   a. The drying—its object.
   b. The separation of the husk.
   c. The sifting.
   d. The grinding.

16. All the subjects given under the first stage may very appropriately be gone over in the second, somewhat in the manner indicated in the example "The Duck." The various parts of the animal —their relations to one another—the structure, and the connection between it and the habits and modes of life, may be thus exhibited more fully than was possible in the first stage; and the lessons thus made the means of communicating much useful information, and of developing the faculty of observation and the power of deducing simple but very important inferences. In addition, however, to the list of lessons already given, we may subjoin as specimens the following:—

The eye—its position and protection.
The manufacture of salt from sea-water.
The manufacture of wool into thread.
The common pump.
The thrashing of corn.
What is smoke—how may it be consumed.
Comparison between hen and duck.
Comparison between cat and dog.
Comparison between lion and tiger.
Comparison between elephant and camelopard, &c.
Glass—of what composed and how manufactured.
Paper—how and from what manufactured.
Tears—their nature and use.
What ought to be the exposure of our gardens.
How to prepare good tea.
Why does a gardener cover his flower-beds with matting in a clear calm night.
What kind of clothing should we wear in winter?
The evil effects of tight lacing—of tight boots, &c.
The beaks of birds—why difference in?
Which is warmer—a sheet or blanket.

The preceding examples will indicate to the young teacher the wide field from which he may cull the subjects of oral lessons.

NOTES OF LESSONS.—STAGE THIRD.

17. In regard to the class of lessons suitable for the third stage we beg to refer the reader to paragraph 7. The train of reasoning is considerably longer in the following specimens than in any of those previously given.

Example I.—The Thermometer.

Meaning of word. Various modes of determining the amount of heat. Effects of heat constant. Expansion furnishes measure of heat. Expansion of liquids most suitable. Mercury commonly employed. Glass Tube. How graduated. The Scale. Centigrade. Fahrenheit's. Reaumur's. How reduced to the same standard.

Means *heat-measure*, an instrument for measuring the quantity of heat in any given substance.

There are various modes of determining the amount of heat, e. g. *the sense of touch;* this is variable in different individuals, and in the same individual in different states of the body. What is warm to one may be cold to another, and *vice versa;* this consequently would not suit—so of other modes.

The effects of heat under given circumstances are constant for all places; one of its effects is expansion. Heat expands bodies, and that uniformly in all countries, according to the amount of it. *Expansion may consequently be assumed as a measure of heat.*

Solids expand under heat, but not to such an extent as to be easily appreciable. Gases expand too much to be conveniently employed. Liquids expand not so much as gases, but more than solids, and more uniformly than either. *Hence the expansion of liquids is employed as the measure of heat.*

Mercury expands very uniformly, and is most commonly employed; and *by observing its expansion and contraction, we have a sufficiently accurate measure of heat.*

For convenience sake, the mercury is confined in a tube, containing a bulb at one extremity, and closed at the other—*tube made of glass*—why? (Exhibit model, or draw one on blackboard.) Show how the tube is formed.

To enable us to read off the different amounts of heat in any substance at different times, the tube *has a scale fixed to it*—how formed? Two points are selected as the extremes, these points are the freezing and boiling points of water—plunge the tube into water when in the act of freezing, and mark where the mercury stands in the tube, (mark it on your drawing,) and you have the freezing point. Again, plunge it into water when boiling, mark where the mercury stands, and you have the boiling point. Call these two points any numbers you choose, say, 0 and 100; divide in this case the intermediate space into 100 equal parts, and *you have the scale.* These equal spaces are called degrees.

Such a Thermometer is called the *Centigrade*—why? *centum* and *gradus.*

The one generally used in this country *is called Fahrenheit's*—why? In it the freezing point of water is marked as 32, and the boiling point as 212. The intermediate space is divided into 212—32=180 equal spaces or degrees. Show why Fahrenheit employed these numbers.

Another one, *called Reaumur's,* has the two points fixed at 0 and 80 respectively.

It is easy to *reduce them to the same standard*, thus, the distance between the two fixed points in the Centigrade is 100, and in Fahrenheit's is 180. They are to one another as 100 to 180, or as 5 to 9, and so with Reaumur's, &c.

Example II.—The Barometer.

Meaning of word. How constructed. Pressure of atmosphere varies Scale. Connection between atmospheric pressure and weather. Connection between atmospheric pressure and height. Marks on common barometer.

Is an instrument for measuring the weight or pressure of the air.

Take a glass tube, closed at one end, open at the other, fill it with a liquid, say mercury, put your finger on the open end, reverse it, and plunge the open end into a vessel containing mercury, taking care that no air gets into the tube. Suppose the tube to be 33 or 34 inches in length, will all the mercury in the tube sink down into the vessel? No. Why not? The pressure of the air on the surface of the mercury in the vessel supports the mercury in the tube. What height of mercury will the atmosphere in ordinary circumstances sustain? About 30 inches. In this case, therefore, we have a space of about 3 or 4 inches above the mercury in which there is no air. (Bring out this point clearly.)

The atmosphere does not in all circumstances exert the same pressure. Sometimes the pressure is greater—sometimes it is less. When the pressure increases will it support more or less mercury? Whether, therefore, will the mercury rise or fall—and so when the pressure is less. Thus, the rise or fall of the mercury in the tube is an index to the pressure of the atmosphere at any given time or place. To enable us to read off the difference of pressure thus exhibited, a scale is attached to the barometer. As the mercury in this country never sinks, at the sea level, below 27, or rises above 31, it is not necessary to have more than these marked on the scale. Where the instrument, however, is employed for meteorological purposes, the scale must descend much lower.

Bring out the connection between atmospheric pressure and the state of the weather. When the weather is good, the pressure is greater than when the weather is bad; hence the mercury will stand higher in good than in bad weather. Before a storm the mercury sinks rapidly; hence it is used to indicate the weather; is called a weather-glass. Show its use to the farmer, the sailor, &c.

Show, also, that as we ascend, the pressure of the atmosphere becomes less, and the mercury sinks; hence it is used as a means of determining heights.

Explain the terms which are marked on the common wheel barometer. Show how unsafe it is to trust to them—they often indicate the very opposite of what actually happens.

Example III.—Dew.

Watery vapor. The earth a good radiator. Radiation cools the surface of the earth. Dew formed. Application.

The atmosphere always contains a certain amount of watery vapor. Its capacity for vapor depends on its heat. Cool the atmosphere it will contain less —increase its heat, it will contain more vapor.

The earth, during the day, when the sun is shining, absorbs a large amount of heat. In the evening, when the sun has set, the earth radiates its heat very rapidly. This radiation soon cools its surface. The air coming in contact with this cooled surface, parts with its caloric to the earth. Its temperature is thus reduced, and, as a consequence, its capacity for watery vapor is diminished.

The vapor it contains is condensed, and is deposited in the form of dew. Illustrate by bringing a cold bottle into a warm room. What happens? The moisture inside the window of a warm room, when it is cold without, &c.

If this be so, where will dew be most readily and most profusely formed? On those substances which radiate heat. Such is the fact. How can you stop the formation of dew? By stopping the radiation. Show how gardeners take advantage of this. Will there be more dew on a clear than on a cloudy night? Why on a clear night?

Example IV.—The Land and Sea Breeze.

Introduction. Land a better absorber of heat than water. Effects produced by its greater absorbing power. Land a better radiator than water. Effects of this. Cause of these breezes.

You have been by the sea-shore—you have been at the bathing. In what direction did you observe the wind blowing in the middle of the day? To the land—from the sea to the land. In the evening, when the sun had set, and when the ground began to cool, in what direction did the wind blow? From the land to the sea.

Bring out clearly the fact that the earth is a better absorber of heat than the sea—that the temperature of the sea remains in all places and at all times far more equable than that of the land. In bathing on a hot day, you must have felt the water cold, and the sand and rocks on the sea-shore almost insufferable hot.

When the sun has risen to some height in the heavens, the earth rapidly absorbs his heating rays, and so becomes warm. The air coming in contact with this heated surface, becomes also heated, is rarefied, and its equilibrium destroyed. How can the equilibrium be restored?—by the accession of cold currents—whence will these come? The sea does not absorb heat so rapidly as the land—its temperature remains more uniform—hence, while the air, resting on the land, is heated and rarefied, that on the sea remains *cold* in comparison—accordingly the cold air from the sea will flow in upon the land to restore the equilibrium.

Again, the earth not only absorbs rapidly, it also radiates its heat very quickly—it parts with it far more rapidly than the sea. Hence, when the sun has set, the earth cools rapidly—becomes colder than the neighboring sea. The air resting on the land partakes of this coldness; and being thus denser than the air resting on the sea, flows in upon the sea, until an equilibrium is restored.

The land and sea breeze is thus produced by the different absorbing and radiating powers of the land and water.

Example V.—Why does Ice float?

Heat expands bodies. Effect of this. Cold contracts, and so renders bodies specifically heavier. We would expect ice to sink. What would happen if ice sunk. Ice floats. Why? The law of contraction is arrested. Wisdom.

Heat expands bodies, and makes them specifically lighter; when, if liquids, they rise to the surface and float. The part of a substance that is lightest floats—thus the cream on milk—the dross in the process of refining, &c.

Cold, on the other hand, as a rule, contracts bodies, and so renders them specifically heavier. Ice is produced by cold, or by the abstraction of heat; and if water continued to contract during the whole process of congelation, the ice, when formed, would be specifically heavier than the under-lying water, and would sink to the bottom. If the cold still continued, a new layer of ice would be formed on the surface, and when formed it would also sink; and so on, layer after layer would form and sink, so long as the cold was sufficient to freeze the water.

Picture out the consequences of this, especially in high latitudes—the rivers and lakes would become one mass of ice, which all the heat of summer would not melt; all life would die, and these part of the earth would become a dreary, icy solitude.

But ice, when formed, does not sink—it floats on the surface of water, like cream on milk, or dross—hence it must be lighter than the under-lying water; but to make it lighter what must have taken place in the process of its formation?—it must have expanded. Here state the remarkable fact, that when water has cooled down to $39\frac{1}{2}^{\circ}$ F., the contracting process is suddenly arrested, and it begins to expand, and continues to expand until it forms into ice—supposed to be owing to the mode in which the crystals of ice arrange themselves.

But whatever the cause of the expansion, the beneficial effects of it are evident enough, and furnish a striking proof of the wisdom and goodness of the all-wise God.

Example VI.—Application of the foregoing Lesson.

HEADS.—1. *a.* Why do water pipes frequently burst in frost?
b. How may this be prevented?
2. Danger of allowing water in winter to get into chinks, etc., of buildings. Why?
3. Show how the principle may account for many of the convulsions of nature.

Example VII.—Locality often determines Custom.

Egypt, its physical features, etc. Seat of empire. Objects of worship. Every people respect their dead. The soil of Egypt unfit for burying in.—Why?—And results of. Entombing in rocks—first results of. Embalming—character of determined by the Egyptian's belief.

Egypt—a long valley formed by opposite ranges of mountains; the river Nile flowing between. Soil naturally dry and sandy. Climate dry and hot—rain seldom falling—its vegetation depending chiefly on the Nile overflowing its banks, thus moistening the soil, and leaving a covering of mud. Its mountains abound with caves, wherein the hyena, jackal, and many other beasts of prey, have their abodes.

Was early, and for a long time, the seat of a great empire. Mention their idolatry—some of the objects of their worship. Many of the native animals, which they embalmed and kept in their temples.

Every people pay great respect to their dead. The Egyptians did so especially. Refer to their belief in the transmigration of souls. The soil, because of its sandy nature, and owing to the dryness of the atmosphere, and prevalent winds, was unfit for the burial of the dead. Why? Wind obliterates the marks of the graves—the hyena and jackal could easily dig up the dead bodies. How the Egyptians would be horrified. Even near cities, which were planted near the Nile, the graves would be obliterated by the mud deposited by the Nile when it overflowed its banks. How would this affect the Egyptians? Set them to find out places of security for their dead. Where could they turn? On either hand mountains looked down on them, displaying caves—lay them there.

They did so. The result—in a few days they could not enter them. Why? the effluvia arising from decomposition caused by the heat of the atmosphere. What then? They must dispose of their dead; and they desired to have them safe, and free from disgusting sights and smells. What then? They knew how to preserve the animals they worshiped—do so with their dead relatives—hence embalming. Train out why they laid out such expenses on embalming—their belief in transmigration of souls. Thus explain the murmuring of the Israelites when Pharaoh's host was behind, the Red Sea in front, and high mountains on either side of them. "Because there were no graves in Egypt, hast thou taken us to die in the wilderness?"—*Exodus* c. xiv. v. 11.

Example VII.—Rice.

Conditions necessary to its growth. Air and light. Heat. Moisture. Where fulfilled Natural region of rice. Mode of culture. Nature of fruit. Nations who live on rice. How prepared for food.

Assume as known the general fact that vegetables require light, air, heat and moisture. In all parts of the earth the first two conditions are fulfilled, and, in so far as they are concerned, all plants might grow every where. But in addition to air and light, rice requires a certain amount of heat and moisture.

It will not thrive well unless there be a summer temperature of at least 73°4 of Fahrenheit. This at once fixes its locality to a certain extent. (Mark off on the map the countries which have this temperature—*i. e.* those lying about 40° on each side of the equator, more or less according to those circumstances which determine climate.)

But even within these limits it will not grow every where—*e. g.* not generally in the west of Asia, in Persia, Arabia, &c. Why? Because, although there is a sufficient amount of heat, there is not sufficient moisture. A great abundance of water is necessary to its growth. This is found in the S. E. of Asia, the Indian Peninsulas, China, Japan, United States, Italy, and certain parts of Africa —hence the rice will grow in these districts.

We have thus the habitat of rice—but even in the districts mentioned, where we have all the conditions specified, rice will grow in certain quarters better than in others. Bring out the fact that each plant has a natural locality, where it flourishes best.

Show how it requires to be covered with water—where the rivers do not naturally overflow their banks, and how is this done? By irrigation. Refer to the vale of Lombardy and the Po. Picture out the scene. Show how long it remains under water—in the ground—mode of reaping, &c.

It produces a greater return in proportion to the ground under cultivation than any other grain, but this is counterbalanced by the fact that it contains a larger amount of starch and a less amount of gluten than any other grain—consequently, bulk for bulk—it is less stimulating and nutritious. It is also destitute of fatty substances, so that, like all substances consisting chiefly of starch, it is not well fitted, if used alone, to support life, although it is very advantageous and economical when forming a portion of the food of man.

What nations live on rice—what is, in general, their disposition? Can you trace any connection between their soft, dull, phlegmatic temperament, and the food on which they live.

This part would, of course, be given to girls—our fair readers can easily supply the necessary notes.

Example IX.—The Cotton Plant.

HEADS.—1. Conditions necessary to its growth.
2. Where fulfilled.
3. How grown.
4. How prepared for manufacture.
5. Its importance to Britain, and the desirableness of having a supply from our own Colonies.
6. In which of them might it be profitably cultivated.

Example X.—Oceanic Currents.

HEADS.—1. Effects of heat on waters of the ocean.
2. Effect of earth's diurnal revolution.
3. Combined effects of these two influences.
4. Effects of interposition of masses of land, &c.
5. Trace these various effects in one known current.

18. We have already, in the chapter on Geography, given a list of subjects suitable for oral lessons in the third stage. Similar lessons should be given on the various points of natural science. We shall specify a few as mere examples.

Lessons on HEAT—
Communication of heat.
Conduction of heat.
Radiation of heat.
What bodies radiate best?
Distribution of heat.
How may heat be distributed?
Absorption of heat.
What kind of clothes most suitable for summer and winter wear?
Expansion and contraction.
Thermometer.
Liquefaction.
Vaporation.
Elasticity of steam—Steam Engine.

Lessons on MECHANICS—
Levers—Practical examples of.
Wheel and axle.
Pulleys—Advantages of.
Inclined Plane } Practical examples of.
Wedge }
Screw }

Lessons on PNEUMATICS—
Elasticity of Air.
Pressure of Atmosphere.
Air Pump—Common Pump—Forcing Pump.
Fire Engine, &c.
Philosophy of draughts—evil effects of—prevention, &c.

Lessons on OPTICS—

Reflection and Refraction of light.
Description of the eye—use of spectacles, &c.
Telescope—Microscope—Magic Lantern, &c.

As examples of lessons of a miscellaneous description, we may subjoin the following:—

Ventilation—of private dwellings—public buildings, &c.
Evils of bad ventilation—dry rot—fire damp, &c.
Why is it dangerous to drink cold water when the body is much heated?
Why is it dangerous to bathe when the body is much heated?
The circulation of the blood.
The connection between health and a constant supply of pure air.
Where ought a bed to be placed—near the floor or at some distance from it.

The earnest teacher can easily find subjects of lessons suitable for every stage of progress. The more common the objects are, the better, as they will thus appeal more directly to the interest of the children, and will tend to make them acquainted with the concerns of every-day life.

III. SPECIMEN NOTES OF LESSONS

FOR COLLECTIVE OR GALLERY TEACHING.

Notes of Lessons, or the orderly preparation and arrangement of the material for a Collective or Gallery Lesson, is now one of the most important elements of school-keeping in the best schools of Great Britain. Its introduction first into Infant Schools, and subsequently into Elementary Schools of every grade. is gradually revolutionizing both the subject matter of lessons and the manner of giving them. It has given a practical importance to the discussion of method, which, till recently, was scarcely recognized in the pedagogical literature of England. The following hints and sketches are selected as specimens of the manner in which the teacher may prepare his notes for a Collective Lesson :—

THE PALM TREE.

It *waved* not through an *Eastern* sky,
Beside a fount of *Araby;*
It was not *fanned* by *Southern* breeze
In some *green Isle* of *Indian* seas;
Nor did its graceful *shadow* sleep,
O'er stream of *Afric lone* and deep.—Mrs. Hemans.

Analysis.

1. Show that *palm* is named from the likeness of its leaves to a man's hand. The word *date* is connected with *dactyle*, a finger, from the shape of that *fruit*.

2. *Eastern*, same as *Oriental*—*Western*, *Occidental*.

3. *Araby*, *Indian* isles, and *Afric* are the native lands or *habitats* of the palm. It is here *exotic*—there, *indigenous*.

4. *Waved* and *fanned* imply gentle winds; while sleeping of the shadow implies a calm.

5. *Green*, Saxon word for *verdant*—"the green" shows it a noun; here it is an adjective.

6. *Isle* is the same as Gælic *Inch* or *Innis* in Inchkeith, Innismore; also same as *island*, from Latin *insula*. Islet a diminutive, meaning a little isle.

7. *Lone* tells that some parts are but thinly peopled.

8. Connect shadow with shade; southern, south—ful, full—stream, streamlet —fount, fountain—fan, fanners—Afric and African—showing the force of the terminations.

PENS.

I. Ancient Pens.

Pens, in olden times, were of two kinds, *iron styles* and the *reed*,—the former was chiefly used for writing on waxed tables, the latter for writing on papyrus with a fluid ink. The reed in size resembled a small round cane or swan's quill. They were obtained from Egypt, Cairo in Asia Minor, and Armenia. Reeds may be obtained around the Persian Gulf, from whence numbers are sent to the east, where they are cut and buried under dung-hills, till they become of a black and yellow color. When ready for use they are *hard*, the *pith* in the inside having been dried up by the heat of the earth, so as to be easily extracted, and so permit the ink to ascend the barrel. The Arabs use reed pens, as they are better than either quill or steel pens, for the formation of their letters.

1. Quill pens, as their name implies, are made from quills got from the goose, swan, crow, and sometimes from the ostrich and turkey; these pens are not in so much demand as they were formerly. The countries from which we get quills, are Russia, Poland, Germany, and the Netherlands. When quills were in good demand, England obtained 27,000,000 of quills in one year from St. Petersburgh. Each wing produces *five* quills, each goose in one year produces *twenty* quills, (because pulled twice.) The second and third quills are the best.

2. Quills, when pulled, are covered with a membrane (soft substance,) are also soft from the oil which they contain, have likewise a soft membrane inside the barrel. By putting the quills into hot sand the outer membrane cracks and is scraped off with a sharp scraper, the inner membrane dries up, and can be easily drawn out, and the oily part is also dried up, and the quills are hard and transparent. By being put into boiling water they are rendered still harder, and are ready for sending off. They are tied up in small bundles and sent to stationers, who sell them to those who wish to use them. The end of the barrel is then cut off, and the barrel is split up by a knife, making each side which forms the pen of an equal length.

Some quill pens are made in the same shape as steel pens, viz., the barrel of the quill is split into two parts, which are fixed in a groove, the edges are then smoothed with a plane, each part is then cut up into three or four smaller parts, which are put into a small cutting press. The knife then makes them ready for use. The ends of some of these pens are tipped with gold, silver, horn, &c., to make them more durable.

II. Modern Pens.

1. The pens chiefly in use in this country since 1803 (when Mr. Wise made steel pens which were fixed in bone cases, so as to be carried in the pocket,) are steel pens. The first kind of steel pens were very costly and did not become very general. Mr. Gillott of Birmingham improved them by using better steel, thinner and more elastic, the slit was made shorter, and the finish and quality of the pen was altogether superior. A gross of this last kind cost little more than *one single pen* of the former. Messrs. Gillott and Perry brought the first kind of steel pen to its present form and make. Other kinds of pens were made, as the *oblique* and *three nibbed slit pens;* but these are not now in use.

2. The steel for making pens is rolled at Sheffield into thin plates; these are cut into slips *four* inches broad, and *three* feet long, and heated; the scales are removed by being placed in oil of vitrol; the strips are rolled again to their proper thickness. Girls are employed to cut the strips into small pieces called *blanks* or *flats*, in the direction of the grain of the steel. The *hole* at the end of the slit is then pierced and the pen smoothed, after which the blanks are again heated and the maker's name stamped on them, (the blanks still being flat.) They are passed to men who make them concave for *nib pens*, and form the barrel for *barrel pens*, by means of a small press; they are then put into a muffle, and heated red hot, and then cooled in oil, which is removed by being moved

about in a tin-plate barrel. They are next tempered and then placed in a revolving cylinder with sand, in order to *brighten* them. The *nib* is next ground with great rapidity by a little girl who picks up each pen by small plyers, and finishes them by a touch on a wheel of emery. The *slit* is next made by a small chisel upon the bed of a press which has a chisel corresponding with the other. The pens are then *colored* brown or blue by placing them in a revolving metal cylinder, over a charcoal stove. The pens are made *brilliant* by being placed in a solution of *lac* in *naptha.* Pens are made at Birmingham.

ROADS.

This Lesson is intended for the upper classes in an Elementary School, containing boys from 12 to 14 years old.

INTRODUCTION.

"Picture out" a desert scene.—An *Eastern Caravan roaming* over the thirsty plain (aided by the patient camel.) Notice difficulty and danger of such a journey (from shifting of sand,) TRACKS SOON INVISIBLE (guided as on sea only by sun and stars.) Supposing the nature of the country admitted, how could these dangers be avoided? (*By road making.*)

I. HISTORY.

At first, forefathers in Asia Minor *content to ramble over plains on camels* (no beaten path.) In *more fertile climes* obliged to *cut narrow paths* (through *woods*, over *mountains*,) &c. *As traffic increased* (these *made wider* and more *durable.*) About this time the *Babylonians*, *Egyptians*, and *Carthaginians* had much improved. These latter *instructed* the *Romans*, whose roads in time became *superior* to *any.* They built,

a. MILITARY ROADS, devoted exclusively to State purposes (principally for the soldiery.)

b. COMMERCIAL ROADS; distinct from the former (devoted to trade and commerce.)

c. BYE-ROADS, or branches from the main or principal roads.

After the conquest of Britain by the Romans it was intersected by roads, or streets, as they termed them, (such as Watling street, Akerma street, &c.)

Some of our roads are founded on the old Roman Works (especially in Kent, Middlesex, Bucks, Lincoln, and Northumberland.)

Recapitulation.—Here all the words in italics should be entered on the blackboard, a map referred to; and great attention given to spelling the words in capitals. Etymology of *street*, *invisible*, *durable.*

II. CONSTRUCTION.

Ròman roads, *straight*, leading direct from station to station (taking *nearest route*—used in their construction *Roman cement* and pieces of *granite*—(this very durable) one now at Lyons, 600 years old, in excellent condition.

In *England circuitous* (thus joining towns that would otherwise be remote from the COMMERCIAL WORLD.) *Improved* by *McAdam* and *Telford*, who cut stones to weight of 6 oz. each, used no CEMENT, but formed solid mass of itself.

London streets excellently paved in some parts with *Aberdeen granite.* Commercial road from Whitechapel to West India Docks, one of the finest in England. Most durable from King William street to London Bridge. Cost of, £2,000.

Wood has been given a trial (but in wet weather, and especially during frost is *too slippery* to come into general use.) Reason why wood adopted (to *diminish* the *noise.*)

In most countries roads are formed by the Government (in England by the people,) a consequence, (more numerous and regularly attended to.)

Recapitulation.—See last note on Recapitulation. The words "circuitous," "station," "diminish," should be *particularly* noticed, as to their *meaning*, *orthography*, and *etymology*.

III. USES.

Endeavor to draw from the class that *blood is carried over the body* by the VEINS and ARTERIES. Compare these with the *roads* of a *country*; and trade, learning, and CIVILIZATION with the blood. (They render the inhabitants of a country far more *accessible* than they would otherwise be, just as the Romans in Britain.

This may be illustrated by the *Allied Armies* in the *Crimea*—transport of material from *Balaklava* to "the *Hights*" since the improvements in the roads.

Recapitulaiion.—Etymologies—arteries, civilization, accessible, transport.

N. B.—(1.) The words enclosed in parenthesis ( ) are those to be drawn from the class—others to be taught.

(2.) Words in italics are those to be written on the blackboard, so as to present to the class an outline of the whole.

(3.) Words in capitals are principally characteristic, and should be spelt individually and simultaneously.

BLACKBOARD OUTLINE.—ROADS.

Introduction.—Eastern Caravan roaming on plain—tracks invisible—danger—avoided by roads (if possible to make them.)

I. *History.*—At first content to ramble on plains—camels—no path. Fertile climes—narrow path; traffic increases, wider and more durable. Babylonians, Carthaginians, Romans. Military, Commercial, and Bye roads.

II. *Construction.*—Roman roads—cement and granite—straight: English roads—circuitous—McAdam and Telford—London streets—Aberdeen granite—wood—too slippery—diminish noise.

III. *Uses.*—Roads of countries similar to veins and arteries of human body—conveying learning and civilization—inhabitants accessible—armies in Crimea—Balaklava and Hights.

WEEKLY EXPENDITURE OF A LABORING MAN—FOOD.

[The following Notes of a Lesson gained one of the prizes offered to the students at Whitelands, by Miss Burdett Coutts.]

I. General Introduction of the Subject.

The children will be told to picture to themselves a cottage in the country (Lancashire) surrounded by a garden, and inhabited by a poor laborer, whose family consists of himself, his wife, and four children. The eldest girl assists her mother and nurses the baby. The two boys attend school. The father's weekly wages are 12*s*. The mother earns 2*s*. 6*d*. a week by going to wash and clean at the neigboring squire's. The eldest boy earns 2*d*. a week by fetching the squire's letters from the post. The children will then mention the probable produce of the garden, which ought to afford sufficient vegetables for home consumption. The rent is paid from the extra wages obtained in harvest and hay seasons. The laborer keeps a pig, the original cost of which was 18s. During the summer the pig feeds upon the refuse of the garden, the wash from the squire's, and acorns from the wood. In the winter on barley meal, &c.

When killed, the prime parts are sold, and bring in weekly 4*d.* gain, besides discharging the previous cost, 18*s.*, and the £2 for fattening. The remainder of the pork is kept for food. The laborer's weekly income is therefore 15*s.* in all.

II. The Weekly Expenditure in Food, &c.

2½ pecks of flour,	5*s.*	8*d.*
2 lbs. of fresh meat,	1	0
Yeast,	0	1½
2 oz. of tea,	0	6
1 lb. of sugar,	0	4
1 pint of milk a day,	0	7
1 " oatmeal,	0	1
1 lb. of butter,	1	0
1 " cheese,	0	6
1 " rice,	0	2
1 pint of peas,	0	2
Pepper, salt, &c.,	0	1
½ lb. of soap,	0	3
½ " candles,	0	3
1 cwt. of coals (Lancashire,)	0	8
Sick club,	0	1
Schooling for the two boys,	0	3
	11	8½

Here we see the weekly expenditure in food, &c., would be less 11*s.* 8½*d*; this taken from 15s. leaves 3*s.* 3½*d.* for clothing.

III. Useful Hints on Expenditure.

The children will here be told to suppose themselves shopping with the laborer's wife. She would consider well, before laying out the money, which would be the most profitable way of spending it; remembering that what many call a "cheap bargain," often turns out to be a dear one. She would bear in mind the proverb which warns us not to be "penny wise and pound foolish." The different ways of testing the quality of the various articles will then be drawn from the children, as tasting the butter, cheese, &c. It is better to purchase plain wholesome food than a few dainties, which only pamper the appetite, and do not nourish the body. It is also important that poor people should pay their way; for even supposing that when they contract a small debt they fully intend to pay it, many unforeseen circumstances may occur to frustrate their designs.

COOKING OF FOOD.

I. Preparations for Cooking.

The utensils which are used should be perfectly clean. A cook should be clean and tidy in her person, and her hands quite clean. Before putting her hands into the dough, &c., she should see that she has all the requisite articles ready; she should also be careful not to throw the flour about the paste-board or table, but should always bear in mind the little maxim, "waste not, want not." Before cooking vegetables they should be cleansed in cold water. Greens should be freed from all tough leaves, and boiled in soft water; the fire must be made large or small in proportion to the amount of cooking. The Sunday's dinner should be cooked on the Saturday.

II. Receipts for Cooking.

1. *Making of Bread.*—Ingredients for $3\frac{1}{2}$ lbs. of bread, $2\frac{1}{2}$ lbs. of flour, 2 tablespoonfuls of yeast, a little salt, and 1 pint of luke-warm water.

Take the flour and put in a pan, mix the yeast with half a pint of luke-warm water and pour it into the pan, and allow it to ferment for one hour; then with another half pint of water and a little salt knead the whole into dough, and put it in a warm place for two hours, in order that it may rise a second time; take up the dough and work it lightly into a loaf; bake for 1 hour or $1\frac{1}{2}$ hours.

2. *To boil Potatoes.*—Take as many potatoes as are required and of nearly the same size; wash, but do not peel or cut them; put them into a saucepan with sufficient cold water to cover them, and a spoonful of salt; let them boil gently till soft; then pour off the water, and allow them to dry for a short time.

3. *To make Milk Porridge.*—To 1 pint of boiling water add 2 spoonfuls of oatmeal, which has been previously mixed with a little cold water; stir them up well and let them boil slowly for 5 or 10 minutes; then add 1 pint of milk, and let the whole boil for a few minutes longer.

4. *To make Pea Soup.*—Take 1 pint of peas and put them into a little cold water over night. In the morning drain off the water and put the peas in a saucepan with three quarts of soft water; or gravy in which meat has been boiled would be still better; let the peas boil for 2 hours; then add 1 or 2 sliced onions, a carrot, turnips, &c., with half a pound of bacon, or any other meat; season with pepper and salt, and let the whole boil for another hour.

5. *The most economical Method of Cooking Meat* is boiling; nothing is lost by this process. It is very extravagant to fry bacon. Time allowed for boiling meat 20 minutes per pound; bacon 25 minutes to each pound.

Lesson II.—(Esther Taylor.)

This lesson contains much practical information. The remarks are very well chosen as to the care and neatness required in preparing food, as are also those against the waste of materials; and the directions respecting the time different dishes of food required in cooking are very useful. The Lesson contains more than could be compressed into one Lesson; but the directions given were complete in themselves, and the class quietly broken up by the teacher, whose manner was excellent as an example to her class, very mild and modest, and well suited to encourage children to ask questions when they did not fully understand all the teacher said.

This Lesson could be made extremely amusing and instructive, when divided into several.

Bread alone would form the subject for an excellent lesson; so would also the Potato: and all the lessons upon Vegetables might be rendered very entertaining, by the anecdotes connected with their introduction into England; such as the story of the Fuchsia, brought by a sailor to his wife, on his return from a voyage; who, during his absence, could scarcely be prevailed on to part with it, though offered a considerable sum by a lover of flowers, who had been struck with the novelty and beauty of the plant. Many of the vegetables now in common use were cultivated in this accidental manner, especially in Cornwall and Devonshire, where the people are fond of gardening, and the climate is favorable to the growth of vegetables and plants. The different modes of preparing food would also give an opportunity for instructive lessons.

Lesson on Climate.

Paragraphs.	Subdivisions.	Notes.
1. Definitions.	1. Relating to a portion of the earth's surface.	Zones — natural divisions — objection: climates — artificial — principle of — half-hour — month — number of — objection: Labrador and Ulster.
	2. To the prevailing state of the weather.	*a.* Temperature: *b.* temp. and moisture: *c.* temperature, moisture, bar. press., purity of air, winds, electricity, &c. Take first of these meanings.
2. Causes.	1. Earth's int. heat.	Constant below surface — isogeothermal lines — no sensible effect — except vol. districts.
	2. Sun's heat.	Total amt. const. — where most effective — when mean. temp. would be reg. distributed — varies as cos[r]. latitude — an. am[t]. strat. in 46 ft. thick.
3. Modifying causes.	1. Latitude.	Direction of rays — diagram: length of day — absorption — radiation: trop. heat through strata to poles.
	2. Elevation above sea level.	Heat decreases as we ascend — rarity of air — effect on man — latent — reflection; snow-line — where highest — why — $80°=0$ — Etna.
	3. Relative position of land and water.	Water bad conductor — "fish" — uniformity of action — evaporation — insular — continental — Edinburgh and Moscow: comp. extent of: N. and S. hemispheres — Baltic — Arctic and Antarctic oceans: former climates — how shown — Lyell. State of Africa arises from?
	4. Surface.	Nature of soil — sandy — clayey — marshes — forests — cultivation — snow-capped mountains — *la bise* in Switzerland.
	5. Aspect.	Towards eq. incr. temp. — N. side of Himalaya the snow-line 4000 ft. higher than on Southern — why — the reverse in very cold climates: direction of mountains — Poland and Hungary: long[de].
	6. Winds.	Prevailing winds — our east cold in spring and warm in autumn — why — west and south warm — why: currents to and from poles: land and sea breezes.
	7. Oceanic currents.	Gulf stream — Columbus — affects climate of America and Europe — British Isles particularly.
4. Gen. Distr[n]. of Heat.	1. Difficulty of ascertaining.	Arises from the numerous modifying causes already enumerated, &c.
	2. Humboldt's plan.	Growth of plants: isothermal, isochimenal, isotheral lines — eq. mean. temp., 81°: hottest part of Globe in Cent. Africa on 11th par. north; two poles of max. cold in N. hem., in America 80° north and 100° west, in Asia 80° north and 95° east. Veg. zones are 1, spices; 2, sugar-cane; 3, olive and fig; 4, wine-grape; 5, oak and wheat; 6, fir, pine, and birch; 7, lichens.

First Lesson on Pens.

1. First Pen.	Pointed iron or other metal: used on stone, bone, sheet lead, wood, bark, palm leaves: hence rude at first: Cadmus knew no other: Solon's laws written with it about 600 B. C.: Mahomet's secretaries: Koran written with it: Bible, parts of, probably (commandments, &c.): Greek stylus (gold sometimes): Roman do. (description): murder with it (by followers of younger Gracchus).
2. Second Pen.	Calamus: used with Egyptian papyrus (latter invn[d]. abt. 4th cent. B. C.): calam.: not yet used in Rome (refer to sedits. of Gracchi abt. 130 B. C.): used in Agus[n]. age there: use further extnd[d]. by invention of parchment (Pergamena charta) mid. of 2nd cent. B. C.
3. Third Pen.	Goose quill: easy trans[n]. to from Calamus: Lincolnshire fens: Somerset best: Irish worst: Russia: Hudson's Bay: crow: swan: eagle: clarification: pen-mak[g]. machine.
4. Fourth Pen.	Return to ancient materials: Birmingham, &c. (manufacture): merits as compared to quill: mode of preserving.
5. Conclusion.	Moral weapon: "mighty instrum[t]. of *little* men:" "in hands of men entirely *great* mightier than sword" (Bulwer): influence on mind: preserver of ancient learning: diffuser of thought and knowledge: destinies of mankind: Napoleon the great (saying of).

Second Lesson on Pens.

Paragraphs.	Notes.
1. History.	Most anc. writing on hard subs. as stone, metal, &c.—thus 2 tables of Law: Chinese wrote with iron style on bamboo: Romans with same on waxed tables (easily effaced): reeds first used for ink writing—cut like pen: quills 6th century: steel pens 1803 (Mr. Wyse): in perfection in 1824.
2. Materials.	*a.* Quills: *b.* Steel: *c.* Other materials of diff. kinds.
a. Quills.	(1.) Adaptation of quills. Quills of diff. birds used: goose quill best: geese fed in great quantities in Russia and Poland for quills and feathers: we get 20,000,000 annually from them: fed also in fens of Lincolns.: quill hollow, hard, and firm for lightness and strength in bird: same qual. useful for pens: split lengthwise: highly flex. and elast.: resist action of ink: in all superior to other materials, and in all approved by—(2.) Preparation of quill, called touching, or clarifying. First moistened by dip. ends in water (cap. attract.): heated them and flattened: scraped: exposed to heat again and regain original form: now fit for use. (3.) Making a pen. Sometimes with little machine at one cut (pens coarse and bad): best made with sharp hard knife, not flat in edge like a razor: quill scraped slightl on back for a clean slit: slit to be fair and straight must be in middle: slit stopped where you like by thumb of left hand to prevent waste: chief defect of beginners, nib short, stunted, and too fine: two sides of nib =, or the right one a little stronger: last cut *straight* across: after use pen must be cleaned and not left in ink: every boy shd. learn to make his own pen.
b. Steel.	(1.) Adapt. for pens. Best material next to quills: superior in durability—no mending: ink acts too on steel, but a good deal prevented by cleaning pen *dry* after use. (2.) Mode of manufacture. Steel must be very thin to be elastic: first pens very coarse and thick: steel well tempered and pressed into sheets $\frac{1}{100}$ or $\frac{1}{200}$ inch: these cut into strips $2\frac{1}{2}$ inch. long: from these pieces are cut off for pens: strips annealed for 14 hours to remove hardness occas. by rolling: then cleaned: maker's name stamped: slit by a very fine edged instrument which cuts $\frac{2}{3}$ thro': shaped by a punch: heated red hot and dipped in oil: polished by being shaken togeth. in a cylinder (called a *devil*) for 8 hours: heated *blue* and slit completed with pincers: cooled and fit for use, but sometimes bronzed: London and Birmingham manuf.: in England 120 tons of steel = 200,000,000 pens manuf. annually.
c. Other materials.	Silver, as in *fountain* pen, which took a large quantity of ink at once: sometimes brass: occasionally metallic nibs on quills (expensive): sometimes precious stones on nibs, thus a ruby set in *fine* gold: such as these still sold and it is said will last 5 or 6 yrs., but expens.—£1: gold nibs on steel now common:—why gold?
3. Uses.	Before printing quite necessary to preserve writings: all books *written* then and ∴ very scarce: penmanship then carried to greater perfect. than now—witness illuminated manuscripts in Trin. College and many other places: still as necessary since every thing must be written before being printed: correspondence: "pen" has come to signify power in writing, as "A powerful pen"—"The grey goose pen, that mighty instrument," &c.
4. Lesson.	Thankfulness to Providence for diffusing so plentifully, quills and steel, the two most necessary materials: especially quills, tho' for use of birds, as perfectly suited for pens as if made for that special purpose: without quills writings of many ages probably lost: small things are often the most important in giving extended employment to people, and in developing ingenuities of clever men.

Third Lesson on Pens.

1. Necessity.	Some means of recording events, &c., required. Ancients used for this purpose to plant trees, erect stones, pillars, altars, &c.: pictures, statues: all highly inconvenient.
2. Nature.	This depends on material emp. for writ. on. The first materials were stone, brick (Babylon), tiles, oyster-shells (ostracism), wooden blocks, ivory, blade-bones of sheep (Mahom.), lead (Job), bronze (Claudius), brass (Rom. laws), copper (Bengal), walls and chairs (Icelanders), boards covered with beeswax. All these required a hard sharp instrument, as the *style*. Shepherds wrote their songs on leather with *thorns*, and wound or rolled (volumes) this round their crooks. Bark (library), leaves (folio), papyrus (paper), parchment, required a different sort of writ. instrument, and ink.
3. Diff. kinds.	Calamus: quills (pen), bone pens: metallic pens.
4. Quill pens.	Goose, crow, &c. Lincolnshire, &c.
5. Metal. pens.	Materials used—process of manufacture—localities—statistics.

IV. GALLERY TRAINING LESSONS,

ORALLY CONDUCTED IN NATURAL SCIENCE AND COMMON THINGS.*

BY DAVID STOW.

ORAL training lessons, in natural science and the arts, are found to be not merely a highly intellectual exercise, but are valuable to persons in every rank of society, whether master, servant, or workman. While they are particularly valuable to persons in the humbler walks of life, in fitting them for manual and other labor, they are also important as the foundation of a more extended knowledge of science, to those whose circumstances may enable them to prosecute their researches still further. To the former, these school exercises may be nearly all the theoretical knowledge on such subjects they can ever receive. To the latter, a thoroughly analyzed or *pictured out* training lesson, day by day, will be found an elementary exercise greatly superior to the ordinary mode of merely reading lessons or lectures, even when accompanied by explanation.

The teaching of science by gallery lessons, and conducted orally, without book, is a new and additional branch in popular education, and that it ought to form a distinct feature in schools, even for the children of the poor and working classes, will appear, when we consider the importance of servants, (male and female,) workmen, and mechanics, having a correct idea of things and of scientific terms. The workman, in consequence, would know better the meaning of relative terms, even in the drudgery of manual labor, and he might be left to execute much by a simple order scientifically expressed, which he can not now do without very close watching and superintendence; and although the mechanic must have acquired a practical knowledge of his particular profession, yet early school training in science and scientific terms would have expanded and exercised the mind of many a man, humble in rank, but of powerful intellect, so as to have produced many more James Watts, Arkrights, and Henry Bells, than we now have, whose genius and discoveries might have enriched mankind, and added to the domestic and social comfort of all. How difficult is it to get a workman out of a beaten track, or, if he be a

---

* Stow's "*Training System of Education.*" Eleventh Edition. Chapter xxviii.

genius, to fix him in any track at all! These considerations induced me, at the earliest establishment of this system, to introduce, as the first exercise each afternoon in our model practicing school, oral training lessons on science *without book.*

It is evident, that although some points of science, from observation, reading and conversation, do force themselves upon the young mind, and may be made available when a person attends a course of public lectures in after-life, yet the fact of his knowledge having been gathered up at random, without arrangement or system, leaves him very much in the dark as to the basis on which all, or any science rests.

Had the sons of tradesmen and workmen, as well as professional men, acquired in school a clear outline of the various natural sciences—the question is, should such a sum require to have been expended on our new Houses of Parliament in regard to the proper arrangements of sound (acoustics) and healthful ventilation? also, as is now required for sanitary improvements in our rivers, and in our cities, and smaller towns throughout the kingdom? What the more learned superintendents may have overlooked, might have been suggested, no doubt, by some one or other of the intelligent humble workmen.

Visitors sometimes say, "What have the children of the poor to do with science? let them learn to read their Bibles, and repeat their Catechism; that's the education suitable for the poor." Science, however, is valuable alike to the mechanic and the man of business, in promoting the arts of life so indispensable to the wealth and comfort of all ranks of society. If the bold and clear outlines of science be given to all ranks, each may maintain his proper place in the scale of its ascension. The poor man, if he chooses, may advance beyond the limited period of his elementary school education, and the man of leisure and scientific research may rise as high as he pleases; whilst the genius, of whatever grade, acquires enough to enable him to prosecute his studies, and take his just place in society. But the trainer rises a little higher in his oral training lessons, and uses scientific terms, expressive of scientific principles, such as are used by lecturers on natural philosophy, in consequence of which, it is still urged by some, WHY TEACH SCIENCE to children in an elementary school? What can they understand of latent heat, the radii of a circle, centrifugal and centripetal forces, gravitation, electric fluid, and innumerable other more complex terms? Now we have to say, that all such terms may be simplified, and when reduced to simple terms, they can be understood by children of a few years old. Having these outlines clearly analyzed *by familiar illustrations*, so as to communicate the idea in the first instance, they can then be made to understand the most complex terms, expressive of the most complex movements and conditions. For example, the motion of a child round the circular swinging-pole in the play-ground, may illustrate, in some measure, how the moon keeps in its orbit round the earth, and the latter, or any other planet, round the sun; in other words, what is meant by the centrifugal and centripetal forces. The proper course of education in science has too generally been reversed; and the reason why so many adults stop short in their progress, and can not educate themselves (for education ought only to close with life,) is, that they have committed to memory technical terms, which, *not having been pictured out* and illustrated, are not understood; and, also, that the minute points of science have been given before the great outlines were drawn.

The philosophical terms which a public lecturer finds it necessary to use, are seldom thoroughly understood by his audience; they have not been explained, far less pictured out to the mind's eye. They do not therefore *see* the bearing of each point of the premises laid down, or the conclusions at which the lecturer arrives, and at the close are found oftentimes to have acquired no distinct impression of the actual lesson, which otherwise might have been received. They may applaud the lecturer as being a very *clever man.* "It was an excellent lecture!" "What beautiful experiments he performed?" "How remarkably bright he made the gas to burn, and what an explosion it produced!" But the lecture itself has not been comprehended. This is the every-day experience of the young and the old in attending public lectures on natural science. It would have been otherwise after a course of early school training.

The lessons during the first stage, or the outlines, at whatever age the child commences his course, ought to be exceedingly simple, and should comprehend a number of the more obvious things in nature and in art, which every child ought to know in their great outlines, before he is perplexed with minute points, or the use of technical terms; a knowledge of which he gradually acquires as he advances from stage to stage.

As a child, I wish to know what wheaten bread and oaten bread are; the distinction in quality, and how they are made; how butter and cheese are made; what salt is; how wine is made, and of what composed; what brown and loaf sugars are; the nature of tea and coffee, with the places where they are produced, and how they are brought to the condition in which they are found when used at home at the fireside; the distinction between wool, cotton, flax, and silk, both how they are produced, and why more or less warm.

The child ought to be made acquainted with articles of furniture. These are continually presented to his notice, and they afford the means of exercising his powers of observation, and training him to think. Their nature and relative qualities ought to be made familiar to him.

The natural history of the more common animals, domestic and foreign, is also an object of interest and a means of enlargement to the young mind, particularly when united with a short history, not merely of the habits of the animals themselves, but of the countries and inhabitants in and among which Providence has placed them, and the peculiar adaptation of each to its own particular circumstances, all proving the wisdom of their great Creator. As a child, I wish to know why the swallow is not seen during winter: why the hen has open feet, and the duck webbed; with other more minute points of the formation of animals; why the butterfly is seen in the summer only; from what origin it has sprung. What are all these? the child naturally inquires, and whence do the wings of the latter derive their pearly whiteness? Of what use rats and mice are, seeing they are so troublesome in our dwellings, and why and when they may be killed, without our being chargeable with cruelty; how the foot of the reindeer is suited to the frozen regions of Lapland, that of the horse to our own, and the camel's to the sandy deserts of Arabia. From each and all of these training lessons, the children may learn something of the power, and wisdom, and goodness of God to all His creatures; and such lessons should uniformly be drawn from the children by every trainer during the daily lessons.

The child sees himself surrounded on every side by men of trade and handicraft, and he wishes and ought to know not merely the qualities of things and the materials in use, but how they are molded, or joined, or mixed, or decomposed, so as to render them serviceable. He sees the smith form a nail or a horseshoe; why does he heat the iron in a furnace before laying it on the anvil and striking it with the hammer? The uses of the pulley, the screw, and the lever, ought to be pictured out to him by analogy and familiar illustrations. The child sees paper; why not woven as a piece of cloth, and why more or less impervious to moisture?

The child breathes air, drinks water, sees steam, dew, hail, and snow. What are all these? the child naturally inquires; and why is the last *white*, and when melted turns into water? What are thunder and lightning, and are they of any use? The sun to him appears always round, not so the moon—why so? The principal parts of his own body, and those of other animals, with their relative functions, ought to be known; the qualities and names of the more common minerals, and the great outlines of botany, causes of the tides, etc., etc. Such oral training lessons should be commenced in their outlines in the initiatory school, and carried forward more minutely in the juvenile and senior departments.

Much of the bewilderment felt by men of all degrees of acquirement rests in the fact, that scientific terms have not been analyzed or or pictured out by *familiar illustrations* as a first step in their early education. Complex subjects, and complex terms, which ought to have been the last, have generally been made the first stage; consequently blindfoldedness, to a considerable extent continues, these first and natural steps not having been traced. The acquirement of these primary steps, therefore, is an ordeal to which every student who practically studies in the seminary is subjected, before he can communicate what he knows to the children in the model or practicing schools.

In the industrial department, there are many important points with which the girls ought particularly to be made acquainted, and which may be carried into domestic and social life; such as, the scientific reasons why a room is better aired by opening the top of a window than the bottom—how to sweep a floor without "watering," and without raising the dust—the effect of making tea with water just brought to the boiling point, and water which has boiled for some time—how to make or mend a fire, so as to save fuel, and whether the top or bottom of the fire ought to be stirred, in rendering it what is termed either a good or a lasting fire—the philosophy of combustion, and whether smoke ought to exist at all, or to what extent, and how it may be cured or prevented—the scientific and practical effect of toasting bread, and laying one slice above another—and the effects, practically and scientifically, of fire on woolen, cotton, linen, and silken cloths. These, in addition to those previously mentioned, and a number of other practical matters, may be rendered highly useful to females in after-life.

Children, of both sexes, should be exercised daily on some point of science or the arts, particularly in relation to ordinary life and common things. Whatever is done should be well done. Analyze one point clearly, rather than a dozen points imperfectly. Variety does not dissipate the mind, or render knowledge superficial; it is only so when the mere surface is presented, without a proper analysis and *picturing out*. The child is fatigued and disgusted when kept too long on one subject, or course of subjects, whereas each power of the mind is strengthened by frequent and varied exercise. The natural process on entering a garden, or green-house, for example, is first to look at every thing within its four corners; but the plan generally adopted by the lecturer is to spend, as it were, a week at the door of entrance, analyzing the first few plants met with. Let the mind see the whole outlines of each department it enters upon in the first instance, and then with interest and intelligence it will patiently investigate each step in its progress.

When objects are within our reach, we make use of them in conducting the lesson as a sort of text, or starting-point; but whether within reach or not, our principle is to picture out the whole lesson, and every point of the *subject-matter* of which it is composed. Facts of which the pupils prove themselves ignorant are, of course, stated by the master—the lesson is then drawn, and given at the time by the children themselves in their own language. Their ability to do so, is the test whether the subject has been simply and properly pictured out—for if so, they must understand what they mentally see—keeping in view that we do not know a thing until we *see it* with our mental eye. For example, if separate lessons have been previously given upon the properties of heat, and water, and steam, and air, and the condensing influence of cold, and the screw, and the pulley, and the inclined plane, and the lever and the centrifugal force; and if all these and other forces be pictured out, as combined in one machine, the children will readily understand what a steam-engine is, in their minds, and tell the trainer the effect of its power upon the shaft that may move spinning machinery, raise water, or propel a steam-vessel or railway train.

These oral gallery lessons are conducted daily on precisely the same mode with Bible training lessons. Whilst the Bible lessons are uniformly read from the Bible itself, the secular oral gallery training lessons are taken from such subjects as are given in a subsequent chapter. The Bible lesson ought to be the first in the morning, and the oral secular gallery lesson the first in the afternoon, although only twenty minutes or half-an-hour be occupied in conducting it.

There are *very few* good text-books on science and secular subjects, which can be read by the children before and at the moment the daily secular lesson is given, both because they are generally too lengthy or incomplete, and because nine-tenths of the points to which our oral training lessons refer are less abstract, and of more practical advantage, than the subjects to which these treatises refer, and must of course be given by the master. Oral secular training lessons, as a distinct branch, therefore, are conducted by the trainer *without book.*

This, however, does not prevent the master elucidating any point he chooses to fix upon during the ordinary reading lessons of a school book.

By some strangers we are complained of as being too simple, by others as being too lofty, in the subject-matter of our lessons, and that the terms used while analyzing them are too simple, or, on the other hand, too complex; they would thus place us "between two fires." Our desire, however, is, that the pupils *see* every step of the progress of picturing out, whatever the subject may be. Our practical students at first uniformly complain of the difficulty of simplifying every subject; but, eventually, they become fully convinced, from experience, that ***simplicity is the last and highest attainment of a trainer of youth.***

PRACTICAL EXAMPLE I.

Early Stage—Initiatory Department.—The Camel.*

Now, children,† you see this picture (presenting the picture of a camel, if you have one, but if not, you must describe its comparative size with some animal they are acquainted with, noticing also the peculiar hunches upon its back.)

What is the name of this animal? *The Camel.* Camel is the name of...*this animal.*‡ The camel, children, lives in hot countries, such as Arabia. Arabia is a very hot country in Asia, where there are hot sandy deserts, in which there are neither trees nor...*grass.* The camel has feet and legs, and...(pointing to the parts) *a head,* and...*a back,*—as every animal has. *What a lump on its back, master!* This is what is called a...*lump.* Do you remember the name I gave to that lump? I called it a hunch. A great...*hunch;*—that, then, is a...*hunch.* Tell me how many hunches it has got. *Two.* It has got...*two hunches on its back.* This one is on... Where is this one near? Supposing this boy were to walk on all fours, that is on his hands and...*feet,*—and a hunch were above this place. What do you call this place? *Shoulders.* The camel, then, has a hunch upon...*its shoulders,*—or close behind...*its shoulders,*—and another upon... What is this? *Tail.* Is this the tail? *Back, Sir.* It is upon...*its back,*—near...*the tail,*—but not...*upon the tail.*§

Now, then, children, I shall tell you something more‖ about this wonderful animal. *It has got crooked hind legs, Sir.* Very right, my little girl; the camel has got very broad strong...*hind legs,*—which look as if they were...*crooked,*—

*In every stage of the child's progress, ***questions and ellipses*** must be judiciously and naturally mixed. Three dots thus...mark the ellipses—Italics—the answers of the children.

†No lesson is proceeded with until the children are physically and intellectually drilled into order. (See Notes, Stage I., "A Stay," and "Man with the withered hand.") At the end of every point of the lesson, also, some slight physical movements are requisite, such as stretching out arms simultaneously twice or thrice, rising up and sitting down, etc., varied according to the age and condition of the feelings of the children. Some of these are absolutely requisite ***before and during the progress*** of every lesson, but one of the most powerful means for securing the attention are the trainer's actions and ***variation in the tones of his voice.***

‡Inverting the sentence.

§The younger the children are, there must be more ellipses and fewer questions.

‖Some slight physical exercises may now be necessary.

and in the next lesson we have upon the camel, we shall say something about the use of what appears a crook in its...*hind legs*,—and you will be better able to understand the reason then than you would just now.* Let me tell you, that the camel has got on his body very fine hair of a light brown color, called... What would you call the hair that grows upon the camel? (No answer.) What would you call the hair that grows upon a cow? *Cow hair.* What would you call hair that grows upon the camel? *Camel hair.* This hair, children, is made into cloth, and makes very pretty...*jackets.* I have no doubt that cloth made from camel's...*hair*—would make a jacket, as this boy says, but it is made chiefly into cloaks or...*mantles.* The climate† is too hot for jackets, that is to say, the sun is too hot in the country where the camels...*live*—for the people to...*wear jackets.* People in hot countries generally prefer loose wide clothes, not clothes that fit tightly like...*a jacket.* Why? *Because they are cooler.* The body is kept cooler, or at least pleasanter, when the clothes are loose than when...*they are tight.* What part of the world are we speaking about? You will remember I told you at the beginning of the lesson. What was the name? *Arabia.* This girl is right; don't forget the name of the country where camels chiefly live...*Arabia.* Very well, the camel's hair is made into...*cloaks*—and *mantles.* Do you remember, in one of our Bible lessons, who was said to have worn a garment made of camel's hair? *John.* John the...*Baptist.*‡ Very well, children, you have said that the camel lives in... *Arabia*—that it has two...*hunches on its back*—one as large as you see, and the other...*small*—or...*smaller;* that its hair is of a...*light brown color*—and very...*fine.* And what do the people make of its hair? *Cloth*—cloth for...*mantles.*§

Look what a nice place that would be for a ride, children. That place is something like a... What is put as a seat on a horse's back? *A saddle.* What do you think that place is like between the two hunches? *A saddle, that would keep us from falling, Sir.* Very right, boy, the hunch behind would keep you from...*falling back*,—and this one near...*the shoulder*—would keep you from... *falling.* Where? *On its neck.* But perhaps you might fall by its sides. *The stirrups would keep me up.* O then, you are for stirrups, my boy! You would ride very safely on the camel's back, if you had...*stirrups*—between these two large...*lumps.* Lumps! *Hunches, Sir.*

Now, I must tell you something more about this wonderful animal, and then you will tell me what you think of it. The camel is a very tall animal, as high as six feet, that is, from the...*floor*—to a little above my...*head.* (The master pointing first to the floor and then to the top of his head.)‖ Supposing I wished to take a ride on such a high animal, how would I get on its back? *You might take a stool.* But suppose I could not get a stool, and were in the desert of Arabia? *I would jump.* Could you jump as high as yourself, think you?

* We give the outline first. See *passim.* At the same time acknowledging one or other of the answers and observations of the children.

† A word they can scarcely as yet understand, but being expressed, the trainer must break it down.

‡ Of course the trainer remembers that this fact occurred in a Bible lesson, otherwise the question would not be put at this time.

§ The children, of course, make many mistakes, which must be corrected by training, not *telling;* but to exhibit which on paper would render the perusal intolerably tedious.

‖ Action suited to the words is important in training, as it is in all public speaking. The attention of the old as well as the young is arrested by it, and it even partially pictures out the subject.

Yes, Sir. Try it. *No, Sir, no.* Now, I'll tell you how it is done. The keepers of the camels *train* them when they are young to kneel...*down*—upon...*their knees.* By training, I mean they make the camels...*kneel down;* that is to say, when the keepers train the young camels to kneel, they make them...*do it.* When the camels are trained to...*kneel*—on the...*ground,* they...*do it.** The keeper whistles, or makes some particular...*sound,*—and the moment the camels hear the...*whistle*—they... What do they do? *They kneel.* And when they kneel, any man can...*jump on its back,*—and after a person is on its back, and the camel rises up... What might they do? *Take a ride.*

Now, then, the camel rides with a man, or any burden, on...*its back,*—just like... What animal do we use for riding in this country? *A horse.* But it is much stronger...*than a horse.* It can carry a greater weight, where? *On its back,*—than...*a horse.* How long do you think a horse could go without water to drink? *Don't know, Sir.* Do you think a horse could want water a whole day? *My father's cart horse drinks every morning and every night.* Not oftener than morning and evening? *Yes, Sir, at meal hours.* Your father's horse takes water, you say, several...*times a-day.* Well, let me tell you that the camel can travel through... What sort of places did we say it traveled through in Arabia? *Hot sands.* Dry, burning...*sands,*—burning with the...*heat of the sun,*—for a whole week together, without taking a drink. *Does it get no water, master?* I'll tell you about that just now, children. There are no wells, or rivers, or . *ponds,*—or water of any kind in these deserts, and God has so made the stomach of this... *animal,*—or rather God has given it two stomachs. You know the stomach is where...*we put our meat in.* And what else? Where do you put your drink in? *Our mouth.* And where does the water go after that? *Into the stomach.* Well, as the camel requires to carry heavy...*men* and *women,*—and what have men and women with them sometimes? *Things—goods.* The camel has goods and other...*things*—to carry besides men and women, which are a great burden, through the... Where? *The sandy deserts,*—sometimes for a whole week together, without coming to a place where they could get...*water,*—so God, out of his goodness, has provided them with a large... Where does an animal put the water it drinks? *Its stomach.* God has provided it with two...*stomachs,*—so large that it can take in as much water in one of its...*stomachs*—before it starts on the journey as serves it the...*whole time.* This boy's father's horse† requires water every...*day.* How often? *Several times a-day,*—and there is plenty of water in this...*town.* What would a horse do in the sandy deserts of Arabia, think you? *Die.* Die for...*want of water.* It would be so thirsty from want of water that...*it would die.* You say the horse would die there. Would the camel die? *No, Sir.* Why? *It has a great quantity of water.* Where? *In its inside,*—that is...*in its stomach,*—which serves it perhaps for seven or eight days, when it is crossing, that is, when it is walking through...*the deserts,*—and burning...*sands*

* DOING is the principle of the Training System intellectually, as well as physically and morally.

† While he acknowledges the answers of all, from time to time, and thus stimulates all—the master, as a moral trainer, must take care not to be partial, and that while he acknowledges the answers of the forward and warm-tempered children (*who are always ready and willing to make a show-off in school,*) he as often notices and comments upon those offered by the more gentle and timid, whose answers are generally no less correct, but who require encouragement to express them, and the particular notice of whose answers, *in turn,* also acts as a check on the too great forwardness of the other parties. The practical exercise of this principle stimulates all alike, protecting and encouraging the timid, whether male or female and regulating and molding, by degrees, the spirit of the forward.

of Arabia. The horse, such as we were speaking about, you say, would not do for...*Arabia,*—but the camel will do to ride across the...*sandy deserts of Arabia.*

We have a number of things to say about this wonderful animal, which I must tell you at next lesson, but I wish to speak about another thing at present. It is about its feet. The camel has very wonderful...*feet.* They are broad, large feet, and very soft and spongy, like a piece of... Mention any thing you know to be soft. *Mutton, bread, butter, beef, my cap, flesh, my hand, twopenny loaves, Sir.** Enough children. One boy says† that the feet of the camel are as soft as his hand. Tell me why do you think God has made the feet of the camel soft. (No answer.) How has God made the horse's feet? Attend, children. What kind of ground does the horse walk upon? *Soft ground.* Is the ground always soft? Where does it walk when carrying a burden, or when a man rides it? *On the road.* And when in towns? *On the streets.*‡ What would take place were the horse's feet as soft as the camel's? *They would be hurt.* Our roads are covered over with...*hard stones*—and a soft foot like the camel's would...*be hurt.* The horse's feet are...*hard*—and the farrier—that is the man who shoes horses—the farrier makes something hard for them. What does he make? *Shoes.* What sort of shoes? *Iron shoes.* You and I wear... *leather shoes.* The horse wears...*iron ones.* In walking upon sand, how do you find it under your feet? *Soft.* Were the horse to ride with a heavy burden on its back on the sands of Arabia, what would happen? *It would sink.* Its hoofs or feet would...*sink in the sand*—and then it would not...*get on*—its...*journey*, when walking on the...*soft sand.* And what would happen to its feet? Do you know what its hoofs are made of? *Hard.* True, they are hard, but many things are hard. This table is...*hard.*—*Bones, Sir.* Not bones, but almost as hard as...*a bone.*§ If the hoofs or feet of a horse are hard and dry like a bone, what would happen them in the hot sandy deserts? *They would be birseled.* What do you mean by birseled? *Burnt.* Not quite burnt, but...*half-burnt.* Then, you think the horse would not do for the hot...*sands*—of...*Arabia*—but it does very well for...*this country.* What kind of feet did you say the camel has? *Soft.* Very spongy—and...*soft*—like a lady's...*hand*—not dry like the... *horse's feet*—but soft and full of moisture, like the palm of my...*hand.*‖ What has the camel to walk upon, little girl? *Sand*—and therefore God has made its feet... How? *Soft.* Soft to walk over the fine...*sand,*—and full of sap like oil,

* Too wide a question (in fact a guess ;) the trainer consequently receives too many answers, and must concentrate their ideas upon one point. He seizes upon one of the answers as the nearest, and trains the children to the correct one he wishes to reach.

† The moment the master fixes upon any one answer, all are silent, to hear what is to be said upon it. This does not depend on its being right or wrong. They are satisfied that some answer is attended to.

‡ During the next lesson, or in Stage II., the reindeer may be brought in as a comparison, but the horse, an animal with which they are *familiar*, is enough at present. In future lessons the comparison of the reindeer in the snows of Lapland, the horse at home, and the camel in the deserts of Arabia, and the adaptation of each to its peculiar circumstances, may then be pictured out, and from which a lesson may be drawn on the wisdom of the great Creator.

§ It would not do at this early stage, when nearly every fact is new to the *children* to divert their attention from the direct course, by giving the analogy between the construction of the hoof of the horse, with other substances, such as horns, whalebones, etc. This should come under its own particular head, or secular gallery lesson on horns, whalebone, etc.

‖ The trainer showing and pointing to the palm of his hand. The child in this way adds, *incidentally*, another word to its vocabulary, viz., *palm*, the idea and the word representing the object being combined.

that never dries up any more than my foot or...*hand.* Now, tell me, why are they full of sap? That they may be...*able to walk in the deserts*—a...*long time*—without their... What would happen to their feet if they were as dry as the horse's feet? *Dry up.* The camel's feet, then, do not...*dry up*,—although they should be walking through hot...*sand*—for many...*weeks.* Why are they large? What use have they for large feet? *Don't know.* If you wish to walk through deep snow, whether would you use stilts, as boys sometimes do when crossing a stream, or would you put on snow shoes, like the Laplanders? (Silent.) You will remember we were speaking about the snows of the north the other day. Whether do you think the stilts or the snow shoes would sink the farther? *The stilts.* The stilts would...*sink very deep*,—the snow boots do...*not sink*—they do not sink very...*much*—because they are... What size are they? *Large.* The snow shoes are...*large*—and...*broad.* How broad? I shall tell you—they are broader and longer than a man's...*boot.* Tell me why the feet of the camel are large? *That they might not sink*—in the...*deserts.* Horses have hard hoofs or...*feet*—which suit them to travel in...*this country*—or any...*country*—where their feet...*would not sink*—but...*not in the deserts of Arabia.* I must tell you that there are plenty of horses in Arabia, beautiful horses, for there is hard ground in Arabia as well as...*sandy ground*—but then Arabian horses won't do for the... What were we speaking of? *Sandy deserts*—where their feet would...*sink*—and where there is...*no water to drink.*

But the camel's feet do not...*sink in the sand*—being...*soft and big.* And what does it do for water? *It carries it in its stomach.* In one...*of its stomachs.* And what does it do with the other. *It digests its food.* God, then, who made all things very...*good*, has made the camel to suit the...*sandy deserts.* Very well, children.*

Now, I fear you are getting tired. Let us have a little exercise. Heads up—shoulders...*back*†—chin...*in*—heels...*close*—toes...*out*—hands on...*lap.* Now, perfect silence.‡

Revisal.—In case too much be occupied at one time, the following Revisal may commence some subsequent lesson on camel.

We shall have done immediately. Let me see if you remember what we have said. The camel is an animal... How high? *As high as you, Sir.* How many feet? *Six feet.* I am not quite six feet high, therefore it must be...*higher than you.* I forgot to tell you that the camel is about ten feet long, that is, as long as that...*desk.* Six feet...*high*, and about...*ten feet long.* It has two large...*lumps.* Remember the name I gave you...*hunches.* Where? *On its back*—which makes a...*nice saddle to ride on.* How many stomachs has it? *Two, Sir.* One of them is...*large.* For what purpose? *To keep water in it.* A curiously formed stomach, that contains as much...*water*—as serves it...*on its journey.* Where? *Across the sandy deserts of Arabia*—for unless it had a

* *Repetition* of the idea in different forms of expression is absolutely necessary during the first and second stages of training.

† When the children fill up the ellipses they naturally perform the action. Were the master simply to tell them what to do, he could not so readily secure the attention of all.

‡ Rising up, and sitting down, simultaneously, not by a stamp of the foot, which is clumsy, but by following the motion of the master's hand, from the horizontal, slowly or quickly to the perpendicular, and again to the horizontal, which may be repeated. The eye being necessarily fixed on the trainer, secures the attention, and this, and every similar exercise, establishes the habit of obedience and order.

quantity of water...*in its stomach, it would die*—for want of water—or from... *thirst.* Why? *On account of the heat*—and dryness of...*the sandy deserts.* You also told me that the camel's hair was...*fine*—and what color? *Brown*—a light...*brown color*,—and that the people make it into...*cloth*—for...*mantles and cloaks.* And what did we say about its feet? What sort of feet has the camel? *Soft and spongy;* and what else? *Large.* Why soft? *To tread the sand.* And why are they broad? *That they may not sink in the sand*—when the camel has... *a large burden on its back.* The camels go in great numbers through the deserts, with men, women, and...*children*—on...*their backs*—and also a quantity of... *goods;* but we must speak about these things again. It is time now to get out to the play-ground for a little.

I am thinking, children, of the camel's feet. Whether is the foot of the horse or the camel the softer? *The camel.* The camel walks so gently on its soft feet, that were one to walk along this floor, you would scarcely hear...*it was walking.* It would scarcely disturb little Henry, here, who is beginning to...*sleep.* Henry is not...*sleeping*—but just a...*little sleepy;* he must, therefore, get out soon into the play-ground, else he will get...*fast asleep.** So you think the soft gentle walk of the immense camel, passing the gallery, would disturb a half-sleeping boy? *No, Sir.*

Now, children, prepare to march to the play-ground. We shall sing the song, "Now, since our lesson's o'er." March prettily—make little noise—do not scrape or beat the floor with your feet. Go on.

To many persons who are unacquainted with the Training System, this example may appear absurdly tedious. Slow, however, as the process is which we have exhibited, many points, even of the few that have been pictured out, are too abrupt. The whole, no doubt, might have been told the children by *explanation*, and embraced in half-a-dozen sentences; or by the question and answer system in a couple of pages; but mere external objects, however varied, or explanation by the master, never can secure an equal amount of understanding as does the principle of *picturing out* in words by familiar illustrations—questions and ellipses mixed, etc.

A trainer who can conduct the first stage or outlines properly, finds no difficulty whatever in conducting the subsequent stages—each succeeding exercise also, on any subject, finds the pupils more capable of bringing out the lesson, so that what would occupy a fresh trainer and fresh scholars one hour to picture out, so as to draw the lesson, will be eventually more easily done in twenty minutes.

PRACTICAL EXAMPLE II.

Stage I.—(Children, who may have been One or Two Years under Training.)

The Mole.

Tell me children, where the mole lives? *In the earth*—under†...*the ground.*

---

* Long before the speech is ended, little Henry, of course, is quite lively. A pull, a push, a scold, or a touch with the rod, whatever effect such may have at the moment, is not so lasting as a general appeal to the understanding and feelings.

† Three dots ... mark the ellipses. Italics the answers of the children.

How many feet has the mole? *Four.* And it is therefore called...*a quadruped.* Where do most quadrupeds live? *Above the ground.* Right. What sort of fore-legs has the mole?—long or short? *Short.* Now, since animals live in such different situations, what should you expect them to be? (No answer.) Do you remember the lesson we had lately on birds? *Yes, Sir.* Well, what was said about land and water birds? *The water ones had webbed feet.* And why? *That they might swim.* But besides the swimming ones, there are some that go to the water and...*wade.* And what have they? *Long legs.* And besides, they have very...*long necks*—and...*short tails.* What would a pheasant or a peacock's tail be to them if they were wading in the sea or a river? *It would trouble them.* It would be...*cumbersome.* Without such a tail they are much more...*comfortable.* When you look at a land bird and a water one, and compare them, what do you notice—do you observe any difference? *A great difference in the way in which they are made.* What was the word that was formerly given, instead of the way in which they are made? Try to remember. *Structure.* Quite right; and they are made differently, or have a different...*structure*—because they differ in their...*ways of living*—or their... Who remembers the word that means ways of living? *Habits.* Now, all sit upright and attend. When you find an animal of a particular structure,* what will you be led to think about it? *That it has particular habits.* And if you are told that an animal lives in an uncommon place, or has particular habits, such as the mole, what will you expect it to be? *Of a particular structure.* All will now answer me. The form or structure of an animal is always well...*fitted to its way of living.* All again. The habits and structure of the animal always...*agree—suit one another very well.* We'll now hear this boy in the lowest seat repeat it... Quite correct.†

Many of you, I dare say, have seen what the mole makes in the fields? *Mole-hills.* If you take away the earth, what will you find below? *A round hole.* What size—large or small? *Like the hole in our water-pipe.* And out of this hole it has...*thrown all the earth.* In what direction does the hole go? *Downwards.* Yes, for a little, and then it goes far...*along.* I perceive most of you have seen mole-hills. Now, hands up all who have seen a mole. (Only two or three have seen the animal itself.) You who have seen a mole will tell about what size it is? *A rat.* Well, let us try to find out then, what kind of body would be best...*fitted*—for its...*place of living*—and its way...*of living.* What does it feed upon, do you think? *Worms and insects.* And what must it do to get them? *It must dig through the earth.* Just like a... Tell me any sort of people who dig along below ground—below the earth. *Miners*—or...*colliers.* But then the miner, when he makes his way under ground, what has he to work with? *Picks and shovels.* What does the mole use? *Its feet—its nose.* When this boy speaks of its nose, what other animal is he very likely thinking of? *A pig.* And if it uses its nose, what should it be? *Sharp and strong.* Just like...*the pig's*—which uses its nose for the...*same purpose*—for the purpose of...*digging.* It digs for...*roots.* But as the mole has more digging than a pig,—besides its nose, what will it also use? *Its feet—legs.* Which? *Its fore feet.* It will chiefly use its...*two fore feet*—for the purpose of...*digging*—because they are...*thick*—and...*short.* What do you observe on the toes of animals? *Nails, claws.*

* However complex the word may be, when clearly pictured out, it may be used ever afterwards.

† Inverting or reconstructing the sentences, more especially in regard to juvenile children, is of great importance, for obvious reasons, as we have already stated.

Since the fore feet have so much more work than the hinder ones, you would expect them to be—stronger or weaker? *Stronger.* Quite correct. They are very...*strong*—and you would say, such strength is...*very necessary.* What kind of legs do you think will be most convenient under ground? *Long, short...* Whether will a tall or a short man get along a coal mine more easily? *A little man.* But the mole, if it had long legs, might make its hole...*larger*, says a girl. That is quite true, and in a large hole or gallery, a long-legged mole would go along as...*easily*—as a...*short-legged one*—would do in a...*small one.* But if the mole were to make a large hole, it would have more...*work*—and if more work, it must take a...*longer time.* Now, if moles are like children, they will be anxious to save their...*labor.* Which legs, then, will best fit the mole to save labor and time? *Short ones.* Short ones will be more...*convenient.* With short legs their work...*will be less.*

When a dog scrapes away the earth, where does it put it? *It throws it under his body.* Yes—between its body and the ground there is plenty of...*room*, because its legs are...*long.* But with legs very short, the lower part of the mole's body almost...*touches the ground.* And if it touches the ground, in what way will it be better to throw the earth? *Away by the sides.* All will repeat. The earth will be...*thrown back*—not under its...*body*—but...*by the sides.* And why? *Because of its short legs.* As it throws the earth back with its feet, what do they answer for? *A shovel.* Right; and a shovel is...*broad.* When it digs, it uses its...*feet*—like a... What do laborers use to break up hard ground? *A pick.* Therefore its feet must be...*sharp*—and... What else? *Strong;* and when the earth is loosened, it uses them for a...*shovel*—therefore the mole's feet should be...*broad.*

You told me before that the nose was...*sharp*—and round the shoulders how do you think it will be? *Thick.* How will the body be toward the hinder parts? *Smaller—Thicker.* Some say thicker, and one says smaller. Let us see. If this were the hole (drawing it on the blackboard, or forming the shape with your two hands,) and the body of the mole were large behind in this way—if it were to throw the soil back, what would happen? *It would not get past.* What would not get past? *The earth would not get past*—past the...*hinder part of the mole.* Surely; and then the mole could not...*get forward.* When it has got a quantity of soil past its body, what will it do with it? *Push it all back.* Yes, out of the...*mouth of the hole.* All will now tell me the shape the mole should be of. You have heard that its nose should be...*sharp and strong*—its feet...*broad*—its shoulders...*thick*—and its body growing rather...*smaller behind.*

What do you think the body is covered with? *Fur.* And whether should it be soft or stiff? Suppose an enemy of the mole to meet it in front, what would the mole do? *Run away.* But before it could run, what must it do? *Turn in the hole.* But you remember the hole is just about the width of its body—what must it do? *Go backwards.* Yes, it will run backwards till it comes to some...*opening*—or...*hole below*—and then it will run... How? *Forwards.* When it runs backwards, the hair would...*rub against the sides of the hole*, and the hair would be...*raised*—or...*ruffled.* And if it were stiff, it would be just like a... What do we use to take off the dust from our clothes? *A brush.* What, then would be done if it were to be brushing all the way backwards? *The earth would tumble in.* Right; and it would get into...*a heap*—and the poor mole would be...*stopt*—and... What would happen to the mole? *It would be caught.* Now, what kind of hair would be most suitable? *Soft.* Right; and if very soft, when you draw your hand along the back from the tail to the head, how will it be? *Nice and soft*—it will be nearly as smooth as when you...*draw it the other way.* Besides, if it were stiff, when the earth is moist, the animal would become... How? *Dirty*—the soil would stick on the...*stiff hairs;* but if it were soft, the soil or earth would...*fall off again,* and it would still be...*clean.* The hair of the mole is very soft, and is called...*fur.* God therefore has given the mole... what sort of hair? *Soft*—that can move as easily...*backwards as forwards.*

When earth or dust is falling all round us, as it will be when the mole is digging, what are we afraid of? *Our eyes.* Quite right; our eyes are very...*easily hurt.* There are some animals, like the hare, that have very large eyes, but besides being large, they are very... Do you remember what we said about the hare some weeks ago, when we had a lesson on that animal? *The eyes stand out.* Another word for standing out? *Prominent.* All will repeat the word that means standing out? *Prominent.* The hare's eyes are large and...*prominent.* And if the mole had such eyes, what would you say? *They would be hurt—they would be in the way.* What must we have besides eyes that we may see? *Light.* And where does the mole chiefly live? *Under ground.* And, under ground it is...*very dark.* When a collier goes down the pit, he takes...*a lamp;* but as the mole has no lamp, having eyes in the dark would...*be useless.* Will it have any need of eyes at all? *No, Sir.* This boy, perhaps, remembers hearing people say to others, You are as...*blind as a mole.* I must tell you that sometimes the mole comes above the ground, then eyes will be...*useful.* But as it is oftenest under ground among falling earth, you say they need not be...*large*—and especially they should not be...*standing out*—or...*prominent.* All will now repeat; the eyes should be...*small and low*—that is, sunk in... Where? *A hollow place.* And if sunk in a hollow place, what would happen? *They would not be easily hurt.*

We shall now go over the chief points once more, all answering. You think it should have its nose...*sharp*—and...*strong*—its legs...*short*—feet...*broad*—to make its way...*through the earth.* Its body thick at...*shoulders*—towards the tail rather...*smaller*—that earth may get... How? *Easily past.* Its fur would require to be...*very soft*—and its eyes prominent, or how? *Small*—and...*sunk in the socket.*

Now, look at this stuffed mole, and compare it with what you have told me. Every thing that you could think of, and a great...*deal more*—has been given by... *God*—to make the mole...*happy*—and to add to its...*comfort.* At once you see here the Creator's *wisdom*—and...*power*—and... What else? *Goodness*—to suit it for the kind of life God desired it should...*live in.*

PRACTICAL EXAMPLE III.

Stage III.—Air a Conductor of Sound.

Children, we are to have a lesson to-day upon sound.* What do you mean by sound, children? *Noise.* What is a noise? You hear my voice just now; do you call it noise? *Speaking.* True, I am speaking, and you hear me...*speaking just now;* but would it be possible for me to speak without you hearing me? *No, Sir.* Think for a moment. Am I speaking just now? *Yes, Sir, you are speaking to yourself.* I am speaking, you think, but you...*do not hear.* Now, why is it you do not hear? When you hear me or any one speaking, you...*hear*

* It is well to tell the children at once the subject of the lesson.

a sound; or if I strike my hand on this...*desk*—you...*hear a sound.* You know what I am saying when you hear the sound of my...*voice*—and you know what I am doing by the sound of...*the hand.*

I wish to know why it is that I can move my lips without your hearing me speak, or lay my hand on this desk without hearing a sound? Tell me what sound is. I suppose I must tell you.* You all know what air is? *Wind.* Wind is certainly air—air in...*motion*, but if not in motion it still would—be... *air.* Air, you know (from former lessons) is a...*substance;* and however light air may be when compared with the...*desk*—still it is...*a substance.* We say "light as air," air, however, has...*weight.* Do you remember how heavy atmospheric air is? *It presses on all sides with a weight equal* to about 14 lbs. *on the square inch.*† It presses this way, and...*that way*—and...*every way*—equal to about...14 *lbs. to the square inch.* There is something substantial in any thing that may be beaten, or...*squeezed*—or...*pressed.* If I turn this slate on its broad side slowly, do you hear any thing? *No, Sir.* Now, I shall move it smartly, what do you hear? *A sugh.* What is a sugh? *A sound.* Is sugh the proper word, children? *No, Sir; sound.*‡

Now, children, tell me how is it that you hear me speaking? *By the air.* When I strike my hand on the desk, what happens? *There is a sound.* True, there is a sound; but how is the sound produced? We shall see how it is. When I strike my hand upon the top of this desk, it makes the desk... What does it make the desk do? *Sound.* Observe; I shall strike my hand upon this... *wall*, and then upon the desk, and you will tell me which gives the greater sound. Which? *The desk.* Why so? *It shakes more and vibrates.*§ You think the stroke made on the top of the table vibrates more than...*the wall.* Very well, then, why was there a greater sound from the table than from the wall? You told me that you heard me speaking by...*the air.* How do you think you can hear the sound of my striking the desk? *By the air.* And the sound from the wall? *The air.* Then why should there be any difference between the loudness of the sound from the table and the wall? (You don't know, I see.)

You told me that the atmospheric...*air*—the air that is in this...*room*—is...*a substance.* You saw me strike the air which you say is...*a substance*, very smartly with the...*slate*, and you heard...*a sound.* Now you also told me that the table vibrated that is...*trembled.* By vibrating, what do you mean? *Trembling or quivering;* that is to say, if the top of the table trembled or...*quivered*—it was set...*a moving*—or...*in motion.* The top of the table was not at rest, but... *in motion*—moving very...*quickly.* What did the top of the table strike against, for you know if the top of the table moved‖ it must move against something? When the top of the table vibrated like the top of a drum, what did it strike against? *The air.* The air being a substance, and filling every part of...*this room*—was struck quickly. How? *By the vibratory movement*—of...*the top of*

---

* The trainer has developed or ascertained the amount of the children's knowledge. They knew the facts, but not the reason.

† The children are understood to have had lessons on air before, but none on sound.

‡ In many quarters of the United Kingdom, provincialisms will be given by children in the course of training; and this mode may be adopted to correct them.

§ This term, of course, had been pictured out during some former lesson on motion, and therefore is now used.

‖ Although the whole body of the table may vibrate, it is preferable to confine the attention of the children to one point, so long as your statements involve nothing erroneous or contradictory.

the table. And... What did the trembling or vibratory motion produce? *A sound.* The air was moved up and down quickly from its place. Where? *On the table;* and this rapid...*motion*—of...*the air,* which is...*a substance*—produced... *a sound.* Whether will there be a greater sound when I strike my hand smartly or softly upon the table? *Smartly.* Why? *Because it will vibrate the more.* The top of the table will rise up and...*down more*—and, therefore, it will... What will it do? *Sound the more.* You will hear a greater...*sound*—because the air is disturbed or shaken more by the greater vibration, than...*the little one,*—than by the less...*vibration.* But why does the wall, when I strike it with my hand, not make as loud a sound as when I strike it upon the table? *The wall does not shake the air so much*—being...*harder*—or rather, not so easily...*shaken.*

Tell me now, children, whether the air will sound when it is in motion or at rest? *When in motion.* Wind, you know, is...*air in motion.* You say you hear the wind when...*it blows*—that is, when the air is in...*quick motion;* and when it can not easily pass a house, or a...*tree*—it makes a...*noise,* or...*a sound,* and you say, O what a noise the...*wind is making!* but when the air is not in motion, or moving only very...*slowly,* you say, There...*is no wind.*

Now, children, tell me what air in motion is? *Wind.* You tell me, wind, or...*air in motion*—striking against a house or a man, makes...*a noise,* and a noise is...*a sound.* Well, if I strike my hand on the slate this way, against the air, what will it produce? *A sound.* And what does it do to the air? *Sets it in motion.* My hand, or this...*slate,* or any thing I strike the air with, moves it... *out of its place.* And where does the air go to that has been moved out of its place? *To another place.* And where does that air go to? *To another place,*—and so on, still to...*another place;* and thus—the whole air in the room will be... What will it be? *Set in motion.*

We might extend the subject of this lesson, and proceed to picture out whether sound travels in straight lines as light does; for example, as in the case of the flash from the firing of a gun to the eye, or the report of the same to the ear, and why the sight and the sound are not simultaneously seen and heard. Also, by a shadow intercepting the light. Further, that light is not seen at all through an opaque body like a wall, and yet sound is heard through it although faintly. Why so? Again, small waves visibly come in circles direct to the person who may be bathing in the sea, but do not stop here, but come round to the opposite side of his body in smaller circles, diminishing in hight as they increase in diameter. This appears more plainly from a stone being thrown into a pond, each wave being succeeded by another, until they reach the side.

From all these points, when pictured out, the children will come to the conclusion, and tell you that light travels more quickly than sound, and in a different form—that light passes through the air in (pretty nearly) straight lines—that SOUND is not only conveyed by the air, but that it must move in circles. Thus we may trace the wisdom and goodness of God to us his intelligent creatures, in the varied effects of light and sounds upon the eye and ear.

It is the experience of almost every trainer, after conducting training lessons, that he has acquired for himself some minute points of knowledge of which he was formerly ignorant, or which had escaped his observation; and at the same time, established others of which he may have had only a very indefinite conception—practice, therefore, adds knowledge to the trainer as well as to his pupils.

SELECTION OF SUBJECTS FOR ORAL GALLERY TRAINING LESSONS ON NATURAL SCIENCE AND COMMON THINGS.

The trainer, whether conducting an Initiatory school or a Juvenile, may choose one particular lesson for each day, or he may take them progressively as they appear on the following lists. These lists are not presented because they are either complete or the best that might be selected, but simply as suggestive of such a useful course as that over which a master might successfully conduct his pupils in a shorter time than may be anticipated. The list No. I. should be considered more as initiatory and preparatory to No. II.; and therefore the subjects therein specified, when taken up for the first time with children of whatever age, are intended to be treated more generally. *The broad outlines* being pictured out first to serve as a solid foundation, and the more minute points, save such as may likely be interesting to the pupils at the time, being reserved to a period when their minds are better prepared to receive them. And in no case should a technical term be employed till the children have first had conveyed to them a clear perception of the idea therein involved.

The subjects contained in either list, more especially those in the first, are not designed to be taken up consecutively. The time for selecting a particular lesson can not be prescribed; it should rather be suggested by circumstances, particularly in an Initiatory Class—as by the season of the year, events of the time, nature of the weather, what the children may have seen or met with in their walks, any object exciting their curiosity or observation, what they may have heard that interested them, by their toys and by their games, at home or in the play-ground, etc., etc.

The lessons will thus prove greatly more natural, pleasing, and efficient, than if given in any connected course, however well arranged; as in the earlier periods of life, and even considerably beyond it, a mind free to be guided by the natural expansion of its faculties resents whatever is continuous. Here a little and there a little, is the natural principle of action. Any subject, therefore, however interesting, will prove tiresome if prolonged beyond due bounds.

List No. I.—Initiatory or Infant Department.

In drawing out these lists, as well as those of the Bible lessons, our greatest difficulty has been to limit the numbers, and yet present a sufficient variety of points for the school trainer to picture out as daily lessons, each occupying from twenty minutes to half an hour. One or other of such lessons as appear in Lists I. and II. form the basis of a daily Oral Secular Training Lesson both to pupils and Normal students.

1. *Grass*—Why the earth covered with it.
2. *Corn*—Its varieties, and the comparative amount of nutriment possessed by each sort.
3. *Peas*—Mode of supporting stalks.
4. *Potato*—Its history and qualities—contrast with bread.
5. *Plowing*—Uses of.
6. *Harrowing*—Wherein different from Plowing.
7. Advantages of Punctuality and Order—picture out—give illustrations.
8. Cleanliness and neatness in person.
9. *Bread*—Different kinds—how made.
10. *Tea and Coffee*—Where grown, and their use.
11. *Sugar*—Where grown, and mode of culture.
12. *Refining* of Sugar.
13. *Molasses*—What, and how prepared.
14. *Milk*—How obtained, and its uses.
15. *Butter*—How made, and how preserved.
16. *Bee*—Outlines of its habits—Industry.
17. *Foot of Fly and Boy's Sucker*—Compare—Philosophy of these.
18. *Honey*—What is it, and how obtained.
19. *Bee's Wax*—How formed.
20. *Wisdom* of Bee displayed in construction of cells.
21. *Spider*—Nature and habits—food.
22. *Spider's Web*—How formed.
23. *Ant*—Its nature and habits.
24. *Ant*—Different kinds of.
25. *Caterpiller*—Its transformation.
26. *Silk-worm*—Its natural habitat—on what fed—how kept in colder climates.
27. *Silk*—Whence and how obtained.
28. *Silk*—Contrast with cotton and sheep's wool in the formation of yarn or thread—comparative strength—why.
29. *Covering of Birds*—Admirable adaptation to their mode of life.
30. *Nests of Birds*—Why of different colors, and why instinctively placed in different positions.
31. *Covering of Waterfowls*—Contrast the hen with the duck as suited to their particular mode of life.
32. *Web-footed Birds*—Enumerate—why webbed.
33. *Beaks of Birds*—Contrast the hawk with the raven and swallow.
34. *Waders*—The Heron, etc.
35. *The Camel's Foot*—and the reindeer's—wisdom in their formation—habits.
36. *The Dog and the Cat*—Compare their nature, habits and uses.
37. *Elephant's Proboscis*, and the Cameleopard's long neck in relation to their habits and mode of life.
38. *Hooked Bills and Claws*—Contrast—why so formed—compare with the Sparrow or Lark.
39. *The Sloth and the Hedgehog*—Means of defence—habits.
40. *The Lion and the Bear*—Nature—habits—means of attack and defence.
41. *The Hare and the Partridge*—Means of defence—habits.
42. *The Whale*—Where found—habits, size, how defended from cold.
43. *Sheep's Wool*—Why different in texture in different countries—advantage of this to the animal, and to manufactures.
44. *The Mole*—Its habits—mole-hills—fore-feet—means of defence—nature of its hair or fur, compare it with that of the dog or sow.

45. *The Structure of the Mole.*

46. *The Beaver*—Its teeth and tail—habits, mode of constructing its habitation—use of its fur.

47. *Rats*—Are they of any use—may they and such vermin be killed—and when—(nothing made in vain.)

48. *Clothes*—Of what use—would certain sorts be equally suitable in all climates.

49. *Dwelling-Houses*—Effects of overcrowding.

50. *Imperfect Drains*—Picture out consequences upon health.

51. *Water*—Weight—composition and uses.

52. Why does water rise in pipes to the level of fountain from which it is taken—picture out the philosophy of this.

53. *Perspiration*—Sensible and insensible—picture out the uses.

54. *Waterproof Clothes*—Picture out their effect on health.

55. *Reaping.*

56. *Winnowing of Corn*—Various modes of.

57. *Nostril*—Position and use.

58. *Weaving*—Picture out the principle, and compare it with sewing.

59. *Felted Cloth*—Picture out the principle, and compare it with woven cloth.

60. Compare the teeth of a Cow with those of a Beaver.

61. Various modes of catching fish.

62. *Frog*—Nature—habits—if of any use—(nothing made in vain.)

63. Compare the foot and feathers of the hen and duck in respect of their habits.

64. *Coral*—How produced—where—results.

65. *Oyster*—Its shell—habits.

66. Mode by which shell-fish attach themselves to rocks.

67. *Leech*—how it inflicts a wound—uses.

68. *Earth-worm*—Its use to the farmer.

69. *Bat*—Its habits—construction.

70. *Nettle*—Its uses—where generally found.

71. Mode by which animals defend themselves—horns—feet—speed, etc.

72. Lead and iron—compare qualities and particular uses of each.

73. Beat iron and cast-iron—how made—compare qualities and uses.

74. Compare the screw, pulley, and saw.

75. Teeth of animals—distinguish the variety and adaptation to their mode of living.

76. Flesh of the different animals used as food by man—compare beef, mutton, lamb, pork, venison, fish, and fowl.

77. Compare cold and warm-blooded animals.

78. Herring—habits—vast numbers, etc.

79. Compare clay, sand, lime, and other soils—uses.

80. Needle-making and pin-making—with their different forms and uses.

81. Greatness and goodness of God perceptible in the least things.

82. Comparative use of roots, barks, stem, and leaves of plants—circulation of the sap—how new wood deposited, etc.—wisdom displayed in all these.

83. The distinction between boiling, roasting, and stewing.

84. Yarn and Thread—Picture out the process of making each.

85. Warp and Weft—Is there, or should there be a distinction in strength.

86. The Cotton Plant—mode of preparation—why not grown in this country.

List No. II.—Juvenile Department.

1. *Heat*—Its nature—sources of.

2. Effects of heat on solids.

3. *Conduction of Heat*—Application to clothing—compare woolen and linen clothes—why a difference.

4. *Heating of apartments by Steam*—Do black or white pipes radiate best.
5. *Why does ice float*—Train out the advantages of this in regard to lakes, ponds, etc.
6. *Evaporation*—What is it—and how caused.
7. Why do we water our streets in summer.
8. *Wind*—What is it—and how produced.
9. Philosophy of drafts and air-currents.
10. *Land and sea-breezes*—How produced.
11. *Air*—Component parts and uses.
12. *Water*—Component parts and uses.
13. *What is meant by a vacuum*—and how produced.
14. Picture out simplest form of barometer.
15. Why does the barometer sink as we ascend a hill or in the atmosphere.
16. *Rain*—How produced—general form of the drops—why—where should rain be most abundant—and why.
17 *Formation of Clouds*—How kept buoyant in air.
18. Reason for winter clothing.
19. *The Quill Pen*—Its history.
20. Use of the pores of the body.
21. *The Eye*—Its position and construction—wisdom displayed—what effect if otherwise placed.
22. *Tears*—Their nature and use.
23. *Nails of the fingers and toes*—Compare with horns, hoofs, etc.
24. *Position and use of the thumb*, *and little finger*—Picture out wisdom in the various lengths of the fingers.
25. *Mortar*—How formed—why mixed with hair.
26. *The Roots of Trees*—Nature and use—comparison between that of the Italian poplar and the oak.
27. *Engrafting*—Picture out the principle of.
28. *India-rubber*—How and where obtained—uses.
29. *Gutta-percha*—How obtained—its uses.
30. Why does an iron vessel float.
31. Paving of streets, and of what materials.
32. *Glass*—Of what composed, and how manufactured.
33. Effect of pouring hot water into a glass suddenly—picture out the philosophy of this.
34. *Making of Shot*—Why round.
35. *Horseshoes*—Why does the animal require them.
36. How are we enabled to fix horse's shoes without inflicting pain.
37. *Paper*—How and from what manufactured—when first made for common use.
38. *Printing*—Picture out principle of, and when discovered.
39. Given the river system of a country to determine its mountain system, or *vice versa.*
40. Refining of gold, silver, etc.
41. *Gunpowder*—Whence formed.
41. Why does gunpowder propel.
42. The philosophy of keeping the body clean by water and rubbing.
43. Why does the firing of a musket produce a report when an air-gun does not.
44. *Air-gun*—Principle of.
45. Exhausting Syringe.
46. *Syphon*—Nature and uses.
47. *Intermittent Springs*—Why does not the water flow continuously.
48. *Magic-Lantern*—Principle and uses.
49. *Bramah Press*—Picture out principle of—uses.

50. Picture out the simple principle of distillation.
51. *Candles*—Of what formed and how.
52. *Soap*—Of what is it composed—and how manufactured.
53. *The Sun-Dial*—Principle of.
54. *Common Clock*—Construction of.
55. *Umbrellas*—Why so formed—when first used.
56. *Coal*—Its origin and how obtained—uses.
57. *Gas*—How formed—when first or generally used.
58. How is gas transmitted through our towns.
59. The Lightning Conductor.
60. Best mode of kindling a fire, so as either to have what is termed a brisk or a slow fire—philosophical mode of placing the coals so as to have either.
61. Why is snow white.
62. Picture out the uses of snow in protecting ground from severe frosts, and in supplying moisture, (in Siberia temperature of *air* is often below Zero, whilst the *ground* covered with snow is not much below freezing point.)
63. Picture out the reason why snow melts so slowly, and the beneficial effects of this, contrasted with what would happen if the contrary were the case.
64. *Snow-line*—Why does it rise as we approach the equator.
65. *Effect of light upon Vegetation*—(A vegetable which grows in the shade is pale and sickly.)
66. The reasons for the various forms of the external ear.
67. Why does fruit ripen more quickly against a garden wall, than if standing alone.
68. *What is Smoke*—Should any smoke be permitted to ascend the chimney—can this be avoided—picture out the philosophy of the principle of preventing smoke.
69. Why does a gardener cover his flower-beds with matting in a clear calm night.
70. *Circulation of Sap in Trees*—How effected.
71. Preservation of seeds of plants.
72. *Dispersion of seed*—How effected.
73. *Leather*—What is it, and how manufactured.
74. *Twilight*—How produced.
75. Why is there longer twilight at the poles than at the equator.
76. Why should we not eat the rind of fruit.
77. *The flying of Birds*—How effected.
78. Why are drops of water, mercury, etc., globular.
79. Thunder and lightning—distinguish the causes and effects.
80. Compare vapor, rain, dew, hail, and snow—outlines of, how produced.
81. Why can you put salt into a tumbler filled with water, and yet the water does not run over.
82. Why does one's image appear as far behind a plane mirror as he is before it.
83. *Barometer*—Principle and uses.
84. *Thermometer*—Picture out principle of.
85. *Pendulum*—Effect of heat and cold upon it.
86. Show how you would give children an idea of a map.
87. *What is money*—Why have coins.
88. *Circulation of Blood*—Compare with the circulation of juices in plants and trees.
89. *The Condensing Syringe.*
90. *The Air-pump*—Construction—uses.
91. *Davy's Safety-Lamp*—The philosophy of—uses—the radiation of heat. Why do we see the flash of a gun when fired before hearing the report—the philosophy of both.

92. By what means do fishes breathe.

93. Picture out the best means of ventilating a room, so as to have in it warm air and yet fresh.

94. The philosophy of making good tea, and whether water long boiled or just come-a-boil, is preferable.

95. Causes and cure of dry rot.

96. Whether will a ship sink deeper in the salt sea or in a fresh water river—the reason.

97. Picture out why the earth and moon keep in their orbits round the sun.

98. Why the length of day varies from the equator to the poles.

99. Gold and lead—compare qualities, malleability, value, ect.—uses.

100. Rope—compare relative strength of one made from cotton, flax, and sheep's wool.

101. Candle—why does the flame ascend—philosophy of this.

102. Rainbow—picture out the cause.

103. Particles of air and water—prove what form the particles are of.

104. Prove that air has weight—changes of weight.

105. Dyeing—picture out why wool is difficult of being dyed an engrained color.

106. Hairs—why are we apt to catch cold when our hair is cut—construction or form of hairs.

107. Steam-engine—picture out the parts and principle.

108. Balloon—cause and principle of its ascension.

109. Mineral strata—if any advantage by being placed in a slanting and not perpendicular direction—design and wisdom.

110 Why may a candle be shot through a wooden door—give the philosophy of this.

111. Lever—principle and use.

112 Volume and power of water when turned into steam—illustrate this by examples—tea kettle, etc., etc.

113. Phases of the moon—causes.

114. Sun or moon—causes of an eclipse.

115. Why fish die when taken out of the water—why a dead fish turns on its back in water—why blood cold, and of a blue color.

116. Sponges—whence derived.

117. Beneficial influence of the sun upon the creation.

118. Contrast iron and gold.

119. Means of supplying water to a city—how the water made to rise, etc.

120. Flowers—stem, flower-cup, petals, stamens, pistils—why some droop—difference in structure of those and upright ones, etc.,—abundance of flowers—use of same in pasturage.

121. Is vegetable life favorable to animal—picture this out philosophically.

122. Bring out the fact that the elastic force of air is proportioned to its density.

123. Train out the mode of determining latitude by the elevation of the Pole.

124. Bring out the ordinary method of determining longitude.

125. Different modes of noting time.

126. Center of gravity—which is safer, to rise or sit in a high-seated carriage, should the horses run off, and why.

127. Distinguish between wind, storm, hurricane.

128. The principle of Bramah's Press.

129. Picture out the principle of operation between a knife and a saw.

130. Electric Machine—the principle.

131. Galvanic Box—the principle.

132. The Sun—distance—velocity of its light—how ascertained.

133. Planets and Fixed Stars—distinguish—how—distances.

134. Comets—wnat supposed to be—velocity.

135. The Hand—principle of its motion—why fingers and thumbs of different lengths and thickness.

136. Gas--Effects on health--of permitting more to escape than can be consumed in ordinary burners—the principle of this combustion.

137. Steam Engine—effect of filling the box with steam, and condensing it alternately.

138. Distinguish the difference in fiber or staple between wool, cotton, silk, and flax—whence derived.

139. Dry-toast—effect of laying one slice above another.

140. The Human Frame—what latitudes most favorable to vigorous development.

141. Is light material, or immaterial—prove this.

142. Distillation—philosophy of—why is the spirit evaporated and then condensed.

143. The uses of Lakes—*regulators* of rivers.

144. Hoar-Frost—what is it—how formed—wherein does it differ from dew.

145. A laundress drops a little saliva on her smoothing iron to test its heat—on what principle.

146. The *Wedge*—the principle of.

147. The *Inclined Plane*—uses in every-day life.

148. Where should a bed be placed—near the floor, or at some distance from it, and why—picture out the effects upon health.

149. The *Telescope*—in its simplest form, what is it.

150. The Microscope—in its simplest form, what is it.

151. Why is it dangerous to drink cold water when the body is much heated.

152. Bathing—whether should a person bathe when the body is perfectly warm, or when cold—picture out the effect in both cases.

153. Why is it dangerous to bathe when the body is heated after much exertion.

154. Why is the horse fitted for bearing burdens, and the ox only for drawing.

155. Where are flies and other insects during winter.

156. How is a fly enabled to walk on the ceiling.

157. The helm of a ship—on what principle is it constructed—compare with the tail of a bird; for example, the swallow.

158. Bird's nests—Their position and color.

159. Why is a house built of stone warmer in Winter and cooler in Summer than one built of brick.

160. Windmill—what is the best position of the arms to secure the greatest amount of pressure from the wind.

161. The adaptation of food plants to climate.

162. Why is it colder with us in Winter than in Summer, though we are nearer the sun.

163. Effect of oceanic currents on temperature.

164. Instinct and Reason--illustrate and picture out.

165. Distinguish between a mineral, a plant, and an animal.

166. Why is the west of Europe warmer than the east.

167. The Snow Line—what causes it to ascend or descend.

168. Compare the foot and bill of the hen and duck in regard to their mode of life.

169. The philosophy of stirring a fire.

170. Why does gas or candle lights burn dimly sometimes in a crowded church.

171. The philosophy of airing a room from without. If by a window, whether top or bottom.

172. Why do the waves from the paddles of a steam vessel continue to roll till they reach the shore.

173. Prove how light travels—the rays of the sun for example.

174. Prove how sound travels—straight, curved, or how, by examples. The philosophy of this.

175. The philosophy of *deafening* the floors and walls of a house.

176. The philosophy of a boy's sucker.

177. The principle of a pop-gun.

178. Why does water rise to its source.

179. Compare lead and iron—qualities and uses.

180. Why do servants not clean or clear up windows properly with a dry cloth.

181. Picture out the operation of the axe and the saw, philosophically.

182. Picture out the chemical process, and effects of boiling, baking, and roasting.

183. The philosophy of preserving eggs *fresh* for weeks or months—we have here the pores in the shell—the principle of evaporation through these pores—why, when long kept and shaken, they may give a rattling noise. Effect of stopping up the pores by melted butter, lime, etc.

184. Effect of snow during winter on the surface of the ground, and on plants.

185. Much of the earth's strata—mineral ores and coal—are placed obliquely, at least not horizontally. Is this an advantage or disadvantage to man.

186. How earth and moon kept in their orbits.

187. The science of the tides.

188. Trade winds—how regulated.

189. The principle of the common bellows.

190. Why does the flame of a candle ascend—the philosophy of this.

191. Prove, by illustrations, of what form are the particles of air and water.

192. The use of the root of a tree, shrub, or vegetable—with their comparative size and shape to the plant itself.

193. Distinguish the difference of the bills, claws, and teeth of various animals, in regard to their mode of procuring food.

194. The philosophy of a glass being apt to break when hot water is suddenly poured into it.

195. The principle of the Lever, in its simplest operation.

196. What is electricity—how produced—(sealing wax—a cat's back when rubbed in the dark, etc.)

197. Lightning—how communicated—lightning-rod.

198. The electric machine—its construction and use.

190. The best mode of sweeping a floor so as to keep down dust.

200. Glass—of what formed—why transparent—when was it first used.

201. The effect of rivers as leveling agents. Illustrate—the Rhone—Nile, etc.

202. Why do rock cuttings in railways gradually crumble—(effect of air and water.)

203. Picture out the difference between thread and yarn—how made.

204. Why is sheep's wool more elastic than cotton wool.

205. What is smoke—The philosophy.

206. Why is the sea not increased notwithstanding the quantity of water that runs into it.

207. The atmosphere—what is it.

208. What is coal—where found—in what form are the strata generally found. *Wisdom.*

209. In placing coals for a brisk or a slow fire—picture out which way you would place the strata of the coal for either.

210. Compare weaving and sewing.

211. The Ant—habits.

212. The Beaver—habits.

213. Caterpillar—transformation.

214. The principle of turning water into steam.

6

215. The comparative nutriment in potato, flour, and oatmeal.

216. Picture out the principle of engrafting.

217. Picture out the different effects of a screw nail and a common nail.

218. Picture out the difference, if any, in water just "come-a-boil," and water that has been boiling a quarter or half-an-hour, in making tea.

219. Compare the science of the telescope and the microscope.

220. The philosophy of the motion of the circulating swing in the play-ground, comparing it with the sitting-swing, and their effect on health (the one throws the blood toward the head, and the other toward the feet.) Gravitation, capillary attraction, and centrifugal and centripetal forces—all involved in this.

The master trainer will keep steadily in view that every point of research in an oral training lesson has its less or more intimate associations with other points in science, however common or familiar the object—the hand, eye, and tongue with the brain—the foot with the knee—and the vacuum with atmospheric pressure, as in "*The Boy's Sucker*," etc.

The foregoing points, each forming a training gallery lesson, and pictured out in their outlines and more common uses, will prepare the pupils to advance stage by stage, and step after step, to other more minute practical points.

List No. III.—Senior Department.

The following has been gone through most intelligently, twice or thrice, with a class of forty pupils (boys and girls,) in one of the training schools in Glasgow:—

Matter—What signified by the term—its general laws and properties, impenetrability, extension, figure, divisibility, and inertia—resolution of forces, etc., etc.

The earth—Its form—how proved—measurement and magnitude—proportions of land and water on its surface. Explanation of the terms, latitude, longitude, equator, ecliptic, tropic, arctic, antarctic, zones and poles, horizon and cardinal points.

Its Motions—Their causes and effects—the alternation of the seasons, and of day and night with evening and morning twilight.

Inequalities of the Earth's surface—Mountains, valleys, table-lands, and plains, under the various names of blanos, pampas, savannahs, prairies, and steppes, with their properties and uses.

Causes of change in the Earth's surface—Coral insect—volcanoes, active, intermittent, and extinct—earthquakes—the theory of volcanoes and earthquakes, with their varieties and an outline of the volcanic world, with the changes being there produced—detrition of rivers and their deposits in lakes and seas—action of tides—and the degradation of mountains by the influences of frost, air, and water, etc.

Varieties of Climate—In different latitudes and at different altitudes—in the same latitude and at the same altitude—circumstances affecting it, such as soil, shelter, inclination of the land, insular or continental position, proximity to frozen regions of arid deserts, etc., etc.

Rivers—Their origin, increase, and destination—watershed of a country—why does the middle of a stream move more rapidly than the sides—the motion of a fluid how accelerated in a confined channel—whirlpools—rapids—cascades and cataracts—how tracing the direction of rivers on a map gives the inclination of the land—their classification as to length—how the extent of their course generally determines as to their being navigable—streams, temporary and perennial—the properties and uses of rivers.

Lakes—Salt and fresh—their various classes and elevations—their properties and uses.

Seas and Oceans—Their varieties of temperature and depth—advantages derived from the sea—why salt—why in constant agitation.

Water—Salt and fresh—why former more buoyant than the latter—why some bodies sink and others swim—specific gravity of bodies—mineral waters—why purest water insipid—springs, their sources—permanent, intermittent, and thermal springs—ancient and modern modes of conducting water—its properties and uses.

Tides—How produced and regulated—phases of the moon—eclipses and causes—harvest moon.

Currents—In the ocean—polar, equatorial, contrary, and under-currents, with examples, and how proved to exist—how temperatures of seas thus effected—how drift-wood, seeds, etc., thus carried unerringly to distant shores.

Atmosphere—Its hight—its composition—oxygen, nitrogen, hydrogen, and carbonic gasses—means appointed by Providence to preserve the air in a state capable of sustaining animal life—whether more wholesome to have growing plants in a sitting room by day or by night—why the air of cities more impure than that of the country—the general properties of air and its important uses both to the animal and vegetable creation—breathing and burning compared—construction of the air-pump.

Heat—Natural and artificial—latent heat made manifest by friction, percussion, compression, and produced chemically—spontaneous combustion, conduction, diffusion, radiation, reflection, and absorption of heat—colors which absorb and radiate best—its expansive effects on various bodies—on the air, rarifying it and producing currents or winds.

Winds—Permanent, periodical, variable, and local, how accounted for—whirlwinds and hurricanes—various velocities, temperature, and names of winds—why a gale in winter heavier than one in summer—uses of storms—application of the winds by man.

Effects of Heat on Water—Producing vapor—tendency of vapor to ascend—formation of clouds—condensation of vapor by cold—descent of rain—why in globules—formation of snow—why white—of hail, of fog, of dew, and of hoarfrost—explanation of the forms they assume—the rainbow—how produced.

Thermometer, *Barometer*, *Diving-bell and Apparatus*, *Syphon*, *Balloon*, *and Water-pump*—Principles of construction.

Distribution on the Earth's surface of Vegetables, Animals, and Man—What is meant by an Organic and what by an Inorganic substance.

Difference between a *Mineral*, a *Plant*, and an *Animal.*

Distinctive Characteristics of Man.

Divisions and *identity* of the *Human Race.*

Wisdom of God in connecting the different parts of Nature.

Mineral Kingdom—Mines in Great Britain, why superior to those of any other kingdom, though not supplying the precious metals—Iron—Tin—Copper—Lead—Mercury—Zinc—Silver—Gold—Platina—Sodium—Magnetic Ore, etc., with their properties, process of manufacture, and uses to mankind.

Rocks—Different formations, granite, limestone, flint, freestone, slate, alabaster, mica, asbestos, petrifactions of various kinds, and a few of the more common and remarkable crystals—clay and soil—fossil remains of animals and plants, etc.

Coal—Its formation—manner of deposit—varieties—association with iron ore—manufacture of coal gas—best position for the gas works of a city, etc.

Salt—As found in mines, and manufactured from sea water or salt springs—its general distribution in nature, and valuable qualities.

Naphtha, *Nitre*, *Tar*, etc., etc.

Sulphur—Its properties, and in what kind of countries to be principally found.

Vegetable Kingdom—General physiology of plants, aquatic and terrestrial—

their divisions—organs, roots, stems, branches, and leaves, with their various functions—the sap, flower, and fruit—varieties in the manner of the growth of trees—changes of vegetation, with the varied condition of climate—air plants, parasites, moss, fungi, fern, lichens, sea-weed, etc., etc.

Vegetable Productions—How those of hot, cold, and temperate countries may all be found in the same latitude—their preservation, and the various natural agencies contributing to their diffusion, as the currents of the ocean, winds, and migratory birds—man a voluntary agent in effecting the same object—adaptation of food plants to climate reflecting the design of the all-bountiful Creator as to the diffusion of the human family.

Animal Kingdom—Animal life, its effects—divisions of the animal kingdom—the integuments of the animal body—pores and their uses—bones, cartilage, muscles, lungs, heart, and vessels of the human body—respiration—circulation of the blood—why warm in some animals, and cold in others—blue and red blood, how these colors alternate—the teeth—the eye, its construction and adaptation to the wants of various animals, as in the case of fish, birds, insects, animals of the chase, and those of nocturnal habits—organs of support and motion—animal mechanics—nervous system—human brain, its protection and position, and its size compared with that of other animals—organs of sense and voice—difference in the form of man and that of other animals—instinct of man and animals—clothing of man and other animals, that best suited for different climates—effects of climate upon animal clothing—uniform heat of the human blood in all latitudes, circumstances accounting for the same—change of food and clothing requisite for various seasons and situations—how man fitted to be an inhabitant of all climes—wherein man superior to the animal creation—reason—beauty and perfection of mind and body—preservation of health, influence of cold upon it, of exercise and rest, pure air, and the regulation of the temper and passions—man's mental and moral nature—his high responsibility.

Miscellaneous Subjects.

Attraction of Gravity and Cohesion—Chemical, capillary, magnetic, and electrical attraction—attraction which all masses of matter have for each other—disintegration and decomposition of bodies—their integrant and constituent parts—center of gravity—condition of standing bodies—an arch, the keystone, etc.—centrifugal and centripetal forces—pendulums, principle of motion—various kinds—adaptation to different latitudes—influence of heat and cold upon them—mechanical powers—their various combinations in different kinds of machinery—the advantages and power of steam in working the same—principle and construction of the various kinds of steam engine at different times in use, and of that at present employed—invention of the screw, and its application to the propelling of ships.

Magnetism—Discovery of the magnetic ore, and origin of the name—its properties—power of communicating its attractive influence without loss of strength—different modes of making a bar magnet—discovery of its polarity—its earliest employment as an indicator of the cardinal points—when, how, and by whom first applied to navigation—construction of the magnetic mask and mariner's compass—deranging influences to which the latter is subject—necessity of adjustment, generally after lengthened voyages or long detention in harbor—the earth a magnet—its power of magnetizing iron fixed in contact with it for a lengthened period, as iron palings, etc.

Electricity—From what substances first obtained, whence the name—electrics and non-electrics—various means of collecting it—electrical conductors and non-conductors—insulators—Leyden jar—dischargers, etc.—electric eel—production of electricity by the escape of steam through a narrow aperture—principle and construction of the ordinary electrical machine, and of the hydro-electric machine—identity of electricity with lightning—lightning conductors, why made to terminate in the ground and generally in a well—effect of the fluid when discharged into a vegetable or animal—thunder, how produced—auroræ boreales vel australes.

Galvanism—Its discovery, and the origin of its name—connection between galvanism, electricity, and magnetism—construction and principle of the galvanic battery—conducting of galvanism—its effect upon the animal body, and how transmitted—its application as a medical agent—principle and arrangement of the electric telegraph.

Sound—How produced and conveyed—echoes—bells—speaking trumpets, etc.

Light—Natural and artificial—effects of light on vegetation—various sources of artificial light—its mode of traveling, wherein different from that of sound—refraction—colors—bleaching—reflection—mirrors, principles and construction of plain and convex—concentration of heat and light—prisms, burning glasses telescopes—the daguerreotype.

Ventilation—Of private dwellings, places of public assemblage, coal-pits, etc., etc.—evils of bad ventilation—fire-damp—dry-rot, how originated, the cure—pestilence, etc., etc.—Sir H. Davy's safety lamp, principle and construction.

Smoke—What is it—must it of necessity exist—why it ascends the chimney curling in its ascent—what becomes of it—what is meant by a draught—why do some chimneys smoke, and how best prevented—why does a paper held in front of a fire increase its intensity, why are fires and stoves placed near the floor and not near the ceiling—why kept black—how heat may be conveyed from one apartment to another with little loss, etc., etc.

Ice—Process of congelation—why ice lighter than water—why formed on the surface of a pond and not at the bottom—why shallow water freezes sooner than deep—why water pipes liable to burst during frost—use of frost in the economy of nature—icebergs—ice-islands—ice-flows—drift, sliding, creeping and ice avalanches—extraordinary effects of the last—snow mountains and glaciers—line of perpetual congelation.

Boiling—Why a boiling fluid in continual ferment—why heat applied to the bottom of the vessel—why a dense fluid, or water slightly mixed with oil, retains heat longer than plain water—why hot water melts salt, sugar, etc., sooner than cold—the best method of melting such substances as sugar in a liquid—the degree of heat at which different fluids boil at the level of the sea—why they boil at a less degree on the summit of mountains—how so great a loss of heat in cooking at such an altitude as the Hospice of St. Bernard.

Solar System—Sun's distance from the earth—beneficial influence upon creation—apparent path—zodiac—tropics—nodes—solstices—aphelion and perihelion—why sun's warmth more felt in northern latitudes when the earth is in aphelion—sun's eclipse, equinoxes, etc., etc.

Moon's distance from the earth—influence on the sea—tides—lunar eclipse, etc.

Fixed stars—planets—comets—polar star—the galaxy, etc.

A class that has been carefully conducted through such a list of subjects as the preceding, will be prepared to enter upon a more consecutive course with advantage. We therefore present the preceding lists, by no means recommending that they should be strictly adhered to, but that the order of the subjects should somewhat vary according to circumstances. Whatever may be the order, however, in which the several lessons follow, we consider that to more advanced pupils a proper classification of the subjects afterwards will prove beneficial. The repetition of a lesson under the same head is no objection whatever, as it is impossible to exhaust all the points of any one subject with young children. The trainer will therefore, of course, *according to the system*, revise and proceed upon the previously acquired knowledge which he ascertains that his pupils possess.

Technical terms employed in describing the various departments of na ture and art are acquired to a large extent in the ordinary process of picturing out such lessons, and thus the student is prepared for proceeding with a more consecutive and extended course—also for apprehending more fully the phraseology of books and lectures on the different branches of science.

Each of the preceding points may be pictured out as a Training Gallery Lesson in school on Natural Science and Common Things, and may occupy from twenty minutes to half-an-hour daily.

Thirty years ago, so far as we know, we were the first to introduce Training Lessons on Natural Science suited to ordinary life and things. In the Model Schools of this Normal Seminary, it has been the practice ever since. The students have also been trained to practice it in the various schools to which they were appointed. The liberty of doing so, however, has not always been granted by Directors, who themselves had not been so instructed and trained. I trust this thoroughly intellectual, and highly useful *practical* principle will now be more heartily and systematically followed in our schools and colleges than it has hitherto been.

The simple reading of some point in Natural Science—a few only of which are to be found in school-books, and from which the teacher may put a few questions on the facts stated, is by no means sufficient to a clear and edequate perception of the subject. Questioning, it is evident, amounts merely to an examination—not training;—and is not an addition to the knowledge already possessed by the pupils. It exercises their memory of facts, but does not prepare their minds to draw the lesson or give the deduction. Besides, no extract on science in a schoolbook can convey one-tenth of the knowledge that may be, and actually is communicated by a practical schoolmaster during an Oral* Training Lesson. Sections III. and IV. present the theory of the principle—Section V. the practical working.

Be content with analyzing, illustrating, and thus picturing out in words to the mind's eye of your pupils, *one point* at a time *thoroughly*, rather than several points *imperfectly*. Condescend to use their simple words in the first instance, and rise progressively to the use of more complex terms—each term being pictured out to the understanding before being used. Do not forget *to invert* the sentences in the progress of the lesson which you accept as correct answers, forming one or two ellipses; you may then demand and expect a simultaneous answer from every child in the gallery.

---

* When we say GALLERY (Lesson) we mean this. Although the Training Lesson to one pupil is the same as to fifty or a hundred, yet the conducting of it with one is less efficient than with five—five also is decidedly less so than with fifty, arising from *the sympathy of numbers* (see Chap. XI.:) and fifty can not be so conveniently seated for every purpose and variety of instruction and training as in a Gallery

Many persons object to the Training System because they find it can not be adopted at once, by a highly-educated individual, having read a treatise on the subject, or having observed the practice in a Model School. We are not acquainted with any art that can be so adopted, without *training.* Most certainly this system of cultivating the whole child, in his threefold capacity, can not. Intellectually, even we can not. Every one must train himself *by a long*, or be trained by masters by *a much shorter* process. Who is it that can write, read, fence, ride, compose an essay, or preach, without previous preparation or practice? Who can make a shoe, or watch, or a steam engine, without training?

The Human Body and its Health.

In conducting training lessons on various portions of THE HUMAN BODY, and their relation to HEALTH, the lessons must not be too minute or complicated at the first, but simply outlines of their various forms and obvious uses, also the natural dependence of one upon the other—words alone may convey to children a sufficient idea of these relations, *without the presentation of any human skeleton.* The minute points of analysis may, and should be left, to subsequent and professional study.

As each child visibly has Head, Arms, Legs, Eyes, Ears, Ankles, Wrists, Hands, etc., and may also have had a lesson on the circulation of juices in plants—without the presentation of a brain, skull, heart, foot, lungs, liver, etc.—the actions of each, and their relation to each other, may be easily pictured out in words by a trained schoolmaster or mistress, assisted by the blackboard.

In order that the young mind may not be tired or disgusted by too consecutive a course of secular lessons, just do as in Bible training—vary the subjects daily. Thus, one lesson on the human body may be taken up weekly, and the remaining four lessons per week as part of the afternoon exercises, on some point of the various subjects of natural and economic science.

At each point of any lesson, not merely on the physiology of the human body, and its relations to health, but, as much as possible, at the close of every lesson on natural or philosophical science, let the wisdom and goodness of the great Creator and Preserver of all things be brought out from the pupils by the trainer, and in such language as is actually within their attainments.

1. HEAD—Bring out from your pupils—The brain as the seat of thought, with all the other obvious parts, such as—eyes, ears, nose, mouth, teeth, skull, etc., with some of their uses. This as a first stage—particular parts during subsequent lessons, and at different times, as may be. If too minute, the children will get tired, and even disgusted with the course.

2. TRUNK OF THE BODY—The most simple outlines of the uses of the spine and backbone, ribs, chest, heart, stomach, bowels, muscles or flesh, skin, nails.

3. LEGS—Picture out the most obvious formation and uses of the limbs above and below the knee—bones, muscles, sinews, skin, knee-joints, ankle-joint, foot,

with heel, toes, etc. The simple outlines of their most apparent uses individually and relatively.

4. ARMS—Single bone above, and double below the elbow—Why? Elbow-joint, wrist—union with hand.

5. HAND—Formation—Bring out, by familiar illustrations, the marvelous wisdom in the formation of the thumb, and different sizes, lengths, and position of the fingers, and the use of the hand as a whole.

6. EYE—The trainer will bring out, during the first lesson, from the children—where placed—in a sort of socket, surrounded by bone, and even partially protected by the nose from injury by a blow—of course more tender than even it; uses of eyebrows, eyelids, eyelashes, general form, having white sides and dark center, called the pupil or apple of the eye, by which we see. The center more easily injured, and therefore partially protected by the white side, where sand or dust is more generally received than in the middle of the eyeball, which is the organic point of sight. Having proceeded thus far with the outlines, a second lesson may be conducted on the various portions of the eye—WISDOM.

7. INTERNAL CONSTRUCTION OF THE EYE—Impression of objects on the retina, vision, optic nerve, etc.

8. EARS—Use, form, nature and use of the parts outside, and could they be better or more easily placed in the head, or elsewhere? Illustrate the wisdom of their position, shape, etc.—then internal construction.

9. HAIR ON HEAD—How grows, how colored—use in all climates.

10. CIRCULATION OF THE BLOOD—in veins and arteries—uses.

11. THE HEART—Its action—vitality—sensitiveness. The mere outlines during the first training lesson. Ample opportunities are afforded during other lessons on the connection of the heart and liver, etc., of bringing out more minute points, and action.

12. LUNGS—Picture out the action of the air on them, and then to whole life of the body—effect on the blood of the decomposition of the air—what portion of the air is repelled—what portion is retained, necessary, and conducive to life and health.

13. THE LIVER—The outlines of its action—blood vessels—and marvelous construction.

14. STOMACH, BOWELS—Deposit for food—digestion necessary for life and health—attention to what we eat and drink necessary—and that the bowels be kept in a proper state, free from extremes.

15. NERVES—Where placed—terminating generally in the brain—feeling of pain and pleasure through them—nerves in fingers, tongue, nose, etc., may be brought out from the children as examples (in their own terms.)

16. NOSE—Nerves—important use of the sense of smelling—familiarly illustrated.

17. TONGUE—Bringing out its connection with the palate, throat, etc., and through the quantity of nerves in this organ, its great importance, in the use of food and drink.

18. THE HUMAN BRAIN—Its position and protection.

19. PERSPIRATION, SENSIBLE AND INSENSIBLE—Through what medium—for what purposes.

20. Picture out the different effects on the human body of too little and too much exercise.

21. The philosophy of washing the skin of the whole body, and its effect on health. Give, or bring out illustrations.

22. The effect on health of sleeping in a small, ill-ventilated room. The philosophy of this, with facts.

23. Picture out whether it is preferable for health to have our bed placed near to the ceiling, or near the floor, or where.

24. Picture out—Why we are apt to catch cold after our hair is cut.

25. The effect of tight M'Intosh or water-proof clothes upon health.

26. Bring out scientifically the effect of cold feet upon health.

27. Whether is white or black woolen cloth the warmer in winter.

28. Illustrate the effect of square and rounded shoulders—also tight-lacing on health.

29. In bathing or washing the body—Picture out the effects of the cold water being applied, in the first instance, to the head or to the feet.

30. In what state should we use a cold bath—cold, warm, relaxed from fatigue, or how—(Too cold or too hot dangerous.)

31. Application of wine to medicinal purposes.

32. THE PHILOSOPHY OF AIRING A ROOM—If by a window—top, bottom, or how.

33. DIGESTION—Effect of eating slowly or quickly.

34. The philosophy of mastication—varied uses of the teeth, names, etc.

35. Picture out the causes and prevention of toothache.

36. Bring out the philosophy of whether an invalid is more apt to catch cold by sitting in front or at one side of the fire—supposing the doors and windows of the room are properly placed.

The trainer will remember that no one organ stands alone, but has others associated with it—which, of course, will be attended to in the progress of the lesson, The hand, with the arm, elbow, wrist, etc., and all with the brain.

If all classes of the community, in town and country, were trained from infancy to a knowledge of Natural Science in common things, as a part of their school education, what additional health and comfort would not mankind experience, especially in towns. The better arrangement of streets and squares—common sewers—chimneys for smoke—ventilation of houses—economy in fuel—"eatables and drinkables"—ventilation and heating of churches and halls for public assemblies. Should architects and overseers even be unacquainted with the natural and proper mode of arranging any particular matter, some of the workmen so trained no doubt would suggest the idea.

Many of the lessons which appear in these Lists might perhaps be better and more easily pictured out with the children if subdivided into two or three parts.

Very many of the minute yet essential practical parts of science, applicable to common life and things, the teacher will only gradually acquire for himself, during the process of picturing out the daily training lessons. Those who have passed through an extended University course of Natural Philosophy confess this to be their experience.

Apparatus, Diagrams, etc.

A trainer, possessing an accurate knowledge of Natural Science, may have an opportunity, in conducting his pupils through these several courses, of rendering the subjects doubly interesting, by means of simple apparatus of no very expensive kind, and of giving much useful instruction illustrative of every-day life. We strongly recommend, therefore, that where funds can be procured, every juvenile and senior school be provided with a few or more of such articles as are enumerated at the close of this chapter; but we consider, at the same time, that these should only be obtained and added to, as the acquirements of the particular school may suggest, lest expense be incurred in the purchase of things which the master might not be able to turn to good account. In such matters very much indeed depends on his own ingenuity in devising interesting and profitable experiments and such as he can render perfectly intelligible to his class, and use also as a basis in explaining the various phenomena of nature—much, likewise, depends upon his dexterity in the various manipulations, and in the improvement and repair of his apparatus. Whilst such appliances, however, are valuable assistants, they are by no means indispensable. On the intelligent and palpable picturing out of the particular subject in words mainly depend the success of the lesson. Devoid of this, apparatus and experiments, as well as objects, may serve for show, but answer little if any practical purpose. Students complain that they can not find books on science and the arts from which they can derive a knowledge of the points required to be pictured out in the daily training lessons, without an extent of reading which they can not accomplish, and a variety of voluminous works which are beyond their reach. They also equally complain that while Bible Commentaries in general give a good doctrinal or practical lesson, yet they do not present the natural picture, or analysis of the emblem, on which the lesson rests, so uniformly presented in the Bible itself.

Our answer is this, bring up the children to your own attainments, whatever these may be, *which the system of communication enables you to do*, and that will be greatly higher than any class of children that may be placed under your charge; and you and they, by this exercise, will mutually acquire a power of analyzing terms, and picturing out ideas, that will render folio volumes less and less necessary. Your own mental powers will get so sharpened up as to analyze more and more easily during the ordinary process of reading such books as are within your reach, which, coupled with the increased power of observation that practice bestows, will enable you to rise to a hight of knowledge, certainly as high as can be demanded in any initiatory, juvenile, or senior elementary school.

Institutions for the Deaf and Dumb.—In institutions for the deaf and dumb, the idea uniformly must accompany the term, otherwise the pupils can not advance one step. Hence the surprising *substantiality* in the knowledge acquired by these interesting unfortunates. It would be well were every master to adopt this natural process with ordinary pupils who are not deprived of such organs of acquiring information.

The Deaf and Dumb Institution of Glasgow, with its accomplished teacher and superintendent, Mr. Anderson, at its head, we would recommend as an excellent model of intellectual, religious and moral training to students; having in view the conducting of ordinary schools, with pupils perfect in all their faculties.

Simple Apparatus for a Senior or Juvenile School.

We now append a brief list of apparatus which may be rendered highly useful. But it must be remembered that the instruction is *not* in the instruments themselves. Many other things too tedious to enumerate might be added, but they will not fail to suggest themselves to a school-trainer as he proceeds :—

A gutta percha tube, twenty-five or thirty feet long, fitted to show how water seeks its level, and how sound can be more readily conducted than through the air.

A glass tumbler, containing about sixteen ounces, and graduated so as to explain liquid weights and measures. It will also serve to illustrate the principle of the Diving-Bell—the pressure of the atmosphere—oxygen as a supporter of combustion, and the amount of it existing in a certain volume of common air, etc., etc.

A Florence flask and spirit lamp, to illustrate the diffusion of heat in a liquid—expansion of water by heat—formation of vapor—process of ebullition—how water rises into a vacuum—the principle of Savery's engine, etc.

A water-hammer, to explain how bodies would fall *in vacuo.*

A glass globe, with a tube attached, and a small aperture below, for illustrating the principle on which a liquid flows from a cask and water from springs, etc., etc.

A glass syphon—a water-pump model—an air syringe and a water syringe.

A few glass tubes of various diameters and lengths, and some hermetically sealed at one end, fitting them to illustrate capillary attraction—the simplest construction of the barometer and thermometer—glass-blowing—the development of electricity by simple means—and the producing of musical notes by means of an ignited jet of hydrogen gas, etc., etc.

A barometer and thermometer consisting simply of the tubes filled with mercury, and a graduated card.

A differential thermometer or pulse-glass—a prism.

A gonigraph—a Gunter's chain—a tape-line—a yard rule.

A horseshoe magnet and a couple of bar magnets.

A magnetic needle balanced on a simple stand.*

* Such an arrangement is much superior to a regularly fitted Mariner's Compass. It illustrates the principle and use of the Compass, and serves for many other purposes in lessons on Magnetism.

A magnetic and an index needle arranged on opposite sides of a wooden dial, to illustrate the working of the electric telegraph.

An electric machine with Leyden jars, dischargers, insulated stool and the different articles requisite to the performance of a variety of experiments with the machine.

A microscope—an air-pump.

A magic-lantern.

In addition to the preceding articles, and where many of them are not available, diagrams, of which there are now a great variety published at cheap rates, including sections of steam engines, and other machinery, would be of great service. Prints in natural history, animate, and inanimate, are, of course, always useful.

Every trainer should provide himself, at all events, with geological specimens from the particular neighborhood in which he is located—with a variety of dried plants—and with fossils and petrifactions where practicable; and likewise encourage his pupils in making similar collections.

V. KNOWLEDGE OF COMMON THINGS;

AND PRIZE SCHEMES FOR ITS ADVANCEMENT.

"God hath framed the mind of man as a mirror or glass, capable of the image of the universal world, and joyful to receive the impression thereof, as the eye joyeth to receive the light; and not only delighted in beholding the variety of things and vicissitudes of times, but raised also to find out and discern the ordinances and decrees which throughout all these changes are infallibly observed."—*Bacon.*

"Man is approaching a more complete fulfillment of that great and sacred mission which he has to perform in this world. His reason being created after the image of God, he has to use it to discover the laws by which the Almighty governs his creation; and by making these laws his standard of action, to conquer nature to his use—himself a divine instrument."—*Speech of Prince Albert at the London Mansion House, March* 21, 1850.

The following Papers will exhibit the direction in which the friends of popular education in Great Britain are aiming to direct the labors of teachers and pupils, as well as the measures by which these labors are made effective.

EXAMINATION IN "KNOWLEDGE OF COMMON THINGS,"

Held at Belfast in 1854, *for the award of Dr. Sullivan's Premiums.*

The following extract from a letter addressed by Prof. Sullivan in February, 1854, to the Secretaries of the Board of Commissioners of National Education, sets forth the origin and object of his scheme:—

In the month of November last I requested you to intimate to the Board, that, if it would not be considered irregular, I would feel great pleasure in placing funds to the amount of £20 per annum in their hands, to be given in premiums to the teachers of National Schools in the counties of Down and Antrim, who should be found by our Inspectors, at the general examination held each year in Belfast, to be best acquainted with "*the knowledge of common things.*"

At the same time I stated that the Dean of Hereford (who has done so much to promote popular education in England, and, above all, to make it *practical* and *utilitarian* in its objects) intended to offer similar premiums to the teachers of elementary schools in the county of Hereford. In fact, the idea—and I consider it a happy one—originated with the Dean, and I am merely following the good example which he has set; and I feel great pleasure at being able to add, that several persons of influence and consideration are also following his example—among others, Lord Ashburton, whose admirable speech on the subject you must have read. In fact, this speech far exceeds in value even the munificent prizes offered by his lordship.

To return to the subject of my letter. As you informed me that the Board would feel great pleasure in having my premiums distributed by their officers in the way which I had proposed, I now beg to inclose the sum of £20 for the present year; and for the next, and each succeeding year, the same amount for the same purpose will be permanently provided by me. Perhaps I should mention that I have *personal* reasons for limiting my premiums to the counties of Down and Antrim. But even if I had not, I would, in order to make them of some value, confine them to a particular county or district; and it is to be hoped that many other persons will follow the example of the Dean of Hereford, and that similar premiums will soon be offered to the national teachers in every county in Ireland.

The useful information contained in the school-books published by the Board, will probably form the principal part of the examination for the present year; and as I consider the education of girls of equal, and, indeed, of *greater importance* than that of boys, I will suggest to Mr. M'Creedy to divide the premiums equally between the male and female teachers. In addition to an examination in the national school-books, the female teachers should be asked some questions in domestic economy. Some questions should also be taken from Dean Dawes' "*Suggestive Hints.*"

In pursuance of this plan, W. M'Creedy, Head Inspector, held an examination at Belfast on the 7th and 8th of December, of twenty-six male teachers, and on the 11th and 12th of the same month, of sixteen female teachers, on the questions printed below. We give a few extracts from his report to the Board.

The examination was in part written, and in part oral; the first three hours, from ten to one o'clock of each day, being given to the former, and from two to five o'clock each afternoon to the latter.

The nature of the written examination may be judged of by the questions which follow; but of the oral, want of space forbids me from submitting the same sure and simple means of judging, and I can no otherwise describe it than by saying that it embraced a full, searching, and minute inquiry into all those parts of the Board's series of school-books which at all treat of that large and miscellaneous class of subjects falling under the head of "common things." The men had twenty rounds of questions addressed to them, or five hundred and twenty in all; and the women, who were fewer in number, and whose written exercises were shorter, had not less than thirty-five rounds of questions put to them on those parts of the same course which it was thought more peculiarly incumbent on them to know.

The general answering in both kinds, and by both sexes, was excellent, and evinced a most respectable acquaintance with the various subjects touched upon. None exhibited any thing like a reproachful degree of ignorance or unpreparedness; and of those even who fell short of the prizes, many acquitted themselves in a highly creditable manner; while the successful competitors again displayed such a compass of knowledge, and expressed themselves, especially in their written exercises, with such accuracy and precision, not to say elegance of language, as surprised fully as much as it gratified me.

The names of the successful candidates, with the prizes awarded them, were as follows:—

Males.			Females.		
1st Premium,	Robert Irvine, . .	£5	1st Premium,	Cath. Mulholland,	£5
2nd "	John Browne, . .	3	2nd "	Susan Irvine, . .	3
3rd "	Mann Harbison, .	2	3rd "	Mary Bell, . . .	2

On the whole, the results of this examination were most satisfactory and promising, and such, I firmly believe, as would fully justify the commissioners in following the example thus set them, and so honorably for himself, by one of their oldest and most distinguished officers, by taking up and adopting for themselves the experiment, and extending it to a much wider sphere of action.

One thing, however, our teachers must ever bear in mind—that whatever *facts*, whether of art or nature, they communicate, they are to communicate in connection with the knowledge of the *law* which governs them, or the *principle* from which they spring, as by such teaching alone can acquaintance with the facts themselves be rendered lastingly interesting, or even in any high degree useful. For, without a knowledge to some extent of the laws which serve to explain, or intelligibly connect, their relations of coexistence or of sequence, the facts or phenomena of nature, like the characters of a strange cipher to one who has not the key, have no instructive interest for the observer; and, however much they may excite his fear, wonder, or surprise, serve rather to bewilder than rightly to inform his intellect. Facts in themselves, and isolatedly viewed, are dead things; it is only when united with principles they become living and productive. As has been finely said: facts, which, consigned to the minds of the unintelligent, are like seeds in a granary, unquickened and inert, imparted to those of informed and cultivated understanding, are like the same seeds when committed to a prepared and congenial soil, where they spring up into luxuriant vegetation, and bear useful fruit. "Do not," says Dean Dawes, in his excellent tract on the mode of teaching common things, "attempt to explain any common thing, until the children understand the law; and if you would have your lessons to be effective, be sure you perfectly understand the subject you are about to teach. In this part of your teaching, as in arithmetic and every other thing, let principles, be understood before you attempt to lay down rules and then the children will understand the grounds on which the rules are based. You must bear in mind it is the office of all such educational helps as have been brought before you in this* exhibition, 'to teach men to think, not to save them the trouble of thinking.' In this way I believe a vast amount of information might be imparted in our elementary schools, which would lead the children to take a great interest in what they are learning, and which would give a practical turn to their minds that no other kind of teaching could give. But I would have every teacher to bear this in mind, that it is better to teach a few things well, than a great many ill."

And to the same effect the Rev. M. Moseley:—"That," says he, "which is valuable in this kind of teaching is not, I apprehend, the knowledge of the "common things" professed to be taught, but the *science* of them.

"What is chiefly to be desired," says Mr. Bowstead, like Mr Moseley, one of her Majesty's Inspectors of Schools for Great Britain, "is, that this department of school-work should be handled more systematically, that the details of ordinary processes should always be accompanied by clear and simple explanations of the principles which govern them, and that teachers should aim not so much to store the mind with facts as to communicate to their pupils a power of reasoning upon and analyzing the phenomena around them."

Thus taught, the importance of such knowledge for all classes of the community can hardly be overrated; for by such a course of instruction our youth, when grown up and entered upon the world, would be fitted not only to view with intelligence the greater glories of creation, but to look with interest on the varied phenomena of social intercourse, *the things that before us lie in daily life*, to know which, as Milton has it, "is the prime wisdom;" and be prepared, too, as another equally great poet has expressed it—when in their daily walks, whether meant for harmless pleasure or healthful recreation—to find

"Tongues in trees, books in the running brooks,
Sermons in stones, and good in every thing."

And might we not further hope that, with their minds thoroughly imbued by such studies, and their perceptions thus made *quick to recognize the moral properties and scope of things*—to discover in every part of Nature's works, the meanest as well as the highest, the traces of law, and order, and wise and beneficent design—they would, not seldom, mount up in thought to Him—"the first Fair, first Perfect, and first Good"—whose bosom is the primal seat of law,† and the everlasting source of wisdom, harmony, and goodness; so that, in their case, as ever, science would prove to be the handmaid of religion!

Rev. F. Temple, now Head-master of Rugby Schools, in a letter on this subject—"the Teaching of Common Things"—remarks:—

On the whole, it seems to me that the title of "common things" is not very easily intelligible by itself. In order to understand it, I suppose I must have recourse to the books in which this knowledge is said to be found, and the examination questions in which it is contained. And it would then appear to be nothing else than the elements of physical science and political economy. But this definition is not yet precise enough; for if it were, there seems no reason

* Educational Exhibition of the Society of Arts, 1854.

† "Of law there can be no less acknowledged than that her seat is the bosom of God, her voice the harmony of the world; all things in heaven and earth do her homage—the very least, as feeling her care, and the greatest, as not exempted from her power. Both angels and men, and creatures of what condition soever, though each in different sort and manner, yet all with uniform consent, admiring her as the mother of their peace and joy."—*Hooker*.

why the phrase "common things," an ambiguous and rather ambitious phrase, should be used instead. Nor, indeed, would the promoters of the movement feel quite satisfied to identify their new branch of elementary education with any thing so old and familiar as the rudiments of physical science. Lord Ashburton evidently means to encourage the instruction of the children of the peasantry, not merely in certain subjects, but in accordance with a certain method. He does not mean merely that the children should be taught the principles of chemistry, of mechanics, of pneumatics, and the like, but that the teacher should, as far as possible, take nature for his laboratory and demonstration room; should make all his science immediately practical and real; should compel his pupils to feel that the knowledge which they were acquiring, was not some recondite mystery, with which their lives had little to do, but a matter of the most ordinary experience, and one in which their concern never for one moment ceased. The science of common things is not to be defined, the rudiments of physical science and of political economy, but these rudiments as illustrated in daily life.

As bearing on this subject, we can not here forbear quoting, from the greatest of our modern poets, the following noble lines on the union of knowledge with religion:—

"Trust me that, for the instructed, time will come
When they shall meet no object but may teach
Some acceptable lesson to their minds
Of human suffering or of human joy.
So shall they learn, while all things speak of Man,
Their duties from all forms; and general laws,
And local accidents, shall tend alike
To rouse, to urge; and, with the will, confer
The ability to spread the blessings wide
Of true philanthropy. The light of love
Not failing, perseverance from their steps
Departing not, for them shall be confirmed
The glorious habit by which Sense is made
Subservient still to moral purposes,
Auxiliar to divine. That change shall clothe
The naked Spirit, ceasing to deplore
The burthen of existence. Science then
Shall be a precious Visitant; and then
And only then, be worthy of her name.
For then her Heart shall kindle: her dull Eye,
Dull and inanimate, no more shall hang
Chained to its object in brute slavery;
But taught, with patient interest, to watch
The processes of things, and serve the cause
Of order and distinctness, not for this
Shall it forget that its most noble use,
Its most illustrious province, must be found
In furnishing clear guidance, a support,
Not treacherous to the Mind's *excursive* Power.
—So build we up the Being that we are;
Thus deeply drinking-in the Soul of Things,
We shall be wise perforce; and while inspired
By choice, and conscious that the Will is free,
Unswerving shall we move, as if impelled
By strict necessity, along the path
Of order and of good. Whate'er we see,
Whate'er we feel, by agency direct
Or indirect, shall tend to feed and nurse
Our faculties, shall fix in calmer seats
Of moral strength, and raise to loftier hights
Of love divine, our intellectual soul."—*Wordsworth.*

DOCTOR SULLIVAN'S PREMIUMS, 1854.—SCHOOLMASTERS.

First Day.—Three hours allowed for this paper. Three questions to be answered out of each section, and others as time may permit.

SECTION I.

1. Name and define what are called the general properties of bodies.
2. Name and describe the several mechanical powers.
3. Explain what is meant by the specific gravity of bodies, and show how it is estimated.
4. What is meant by the center of gravity of a body? Show how the center of gravity of an irregular block of wood may be found.
5. Distinguish between the terms *heat* and *caloric;* enumerate the several ways in which the latter is produced, and explain the difference between *latent heat* and *free caloric.*

SECTION II.

1. What is meant, *technically* taken, by the term *value?* Enumerate and explain the constituents or elements of value, and show, by examples, that the possession of the union of all these, and not of one or two alone, is necessary to an object to constitute it an *article of value.*
2. What is meant by *division of labor?* Show how such an arrangement naturally arises in the progress of society, and enumerate its several advantages, and, if you suppose it to have any, its disadvantages.
3. Are improvements in machinery, by which a few men are enabled to do the work of many, in the end, and judged by their total results, beneficial or otherwise to the working classes? If beneficial, show why, and illustrate by examples.
4. What is the nature of the connection between high rents and high prices?

a. Show that the high price of agricultural produce is not caused by high rents.

b. Show that the abolition of all rent would not necessarily tend to cheapen agricultural produce.

5. Define *taxes*, and explain what it is the subject receives in exchange.

a. Show in what respect the payment of a tax is like any other legitimate exchange or payment.

b. Show in what *two* respects it differs from other exchanges, and explain why it should do so.

c. Show that, generally speaking, and under almost any form of government, what the people receive in return for the tax is, on the whole, a fair equivalent.

SECTION III.

1. Explain the principle of the barometer, and the uses to which it is applied.
2. How is the formation and deposition of dew accounted for?

a. Why more copious in summer than in winter?

b. Why more copious on clear than on cloudy nights?

c. Why not deposited equally on grass and gravel, on broken and on unbroken ground?

3. To what hight can water, ordinarily speaking, be raised by the common suction pump? Explain its mode of action, and illustrate the principle by reference to other kindred phenomena.
4. How many sorts of levers are there? Describe the relative positions of the *weight, power,* and *fulcrum* in each, and give familiar examples of each.
5. Give examples of the various contrivances employed to increase and to lessen friction.
6. How are porous bodies affected by the absorption of moisture? To what practical account has the knowledge of this fact been turned in some parts of France?

SECTION IV.

1. What are the organs of respiration in man and the higher order of animals; Describe them, and explain their functions.

a. Describe the peculiarities of the respiratory system in birds.

b. Also in fishes.

2. Explain the composition of the atmosphere, and describe its several uses.

3. What is meant by the conduction of heat? Give familiar examples of good and bad conductors; and illustrate the value of the knowledge of such phenomena by reference to the arts and life.

4. Explain the formation of clouds and rain.

5. What are the necessary requisites of a correct balance?

6. Why will a glass sometimes break by pouring hot water into it?

7. Why will a heated body, if suddenly cooled by pouring cold water on it, sometimes crack? How has the knowledge of this fact been sometimes applied for the economy of labor?

Second Day.—Three hours allowed for this paper. Three questions to be answered out of each section, and others as time may permit.

SECTION I.

1. Define what is meant by *wages*, and say on what the *rate* of wages naturally depends.

a. Show that it does not rise and fall, as some suppose, with the price of provisions.

b. Show that any attempt on the part of the Legislature to determine this rate must be inexpedient and inoperative, whether the aim be, first, to fix it *higher*, or, second, to fix it *lower* than that which it would be the interest of employers to offer, or which the circumstances of the *labor market* would alone render legitimate.

c. Again, supposing the Legislature would concede, not alone to one or a few classes of workmen, which would be manifestly partial and unjust, but to all, which would alone be fair and equal, the right of fixing each their own rates of wages, and of enforcing their payment, show how the laborer, who is not only a *seller* of labor, but, almost invariably to a like extent, a *purchaser* of labor, would, in this latter capacity, be affected by such legislation?

d. Enumerate the causes which go to explain the inequality of wages in different employments; in other words, explain why, at the same time and in the same place, all workmen do not receive the same wages.

2. How is capital divided? Characterize the two kinds, and enumerate the things which, in the case of a farmer, for instance, fall under each respectively.

3. The interest of the corn dealer is supposed by many to be opposed to the public interest; now, take the two cases following, and state what you think the just inference on this point:—

1st. Suppose a corn dealer who, in anticipation of a scarcity, may have made large purchases of provisions, to have been deceived in his expectations, who are the parties to suffer most by his miscalculations?

2nd. Suppose, on the contrary, that he has not miscalculated, and that he has been right in his anticipation, who are the parties to be benefited?

4. In what way is security of property necessary to the growth of wealth?

a. Show that *inequality* of fortunes must *necessarily* arise with security of property.

b. Show that the robbery of the rich, and the equal distribution of their wealth among the poor, would not prove beneficial to a people.

c. Show that, however he may live, every man, rich or poor, spends his income, whatever it may be, or allows somebody else to spend it for him; and that the less he spends on himself, the more remains for others.

SECTION II.

1. Describe the structure of the eye in man, its humors, coats, &c., and explain how it adapts itself to different degrees of light, and the varying distances of objects.

a. Explain the offices of the eyebrows, eyelids, and eyelashes.

b. Explain the defects of short-sightedness and its opposite, and the remedies for each.

2. Describe the structure and action of the heart, and the course of the blood through the arterial and venous systems.

a. Note the difference of office between the auricles and ventricles.

b. Note the difference of office, structure, and position of the veins and arteries.

c. Note the difference between the arterial and venous blood.

d. Note the difference of the pulmonary and the general circulation.

e. Note when, by whom, and by *what steps*, the discovery of the circulation of the blood was made.

3. What is the distinction between *animate* and *inanimate* bodies?

4. State, with examples under each, the *five* important points, as mentioned in the Fifth Book, in which the vital principle appears to counteract the laws of general physics.

5. Explain the several steps or processes through which the food of ruminants ordinarily passes before its conversion into *chyle;* and state whether there is ever any departure from this order. Note the peculiarity of structure in the stomachs of the lama and camel.

SECTION III.

1. Of what substances do soils chiefly consist?

a. How are soils named?

b. What is meant by heavy lands?

c. How may such be rendered lighter?

2. What are the four things necessary to the healthy growth of plants? Illustrate your answer by examples.

3. What are the processes to which, after inclosure, and before cropping, it may be desirable to subject the land?

a. Explain what lands most need draining.

b. Enumerate in their order the several advantages of draining.

c. Explain the difference between subsoiling and trenching, and point out what is the most appropriate season for this latter operation.

4. What are the various modes by which plants are propagated?

5. On what principle is the *rotation of crops* founded?

6. What is the *twofold* division of manures mentioned in the "*Agricultural Class-Book?*" Enumerate those which would fall under each respectively.

a. What other threefold division of manures has been made?

b. What other *twofold* division is made?

c. Of the last, which is the more neglected?

SCHOOLMISTRESSES.

First Day.—Three hours allowed for this paper. Three questions to be answered out of each section, and others as time may permit.

SECTION I.

1. Describe the two chief defects of sight, and explain how they are remedied.

2. Describe the process of digestion, and the course of the food from its mastication until its conversion into chyle.

a. Note by what agency mastication is aided.

b. By what contrivance the food is prevented in its passage from the mouth to the gullet, from entering the larynx.

c. Offices of the crop and gizzard in birds.

d. What is observed of the crop in birds of the dove kind?

3. Describe the structure of the teeth in man, distinguishing the *temporary* from the *permanent*, and noting the number and divisions of each set. What are the advantages of cleaning the teeth daily?

4. State the marks of design in the structure of birds, and in the human spine.

5. Enumerate the differences between birds and beasts, as given in Sequel, No. 2.

SECTION II.

1. Describe the processes gone through in the manufacture of pins, as given in the Second and Third Book of Lessons.

2. Describe the processes gone through in the manufacture of ordinary sewing needles, as given in the Girls' Reading Book.

3. Give the substance of the lesson on the prognostics of the weather, as explained in the Supplement to the Fourth Book. Write out also as many of Dr. Jenner's "*Lines on the Signs of Rain,*" given in our Second Book, as you can recollect.

4. What are the general properties of metals? Write down in order, one under the other, the names of all metals treated of in our Fourth Book, and note some of the distinguishing qualities of each.

5. Why is the presence of flowers and living plants in a bedroom during the night thought injurious?

6. Write out the substance of the lesson on "Bread," given in the Girl's Book.

SECTION III.

1. Give a few examples to show how economy in the use of the raw materials tends to cheapen the chief manufactured product.

2. Why have kettles and tea-pots wooden handles?

3. Enumerate the capitalists and laborers whose capital and labor have contributed to form the cotton gown you ordinarily wear.

4. Name the countries from which we derive our chief supplies of the following commodities, viz.:—tea, coffee, rice, sugar, spices, pearls, cotton, tobacco, rum, brandy, iron, hides, timber, fruit, port wine, sherry, claret, mahogany and other hard woods, flax, hemp, and tallow.

5. Explain why it is that, in this country, ground which has a south-western aspect is preferred to that which has a north-eastern?

6. Write out the substance of the extract from Addison, on the "*Results of Commerce,*" as given in the Girls' Book.

Second Day.—Three hours allowed for this paper. Three questions to be answered out of each section, and others as time may permit.

SECTION I.

1. Of what country is the sugar-cane a native, and when and by whom was its cultivation first made known to Europeans? Describe the process of the manufacture of sugar.

2. Where is the nutmeg tree to be found? Describe the fruit, and mention the uses of its several parts.

3. Between what parallels of latitude is tea cultivated? Describe the plant, and how it is cultivated; when its leaves are plucked and how; and in what way they are prepared for the market.

a. By whom first introduced into Europe?

b. Into England?

4. In what way would you instruct your pupils to distinguish the four cardinal points of the heavens?

5. From what is paper manufactured? Describe the several processes through which it passes until it reaches the hands of the consumer?

SECTION II.

1. Mention the parts of plants essential to their growth, perfection, and propagation.

2. What are the various means provided by nature for the preservation of the seeds of plants, as described in our Fifth Book? What are the means provided for their dispersion?

3. Why is attention to the right ventilation of our apartments of such essential importance? Enumerate some of the ways in which the air of our dwelling rooms may become vitiated, and say in what way it may be purified.

4. When a female discovers her dress to be on fire, what should she do?

5. Enumerate briefly, as given in the Supplement to the Fourth Book, the things to be attended to, and the rules to be observed, by those who wait upon the sick.

SET OF QUESTIONS AT THE EXAMINATION FOR THE ASHBURTON PRIZES.

For proficiency in the teaching of "Common Things"—held for schoolmasters at Southampton, by the Rev. W. H. Brookfield, H. M. Inspector: and for schoolmistresses, at Salisbury, by the Rev. W. P. Warburton, H. M. Inspector—21st April, 1854.

SCHOOLMASTERS.

Morning—Three Hours allowed for this Paper.

Two questions to be answered out of each Section, and others as time may permit.

SECTION I.

1. Define the following words and phrases, and illustrate your meaning by their usage in matters of social life:—skill—industry—economy and forethought—wealth—money—value—price—laborers and employers of labor—capital and capitalist.
2. What is the usual consequence of an abundant or deficient harvest upon the price of food? and upon the wages of labor?
3. What is meant by division of labor? and show the importance of this in advancing the wealth and well-being of a nation.
4. What are the principal conditions of industrial success among the laboring classes, and what kind of training in early life is most likely to lead to it?
5. What are the necessary qualities of the food of a people, in order that the supply may be permanent? and how do foods for man and beast vary in this respect?
6. What metals are the most useful? Mention the particular properties which make them so; and give the outline of a lesson on iron or lead, and its uses, from the state of ore up to a knife-blade, or sheet-lead

SECTION II.

1. Point out the different ways in which the air in a dwelling-room is rendered impure, and the best way of ventilating the room.
2. What are the best materials for building a cottage; the necessary conditions of health with reference to the building; and which is preferable, a slated or thatched roof, and why?
3. What vegetables are usually cultivated in a garden? Which do you consider the most nutritious? and why? What rotation of crops would you recommend in a garden of one rood in extent?
4. What is the difference between porous and retentive soils, and how would you treat them? Explain the principle on which soils pulverize after frost, and the advantages of this.
5. Explain what is meant by a proper rotation of crops—by exhausting and non-exhausting plants. How would you ascertain what substances plants draw from the soil? and, having done this, how would you manure the land?

SECTION III.

1. What are the essential properties of matter? Define and explain some of them.
2. Explain what is meant by the attraction of cohesion and gravitation, and exemplify by giving instances of each.
3. Give Newton's three laws of motion, and illustrate the last by experiment.
4. What is meant by centripetal and centrifugal forces? and show how in different latitudes the weight of bodies is affected by the latter.
5. A body let fall from the top of a tower is three seconds before it reaches the ground; how far did it fall in each second? and what was the hight of the tower? If the action of gravity ceased at this point, how far would it fall in the next three seconds?

SECTION IV.

1. To which of the mechanical powers do the following implements belong:—a spade and fork in digging—the plow—the saw—the axe—a pair of scissors—a pump handle—the screw? Give your reasons in each case.
2. Explain the principle of a pair of scales, and of a common steelyard.

3. Explain the principle of the wheel and axle, and show how it is applied in raising up water from a well.

4. Show the use of the plumb-line, the square, and the spirit level to the bricklayer and carpenter.

SCHOOLMASTERS.

Afternoon—Three Hours allowed for this Paper.

Two Questions to be answered out of each Section, and others as time may permit.

SECTION I.

1. What are the principal bones of the human skeleton? How are they kept together at the joints; and of what substance are they composed?

2. Explain the construction of the spine, or of the hand, and the mechanical contrivances for the different movements which they are intended to perform.

3. How would you judge of the habits and food of animals from their jaws and teeth? Illustrate your answer by examples.

4. What are muscles and tendons, and their uses in the animal frame? And in the movement of one bone against another in the joints, how is it they are not worn away?

5. What is the cause of a defect in vision in what are called short-sighted and long-sighted persons, and what kind of glasses are required to correct it in each? What are the purposes of the eyelids and eyelashes?

6. Point out any differences in the eyes and ears of animals which show adaption to their respective wants.

SECTION II.

1. What is the difference between an artery and a vein, between arterial and venous blood; and why is the cutting or rupture of an artery more dangerous than a vein?

2. Give your reasons for thinking that exercise is necessary, and generally beneficial to all the animal functions.

3. What is meant by respiration? Explain how the chest expands and contracts in this process? And in what does the air breathed out from the lungs differ from common atmospheric air? What experiment would shew this?

4. Does the blood undergo any, and what change in circulating through the body? And explain the functions of the heart, arteries and veins in this circulation.

5. What are the properties of milk as a food, and the substances it contains? Is it equally good at all periods of life?

6. What analogy is there between the blood of animals and the sap of vegetables? In each case mention as many substances as you can for forming which they must contain the materials?

SECTION III.

1. What are the constituent parts of the atmosphere? How are they combined, and in what way are they subservient to the wants of animal and vegetable life?

2. What is meant by specific gravity of bodies:—and under what conditions is water taken as the standard? How would you ascertain the specific gravity of substances heavier and lighter than water?

3. Explain the principle and construction of the common barometer; when the mercury stands at 28–7 inches, at what altitude would the water stand in a winter barometer?

4. Describe a common suction pump or syphon; and explain the principle of their action?

5. A vessel will float on water whose specific gravity is 1, with a burden of 200 tons; what weight of cargo would it carry if floated on sea water whose specific gravity is 1.035—or on mercury?

SECTION IV.

1. What is meant by the terms "warm" and "cold;" and why do not all substances of the same temperature feel equally so when touched?

2. What is the general effect which heat has upon matter; and what are the different ways in which solid and fluid bodies are heated?

3. What are the phenomena attending the melting of ice and heating the water till it boils away in steam?

4. Explain how dew is formed, and its effects on vegetable life. Why does it not fall equally on grass and gravel?

5. What is meant by the number of inches of rain which fall during the year at any particular place; and how is this ascertained?

6. What is meant by the solvent power of water? Enumerate the substances you know to be solvent in it. How does it affect the group of plants and animals?

SCHOOLMISTRESSES.

Morning—Three Hours allowed for this Paper.

Two Questions to be answered out of each Section, and others as time may permit.

SECTION I.

1. Define the following words:—skill—industry—economy and forethought —wealth—money—and illustrate your answer by their application in matters of social life.

2. What are the principal conditions of industrial success among the laboring classes, and what kind of training in early life is most likely to lead to it?

3. What are the advantages of paying ready money in your dealings, and the disadvantages of the contrary practice?

4. What are the advantages of clothing clubs for the laboring classes, and how ought they to be conducted?

SECTION II.

1. What are the neccessary conditions of a cottage, in order that it may be healthy and comfortable? What is the use of a fireplace in a bedroom?

2. Give some of the various ways with which you are acquainted of preserving meat or vegetables, so as to lay them up in store for future use.

3. Of the modes of cooking animal food—roasting, boiling, stewing—which do you consider the most economical, and why?

3. What are the nutritive properties of milk? Explain the processes of making butter and cheese, and the way in which they must be treated in order to make them keep.

5. What do you consider a proper and economical diet table for a week for a family, consisting of a man, his wife, and 4 children earnings 12 shillings a week?

SECTION III.

1. What is the difference between an artery and a vein—between arterial and venous blood?—and why is the cutting or rupture of an artery more dangerous than a vein?

2. Does the blood undergo any and what change in circulating through the body; and explain the function of the heart, arteries, and veins in the circulation.

3. What are the muscles, tendons and nerves, and their uses in the animal frame?

4. How would you treat a scald or a burn?

5. Give your reason for thinking that exercise is necessary and generally beneficial for health.

6. What are the advantages of cleaning the teeth daily? and what are the disadvantages of losing them or of their decaying in early life?

SCHOOLMISTRESSES.

Afternoon—Two Hours and a Half allowed for this Paper

Two Questions to be answered out of each Section, and others as time may permit.

SECTION I.

1. Draw out a series of lessons on domestic economy, such as you think would prove useful to the elder girls of your school, and describe one lesson in the way you judge necessary to impart it.

2. In what respect do you perceive the homes of your scholars to be deficient, and the teaching of your school to act as a remedy?

3. Describe the manner in which you conduct the needle-work of your school. What distinction do you make between the useful and the fancy work which the children do?

4. Give an outline of a lesson on soap, and its uses.

5. Give your reasons (if any) for regarding a popular knowledge of the atmosphere, water, heat, gases, animal economy, &c., as not unsuited to girls.

SECTION II.

1. What is meant by "hard and soft" water? what is the cause of it? and what are the effects of hard and soft water in cooking and washing?

2. What kind of substances are removed by filtering and by boiling water? Explain the process in both cases.

3. Why do woolen things shrink when washed?

4. What are the advantages of woolen and cotton things as clothing for the laboring classes over linen? and why is cotton preferred in warm climate?

5. What is the best tea-pot to use, and why?

VI. ELEMENTARY INSTRUCTION IN ECONOMICAL SCIENCE.

The Companion to the British Almanic for 1860, contains a valuable paper by Charles Knight, on "*The necessity for Elementary Instruction in Political Economy*," suggested by the extensive and disastrous combination of workmen, engaged in and around London in building, for higher wages. The cure for this and similar "strikes," suggested by this veteran laborer for popular enlightenment, is the general diffusion through schools and mechanics' institutions, of the elementary principles which underlie the phenomena of industrial life, and determine the conditions of industrial success. We give the closing portion of this paper—as affording good specimens, both of subjects and treatment, of lessons on Common Things, and exhibiting the progress and direction of popular education in Great Britain.

It is easy to understand why, some thirty years ago, when there still existed in many quarters an indisposition, if not a strong objection, to teach the mass of the people any thing, there should have been an especial objection to teaching them political economy. There was peculiar ignorance at the root of this objection—the same sort of ignorance that was opposed to instruction in geological science—the ignorance of cowardice. Dr. Chalmers in 1826 thought that, "in deference to a general but ill-founded alarm, the education of workmen in political economy should be kept out of mechanics' schools." The alarmists believed that "a lecture upon this subject in a school of arts" would be like "a demagogue in the midst of his radical auditory."* Against these prejudices Dr. Chalmers maintains, what scarcely any one now doubts, that "political economy, the introduction of which into our popular courses has been so much deprecated, will be found to have pre-eminence over the other sciences, in acting as a sedative, and not as a stimulant, to all sorts of turbulence and disorder; will afford another example of the affinity which exists between the cause of popular education and that of public tranquility."† In 1831, Dr. Whately, now Archbishop of Dublin, in a course of lectures delivered in his capacity of Professor of Political Economy in the University of Oxford, adverted to the same prejudice, and proclaimed that political economy ought to be taught, and could easily be taught, to *all*. "There are some very simple but important truths belonging to the science we are now engaged in, which might with the utmost facility be brought down to the capacity of a child, and which, it is not too much to say, the lower orders can not even safely be left ignorant of."‡ With the

* "*Civic Economy*," vol. iii. p. 382. † Ibid., p. 407.

‡ "*Introductory Lectures*," p. 217.

sanction of such authorities, we may fairly ask the most timid person—one who may still believe that "political economy" means "politics," or that "social economy" means "socialism"—to follow us to a school where "political economy" is intelligently taught—not "brought down to the capacity of a child" by evasions or dilutions of the truths which the philosophical student receives as axioms; but by leading "the capacity of a child" to recognize, step by step, and to expound himself as he goes on, the whole "phenomena of industrial life," and the "conditions of industrial success."*

In the south-eastern district of the metropolis is the largest of the schools known as "Birkbeck" schools. These Birkbeck schools have, with the exception of that of the London Mechanics' Institute, been established at the expense of Mr. William Ellis. Upon the school at Peckham, which we are about to describe, Mr. Ellis has expended about five thousand pounds. It may be interesting to our readers to know who and what is the person making such individual efforts for the promotion of education,—one who has been selected by the Queen to teach her own children the elements of all individual and national prosperity, which he has for some years been striving to teach, and to procure to be taught, to many amongst the children of her Majesty's subjects who are accustomed to be spoken of as "the lower orders." There must be something, it may be thought, very remarkable in this teaching, and equally of the nature of discoveries in the subjects taught, which makes the teaching as attractive, and the knowledge as indispensable, to the prince as to the peasant. The mode of teaching is as old as the days of Socrates: the subjects taught date from the birth of civilization. We extract from "*The English Cyclopædia of Biography*," a brief notice of the founder of Birkbeck schools:—William Ellis "was born in the vicinity of London in 1800. The son of a gentleman engaged in commercial pursuits, he was early placed in a mercantile office, and soon acquired such a position among commercial men, that at the age of twenty-six he was appointed manager of a marine-insurance office—a post he has ever since held, the office under his management having become one of the most successful establishments of its kind in the metropolis. But commercial pursuits did not at any time entirely engross his thoughts. His attention was in early life drawn to the subject of political economy by the circumstance of his copying for Mr. Tooke (who was a friend of his father) the manuscript of his work on Prices; and it was for Mr. Ellis a fortunate circumstance that, while involved in the difficulties which that mass of facts was sure to present to a young inquirer, he found no less able a guide than the late James Mill, under whose advice he prosecuted the study with great ardor and with corresponding success. And here perhaps it may be worth while to call attention to one fact in Mr. Ellis's history, which, besides exercising probably a very powerful influence in the molding of his opinions, both on literary and political subjects, has certainly impressed a marked character upon his educational efforts. The study of economic science in early life, like his teaching of it in his riper years, was not a thing of books merely. Not undervaluing books, yet not content to rest his belief on authority as such, he investigated for himself, and so conducts his lessons that boys do really investigate for themselves. The conclusions of the writers on political economy were in his hands propositions for investigation. He tried them against the phenom-

* The admirable little book by Mr. William Ellis, edited by the Dean of Hereford, is entitled, "*Lessons on the Phenomena of Industrial Life, and the Conditions of Industrial Success.*"

ena of industrial life, as his daily commercial experience gave him opportunity; and the knowledge so gained has rendered him one of the discoverers in the science, as well as perhaps one of its most zealous and able advocates. And when we call to mind the great social changes of the present century, it will not be difficult to understand how large the field, and how important the subjects, on which Mr. Ellis's observation has been exercised. In his boyhood Mr. Tooke put him in possession of all that was then understood of Bank Restriction Acts and a depreciated currency. Since then he has seen our currency, as at present established, assailed in every panic from that of 1825 to that of 1848; and during the same period there have passed under his scrutiny all the great strikes by which workmen have been deluded into the hope of alleviating the sufferings incident to insufficient wages. These evils induced Mr. Ellis to make some attempt at removing them; and further impelled, it may be, by the kindly feelings toward children which form a prominent feature in his character, he determined, if possible, to introduce into schools such instruction as should send boys into the world furnished with intelligent thoughts upon all the great questions relating to industrial life. With this view, he began in 1846 a serious of lessons to the elder boys of a British school, to which for some years previously he had been accustomed to render assistance; and about the same time he also gathered round him a group of schoolmasters, with whom he went over the course of inquiry which will be found in his '*Progressive Lessons;*' and these 'Lessons' will also furnish a good illustration of the mode of teaching adopted. The boys had no tasks to learn by rote; but the whole of the subjects brought before them, with the exception of things merely technical and arbitrary, were, so to speak, developed by the boys themselves, they being guided in their inquiries, of course, by the questions of the teacher. Thus these lessons came to be something more than the mere teaching of dry academical political economy. They assumed, in fact, the character of *moral* lessons. For, thus taught, not only do children learn as a matter of fact about what is going on as the every-day work of industrial life, but they are continually invited to investigate what ought to be the rule of conduct of those who are engaged both in production and distribution."

The Peckham Birkbeck School, founded in 1852, is a large isolated building on the bank of the Surrey Canal, not far removed from a great thoroughfare and the abodes of a dense population, but accessible by very indifferent roads, and surrounded by cabbage-gardens and other large portions of land not yet brought under subjection to the empire of brick and mortar. Through the miry ways some five hundred boys and girls trudge every morning, to receive a better education, at a lower price, than they can obtain at many schools denominated first-class. These are the sons and daughters of artisans, clerks, shopkeepers, and we may add of gentlemen. There is a large room appropriated for the particular instruction of girls, a much larger room for boys, and a large room where boys and girls assemble together, for instruction in certain branches of knowledge common to both. When we entered in the morning, a considerable portion of the boys were engaged in writing on paper from copies set before them. This is all we could observe in the school of the ordinary mode of instruction. None were occupied in learning lessons in spelling or grammar. There are no books used in the school. We learnt that another moiety of the male scholars were occupied in a class-room, where oral instruction was going forward. In a short time the boys we had seen engaged in learning writing had finished their task. At the word of command of "attention," they stood up; "right face,"—"mark time"—"march"—and, in as perfect order as a company of soldiers in Hyde Park, they proceeded to the class-room, where they took their seats without noise or hurry. A file of girls entered, and took the front row before the raised table of Mr. Shields, the master of the school; and thus about a hundred and fifty children, from ten to thirteen years of age, were engaged for an hour in a lesson in arithmetic. This was not taught by the ordinary method of the school-books, but by that higher method which calls out the mind to understand the *rationale* of figures. The problem was worked out upon a slate, the boys constantly giving the calculations, and the teacher writing down the figures. A lesson on chemistry succeeded, in which the teacher showed many experiments upon the flour of wheat, of rice, and of potatoes, to exhibit what constituted starch, and its chemical constituents. In both these lessons many questions originated with the boys themselves, and the solutions of their difficulties impressed the knowledge upon them in a manner they would not be likely to forget. We may observe, that whenever a difficult word, such as hydrogen, or oxygen, or isomeric, occurred, the teacher called upon the class to spell it. Each volunteer thrust out his hand, to show that he was competent to do so. The word was written on the slate; and thus spelling was learnt without books.

These processes were the ordinary routine of the school; and we mention them here to show that in the political economy class, which we attended in the afternoon, there was nothing exceptional to the general system of education pursued daily in this establishment. But having taken notes of this lesson, which was also conducted without any previous knowledge acquired by the scholars from books, we shall endeavor, as literally as we can, to give an idea of the mode in which an hour's instruction was conducted. There are about a hundred and twenty boys seated before the master, and he thus begins. We indicate the questions by *Q.*, and the answers of the pupils by *A.*:—

Q. When a boy goes to work, what does he expect to receive?

A. (from twenty at once.) Wages.

Q. When a boy goes to work for wages, from whom does he expect to receive the wages?

A. A capitalist—a man who possesses capital.

Q. What does a capitalist look for in this expenditure?

A. Profit.

Q. Whilst the capital is thus employed to produce more wealth, what happens to it?

A. It is being consumed.

(The teacher then gave several illustrations:—how when a farmer employs capital in feeding laborers, food is consumed: in clothing them, clothes are consumed—which they replace by wages, as regards themselves.)

Q. If a portion of the farmer's capital is thus consumed, and if the seed sown in the ground is also consumed, there must be an interval before there is profit. When will profit come? Several answers were given, which resolved themselves into—

A. After next harvest. (*Remark.*—Laborers working for wages are thus paid out of capital. When working men meet together and talk about wages, some say—perhaps some of you may have heard it said—wages are paid out of profits. This is a mistake. A workman can't wait for profits. He goes to the capitalist and says, "Give me wages out of what you have stored up in the past: I will work to produce more for the future.")

Q. Would you rather, then, have capital abundant or scarce?

A. Abundant.

Q. Why?

A. Because there will be more wages to be paid out of capital.

Q. Suppose a capitalist, in employing his capital, makes large profits, would that harm the working man?

A. No. There would be more capital to pay wages.

Q. Which is best, that capitalists should be saving or wasteful?

A. Saving.

Q. Why?

A. (After several attempts, a boy said,) If wasteful men, they would consume, and have less capital.

Q. But if they were not wasteful, what would happen?

A. There would be more capital to earn capital hereafter.

Q. Are you sorry, then, that capitalists should have great profits?

A. Glad.

Q. Sorry that they should be saving?

A. Glad.

Q. Do all workmen get the same wages?

A. No.

Q. Does a boy always get wages when he first goes to work?

A. No. He sometimes goes to work without wages.

Q. His parents or friends, therefore, provide for him till he is capable of earning wages. But do all men get the same wages?

A. No. (An example is then given of the difference of wages to a foreman and a laborer, using the word "laborer" not in the general sense in which all who work for wages are called laborers.)

Q. Why does the foreman get more than the laborer?

A. Because the foreman's work is of more value than the laborer's. The foreman is a skilled man.

Q. There are differences of character as well as of skill between two workmen. Why do capitalists run after men, and will give them very high wages for skill, and a combination of good qualities?

A. Capitalists give wages to workmen in proportion to their productiveness. (The word "productiveness" is then spelt and written on the slate, and the inference is urged, that if they prefer high wages to low wages, they must try to be productive.)

Q. What is there in the character of a workman besides his skill that goes to make up productiveness? (a pause.) Which would be most productive, a sober or a drunken workman?

A. A sober.

Q. One getting knowledge or one dissipated?

A. One getting knowledge.

Q. One frank and truthful, or the contrary?

A. One frank and truthful.

Q. When a master engages a fighting and quarrelsome man, what does that matter as long as he does not fight the master?

A. The master knows that he is a questionable man.

Q. How does the possession of bad qualities like these interfere with a workman's productiveness? (A pause.) If a master bricklayer engages two bricklayers—one sober, one drunken—and gives them each five shillings a day, we say they are earning the same wages. But a man living by wages lives through them all the year. If the sober bricklayer has worked fifty-two weeks of the year, and the drunken forty-two, which has the higher wages?

A. The sober.

(Lay, then, to heart this truth—that the capitalist distributes wages according to the productiveness of the workman, and that the amount of his productiveness is determined by industry, skill, sobriety, truthfulness.)

Q. Were any capitalists ever laborers?

A. Yes.

Q. If there are two boys starting in life, one the son of a man who has accumulated capital, the other of a man who has not, shall I be right in saying that the boy without this advantage can never be a capitalist?

A. No.

Q. But what is to make him a capitalist?

A. Saving.

Q. How are wages usually paid?

A. In money.

(The teacher then proceeded to some elementary questions regarding money-wages, and the fluctuating prices of commodities: but as the time for the political economy lesson was nearly at an end, he left that subject, to be resumed on a future day.)

We give this plain transcript of our notes, as near as possible in the words of the teacher and the pupils, not only for the purpose of enforcing the principles by which the popular ignorance of economical truths is to be met; but to invite attention to the mode of teaching pursued with great success in the Birkbeck schools. It is true that these schools have the especial advantage of the general superintendence of their founder; and that the Peckham school, in particular, has the very rare benefit of a master possessing, in the highest degree, the educational talent—the power of imparting knowledge to others by leading their minds, step by step, to work out their own instruction. The transcript of our notes can give no notion of the interest of this lesson on wages; of the rapt attention of a hundred and twenty boys to what most children would shrink from as a dry and difficult subject; their eagerness to answer; their desire to answer in the clearest manner, and by the use of precise terms to avoid exhibiting what their teacher called "a sloppy state of mind." The same intelligent instructor gives a lesson on social economy twice a week, at the London University College, to elder and more advanced students than these Peckham boys. But although the course for the better-prepared pupils may embrace a wider range and include more subtle points, it must rest upon the same facts, and be developed in the same process of reasoning, as that of which we have furnished an example.

If teachers could be readily trained to the work which Mr. Shields performs with remarkable success, we should have no doubt of the rapid spread of such "elementary instruction in political economy" in schools for every class. A step has been made towards this end, in "A Course of Six Lectures on Social Science as a branch of School Instruction, especially addressed to teachers," which Mr. Ellis has just delivered in the lecture-theater, South Kensington, under the direction of the "Science and Art Department of the Committee of Council on Education." To these lectures four hundred schoolmasters, schoolmistresses, and pupils, have been admitted gratuitously. The syllabus is a very suggestive outline of what "social science" here means:—

Lecture I.—Introductory. Necessity of Social Science as a branch of school instruction. Preparation of schoolmasters and pupil-teachers for teaching the science.

Lecture II.—Form in which the subject should be presented to children. Method of opening and conducting the instruction. Dependence of children on parents. Condition of each generation principally determined by the conduct of preceding generations. Conduct necessary to preserve the advantages bequeathed by preceding generations, and to add to them. Industry, knowledge, skill, and economy, as sources of wealth and well-being.

Lecture III.—Different ways of attempting to obtain possession of wealth. Which to be encouraged, and which discouraged, and why? Protection to property. Respect for property. Precautions for guarding against a diminution of the store of wealth, and arrangements for promoting its increase. The function of capital. Nature of the engagements between capitalists and laborers, employers and employed, masters and servants, and between capitalists and capitalists.

Lecture IV.—Wages, or the share of the produce of past labor obtainable by laborers. How distributed among laborers, and by whom? Wages hitherto inadequate, and why? Means for obtaining an increase of wages. Profit, or the increase obtainable by capitalists, and why more by some than by others. Capitalists and laborers not two entirely separate classes. The former constantly recruited from the latter. Some laborers possessed of larger capitals than many administrators of capital.

LECTURE V.—Division of labor. New responsibilities incurred by the adoption of division of labor. Interchange. How administrators of capital are warned against producing what society does not wish for, and stimulated to produce what it does wish for. Value and its fluctuations. Supply and demand, and the fluctuations in them. Cost of production.

LECTURE VI.—Contrivances for facilitating and expediting interchange. Measures and weights. Money. Prices. Causes and consequences of fluctuations of prices. Wealth, capital, wages, and profit, as estimated in money. Full advantage of these contrivances not to be enjoyed without trustworthiness and fidelity in the performance of contracts; and these and other good qualities scarcely to be expected without the schoolmasters' assistance.

We have thus indicated two modes of conveying elementary instruction in political economy. The mode pursued in the Birkbeck schools is "the indirect dialogical method which Socrates invariably adopted; and which may be considered as his method of extracting scientific truth from the mass of semblances and contradictions by which it was surrounded," ("*English Cyclopœdia*," *Article*, "*Socrates*.") The other method is the more familiar one of lectures. The comparative efficiency of either method must very greatly depend upon the individual power of the teacher. But with two men of equal knowledge and equal capacity of exposition, there can be no doubt, we think, that the Socratic method would be productive of the most permanent advantage to learners—whether young or adult—whether coming to be taught with unbiased minds, or with minds choked up with the weeds of popular ignorance, which must be removed before good seed can germinate.

Of the one hundred and twenty pupils that, under the guidance of a most intelligent master, we saw at Peckham, working out their own instruction in political economy, the ages may be taken at from nine to fourteen years. Taking the whole school, the average age would be above that of our National and British schools, in which the period of education rarely extends beyond the age of twelve or at most thirteen, from three or four years of age. It is possibly from a belief that political economy can not be made intelligible in these schools, or even in the "training colleges," that in the last annual report of the council of education we find not the slightest mention of this branch of instruction. We may ascertain the number of schools in which the bulk of the pupils of both sexes are instructed in the Holy Scriptures, in reading, writing, arithmetic; and some in English grammar, geography, and history. In a few schools, modern languages, mathematics, drawing, and music, are professed to be taught. In very many of these public schools the pupils are also trained in industrial occupations. Might it not be salutary to give some instruction in a knowledge of the principles on which business transactions are conducted, and the conditions of success in industrial life? Would it not be wise, in a country where about four hundred masters and two hundred and fifty mistresses are annually prepared in training schools for the performance of their duties as teachers, that they should be trained in that knowledge which, if judiciously imparted, would go far to produce a happier and a more contented population—certainly to put an end to that chronic state of feverish hostility between capitalists and laborers which is constantly lessening the productiveness of industry by diminishing the funds for the support of labor? In the absence of any such provision for education in our public schools that receive the assistance of the state, let us see whether there is not a large field for such teaching in those institutions where the imperfectly-educated boy or girl, grown into an adult, may continue the course of early instruction, to carry forward its benefits, or repair its deficiencies.

The number of institutions in the kingdom, whether called Mechanics' Institutions, or Literary and Scientific Institutions, has been roughly estimated at one thousand. It is not necessary to be very precise as to the number, with reference to our present purpose: we may broadly affirm that, in none of these is political economy systematically taught. No doubt in a very small number of these educational establishments a few lectures have been occasionally given, as at the Liverpool Institute—a noble foundation "for the instruction of the working classes in the principles of the arts they practice, and in the various branches of the science and useful knowledge connected therewith." No definition could more distinctly include political economy, as a science to be most especially taught where fourteen hundred such pupils are in daily attendance. At a public meeting held on the 7th of October last, "to inaugurate a greatly extended scheme of instruction in the evening-school of the institute," the Rev. Stowell Brown, in moving one of the resolutions, thus expressed himself with reference to what he considered an omission in the list of subjects to be taught under this comprehensive scheme:—

I have looked over the list, and have felt disappointed at one thing, because I rather fancy there is an omission here; I hope I may be pardoned for referring to it, and asking whether it is possible to have the omission supplied. There is a science which is of very vast importance; a science in which all classes of the community are very greatly concerned; a science which has been strangely neglected in educational institutions to a very great extent, and from which neglect the country is suffering, will continue to suffer, and must suffer, until such science meets with careful cultivation; that science is political economy. I don't think in an assembly like this, composed to a great extent of mercantile men, presided over by a merchant known every where, and honored wherever he is known, that there can be any necessity for stating, and for proving, that political economy is not politics, or that political economy is something a great deal better and higher than all politics, and is not based upon feeling, opinion, and prejudices, but upon facts, calculations, and reasoning; nor can there be any difficulty in showing the necessity of this science. I say that the social condition and the moral character of the nation is very greatly involved in the matter. All, from the lord of ten thousand acres to the tenant of a cellar—from the speculator in the funds down to the man who cries oysters in the street—all are interested in the matter. If you want proof of it, you may see it in the metropolitan building strike, in the Preston strike, and other disagreements between employers and the employed, arising in consequence of the ignorance of those great principles which must regulate the relationships of capital and labor. And, whatever may be your predilections or prejudices, gentlemen; whatever be your hopes or fears, you know this, that it is at least perfectly possible that many thousands of those men who have been manifesting such ignorance of those great principles, will shortly be put in possession of the political suffrage, and, under those circumstances, it is a matter of very great importance that those principles should be well inculcated upon the people. Is not this science as useful at least as ancient history? Is it not as important as freehand drawing? Is it not of at least as much consequence that the working man should know the philosophy of the price of the quartern loaf as the problems of spherical trigonometry? And is there no wise man amongst us, who, looking down with disdain upon all political sects, can deliver wise and weighty maxims upon this subject to those great classes of the community whom we seek to bring within the pale of this institution, whose manual skill is England's strength, but whose mental darkness threatens to be England's danger?

The speaker was told that the directors had not overlooked the necessity of instruction in political economy; "and if they could add political economy to the present course, they would most certainly do so at the earliest opportunity." Is it the want of teachers that constitutes the difficulty? The "Science and Art Department of the Committee of Council of Education" have announced by their Minute of the 2d of June, 1859, that they "will hereafter assist the industrial classes of this country in supplying themselves with instruction in the rudiments of practical and descriptive geometry, physics, chemistry, geology and mineralogy, and natural history, by augmentation grants in aid of salary to competent teachers," &c. Not a word of the science which involves "the social condition, and the moral character of the nation." The "programme of examinations for the Society of Arts' Union of Institutes," has "political and social economy" as one of fourteen subjects, in which candidates for prizes are to be examined. May we ask if any one candidate ever appeared, and if any prize was ever awarded in that department of knowledge?

A faint notion has begun to develop itself amongst the directors and friends of "institutions," that something more than the ordinary course of rudimentary instruction requires to be provided for the "evening classes," that, in the populous manufacturing districts are now commonly attached to such institutions—something more, even, than the occasional lecturer, who has rather gone out of fashion. In the "Second Report of the East Lancashire Union of Institutions having Evening Schools," issued in August last, we find this statement:—

> The promoters of the East Lancashire Union seek to ascertain in what way not only the humble learning of the elementary school, struggling with obstacles at present insurmountable, may be completed, but habits of self-culture formed in our youth between thirteen and manhood. They found in this Union only one or two evening-schools connected with inspected day-schools. But in every considerable village existed evening-schools, unconnected with day-schools, open to the members of every religious communion, and associated with libraries and news-rooms. This group was commonly called a mechanics' or literary institution. Experience had shown that its vital parts were the night-school, the library, and the news-room. The occasional lecturer, employed as an expedient to excite the curiosity of the people as to objects of intellectual pursuit, had ceased to have any permanent attraction for those of our sagacious workmen who sought amusement less than instruction.

The promoters of the East Lancanshire Union seek to realize the original design of mechanics' institutions—that they should be "colleges for working men." To accomplish this object, they say that "there are two plans to be carried out." The first would be "to supply, or complete, a thoroughly sound course of rudimentary instruction." The second plan proposed shows that these intelligent promoters of knowledge, amongst a scattered agricultural and a dense manufacturing population, are not insensible to the necessity for the cultivation of one large plot of the field of science yet lying waste:—

> The second is to rear upon the firm basis of a solid elementary education habits of self-culture, extending through youth to manhood, and to lead the artisan to such a knowledge of the principles on which our social relations are based, and of our political history, as may give increased stability to society; to such a familiarity with the laws of health as may increase his well-being; and to such an acquaintance with the applications of science to arts and industry as may promote material wealth and prosperity.

In this report of the East Lancashire Union, we see the evidence of a more philosophical estimate of the objects and the means of popular instruction than we usually recognize in local reports. For example—nothing can be more useful, and more worthy of imitation than their prizes to naturalists.

The Council have ascertained that there are, scattered through the East Lancashire Union, a class of men supported by manual labor, more or less literate, who are humble but reverent students of nature. Some of these have been successful collectors of fossils, and have acquired a considerable knowledge of our coal measures. Others have studied the native wild flowering plants, ferns, mosses, and algæ of the district. Some are well acquainted with its purely physical features. It may be that others have explored the natural history of birds; that others are entomologists; and others meteorological observers, and keep records of rain-gauges, thermometric, hygrometric, and barometric changes, the state of the sky, the weather, &c. To none of these forms of natural observation are the Council indifferent; they may all be to no mean extent cultivated by men supported by manual labor, and in every case will tend to refine, elevate, and purify the student.

The Council, therefore, offer prizes in the first instance, to self-taught botanists for the best herbarium of native plants, growing within ten miles of Burnley; for the best collection of fossils from the coal measures within the same distance; and for the best model of the physical geography of the Burnley district. Each institution might obtain, by the labors of these local naturalists, valuable collections in natural history.

Pursuits such as these, it may be said, will have far more attractions for those pursuing their secondary education from youth to manhood, than the dry facts of political economy. Are these necessarily dry? are the lessons to be derived from them unavoidably abstruse? Let the facts of industrial occupation, in a particular neighborhood, be observed and collected, like its plants and its fossils. Let a student in one of these institutions record the ordinary rate of wages amongst agricultural laborers, the skilled and the unskilled; and compare them with the wages of the greater varieties of the employed in mines and manufactories, and the relative amount of their earnings. Let him note what are the machines in use; and learn from his elders whether they have displaced labor; and to what extent the division of labor is carried, compared with past years. Let him record the fluctuating prices of provisions, varying in different seasons of the same year. Let him, without prying into the affairs of his neighbors, observe how of two men working at the same wages, one will live upon his earnings or his savings at a dear time, and the other look to the assistance of public or private charity. Let him note the differences in price to those who pay ready money at the grocer's shop, and those who buy upon credit. Let him mark the variation in the rate of wages given to those who carry on dangerous or unwholesome employments, and those engaged in safe and healthful occupations. Let him observe the number of men who are constantly going out of the laboring class into the capitalist class, and what are the conditions of individual character which appear to contribute to this social advancement. Let him take note of the difference of rent of land in the same district, varying according to degrees of fertility; and of houses in the same town, equal in accommodation, but differing in situation. Let him observe the means of communication in his district—the canals, railways, roads—and mark how, with facility of communication, prices are equalized and supply readily follows upon demand. If a fire takes place, let him inquire if the house or furniture was insured, and mark the different results to the insured or the non-insured. If any neighbor emigrates to a foreign country, let him inquire into the reasons of his emigration—whether he goes with capital or without—whether he goes to be a shepherd and cultivator, or a digger for gold. Whenever he hears of a combination, or a strike, or a lock-out, let him endeavor to ascertain the causes of difference between the employers and the employed; and reason upon them, in connection with the whole range of economical facts that he has accumulated. Now, we do not mean to say that if an observing youth does nothing more than observe these phenomena of industrial life, he will become a political economist. But he will have acquired valuable materials as the foundation of economical knowledge; and by the very process of observation he will be calling out the reasoning faculty, and be arriving, probably with some admixture of error, at the recognition of elementary truths. But give him an intelligent teacher in his evening class, to marshal his statistics into a system—to make his facts the stepping-stones to principles—and he will see light gathering round obscurity, and find a sure guide through the social labyrinth, in a knowledge of the real conditions upon which all the industry of the world must be carried on, if the productiveness of capital and labor is to replace the never-ceasing consumption occasioned by human wants.

In concluding this paper, we would call especial attention to the necessity for rendering "elementary instruction in political economy" a course of practical lessons on individual conduct. Our readers can not fail to have observed that this is the mode of teaching in the Birkbeck schools; that it is kept constantly in view by Mr. Ellis in his lectures. Propose to an uneducated youth to inform him on the theories which are held to regulate "The Wealth of Nations," and you appear to be leading him to a knowledge which, like a knowledge of Law, is for him to respect and obey rather than to learn and practice. But propose to him that he should obtain by your teaching a mastery of facts and principles which are the true foundations of his personal good in the industrial relations of life, and he will quickly come to perceive that in the proportion in which *all* have a knowledge of political economy, as units of society, will also result that welfare of millions which we term "The Wealth of Nations."

VII. EDUCATION, A PREVENTIVE OF MISERY AND CRIME.

[From a Prize Essay by Edward Campbell Tainsh.]

NUMEROUS and complicated as are the forms that misery and crime assume when arrived at full maturity, they are comparatively simple in their beginnings, and arise from causes not difficult to be traced by the careful observer. How far they act upon each other—to what extent misery, while the offspring of crime, may also reproduce it,—though interesting in the extreme, it is not our province to inquire. But what are the causes of both it is essential to know, before we can hope successfully to apply the remedies.

We can not do better than take a look into real life, and endeavor so to ascertain the causes of misery and crime. Some one of the wretched courts, so abundant in our towns, will supply us with facts ready prepared for our inspection.

Enter the first house, one room of it—you will not soon forget its close atmosphere (and indeed that of the whole house.) The furniture, what there is, is dilapidated and dirty; the floor bare, the children are in rags, and moaning with hunger. In one corner is a sick child lying on a heap of rags, pale and wretched. The mother is out, earning the shilling for which the miserable children are impatiently waiting to supply them with food. Sitting over the fire is the father. He is ill, surely? No! Why at home then? Where else should he be! But why not at work? He has none to do. How long has this been the case? Several weeks. Why did he leave his last employment? Well, he happened to be late once or twice, and when the slack time came he was turned off first. But why not looking for more? He did look till he was tired, and found none; at least, he had one job, but it was so far to go, and the hours were so long, that he gave it up. *That* will do. You need not question any farther, the man is *idle*, and this scene of misery is explained.

Go on to the next house. But stop; wait till midnight, then go in. The state of the room is not greatly different from that of the last in its forlorn wretchedness. The children are asleep on some filthy bedding, near the remains of the fire, huddled close together to keep themselves as warm as possible. Look at them and you will perceive by their moist cheeks, their red eyes, and broken sobs, that they have cried themselves to sleep. Poor things! the sad looks remain, though consciousness has gone for a time. The mother is up and trying to soothe the shrivelled infant in her arms. She herself is wasted to a shadow, and weeps bitterly over her own sad fate, and the sufferings of her children. Your heart melts for her, and you are just about to ask the cause of her unhappiness, when you hear a heavy foot stumbling on the stairs. A man enters the room swearing, and strikes the mother for being up. It is the *husband* and *father*, and he a *drunkard!* The key is found to *this* scene of misery.

We enter another house. The place bears marks of poverty, but not so abject as in the other cases. There are indications of the inmates having seen better circumstances. Still, no doubt, they are in great want; all look pale, and weak, and sad. The husband lies ill, the wife is exhausted through nursing and want, the children are pinched with hunger. In conversation you learn that the father has had regular work for some years, that he has no such habits as idleness or drunkenness, and that he bears a good character with his late employer; but by an illness which has already lasted some weeks, he and his family are plunged into distress. Here is a case, which, at first sight, might seem like one of pure *misfortune*, for which the man could not be blamed. But a moment's thought must correct this opinion. He has had regular work for many years, during which time he has saved nothing; he has been *extravagant;* that is, he has spent his means regardless of the wants and claims of the future, and, by so doing, has involved himself, and those whose well-being it is his especial duty to care for, in destitution and misery.

Such are but feeble examples of the ever-varying phases of misery, resulting from these prolific causes—Idleness, Drunkenness, and want of Forethought. The legitimate results of each are here pictured singly for the sake of perspicuity; but it is by far more frequently the case that the evil qualities exist, and consequently act together, thus intensifying the misery that is produced. Who can wonder if such homes turn out to be not only scenes of misery, but hotbeds of crime?

Instances of misery, as the result of ignorance, are everywhere to be met with. Ill-ventilated dwellings producing sickness; bad domestic management making the scarce food scarcer, and the comfortless home still more uncomfortable; the choice of unwholesome instead of wholesome food; the indulgence of habits injurious to the health; low wages obtained by a laborer not disqualified by bad habits; destitution resulting from a strike which was engaged in with a view of bettering the condition:—these, and innumerable other instances, are every day occurring, illustrative of the baneful effects of ignorance.

The history of many a man convicted of embezzlement, burglary, forgery, or some other of the various forms of dishonesty, would furnish the teacher with an instructive explanation of the beginnings of crime. Not all at once did the criminal become capable of the act for which he has been condemned. Time was when his character gave promise as fair as most. A false excuse for being late at school offered to avoid the consequence of having loitered on the way; a sum shown up as his own, which had been done by another boy; an apple taken from a neighbor's desk; a penny kept back from some change; the wasting of an employer's time; the money *borrowed* from the till to gratify some otherwise unobtainable pleasure; the increased distaste for steady work; the more wholesale abstraction of money; the alteration in the books to correspond with the deficiency of cash; the forgery, or some such climax:—these are gradations, easy, almost insensible, when the first steps have been taken undiscovered, or have been improperly dealt with. The *flagrant crime* is the legitimate fruit of the so-called *petty falsehood or dishonesty*.

The condemned murderer was once, perhaps, just such a one as you, teacher, now have under your charge. You must watch that boy at play if you would learn his character. You will find things in it demanding your serious attention, and which, if allowed to go unchecked, may ripen into the worst crimes. One time you will see him amusing himself with the sufferings of a fly, whose limbs he has torn off; at another time teazing and ill-using a younger boy, whom he has selected to annoy; he prefers scheming to working, and is cunning in compassing an end, and unscrupulous in sacrificing the happiness of a school-fellow to his own; he is passionate and overbearing, and long remembers an injury done him; he is the subject, and may be the victim, of ungoverned passions.

The teacher who would successfully strive to prevent the growth of the causes of misery and crime, must thus study character; he must learn to detect a bad habit or an evil passion in its beginning, and to perceive to what that beginning may lead if unchecked; to see, in an equivocation, the germ of a forgery, and in a revengeful blow the first step to murder. Then, and only then, will he be capable of selecting and judiciously applying the means of prevention.

Such, then, are some, perhaps the most important of the causes of misery and crime—Idleness, Drunkenness, Want of Forethought, Extravagance, Dishonesty, Ungoverned Passions, and Ignorance. To prevent the existence of these causes is to prevent their results; to set in operation opposite causes is to produce opposite results.

The schoolmaster's question is, How can he best accomplish these ends? how can he best prevent these qualities appearing, and cultivate the opposite qualities—Industry, Forethought, and Economy; Sobriety, Honesty, Self-government, Knowledge, and such other qualities as shall conduce to a state of wellbeing?

It is of importance to remember, that in the cultivation of a good quality there are two distinct things to be done; to produce conviction of its propriety, and to form the habit of exercising it. The former may easily exist without the latter, while the latter is not sufficiently strong without the former. Many an inveterate drunkard will, in his sober moments, confess that he feels how dreadful a thing drunkenness is, and that the misery it produces by far exceeds the pleasure he feels in it; but the *habit* is too strong for him. And, on the other hand, many a young man brought up in habits of sobriety has yielded when temptation came, because his conviction of its importance was not sufficiently strong and ready for use.

The question becomes then, What kind of teaching is best adapted for producing *conviction* upon the various duties necessary to a state of wellbeing, such as just indicated? And what kind of training is best adapted for forming *habits* in accordance with those convictions?

To any thoughtful mind directed to the subject, suggestions will present themselves; among others, perhaps the following.

We may suppose the teacher with a class of boys before him, and shall attempt to follow him through a course of teaching. He begins by asking:—

Have you any wishes for the future, when you are men?

Carefully followed up, this question may afford abundant matter for a useful lesson. The teacher will find some of his pupils wishing for impossibilities; the nature of such wishes should be pointed out, and also the folly of allowing the mind to dwell upon them. Others he will find wishing for things, to their minds desirable, but which he will be able to show undesirable. But in all their thoughts and hopes, wise or unwise, he will find one leading thought—happiness. He proceeds—

Are you sure to be happy when you are men? If not, upon what does it depend?

Such things as chance, luck, undue reliance upon friends, are the errors that will show themselves here, and which will need to be wisely dealt with.

Will it depend upon yourselves at all?

The skillful teacher will find little difficulty in making his boys perceive how greatly it depends upon their *conduct*.

What kind of conduct will it be necessary for you to adopt, in order to be happy?

Among the many answers sure to be given to this question, the teacher will be able to select as he pleases to begin with, only *post-poning* the examination of the others. Suppose him to choose the answer, "We must be industrious."

What do you mean by being "industrious?"
Why must men work at all?

From this question might arise a series of lessons upon the various necessaries and comforts by which we are constantly surrounded, affording the opportunity of conveying a large amount of useful information, still always bearing upon the primary object of the lesson, namely, to show that the great majority of the comforts and necessaries of life are to be obtained only by labor, and *therefore*, men must work

The following may serve as an illustration:—

From whence did your parents obtain the bread off which you breakfasted this morning?

How did the baker obtain it? and was it bread when he received it? What did he do to the flour?

From whom did the miller have the flour? Was it flour when it came to him? How did he obtain flour from corn? How did the farmer obtain the corn?

Give me one general name for all the operations performed by the farmer, the miller, and the baker.

If the farmer, the miller, and the baker had not worked, how would you have fared for bread?

Suppose no men worked at farming, grinding, baking, etc., what would be the consequence?

If those who do work, worked less industriously, how then? or more industriously?

Who beside himself is benefited by the industrious man's industry? and damaged by the idle man's idleness?

Lessons of this kind, constantly forming part of the school work, varied according to circumstances, filled up, and the "breath of life" *infused into them* by the teacher, can not fail to work into the mind the conviction of the necessity of industry. Of subjects there can be no lack: other articles of food; clothing; fuel; buildings; books, and a host of other things, form an inexhaustible fund, replete also with interest on account of the valuable knowledge *of other kinds* connected with them.

But the teacher will not rest satisfied with producing conviction of the necessity of industry; he has more to do; he proceeds:—

How does industry assist in producing happiness?

Who is happier, the industrious or the idle man?

Then if the idle man were compelled to work, would he at *once* be happier? and why not?

If the industrious man were compelled to be idle, would he be happy? and why not?

Had these men always the habits that now distinguish them? When did they begin to form them?

If you would be industrious men, when must you begin to form the habit? How can you do this?

Does your happiness when you are men depend at all upon your conduct now?

Such teaching, not merely given at set times, but constantly recurring when opportunity offers, and given by the teacher who feels the importance of what he is teaching, can not fail to arouse in a boy's mind the determination to strive to form in himself the habit. But *this* is not all. The teacher knows he has to *train* as well as teach—to assist his charge in their endeavors, as well as to incite them to make the effort. The means at his command for carrying out this training are numerous. Viewed in this light, the school work assumes additional interest and importance. While it is essential for the sake of the knowledge to be obtained, that the work should be *done*, and done *thoroughly*, it becomes doubly important when it is remembered that if done, *so* much is accomplished towards the formation of the habit of industry; if neglected, *so* far is idleness encouraged. The sums, the copy, the drawing, the reading—all, to their own importance, superadd that of being means for the formation of habits. In every lesson, the teacher will say to himself, not only "I want to make the boy a good reader or writer," and so on, but, "I want to make the boy industrious." Whenever a disinclination for steady work shall show itself, the gentle pressure of the teacher's authority, backed by such teaching as has been indicated, repeated whenever occasion calls for it, "line upon line, precept upon precept," and wisely administered in all earnestness and love, will surely not fail to send back the waverer with renewed and strengthened purpose to resume his work. By such means the teacher may hope gradually, but surely, to develop in his children habits of industry that shall stand the brunt of any future temptation.

He proceeds another step.

Do you expect always to be able to work?

Will your wants be as numerous when you are unable to work as when you are able?

How can they be supplied?

How should the wants of those too old to work be supplied?

If what a man can earn when able to work be barely sufficient, or even insufficient to support him in comfort, ought he *then* to save?

What would be the state of a people of whom *none* saved?

Among a people of whom some save and others do not, how are the wants of the unsaving supplied when they are unable to work?

What do we call the man who saves out of his present means for the wants of the future? and the man who does not?

Who is benefited by the economical man's economy, and damaged by the extravagant man's extravagance?

Then what kind of quality shall we call economy? and extravagance?

How are the wants of the young supplied?

Would it not be better for them to be set to support themselves while still young? and why not?

How must they act while young in order to be able to more than compensate when older for the time spared them from work?

Who provides for them while they are preparing for work, and how should they behave to their parents in return?

What must be the consequence of parental neglect or incompetence?

Then before assuming the parental duties, what should each one do?

Are economy and forethought easy to every one? and why not?

When should the formation of these habits be begun?

How can you best aid in forming these habits in yourselves? and how can others help you?

In endeavoring to train in habits of Economy and Forethought, the cultivation of the power of *self-denial* will deserve the first consideration. Indeed, economy is but one form of self-denial. The boy who can resign a pleasure for the sake of giving pleasure to another, will also be able to give up a present gratification when his judgment is convinced that the wants of the future demand it, and that it is his duty to provide for those wants. The boy accustomed to devote part of his evening leisure to the preparation of school-work for the next day, will be in training to form the man able to set aside part of his means of present enjoyment, or to forego some pleasure or relaxation, in order to be able to fulfill his duties in the future. The boy trained to consider the happiness of his fellows as well as his own in his plans, may well be expected to ripen into the man who will see himself qualified to fulfill before he undertakes duties to others.

The manner in which the school materials—pens, ink, paper, and so on—are used, will not be beneath the teacher's notice, nor will the way in which the boy disposes of his pocket-money, inasmuch as it is by *little* things the habits are mainly formed, and little things *only* are at his command.

The man of economical habits will scarcely be a drunkard; all the reasons against ordinary extravagance militate equally against drunkenness, besides which, it has peculiar evils attending it. The teacher will endeavor to bring these strongly before the minds of the boys. It might be done thus:—

We have seen that under certain circumstances men should abstain from consuming as much as is necessary to their comfort, in order to provide for the wants of the future. Can you think of any case in which a man should consume *more* than is necessary for his comfort?

What effect has the consumption of more food than is necessary upon the health?

What is a drunkard?

What effect has drunkenness upon the health?

Would you expect to find a drunkard industrious, economical, etc.?

Will he be a good workman? or a good master?

What sort of husband and parent will he be?

Is the drunkard happier than the sober man? if not, would he *at once* be happier if compelled to be sober? and why not?

Is there usually any strong temptation to *begin* habits of intemperance?

What would you think of the man who "to drown sorrow" became a drunkard?

Which is easier, for a sober man to remain so, or for a drunkard to become a sober man? and why?

What kind of men are most likely to become drunkards—the industrious or the idle? the economical or the extravagant? the intelligent or the ignorant? the comfortable or the wretched?

Are there any habits a boy can form which will make him likely to become a drunkard? or any that will tend to prevent it?

How should you act *now* in order to place yourself as far as possible out of the power of this temptation?

With facts from life illustrating and confirming the conclusions arrived at, the teacher will, after such a lesson, find his class impressed with the dreadful effects of drunkenness upon its victim's health and morals; upon the happiness of his wife and children; upon his character as a workman, and his efficiency in any position in life. They will see that he ceases to be useful to any, a disgrace to himself, and a burden to all connected with him—a plague to society, leaving little to hope for but his absence. They will be led to notice what are the habits and condition of mind most likely to lead to drunkenness, and will be warned to avoid those habits, and to store their minds with matter that shall prevent vacuity, and save them from the necessity of "drowning thought" or "killing time." They will also have learned to hold in just contempt that cowardly shirking of trouble which prefers the lowest degradation to the brave and manly endurance of misfortune. And, perhaps, it is not too bold to hope confidently that the firm resolve will spring up in their minds to shrink from the first beginnings of a vice so easy to be resisted *in* its beginnings, and so almost omnipotent when it has once become a habit.

The kind of training adapted for guarding against this fearful habit of drunkenness is obvious. Training in industry, economy, and such habits, is also training against drunkenness. *In the boy* the vice has not to be cured or checked, its place has but to be pre-occupied by qualities the presence of which forbids the intrusion of drunkenness, and the mind impressed with vivid pictures of the dreadful fate of the drunkard. At the same time, any disposition to undue indulgence of the appetite, to purchase present pleasure at the cost of future suffering, or to yield to temptation from fear of the ridicule or annoyance of companions, will deserve serious attention, as habits tending to weaken the power of resistance.

There is no part of his work which will require more care and attention on the part of the teacher, or that will more richly reward him for his exertions, than the cultivation of *Honesty* in his pupils. While the phases of the virtue are various, possible aberrations from it are equally numerous and subtle, and the consequences of failure most serious and almost irreparable. The following may illustrate the teaching that might be employed:—

Why do men work? why do they save?

If a man, having worked and saved, should lose his savings by some accident not likely to occur again, what would he do?

If he lost them by means likely to occur repeatedly, what would he be disposed to do?

In order, then, for men to continue to work and save, of what must they feel secure?

How do thieves affect this feeling of security? and what effect has their conduct a tendency to produce upon industry and economy? How much do they themselves produce?

Do they consume any?

Then, in how many ways do they help to prevent the accumulation of wealth?

What means does society adopt to prevent the consequences that would otherwise arise from the want of honesty in some of its members?

What would be the result if society either neglected or were unable to do this? Who would prosper? Would thieves even?

Can laws, however good, prevent all the evil effects of dishonesty?

Which would be better, to prevent dishonest men from stealing, or to prevent men from becoming dishonest?

How can this latter be effected?

Are there any other forms of dishonesty besides stealing?

If a man have entered into an engagement which he afterwards finds to be to his disadvantage, how should he act?

During the time that a workman has engaged to give to his employers, how should he work?

How is unpunctuality a form of dishonesty?

How should a promise be regarded?

What is a lie? Is it possible to lie while speaking words *literally* true? or without speaking at all?

If a case occurred in which by telling a lie there appeared to be some great advantage to be gained, without detriment to any one, should the lie be told?

Were confirmed thieves and liars always such? How did they become such?

When will these bad habits, or the opposite good ones, begin to be formed in you?

What can you do *now* to insure that the good and not the bad habits shall be found in your characters?

By such teaching the boys will be led to discover the usefulness of the institution of property, the evils arising from a want of respect for it, and the means society has taken, and is taking to enforce this respect wherever any inclination to disregard the rights of property shall manifest itself.

They will also perceive that conduct not usually called dishonesty is still of the same nature, and attended with similar results. The evils of flagrant dishonesty and positive falsehood they will readily discover; the teacher will have to dwell most on the less palpable forms, such as shirking of engagements, unpunctuality, and equivocation. Thus he will lead them to scorn the dishonor that would escape from the fulfillment of a contract by means of some legal quibble, or because the agreement was only tacit, and therefore not provable; to form a tproper estimate of that sham truthfulness which is content to convey a false impression so that no words are used which could be marked as positively and literally untrue; and to feel that "a lie is an *intent* to deceive."

Perhaps nothing is more striking in its way than the confusion, inconvenience, and loss, which an unpunctual person may cause. This should be vividly brought before the minds of the children, with the damage and inconvenience often caused to the person himself; nor should the ease with which the habit of punctuality may be acquired be passed unnoticed.

The children will then discover how these bad habits commence, how they grow upon their victim, and what *they* must do to guard themselves against their encroachments.

Opportunities for training in honesty will be constantly occurring. Late arrivals at school—so annoying on account of the interruption caused to the school-work—will deserve still greater attention on account of the training in the matter; lessons unprepared become unfulfilled engagements; school-time wasted, the first step to the wasting of an employer's time; and a sum done by another boy, and shown up as the exhibitor's own, a practical lie.

It is lamentable to see how little wisdom is frequently displayed by those who have the charge of young children in the matter of truthfulness. The "See what I've got for you!" when there is nothing for the child, is practical teaching in deception. Let the child, a year or two later, convey the same kind of deception in the form of a proposition, and every one is shocked at its want of truthfulness. Children are taught to look too much at the form of words, and too little at the intention with which the words are spoken. But the lie conveyed in the mere shrug of the shoulders is not lost upon a child, however it may fail to touch the conscience of the perpetrator. If parents and teachers would have their children truthful, they must show by their conduct that they consider an *intention to deceive* to be a lie.

The experienced teacher knows how certainly his boys' minds are moulded after his own—how *they* are affected by traits of character almost imperceptible to *himself*.

Now, a teacher is not a walking encyclopædia, neither need he be ashamed of not being one. Some teachers, however, have so great a horror of "I don't know," that they prefer equivocation, or, at least, mystification to saying it, if a pupil happen to propose a question they are unable to answer. The effect of such shuffling upon the boys' characters is certain and unmistakable. The teacher *must* be unreservedly honest or his boys never will be.

If ever a boy be found to have lied or pilfered, all the teacher's wisdom will be called into requisition to deal properly with the occurrence. Such an act may form a crisis in a boy's life; his future may depend upon the judgment, faithfulness, and love, with which it is met.

The dreadful consequences arising from ungoverned passions, the duty of governing them, and the way in which the power of self-government is to be attained, will have to be the theme of many a lesson, and the subject of frequent reference. It *is* possible to make the school a nursery (in efficiency second only to a good home) for all the best and tenderest feelings of our nature; but this can only be done when the best energies of a good teacher are influencing the school.

If envious feelings on account of the superior attainments or reputation of a school-fellow should show themselves, the teacher will lead his children to see how contemptible such feelings are; what malice there is in them; how, instead, kindly admiration and emulation should be awakened; how that no good could arise to *any one* if the envious wish were realized, but harm and loss; while, on the other hand, by emulation instead of envy, double good may be effected.

The fearful effects of *jealousy*, the absence of all power of self-government in its victim while under its effects, the increasing power it gains over him who indulges it, can not be too strongly painted.

Acts of wanton *cruelty* have but to be brought to light to produce a feeling of burning shame in the culprit not "hardened in sin," and strong disapprobation in the witnesses. The skillful teacher will know how to awaken and to avail himself of these feelings; to show what a despicable character that is, in which cruelty has become habitual, and to what dreadful crimes it may lead. In a school where such teaching is constantly recurring, a boy tormenting an animal or ill-treating another boy will be a rarity.

There is, perhaps, no evil passion that a boy is so inclined to justify as *revenge* under various forms and names. "Served him right!" "I'll pay you;" "He did it to me, and I'll do it to him," are expressions often believed to convey defensible sentiments. The boy who would be ashamed of an act of unprovoked cruelty would often not be ashamed of a revengeful act. Suppose a case of the kind to have occurred in a school, it might be dealt with thus:—

Did you like the pain he gave you?

Will it diminish your pain to inflict pain on him?

Do you take pleasure in giving him pain? and if you do, is that a feeling you would like to check or encourage?

Is it any reason for your being cruel, that he was?

What sort of man will you become if you encourage such feelings?

Which do good men take most pleasure in, forgiveness or revenge?

Even if your motive were to prevent him hurting you again, did you take the best means?

Would an act of kindness have been more effective?

Is it an easy thing for a boy accustomed to indulge revengeful feelings to check them?

Will it be easier or more difficult the second time than the first? When will it become quite easy?

Which feelings will you try to cultivate in yourselves, the revengeful or the forgiving?

It would be almost impossible to leave such a case as this, without referring to the beautiful example of the Redeemer, who, "when he was reviled, reviled not again;" but "loved his enemies," and "did good to those who hated him."

So much may suffice in illustration of the way in which the first buddings of evil passions may be dealt with, and the first endeavors after a kind and forgiving spirit encouraged. He who has taken the trouble to observe the amount of misery and crime resulting from ungoverned passions will think no amount of attention too great, if, peradventure, he may prevent their growth.

It is more than possible that among the parents of the boys subjected to this kind of teaching and training, there may be one, who, when he finds the teacher endeavoring to make his son honest otherwise than by the iteration and reiteration of the command, "Thou shalt not steal," will begin to make use of such expressions as "enlightened selfishness," "anti-religious," and so on. Even teachers are not wanting to urge the same objection. Such a feeling, however unfounded or absurd, must be met and answered; for it is of the highest importance that no such under-current should exist in the boys' minds, to weaken or neutralize the effect of the teacher's work. Suppose such a notion to leak out, it might be met thus:—

Why, have we seen, should men be industrious, sober, honest, forgiving?

What name do we give to the men who possess these and such qualities?

Suppose it could not be *proved* to be good for society that men should possess these qualities, would it *then* be a duty to practise them nevertheless? Why?

What name do we give to men who obey the commands of God?

With what design are God's commands given?

If certain conduct not included in the commands of God could be proved to be conducive to the wellbeing of society, would it be the duty of a religious man, as such, to adopt that conduct? and why?

Then, what shall we say should be the test of conduct with *all* good men?

By such a lesson the children could be led to see that a "moral" man is one whose conduct is in conformity with that ascertained to be conducive to the wellbeing of society, as far as such has been ascertained; that a "religious" man is one whose conduct is in conformity with the will of God, as far as that will is expressed, and beyond, with such conduct as agrees with the evident intention of God's expressed will, namely, the wellbeing of society; that, therefore, the test of conduct with the man called "religious," is the same as that of the man called "moral," and that therefore the notion of antagonism is absurd.

That *knowledge* is one, and an important one, of the causes of wellbeing few will doubt. Many educators, so called, seem to act as if it were *the* one condition of wellbeing. To the neglect of all training in good habits the whole school routine seems framed, in some cases, with the sole view of imparting knowledge. In order to act wisely in this matter, two things must be borne in mind, first, that knowledge *alone* will not make a good, useful, and successful man; and, second, that not all knowledge is equally useful, nor all useful knowledge equally applicable in the school-room. But while bearing in mind these facts, the teacher will most anxiously strive to work into his boys' minds a respect for knowledge, a conviction of its effect upon the wellbeing of society, a thirst for it, and a determination to gain as much as possible, while at school, and to continue their efforts when they enter the wider school—the world. As tending to accomplish this end, such teaching as the following may serve:—

Why must men be industrious in order to be in a state of wellbeing?

Would an industrious Hottentot be able to produce as much of the necessaries and comforts of life as an industrious Englishman? and why not? How does knowledge assist industry?

What kind of crops would the farmer reap if he were ignorant of the nature of different kinds of soil, and the soils best adapted to different seeds?

Why did not the ancient Britons use ploughs of the same kind as those now used?

Why is the steam-mill in many cases superior to the windmill? and why were steam-mills not always used?

How has the introduction of steam affected the facilities for travelling?

Why was not steam always used for the same purpose?

Why are our streets lighted with gas? and why were they not always?

Are calico and stockings manufactured with greater or less facility now than formerly? and why?

How was the stock of knowledge at present in existence accumulated? and how must it be increased, if increased at all?

When did you begin to acquire knowledge? and how will your present efforts to gain it affect your power of increasing your stock in the future?

What must be the condition of the man who neglects to gain knowledge?

But part of the teacher's duty is to impart knowledge. What among the immense stores before him shall he select for his use? Which will best serve the purposes of education? Which be most likely to be useful to the children in their future course? This is a serious question. He will teach them to read, of course; and write, most certainly; and teach them thoroughly too. But it *is* possible to put these *instruments* into a boy's hands, and yet leave him perfectly incapable of using them to any good purpose. People who can read are not always readers, and readers do not always read intelligently, and, consequently, with profit. A boy can scarcely be said to be able to read who simply has the power of deciphering words; he must, in addition, have the power to comprehend the *meaning* of a set of words, the connection between two sets of words, and to form a judgment for himself upon what he reads. Without this, his so-called ability to read will avail him little.

No one can know everything; no one need be the worse off for not knowing everything. There is a great deal of knowledge, which it is quite sufficient for the good of society, if *some* of its members possess. For instance: all need not know how to make a steam-engine, to navigate a ship, to calculate the distances of the fixed stars, to work a mine, to demonstrate a proposition of Euclid, to tell the number of square miles on the surface of the earth, the length of the longest river, the height of the highest mountain, or the area of the smallest county in England.

But there *is* knowledge which none can lack, without serious detriment to himself and to society. What this knowledge is, and how it can be best imparted, will be questions of the highest importance to the teacher.

In general, this indispensable knowledge may be expressed as *a knowledge of the relation in which each one exists to the beings and influences around him, and of the conduct necessitated by this relationship.*

For instance, the boy should know that he is an organized being, surrounded by agents, some of which act beneficially, others injuriously, upon him. He should know the nature and effects of, at least, the most common of these, and that some of them, beneficial in their action in certain quantities, are injurious in other quantities; he should know the nature of his own organization and the conditions of its healthy working.

He should know that he is a social being, and that his wellbeing is thereby made to depend upon the success with which he strives to promote the wellbeing of the society of which he is a member. He should know the duties attaching to the various forms of social relationship, and should be prepared or preparing to fulfill them. Thus:—

As a *parent*, he should be prepared to fulfill before he undertakes duties to others. He should provide for the physical health and comfort of his children. He should watch and direct the formation of their characters—check their faults, and encourage their efforts after good. He should prepare them to provide for themselves, when he is no longer able to provide for them.

As a *capitalist*, he should so employ his capital as to produce that which society most wants in the greatest possible quantities, and at the smallest possible cost. He should select those laborers who can best help him in making his capital productive, those whose qualifications are the highest, who can produce most in proportion to the wages paid them. He should endeavor to turn their labor to the best account, availing himself of every aid that lies within his reach. In so doing he will be the benefactor of society by efficiently supplying its wants, by encouraging among his laborers those qualities upon which their happiness and usefulness depend, and by enabling them to obtain knowledge and skill, which, but for his vigilant direction, they could not attain. As his own special reward he will obtain large profits.

As a *laborer*, he should endeavor to cultivate in himself those qualities, to attain that knowledge and skill which will make his services most acceptable to the capitalist. He should serve his employer faithfully, bringing all his intelligence to bear upon his work. He will then serve society by making the capital upon which he is employed as productive as possible, and will earn for himself the reward of high wages. If his wages be lower than desirable, he should seek for the means of obtaining higher, taking care, at the same time, not to engage in strikes, or any other such means, whose real tendency is the opposite of the one sought for. Should there be no means of *immediately* obtaining higher wages, he should endeavor to increase his productiveness as the only means of increasing the store out of which wages are paid, and of obtaining for himself a large share of that store.

These examples, not thought to be comprehensive, but only illustrative, of the kind of knowledge not to be dispensed with, must suffice. Enough if they serve as indications. Other points, no way inferior in importance, are sure to suggest themselves. The teacher has to remember that his work is to send the boy out, *fitted for the duties of life.* He must not rest satisfied without sending his teaching right home to the hearts of his boys, so as to lead to actual living results.

The knowledge that shall be imparted beyond what is here indicated, must depend upon circumstances, and need scarcely be discussed now. With the boy who is able to remain at school five or six years, of course more can be attempted than with him whose time is but two years. Few will complain of too *much* knowledge, but all have a right to complain when indispensables are neglected for the sake of things of doubtful or inferior importance. The intelligent educator will throughout select those materials which either have the most direct bearing upon the boy's future wants, or most efficiently aid in the formation of the judgment and character.

Our *question* was, "What are the best means for making the schoolmaster's functions more efficient than it has hitherto been in preventing Misery and Crime?"

The foregoing remarks proposed as an answer to this question, may be briefly summed up thus:—By the schoolmaster's making himself better acquainted with the causes of these evils, in their first beginnings especially; by working into the minds of his boys the conviction of the duties devolving upon them; by training them in habits corresponding with those convictions, and by imparting knowledge calculated to enable them to act up to their convictions.

It need scarcely be said that the subject is not thought hereby to be exhausted, or that the sketches of lessons that have been adventured pretend to be nothing more than skeletons, depending for their value upon the living teacher.

There will not be wanting objections to the proposal to attempt this kind of teaching and training. "To do this we must neglect other things," is one common objection. Be it so, if necessary, unless those "other things" can be shown to be of greater, or of equal importance. What amount of "other things" can compensate for habits of idleness, dishonesty, and extravagance—for passions unchecked, and a mind unstored with the knowledge necessary to the performance of the great duties of life; and that this knowledge and these habits do not come spontaneously, is a matter of experience.

Another objection is—"There is not time to do it perfectly, the children do not remain long enough at school." Well, then, do it *imperfectly;* do it as far as you can. No one will say that a little honesty, industry, economy, or even knowledge *of this kind* is "a very bad thing." That teacher must do his work very badly who sees a boy leave his school, even after a three months' stay, without some useful thoughts, some good resolves, and some insight into the duties of his future career.

If the time be short, why, then, work the harder! and, *perhaps, you will find in this effort and this direction of it, the means of detaining the boy longer in a school where himself and his parents will feel he is gaining something worth making a sacrifice to obtain.*

Whether, by incorporating productive labor with the school work, it is possible in some cases to retain the children longer at school, or more efficiently to cultivate the industrial qualities, is a question that, perhaps, deserves more attention than has yet been given to it.

It is strongly insisted upon by some, that owing to peculiar organization certain individuals are predisposed to particular vices, and that this predisposition requires particular attention. It is a fact that in some cases, children, under the influence of bad example, very early acquire habits which will need the greatest attention for their cure. Now, if the first case be a true one, still, for all practical purposes, the two cases may be looked upon as one. Both call for special attention; to the work of prevention is added that of cure, to some extent, in both cases. Careful watching for the display of the bad habit; constant checking of it; kindly encouragement whenever improvement is attempted: these are the means called for.

Such, then, the work, and now a word in conclusion upon the workman. How much depends upon him! It is not enough that he has plans and theories in any quantity stored in his head; he must be devoted to his work; fully aware of the difficulties he has to overcome; well acquainted with the implements he is using; thoroughly alive to the immense importance of the results he is aiming at; full of love for the tender beings under his charge, and of faith in the efficacy of his mission; enthusiastic and willing to be spent in his work, and, if necessary, to find his whole reward in the consciousness of being the means of moulding the children committed to him into good, useful, and happy men. When such are the men to whom the teaching and training of the young is committed, we may hope for results till then impossible.

The foregoing Essay received the prize of $100 offered by the United Association of Schoolmasters of Great Britain, "*On the best means of making the schoolmaster's function more efficient than it has hitherto been in preventing misery and crime.*" The reading of the Essay in a meeting of the Association, called forth a discussion of the argument, which was thought by Mr. Tate, "to be clear, simple and argumentative," but not exhaustive. "He had no fault to find with what the essayist proposed to do; he had only to find fault with what he did not propose to do. He would advocate the introduction of social science in schools, but he would make it supplementary to the authority of revelation. He would invert the order in which the essayist proposed to proceed. He should not begin with the principles of social science, and end with the dictates of revealed religion; but he would begin with revelation, and end with the arguments to be derived from social science. Let them take an example. It was a common observation—'Honesty is the best policy.' All would admit that axiom. But before he would expound this axiom, as derived from moral philosophy, or from social science, he should first give the child the Divine authority for the law—'Thou shalt not steal.' The child was to obey the command of God from love—love towards his good and beneficent Creator."

After remarks by Mr. Tilleard and other members, Mr. Tainsh said, "He *did* consider the religious teaching, commonly given in our schools, a palpable sham, as Mr. Tilleard had represented it, for his own observation had led him to that conclusion; yet he did not think he would better have fulfilled his task by attempting to expose the sham, or to alter the system. He thought he had pointed out the *best* means for preventing misery and crime, inasmuch as the means suggested were those which struck directly at the root of the evils. He had not attempted to traverse the whole range of school appliances and teaching, and among other things had omitted what was called religious, or, more properly, theological teaching. He discovered throughout the whole of the objections, one leading thought, which appeared to him a radical error, viz., the supposition of antagonism between social economy and religion: that social economy took as its motive—*interest*, while religion took the higher motive—*duty*. He suggested that this notion arose from a misapprehension of the nature of social economy, which was indeed but the practical application of the religion of the Redeemer."

PART II.

ELEMENTARY INSTRUCTION IN IRELAND.

PAPERS VIII.—X.

VIII. ELEMENTARY EDUCATION IN IRELAND.

HISTORICAL SKETCH.

THE checkered experience of Ireland,—its dark and its bright sides,—forms one of the most instructive chapters in the history of popular education. It commences, according to the testimony of the earliest chroniclers, with institutions of learning, not only of earlier origin, but of higher reputation, than any in England or Scotland,—institutions which were resorted to by English youth for instruction, who brought back the use of letters to their ignorant countrymen. According to Bede and William of Malmesbury, this resort commenced even so early as the seventh century, and these youth were not only taught, but maintained without service or reward. The great college of Mayo was called "the Mayo of the Saxons," because it was dedicated to the exclusive use of English students, who at one time amounted to no fewer than 2000. Bayle, on the authority of the historian of the time, pronounces Ireland "the most civilized country in Europe,* the nursery of the sciences" from the eighth to the thirteenth century, and her own writers are proud of pointing to the monastery of Lindisfarne, the college of Lismore, and the forty literary institutions of Borrisdole, as so many illustrative evidences of the early intellectual activity and literary munificence of the nation. But Ireland not only abounded with higher institutions, but there were connected with monasteries and churches, as early as the thirteenth century, teachers expressly set apart "for teaching poor scholars gratis." When the country was overrun by foreign armies, and torn by civil discord, and governed by new ecclesiastical authorities, set up by the conquerors, and not in harmony with the religion of the people, a change certainly passed over the face of things, and there follows a period of darkness and educational destitution, for which we find no relief in turning to the history of English legislation in behalf of Ireland. Indeed there is not a darker page in the whole history of religious intolerance than that which records the action and legislation of England for two centuries, toward this ill-fated country, in this one particular. Even the statute of Henry VIII., which seems to be framed to carry out a system of elementary education already existing before the new ecclesiastical authorities were imposed upon the country, was intended mainly to convert Irishmen into Englishmen. By that

* These facts are stated on the authority of a speech of Hon. Thomas Wyse, in the House of Commons, in 1835.

statute, every archbishop and bishop was bound to see that every clergyman took an oath "to keep, or cause to be kept, a school to learn English, if any children of his parish came to him to learn the same, taking for the keeping of the said school such convenient stipend or salary as in the said land is accustomably used to be taken;" and both higher and lower authorities, archbishops and their beneficed clergymen, are subjected to a fine for neglect of duty. The fatal error in this and in all subsequent legislation and associated effort for education in Ireland, until the last twenty years, was its want of nationality; the schools were English and Protestant, and the people for whom they were established were Irish and Catholics, and every effort, by legislation or education, to convert Irishmen into Englishmen, and Catholics into Protestants, has not only failed, but only helped to sink the poor into ignorance, poverty and barbarism, and bind both rich and poor more closely to their faith and their country.

Every system of education, to be successful, must be adapted to the institutions, habits and convictions of the people. If this principle had been regarded in the statute of Henry VIII., Ireland, which had the same, if not a better foundation in previous habits and existing institutions, than either Scotland or Germany, would have had a system of parochial schools recognized and enforced by the state, but supervised by the clergy. This was the secret of the success of Luther and Knox. What they did was in harmony with the convictions and habits of the people. So strangely was this truth forgotten in Ireland, that until the beginning of this century, Catholics, who constituted four-fifths of the population, were not only not permitted to endow, conduct, or teach schools, but Catholic parents even were not permitted to educate their own children abroad, and it was made an offense, punished by transportation, (and if the party returned it was made high treason,) in a Catholic, to act as a schoolmaster, or assistant to a schoolmaster, or even as a tutor in a private family. Such a law as that in operation for a century, coupled with legal disabilities in every form, and with a system of legislation framed to benefit England at the expense of Ireland, would sink any people into pauperism and barbarism, especially when much, if not most, of the land itself was held in fee by foreigners, or Protestants, and the products of the soil and labor were expended on swarms of church dignitaries, state officials, and absentee landlords. But even when these restrictions on freedom of education and teaching were removed in 1785, the grants of money by the Irish and Imperial Parliaments, down to 1825, were expended in supporting schools exclusively Protestant. Upward of $7,000,000 were expended on the Protestant Charter Schools, which were supported by a society which originated in 1733, on the alleged ground "that Protestant English schools, in certain counties inhabited by Papists, were absolutely necessary for their conversion." By a by-law of this society, the advantages of the institutions were limited exclusively to the children of Catholic parents. On the schools of the "Society for Discountenancing Vice," which originated in 1792, and which was soon converted into an agency of proselytism, the government expended, between 1800 and 1827, more than a half million of dollars. In 1814, the schools of the "Kildare Place Society," began to receive grants from the Parliament, which amounted in some years to £50,000, and on an average to $25,000, and in the aggregate to near $2,000,000; and yet the regulations of the Society, although more liberal than any which preceded it, were so applied as practically to exclude the children of Catholics, who constituted, in 1830, 6,423,000, out of a population of 7,932,000.

In 1806 commissioners were appointed by Parliament to inquire into the state of all schools, on public or charitable foundations, in Ireland; who made fourteen reports. In their last report, in 1812, they recommend the appointment of a board of commissioners, to receive and dispose of all parliamentary grants, to establish schools, to prepare a sufficient number of well-qualified masters, to prescribe the course and mode of education, to select text-books, and generally to administer a system of national education for Ireland. To obviate the difficulty in the way of religious instruction, the commissioners express a confident conviction that, in the selection of text-books, "it will be found practicable to introduce not only a number of books in which moral principles should be inculcated in such a manner as is likely to make deep and lasting impressions on the youthful mind, but also ample extracts from the Sacred Scriptures themselves, an early acquaintance with which it deems of the utmost importance, and indeed indispensable in forming the mind to just notions of duty and sound principles of conduct; and that the study of such a volume of extracts from the Sacred Writings would form the best preparation for that more particular religious instruction which it would be the duty and inclination of their several ministers of religion to give at proper times, and in other places, to the children of their respective congregations."

In 1824, another commission was instituted to inquire into the nature and extent of the instruction afforded by different schools in Ireland, supported in whole or in part from the public funds, and to report on the best means of extending to all classes of the people the benefit of education. This commission submitted nine reports, concurring generally in the recommendations of the committee of 1805.

In 1828, the reports of the commissioners were referred to a committee of the House of Commons, who made a report in the same year, in which they state their object to be "to discover a mode in which the combined education of Protestant and Catholic might be carried on, resting upon religious instruction, but free from the suspicion of proselytism." The committee therefore recommend the appointment of a board of education, with powers substantially the same as possessed by the former commissioners. The following resolution presents their views on the matter of religious education

"That it is the opinion of this Committee, that for the purpose of carrying into effect the combined literary and the separate religious education of the scholars, the course of study for four fixed days in the week should be exclusively moral and literary; and that, of the two remaining days, the one to be appropriated solely to the separate religious instruction of the Protestant children, the other to the separate religious instruction of the Roman Catholic children. In each case no literary instruction to be given, or interference allowed on the part of the teachers, but the whole of the separate religious instruction to be given under the superintendence of the clergy of the respective communions. That copies of the New Testament, and of such other religious books as may be printed in the manner hereinafter mentioned, should be provided for the use of the children, to be read in schools, at such times of separate instruction only, and under the direction of the attending clergyman:—the established version for the use of the Protestant scholars, and the version published with the approval of the Roman Catholic bishops for the children of their communion."

In 1830, the subject was again considered by a select committee of the House on the state of the poor in Ireland, and the hope expressed that no further time would be lost in giving to Ireland the benefit of the expensive and protracted inquiries of the commissioners of 1805 and 1825, and of the committee of 1828. In September, 1831, Mr. Wyse, author of the able volume entitled "Educational Reform," a member of the House from Ireland, brought in a bill to establish a system of national education for Ireland, but it was not acted upon on account of the adjournment.

In October, 1831, Mr. Stanley, then Secretary for Ireland, announced, in a letter to the Duke of Leinster, Lord-lieutenant of Ireland, the intention of the Government to appoint a Board of Commission of National Education. The Board were soon after appointed, consisting of the Duke of Leinster, the Protestant Archbishop of Dublin, the Catholic Archbishop of Dublin, Rev. Dr. Francis Sadleir, Rt. Hon. A. R. Blake, and R. Holmes, Esq.,—three Protestants, two Catholics, one Presbyterian, and one Unitarian.

The Board of Commissioners have now been in existence about eighteen years. During that time they have encountered bitter opposition from able but ultra zealots in the Protestant and Catholic churches; but, sustained by the Government under the administration of all political parties, they have gone on extending their operations, and accomplishing results which are worthy of the attentive study of every statesman and educator. The fruits of their labors are already visible, but they will be "read of all men" when another generation comes on the stage.

The following are among the results of their measures:

I. The Board have succeeded in establishing a system of National Education, or have made the nearest approach to such a system, which knows no distinction of party or creed in the children to whom it proffers its blessing, and at the same time it guarantees to parents and guardians of all communions, according to the civil rights with which the laws of the land invest them, the power of determining what religious instruction the children over whom they have authority shall receive, and it prohibits all attempts at enforcing any, either on Protestant or Roman Catholic children, to which their parents or guardians object.

"For nearly the whole of the last century, the Government of Ireland labored to promote Protestant education, and tolerated no other. Large grants of public money were voted for having children educated in the Protestant faith, while it was made a transportable offense in a Roman Catholic (and if the party returned, high treason) to act as a schoolmaster, or assistant to a schoolmaster, or even as a tutor in a private family.* The acts passed for this purpose continued in force from 1709 to 1782. They were then repealed, but Parliament continued to vote money for the support only of schools conducted on principles which were regarded by the great body of the Roman Catholics as exclusively Protestant, until the present system was established."

"The principles on which they were conducted rendered them to a great extent exclusive with respect either to Protestants or to Roman Catholics; Roman Catholic schools being conducted on Roman Catholic principles, were, of course, objectionable generally to Protestants; while Protestant schools, being conducted on Protestant principles, were equally objectionable to Roman Catholics; and being regarded by Roman Catholics as adverse establishments, they tended, when under the patronage of Government, and supported by public money, to excite, in the bulk of the population, feelings of discontent toward the state, and of alienation from it."

"From these defects the National Schools are free. In them the importance of religion is constantly impressed upon the minds of the children, through works calculated to promote good principles, and fill the heart with a love of religion, but which are so compiled as not to clash with the doctrines of any particular class of Christians. The children are thus prepared for these more strict religious exercises which it is the peculiar province of the ministers of religion to superintend or direct, and for which stated times are set apart in each school, so that each class of Christians may thus receive, separately, such religious instruction, and from such persons, as their parents or pastorsmay approve or appoint."

The following Regulations will show the manner in which the Board have aimed to avoid the difficulty of religious instruction in schools composed of different denominations, as well as the prejudices of political parties:

As to Government of Schools with respect to Attendance and Religious Instruction.

"1. The ordinary school business, during which all children, of whatever denomination they may be, are required to attend, is to embrace a specified number of hours each day.

2. Opportunities are to be afforded to the children of each school for receiving such religious instruction as their parents or guardians approve of.

3. The patrons of the several schools have the right of appointing such religious instruction as they may think proper to be given therein, provided that each school be open to children of all communions; that due regard be had to parental right and authority; that, accordingly, no child be *compelled* to receive, or be present at, any religious instruction to which his parents or guardians object; and that the time for giving it be so fixed, that no child shall be thereby, in effect, excluded, directly or indirectly, from the other advantages which the school affords. Subject to this, religious instruction may be given either during the fixed school-hours or otherwise.

4. In schools, toward the building of which the Commissioners have contributed, and which are, therefore, VESTED in trustees for the purposes of national education, such pastors or other persons as shall be approved of by the parents or guardians of the children respectively, shall have access to them *in the school-room*, for the purpose of giving them religious instruction there, at convenient times to be appointed for that purpose, whether those pastors or persons shall have signed the original application or otherwise.

5. In schools NOT VESTED, but which receive aid only by way of salary and books, it is for the patrons to determine whether religious instruction shall be given *in the school-room* or not: but if they do not allow it in the school-room, the children whose parents or guardians so desire, must be allowed to absent themselves from the school, at reasonable times, for the purpose of receiving such instruction ELSEWHERE.

6. The reading of the Scriptures, either in the Protestant authorized, or Douay version, as well as the teaching of catechisms, comes within the rule as to religious instruction.

---

* See 8th Anne, c. 3, and 9th William III. c. 1.

7. The rule as to religious instruction applies to public prayer and to all other religious exercises.

8. The Commissioners do not insist on the Scripture lessons being read in any of the national schools, nor do they allow them to be read during the time of secular or literary instruction, in any school attended by children whose parents or guardians object to their being so read. In such case, the Commissioners prohibit the use of them, except at the times of religious instruction, when the persons giving it may use these lessons or not, as they think proper.

9. Whatever arrangement is made in any school for giving religious instruction, must be *publicly notified* in the school-room, in order that those children, and those only, may be present whose parents or guardians allow them.

10. If any other books than the Holy Scriptures, or the *standard* books of the church to which the children using them belong, are employed in communicating religious instruction, the title of each is to be made known to the Commissioners.

11. The use of the books published by the Commissioners is not compulsory; but the titles of all other books which the conductors of schools intend for the ordinary school business, are to be reported to the Commissioners; and none are to be used to which they object; but they prohibit such only as may appear to them to contain matter objectionable in itself, or objectionable for *common* instruction, as peculiarly belonging to some particular religious denomination.

12. A registry is to be kept in each school of the daily attendance of the scholars, and the average attendance, according to the form furnished by the Commissioners."

II. The Board have done much to improve the literary qualifications, and professional knowledge, and skill of teachers, as well as their pecuniary condition, and by a judicious system of classification in salaries, and rewarding cases of extraordinary fidelity and success, to diffuse a spirit of self-education throughout the whole profession. The main defect in the schools of Ireland at the institution of the Board was the incompetency of the teachers. They were in general extremely poor, many of them were very ignorant, and not capable of teaching well even the mere art of reading and writing; and such of them as could do so much, were for the most part utterly incapable of combining instruction in it with such a training of the mind as could produce general information and improvement. One of the first and main objects of the Board was, and continues to be, to furnish an opportunity to deserving persons of the right character, to qualify themselves properly for teaching, and then, by a fair prospect of remuneration and advancement, to devote themselves to the business for life, with a holy national and catholic spirit. A brief notice of the successive steps by which the present system of training and aiding teachers in Ireland was reached, will be appropriate to the design of this work. The earliest indication of any movement in the educational history of Ireland, for the professional training of teachers, was in 1812.

In their thirteenth annual (for 1812) report, the "Commissioners for inquiring into the state of all schools on public or charitable foundations in Ireland," recommend the appointment of a Board of Commissioners as the first step in a system of National Education, with power to establish a number of additional or supplementary schools to those already in existence, and that they be "directed and required to apply themselves immediately to the preparing a sufficient number of well-qualified masters to undertake the conduct of such supplementary schools as they should from time to time proceed to endow."

"We have already adverted to the deplorable want of such qualification in a great majority of those who now teach in the common schools, and to the pernicious consequences arising from it; their ignorance, we have reason to believe, is not seldom their least disqualification; and the want of proper books often combines with their own opinions and propensities in introducing into their schools such as are of the worst tendency. Even for schools of a superior description, and under better control, there is a general complaint that proper masters can not be procured without much difficulty; and we are persuaded that a more essential service could not be rendered to the State than by carrying into effect a practicable mode of supplying a succession of well-qualified instructors for the children of the lower classes."

The recommendations of the Commission were not acted upon, but annual grants were subsequently made to the Kildare Place School Society, which were applied in establishing two Model Schools in Dublin, in which teachers, intended for their employment, were practised in the mechanism and methods of the particular system of teaching encouraged by that society. The period of instruction, or rather of observation and practice, was brief, and the instruction itself amounted to but little more than a knowledge of the forms and evolutions of the monitorial system of Dr. Bell.

In 1828, R. J. Bryce, Principal of the Belfast Academy, in a pamphlet entitled "*Sketch of a Plan for a System of National Education for Ireland*," pp. 58, presents a very elaborate argument in favor of legislative provision for the education of teachers, as the only sound basis on which a system of public instruction for Ireland could be raised. He sums up his discussion of this branch of the subject in the following manner:

1. It is commonly supposed, that a man who understands a subject must be qualified to teach it, and that the only essential attribute of an instructor is to be himself a good scholar.

2. Even those who are aware that there often exists a difference between two teachers as to their power of communicating, conceive this difference to be of much less importance than it really is; and, if ever they take the trouble to think of its cause, they ascribe it to some mechanical *knack*, or some instinctive predisposition.

3. On the contrary, we maintain, that when a man has acquired the fullest and most profound knowledge of a subject, he is not yet half qualified to teach it. He has to learn how to communicate his knowledge, and how to train the young mind to think for itself. And, as it usually happens that children are placed under the inspection of their instructors, who become in a great measure responsible for their morals, every teacher ought also to know how to govern his pupils, and how to form virtuous habits in their minds. *And this skill in communicating knowledge, and in managing the mind, is by far the most important qualification of a teacher.*

5. Every teacher, before entering on the duties of his profession, ought therefore to make himself acquainted with *the Art* * *of Education*; that is, with a system of rules for communicating ideas, and forming habits; and ought to ob-

* The author thus refers to an article in No. 54 of the North American Review, devoted to Mr. Carter's Essay, which will be found in another part of this work.

"The necessity of some regular provision for instructing teachers in the Art of Teaching, has begun to be felt by all those who take an enlarged and rational view of the subject of education. The first rude essay was made in the model schools of Bell and Lancaster. But reflecting people soon saw the utter inefficiency of this mere mechanical training, which bears the same relation to a true and rational system of professional education for teachers, that the steam-engine of the Marquis of Worcester bears to the steam-engine of Watt. Hints to this purpose we have met with in various places; but the first regular publication on the subject that we have heard of, is one by Mr. J. G. Carter, an American writer, with which we are acquainted only through a short article in No. LIV. of the North American Review. * * *

In short we recommend the whole of this article to the careful perusal of the friends of *real education* in Britain and Ireland."

tain such a knowledge of the philosophy of mind, as shall enable him to understand the reasons of those rules, and to apply them with judgment and discretion to the great diversity of dispositions with which he will meet in the course of his professional labors.

6. No man is qualified for the delicate and difficult work of managing the youthful mind, unless his own mental faculties have been sharpened and invigorated by the exercise afforded to them in the course of a good general education.

7. Therefore, a legislature *never can succeed* in establishing a good system of national education, without making some provision for insuring a supply of teachers possessed of the qualifications specified in the two last articles; in order to which, it is indispensably necessary, that Professorships of the Art of Teaching be instituted; and that students, placing themselves under the care of such professors, be required to have previously attained a good general education, and, in particular, a competent knowledge of the philosophy of the human mind.

In 1831, the Board of Commissioners of National Education in Ireland was established. In a letter from Hon. E. G. Stanley, Chief Secretary for Ireland, explaining the powers and objects of the Board, one of the objects is declared to be "the establishing and maintaining a Model School in Dublin, and training teachers for country schools," and it is made a condition on which pecuniary aid shall be granted to any teacher, that "he shall have received previous instruction in a Model School to be established in Ireland."

In April, 1833, two Model Schools, one for males and one for females, were established by the Board, and two courses of instruction provided for teachers in each year, to continue three months each. In 1834, steps were taken to extend both the Model Schools and the Training Establishment, as set forth in their Report for 1835.

"If we are furnished with adequate means by the State, not only for training schoolmasters, but for inducing competent persons to become candidates for teacherships, through a fair prospect of remuneration and advancement, we have no doubt whatever that a new class of schoolmasters may be trained, whose conduct and influence must be highly beneficial in promoting morality, harmony, and good order, in the country parts of Ireland.

It is only through such persons that we can hope to render the National Schools successful in improving the general condition of the people. It is not, however, merely through the schools committed to their charge that the beneficial effects of their influence would be felt. Living in friendly habits with the people; not greatly elevated above them, but so provided for as to be able to maintain a respectable station; trained to good habits; identified in interest with the State, and therefore anxious to promote a spirit of obedience to lawful authority; we are confident that they would prove a body of the utmost value and importance in promoting civilization and peace.

Formerly, nothing was attempted in elementary schools further than to communicate the art of reading, writing, and arithmetic, with some knowledge of grammar, geography, and history. Latterly, teachers have made use of the reading lessons to convey information. Writing has been made subservient to the teaching of spelling, grammar, and composition, and also to the fixing of instruction on the memory. Arithmetic, instead of being taught by unexplained rules, has been made the vehicle for conveying the elements of mathematical knowledge, and training the mind to accuracy of thinking and reasoning. Reading-books have latterly been compiled on these principles, the lessons being so selected as to convey the elements of knowledge on a variety of subjects. And this introduction of intellectual exercises into the teaching of these elementary arts, has been found to produce a reflex effect upon the progress of the pupils in learning the arts themselves. Children are found to be more easily taught to read when, while they are learning to pronounce and combine syllables and words into sentences, they are receiving information. Their writing proceeds better when, while they are learning the mechanical art, they are learning the use of it; and they become better arithmeticians when the principles on which arithmetical operations are founded are gradually developed to them.

To teach upon this principle, it is absolutely necessary that the teacher not only be able to read, and spell, and write well, and be a good practical arithmetician, but that he be a person of general intelligence, having an extensive and accurate knowledge of the subjects treated of in the reading lessons. He must know much more than is expressed in the lessons themselves, or he will be totally unable to explain them familiarly, to correct the mistakes into which his pupils fall, and answer the innumerable questions that will be put to him as soon as the understanding of his pupils begins to be exercised on any subject.

It is therefore necessary that teachers should not merely be able to teach their pupils to read, write, and to conduct schools upon an approved system of discipline, but that they be able to aid in forming the minds of children, and directing their power of reading into a beneficial channel. The power of reading is frequently lost to children, and even becomes a source of corruption and mischief to them, because they have never been directed to the proper use of it; and it is consequently of the highest importance that, while they are taught to read, their thoughts and inclinations should have a beneficial direction given to them. To effect this, manifestly requires a teacher of considerable skill and intelligence.

To secure the services of such persons, it is material that suitable means of instruction should be provided for those who desire to prepare themselves for the office of teaching, and that persons of character and ability should be induced to seek it by the prospect of adequate advantages.

With these views, we propose establishing five Professorships in our training institution. I. Of the art of teaching and conducting schools. The professor of this branch to be the head of the institution. II. Of composition. English literature, history, geography, and political economy. III. Of natural history in all its branches. IV. Of mathematics and mathematical science. V. Of mental philosophy, including the elements of logic and rhetoric. We propose that no person shall be admitted to the training institution, who does not previously undergo a satisfactory examination in an entrance course to be appointed for that purpose; and that each person who may be admitted shall study in it for at least two years before he be declared fit to undertake the charge of a school; that during this time, he shall receive instruction in the different branches of knowledge already specified, and be practised in teaching the model school, under the direction of the professor of teaching.

We are of opinion that, in addition to the general training institution, thirty-two district Model Schools should be established, being a number equal to that of the counties of Ireland; that those Model Schools should be under the direction of teachers chosen for superior attainments, and receiving superior remuneration to those charged with the general or Primary Schools; and that, hereafter, each candidate for admission to the training establishments should undergo a preparatory training in one of them.

We think the salary of the teacher of each Model School should be £100 a year, and that he should have two assistants, having a salary of £50 a year each.

We consider that the teacher of each Primary School should have a certain salary of £25 a year; and that the Commissioners for the time being should be authorized to award annually to each a further sum, not exceeding £5, provided they shall see cause for doing so in the Inspector's report of his general conduct, and the character of the school committed to him. We are also of opinion that each teacher should be furnished with apartments adjoining the school."

By the parliamentary grants of 1835 and 1836, the Board were enabled to proceed with the erection of suitable buildings, and the establishment of the Model School, and Training Department, in Marlborough street, Dublin, which were completed in 1838. To this, in 1839, was added a Model Farm, and School of Agriculture, at Glasnevin, in the neighborhood of Dublin, where the male teachers are lodged, and where they receive a course of instruction in agricultural science and practice.

The training department was at first intended for schoolmasters; but in 1840, through the munificent donation of £1000, by Mrs. Drummond, for this special purpose, and an appropriation of a like amount by the Government, a suitable building was erected in connection with the Model School in Marlborough street, for the training of female teachers. In addition to the ordinary course of instruction in the theory and practice of teaching, schoolmistresses are instructed in plain needlework, in the art of cutting out and making up articles of female wearing apparel, in the arts of domestic economy, such as cottage cookery, washing, ironing, mangling, and other useful branches of household management.

The Commissioners have recently erected in Dublin subsidiary Model Schools, where temporary courses of instruction are given to teachers already connected with National Schools.

In connection with, and in extension of the plan of the central Training Establishment, a system of Primary Model Schools in each district into which the country is divided, is commenced. To several of these schools a residence for the teacher, and land for a Model Farm, are annexed. It is in contemplation to make these District Model Schools the residence of the inspector, and depots for a supply of school books, apparatus, and requisites for the schools of the district. Respecting these Model Schools and Training Department, the Board remark in 1848:

"Our training establishments continue in a prosperous state. We have trained, during the year, and supported at the public expense, 224 national teachers, of whom 137 were males and 87 were females. We also trained 14 teachers not connected with National Schools, and who maintained themselves during their attendance at the Model Schools. Of the 224 teachers of National Schools trained during the year, 9 were of the Established Church, 37 Presbyterians, 3 Dissenters of other denominations, and 175 Roman Catholics. The total number of male and female teachers trained, from the commencement of our proceedings to the 31st of December, 1847, is 2,044. We do not include in this number those teachers who are not connected with National Schools.

With reference to the training of teachers we have to observe, that the experience of each successive year strengthens our conviction of its importance. It is vain to expect that the National Schools, established in all parts of Ireland, will ever be effectively conducted, or the art of communicating knowledge materially improved, until a sufficient number of well-paid masters and mistresses can be supplied, thoroughly qualified, by previous training, to undertake the office of teachers, and feeling a zealous interest in promoting the great objects of their profession.

We have observed, with satisfaction, a marked improvement in the appearance, manners, and attainments of every successive class of teachers, who come up to be trained in our Normal establishment. With reference to the two last classes, we have ascertained that 34 teachers in the last, and 73 in the present, had been originally educated *as pupils* in National Schools. It is from this description of persons, to whom the practice of instructing others has been familiar from their childhood, that we may expect to procure the most intelligent and skillful teachers, to educate the rising generation of Ireland.

It is a gratifying fact, that the good feeling which has always prevailed amongst the teachers of different religious denominations residing together in our training establishment, has suffered no interruption whatever during the last year of extraordinary public excitement.

Whilst every attention has been paid to the improvement of the children in our Model Schools, in the various branches of their secular education, the paramount duty of giving to them, and the teachers in training, religious instruction, has not been neglected by those intrusted with that duty. Upon this subject we deem it expedient to republish the statement made in our Report of last year, which is as follows:—"The arrangements for the separate religious instruction of the children of all persuasions attending these schools, and also of the teachers in training, continue to be carried into effect every Tuesday, under the respective clergymen, with punctuality and satisfaction. Previously to the arrival of the clergymen, each of the teachers in training is employed in giving catechetical and other religious instruction to a small class of children belonging to his own communion. These teachers attend their respective places of worship on Sundays; and every facility is given, both before and after Divine service, as well as at other times, for their spiritual improvement, under the directions of their clergy.'"

III. They have not only increased the number of ordinary elementary schools, but they have established and aided a number of special schools of different grades, pre-eminently calculated to benefit the people of Ireland.

1. *Evening Schools.* The experiment was commenced at Dublin, under the direct inspection of the Board, and was conducted to their satisfaction. They thus refer to the subject in their report for 1847:

"The average attendance of the Evening School on our premises in Marlborough street, Dublin, during the past year, was about 200, composed partly of boys who could not attend school during the day, and partly of adults.

The anxiety evinced by boys, and by young men from eighteen to twenty-five years of age, to participate in the advantages afforded by this school, confirms our opinion that such institutions, if well conducted, will be of incalculable benefit to the working classes; and that, if established in large towns, or in populous localities adjoining them, they will form an important step in the education of the artisan between the common National School and the Mechanics' Institution. After the toils of the day, the humble laborer and the tradesman, will find in Evening Schools the means of literary and moral improvement, and a protection against temptations to which, at their age, this class of persons are peculiarly exposed.

We received during the year numerous applications for aid to Evening Schools, the majority of which we rejected, being of opinion that our grants for this purpose should as yet be confined to large towns, in which trade and manufactures are extensively carried on, and where alone we at present possess the means of inspection. We made grants to twelve Evening Schools in the course of the year. It is probable that the number of applications for assistance will gradually increase. Should this be the case, we shall take the necessary steps to ascertain that the Evening Schools are properly conducted, and that the system of education carried on in them, is adapted to the varied occupations of the artisans, mechanics, and others, who are desirous of obtaining the special instruction which their several trades and avocations require."

2. *Workhouse Schools.* The children of families provided for in workhouses, under the Poor Law Commissioners in Ireland, are gathered into schools under the care of the Board. In 1847 there were 104 of these schools, for which the Board propose the following vigorous measures of improvement:

"1. That the minimum rate of salary to male teachers, in addition to apartments and rations, shall be £30 a year; and to female teachers £25, exclusive of any gratuity from the Commissioners of National Education.

2. That no teacher shall be required to undertake the instruction of more than from 80 to 100 children; and that assistant teachers be provided, at lower salaries, when the daily average attendance considerably exceeds 100.

3. That in female schools, when the number of pupils considerably exceeds 100, a work-mistress be engaged, in addition to the principal teacher, to instruct the children in the various branches of plain needlework, and in the art of cutting out, and making up articles of female wearing apparel.

4. That the whole time of the teachers shall be devoted to the literary, moral,

and industrial education of the children, and to the superintendence of them, during the hours of recreation and manual labor.

5. That Evening Schools be opened for the instruction of the adult paupers, and of such of the pupils of the day schools, as it may be practicable and desirable to have in attendance for two hours each evening. The Evening Schools to be conducted by the teachers of the day schools.

6. That the number of children to be accommodated in each school-room be so regulated, as that a space of at least six square feet be allowed for each child.

7. That every Workhouse School, in connection with the Commissioners of National Education, be supplied with suitable furniture and apparatus, according to models to be furnished by them.

8. That each Workhouse School, on its coming into connection with the Commissioners of National Education, be gratuitously supplied with a complete outfit of books, maps, stationery, &c., and that a further supply be granted afterward, at stated periods.

9. That two of the local Guardians be requested to visit the schools weekly, and report once a month to the Board of Guardians. This duty might be rendered less onerous, if undertaken by the members of the Board in rotation.

10. That in order to provide industrial training for pauper-children, a sufficient quantity of land be annexed to each Workhouse, to be cultivated as farms and gardens by the pupils of the schools; and that, for this purpose, Agriculturists be appointed, to the most deserving of whom the Commissioners of National Education will award gratuities not exceeding £15 each.

11. That it is advisable, under particular circumstances, to consolidate two or three Unions, and to establish a Central Agricultural School, to be attended by the children of each."

3. *Industrial Schools.* The Board have extended aid to a class of schools which gather in children who can not ordinarily be induced to attend the regular day schools, and who need special care and training. The results are shown in the following extracts from the Reports of the Inspectors appointed by the Board:

"*Claddah Fishing School, County Galway.*—The attendance has been, sometimes, over 500, and the average for six months has been nearly 400. I regret that the apparatus requisite for giving an extensive course of instruction on practice of navigation has not been provided, and that there are no funds available for this purpose.

Since the opening of the female schools, 36 girls have been employed in the industrial room at spinning and net-making; and in providing materials and making trifling donations to children, £66 1*s.* 6*d.* have been nearly expended. The schools are in a much better state than I expected them to be, the merit of which must be attributed to the praiseworthy assiduity and attention of the manager, and rev. gentlemen of the Caddah convent."

4. *Agricultural Schools.* In accordance with the wise policy which has characterized all the measures of the Board, of trying all new experiments under their own inspection, and of exhibiting a working plan, the Board first established a Model Farm and Agricultural School at Glasnevin, in connection with the Training Establishment in Dublin, and afterward attached an ordinary National School to the establishment at Glasnevin, to ascertain to what extent industrial training suited to the wants and circumstances of the locality, could be united with literary instruction. As to the results the Board remark:

"It has proved that literary instruction and practical instruction in gardening, together with some knowledge of agriculture, may be successfully communicated to boys in a National School by one master, provided he be zealous and skillful. No difficulty has been experienced in inducing a limited number of the advanced boys to work in the garden two hours each day, after the ordinary school business. The scholars composing the Industrial class are paid sixpence a week each for their labor; and the produce of the garden is valued to the Commissioners, at the current market prices, for the use of the teachers and domestics, in the male and female training establishments: an account is kept by the teacher of the receipts as well as of the expenses of cultivation. Our masters in training have thus an opportunity of seeing a model of what a small village school ought to be in a rural district, and how far it is practicable, under one and the same master, to unite literary and industrial education. The boys employed in cultivating the garden attend daily, together with the teachers in training, a course of lectures on the elementary principles of agriculture, as well as of gardening. The practical information they thus acquire, and the habits of industry to which they become accustomed, can not fail to be highly serviceable to them in after life. It will be a subject for future consideration, whether this arrangement for the regulation of the labor of the garden might not be so altered, as to place under each of the pupils a small allotment, which he shall be required to cultivate, being permitted to receive a portion of the profit derived from his industry.

We conceive that no greater boon could be conferred upon Ireland than the establishment of similar schools in every country parish. They would not only be conducive to the improvement of the laboring classes themselves, but would tend materially to remove the prejudices existing amongst many respectable farmers, against the mere literary education of the peasantry. Schools of this description would prove, by the combination of intellectual with industrial training, that not only are the understandings of the young developed by this species of education, but their bodies formed and disciplined to habits of useful and skillful labor."

After training up teachers competent to conduct Agricultural Schools, and showing them a working model of such a school, and also of an ordinary school in which agriculture was introduced as a study and an exercise, the Board proceeded to establish Model Agricultural Schools, publish Agricultural Class Books, and promote the study of agriculture in all the schools under their care, in appropriate situations. In their Report for 1847 they remark:

"We had in operation on the 31st of December, 1847, seven Model Agricultural Schools; and we have made building grants of £200 each to ten others of this class, some of which are in progress. In addition to those schools, there are twelve other Agricultural Schools to which small portions of land are attached; and to the masters of these we pay an additional salary of £5 per annum for their agricultural services; and other emoluments are secured to them by the local managers. Since the commencement of the present year, several applications have been received for aid both to Model and ordinary Agricultural Schools; so that we hope to announce, in our next Report, the establishment of a greater number.

We have published an Agricultural Class Book for the use of the advanced pupils attending the National Schools, which it is intended shall be read by all the pupils capable of understanding its contents. The object of this little work is to explain, in as simple language as possible, the best mode of managing a small farm and kitchen garden. Appended to it are introductory exercises, in which the scholars should be examined by the teachers. In order to render the lessons attractive, they have been thrown into the form of a narrative, calculated to arrest the attention of young readers. This reading book is not, however, designed as an agricultural manual for our teachers. We propose to supply this want by the publication of a series of agricultural works, rising from the simplest elementary book, to scientific teaching of a high character, and comprehending various branches of practical knowledge, bearing upon the subjec of agricultural instruction. We distributed last year, amongst our teachers, a variety of cheap and useful tracts, relating to the best modes of cultivating the soil, and providing against the dearth of food; and we are now engaged in circulating, amongst our masters, several other elementary treatises on husbandry, recently published under the direction of the Royal Agricultural Society, and containing much valuable information.

In a limited number of *large* National Schools, situated in rural districts, we intend to introduce agricultural instruction, subject to the following conditions

If the manager of a National School of this description, or any respectable person of whom he approves, shall annex to it a farm of eight or ten acres, and erect the necessary farm buildings thereon, without requiring any grant from us toward building, repairs, the purchase of stock, or the payment of rent, we propose in such cases to pay the Agricultural teacher a salary not exceeding £30 per annum.

We shall leave the appointment of the teacher and the superintendence of the farm to the proprietor of the land, or to the manager of the school, should he also be the owner of the land. All we shall require will be, that the teacher be competent, in the opinion of our Agricultural Inspector, to manage the farm according to the most improved system; and that he shall instruct daily, in the theory and practice of agriculture, a sufficient number of advanced boys, who shall be in attendance at the adjoining National School. Our Agricultural Inspector will be required to report half-yearly whether the farm has been conducted to his satisfaction, and whether the regulations which we shall prescribe for the agricultural instruction of the pupils have been strictly adhered to.

The plan we have now explained can not be effectually worked by our ordinary inspectors. It will be necessary, therefore, that our Agricultural Schools, including our Model Farm at Glasnevin, should be under the superintendence of a person, practically conversant with agricultural operations, with plans of farm buildings, and the best method of keeping farming accounts; and who shall be competent to examine and report on the system of agricultural instruction adopted in schools of this description. We have, accordingly, determined upon appointing an officer to discharge those important duties. With his assistance, we shall in future be able to make full and satisfactory reports to Parliament of the agricultural branch of our system.

In order to supply the demand for persons qualified to conduct farms and Agricultural Schools, we have resolved upon increasing, from twelve to twenty-four, the number of agricultural pupils, who compose the free class, at our Model Farm, Glasnevin; also, upon increasing to the same extent the number of agricultural teachers at our training establishment there. We shall thus have a total of forty-eight pupils and teachers, who will be all under instruction at the same time.

Our agricultural pupils are selected from the best qualified of our pupils attending our several Agricultural Schools throughout Ireland; and our agricultural teachers who come up to be trained, are chosen from among the masters of ordinary National Schools. This arrangement is calculated to accelerate the diffusion of agricultural instruction throughout our schools, and, generally, amongst our teachers.

Though convinced that, by means of these and other arrangements, we may become instrumental in promoting the cause of Agricultural Education in Ireland, we feel bound to state that we can accomplish little, unless our efforts be cordially sustained by the co-operation of the landed proprietors of the country. The Agricultural Schools must, in almost all cases, be created by them, and conducted under their directions. It will be necessary for them to expend much money, and bestow constant care upon them. The salaries, training, and inspection, furnished by the state, are indispensable; but they will be unavailing if local expenditure and exertions do not supply the groundwork upon which the assistance of Government is to be brought into operation."

5. *School Libraries.* From the following extracts, it will be seen that the Board are about to adopt the educational policy of New York and Massachusetts in extending the means of self-education out of school hours, and beyond the period of school attendance.

"The want of School Libraries for the use of the children attending our schools has been long felt. To compile a series of instructive and entertaining works adapted to this purpose, would occupy a very considerable time, and require the assistance of many individuals well qualified for compiling books suited to the minds of children. Under these circumstances, we have adopted the necessary steps for the selection of a sufficient number from those already published. Care will be taken that they are unobjectionable in all respects, to the members of every religious denomination. We shall buy them from the publishers at the lowest cost, and sell them at reduced prices to such of the managers of our schools as may approve of their being lent to their pupils. We shall also frame regulations for managing the School Libraries when formed, which will insure a regular delivery and return of the books."

IV. The Board have aided in the erection and fitting up of more than 3000 school-houses in different parts of Ireland, by contributing an amount, not more in any case than two-thirds of the sum actually expended. The expenditure in Ireland for school-houses, in connection with the Board, up to 1850, has been estimated at $2,500,000. The Commissioners must be satisfied as to the site, size, furniture, material, and workmanlike manner of the work done, before the payment of any grant.

V. The Board have succeeded in publishing and introducing a valuable series of text books, maps and school requisites, prepared with great care, and furnished for a first supply, and at the end of every four years *gratuitously* to each school, and at other times *below cost*. Great pains have been taken to exclude from all books published or sanctioned by them, every thing of a sectarian or party character, the upper and the nether millstone between which Ireland has been for two centuries crushed. The publication of this "Irish National Series of School Books," has had the effect already to reduce the price of all school books in England and Scotland, and to lead to the revision of most of the standing text books, in order to compete with this new competitor in the market. In their Fourteenth Report (for 1847) the Board remark:

"We have the gratification to state that the demand for our school-books, in England and Scotland, is progressively increasing. Many of our colonies, too, have been supplied during the year with large quantities; and in some of them a system of public instruction for the poor, similar in its general character to that of the national system in Ireland, as being equally adapted to a population of a mixed character as to their religious persuasions, is likely to be established. We have sent books and requisites to Australia, British Guiana, Canada, New Brunswick, Newfoundland, Nova Scotia, Gibraltar, and Malta. A complete series of our National school-books was also sent to Lord Seaton, the Governor of Corfu; and it is not improbable that they will be translated, at no distant period, into the Greek language, for the use of children attending schools in the Ionian Islands."

VI. The Board have subjected their schools to a system of thorough, periodical and intelligent inspection, by which all abuses and deficiencies are detected, and at once corrected or supplied, and a stimulus of the most powerful character is brought to bear on all of the teachers in any way aided by the Commissioners.

Besides three head inspectors residing at Dublin, for local duties and special business abroad, there are thirty-four district inspectors, who devote their whole time to the services of the Board, under the following regulations:

"1. The commissioners do not take the control or regulation of any school, except their own model schools, directly into their own hands, but leave all schools aided by them under the authority of the local conductors. The inspectors, therefore, are not to give direct orders, as on the part of the Board, respecting any necessary regulations, but to point out such regulations to the conductors of the school, that *they* may give the requisite orders.

2. The commissioners require that every National School be inspected by the *inspector of the district*, at least three times in each year.

3. The district inspector, on each inspection, is to communicate with the patron or correspondent, for the purpose of affording information concerning the general state of the school, and pointing out such violations of rule, or defects, if any, as he may have observed; and he is to make such suggestions as he may deem necessary.

4. He is to examine the visitors' book, or daily report book, and to transmit to the commissioners copies of any observations made therein which he may consider to be of importance.

5. He is not to make any observation in the book except the date of his visit, the time occupied in the inspection of the school, showing the precise time at which it commenced and the precise time at which it terminated; and also the number of scholars present.

6. Upon ordinary occasions, he is not to give any intimation of his intended visit; but during the middle term of the year, from the 1st of May to the 31st of August, when the inspection is to be public, he is to make such previous arrangements with the local managers, as will facilitate the attendance of the parents of the children, and other persons interested in the welfare of the schools.

7. He is to report to the commissioners the result of each visit, and to use every means to obtain accurate information as to the discipline, management, and methods of instruction pursued in the school.

8. He is to examine all the classes in succession, in their different branches of study, so as to enable him to ascertain the degree and efficiency of the instruction imparted.

9. He is to examine the class rolls, register, and daily report book; and to report with accuracy what is the actual number of children receiving instruction at the school, and what is the daily average attendance.

10. He is to receive a monthly report from the teacher of each school, and also to make one quarterly himself to the commissioners, in addition to his ordinary report upon the school after each visit.

11. He is also to supply the commissioners with such local information as they may from time to time require from him, and to act as their agent in all matters in which they may employ him; but he is not invested with authority to decide upon any question affecting a National School, or the general business of the commissioners, without their direction.

12. When applications for aid are referred to the district inspector, he is to communicate with the applicant so as to insure an interview, and also with the clergymen of the different denominations in the neighborhood, with the view of ascertaining their sentiments on the case, and whether they have any, and what, objections thereto. He is also to communicate personally, if necessary, with any other individuals in the neighborhood.

13. The district inspector is to avoid all discussions of a religious or political nature; he is to exhibit a courteous and conciliatory demeanor toward all persons with whom he is to communicate, and to pursue such a line of conduct as will tend to uphold the just influence and authority both of managers and teachers.

VII. They have, by their wise and successful measures, induced the British Parliament to increase their annual appropriation in aid of National Education in Ireland. The sum appropriated in 1831 was £4,328; in 1835, £35,000; in 1840, £50,000; and in 1847, £90,000. The whole sum expended by the Board in 1847 was £102,318. To the amount received from the Treasury was added the sum of £8,500, realized from the sale of books, published by the Board. The sum appropriated by the Board is made the condition and inducement of a still larger sum being raised by local and parental effort. The following account of the expenditures of the Board for 1847, will indicate the objects which they aimed to accomplish:

THE DISCHARGE.	£. s. d.	£. s. d.
NORMAL ESTABLISHMENT:		
Salaries and Wages,	861 0 0	
General Expenditure,	23 0 10	
MALE TRAINING DEPARTMENT, GLASNEVIN:		
Salaries and Wages,	126 2 4	
Maintenance and Traveling,	1,218 15 5	
General Expenditure,	312 16 8	
MALE TRAINING DEPARTMENT, GREAT GEORGE'S-STREET:		
Salaries and Wages,	119 7 8	
Maintenance and Traveling,	928 12 9	
General Expenditure,	248 7 5	
MALE TEMPORARY DEPARTMENT, 27, MARLBOROUGH-STREET,	307 16 0	
FEMALE TRAINING DEPARTMENT;		
Salaries and Wages,	183 0 0	
Maintenance and Traveling,	1,139 0 8	
General Expenditure,	306 1 8	
MODEL SCHOOL DEPARTMENT,	852 19 10	
EVENING SCHOOL, MARLBOROUGH-STREET,	101 9 10	
MODEL FARM DEPARTMENT, including the Board and Lodging of Agricultural Pupils and Teachers, Rent, Permanent Improvements, Salaries, Wages, &c.,	921 19 8	
Purchase of Farm Stock and Agricultural Implements, from Mr. Skilling, in November,	916 2 7	
GLASNEVIN NATIONAL SCHOOL:—Completion of Building, Fitting-up, &c.	744 18 9	
GLASNEVIN EVENING SCHOOL,	21 16 6	
		9,333 17 7
BUILDING, FITTING-UP, REPAIRING, &c., SCHOOL-HOUSES,	3,956 7 10	
Do. Do. AGRICULTURAL, INDUSTRIAL AND OTHER SCHOOLS,	399 8 9	
		4,355 16 7
SALARIES TO TEACHERS AND MONITORS,	—	50,209 6 1
DISTRICT MODEL SCHOOLS:—		
Purchase, Rent, toward Building, Furnishing, &c.,	520 0 0	
Salaries and Allowances to teachers,		
General Expenditure,	232 13 0	
		752 13 0
INSPECTION,	—	9,322 1 7
BOOK DEPARTMENT:—		
Her Majesty's Stationery Office, for one year ending 31st March, 1847, for Paper, Printing, Binding of National School Books, including Slates, Pencils, and other School Requisites,	14,064 8 5	
For Books and Requisites purchased from Publishers, and sold to the National Schools at reduced prices, Salaries, &c.,	3,339 4 9	
		17,403 13 2
OFFICIAL ESTABLISHMENT IN MARLBOROUGH-STREET,	—	4,961 3 8
REPAIRS AND WORKS AT MARLBOROUGH-STREET, including Purchase of ground in Rere, for New Male Training Establishment,	1,100 0 0	
Building and Fitting-up New Book Stores,	1,500 0 0	
Sundry Repairs and Alterations in various Departments,	1,412 4 2	
		4,012 4 2
MISCELLANEOUS:—		
Rates, Taxes, and Insurance,	301 11 6	
Coals, Candles, Gas, &c.,	435 9 0	
Postage,	380 5 0	
Stamps,	136 15 0	
Incidents, { Law Costs, £424 13 2; Sundries, 165 2 3 }	589 15 5	
		1,843 15 11
Gratuities to Monitors, from Model School Fund,	....	124 2 8
JAMES CLARIDGE, *Accomptant.*		102,318 14 5

VIII. The success which has attended the efforts of the Board even under the extraordinary and peculiarly difficult circumstances of Ireland, has had a powerful influence on the cause of educational improvement in England, and other parts of the British Empire.

Much has been done within five years past, and more is now doing in the Province of Upper Canada, by the Government, to establish a system of common schools than in any one of the American States, not excepting even New York, or Massachusetts. The action of the enlightened and indefatigable superintendent of schools, the Rev. Egerton Ryerson, D. D., has been guided more by the experience of the National Board of Ireland than that of any other State.

The following survey of the operations of the National Board of Education for Ireland appeared in the "*Westminster Review*" for July, 1860.

It was no part of the design of the National Board to monopolize educational activity, or throw obstacles in the way of the freest development of private enterprise engaged in the same task. The functions which they undertook to discharge were not to supersede, but to supplement, to aid, and to improve—to supply schools where schools were wanting, to assist them where they were in operation, and above all, through the example of their own models, to raise the general character of education. Agreeably with this design, the Board framed its rules upon a threefold plan, under which three distinct classes of schools were established—the model, the vested, and the non-vested schools.* In the first of these the Board supplied all the funds, and exercised in return exclusive control, appointing the teachers, selecting the books, and regulating the courses of instruction. Of these model schools it was originally intended, though the intention has as yet been but partially realized, that one should be placed in every county in Ireland, with a view, as the name indicates, not merely of supplying education, but still more of serving at once as rivals and models to stimulate and direct the existing educational machinery. In the case of the vested schools the assistance was more limited, as was also the authority exercised. The state supplied to them, as a maximum, two-thirds of the expense of the original foundation, requiring the remaining third to be made up by local exertions; and further contributed to the current yearly expenditure according to the exigencies of each case. In return for this assistance it exacted an adherence to the fundamental rules respecting religious teaching, and claimed a general superintendence over the school, but left to local patrons, subject to the approval of the commissioners, the appointment of the teachers, and the regulation of the details of instruction. Lastly, in the case of the non-vested schools, the connection with the board was of a still slighter kind. In this case, what may be called the "capital" of the undertaking was supplied entirely by local parties, the state merely contributing in the way of salaries and books; while the control was limited to a general veto on the books and teachers employed, the right of inspection, and a prohibition of all compulsion in imparting religious instruction.

Such was the machinery by means of which the Board, established in 1831, proposed to carry out the important task of national education, and the success of the scheme has been commensurate with the wisdom with which it was framed. The commissioners had, from the commencement of their labors down to March, 1858, trained nearly 5,000 teachers. At that date they had under their control 5,308 schools; and these schools were attended by 569,364 pupils. These numbers speak for themselves.

---

* That is, schools vested in the commissioners as trustees for the public, and schools not so vested, but remaining the property of those by whom they were erected.

They leave no doubt as to the magnitude of the operations of the board; it is instructive to compare them with the futile results of former systems. It is further curious to observe, that the number of children in attendance is as nearly as possible that for which the commissioners originally estimated that the aid of the national schools would be required. Their estimate was, that ultimately 570,000 children would need to be brought under public instruction. No less unquestionable is the excellence of the education given. We but express the concurrent opinion of all who have examined the subject, when we say that the primary education of Ireland is not surpassed, if equalled, in any portion of the empire. When we add that the National Board do not confine their attention to literary and scientific training, but are disseminating, with the happiest effect, a sound knowledge of the principles and practice of agriculture in one hundred and sixty establishments in various parts of the country; and that the Parliamentary grant by which all this is achieved does not much exceed £270,000, we may confidently assert that never were grander results brought about by a smaller outlay. So much for the first criterion of the system's success—that afforded by the extent of its operations. Let us now apply a second test to which in fairness it must submit. It professes to be a *mixed* system; how far has it succeeded in bringing together children of different religious persuasions for common instruction?*

We have been favored with official returns made up to March, 1858, which prove incontestably that, even regarded as a mixed system, the national system of education has been reasonably successful. We shall place some of these results before our readers.

It appears, then, that of 5,222 schools from which returns had been received on the 31st March, 1858, 2,929, or more than fifty-six per cent. of the whole had, in point of fact, a mixed attendance. Nor were these schools in isolated districts, but diffused through the whole country, apparently in fair proportion to the geographical distribution of religious sects. Thus, according as the humbler classes, from which the national schools derive their pupils, were more divided in religious persuasion, the number of mixed schools increased, while it fell in proportion to the prevalence of some one form of religious belief. In several of the counties of Ulster, for example, where the various religious sects are fully represented, the proportion of mixed schools was above ninety per cent., and in the whole province it was eighty-four per cent.; while in some of the Roman Catholic counties it fell as low as thirty per cent. It is, however, satisfactory to think, that in two counties alone in the whole of Ireland did the proportion fall below this per centage, and still more so, that the proportion is increasing. The return from which we quote exhibits an advance of two per cent. on a return made in 1853. How, in the face of facts like these, the national schools can be said to have failed in bringing

* The principle of this Board is, that the national schools shall be open alike to Christians of all religious denominations, and that accordingly no child shall be required to be present at any religious instruction or exercise of which his parents or guardians may disapprove; and that opportunities shall be afforded to all children to receive separately, at particular periods, such religious instruction as their parents or guardians may provide for them.

together for common instruction the children of the various religious sects, we are wholly at a loss to conceive. They have succeeded in this object to an extent which, looking at the numerous obstacles they have had to contend with, may well excite surprise.

But there is a third test by which the system may be tried, and according to which it has been again pronounced a failure. It is admitted—for this point appears to be too clear for cavil—that the national schools have succeeded so far as the Roman Catholics are concerned; but it is maintained that this is the limit of their success, and that the Protestant portion of the nation derives no adequate benefits from the system. Let us for a moment inquire how far this charge is consistent with the facts of the case. As we have already seen, the number of children on the rolls of the national schools for the year ending March, 1858, was 569,-364. To this aggregate the different denominations contributed in the following proportions:—

Roman Catholics,	481,000
Presbyterians,	57,018
Established Church,	29,130
Other Protestants,	2,216

It hence appears that the Presbyterians contribute considerably more than their quota to the total sum;* on the other hand, it must be admitted that the numbers contributed by the Established Church are below their due proportion; but we shall not find much to wonder at in this, when we remember how much more wealthy the Protestants are than the Roman Catholics, and consequently how much better able to provide education for themselves; as in fact they do through the schools of the Church Education Society.†

Thus much for the pupils. It is interesting to observe that amongst the teachers the various creeds are represented with equal fairness. From returns which lie before us it appears that while the proportion of Protestants of the Established Church on the school rolls is five per cent., the proportion of teachers of the same communion comes out six per cent. The Roman Catholic pupils make up eighty-four per cent., and the

* In the last census, in which the religious denominations of the population of Ireland were noted, the Presbyterians were less than one-tenth of the Roman Catholics.

† It is further to be observed that the number of Protestants has in recent years largely increased. If we again compare the returns given above with those of 1853, we find that of the gross number of pupils on the rolls in that year (490,027) there were:—

Of the Established Church,	23.629
" Presbyterians,	39.751
" Other Protestants,	2,083

making a total of 65,463 as against 88,364 of the year 1858. We have thus an increase of 35 per cent. In favor of the latter year, an increase shared by all the items of the calculation. Surely, if there is any faith to be put in statistics, these figures show that the national system is largely and increasingly acceptable and beneficial to Protestants. We may add that in the model schools, where the highest class of education is given, the Protestants of the Established Church considerably exceed their due proportion, making up one-third of the entire number of pupils in attendence. This fact confirms our impression that the deficiency of members of this communion in the ordinary schools is due to other causes than hostility to the system.

proportion of Roman Catholic teachers is eighty per cent. Lastly, the Presbyterian pupils number ten, the Presbyterian teachers twelve per cent. This correspondence, amazingly exact, considering that it was undesigned, and in fact accidentally brought to light by a hostile critic, admirably illustrates the skill with which the rules of selection have been made, and the fairness with which they are administered by the National Board.

On every ground, then, whether we regard the admixture of children in particular schools, or the aggregate numbers of the great religious denominations which divide the country amongst them, or again the representation of the several creeds in the staff of teachers, we assert that the national system of education in Ireland is fairly entitled to be called a mixed system; and that in this respect, no less than in the extent to which it has been instrumental in diffusing education, it has fairly vindicated its claim to success. It might have been thought that success so complete would have silenced all opposition: and so it would, were the education of the people the primary object of religious parties. This, however, is far from being the case, and consequently the success attending the scheme, instead of disarming, has, it is to be feared, in some instances inflamed the hostility of its opponents. These comprise, on the one hand, the bulk of the clergy of the Established Church, and, on the other, the ultramontane party in the Church of Rome; and are represented respectively by the Church Education Society and the Roman Catholic prelates.

The main objection of the Church Education Society to the national system is that the reading of the Scriptures is not made compulsory on all the children who attend the schools.

To use their own language:—"They conceive that no system of education can be sound in principle, or prove beneficial in its results, which exempts any portion of the pupils it admits into its schools from instruction in the inspired volume. Whatever such a system may be, as regards those whom it permits to *receive* such instruction, it is essentially defective as regards those whom it permits to refuse it."

The demands of the Roman Catholic prelates presents themselves in a more specious guise. "It is the denominational system which is in force in England; it has been found to answer there; and why should not the same measure of justice, and the same rule of expediency, be applied to both countries?"

In the first place, then, we must observe that the educational institutions of the two countries differ in other respects than those in which the Roman Catholic prelates require assimilation, and further that the particulars in which they differ are of the essence of the case. In Ireland, as we have seen, the expense of elementary education is supported principally by the state. In the Model Schools the expense is exclusively borne by the Government, if we except the small sum derived from pupils' fees; in the vested schools it sustains perhaps three-fourths of the expense; and even to the non-vested schools its contributions are considerable; while the training of teachers is conducted exclusively at the public expense. On the other hand, in England, the principal weight of the charge falls upon the local subscriptions and pupils' fees: it is estimated that over the whole country the sources derived from voluntary effort bear to those derived from the state the proportion of three to two. With this difference in the mode in which the schools in the two countries are supported, it does not seem strange that there should be a difference in the mode of imparting religious instruction—it is not strange that, while in England schools which are called into existence, many through voluntary efforts, take their religious tone from the localities in which they are founded, those in Ireland, which are supported chiefly by the state, should exhibit, in their mode of dealing with religion, somewhat of the comprehensive character of the source from which they derive their origin.

What the Roman Catholic prelates really desire, in appealing to the precedent of England, is to obtain all the privileges possessed by the various denominations in England, without making the sacrifices with which those privileges have been purchased. They wish to dispose of the funds of the state with as much freedom as the English enjoy in disposing of their voluntary subscriptions. Their demand is, not that they may be placed on the same footing with the English—for we have had no intimation of a desire to undertake the English share of the expense—but that they may be permitted to deal with the national funds according to their uncontrolled discretion—that they may be intrusted with prerogatives which have never yet been intrusted to any religious party, not even to the national Church.

We would recommend those who are doubtful of the capabilities of the combined system for inculcating religion, to read the reports of the various ministers attending to the spiritual wants of the Belfast Model School. The catechist of the Established Church, after stating that the bishop, in whose presence the annual examination was conducted, expressed his entire satisfaction with the proficiency of the children in the various subjects in which they were examined, goes on to say; "The Rev. Professor Reichel, who examined the senior class in the Evidences of Christianity (a subject which was entirely new to the children, not having been taught in any of the Church schools in Belfast,) has permitted me to say that he never met so good answering, in a subject of corresponding difficulty, in any school in which he had previously examined." Again the Roman Catholic clergyman says, "The progress of the children in the knowledge of their religious duties, always steady, has been, in many instances, most astonishing—a fact which I attribute partly to the very abundant time set apart for such purposes, and partly to the zealous energetic coöperation of the Catholic teachers." Lastly, the ministers of the Presbyterians say, "that the answering of the children at the examination called forth repeated expressions of admiration from the visitors present."

IX. SUBJECTS AND METHODS OF EARLY EDUCATION.*

BY THOMAS URRY YOUNG.

I. NECESSITY AND NATURE OF THE INFANT OR PRIMARY SCHOOL.

The idea of collecting very young children for elementary instruction is not new; schools for infants have long existed under the name of *Dame Schools*. Indeed the embarrassment arising from the union of children widely differing in age generally led either to the separation of the younger portion, or to their entire neglect. Very little observation and reflection are required to convince us of the marked disparity in the state of mind in children of various ages, which, when we address them familiarly, we involuntarily admit, by bringing our language and ideas to their level; and they themselves generally divide into groups, according to their age for conversation or play. No judicious teacher overlooks this fact, or attempts to unite in one class pupils of five years of age with others of ten and twelve. It is not, therefore, in the mere collecting of young children together, but in the kind of instruction given, and in the mode of communicating it, that the infant school system differs essentially from any previous form of elementary teaching. Under the old system, little was attempted until the child had learned to read; and, during this long and painful interval, the monotony of the school-room was seldom varied by any thing to interest or amuse the little pupil. No physical exercises relieved the wearied body, but all was starched formality, and what was called good order. Immured in a close dull room—all the joyous freedom of infancy repressed—the eyes vacantly poring over the unexplained mysteries of learning's first page, the only motives to exertion being the dread of the fool's cap, or of the

> "Tway birchen sprays, with anxious fear entwined;
> With dark distrust and sad repentance filled;
> And steadfast hate, and sharp affliction join'd,
> And fury uncontroll'd, and chastisement unkind."

With such a system, was it wonderful that the little sufferer longed to escape from school as from a prison house—that small progress

---

* Extracts from "*Young's Infant School Teachers' Manual.*"

was made—and, worst of all, that the temper and disposition were too often irremediably injured? But, with the advancing intelligence of the present century, it began to be perceived and felt that something more was required for the happiness and good of infancy than this, at best, negative system; that, in fact, much could be done in the formation of character and good habits, as well as in the development of the intellectual and physical powers, even with children in the earliest stages of life: hence, infant schools, arising in an age of high intelligence, have had impressed upon them, at their commencement, enlarged and philosophical principles. Throwing aside, as unfit, all previously existing systems, the infant school legislates for its pupils in accordance with their age and state, basing its plans on the simplicity of nature; taking advantage of those restless instincts which were the terror of former teachers, it makes them subservient to the most perfect training, subduing to cheerful orderly activity that incessant restlessness, which, when suppressed, constantly breaks out into irregularities. That troublesome curiosity which so often annoys us in the young, is made to produce the rapid and apparently spontaneous development of the intellectual faculties; while the ever springing love of infancy opens the heart to receive the seeds of the purest virtue.

The following extract from an eminent Continental writer gives a fair statement of the position and use of infant schools:—

> The vocation of such establishments is not to antedate the true effect of our schools, but to dispose and prepare children to enter them. Well directed, their utility is incalculable. The power of education is inversely as the age of the young; and Montaigne perhaps rightly said, that he learned more from his nurse than from all other teachers besides. Now, the teacher of an infant school carries the work of the nurse on to the age at which development really begins, and where habits are effectually formed. How many parents are there, who, for want of intelligence or leisure, of constancy and patience, are unfitted to watch over this first blossoming of our luxuriant human nature; and how desirable is it that the noble task should be intrusted to those who will regard it not as a trade, but as a profession and high art! Such institutions, too, necessarily facilitate, to a great extent, the operations of the primary schools. Instead of losing their best time, and consuming their best efforts, in bringing children within some order and discipline, in accustoming them to the school, and inducing them to fix their attention, the teacher would then only have to carry on an education already begun in every direction. In existing circumstances, and in places where there is no infant school, the teacher has reason to congratulate himself when the children committed to his care have received no education whatever, but remain very much as when they issued from the hands of nature; for then he has not to cause them to unlearn vicious habits instilled by previous maltreatment; but if good infant schools were universal, he would require only to resume the work they had begun, and to continue what already is considerably advanced. Learning to read, write, and cypher, would then not occupy all the leisure of the children; enough would remain for receiving true instruction, and for the work of education, properly so called.
>
> I do not hesitate to state my opinion, that every primary school open to children from the age of six to fourteen, ought, in its younger classes, to be conducted and disciplined very nearly as an excellent infant school; and that in the

construction of new school-houses, attention should be paid to this special requirement.

To work, then, ye generous minds, who seek but an opportunity to accomplish services for humanity; none can be presented to you more enticing or more easy to be seized! To work, you also, who desire a greater security for your actions, who try your emotions by calculation, and consent to be charitable only when you have proved that thus also you shall be useful and just! The good now in question is in every way manifest, for the education of the people will not be truly provided for until infant schools are established every where; and the success of primary instruction itself can not fully be obtained unless through their establishment.

Arguments in favor of infant (or primary) schools are scarcely needed. Their extensive popularity and usefulness in Europe and America are the best proofs of their utility. The necessity of providing for the care of young children while their parents are engaged in their daily occupations—the importance of removing them from the moral contamination, as well as from the physical dangers, of the streets—the duty of inculcating, at the age most susceptible, pure moral and religious principles—the immense saving effected in their future education, by employing their otherwise valueless time in the acquisition of elementary knowledge—all plead for the establishment of these institutions wherever practicable.

As the passions and affections of our nature furnish the first impulses to action, it is important that we address ourselves to the task of moulding and directing them at the age at which they are most yielding and susceptible.* And as examples of good and evil are presented to the mind as soon as it is capable of intelligent observation, it is not sufficient that we ourselves set a good example, but it also becomes necessary to explain to the opening mind of the pupil the nature and tendency of the actions he may witness, or in which he participates.

The acquisition of knowledge suited to the age and state, by occupying the mind, prevents it from receiving evil, and prepares it for the reception of good. Children can not be effectively trained without the society of those of their own age. Constant and skillful treatment is required to form the character and develop the powers. Parents rarely possess the requisite knowledge, or can spare the time required for this important work, and consequently infant schools are necessary for the future welfare of the rising generation.

It must never be forgotten, that the tender age of the pupils renders constraint and severity alike unnecessary and prejudicial. The habit of study and fixed attention is of slow growth, and consequently all long continued lessons are useless and injurious. No lesson is

* A child is a being endowed with all the faculties of human nature, but none of them developed; a bud not yet opened. When the bud uncloses, every one of the leaves unfolds, not one remains behind. Such must be the process of education.—*Pestalozzi.*

good unless it is pleasing to the children. The lessons should be such as arise out of the spontaneous action of the perceptive faculties, directed by the teacher to a certain end.

The paramount importance of physical development must never be lost sight of, and a pleasant alternation of exercise and repose must be kept up.

And lastly, as the teacher stands for the time in the place of the parent, he must set a good example to his little ones, and lead them to virtue by encouraging every good impulse, and constantly watching for and repressing evil tendencies.

Moral Education.

It is more particularly for the first formation of moral character that infant schools are valuable; for, by commencing at so early an age, and before bad habits are formed, we have not only little to undo, but we have the immense advantage of making first impressions on the opening mind.

Every event in the life of a child must be made subservient to this end; nor can any of its acts be considered unimportant, since they all leave their traces on its future character. The watchful eye of the teacher must ever follow the child. It is the play-ground which first introduces it into social life; there the free play of the limbs is accompanied by an equally free development of the passions; each individual disposition stands out in bold relief, and all the hidden springs of action are revealed, thereby enabling the teacher to apply to each that mode of treatment which is best suited to its nature. No interference which is not positively necessary, should take place with the freedom of the child; but each incident requiring comment ought to be observed and stored up for future instruction in the quiet of the school-room.

The selfish principle is the great obstacle to moral training. All goes on smoothly so long as there is no *bone of contention;* for even in the merest infant we may trace almost every outbreak of the evil passions to a desire for the possession of some real or fancied advantage. To moderate this strong instinct, to teach self-denial and self-control, must be the first care of the teacher. We give the following extract on this subject from Simpson's "*Philosophy of Education:*"—

Moral education embraces both the animal and moral impulses; it regulates the former and strengthens the latter. Whenever gluttony, indelicacy, violence, cruelty, greediness, cowardice, pride, insolence, vanity, or any other mode of selfishness, shows itself in the individual under training, one and all must be repressed with the most watchful solicitude and the most skillful treatment. Repression may at first fail to be accomplished unless by severity; but the instructor, sufficiently enlightened in the faculties, will, in the first practicable moment, drop the coercive system, and awaken and appeal powerfully to the higher faculties of conscience and benevolence, and to the power of reflection. This done with kindness, in other words, with a marked manifestation of benevolence itself, will operate with a power, the extent of which, in education, is yet to a very limited extent estimated. In the very exercise of the superior faculties the inferior are indirectly acquiring a habit of restraint and regulation; for it is morally impossible to cultivate the superior faculties without a simultaneous, though indirect, regulation of the inferior.

But in order to carry on this training without impairing the happiness of the child, every reasonable pleasure must be allowed, and above all, those simple enjoyments promoted, which, by exercising the bodily powers, encourage cheerfulness and predispose to good humor.

Every thing that can please, attract, or interest, and thereby draw away the mind from low desires, should be sought. Perfect cleanliness and order must pervade the school and play-ground. Flowers, shrubs, and simple ornaments, as shells, models, natural objects, and pictures, all afford great delight to the young, and create pleasant associations in the mind with the idea of school. The aim of making school agreeable should pervade every arrangement. Unless the children love the teacher, the school, their lessons, and their companions, they will not be happy; and love, like every feeling, must have a cause.

But besides that kind of moral training which arises out of the actions and events of the day, another important mode is open to us. Children are universally fond of *office*, and it is both reward and excellent training to employ them in regular duties. The trust thus reposed, elevates and strengthens the character, and even the faults arising from an abuse of trust give rise to excellent opportunities for explaining and confirming moral principles. On these grounds, various offices are created amongst the children, which are frequently transferred from one to another, so as to try the character of each. It will also be found that different children are fitted for different duties, and thus the waste energies of all can be made useful. For instance, a very restless and active child will make a good monitor of order. Some children from their love of order are happy when employed in keeping the school neat and putting every thing in its place. Others delight to guide and assist the very little children, and are pleased when one is committed to their care. Some, from their steadiness of character, may be intrusted with the books, clothes and bread, of their respective classes, while the busy intellects can be employed to teach simple lessons to the little ones.

To carry out the training of the child it is necessary that parents and teachers should act in concert. It is comparatively of little use for the teacher to pursue one system at school, whilst a counteracting one is going on at home. This latter must be changed.

This is plainly the teacher's duty, as well as to keep up a friendly relation with the parents generally, by which means the ideas of school and home will become connected, and the child prevented from assuming two characters, which is too often the case. Both school and home will benefit by this mutual influence, and a greater consistency of conduct be obtained. A child who has been visited in sickness by its teacher will never forget the kindness, and I have known more improvement arise in the conduct and studies of some children, from having called at their homes, and spoken of them in an encouraging, hopeful manner, than by any other means; while in all cases the home influence is the most useful and natural auxiliary on which the teacher has to rely.

As an inseparable adjunct of moral training, outward amenity and delicacy of demeanor must be carefully cultivated. Coarseness, vulgarity, and rudeness, debase and brutalize; while refinement of manner and consideration for the feeling and comfort of others, not only render the intercourse of life delightful, but promote internal purity and elevation of feeling. It is plain that one means of improving the manners of the children, is for the teacher to show an example of gentleness and propriety, which will be insensibly imitated by them. But this is not entirely sufficient; errors and habits must be corrected in individual cases, and, when general, made the subject of lessons to the whole school. No more should be said to the children on these subjects than is actually necessary, as frequently remarking their behavior will make them nervous and unnatural. A good tone of manners once established can be kept up quietly without calling much attention to it. Consider that personal habits are generally acquired more *by habit* than by direct teaching. Cleanliness, for instance, is (as far as the child is concerned) easily acquired, if care be taken to notice a child when clean with approval, and gently to admonish it for any willful neglect, in unnecessarily soiling either its person or its clothes.

Obedience to the teacher's commands must of course be secured, but, as a general principle, it should be a willing obedience. To obtain this, the teacher must first gain the affections of the child, and take care to require only what is just and reasonable.

Truth.—Infants have at first very vague notions about truth and falsehood, and we must be careful not to attribute the wanderings of the imagination, or the momentary effects of timidity, to deliberate intention. We have often known children indulge in a kind of romance, and tell long histories, as if true, which never occurred, without being aware they were doing wrong until it was pointed out to them. *Fear* also is so very likely to lead to concealment that every inducement to candor should be held out, and when a little child once *confesses* a fault, it is questionable whether punishment should ever be inflicted.

Gentleness.—The exciting causes being as much as possible removed, outbreaks of anger will diminish, and the passion come under control. When *rights* are clearly defined and rules for the conduct of each established, quarrels will no longer be frequent; and as every case of wrong or injury is investigated, and just judgment given, a positive check will be put to such occurrences, and a gentleness of manner be induced.

Generosity.—Every thing that is ungenerous, such as a disposition to report and magnify the faults of others, or to depreciate them and to exalt self, must be discouraged, and a liberal, generous spirit cultivated and encouraged; for by this alone can the intercourse of the children be rendered happy.

Ridicule.—Children are so keenly sensible to ridicule, that the worst effects would flow from allowing them to deride each other, and the disposition to do so should be carefully repressed.

Pride.—In our anxious endeavors to encourage virtue or merit of any kind, we must be careful not to nourish pride. Children should be encouraged as far as possible to learn for learning's sake, to deny themselves for virtue's sake, and always to act from a sense of duty. The dangerous stimulus of public reward or praise should be administered with care; and above all things, the teacher must avoid making *show-children*, either for talent or virtue. To do so is often the greatest injury to those whom we think to benefit. For this reason also, offices of trust ought not to be confined too exclusively to a small number of children, however meritorious, as they will come to look down on the less favored, and believe themselves superior in nature and abilities; even to confine singing, drawing, or any accomplishment to a small class is often an injury to them. If possible, every one should have the same chance of learning; there will still always be difference enough arising from unequal natural abilities.

Tyranny and exclusiveness.—A few individuals in a school will generally try to tyrannize over the rest, and to monopolize the amusements which should be common to all. The remedy is very simple. Rules securing freedom and justice to all must be made, and strictly enforced, and, when necessary, lessons given explaining the evil tendency of such faults.

Cruelty to animals, and destructiveness.—Many children seem to delight in destroying insects, and ill-treating animals; and this habit, if allowed to strengthen, would undoubtedly lead to an unamiable disposition, and should be counteracted by proper lessons explaining the suffering they cause to animals, and the wrong they commit by ill-treating them. With regard also to inanimate objects, a careful, conservative spirit should be inculcated, which is best done by giving them an interest in, and teaching them to examine and admire works of art and natural objects.

Mutual love and benevolence.—Every opportunity should be sought for cultivating the higher feelings. The elder children should be taught to succor and assist the younger ones. When a child is hurt, or ill, or in any trouble, the teachers should hasten to set an example of kindness, by doing all in their power for its comfort and relief. Anecdotes and histories illustrative of kindness may also be frequently related in the gallery with a similar view.

Courage.—Many children are timid from constitutional causes, others are rendered so by injudicious treatment at home, while some have vague terrors at sight of some particular object, or in the dark, &c., &c. From whatever cause fear arises, it should be counteracted by kind and judicious reasoning, and by encouraging the child to overcome its terrors. The mere association of many children together has a tendency to give to each a degree of fortitude and self-support.

Intellectual Education.

"I began with children," says Pestalozzi, "as nature does with savages, first bringing an image before their eyes, and then seeking a word to express the perception to which it gives rise."

This appears to be the true way to commence, since our ideas are first derived from nature; and as books merely represent this knowledge, it is plain that they instruct us only as far as we are able to connect the words they contain with the ideas those words represent.

We must begin by teaching real sounds, real forms, real colors, and real things. Before we use the word purple, we must distinctly impress upon the eye the color purple. If we would speak of a thing being square, we must take care first to impart the true notion of the form; and, when using the words rough or smooth, we should have previously made the mind acquainted with those sensations. The more we spread and enlarge these roots of knowledge, the more rapidly the future tree will grow, and the more vigorous will be the fructification. A child thoroughly drilled in real arithmetic by counting and arranging objects, will carry clearness and vigor into the artificial processes of figures; while a thorough comprehension of the qualities of common things will enable the learner to understand the descriptions met with in history and geography, in a manner impossible without this elementary knowledge.

The spirit in which intellectual instruction should be carried on is of so much importance, that we are tempted to give the following clear and enlightened passage from Pestalozzi:—

The interest in study is the first thing which a teacher should endeavor to excite, and keep alive. There are scarcely any circumstances in which a want of application in children does not proceed from a want of interest; and there are perhaps none under which a want of interest does not originate in the mode of teaching adopted. I would go so far as to lay it down as a rule, that whenever children are inattentive, and apparently take no interest in a lesson, the teacher should always look to himself for the reason. When a quantity of dry matter is before a child, when a child is doomed to listen to lengthy explanations, or to go through exercises which have nothing in themselves to relieve and attract the mind, this is a tax upon the spirits which a teacher should make it a point to abstain from imposing. In the same manner, if the child, from the imperfection of his reasoning powers, or his non-acquaintance with facts, is unable to enter into the sense, or follow the chain of ideas in a lesson; when he is made to hear or to repeat what to him is but "sound without sense," this is perfectly absurd. And when to all this the fear of punishment is added, besides the tedium which in itself is punishment enough, it becomes absolute cruelty.

The first thing to be considered then is—how to create an interest in study, so as to cause the mind to receive and retain the necessary information. Knowledge may be divided into—first, that derived from the involuntary action of the senses, impressed by some outward object or event, which by its novelty or interest makes a distinct and permanent impression on the mind; and secondly, such as is obtained designedly by compelling the attention of the perceptive and reasoning powers to some subjects with which we wish to become acquainted. The first merely wants to be directed to become a fruitful source of improvement, but no child will adopt the second without some motive. It is of the highest importance to determine what that motive is to arise from. Two stimulants were much in vogue in the old system, *fear* and *ambition;* fear of the rod; and ambition to be considered clever, with a mingling of envy of the more gifted.

But will not *love* do more than fear? Will not the desire to acquire knowledge for its own sake, once awakened, do more than the wish to excel others? The answer is not difficult; and the choice once made, minor details will follow.

Mr. Wilderspin thus states his views of intellectual education:—

The error of the past system (for such I hope I may venture to call it) as to mental development was, that the inferior powers of the mind were called into activity, in preference to its higher faculties. The effort was to exercise the memory, and store it with information which, owing to the inactivity of the understanding and the judgment, was seldom or never of use. To adopt the opinions of others was thought quite enough, without the child being troubled to think for itself, and to form an opinion of its own. But this is not as it should be. Such a system is neither likely to produce great nor wise men, and is much better adapted to parrots than to children. Hence the first thing attempted in an infant school is, to set the children thinking—to induce them to examine, compare, and judge, in reference to all those matters which their dawning intellects are capable of mastering. It is of no use to tell a child in the first place, *what it should think*,—this is at once inducing mental indolence, which is but too generally prevalent among adults, owing to this erroneous method having been adopted by those who had the charge of their early years. Were a child left to its own recources, to discover and judge of things exclusively by itself, though the opposite evil would be the consequence, namely, a state of comparative ignorance, yet I am doubtful whether it would be greater or more lamentable than that issuing from the injudicious system of giving children dogmas instead of problems, the opinions of others instead of eliciting their own. In the one case we should find a mind uninformed and uncultivated, but of a vigorous and masculine character, grasping the little knowledge it possessed with the power and right of a conqueror; in the other a memory occupied by a useless heap of notions,—without a single opinion or idea it could call its own,—and an understanding indolent and narrow, and from long indulged inactivity, almost incapable of exertion. As the fundamental principle of the system, I would therefore say, let the children think for themselves. If they arrive at erroneous conclusions, assist them in attaining the truth; but let them with such assistance arrive at it by their own exertions. Little good will be done if you say to a child,—*that is wrong*, *this is right*, unless you enable it to perceive the error of the one and the truth of the other. It is not only due to the child as a rational being that you should act so, but it is essentially necessary for the development of its intellectual faculties. It were not more ridiculous for a master in teaching arithmetic to give his pupil the problem and answer, without instructing him in the method of working the question, than it is for a person to give a child the result of reasoning, without showing how the truth is to be arrived at.

It will often happen that the mind of a child remains dull and inert, without any apparent cause; in most cases this arises from our not having discovered the peculiar taste or bias of the individual. While we are knocking at the outer gate, and groping in the dark, the mind is asleep within, and will not awaken until we can establish some means of communication; but once aroused, it is all bustle and activity.

It must be the constant care of the teacher to bring forth the latent powers of each pupil, and to allow to each the credit due to his efforts, although these may not in all cases be equally successful. For this reason the classification of the children should be made with reference to each separate subject. How absurd would it be to prevent a pupil from progressing in arithmetic, for which he may have a peculiar talent, because he is not quick in learning to read; or not to allow him to extend his knowledge of geography, because he is not a good arithmetician! Rather let us encourage the development of peculiar talents in each individual, thereby to give to all the consciousness of successful progress; and the self-respect arising from this feeling, will impart energy and motive to grapple with those studies which are difficult.

Nothing is of more importance than to watch the progress of the pupils, and remove them from class to class, as soon as they are fit. The child who is not advanced in proper time will retrograde. The spirit of learning flags when allowed to stand still, and it is often difficult to recommence the onward movement. The subjects placed before each class should come in a natural order and succession, according to the previous advances of the mind.

The first efforts should be directed to the most simple perceptions. The blending of manual exercises and singing with the earlier lessons, deprives them of their dry character, and assists to keep up the attention, by bringing them to the level of the infant mind. The repetition of very simple rhymes, accompanied by amusing exercises, and rendered instructive by simple explanations, is also of great use in these first stages of instruction.

Whatever is useful and necessary to man, possesses an interest for the child. It wants to know about the food it eats—the house it lives in—the uses of each article of furniture—of tools men use—about its clothes—who makes them, and how—what they are made of—of its own body—of every thing relative to man, as well as the habits and economy of animals and plants; in fact, its curiosity is insatiable, because a knowledge of these things is necessary to its existence and well-being. It is evident that by taking advantage of this propensity, while only gratifying a natural impulse an immense amount of information may be imparted, and at the same time the perception and the judgment cultivated.

Modes of Intellectual Instruction.

The different modes of intellectual instruction may be divided into—

1st. Intuitive teaching, by which the senses and perceptive faculties are trained, and the mind stored with a knowledge of surrounding things. This in an infant school is the first and most important mode.

2d. By Comparison—as when you exhibit two objects or pictures, and lead the pupil to observe the differences between them and guess at their causes.

3d. By Pictures and verbal descriptions—which depends for its success on the first having preceded it.

4th. By Questioning—which is chiefly valuable as it leads the mind of the learner to form conclusions of its own; or when, by questions put to the teacher, the pupil seeks to supply imperfections in his own conception of the subject.

5th. By Ellipses—a most valuable method of securing attention to any historical or descriptive lesson. It consists in interrupting the sense of a passage by omitting some necessary part, and leaving the pupil to discover from the foregone sense the suppressed word or phrase.

6th. By Imitation—as in writing, drawing, music, &c. To these may be added exercises of the memory, as recitation and spelling. We do not mean that these various modes are always to be separately employed; on the contrary, some of them are generally combined with advantage; we only point out the distinct nature of each.

Intuitive teaching embraces all our perceptions of the external world through the senses, as form, number, size, position, motion, texture, color, sound in all its varieties, taste, odor, temperature and resistance. These qualities occurring in varied combinations in nature, it is the teacher's business to separate and present them in a simple, striking manner, so that the pupil may get a clear notion of the nature of each, and be able to trace its existence wherever it occurs, or to understand what is meant when the term expressing it is mentioned. But in imparting this knowledge, frequent recourse to *comparison* is necessary. In colors, for instance, shades of the same color become more evident when compared; differences of weight are more clearly perceived by the same means, as well as degrees of light and sound. Opposite qualities are also rendered more palpable by contrast, as transparent and opaque—solid and fluid.

It is plain that, without this preliminary knowledge, no description can be understood. We may, indeed leave its acquisition to chance and casual observation, but this will take too long for the purposes of education, and after all, will be a most imperfect process. It is better to overcome the difficulty at once by supplying systematically those elements upon which the future education is based. Second only to this direct knowledge of things present, are the notions derived from models and pictures. This is the first extension upwards of the previous foundation, and prepares the mind to receive and comprehend history and description.

Reading and the analysis of words become, from the first, an exercise of the reasoning powers, and should therefore be taught gradually and with care. If a judicious system is followed, the art of reading should be acquired without painful difficulty or overstraining the mind; it is, indeed, often forced on too fast, and then becomes mere parrot-work; the interest in reading will infallibly cease if what is read be not thoroughly understood.

The natural history of living things is exceedingly interesting to children when taught in a manner suited to their age, that is, with full illustration by pictures and by description.

Every thing must be first taught as a whole, without regard to niceties of structure: if an animal, its general form, color, size, motion, habits, &c.: and less striking points may be afterwards brought out by contrasting it with other species.

Geography, treating as it does of such vast subjects, should be very gradually approached. Ideas of time and space arise but very slowly in the mind; and it is only by carefully extending these conceptions that any approach to a just notion of the surface of the earth can be given. It is best to combine natural history and descriptions of the manners and customs of nations, with geographical teaching, so that, from the first, ideas of real things may be associated with names of places, otherwise unmeaning.

Narrative is always delightful to children, and may be introduced as the judgment of the teacher directs, to secure attention to the subject, whether moral or intellectual.

The education of the hand and eye in drawing, and of the ear in singing, not only cultivates the taste and refines the feelings, but also affords a pleasing variety of occupation and a relief from more intellectual studies.

The recitation of simple poetry, while it cultivates the memory, also serves a most important purpose in imparting a correct and pleasing pronunciation. As the first difficulties of reading tend to embarrass and retard speech, some counteracting process is required, and none is so pleasing to the child as repeating rhymes.

The arrangement of these several subjects in such order as shall give to all their due share of attention, and, at the same time, by their judicious alternation, produce the least fatigue to the learner, should be carefully studied by the teacher. Rest, both to men and infants, is often only another name for change of occupation; and it is possible, by a proper management of school business, greatly to lighten the labor of each successive study.

In concluding this subject, we beg to call attention to the following "Hints to Teachers," by an eminent authority, which we have found by long experience to be most useful and important.

Hints to Teachers.

The best mode of teaching any science may mean—

1—The best for the teacher's ease; (such as the books in "question and answer," which the learner is set to get by heart; for him the books are ill adapted, but they are good for the writer and bookseller because they sell; and for the master because they save him trouble.)

2—The best to make the pupil show off at a made-up examination.

3—The best for grounding him speedily and soundly in the science.

All teachers question their pupils, if there is even any attempt or pretense of advancing them properly.

Questioning is of three kinds—

1. Preliminary [or preparatory]* questioning (relates to the future.)
2. Instructive questioning (to the present.)
3. And examination questioning (to the past.)

All three very few persons employ designedly: the last two are used by all who at all deserve the name of good teachers: the third alone is employed by probably the majority.

1. The first consists in asking (orally or on paper) questions relative to what the pupil is about to learn, to try what notions or guesses he may form on each point.

This is an increase of trouble to the teacher, and, in the outset, taxes the efforts of the pupil by compelling him to think. In the end it will be found that he has learned much more rapidly and with more interest, more correctly and more permanently.

This mode is seldom employed designedly; but a man often finds how advantageously he has employed it for himself by accident; when he has learned a subject, for instance, by sitting down to write a book upon it.

If the teacher will have the courage to use this method systematically, by every day putting before his pupils questions relative to what they are next to learn, he will find himself doing wonders.

2. The second consists in asking questions as to the lessons actually before the pupils, to see how far they understand each passage, and can state it in their own words.

3. The third consists in examining them as to what they *have* learned, to try how well they retain it.

These three processes have been compared to the plowing, the sowing, and the harrowing of a field.

N. B.—You will judge from what has been said, what is the best and what the second best mode of advancing your pupils.

N. B.—You should frame examples for them and teach them to do so themselves.

It is not necessary that they should remember quite perfectly and rapidly each lesson before proceeding to the next; but they should clearly *understand* as they go on; and they should not advance far a-head of what they have perfectly learned. In particular, the technical terms and definitions should be as familiarly known as the alphabet; for technical language is an incumbrance to those not quite familiar with it, and a great help to those who are.

* Please to observe that the square [brackets] as distinguished from the common (parenthesis) denote a word or phrase equivalent to one before: and are used to guard the learner against mistaking it for a different thing. It is thus I should speak in geometry of "Trilateral figures," [or "Triangles."]

Physical Education.

All children require sound sleep, regular and wholesome meals, cleanliness, warmth, light, fresh air, and frequent exercise.

Mr. Wilderspin observes—"An inactive and healthy child under six years of age is never seen. * * * Children must exert all their muscular force, and employ all their ingenuity, in order to gratify their curiosity, and satisfy their little appetites. What they desire is only to be obtained at the cost of labor, patience, and many disappointments. By the exercise of body and mind necessary for satisfying their desires, they acquire agility, strength, and dexterity in their motions, as well as constitutional health and vigor; they learn to bear pain without dejection, and disappointment without despondency."

In winter time it is necessary to induce the children to exert themselves, by joining in and promoting their games; and when in the gallery on cold days, their lessons must be interrupted by vigorous manual exercises, to restore the animal heat, and with it cheerfulness and attention; while in summer it is equally important to promote quiet amusements, which do not heat or exhaust the children.

Every school-room should be well lighted, and the means of free ventilation provided. But this alone is not sufficient; relaxation in the open air is also necessary to health, for if kept constantly in the school-room, infants will not remain healthy.

The general rule for infants is, short lessons and frequent exercise. Overstraining the attention and intellectual powers, would infallibly injure the health of the child.

II. QUALIFICATIONS OF THE TEACHER.

> "He, whene'er he taught,
> Put so much of his heart into his act,
> That his example had a magnet's force,
> And all were swift to follow whom all loved."

The person who undertakes the charge of an infant school should be prepared to undergo much labor and anxiety, and to meet with many difficulties. On the other hand, it is a work full of interest, and yielding peculiar pleasures to those engaged in it. The dispositions necessary for success are kindness, gentleness, and patience towards the children, steadiness of temper, a habit of observation, cheerfulness and activity. To the usual branches of education the teacher of infants should add a knowledge of the elements of music, drawing, natural history, and as much general information as possible. The habit of study and observation must always be kept up, whether in the fields, in the town, or at home; a good teacher is always observing and storing up facts for future lessons, by which to attract the attention and inform the minds of his pupils.

Speaking of the first transfer of the children from the mother's care to that of the teacher, Pestalozzi says:—

It will therefore become possible even for a stranger, and one who is a stranger also to the mother, by a certain mode of conduct, to gain the affection and confidence of the child. To obtain them, the first requisite is constancy in the general conduct. It would appear scarcely credible, but it is strictly true, that children are not blind to, and that some children resent, the slightest deviation, for instance, from truth. In like manner, bad temper, once indulged, may go a great way to alienate the affection of the child, which can never be gained a second time by flatteries.

This fact is truly astonishing; and it may also be quoted as evidence of the statement, that there is in the infant a pure sense of the true and the right, which struggles against the constant temptation arising from the weakness of human nature, and its tendency to falsehood and depravity.

In the following passage Mr. Wilderspin points out the error of employing incompetent teachers:—

It is indeed a melancholy truth, that moral training is yet to a very limited extent estimated; and this is mainly owing to its not being understood by the generality of those selected for the office of teachers of infants; nor can it be expected that persons of sufficient intellect and talent to comprehend and carry out this great object can be procured, until a sufficient remuneration is held out to them to make it worth their while to devote their whole energies to the subject. It is a fatal error to suppose that mere girls, taken perhaps from some laborious occupation, and whose sum total of education consists of reading and writing, can carry out views which it requires a philosophical mind, well stored with liberal ideas and general knowledge, to effect. They may be able to instruct the children in the mere mechanical parts of the system; and as long as they confine themselves to this, they will go on capitally; but no farther than this can they go; and though the children may appear to a casual visitor to be very nicely instructed, and very wonderful little creatures, on a closer examination they will be found mere automatons; and then, perhaps without a further thought on the subject, the system will be blamed, not considering that the most perfect piece of mechanism will not work properly in any hands except those who thoroughly understand it.

We must however take this with some qualifications, and not despair of success even with ordinary teachers; for daily experience proves that most persons by devoting their minds steadily to one subject, can attain to a certain proficiency, and this special study will enable a sufficient number to qualify themselves, whose views in life may lead them to devote themselves to the work. But in order to do so, they must at least know what they aim at, and this they can not do without a proper training in some well conducted model school. Perhaps it is more important that the infant school teacher should have received a regular course of training than any other. The plans are such as are not likely to be *guessed* at: when known, they present no insuperable difficulty, but it is necessary that they should be learned to be successfully practiced.

III. SCHOOL RULES AND REGULATIONS.

Good rules are as important for a school as good laws for a country; neither the one or the other will go on well without them. The rules for parents may be printed, and distributed to them when they enter their children. The rules for the internal management of the school should be explained to the children at stated periods.

RULES FOR PARENTS.

Parents are requested to observe the following rules:—

1. Parents wishing their children to be admitted must apply on any morning of the week, ***except Monday.*** The names, residences, &c., of the children will then be registered in a book kept for the purpose, and as vacancies occur, they will be sent for in the strict order of their respective applications—***except in the case of pupils who have been dismissed for irregularity of attendance, who are not to be received again till after all the other applicants shall have been admitted.***

2. No child can be admitted who is under two, or more than seven years of age.

3. The doors are closed every morning precisely at ten o'clock, and the children are dismissed at three, except on Saturdays, when the school closes at twelve o'clock.

4. If any child be frequently absent, or absent five days successively, and the cause be not made known to the teacher before the expiration of the five days, such child will be discharged from the school. If the parents wish the child to be readmitted, they must get the name entered in the application book as at first, and wait till after all the children who have applied for the first time shall have been admitted.

5. The payment is ——— per week, to be paid the first day in each week the child attends; and should any child be unavoidably absent, payment must nevertheless be made weekly so long as the parent wishes the name of the child to remain on the roll.

6. No child having any infectious disease, or who is deficient in personal cleanliness, can be admitted or retained in the school.

MAXIMS AND REGULATIONS TO BE OBSERVED BY THE TEACHER.

1. Endeavor to set a good example in all things.

2. Never overlook a fault: to do so is unjust to the children, since you will, no doubt, soon have to correct them for a repetition of it.

3. Spare no pains to investigate the truth of every charge; and, if you can not satisfy yourself, make no decision. Leave it to the future to develop.

4. Never correct a child in anger. It rarely happens that we know the truth of a case without investigation.

5. Do strict justice to all, and avoid favoritism.

6. Always prepare for your gallery lessons by previous study; never attempt to teach what you do not know thoroughly; and if at any time you are unable to answer a question put by the children, acknowledge your inability.

7. Try to bring forward the dull and backward children. The quick intellects will come on without your notice.

8. Teach *thoroughly*, and do not try to get on too fast; remember that you are laying the *foundations* of knowledge.

9. Never leave the children alone, either in the school-room or play-ground.

10. Attend strictly to the personal cleanliness of the children; and watch against the entrance of disease.

11. Let particular care be taken of the pictures, books, and apparatus, and see that all is kept in working order.

12. Attend to the cleanliness and neatness of the school-rooms and offices, and to the order and neatness of the play-ground and garden borders.

13. Attend to the ventilation and heating of the rooms. In summer keep the windows constantly open, in winter open them when the children go out to play.

14. Never let the children get chilled or overheated.

15. Do not be tempted to give undue attention to the elder, to the neglect of the younger classes. Such a course would be fatal to the general advancement of the school.

16. Take every opportunity of moral training. Consider that it is better to make children *good* than *clever*.

17. Constantly seek self-improvement, and try to enlarge your own stock of information. Remember that *knowledge is your stock in trade.*

18. Let your intercourse with the children be regulated by *love*. Remember that our blessed Lord loved little children, and took them in his arms and blessed them.

SCHOOL-ROOM RULES, TO BE REPEATED BY THE CHILDREN AT THE CLOSE OF THE WEEK.

1. We ought to be kind and gentle in our conduct towards each other, and, when injured in any way, not to revenge ourselves, but seek the protection of the teacher.

2. Always to speak the truth without reserve.

3. Never to speak evil of others.

5. Never to take any thing which is not our own, nor keep any thing we may find belonging to another.

5. Never to covet any thing other children have, nor try to deprive them of it.

6. To obey the teachers in all things, and pay strict attention to their words.

7. To keep silence when in the gallery, except when permitted to speak, and never interrupt either the teacher or any other person who may be speaking.

8. To be strictly attentive to lessons at all times, and always seek an explanation of what we may not understand.

9. To keep our books whole and clean, and never to touch or injure the pictures or apparatus.

10. To come in time in the morning, and with clean hands, face, and clothes.

PLAY-GROUND RULES.

4. To be gentle in play, and careful not to hurt the very little children.

2. Not to be selfish or exclusive in play, but to endeavor to make others happy, as well as ourselves.

3. Never to interfere with or interrupt other children's amusements.

4. Always to try and comfort and assist any one who is hurt or in trouble.

5. To refer every cause of complaint to the teacher.

6. Not to touch or injure the flowers, nor to tread on the garden borders.

7. Each class to use the swings (or other gymnastics) in turn, as appointed.

8. Never to go in the way of the swings, nor interfere with others who may be using them.

9. To form quickly in line when the bell rings for lessons.

Sanitary Regulations.

VENTILATION.

Children breathe more quickly by about one-third than grown persons. A child under seven years of age will render impure nearly three cubic feet of air in a minute. Now if we take as an example a school-room forty feet long, twenty wide, and fourteen high, and say that there are one hundred infants in it at one time, it will give (allowing for the space occupied by gallery, furniture, &c.) about one hundred cubic feet of air for each pupil, and if there were no ventilation this stock would be exhausted in thirty-three minutes; but long before this limit is reached, the air of the room becomes unwholesome, the oxygen or life-supporting part of it being absorbed into the blood, and a deleterious gas (carbonic acid) returned in its stead; if means are not taken to remove this, and admit pure air, the children will become languid and dispirited, and their health will suffer. An air shaft, with an opening near the top of the room, having a sliding lid that can be raised or let down, is a simple and effectual mode of ventilation. Where no other means occur, the top sashes of the windows should be kept down a little, to allow the heated air to escape as it ascends.

CLEANLINESS.

Cleanliness is next in importance to ventilation: for, independently of the unpleasant and demoralizing character of a dirty school-room, the dust raised by so many feet, when taken into the lungs, is highly injurious.

TEMPERATURE.

When the room is heated by an open fire-place, it is well to admit the air for ventilation as near the fire as possible, as by that means a more equal warmth is kept up. It is dangerous to overheat the school-room, as it causes the children to take cold when changing to the play-ground: the temperature should not rise above 70° or fall much below 60° Fahrenheit.

DISEASE.

Although it is the parents' duty to attend to the health of the child, yet in epidemics or sudden illness, it is necessary for the teacher to be able to distinguish the premonitory signs of disease, as he stands for the time in the parents' place.

The following diseases may with certainty be considered as infectious:—Measles, scarletina, mumps, small-pox, and hooping-cough.

The symptoms of measles are sneezing, running from the eyes and nostrils, sickness, cough, together with heat of the skin and quick pulse.

The approach of scarletina is known by alternate shivering and heat, quick pulse, sickness, white tongue; and later, by red spots or patches on the face, neck, and chest.

Mumps are known by painful swellings above the sides of the throat, on a level with the ear.

Hooping-cough comes on like a common cold, but with violent cough, in which a watery fluid is expectorated; watery discharges from the eyes and nostrils; hoarseness and sneezing. The child is generally languid and out of spirits. When much advanced, the symptoms of this disease are so evident as not to require description.

A well-regulated school tends to preserve and improve the health of those attending it, but it is evidently necessary to return to the care of its parents any child who exhibits signs of sickness or disease. Even in case of common diarrhea the child should be immediately sent home.

In inspecting the children for cleanliness, the *head* should be particularly observed; and if there is any appearance of ring-worm or scald-head, the child should be kept at home until the disease has entirely disappeared, as both are infectious and troublesome, as are most cutaneous diseases.

ACCIDENTS.

Accidents rarely occur in a well-regulated school: but as there is a possibility of such things happening, where so many children are collected together, we give a few simple directions for treatment.

In case of a bruise or wound from a fall or other cause, the part should be washed clean, and a piece of old linen or lint dipped in cold water applied.

Sprains require the limb to be kept quite still, and bathed with vinegar and water.*

In case of a cut from any sharp instrument, slate or glass, bring the edges of the cut carefully together and apply a slip of common adhesive plaster.

Should so unfortunate a circumstance happen as that of a child falling into a fit from disease or constitutional causes, the children of the school should not be allowed to witness the painful sight, but the sufferer should be removed from the room, and exposed to the fresh air, with the clothes loosened. No restraint should be used in the convulsion, except to prevent the patient from injuring himself.

---

* His Grace the Archbishop of Dublin has kindly communicated to us the following note:—

"Tincture of arnica is now to be had at any chemist's. For a bruise or strain (when the skin is not broken) six drops to a table-spoonful of water (five for the wound when the skin is broken), make the lotion. A rag wetted with the lotion, and kept wet, to be kept on the place. There is nothing at all comparable to it for all hurts; but the bottle of tincture should be marked 'poison.'"

In conclusion, we may remark that children liable to fits, defective in sight or hearing, or affected in any other way which would require *special* attention from the teacher, should not be in a common school, the ordinary duties of which are arduous enough, without this additional perplexity.

The Play-ground.

With regard to recreation in the play-ground, let it be as unrestrained as possible; nature is the best gymnastic teacher, and little can be done to assist her. Whatever apparatus is introduced should be very simple, as scarcely any is free from danger. A dry floor under foot, a free circulation of air, and a constant gentle superintendence, which, by affording protection to the weak or injured, secures the greatest amount of liberty to each, are the chief requisites; and any one who has witnessed a well-regulated infants' play-ground, must be aware how perfectly the happiness of the assembled group is secured. If we come to inquire into the causes, we shall find that freedom and the gratification of the craving for sympathy and society are the chief. In the large number assembled together, each finds companions whose age and taste suit its own; peculiarities of character find free play. Some naturally take the place of *leaders*, while others are content to serve. If any one wishes to be an architect, he will soon find plenty of builders at his command. Perhaps another is a rider, and he easily persuades some one to be horse; or, if he likes to drive, he may have a whole team! In one place you may see a little knot of exclusives, who would not for the world admit another member to their club; while close by is a laughing face which has formed a dozen associations in the hour! Here the imitative faculty develops itself in a mimic school, including a very fair copy of the teacher (*peculiarities* and all) from which, if he be wise, he may take a lesson in turn. It is true that, in the first formation of the school, many of these different elements will come in collision, but constant moral training will teach them to associate together in harmony and love, and we repeat, *the less interference the better.*

No play-ground should be without a border of flowers, and, if possible, fruit trees. The moral discipline afforded by teaching the little ones to respect these things, is not their only use; they give pleasure to the senses and cultivate a love of nature. The gymnastic apparatus should be carefully watched to avoid accident, and the proper mode of using it be taught to the children.

Time Table.

The time table should be so arranged as to bring those lessons which require mental effort as distant from each other as possible, and to secure frequent relaxation in the play-ground. Those subjects which require special attention should be introduced at the commencement of the day, before the mind is wearied or preoccupied. The general time table is as follows:*—

DAILY TIME TABLE.

Nine o'clock: school doors opened; teacher in attendance; the children, as they arrive, deposit their clothes and bread in the baskets which are placed at the respective class posts, and proceed to the play-ground. Where there is a monitor's class, it is taught at this hour.

Ten o'clock: children assembled in galleries for morning lesson.

Half-past ten: reading, the elder children in classes, the younger in galleries.

Half-past eleven: march to play-ground for recreation.

Twelve o'clock: writing lesson.

Twenty minutes past twelve: drawing.

Twenty minutes to one: march to gallery for midday lesson.

Ten minutes past one: lunch hour.

Thirty minutes past one: dismissed to play-ground.

Two o'clock: in gallery for afternoon lesson, or in circulating classes for picture or object lessons.

Three o'clock: school dismissed.

Synopsis of a Week's Lessons for the Elder Classes.

The object of the following arrangement is to secure, first, the recurrence of each subject at certain intervals; and secondly, to indicate the manner in which its several parts should be taken up in successive lessons, so as to avoid a desultory and confused method of teaching on the one hand, or the neglect of any material point on the other.

MONDAY.

Morning Lesson.—Arithmetic, enumeration of real objects, the ball-frame, notation with blackboard.

Reading.†—Preliminary questions on the subject of the lesson, with explanations. Teacher then reads a portion of the lesson, with remarks upon punctuation, and tone of voice. Children read, classify words in first sentences. Spelling.

Midday Lesson.—Geography, Map of the World, first outlines—cardinal points—circles—climates—division of time and seasons.

Afternoon Lesson.—Developing lesson—form, lines, and plane figures, with illustrations from objects. Teacher draws on blackboard simple outlines, children analyze them. Song, "Geometrical lines."

TUESDAY.

Morning Lesson.—Singing exercises on tone and time, concluding with a song.

Reading.—Children read, questions on the meanings of words, substitution of words, parts of speech, spelling.

Midday Lesson.—Arithmetic, addition and subtraction, with ball-frame and blackboard.

Afternoon Lesson.—Geography, division of land, continents, islands, peninsulas, countries. Song, "The solid earth."

WEDNESDAY.

Morning Lesson.—Developing lesson, color, texture of surfaces, structure, (as laminar, fibrous, &c.)

Reading.—Children read, teacher then reads with ellipses, requiring the children to complete the sense. Questions on the time of verbs, number and gender of nouns, and comparison of adjectives. Spelling.

Midday Lesson.—Singing. Teacher sings the melody to be learned twice or oftener to the children, explains the style and time, then the children sing it with the teacher.

---

* In Ireland the general school hours are from ten until three o'clock, while in England the children attend twice in the day; in the morning from nine until twelve, and, in the afternoon, from two until four or five o'clock.

† The reading classes come up twice, first to read, and then they return to their seats to look over the lesson again for questions and spelling; otherwise the lesson would be too fatiguing. When the subject of the lesson is sacred history, it should not be made the basis of any grammatical teaching.

Afternoon Lesson.—Picture lessons. The monitors should have been well trained previously. The classes must move exactly at the appointed time, and the teacher go from class to class, assisting and directing, so as a keep up the spirit of the lesson.

THURSDAY.

Morning Lesson.—Geography. Divisions of water, oceans, seas, gulfs, lakes, rivers, with explanations of each term.
Reading.—Teacher reads slowly, purposely making errors in punctuation, &c., requiring the children to look on their books and correct them. Children read; classification of words. Spelling.
Midday Lesson.—Developing lesson. Weight, with illustrations of mechanical powers.
Afternoon Lesson.—Arithmetic. Multiplciation and division, with ball-frame and blackboard.

FRIDAY.

Morning Lesson.—Singing. Children sing; teacher listens, corrects, and instructs; gives explanations of the words of the song.
Reading.—Children read, and ask the teacher questions on the subject, and meanings of words. Spelling.
Midday Lesson.—Arithmetic. Mental arithmetic and illustrations of fractional parts by drawing on the blackboard.
Afternoon Lesson.—Natural history of animals and plants, with pictures.

SATURDAY.

Morning Lesson.—Geography. Capital cities, national characteristics and exports
Second Lesson.—Singing. Recapitulation of songs of the week.

The foregoing is only given as a specimen, as each teacher should arrange his own work in accordance with the circumstances of his particular school. It will be seen that no place is given above for religious instruction, as that must entirely depend upon local arrangements; but, as a general principle, the commencement or close of the day should be selected for this important exercise.

Moral lessons will intermingle themselves with all others, and must be taken up as they arise; it is, however, a good practice to defer any important investigation to the beginning of the afternoon gallery lesson.

IV. DEVELOPING LESSONS.

For want of the habit of observing the properties of common things, and the evident conclusions to which such observation must lead, the most lamentable errors are often committed even by those who are considered educated. People are continually committing follies of which an unreasoning animal would scarcely be guilty. We have seen a person deliberately put one foot on the step of a carriage in motion, fully expecting the road to move on to accommodate the remaining foot. How few, when called upon for any muscular effort, know how to economize their strength, or can judge of the weights they are about to move. How few servants or parents think of the nature of the articles of food or of utility under their care, or reason on the cause of smoky fires, ill-cooked food, or ill-ventilated rooms, or could tell why danger lurks in a copper saucepan or a leaden cistern, or distinguish a mushroom from a fungus. To look beyond mere utility, how much intellectual improvement do we lose for want of the habit of observation. To many persons nature is a sealed book. When they walk abroad, the animal and vegetable life around them appears but a hopeless mass of confusion, in which they fail to perceive the order and beauty of Divine wisdom. To them the stars tell no wonders, mark no seasons, and, from a want of this knowledge in the reader, the most accurately written description often conveys but a vague shadow of the reality. To remedy these evils, the education of the perceptive faculties must be commenced in infancy, carried on in youth, and confirmed in manhood.

To cultivate the latent powers of children is the intention of those lessons which, in an infant school, are called developing. If, for instance, the ear be not trained in early life, the power of distinguishing musical sounds remains very imperfect; yet, in a school, all will learn to sing, unless where any positive defect of hearing or voice exists. The same may be said of drawing, which is less difficult in many respects than writing. Take, as a further example, the faculty which enables us to judge of weight or resistance, and observe how it becomes strengthened by education in workmen who have to perform mechanical operations; no doubt there are differences of natural ability in this respect, but most men acquire sufficient skill for the purposes of their respective arts. Now the business of elementary education, in its widest sense, embraces the development and training of every faculty so far as is necessary for the common purposes of life, and, in so doing, it prepares the pupil for special instruction of whatever kind.

From much experience, we have found that it is better to commence by teaching the properties of things separately; so that each may make a distinct impression before the pupil is required to recognize it when in combination. Simple perceptions may be divided into those of form, size, position, number, weight, motion, color, temperature, taste, odor, and sound; all these require cultivation; and as the senses are the channels by which they are conveyed to the mind, their nature and mutual relation must be studied by the teacher. By the *eye*, we perceive form, size, position, motion, number, and color; by the *ear*, all sounds; by the sense of touch we perceive heat and cold, weight, form, motion, texture, size, and number. The senses of taste and smell are very intimately connected with each other, both in their uses and mode of action.

The education of the senses commences with life itself, so that even the youngest child in an infant school has already acquired many ideas; and were it not so, the difficulties of the teacher would be almost insurmountable; as it is, enough remains to be done in establishing a relation between words and things, and training the mind to correct methodical observation, before ordinary instruction can commence. We have found in practice that *form* is the most striking quality of bodies, and therefore the best to commence with; as, from its being capable of clearer definition, it is more easily comprehended than any other.

Form.

The first exercise for the younger children should be to learn to distinguish and name the regular polygons, without entering into any explanation of their properties. The best means of doing this, is for the teacher to prepare a set of models in card or pasteboard, of the required forms, of not less than six inches diameter each, which should be exhibited singly, and the name repeated by the children. If two sets be prepared, it is a good first exercise for the teacher to hold up a form and require the little learner to select a similar one to match it; when, the two being placed on each other, their identity can be shown.

In further explaining the properties of figures, we must advance by slow degrees, and beware of impatience or haste; and, as each definition is given, it should be fixed in the mind by abundant illustration, as the great object is to give certainty and clearness to the mind.

We suppose the children to be seated in the gallery for these lessons, and the teacher furnished with a blackboard and chalk. Each figure required for illustration must be accurately drawn; for although a student far advanced in geometry may be able to comprehend a diagram rudely sketched, because he has in his mind a correct conception of what is intended, yet, in imparting first ideas of form to children, it is indispensable that all representations should be truly and neatly drawn. Should the teacher be unable to do this by hand, a ruler and compasses will smooth all difficulties, and the necessary diagrams may be prepared beforehand, to save time during the lesson. Large compasses constructed of wood, with a chalk-holder, can be obtained; or a very good substitute may be made with a lath, a foot long, having a piece of chalk tied to one end and a common brad-awl inserted at the other, to form a center, by shifting the place of which, circles of different diameters may be accurately delineated. With two centers and a loop of twine, ellipses can be drawn; and the sight of these simple contrivances is instructive to the children.

Another means of illustrating geometrical forms is by the gonigraph, an instrument consisting of ten short rulers or joints of iron hinged together. The facility with which various lines and forms can be represented by this contrivance, renders it very popular in infant

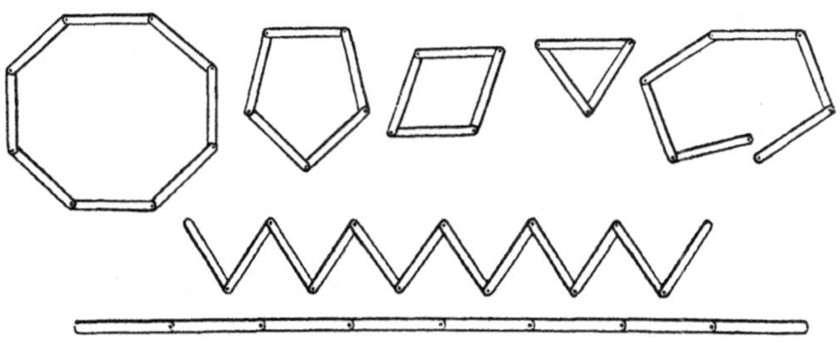

GONIGRAPH.

schools; and it has the additional advantage, that it can be used by the children themselves.

We now proceed to give such hints as are necessary for the order and succession of lessons on this subject, which the teacher must further expand and illustrate.

Length.—The first step is to give a clear conception of extension in one direction. Draw a fine straight line, and explain that it has *length* only; measure it with a string or compasses, and then give various illustrations of length, or distance from one point to another; stretch a string or tape, divided into feet, along the room, and show that the room is so many feet long; remove the string, and explain that the length of the room is still there, and would be the same whether the room was wide or narrow. Make the different children tell where they live, and point out that some have far to come to school, and others a less distance—that in each case we speak only of the *length* of the way, not of its width. Extend these illustrations: as the length of a stick, of a road, a street, a table, the play-ground, a line, and the like. Also draw proportional lines, and compare them. Distance from one place to another is always said to be so far, or so long; and never so broad, or so thick. A road would be just as long whether it was a good road or a bad one; whether we ran or walked along it, or went by a railroad, we should go over the same distance, although in different periods of time.

Length and breadth.—A surface has length and breadth, but no thickness; it is the outside boundary of any thing, as the surface of the floor, of the ceiling, the walls, the play-ground, and so forth. The largest measure of the floor is called length; the smallest, breadth, or width. One child may be made to walk *along* the room, and another *across* it. It may be pointed out, that if either the length or breadth of the room were made less, the *surface* of the floor would be smaller; and if the length of the play-ground were increased, its surface would be greater. The children may be made to point out various surfaces, and show their length and breadth; as those of a card, pocket-handkerchief, blackboard. All surfaces are bounded by lines or edges, and the children should next touch or point to the edges or boundary lines of various surfaces.

Solid bodies have three dimensions, all crossing each other. The largest is called length; the next, breadth; the smallest, thickness. A box, or other object of some size, may be used as an illustration, and its different dimensions measured; and it may be easily explained that it occupies some space, and that many such objects would fill the room. Other illustrations should be given, and the children encouraged to point out solid objects, and guess at their different dimensions. Let the children repeat these definitions together.

A *line* has length only.

A *surface* has length and breadth.

A *solid* has length, breadth, and thickness.

Familiar illustrations should be given of these properties; as, any number of lines put together would not make the thickness of the smallest thread; the whole surface of the floor is no part of the substance of the floor, but only the outside or boundary, and has no weight, or thickness.

Lines.

Lines define the shape and boundary of things, and by lines all things are measured. A line is the distance from one point to another. These points are called its ends. Lines are divided into *right* lines, or the shortest distance between two points, as when a string is stretched tightly; and *curved* lines. Curved lines are of many varieties, as circular and elliptical curves. Illustrations must be given on the blackboard, and the children required to find examples for themselves, in various objects, of *straight*, *curved*, *waved*, *spiral*, and other lines. The *direction* of lines should next be taught, as horizontal, perpendicular, oblique, parallel, converging, and diverging lines.

PARALLELS. CURVED. WAVING.

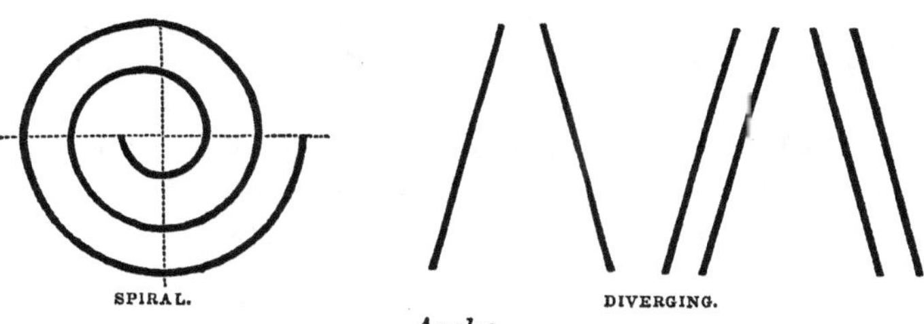

SPIRAL. DIVERGING.

Angles.

When lines meet or cross each other, they form angles or corners. Give examples: as the corner of the room, of a book, a board, a table. Draw on the blackboard the three varieties of angles, right, acute, and obtuse; require the children to point them out frequently,

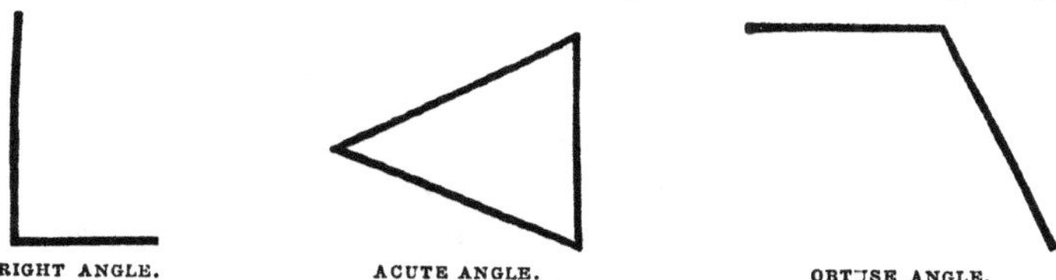

RIGHT ANGLE. ACUTE ANGLE. OBTUSE ANGLE.

and to find other angles or corners answering to them. Make the children form the different angles for themselves with the gonigraph, or draw them on the blackboard, or on slates held in the lap; show how many angles can be formed with *two* lines; with *three, four, five.* These figures should be drawn on a large scale, and the children required to count and point to the different angles.

Plane Figures.

Lines are said to be parallel when they are at the same distance from each other in every part; if ever so long, they will never meet. Two lines in any other position, on the same plane, converge, and will meet or cross each other; but in no case will they form a polygon or enclose a space. This must be easily illustrated with two rulers, or two school forms, which can not be made to enclose a space between them. A farmer could not enclose a field with *two* straight hedges: *two* straight walls would not make a house or room; but *three* straight lines will enclose a space, and form a triangle. Draw an accurate equilateral triangle on the blackboard, measure each side with a string or compasses, and prove it to be equal-sided. Allow some of the children to form the same with the gonigraph, or to attempt to draw it, or to form it with three laths or rulers of equal length. Explain to them that only *one* kind of triangle can be formed with the same sides. A triangle may have only two of its sides equal, and is then called isosceles. Prove to the children the equality of two sides in each of these figures, and lead them to point out their differences, and to distinguish the different kinds of angles. A triangle may have all its sides unequal, and is then called scalene. A similar proof should be gone through of the inequality of the sides, and the children required to point out the acute, right, or obtuse angles, and the longest and shortest sides of each figure.

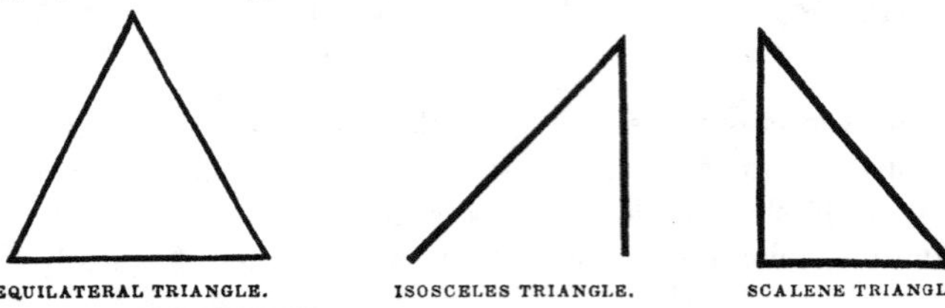

EQUILATERAL TRIANGLE. ISOSCELES TRIANGLE. SCALENE TRIANGLE.

In describing an equilateral triangle to little children, it may be said consist of three equal straight lines, one leaning to the right, one to the left, and one horizontal; it may also be dived into three equal acute angles; one opening downwards, one to the right, and one to the left. All the other triangles should be analyzed in the same simple manner, and representations of various objects in which they occur should be sketched, and the intelligence of the children exercised in distinguishing them.

A square has four equal sides, and four right angles: if its two opposite sides are horizontal, the other two will be vertical. The opposite sides of a square are parallel: the distance from the corner A to the corner C is equal to the distance from the corner B to the corner D. A square may be described as four right angles. If a square is first formed with a gonigraph, and the opposite angles pressed toward each other, a rhomb is produced; the sides are still equal, but the angles are no longer *right* angles, two opposite ones being acute, and the other two obtuse. Many representative figures may now be formed for the amusement and observation of the children, composed of the triangle, square and rhomb.

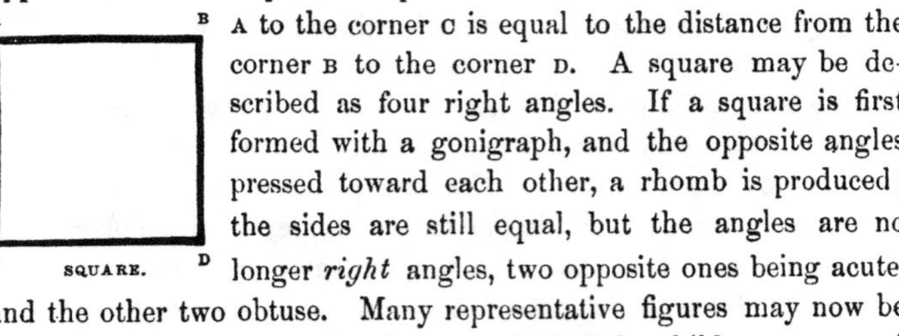

SQUARE.

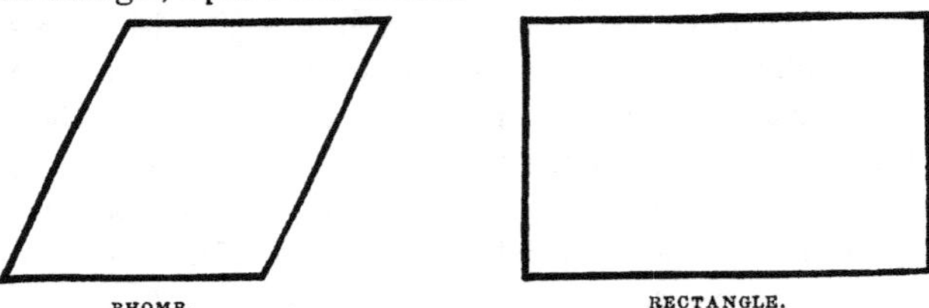

RHOMB. RECTANGLE.

A rectangle has four right angles, and its opposite sides are equal but its adjacent sides may be unequal. It may thus be resolved into four right angles with unequal legs. As this is a form of frequent occurrence, sufficient illustrations may be found in surrounding objects, as windows, doors, slates, books, &c. The oblique parallelogram or rhomboid has its opposite sides and angles equal; but its adjacent angles and sides unequal. It may be separated into two acute and two obtuse angles with unequal legs.

The other four-sided figures are those with three equal sides, with two, and those in which all the sides are unequal: they are called trapeziums. A pentagon has five equal sides and five equal obtuse

HEXAGON. OCTAGON. PENTAGON.

angles, and may be said to consist of five obtuse angles. The other regular polygons are, the hexagon, six sides; heptagon seven sides; octagon, eight sides; nonagon, nine sides; and decagon, ten sides. All these should be carefully constructed before the children, by first drawing a circle, and then dividing the circumference into the proper number of parts, and uniting the points so obtained by lines. These figures can also be formed with the greatest facility with the gonigraph, and should be thoroughly learned and analyzed in every way before we proceed further.

CIRCLE. HALF-CIRCLE.

A circle is a plain figure bounded by a single curved line, called its circumference, every part of which is at the same distance from the center. The diameter of a circle is a straight line passing through the center, and bounded by the circumference. The radias is a straight line drawn from the center to the circumference. The parts of the circle having been repeatedly drawn and explained, it should

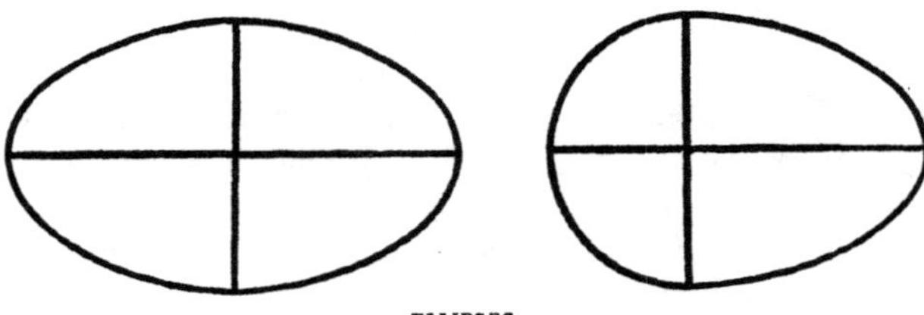

ELLIPSES.

be divided into semicircle, quadrant, segment, and octant. The nature of the ellipse is best illustrated by constructing it before the children, and varying the proportionate axes.

A spiral line may be illustrated by a slip of card rolled up and allowed to uncoil by its elasticity; by a piece of watch-spring; by the tendrils of plants; and its occurrence may be pointed out in univalve shells. The line may be drawn for illustration, by tying a piece of chalk to a string, and winding the string about a fixed spindle as a center, and tracing the line as you unwind it. Waved lines are shown by the moving surface of water, or by a cord shaken, and by drawing.

Solids.—Definitions.

A tetrahedron is a figure bounded by four equilateral triangles. It has six edges, four solid angles, and twelve plane angles.

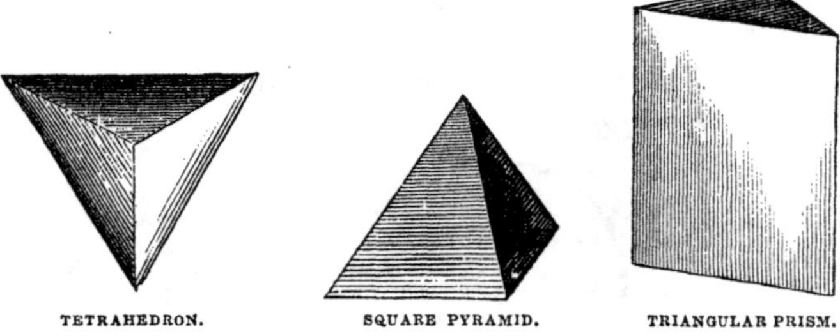

TETRAHEDRON. SQUARE PYRAMID. TRIANGULAR PRISM.

A square pyramid is bounded by four triangular sides and a square base. It has eight edges, five solid angles, and sixteen plane angles.

A triangular prism is bounded by two equal and parallel triangles and three rectangles. It has nine edges, six solid angles and eighteen plane angles.

A cube is bounded by six square sides, and has twelve edges, eight solid angles, and twenty-four plane angles.

A cylinder is bounded by two equal plane circles, parallel to each other, and united by one curved surface.

A cone is a figure having a circle for its base, its side being a curved surface ending in a point, called its apex.

A sphere is bounded by one continued curved surface, which is every where at the same distance from its center.

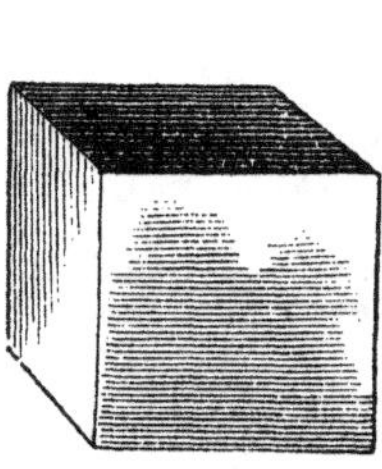

CUBE.

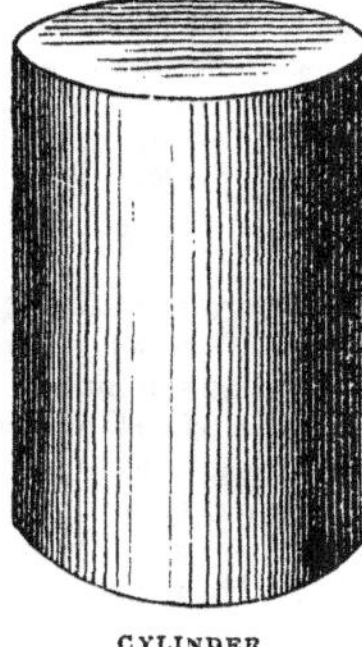

CYLINDER.

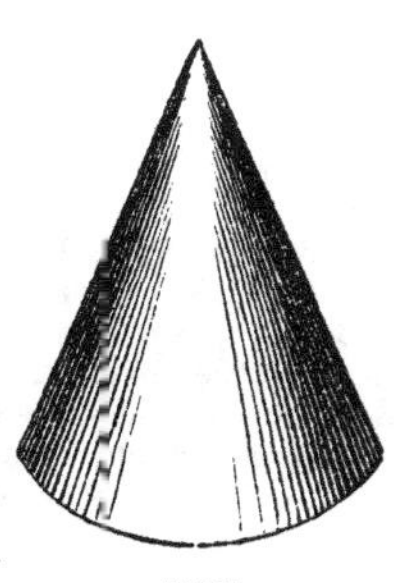

CONE.

A spheriod is a solid formed by the revolution of an ellipse about its axes.

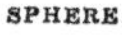

SPHERE.

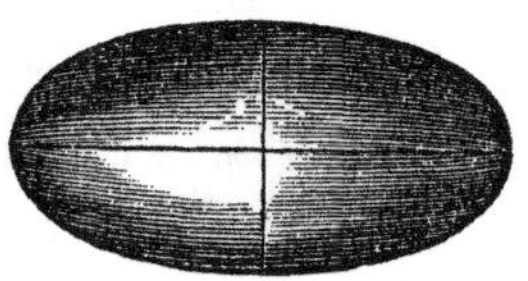

SPHERIOD.

The regular solids made in wood should be first named and distinguished by the children, without explanation; and they should be made to mention as many things as possible which they may happen to know of the same shapes. They should then learn to distinguish and count the edges, sides, corners or solid angles, and plane angles. By drawing the mathematical figures on pasteboard, and then cutting the lines half through, so that the parts can be turned up and brought together, they will represent the first four angular solids, and afford a very useful explanation to children. Also, by means of wire forms, the manner in which the curved solids are generated may be shown; for instance, by suspending a ring or hoop, and causing it to revolve, a sphere is described. In the same manner, a triangle in revolving will describe a cone; an ellipse a spheriod; and a square or oblong a cylinder.

Specimen Lesson on Form.—Solids.

How many objects have I placed before you?

Are they all alike? Are they different in shape or in size? Are they made of the same substance? Repeat their names after me, sphere, cube, cylinder, cone. Repeat the name of each as I point to it. Who will come and point out the sphere? That is right; now look at it, and see if it has a flat side. No; it has only one curved surface. Is it the same in every part? If the surface were not the same in every part would it be a sphere? Repeat with me, "A sphere has one curved surface, every where the same." What part of it do you see, the inside or the outside? What is the outside called? What is the middle of a solid called? What things have you seen of this shape? If a marble or a ball were not exactly a sphere, would it roll evenly? What then is the best form for a ball or marble? Do you know that the earth on which we live, and the sun and moon, are nearly like this ball in shape? Now tell me what part of the earth do you live on? Suppose you lived down in a coal mine, would you live on the surface then?

Which of these two solids will stand where it is placed, the sphere or the cube? Why? Do you know what an edge is? Two sides must meet to form an edge. Some edges are sharp, some square, and some blunt. Has the sphere edges? One of you, little children, come and point to a side of the cube. What shape is the side? Are all the sides of a cube alike? Where three sides meet, they form a corner or solid angle. Show me a corner of the cube. Some one must now come and count the sides of the cube for me. You see they are all flat and square. Repeat, six flat square sides. Now count the corners or solid angles. Three plane angles meet to form one solid angle, and three edges, as well as three sides, meet in each angle. Repeat, eight solid angles or corners, in a cube. Now count the edges; pass your finger along each; say, twelve straight edges. Repeat the parts of the cube again; six square sides, eight solid angles, twelve edges. Now tell me the parts of a sphere; one curved surface, every where the same, and always at the same distance from the center. Name all the things you can which are like a sphere,—now those like a cube. Show me the edges and corners of this box—the surfaces. Can I roll this box along? No; because it has flat sides. Can I roll the ball? Yes, because it is curved.

What figure is this? A cone. Will it stand? Yes, because it has one flat surface. Take it up, and tell me what shape the part is on which it rests. What is this part called? You can not tell, I see, so I must tell you. It is called the base. Repeat, a cone has a flat circular base. How many surfaces do you see, besides the base? It is flat or curved? What does it end in at the top? Say, a cone has one curved side ending in a point. Has it any edges? Now repeat the names of the parts of the cone, as I point to them—one flat circular base, one circular edge, one curved side, one point. Look, I have made a cone of paper. Is it like the other cone? No, they are not alike; for the paper one you see, is hollow, but the wooden one is solid; and as this little child here says, the paper one is longer and narrower; but you see, children, that the parts of both are the same; each has a point, side, edge, and base.

Who will find me the cylinder? Has it one end or two? What shape are they? Repeat, two circular flat ends. How many curved surfaces has it? Say, one circular curved surface. Now think of all the things you have seen of this shape. Are the bandbox and drum solid? You have mentioned a column, a pole, a roller, as being like a cylinder; are *they* solid or hollow? Is the cylinder a good shape to roll along? Yes, and the two opposite wheels of a coach are like a cylinder with the middle part cut away. Will a cone roll along? No; you see it will only roll round in a circle. Which of the four solids before us is most like the stem of a tree? Which resembles an orange? Which is nearest to the shape of the room we are in? Which is like a sugar-loaf?

These questions should be extended and sometimes reversed; as, What is shaped like a cylinder? &c.

The advantage gained by learning first the regular geometric figures is the accuracy and certainty which it gives the learner; but, whatever the lesson may be in which *objects* are used, their forms should be analyzed.

Color.

The most simple means we know of by which to impart an accurate knowledge of this subject is to have the various tints on separate cards, and beginning with the three primitive colors, red, blue, and yellow, to exhibit several shades of each, taking care to impress them separately upon the memory. These various cards may then be thrown together, and the children exercised in selecting particular tints. In subsequent lessons, the colors in clothes, pictures, and other objects may be distinguished, and then the memory exercised by calling to mind absent things in which they occur. The intermediate colors, purple, orange, and green should next be gone through in the same manner; proceeding then to the less pure, as brown and gray. It will be found that very few children have any certain knowledge of colors without this instruction, and that it can be made attractive by constant reference to nature. When the subject is so far learned, it may be extended by teaching the distinction between reflected colors and those transmitted through transparent substances, as glass, fluids, and air. Prismatic colors may be easily shown, by throwing the spectrum of the sun's rays on a wall or ceiling, and by allowing the children to look through the prism.

The colors of thin films are easily shown, by letting fall a drop of oil on the surface of water, or in soap-bubbles. Various other distinctions will occur to the teacher, who should consider that the knowledge of these simple elements is most important to the future progress of the child.

Specimen Lesson—Primitive Colors.

Teacher—I am going to give you a lesson about colors to-day; but first, can you tell me what enables you to see them? If your eyes make you see colors, how is it that you can not see them at night; Well, now tell me how it is that you can see in the day. Yes; that is, without the light you could not see things at all. Are all things colored? No; some things are white, and some are black, and white and black are not colors; the air in the room has no color, nor white paper. If every thing in the world were white, do you think it would be as beautiful as it is? Yet, in winter, when things are covered with snow, we like to see it; but is every thing white *then?* You are right, the sky is still blue, the houses and trees and animals are not altered, except where the snow lies. There are a great many colors in nature, but to-day we will talk about only three. The first I shall show you is *blue;* and see, I have several shades of blue, some light and some dark. Look at them well, and then tell me if you see any thing else in the room that is blue. You say your frock is blue; well, which of these tints is most like your frock? Yes, that is right, it is *dark* blue. What other thing do you see that is blue? Some *eyes* are blue. Well, so they are; some are dark blue and some light blue. Can you tell me any thing else that is blue? Who will find out which of these tints is like the sky? Yes; it is a pale blue. Blue is a very pleasant color to look on, and God has made many things in nature of this color, as the sky, and also the sea and lakes which reflect the color of the sky; amongst flowers, the blue-bell, violet, and iris are of this color, as are *some* stones and shells. If the sky were red instead of blue, it would be most painful to the eye. Sometimes, when a town is on fire, or when a volcano is pouring out lava and fire, the sky is red, and it is then terrible to see; but it is very pleasant to look at the blue sky or the distant sea, and think how good and great God is, who made this beautiful world for his glory and our use.

The next color I have to show you is red. It is very bright, and gives great beauty to many things. Out of all these shades of red, who will show me the lightest or palest red? Yes; that is right. What have you seen of that color? Quite right: the rose and a fair face are of this tint, but some parts of the face are of a darker red. Who will show me the color of the lips? Now who will point to the brightest red? What have you seen of that hue? "A poppy," "a soldier's coat," "a country-woman's cloak." Yes, all these are of a bright red, and many other things we could name; but now we must look for the *darkest* red. What have you seen like that? Very good; many flowers are of this rich color, and so are many kinds of materials, such as silk, satin, cotton, stuff, and various other things. Now repeat the names of the different shades of red. I want you all to shut your eyes, and not open them until I stamp my foot. Now what color am I holding up? Some say golden color, some say yellow; well, yellow is the proper name. When the sun is setting, it casts a rich yellow light over every thing. Now try and think of something you have seen of this tint. "The sand on the sea shore," "some kind of rocks," "the corn when it is ripe," "the leaves of trees in autumn." Yes; all these are of a yellowish color, and the sand in great deserts has this tint too. Can you think of any metals of this color? Now, some fruits? Now, some flowers? Well you have named a great many things, and there are many more, such as sulphur, mustard, the pretty flowers of the laburnum tree, the furze bushes on the hills, the daffodil, and the sunflower. Now you may look at each other's dresses, and find me all the parts that are either blue, red or yellow; first find the dark shades, then the light ones. Now we have found out so many colored things, let us finish our lesson by pointing out all the things that are white, and then those that are black in the room. White is like bright daylight, and black is like dark night. When I put a piece of white paper and a piece of black cloth side by side, they both look brighter by contrast, and so also colors make each other look brighter. The sea seems of a deeper blue when we see it and the yellow shore at the same time; and if red and blue flowers are placed together, it makes them both appear very bright. If all things were of one hue, it would look very dull; but the sky, the trees, the flowers and animals are all distinct and beautiful, because each has its own shade of color.

Size.

It is of little use to make children repeat tables of long and square measure, unless we first make them practically acquainted with the unit of measure upon which they are based. The teacher should therefore begin by teaching what an inch, a foot, and a yard are; and for this purpose a measure should be kept in the school. A five-foot rod, with white figures on a black ground, is best adapted for this purpose, but a common carpenter's rule will do.

When the children are well acquainted with the divisions on the rod or rule, various objects, large and small, should be measured before them, and their dimensions repeated. The children may then be exercised in drawing lines of specified lengths on the blackboard or slates. The next step is for them to endeavor to guess at the dimensions of things placed before them, and then to correct the various guesses by measuring the objects. The sizes of things mentioned in other lessons may be made useful exercises for the judgment of measure, as also the comparative size of objects of the same class.

Specimen Lessons.

We are going to learn to-day to distinguish things by their size. Some things, you know, are small, some great. Children are not all of one size or of one hight. See, I have placed four children in a row before you, will you tell me which is the tallest? How tall should you think he is? Well, we will try how high he is by the measure: count the feet and inches with me; three feet and eight inches, and he says he is six years old. Now, how tall is the least of the four? We shall see who is right. You see she is two feet ten inches high, and *she* is three years old, so you see the hight of children is usually in proportion to their age; they continue to grow until they are as big as men and women, and a *tall* man is six feet high; a woman is not so tall. But some people are large and stout, others are thin, so that one man may be really *larger* than another, though not so tall. Look at this sheet of paper, and this slate; you see that they are exactly the same length and breadth, but which is the larger? The slate. Why? This book is not so long nor so wide as the slate. Which is the larger? The book. Why? It is so much thicker. How high do you think this room is? How long? How wide? How high is the door? Could an elephant get in at the door? No; it was only made for the hight and size of men. If an elephant were in the room, how high would he stand? Ten feet. Look, I now hold up this measure, so that it reaches ten feet from the ground; that is very high for an animal to be; but the giraffe is sixteen feet high; so that a man standing on the back of an elephant would only be raised as high as a giraffe! Can you think how large a whale is? He is seventy feet long! We must measure his length in the play-ground, for we have no room here. The little Barbary mouse is the smallest of four-footed beasts; he could lie in the hollow of a child's hand. How small he would look placed beside a whale!

Progressive Sizes.—A grain of sand is smaller than a gravel-stone; a gravel-stone than a pebble; a pebble than a boulder-stone; a boulder than a rock; a rock than a hill; a hill than a mountain. A mountain compared to the earth is like a boulder compared to a mountain. The earth compared to the sun in size, is like a mouse compared to an elephant.

Sir J. Herschel suggests that, in describing the solar system, the sun may be represented by a globe two feet in diameter; Mercury, by a grain of mustard-seed; Venus, by a pea; the Earth, by a pea; Mars, a rather large pin's head; Vesta, Juno, Ceres, Pallas, by grains of sand; Jupiter, a moderately sized orange; Saturn, by a small orange; Uranus, a full-sized cherry, or *small* plum; Neptune, a *large* plum.

Such things as the following may be shown to the children to illustrate progressive sizes:—

Seeds.—Poppy seed, mustard seed, sweet-pea, garden pea, bean, nut, walnut, cocoa-nut.

A spider line, a fiber of silk or cotton, a hair, a bristle, a thread, a packthread, twine, cord, rope, cable.

Thickness.—Silver paper, writing paper, parchment, card, pasteboard, mill-board, a piece of deal board; gauze, muslin, silk, linen, sheeting sail-cloth, sacking, and carpet.

Order and Position.

In accustoming children to judge of relative position, the number of objects referred to should at first be very limited; two or three will enable the teacher to illustrate most of the positions in a practical manner, which should be done frequently, or until clearly recollected. The teacher may also place several children in a line; or square, in pairs; or threes, singly; or in a group, and so on, to explain those terms.

Make the children name the position of the objects in the room, as the fireplace at one end, the door in the middle of one side, the windows at the opposite side. Let the teacher then sketch on the blackboard a plan of the room, and mark the place of the several objects; the children may copy this on their slates; change the position of light articles, as a stool or chairs, and mark their new places on the plan. Make a similar sketch of one side of the room, and mark the place of the windows, pictures, &c., and let the children do the same on their slates. Make an outline only of the wall or floor on the blackboard, and let the children mark on it the position of secondary objects.

Teach the children the relative position of the parts of the body. Describe and illustrate the meaning of names of collections of things; as a cluster of grapes, a heap of stones, a flock of sheep, a herd of swine, a crowd of people, a group of stars, a bunch of flowers, a wood, a forest, a grove of trees, a fleet of ships, a shoal of fish, a covey of birds, a street, and a square of houses.

Scattered.—The stars appear to be scattered over the sky; corn is scattered over the ground for seed; grain is scattered in the poultry-yard for the fowls to feed on; if a shepherd leave his sheep, they no longer remain as a flock, but become scattered abroad.

Compact.—In a hayrick, or a stack of oats, the stems and seeds are all pressed together in a compact mass. The same may be said of a stack of wood or turf; rocks are compact masses of stone; the leaves of grass in a field stand close together, but the flowers are scattered over the field; in a garden, the flowers are arranged in *order.* Many other terms should be illustrated in the same way.

Make the children well acquainted with the cardinal points as relates to the school-room, and try to extend this knowledge by the relative position of their respective homes. On the blackboard make dots or points in different positions at the top, bottom, right hand, and left. Make points in the position of the angles of triangles, squares, and other figures. Make dots to represent the capital letters, or to suggest the form of any other objects, and let the children describe their positions.

Show a picture to the class, and make them describe the relative position of its parts. Remove the picture, and require them to do the same from memory. Make a simple arrangement of dots or figures on the blackboard; let the children look well at it: erase it, and let some one of the class try to reproduce it, the rest trying to correct him when wrong.

Specimen Lesson.

Let the teacher sketch a small but accurate plan of the school-room on the blackboard, and mark across it two lines at right angles to each other, directed to the cardinal points. First allow the children to point out the different parts of the plan, and particularly the position they themselves occupy on it. If we go out at the front door of the school, what street do we get into? Which way does it lie? Tell me, that I may add it to the drawing. Now it is drawn, one part goes northward and the other to the south. Who lives in this street? I do. Point in the direction of your home; is it north or south from us? What must I put behind the plan of the school-room, or to the east side of it? The play-ground? What shape must I draw the play-ground? Where must I mark the swings? What street is behind the play-ground? Yes, —— street lies north

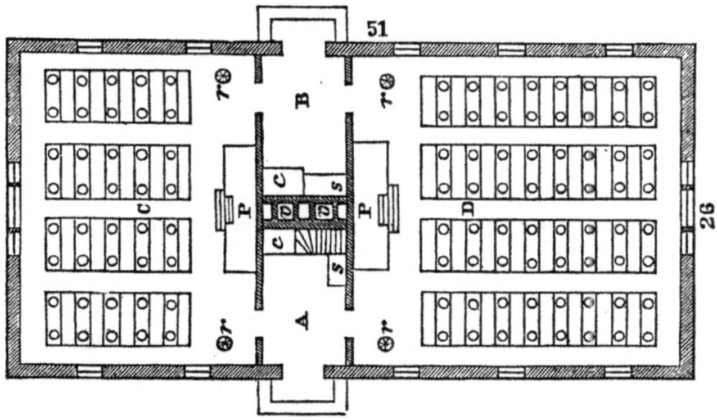

and south. Does any one go home that way? Do you go along any other street besides? Yes, —— street. Then you go to the east; see, I have drawn the two streets that form your way home; first you go so far to the south, then you turn to the east. In the morning, the sun would shine along this street, or from the east. At midday he would shine only on the north side of the street, or from the south. Show me which side of the school the sun is on in the morning? At noon? In the evening?

Of course the above must be varied to suit the locality, but its use in leading to first ideas of geography is obvious, and its gradual extension, as the ideas of the children enlarge, must be left to the teacher. When much more advanced, a large map of the town or neighborhood should be used, and each child required to trace its own way home, and any streets or roads it has been accustomed to traverse. This is a work full of interest and real instruction. Mr. Wilderspin recommends maps on a large scale made in oil cloth, on which the children could walk, and movable models to be placed on them. This is no doubt an excellent plan, but also an expensive one. It might be very useful, however, to chalk a large plan on the floor for the younger classes, as it would possess more reality to them from its size and position than a small map suspended vertically.

Number.

First ideas of number are best communicated by reference to familiar objects, and these should be of several kinds, to prevent the association of the numbers with one class of things only. Let the younger children learn to count cards, books, pence, or any objects which may be at hand. When a large number of units are required, let one child first hold up a finger, then the next, and so on as many as are wanted. Or let them hold up a finger of each hand, then two, then three, or more. One hand may be held up with the fingers spread, while the little class count one, two, three, four, five; another hand leads them to ten, another to fifteen, and as many more as they are able to count. This has the advantage of employing both hands and eyes, and affords amusement. When once the idea of number is acquired, the arithmeticon serves the purpose of giving combinations of number, and of working any arithmetical problem.

Specimen Lesson.

The teacher should be furnished with several sets of small objects.

Teacher.—I have here five books, five pence, and five sticks ; count them with me. Now, I have placed them all on the floor, and I want some little child to bring me two books. That is right. Now who can bring me three books? Quite right; now put them back again. Who can bring me a penny and two books? Now bring three sticks and a book. Now a book, a penny, and a stick. How many are they together? Who can bring me four sticks, five books, and five pence? Who will answer me a question? I will. Well, how many brothers and sisters have you? Try to tell me their names. William, Peter, and Mary. How many together? Who can count the legs of the chair? The bars of the grate? Clap your hands once, now twice, now three times.

This subject is too simple to require further detail; yet it must be taught progressively, otherwise the mind of the learner is apt to become confused. It will be perceived that it is entirely preliminary to arithmetic, and therefore it is best in this stage to keep to small numbers; and when arithmetic is commenced, still to carry on the previous process in conjunction with it, in order to give reality to the value of figures. It is particularly useful to give easy exercises in mental arithmetic, in which the notion of real objects is associated with number.

Weight.

In commencing this subject, the teacher should first call attention to such general facts as the falling of bodies towards the earth, the tendency of water to flow downwards, the difficulty of raising any heavy object up from the ground, and the sensation of weight in the human frame. Cubes or spheres of equal size, formed of lead, stone, wood, cork, or other substances, strikingly different in weight, should be examined and compared by the children. Bodies that are lighter or heavier than water may be distinguished by actual experiment. The resistance of the air to falling bodies may be easily shown by letting fall at the same instant such things as wool, cork, and lead, and watching their unequal rate of descent. The pupils should be allowed frequently to handle and compare objects of different density and size.

The next step is to make the children acquainted with the standard weights, and then to let them judge of the weights of various things, testing the accuracy of their guesses by weighing the objects before them

When a pretty accurate knowledge of small amounts of weight is acquired, it may be extended by degrees to familiar examples of greater quantities; but in this, as in the case of number, it is useless to attempt to expand the idea too rapidly; the process must be progressive, and, if hurried, would lose its reality.

The use of wooden bricks and other mechanical toys in the playground, greatly assists in developing the perception of weight.

Some idea of the nature of the mechanic powers should be given in connection with this subject, and this may be easily done by means of models and by simple experiments.

Specimen Lesson.

The teacher should be provided with several different substances for experiment. Wool, cork, pumice-stone, marble, wood, lead, or such objects as are within reach, may be used for illustration.

Teacher.—You see in my hand two balls of equal size. I want some one to try for me which is the lighter of the two. They are very different in weight; one is a ball of cork and the other of lead. If I let the leaden ball drop from my hand, can you tell me the direction in which it will go? It will fall down to the floor. Yes, for we never see any thing fall up to the ceiling or to one side, but always downwards, because the earth draws all the smaller things which are near it towards itself. The earth draws all you little children towards it, and when you try to climb a hill, you find that lifting your feet from the earth is hard work. Will you watch what takes place when I let the ball of lead fall from my hand? It strikes the floor and makes a loud noise. Now see if the same takes place when I drop the ball of cork. No, it makes only a faint sound. Why is this? The lead is heavy and the cork is light. I have here two more balls, one of wood and one of stone. Who will come and try their different weights? I am now going to place the four balls in this glass of water, and you must observe what happens. Two of them sink and two swim. Why do the cork and wooden balls swim? You can not tell; well, I must explain to you that wood and cork are lighter than water, and so come to the surface; but lead and stone are heavier than water, and sink down in it. A fish swims in the water, because it is about the same weight as water; but an oyster lies at the bottom of the sea, because it has a heavy shell. If things upon the earth had no weight, men and animals would not require to be strong; but the larger an animal is, the more strength it must have, to be able to move about. Could any little child here lift me from the ground? No, I am too heavy, and you are not strong enough. Quite true, but I could lift any of you, because you are all lighter than I am, and I must have strength enough to be able to move my own weight. A horse can carry a man because a horse is larger and heavier than a man, and has more strength. If a little child were to run a great way, would he not be tired? Yes, he would have to carry the weight of his own body all the way he went, and this would tire him. Look at the walls of the school-room. What are they made of? Are they not very heavy? Why do they not fall? Because they are upright or vertical. Would they stand if they were inclined? No, they would then fall; for all heavy things which are not supported will fall straight down. When we stand, we take care to stand upright, or else we should fall. When people fall, we say they lose their balance; that is, they throw more of their weight to one side than to the other, which causes them to come to the ground. Would you stand near a wall that leaned to one side? No, it would be dangerous to do so; it might fall and kill you.

Some things are very light, compared with others of the same size. Will you tell me of all the light things you know? Now name those that are heavy. Will you try to think of things that are bought and sold by weight? I have here a penny and a halfpenny; why is the penny worth more than the halfpenny? Because it is larger and heavier. Yes, metals are valued by weight.

When I put this iron weight into one scale, and this piece of wood in the other, what happens? The scale with the iron sinks down; the other rises. Why is this? Because the iron is heavier. And which is the larger? The wood. What should you then say of the wood? It is a lighter substance than the iron. I now put a package of wool into one scale, and the piece of wood in the other. Which appears the heavier now? The wood. Which is the larger? The package of wool. So we find that wool is lighter than wood in proportion to its size. All things which we see have weight. Even the air has some weight, as you will learn in a future lesson. If it were not so, we should have no power to move or to work; without weight, the workman's hammer would not strike, the water would not turn the mill to grind the corn, or the wind move the great ships over the sea, to fetch us good things from distant countries. Even the rain could not fall from the sky to make things grow, if it had not some weight; so that when we find it difficult and laborious to move about, or carry heavy things, we should remember how useful and necessary it is for things to have weight, and how God, in his wisdom and goodness, made every thing just as heavy as it should be. He made the air light for us to breathe and to move about in, the heavy stones to build our houses, light wool and cotton to make us warm clothes, and heavy metals to make our tools. Let us always think that He has made every thing in the way it should be.

Sound.

First lessons on this subject should not be of a musical character, but chiefly confined to the discrimination of ordinary sounds. The attention of the pupils may be directed to the varieties of the human voice in children and grown persons, in men and women, and in different individuals; also to the different modes of utterance, as speaking, calling, singing, whispering, and so on. Sounds may be produced experimentally, as by the ringing of bells, the noise made by striking various bodies, and by other means; and these should be divided into sharp, grave, loud, faint, or as many varieties as can be exhibited.

The next step is to require the pupils to observe sounds for themselves. Children, when first called upon to mention the sounds they are acquainted with, will not, perhaps, be able to remember more than ten or twelve; but we have known many who, in a week or two after their attention had been directed to the subject, could enumerate upwards of one hundred. It is useful to lead them to classify their observations, as into the voices of beasts, birds, sounds produced by insects, by the footfall of men and animals, by the motion of carriages and machinery, by workmen in performing various mechanical operations, sounds produced by the motion of water, air, and by other natural causes. Sounds may also be divided into kinds, as roaring, rumbling, crashing, crackling, murmuring, rolling, tinkling, echoing, and so on; the intention of such exercises being to connect words with definite ideas, and to cultivate habits of correct observation.

Directions for a Lesson on Sound.

Strike in succession two bells, one much sharper in tone than the other, and call attention to the different pitch in their sounds. Let the children try to produce high and low tones with the voice. Produce sudden sharp noises, as by striking hard substances, by the breaking of wood, or by the children calling out in a high key and stopping suddenly; then sounds of an opposite character, as by the rapid movement of the feet of many children, as they sit in the gallery, by rolling any heavy object on the floor, or by the lower tones of the voice. Call attention to such slight sounds as those produced by the rubbing or striking of various substances, and then let the children listen with closed eyes, and try to determine the causes which produce them. Place several children out of sight and let them speak in succession, while the class try to discriminate their voices. Direct attention to the feelings expressed by the human voice in exclamations of sorrow, joy, pain, terror, mirth, and other emotions, and to the voices of animals expressive of their feelings and wants.

Explain the difference between inarticulate sounds, such as laughing, sobbing, muttering, screaming; and articulate sounds, as speaking and singing.

The kind and amount of instruction given in each lesson must, of course, depend entirely upon the age and advancement of the pupils; the subject may as easily be treated in a way to suit a child of three as of ten years of age, and such preliminary lessons are an excellent preparation for correctness of ear in speaking and singing. Indeed, when developed, the imitative power of children is so great that no refinement of tone or inflections of voice are difficult to them; and hence the importance of a pure pronunciation and correct manner of speaking in the teacher, as defects in this respect are but too readily imitated and bad habits formed.

Developing Lessons on Objects.

When, by the preceding series of lessons, some idea of the general properties of things has been imparted, the observation of particular objects should be commenced; but we must always keep clearly in view the *principle* on which this kind of lesson rests, viz., that the children should discover for themselves the qualities of the object under examination, the teacher merely supplying the words needed to express them; for to *tell* the pupil that such and such qualities exist in it, which we are not able to demonstrate, will not develop his faculties. Hence it follows, that attention should be called only to the more palpable and striking characteristics, and that, if possible, the same quality should be traced through several examples, and even contrasted with its opposite, to render it more evident.

Suppose, for instance, two such substances as glass and india-rubber were chosen for a lesson. The most striking properties of the glass are that it is transparent, hard, brittle, sonorous, rigid, reflective. These are rendered more evident by contrasting them with the qualities of the india-rubber, which is opaque, soft, tough, not sonorous, flexible, dull. The idea of transparency may be rendered more general by reference to water, air, mica, crystals, and other examples, and also by extending the idea of the opposite property of opacity, and so on with the remaining qualities. We will now proceed to an example of this kind of teaching.

Lesson on Coal and Chalk.

Teacher.—Tell me what you observe in the object I now show you. *Children.*—It is white. Is it quite white? Yes, quite white. What else have you seen of the same kind of white? Linen, paper, snow. Tell me the color of this object. It is black. Is it black like this piece of cloth? No, the coal is bright and the cloth is not. But are not both *black?* Yes. Is the chalk bright and smooth? Feel it and try. No, it is quite rough and dull. Now feel the piece of coal. Is it smooth? Yes, in some parts. Does it shine or reflect the light? Yes. Repeat now with me, coal is black and reflects the light; chalk is white and dull. I will make a line on the blackboard with the chalk. How is it that the chalk makes a white mark? Some of it rubs off. Yes, it is friable; that is, it will rub or crumble away. Now we will try to make the coal mark. Has it made any mark? No. I will tell you the reason: the wood is softer than the coal, and so it will not mark. Weigh the two substances in your hands, and tell me are they heavy or light. Try which feels the harder. Listen while I strike each of them, and tell me what you hear. The coal gives a sharper sound than the chalk. Yes, because it is harder; for you will find that soft bodies give a dull, heavy sound, and hard bodies a sharp sound.

I am going to hold the piece of coal in the flame of this candle; will you watch what takes place? The coal burns and gives out smoke. Say, coal burns or is *combustible*. Now, watch if the chalk burns when in the flame. No, it neither burns nor smokes. Say, chalk will not burn; it is *incombustible*. It is changed, indeed, by the heat, but you can not see the change now.

When we wish to break coal into convenient pieces, how do we do it? With a hammer. Can chalk be broken in the same way? Let us try. Yes, both coal and chalk can be broken by a blow, and are therefore called *brittle*. Do you think that coal or chalk is made by men? No; I will tell you: they are both dug out of the ground, and were formed by the power of God, and such things are called natural, while things made by man are called artificial. Is either of these substances transparent? No, most rocks and other things dug out of the earth are *opaque*, that is, no light will shine through them, nor can we see through them. Such things as are neither animal nor vegetable are called mineral, and these are mineral substances. Now let us repeat what we have learned about them: Both coal and chalk are natural, mineral, opaque, brittle, heavy. Coal is also combustible, black, smooth, shining, hard. Chalk is white, friable soft, and will not burn. You know that they are both useful. Will you try to name some of the uses of coal? To warm our houses, to cook with, to drive steam engines, to make gas, and so on. Now some of the uses of chalk? To write and draw with, to make whitewash, to make lime, to manure land. Now you have examined these two substances and know some of their qualities, I will tell you something more about them. Coal is generally found deep down in the earth, and men must dig down to get it. Some of you may have seen a well out of which water is raised, and the entrance to a coal mine is like a very deep well. Up this well or shaft the coal is drawn by a rope or chain, moved by a steam engine, and when the workmen wish to go down into the mine, they get into a box covered with an iron roof, and are let down. If you look on the map of England for the counties of Northumberland and Durham, it is there, on both sides of the river Tyne, that so many coal mines are worked; but there are many other places in England, Ireland, and Scotland, where coal is found.

If you wish to see a coal mine, you would first have to be let down the shaft very far; and then, when you arrived at the bottom, you would find many passages leading in different directions, along which little cars laden with coal are drawn by horses or pushed along by boys; and, in some places you would see the miners digging the coal out of the earth with pickaxe and spade, each with a lantern to light him, covered with wire-gauze; for a kind of gas like that which burns in the street lamps comes out of the coal, and if the flame of a candle or lamp touches it, it takes fire and explodes with a dreadful noise, often killing the poor miners who may be near; but this gas will not pass through the small holes in the wire-gauze, and so can not take fire from the miner's light.

Chalk is dug out of the ground, but it is not so deep in the earth as coal, and is often close to the surface. The men who dig it out are called chalk-cutters, and a great quantity of chalk is used to put on land to make wheat and other crops grow. When chalk is burned, it changes into quick-lime, and is then used for making mortar for building. Sometimes chalk is given to calves to lick, or put into the water which cattle drink. Although chalk is now found in the sides of hills, it was once underneath the sea; for sea-shells are found mixed with it, which must have got in it when it was in a soft state at the bottom of the sea, just as we find shells mixed with the soft sand on the sea-shore now.

Sponge and Bread.

Let us compare these two things, and try to find out their properties. First look at the sponge, and tell me its form; is it of a regular or irregular shape? What is its color? Feel it, and tell me what sensation it gives to your hand. It is rough. Look at it, and tell me if the surface is uniform or every where the same. No, it is full of holes. Things which are so are called *porous*. Try if you can press it into a different shape. Does it remain in the form you pressed it into? No, it springs back to the shape it was in at first. Yes, it is *elastic*. Dip it into this glass of water, and tell me what you observe. It takes up some of the water. Will you try, children, to remember what this quality is called? *Absorbent*. Take the sponge from the water and squeeze it dry. Is any of it gone? No, it is the same as before. That is because sponge will not melt or dissolve in water.

Now let us examine the bread. What is its color? Its form? Is it like the sponge in any thing? Yes, it has holes or pores. Can you press it into a new shape? Yes. Does it spring back to its former shape? No; things which can be pressed or molded into new shapes in this way are said to be *pliant*. If you rub the bread, what happens? It crumbles away. Will the sponge crumble when rubbed? No, it is *tough* and *elastic*. Try if the bread will absorb water. Yes; but you see the water changes the bread into a sort of pulp, so that it must be miscible in water. Try which is the lighter substance, bread or sponge? Sponge. Now tell me what you know about bread. It can be eaten. It is made from flour, and flour from wheat. Then what kind of substance must bread be? Vegetable. Show me the hardest part of the bread? What made the crust hard? When you toast bread, does the surface become hard or soft? Does it change color? What part of the bread is most like the sponge in color? What is sponge used for? Why is it useful for washing and cleaning? Because it is *soft*, *flexible*, *elastic*, and *porous*. Sponge is not a vegetable, like bread, but part of an animal which lives at the bottom of the sea, and men dive down to get it from the rocks on which it lives. Could you eat sponge? No, the qualities which make it useful for washing render it unfit for food. God has given to each thing some purpose to fulfill; and he has made bread wholesome and nutritious to eat, and sponge useful for cleanliness and comfort. Let us think now of all the properties we have found in these two things. They are both light, but the sponge is the lighter. Both are full of holes or pores. Both suck up or absorb water. Both can be squeezed into new shapes; but the bread remains in the shape into which it is put, while the sponge springs back to its first form. When soaked in water, the bread is changed; the sponge is not. The bread is easily broken in crumbs; the sponge is not, it is *tough*. Bread is yellowish white; sponge is brown. Bread is vegetable; sponge is animal. Bread is edible and nutritious; sponge is not. Both are rough to the touch, and of a dull surface. One is in a natural form, the other artificially prepared. If we were to try, we would find out a great many more properties in these simple things; but let us admire the wisdom and power of God, who made all things in so wonderful a manner. The most skillful and learned man could never make a piece of sponge, nor give it life as this once had, or cause a single grain of wheat to grow.

Lesson on a Penny.

What is this? A penny. What is it made of? Copper. What color is it? A reddish brown. Tell me its shape. Round or circular? Have you seen any thing else circular? A ring. Is a penny like a ring? Why not? A ring has the middle part cut away; a penny is solid. How many surfaces has a penny? Count and see. Two flat round sides, and a circular curved part. What geometrical solid is it like then? A cylinder. What kind of cylinder? A very short one. How many edges has the penny? Two circular edges. Are the sides quite flat? No, the edges are raised, and there are figures in the middle. What do you see on this side? The Queen's likeness. And on the other side? A figure of Britannia. Are these figures raised or sunk on the surface? Raised. Yes, they are said to be in relief. Do you know how these figures were formed on the penny? I will tell you; they were stamped by dies of very hard steel, on the surface of the copper, which is much softer than steel. To explain this to you,

I will melt some of this sealing wax, and stamp an impression of the penny on it Now you see I have made a copy of one side on the wax. Is it exactly the same? No; the figures are sunk on the wax, and raised on the penny. Why did the wax receive an impression? Because it was softer than the penny. Tell me what sound you hear when I strike the penny? A ringing sound. That is because it was pressed and made hard by the steel dies. If it were softened again, it would not sound the same; and bad money has generally a different sound from good, either from not having been struck in a die, or from not being made of the same metal. Now we will talk about the penny as *money*. You all know the *use* of a penny. Many of you, no doubt, have been intrusted with money by your mothers, to buy things with. Did you ever think why people are so ready to give their goods for money? Because they can spend the money again. Yes, but what makes a penny of any value? Because it is made of copper. You are quite right; copper is very valuable, and also very useful; it serves to cover the bottoms of ships, to make kettles and saucepans, and many other things. It is made into wire, and also, when mixed with zinc, it forms brass. But how do you think copper is first obtained? You know how many things can be got without much trouble. Common stones, and earth, and wild plants can be easily picked up; but did you ever see copper lying about the ground? Oh no! if it were so common as that, it would not do to make money with, although it would be just as useful for other things. However, much has to be done before the copper to make a penny is to be had. First, men have to search out the veins of ore in the rocks, and then to dig mines down to them, and rend the hard rock with gunpowder, and break it with hammers, and then pick out the bits of ore, which must be heated and pounded fine, so as to separate all the stony or earthy part, and then it has to be melted by great heat, and refined or made pure. All this costs much labor and skill, and employs many different men, who must be paid for their work; so that by the time it is made into pure copper, it is very valuable. But with all this trouble, only a certain quantity of this metal can be got; so that it is rather scarce, and this makes it dearer, and the better suited to make money; for you know that a few pennies, which can be held in the hand, are worth as much as a loaf, or a good quantity of potatoes. If I buy a penny loaf, I give a penny for the bread, because the corn that made the bread took much trouble to cultivate; then the miller must be paid for grinding it, and the baker for baking it; and as the loaf is valuable and useful for food, so the penny is valuable, because copper is useful for many things. Now suppose pennies were made of iron or lead, would they be as convenient? No; for to be of the same value they would require to be much larger, and would be too heavy to carry about. When much money has to be paid, we do not use copper, but silver or gold, which being worth more take up much less space, and are not so heavy in proportion. Shall I tell you a little story before we close our lesson? There was a very clever painter, who lived in Italy a long time ago. He spent much time and thought in painting a picture, and when he went to receive the money which was the price of the work, it was paid to him all in copper coin. The weight was very great, and he had a long way to go home; he was not strong, and the fatigue of carrying so great a weight along the hot road so injured his health as to cause his death. Now, if he had been paid in gold coin, it would have given him no trouble to carry home; for a very small weight of gold would have been as valuable as his great bag of copper.

Moral Lessons.—God.

A few years ago, not one of you little children was alive. Where were you then? Not in any place. God had not made you. Many children come to life every day, and many people die every day. But God was always alive! The world we live in was made by his word; but He lived before all worlds, before all men and angels, and He will continue to live forever. Is God like as we are? No, for *we* are all sinful, and He is perfectly good and pure. *We* know very little; He knows every thing: *we* can only see and hear a little way around us; *He* can see and hear ever so far. *We* can only be in one place at a time; God is in every place at the same time. He is here in this room now, and knows what we are all thinking about, and all that we do and say. He could destroy us all in a moment. Will he do so? No; for He is very kind, and loves us. He has told us how to become good, that we may go to Him, and be happy forever. He sent us his Son Jesus Christ into the world to save us from our sins, and to show us what we ought to do that we may become his children. Although God is present every where, yet Heaven is called his dwelling-place, for it is there that He is pleased to show his glory most; there every thing is good, and pure, and holy; there saints and angels dwell, and those who serve God on earth will go there at last, to live forever in perfect happiness. Can we see God? No; not with our eyes; but we can think of Him in our minds when we see his wonderful works. If one of you saw a clock, would you think that it made itself? Would not you say, some man must have made it? If the clock were going, you would know that some one must have wound it up. A clock is a very curious work; the hands move, and the bell rings to tell the time; and many other things men make are very ingenious, but they are very different from the works of God. If one of you were to lose an arm, could any man make a new arm grow for you? No; for our bodies are the work of God. If you pluck a rose in the garden, can you join it again to the tree? No; for the rose-tree is God's work.

The great globe on which we live is always moving very swiftly on; *who* could move or stop so very large a thing? The bright sun goes on always shining; *who* could make so great a light? All the men and animals on the earth are fed every day; *who* finds so vast a quantity of food as to give all creatures enough? How many things we have to make us happy; from whom do these blessings come? From God. What can we give God in return? Nothing, for *all things* are His; but we should love Him for all his goodness to us, and trust in Him, and give Him thanks and praise for all we have. Let us think what God has done. He made all things. He supports and preserves all things. All his works are full of wonders. He sent his Son to redeem us from sin and death.

Let us think how great God is. He is all-wise, all-powerful. He is in every place; and He is eternal. He had no beginning, and he will have no end.

What comes from God? All life comes from him, and he is the source of love and truth, knowledge and power, justice and mercy. Without him we could not live a moment. Oh! let us love and serve him as long as we live.

Creation.

As I have told you something about God, we will now talk about Creation. Do you know what that word means? Well, I will try to tell you, but you must listen very attentively, and *think*, as it is rather difficult for little children to understand at first. I dare say you often sit upon a chair or stool when you are at home; and when you eat your dinner you sit at a *table* and eat off a *plate* with a spoon, or knife and fork; at night you sleep upon a *bed*, and in the morning when you get up, you put on some *clothes* to keep you *warm*. Now, all these things must have been made by *somebody* and out of *something*. The chair and stool and table were made by a? *carpenter*, and of? *wood*. The plate by a? *potter*, and of? *clay*. The knife and fork by a? *cutler*, and of? *metal*. You see all these things are made by man, but did man make the wood, the clay, or the metal? Oh no! they were all created or produced by the power of God. When you look at this beautiful world, and all the things in it which are given us for our use and pleasure, do you not feel that some great Being whom we can not see must have made all? Yes, dear children, you know it was Almighty God. He called into existence this wonderful world on which we *live*, the *sun* and *moon* and *stars*, which altogether we call Creation or the Universe. I will now begin to tell you the way in which God did this. Do you think He had need of any thing to make the world with? No; he only *spoke* and it was done! Can any one else make things by speaking? No. You are right; it is only Almighty God who can do such a wonderful thing. We are told that at first "the earth was without form and void, and darkness was upon the face of the deep;" that means, that the earth was without any agreeable shape or order, and that it was empty. There were no nice trees or plants to furnish it, nor beautiful lakes and mountains and valleys, nor animals to inhabit it. First of all, God made the light. He said, "Let light be, and there was *light*." Then he made the air and sky, or firmament. Can you see the air? No; but you can *feel* it. Do you know where the air is? It is every where; it covers the whole *earth*. Sometimes water comes down from the clouds; what do we call it? *Rain*. Now, God said, "Let the waters that are under the heavens be gathered together into one place, and let the dry land appear." What did God call the dry land? *Earth.* What did he call the waters? *Seas.* But there was as yet nothing on the earth or in the waters; so God spoke, and things grew out of the ground; trees, with their beautiful leaves and fruit; nice vegetables, and corn, and soft green grass, and lovely flowers, all sprang up at his command. How thankful we ought to be when we remember that God made all these things for us! Next, God placed two great lights in the sky, the greater light to rule the day, and the lesser light to rule the night, and covered the sky with stars. What did he call the great light? The *Sun.* And what the lesser light? The *Moon.* None of these things which God made were alive. At last he made some living things. He filled the water with *fishes*, some very large, and some of them very small. Then He made the beautiful birds to live in the trees, and some to swim on the water, and He made all the creeping things, and the beasts of the earth according to their kinds, and cattle, and every thing that creepeth on the earth after its kind; and last of all He made man, and gave him dominion over the fishes of the *sea*, and the fowls of the *air*, and the *beasts*, and the whole *earth;* and God saw all the things that he had *made*, and they were very good.

Now, let us try to consider what was created on each day. The first day God made the *light.* On the second day, the *air* or *firmament.* The third day He formed the *seas* and the *dry land*, and made the *grass*, *herbs*, and *trees.* On the fourth day God made the *sun* and *moon* and *stars.* On the fifth day, the *fishes* and *birds;* and on the sixth day He made the insects, reptiles and *beasts*, and also *man.**

Life.

Let us think of God's goodness in granting life to all his creatures. When we awake in the morning, and feel that we are *alive*, how pleasant it is to see the bright daylight, and to breathe the fresh morning air! Then little children sit down to their morning meal, and hear their kind parent's voices; and when hunger and thirst are satisfied, they prepare to go to school, there to learn many good and useful things, and to spend an hour in pleasant play; tired at last, they go home to meet their dear parents once more, and then, when the sun has set and darkness covers the sky, God sends sleep to rest our bodies and to give us strength for a new day. How thankful we should be for these great blessings!

But are there no people living except those we have seen? Oh yes. Thousands of thousands of men and women and little children are now enjoying life in many other countries. Some are black, some are white like ourselves, but God supports the life of every one. And are *men* the only living things? No; for the beasts in the field live, and so do birds and fishes, and the little insects. Who could count all the living things God has made? No one could number them, they are so many. Could a *man* cause any thing to live? No; God only could do that. Men can make many wonderful things, such as a watch, to tell the time; in it the wheels keep moving, with a ticking sound; but then, if it is not wound up it will stop; it is not *alive.* What is it in our breasts which beats night and day? It is the heart, which keeps on moving as long as we live. Does any one touch it to make it beat? No; it is alive. We can not stop it or make it move. We may call the heart the life-clock; it will go on beating until we die.

How many wonderful parts the body has, in order to support life. The head is at the top; it turns about on the neck. Inside the head is the *brain*, where we feel; in front is the face, with eyes to see, nose to smell, mouth to taste and speak with. At the sides of the head are the ears to hear with. The head seems to govern the body. Then, inside the chest, besides the heart are the lungs, by which we breathe air to keep our blood pure; and below is the stomach, to digest the food we eat, and change it into nourishment for the blood, which the heart sends to all parts of our frame. Then we have hands and arms to work and get food, and to do many other things. Our feet and legs carry us about from place to place, just as we wish, which is a most useful thing. But we must now think of another wonderful part of life; I mean that it is always changing. You are little children *now*, soon you will grow to be big boys and girls; then your bodies will be larger, and your minds will know much more. At last you will become men and women, and then you will not grow any more, but will change gradually

---

* The words in italics are to be supplied by the children.

to be old people; your strength and your senses will decay, and at last you will die, and new children will grow up to take your places in the world; for this is how God made all living things, both men and animals and plants. When a seed falls into the ground, it swells and grows: at first a little green shoot appears, then, after many years perhaps, it becomes a large tree, and bears flowers and fruit and seed. At last this tree grows old and dies. Will God ever die? Oh no! He is a spirit, and spirits do not die, they live forever. *Our spirits* will not die, only our *bodies*. The angels do not die; but all things which we see on the earth will die; they come to life, and grow, and live, and then die. Some things never had any life; stones and metals never were alive; they are called minerals. But living things could not do without those which have no life. What do we want that has no life? We want air to breathe, and water to drink; without these we should not live a day, and so God in his love has given us both in abundance. The air is every where over the earth; we live in it, and breathe it; so do plants and animals; but there is enough for the use of all. And how plentiful is water! it drops in the rain and dew, it flows in rivers and streams, and the great ocean is full of it. The minerals of the earth serve for the plants to grow in, and the plants serve to feed men and animals; so you see all things help to support life, and all life comes from God. We should thank and praise Him every day for all his blessings.

The Mind.

Some of you, little children, may have observed how many wonderful things animals can do. You may have seen a bird's nest, and noticed how neatly and curiously it is made; or you may have looked at a little spider weaving his web. There is one kind of bird that sews leaves together to form its nest, and for this reason it is called the Tailor bird; and you have all heard of the Beaver, that cuts down trees and builds himself a house and a wall on the river side. But animals do all these wonderful works without being taught; for God has given to them what is called instinct, by which they know just what to do. To the beaver He has given a building instinct, to the spider a weaving instinct, and so on. Yet animals can learn to do some things. Dogs are trained to mind sheep, and horses to draw carriages. Some birds can be taught to sing tunes, or even to say a few words; but no animal can learn like a child; for the same child may be trained to be either a weaver, a tailor, or a builder, or to any other trade. Why is this? You know that many animals have five senses like ourselves; but can any animal learn to speak like a child? Oh no! for God has given the power of speech to man only. When God created the animals, he brought them to Adam for him to give each a name; and you know that we have names for every thing we see or know of, and for whatever we do. When we hear the name of a thing, we think of the thing itself; and when we want to tell what we have seen, we use words only. With words we can tell whatever we feel, or think, or know; and by listening to what others say, we can learn from them. Words stand for things. We think, speak, read, and write in words. Whether we think, speak, or write the word *man*, it always stands for the same thing. We learn to know things through our senses: this is called *perceiving*. When we once know any thing, we can think of it again: this is called *remembering*. How do you know the difference between one object and another? By *comparing* them. Can you tell me which is the taller of these two children, the boy or the girl? *The boy.* Which is the elder? *The boy.* How do you know? Because he is much bigger. Yes; you have observed that children increase in size as they get older, and so you *judged* of their ages by their difference of size. In this way we can judge of the differences of all things, and by reasoning on their qualities we learn to know their uses. We can judge of *actions* as well as of *things*. We all know that to get our food and clothes, some one must work. Little children can not work, but their parents labor for them. Now, when we see people who are idle all day, we say that they do wrong, and that they soon will come to want. Why do we say this? Because we know that much labor is needed to prepare food and clothing for our use; and if men are idle, others will not give them what they want. It is by our *minds*, then, that we are able to tell right from wrong. And God requires us to think on what we do, and to obey his laws. Does He require the animals to reason on what they do? No; for He has not given them speech and reason like man.

Let us think of another power in our minds. We said that by means of our senses we can perceive whatever is around us; but we can sometimes think of things we never saw: this is called *imagining*. Let us try to imagine a palm-tree. I show you this picture to help you to imagine it. Now you must think of a tall straight tree, growing upright, with no branches at the sides, and only one great bunch of leaves at the top. Now look again at the picture; fancy the stem as tall as an elm-tree; the leaves at the top each as long as this room is wide, and a great bunch of fruit in the middle of the leaves. Have you any idea of the palm-tree now? How did you get it? Yes; from the picture, and by what you know of other trees, and by my description. Let us now see how many mental powers we have found out. We can perceive; we use signs or language; remember; compare; judge; imagine. What a wonderful thing is the mind! It is said that God at first made man in his own image; that is, He gave him a thinking spirit or soul, and made him pure and good. Two things our minds can learn about God; how well he has made all things, and how merciful he has been to man, who sinned against him. When we think of these things, it should make us love him more and more every day.

Conscience.

Almighty God has made the great world and all living things, down to the smallest insect, on a regular plan; even the water and air and light obey his laws, and he has put an instinct in every animal, by which it does that which is good and right for it to do. Have *we* the same instinct in us? No, but we have what is much better, a mind which can judge between right and wrong. How do we know what is right? God has given us a law which tells us. Is this law good? Yes; for God made it, and He does all things well. Those who keep this law are happy, while those who break it are unhappy.

The feeling which we have of what is right or wrong in our actions is called *conscience;* and although no one might see us when doing a wrong act, conscience would tell us we were not doing as we ought. We should always listen to conscience. We should always do what we know to be right, not what we see others do. Children often try to excuse themselves when in fault, by saying that they only followed the example of some of their companions: is this right? No; for we should not join in any act without first thinking if it be right to do so. Do you know what you *ought* to do? The great thing is to love and serve God; the next, to love your fellow-creatures, and do them all the good you can. Do you know what it is wrong and wicked to do? Is it right to hate any one, or to try to injure him? Is it right to give way to anger, greediness, and other passions? No; for we should try to govern our minds and obey God's law, and not our own bad feelings. Ought we to say what is not true? No; for God is not pleased with those who lie. May we be rude or disobedient to our parents? No; we are commanded to obey them in all things. Can children serve the Lord? Yes; Joseph, the prophet Samuel, king Josiah, Timothy, and many other holy men, sought the Lord while they were yet children; and he led them all through their lives in the right way; and *we* must try to learn how to be good. We can not do this all at once. Many little children who are naughty when they first come to school, learn by degrees to do what is right. Will *you* strive to improve? You must try very much, and not be discouraged; endeavor always to find out which is the right way to act. I will tell you about a poor American Indian who was among his white neighbors. He asked a white man to give him a little tobacco. The man had some in his pocket, which he gave him. When the Indian came to use the tobacco, he found a piece of silver money in it; so, the next day he came back and brought it to the owner. When asked why he did not keep the money, he pointed to his breast and said, "I got a good man and a bad man here: the good man say, 'it is not yours, take it back.' Bad man say, 'he gave it you; it is yours.' Good man say, 'it is not right; he gave you tobacco, not money.' Bad man say, 'never mind; you got it, go and spend it.' So, I don't know what to do, and I try to go to sleep; but good man and bad man keep talking all night, and trouble me; so I bring the money back, and feel good now." What did the Indian mean by the good man in his breast, who said, take back the money? He meant his conscience, which told him right from wrong. What was the bad man that told him to keep the money? This was the feeling of selfish greediness, which would have had him buy something for his own pleasure with the money.

Not long ago I saw a little girl come into school one morning; she put her own bread away, and then took some out of another child's bag. As soon as she had got it in her hand she hid it under her cloak, and looked timidly around to see if any one was near. I went to her, and asked her where she got the bread then in her hand. She said, from her own bag. Was this true? No; for I saw her take it from another bag which was now empty. What made her hide the bread, and look round to see if any one noticed what she had done? It was conscience. She knew that she had done wrong: in her own bag she had plenty of bread, but she was greedy and wished for more. This was a sad fault, it led her to steal; and then, to hide her theft from me, she spoke what was false. See how one fault leads to another: covetousness to theft, and theft to lying! But I am glad to say, she soon came to see how badly she had acted, and to be very sorry for it. Perhaps she did not think much of what she was doing, but only followed the bad feeling of greediness; yet she knew that she was doing wrong, or why did she try to hide the bread, and then tell an untruth to conceal her fault? Let us always think of what we are doing, and try to act rightly. Even the poor Indian who had not been taught the true way, wished to be honest; and how much more should we who have the law of God.

Hope.

What a delightful feeling is hope! I think we may call it a bright feeling. You may have seen the farmer laboring to plow and sow his fields. Why does he throw the seed into the ground? Is it not that he *hopes* to see it grow up and bear fruit? He waits long, and is not impatient; for he says to himself, "When harvest time comes, I shall be rewarded for all my labor and cost; I will wait and *hope* until then." When a merchant sends out a ship laden with goods over the ocean to a far country, he says, "My goods cost me much, but when my ship comes back, I *hope* she will bring me many more valuable things in return."

If a mother were parting from her son who was going on a long voyage, she would say, "It is, indeed, sad to part, but I will live in *hope* that my child will return, and then what joy I shall feel to meet him again!" Do you, children, ever feel *hope?* When you have a lesson given you to learn, you may perhaps say, "It is rather hard, but never mind, I think I can learn it." If you thought you could not learn it, you would have no *hope*, and be very sad.

When you bid your mothers good-by in the morning on coming to school, you do it cheerfully, because you say, "In the evening we shall meet our dear mothers again." If you had not this feeling, how miserable you would be.

You all wish to walk abroad and play in the fresh air; think how you would feel when shut up in a prison, with strong stone walls and iron-bound doors, so that you could not get out, and only saw the light through one small grated window. Yet, if you expected to be let out in a month, a year, or any fixed time, you would still live in *hope*. Perhaps you might say, "It is very hard to be so long in this dark, cold cell; but, oh! how happy I shall be when the day comes, to go out and breathe the fresh air again." Think, then, of those poor prisoners who have been shut in for life, with no hope of liberty. Oh! how sad their fate must have been! no change, no hope in this world! Some have given way to despair, and even gone mad in their dungeons. Others have trusted in God, and borne all patiently, placing their hope on a better world. Think, then, my dear children, what a blessing hope is; how many happy thoughts it gives us; how cheerful we are, and how much we can do, if we have a hopeful spirit. With this feeling our faces are bright, our hearts are light, and our hands are active and busy; so let us always try to *hope*, and never despond or despair.

The foregoing are merely given to show how these subjects should be simplified to suit the capacities of little children. It is a good plan for teachers, when they intend giving a lesson of this kind, to draw out beforehand an outline of the manner in which they mean to treat the subject. We give an example or two.

Love.

In treating this subject, the first leading idea to be brought out is love to God for all his boundless goodness to us, and for his infinite perfections. Next, love to parents as a duty commanded, as a return for their unbought care and affection, and for constant benefits. The ties of relationship should then be dwelt upon; the duty of brotherly love and of general union in families, with simple anecdotes illustrative of the happiness and beauty of family union. Then duties of humanity in general, and of kindness and hospitality to strangers; with such narratives as Abraham entertaining the angels; the parable of the merciful Samaritan; the story of Mungo Park entertained by the poor African women; the divine command to love our enemies, and to overcome evil with good, illustrated by the example of the Saviour praying for his murderers.

The foregoing principles may be contrasted with examples of the dreadful effects of hatred, and of the misery of quarreling and anger. Inculcate, also, kindness to animals, and frequently show their uses both to man and in the scheme of creation. Also show the cruelty and cowardice of giving pain to weak and helpless things, which are placed by Divine Providence under our protection. Try to cultivate a love for natural objects generally; flowers, trees, and so forth. As children come to perceive and admire the beauty and order of creation, a feeling of love extends itself to every natural object, as exhibiting the power and goodness of God.

Fear.

Show the evil and folly of indulging in unnecessary alarm at common dangers or mere appearances. Try to strengthen the minds of children to meet dangers, by directing them how they should act in such ordinary occurrences as may excite alarm. Explain what is meant by *moral* courage, and show how *fear* is generally accompanied by guilt, and that innocence gives the best feeling of security. Try to induce a constant dependence on divine protection. Explain that the feeling of fear or insecurity in darkness arises from physical causes, such as the impossibility of seeing where to step, and show how the blind overcome this feeling.

Additional Subjects for Moral Lessons.

On the continual support of all things by Divine Power.

Time.—Our experience and knowledge of the *past*, the duties of the *present*, and our ignorance of the *future*.

The design and wisdom shown in the works of creation.

The starry heavens; the idea of distant worlds.

The stages of life, and their mutual relation and duties: infancy; youth; maturity; age.

On the various ranks and occupations of men, and of their mutual usefulness and support.

Love to God—to parents and relations—to companions—strangers and enemies.

Fear.—Physical and moral.

Truth and justice in our words and actions.

Falsehood, dissimulation, and evil speaking.

Obedience.—Explain the difference between *willing* obedience and *forced* obedience.

Contentment, and submission to unavoidable evils.

Patience and perseverence under difficulties.

Gentleness both in *word* and *action*.

Selfishness contrasted with self-denial for the good of others.

Industry and diligence.

Self-control—in sudden alarm or cases of illness—of provocation.

Generosity—covetousness.

Self-conceit, and a spirit of contradiction.

Effects of envy—anger and hatred.

Cruelty to animals.

Cleanliness.

The tendency of one fault to give rise to another.

Respect due to parents—to age—to good and great characters—to office and to rank.

The evil of ridicule. Forbearance and sympathy due to misfortune and deformity.

Punctuality. Destructiveness. Order. Honesty.

Loyalty and love of country.

X.—ORGANIZATION AND INSTRUCTION OF THE NATIONAL SCHOOLS OF IRELAND.

THE following Circular and Time Tables, selected from a Report of P. J. Keenan, Head Inspector, instructed by the Commissioners of National Education in 1855, to hold, what would be called in this country, a "Teachers' Institute," composed of practical teachers, whose business it is to visit different parts of the country for the purpose of assisting in the organization of schools, and diffusing a knowledge of the best principles and methods of instruction, throw much light on the aims and processes of the National Schools of Ireland.

CIRCULAR LETTER explanatory of the nature of SCHOOL ORGANIZATION, and the DUTIES of the ORGANIZERS and INSPECTORS in relation to it.

1. The objects which the Commissioners of National Education have had in view, in establishing the staff of organizers, are two-fold, viz.: —

A.—To bring National Schools into a state of efficiency.

B.—To diffuse amongst the teachers of the country a knowledge of Schoolmastership in all its practical bearings, and also of the leading principles of the Science of Education.

2. To carry out the first great object, (1 A), the organizers will devote themselves, during their stay in a school, to the following, as the main part of their duties.

3. To secure a regular and proper ventilation of the school-room.

4. To improve the lighting of the school-room, if necessary.

5. To make suitable arrangements as to the playground and out-offices.

6. To make every available use of the walls; to provide tablet rails, &c.

7. To arrange maps, charts, and tablets, and show how they can be most profitably used.

8. To provide black-boards, easels, pointers, arithmeticons, &c., and instruct the teachers as to their use.

9. To see that a sufficient number of desks is provided; that they are properly arranged and fixed on the floor; that provision is made for holding the slates; and that the business legitimate to the desks is regularly carried on.

10. To secure sufficient space for the drafts; to denote them by suitable marks on the floor; and to arrange the business proper to the drafts.

11. To classify the pupils, and divide them into convenient divisions and drafts.

12. To make out a time-table suitable to the circumstances of the school, and to test its judiciousness, by experiment, for a number of days before recommending its adoption to the Manager.

13. To see that the pupils, as well as the teacher, understand the arrangements indicated in the time-table.

14. To establish a sound system of monitorial instruction; to see that the members of the monitor class are judiciously selected; that they are sufficiently mature and intelligent for their duties; *that their employment as monitors does not interfere with their business as pupils;* that they be required to teach those subjects only which they are competent to teach; that they receive special instruction from the teachers, in lieu of the time spent by them in teaching; that the business arranged for their special instruction is regularly conducted; that they are instructed in the art of teaching; that they are taught to prepare notes of the lessons which they may be called upon to teach; that they know their duties prospectively; that they teach the same set of children from day to day for an assigned time; that their teaching is effective; that the pupils have sufficient respect for them, and confidence in their abilities; that such arrangements are made as to satisfy the parents of pupils and monitors with the monitorial system, and that the teacher is duly prepared to control and prepare the monitors for their duties.

15. Whilst monitorial instruction, *judiciously* and *moderately* employed, is encouraged, the organizers are to see that all the *essentials* of the education of a child are looked after and cared for by the teacher himself, and that the latter is to be almost constantly employed in the actual teaching of class after class, at the same time that he exercises an active superintendence over all the simultaneous operations of his school.

16. To establish a system of home lessons; to make arrangements for their regular announcement day after day; to see that they are properly heard; that the answering of the pupils is in some form noted; and that the general order of such lessons be kept in correspondence with the ordinary teaching pursued in the school.

17. To arrange for the regular recapitulation or repetition of the home and other lessons.

18. To make arrangements that the parents may be occasionally informed as to the attention of the children to the home lessons and general business of the school.

19. To exemplify before the teacher the different methods of teaching, and to cause him in turn to practise the same.

20. To see that he prepares "notes of lessons" in proper form, on the different subjects taught in the school, and that he teaches the various lessons in conformity with the notes so prepared.

21. To effect as much improvement as possible in the teaching of reading, writing, arithmetic, dictation, grammar, geography, drawing, &c., *and particularly in the teaching of the First Book.*

22. To see that the teacher gives clear evidence that he prepares himself beforehand *for the work of each day*, not only in the notes of the lessons which he is to teach, but also in the general business, including the simplest mechanical details of his school.

23. To drill the children, put them through the simple marching exercises, establish order and discipline, and train the teacher to continue the same course of drill and discipline so established.

24. To see that the business of the school is conducted with the least noise possible.

25. To establish a system of punishment for badly conducted children, and to introduce a system of emulation or reward, to promote good conduct.

26. To improve the manners of the children, and to see that there is a daily inspection as to cleanliness, &c.

27. To see that the children are provided with the necessary books for home study, and that a sufficient sale stock, and an ample supply of school materials and requisites are furnished.

28. To arrange as to the calling of the rolls with all possible despatch; to provide a report slate; to correct and show the teacher how to keep the school accounts, and to cause scroll rolls to be kept.

29. To adopt measures towards improving the attendance of the children, particularly with reference to punctuality in the morning.

30. Finally, the organizer is to lead the teacher into a strict observance of the rules of the Board, but especially the Practical Rules for Teachers.

31. The Commissioners of National Education have decided that no National school can be organized until the Manager express his desire to avail himself of the services of an organizer; and even after so expressing himself, and permitting the organizer to commence operations in his school, it is to be distinctly understood that he is not bound to carry out the plans or to effect the alterations suggested by the organizer.

32. The Inspectors should therefore select those schools only for organization, the Managers of which are likely to exhibit a kind and coöperative spirit to the organizers.

33. Before a school can be organized, the Manager must provide a sufficient sale stock for the use of the children attending it. As already announced to the Inspectors, the Commissioners, on the recommendation of the Head or District Inspector, or the organizer, will make a small grant of charts, black-boards, easels, pointers, &c., proportioned according to the wants and attendance of the school, not exceeding, however, except in special cases, the value of five pounds.

34. When an organizer enters a school, he is carefully to observe the methods of teaching pursued by teachers and monitors; the order, discipline, arrangements, and general organization of the school; and he is afterwards to report, on a form prepared for the purpose, the exact state in which he finds the school in all these respects. This report is called the *Preliminary Report.*

35. When an organizer has completed the organization of a school, he is to make a report of the order, discipline, system, &c., established by him; to detail the exact state in which he leaves the school; and to record the general results of the organization. This report is called the *Final Report.*

36. The organizer is then to forward the two reports just referred to, to the Inspector of the district in which the school is situated.

37. After a period of not less than three weeks, and not more than six weeks from the completion of the organization of the school, the Inspector of the district is to inspect the school, with a special view of ascertaining the effectiveness of the organization, and of examining and checking, in detail, all the points and statements contained in the organizer's final report.

38. The District Inspector is then to forward this report, along with the organizer's Preliminary and Final Reports, to the Head Inspector of the District, who will afterwards transmit them to this office.

39. During the time that a school is under organization the Inspector is not to make a formal inspection of it, nor sooner after the organization is completed than the time mentioned in paragraph 37; and it is the express wish of the Commissioners that the employment of an organizer in a district *may interfere as little as possible with the usual and regular business of inspection.*

40. It is, however, exceedingly desirable that the Inspector should make as many *incidental* visits as possible to a school under organization, to see that the work is proceeding with regularity and vigor; to confer with the Managers, and stimulate them to a hearty co-operation with the organizers; to assist in removing local difficulties or impediments, and to extend, as much as lies in his power, the advantages accruing to the National system from the operations of the organizers.

41. No organizer should, for the present, be sent to any place where there are not, *at*

least, four National Schools within a circuit of three miles from it, the Managers of which are desirous that their schools may receive the advantages of organization.

42. No less than four, or more than eight, schools are for the present to be organized by the same organizer in any particular locality.

43. As a general rule, the time spent in the organization of a school is not to exceed a fortnight; but the organizer is to return for a day or two, if necessary, before he leaves the locality in which the school is situated, to observe the results of the organization, and give such further instruction to teachers and monitors as the state of the school may at the time suggest as necessary and important.

44. The two weeks which may be spent by an organizer in a school are not to be consecutive; a week, in all cases, is to elapse between the first and second parts of the organization. For instance, where four schools, A, B, C, D, are to be organized, the following may be the order of organization:—

First week	A		Next week	C	
Next week		B	Next week		D
Next week	A		Next week	C	
Next week		B	Next week		D

45. The second great object which the Commissioners of National Education have had in view in establishing the staff of organizers, as already stated in paragraph 1 B, is "to diffuse a knowledge of schoolmastership in all its practical bearings, and also of the leading principles of the science of education amongst the teachers of the country."

46. To carry out this great object each organizer will deliver a course of lectures to the teachers who live in the neighborhood of the school in which he is engaged, upon method, order, discipline, school accounts, employment of monitors, construction of time-tables, arrangement of school furniture, use of charts, tablets, and apparatus, industrial education, and upon organization generally.

47. These lectures will take place on Saturdays, at whatever hour may be most convenient to the organizers and the teachers.

48. The District Inspector is to invite all teachers living within a reasonable walking distance—four or five miles—to those lectures; and whilst attendance is, under no circumstances, to be considered as compulsory, it is to be understood that the Commissioners will regard with satisfaction the conduct of those teachers who attend the instructions.

49. None but schoolmasters and monitors in their fourth year, are to attend the lectures of male organizers, and none are to attend the instructions of the female organizers but schoolmistresses and monitresses in their fourth year.

50. Teachers, whether trained or not, are eligible for admission into the organizers' classes; for it is hoped that both the trained and the untrained will derive such advantage from the instructions as to qualify them the better for a skilful and efficient discharge of their duties.

51. The organizers will keep a roll of the attendance of the teachers, and submit it at the end of the course of instruction to the District Inspector.

52. The organizers will require the teachers who may attend to take such notes during each lecture as will enable them to write out an abstract of it before the day for the following lecture; those abstracts and whatever other written exercises the organizers may require the teachers to prepare for them are to be examined and noted by the organizer, and submitted from time to time to the District or Head Inspector, to be afterwards, however, in the corrected state, returned to the teacher.

53. A statement will be made at the end of each course of lectures by the organizers, for the information of the Inspectors and Commissioners, of the attention paid by each of the teachers to their instructions, and of the proficiency which each of them shall have made.

54. As the duties of an organizer, when organizing a school, will be such as to prevent him from doing much more, in reference to methods of teaching, than exemplifying and carrying into practical effect the instructions contained in his lectures, no school can be organized, the teacher of which does not attend, or shall not have attended, a course of lectures either from him or some other organizer.

55. The Commissioners desire that the Inspectors should devote as much attention as possible to the arrangement and superintendence of those weekly meetings; and they also desire that the Inspectors should sustain and encourage the organizers on those occasions, uphold their authority, give weight to their position, and contribute by every means in their power to their success.

56. Before an organizer commences operations in a locality, the Inspector should have all necessary arrangements with Managers and teachers completed, as to the schools to be organized and the teachers who are to form the Saturday class for practical instruction.

57. Whenever a District Inspector feels that the services of an organizer are required for any particular group of his schools, all the conditions already announced being either fully complied with, or in a fair way of being so, he is to communicate with this office, giving information on the following points:—

(*a*) As to the centre which he proposes for the residence of the organizer, selecting, of course, no place in which a suitable lodging cannot be procured for him and his family.

(*b*) As to the schools which he recommends for organization and the distance of each from the proposed residence of the organizer.

(*c*) As to the number of teachers who would likely attend the lectures of the organizer upon Saturdays.

58. Each District Inspector is requested to inform this office, within a week after the receipt of this circular letter, upon the points enumerated in the previous paragraph.

59. The office, on receipt of those communications, will advise them to the Head

Inspector, whose duty it will be to select the schools proposed to be organized, to instruct the organizers as to the schools assigned them, and the time of the commencement of the organization, and immediately to advise the office as to the steps thus taken.

60. In order to place the object and details of the system of organization, and the machinery by which it is worked, as fully and clearly as possible before the Inspectors, the Commissioners append printed copies of the reports referred to in paragraphs 34 and 35. These reports, printed verbatim from the copies furnished by the organizer, are selected principally because the school to which they refer, from being one of the worst town schools in connection with the Board, has become, since its organization, distinguished for the neatness and completeness of its arrangements, and the general excellence of the order, discipline, and methods of teaching pursued in it. The Inspectors should peruse these reports carefully, inasmuch as they exhibit, with considerable precision, the chief points and details in the organization of a school.

61. The District Inspectors are requested to circulate, as extensively as possible, amongst Managers, teachers, and the public generally, information as to the object, scope, and leading features of organization; to let Managers understand that the presence of an organizer in their schools neither affects their privileges nor interferes with their functions; to inform teachers that organization is intended to diminish, in no way, their authority in their schools, or to degrade them in the estimation of their pupils or the parents; to acquaint all classes interested in the education of the people, that an organizer has nothing whatever to say or do in relation to the arrangements for religious instruction; that, on the contrary, it is the aim of the Commissioners, in the measures now taken by them for the improvement of their schools, to uphold the rights of Managers, to strengthen the power of the teachers, by rendering them more skilful servants of the public, and to realize what the Board have long desired to attain, a scheme of organization which, by combining all that educationists approve in the matter of instruction and commend in school keeping, will give a distinctive stamp and uniform character to the schools conducted on the National system.

The following extracts from Mr. Keenan's Report (1856) illustrates some of the above points.

School Organization.

In organizing an ordinary National School, the teacher should divide the school into two divisions; and he would arrange that the divisions should move alternately from floor to desks, desks to floor, and so on. He would appoint specific business for each division for every moment of the day, whether in the desks or on the floor, and the spirit of the whole organization would consist in the unflagging nature of the work from morning to evening. On the floor there would be the active *viva voce* lessons in reading, grammar, geography, arithmetic, spelling, geometry, algebra, mensuration, &c.; in the desks there would be the quiet work, requiring only superintendence and occasional examination or instruction, as writing on slates and paper, dictation, composition, drawing, slate arithmetic, lesson exercises, book-keeping, and,industrial work. "Lesson Exercises" is a name which I have given to any exercise on paper or slate, which refers to some lesson previously learned. For instance, if it refer to grammar, the exercise may be to classify columnarly the parts of speech of the words of a sentence, to write out the derivations of a number of words dictated to them, &c.; if it refer to the Lesson Books, the exercise may be to write out the substance of the lesson read a little previously upon the floor, or to summarize the lessons of a section of one of the books, &c.; if it refer to geography, the exercise may be to write down the manufactures, population, imports, exports, &c., of some country, or to draw an outline map of it; and no matter, in short, what the subject may be, it will afford material for this very useful and interesting exercise, which has the advantage of being always an appeal to the judgment as well as to the memory.

The organizer takes care that there shall be no "preparing lessons," home being the place for that, the suitable place where even if there were no improvement on the hour and forty minutes' plan, it would be still desirable to enforce habits of reading and study and of preparation for the business of the school. The arrangement into two divisions — the rotation being from desk to floor and floor to desk throughout the day — would be called a bipartite organization; but if the school were large and possessed the convenience of a gallery or class-room, the arrangement might consist of three divisions, the rotation being from desk to floor, floor to gallery, gallery to desk, it would be called a tripartite organization. The result of these arrangements is, that there are either two or three distinct courses of business going on at the same time, each course of business being regularly arranged and properly defined, and having strict reference to the gradual development of the education of the children in the school. There can be no haphazard work, no fortuitous employment; every one must be constantly engaged, the master teaching and the pupils learning. In Holland, one of the state laws declares — "The instruction shall be communicated simultaneously to all the pupils in the same class, and *the master shall take care that during that time the pupils of the two other classes are usefully employed.*"

Tripartite System.

If the school be large, the teaching power sufficient, and a class-room or gallery at his disposal, the organizer decides upon the tripartite system, and arranges the school into three divisions, the junior, the middle, and the senior. The junior division may be composed of the first class, the middle division of the second and sequel classes, and the senior division of the third and fourth classes. Sometimes it may be necessary, although to be avoided if possible, to break up a class and place the lower portion of it in one division, and the higher portion in another. For instance, the lower section of Second Book might be placed in the junior division; the middle division might include the higher section of second and the sequel class, and the senior division, as before, might contain the third and fourth classes. The head master might possibly have *special* charge of the senior division, the assistant master of the middle division, and a paid monitor might have the care of the junior division. The routine working of the tripartite system is very simple. The business of the day, say, commences with the senior division upon the floor. The head master, having a monitor in each draft of it, goes from draft to draft, revising what has been done by the monitors, and giving the substance of the lesson for the time being to each class as he passes along. The middle division is at this time, say, in the gallery, receiving a simultaneous lesson from the assistant master on some subject appropriate to the gallery; and the junior division is in the desks under the monitor, engaged in some befitting desk occupation. The head master, although having special charge of the senior division, is yet master of the whole school, and he must so contrive his duties, that whilst he teaches his own division, his influence and superintending function shall be felt and exercised in each of the other divisions of the school. Accordingly, whilst the divisions are disposed of as I have represented them, for the first lesson of the day, he must, in addition to the immediate instruction which he gives his own division, turn to the junior division in the desks, see how the monitor is managing it, take a momentary part in the teaching, and make a cursory inspection of what the children are employed at. This must be done without causing gaps or incoherency in the teaching of his own division, every draft of which must receive its share of his services, and every monitor in which must account to him for all that he is doing and for the proficiency of his pupils. He must also pay an occasional visit to the gallery, to see that his assistant is instructing the middle division with intelligence and effect, and that he exhibits evidence of having carefully prepared himself for the lesson. The order of the whole school is to be watched; a monitor inclined to rest upon his oars is to be aroused; a child disposed to idle is to be admonished. Every one must be employed; every monitor must be in earnest; every blackboard must show that work is being done. The quality of the instruction must be looked after; there must be no lounging or yawning or talking or whiling time away. He must know the extent of the instructions which have been given in the desks and in the gallery. The lesson has now lasted for thirty minutes; the bell announces the time up for a change, and in a moment the three divisions are simultaneously in motion. In less than half a minute they have all changed places. The senior division has gone from the floor to the desks; the junior from the desks to the gallery; the middle from the gallery to the drafts on the floor. There is no noise or confusion in the movement, no roaring out the orders; the stroke of the bell by the monitor of order, or the head master, is sufficient to announce the change. Immediately that the divisions reach their places, business is resumed. The head master starts his division at once to work in the desks; the assistant is going through a course with his drafts on the floor, similar to that pursued by the head master during the previous lesson; and the monitor is busy with his division in the gallery. The head master has more leisure now to pay attention to the junior and middle divisions, for his own division is engaged at some silent occupation in the desks, which only requires superintendence and occasional examination. He may possibly exchange with the monitor, and give the simultaneous lesson to the junior division in the gallery, or he may go from draft to draft through the middle division, and confer with his assistant as to the state of each draft, the industry or the ability of each monitor, and the whole scheme of the instruction of the division. It requires only an occasional minute to pass through the desks and overlook and correct the exercises of his own, the senior division, or he may spend four or five minutes with it consecutively, in explaining the principle of what it is engaged at, whether writing, or drawing, or book-keeping, or composition, or whatever else the lesson may happen to be. The same activity and the same watchfulness prevail during the second lesson, as during the first; and when the allotted time, thirty minutes, more or less, is up, the bell again rings, and again the simultaneous movement is made. As before, there is no noise; no confusion; no trampling of feet; no blundering; in silence and order each division reaches its new place. The junior division has moved from the gallery to the floor; the middle division now occupies the desks; and the senior division has marched to the gallery. Business has again commenced. The head master is giving a simultaneous lesson in mechanics, geometry, geography, or some other gallery subject; the monitor is engaged with his junior division on the floor; the assistant has the copies or slates, or pens or pencils, distributed in the desks, and his division is soon in full work. Every body is engaged. The change of place has relieved the minds of the pupils, the change of subject and position has protected the teachers from tedium or fatigue. Already much solid business has been done, much permanent good accomplished. The assistant has now time to turn for a moment from the desks to the junior division, and to coöperate with the monitor in instructing his drafts. He controls and directs the monitor whilst he aids him, keeps an eye to the general order of the room, and reports to the head master how matters proceed during his absence in the gallery. If the lesson which is being given in the gallery, admits of a break or rest in the middle, or in any part of it, the head master may take a brief glance at the principal school, have a word with the assistant or the monitor, and return to finish the lesson with his division, or, in order that he may occasionally have an opportunity of examining the pupils of the junior division in their drafts upon the floor, and those of the middle division whilst they are engaged at some desk occupation, he may change places with the assistant master, having previously given him notice of his intention, allowing the latter to give the gallery lesson to the senior division, whilst he himself takes charge of the divisions in the principal room. And thus in a quiet orderly rotation of this kind, in a life-like series of changes, with every body busy, every body happy; the head master guiding and inspiriting his assistant and his monitors; his influence every where; the instruction progressive; results, sterling and impressionable, produced at every lesson, is a school conducted on the tripartite system of organization.

Bipartite System.

By the Bipartite System the school is arranged in two divisions, the junior and the senior; and even without the assistance of a paid monitor, a teacher following the system laid down by the organizers could conduct a school with the same energy and effect, as that which I described in the case of the school organized on the tripartite system. The master of a bipartite school has always one division in the desks, another on the floor; the rotation is from desks to floor, and floor to desks. It does not require the same exertion to teach and superintend a bipartite, as a tripartite school. The master has a limited number of children; the operations of the school are concentrated into one room; he never quits the gaze of the main body of his pupils; the changes are easily made; and he has but to labor assiduously to insure success. The pupils of a tripartite school have the advantage of gallery instruction, which is not embraced in the bipartite system; but in other respects, the latter is just as effective as the former. By omitting what relates to the gallery, from the illustration which I gave of the tripartite system, and by substituting an intelligent paid or unpaid monitor for the assistant, the description would answer just as accurately for the simple operations of a bipartite school. I need not, therefore, describe the order of procedure in a school of the latter kind. The golden rule of either system is, that the teacher as well as the pupil is constantly employed; that he has a special duty for every moment of the day; and that he discharges this duty in such a way that he can superintend the whole of the operations of his school.

Modified Monitorial Teaching.

The Commissioners of National Education have always encouraged monitorial teaching; they have seen that a child who is employed, at stated times, in the teaching of a class of his fellow-pupils, is rendering most valuable assistance to the master, is improving himself in knowledge, and is obtaining a taste, and undergoing the best possible training for becoming a teacher. They approached the consideration of the question with the greatest care. They never contemplated conducting a large school solely by monitorial assistance; nor did they ever permit their monitors to forget that they are pupils. The first regular monitors in the service of the Board, were those in the Model Schools, Dublin, so far back as March, 1833. Some were paid, and others acted gratuitously. One of the greatest prizes and highest distinctions in the school was to attain to a monitorship. At one time during school hours the monitors taught some of the classes, and at another time they were themselves instructed; and, before school hours, there was a special course of instruction always given them.

The Commissioners, in their Report for 1837, refer to a new system of remunerating this class of young persons, in the Model Schools they were intending to establish throughout the country, which shows the permanency of the monitorial system at that early period in the history of the Board. They say, "that the money, so paid (in school fees), shall constitute a school fund, and that it shall be divided into such proportions, as we may determine, between the head master, his assistant, and the most advanced of the monitors whom he may employ." The system was always worked with moderation; it was free from the wild pretensions of the plans of Bell and Lancaster; and the pupilary and the monitorial functions were happily coalesced. It was the first rational trial, in my mind, which was given to monitorial teaching in these countries. In their Report for 1846, the Commissioners refer to the fruits of the system; they develop its organization, and they announce their determination to extend it to the Ordinary National Schools throughout the country. Each monitor was to serve for a period of four years; at the end of each year there was a sifting examination as to his proficiency; his teacher was required to employ him moderately as a monitor, and freely as a pupil; and his income increased each year up to the last of his service.

The system received a further development by the institution of a small staff of pupil-teachers in each of the Model Schools, who, in most cases, were the elite of those monitors who had completed their fourth year of service. It should be remembered, that the functions of the pupil-teacher and the monitor are very different; the former is more fo a teacher than a pupil; the latter more of a pupil than a teacher.

In 1855, the monitorial system received a still further extension of its usefulness, by the appointment of a number of junior paid monitors, commencing at eleven years of age, and serving for three years; to receive £2 for the first year, £3 the second, and £4 the third. If the conduct and attainments of a junior paid monitor be satisfactory at the end of his period of service, he is then drafted into the ranks of the senior paid monitors, to serve for four years more, and receiving respectively each year, £5, £6, £8, and £10. The paid monitor is now eighteen years of age, and should he persevere in his intention to become a teacher, and exhibit the necessary qualification, he may then be appointed to a pupil teachership in a District Model School, in which he remains for twelve months or two years. In this last stage, his professional education is carried to such a degree, as to qualify him in the most superior way for the offices of teaching; and at the expiration of his stay in the Model School, he is very likely at once nominated to the charge of an Ordinary National School. After serving a year or two as teacher of a school, and becoming acquainted with the difficulties and the responsibilities of the position, he is then brought up to Dublin to receive a final course of training in the Central Institution, Marlborough Street.

Elaborate and well designed as each step in this gradation of monitorial training really is, and superior as have been the results flowing from it, there yet remained a gap in it, the want of a regular scheme of unpaid monitors, which has been filled up by the system of organization, and which has tended to make our monitorial system still more comprehensive and perfect. When a school is being organized, the organizer selects a class which is called "the monitor's class," from amongst the most deserving and intelligent children of the school; he admits as many as possible into the class, in order that the duties may be distributed amongst them and be light upon each; he impresses upon them the importance of their new position and the extent of the distinction which is conferred upon them; and he then arranges that in lieu of the hour a day during which, on the average, they will be called upon to teach, they shall receive an hour's extra special instruction before or after the regular school business. Wherever practicable, it is better that the instruction should be given before school hours, as the minds of the children are fresh and the teacher himself is vigorous. The subjects which are specially taught during the time for extra instruction, are those which bear most upon the duties of the monitor, the preparation of notes of the lessons, and the art of teaching; and care is taken that this instruction supplementalizes and completes the course of business of the day. In order to encourage the teachers to take an interest in the instruction of their monitors, and as a recompense for the additional duty imposed upon them, the Commissioners grant an annual gratuity of £1 for each paid monitor of the first year, £1 10*s*. for each paid monitor of the second year, £3 for each paid monitor of the third or fourth year, and £4, as I have already stated, for the careful instruction of an unpaid monitor's class in any school which is organized. Every school that is organized will thus have its staff of unpaid monitors. Some of them, in the course of time, will be placed on the list of junior monitors, be again drafted into the class of senior monitors, and be finally appointed as pupil-teachers in a District Model School. During each stage they are pupils one hour, monitors the next; blending the didactic with the studious; rising in powers of thought and expression with their daily experience in teaching, and feeling the counterpoising and disciplinal influences of submission and authority.

SPECIMENS OF TIME TABLES.

No. 1.—Boys' School.—Tripartite Organization.

Time.	Junior Division.	Middle Division.	Senior Division.
10½ to 11	Home Lessons & Reading alternately. Floor.	Drawing. Desks.	Geography & Grammar alternately. Gallery.
11 to 11½	Writing. Desks.	Geography & Grammar alternately. Gallery.	Home Lessons. Floor.
11½ to 12	Geography & Grammar alternately. Gallery.	Home Lessons. Floor.	Writing. Desks.
12 to 12½	Arithmetic. Floor.	Writing. Desks.	Reading. Gallery.
12½ to 1	. . . .	Recreation in Playgr'd.	. . . .
1 to 1½	Theory of Arithmetic, Object Lesson, & Singing, alternately. Gallery.	Arithmetic. Floor.	Dictation. Desks.
1½ to 2	Reading and explanation. Floor.	Dictation. Desks.	Theory of Arithmetic, Object Lesson, & Singing, alternately. Gallery.
2 to 2½	Dictation and Drawing alternately. Desks.	Theory of Arithmetic, Object Lesson, & Singing alternately. Gallery.	Arithmetic, Algebra, &c. Floor.
2½ to 3	Tables and Mental Arithmetic. Gallery.	Reading. Floor.	Drawing. Desks.
3 to 3½	Dism	issed.	Algebra (M.), Mens. (T.), N. Phil. (W.), Geometry (Thurs.), Book-keeping (F.)
3½ to 4	Dism	issed.	Geometry (M.), Book-keeping (T.), Algebra (W.), Mens. (Thurs.), Nat. Philosophy (F.)

Religious Instruction from 10 to 10½ o'clock.

No. 2.—Girls' School.—Tripartite Organization.

Time.	Junior Division.		Middle Division.		Senior Division.	
H. M. H. M.	1st Class.	2d Class	Sequel.	3d Class.	4th Class.	5th Class.
10 30 to 10 55	Geography and Grammar. Gallery.		Dictation and Drawing. Desks.		Home Lessons. Floor.	
10 55 to 11 20	Dictation and Drawing. Desks.		Home Lessons. Floor.		Geography and Grammar. Gallery.	
11 20 to 11 45	Home Lessons. Floor.		Geography and Grammar. Gallery.		Dictation and Drawing. Desks.	
11 45 to 12 15	Reading. Gallery.		Writing. Desks.		Arithmetic. Floor.	
12 15 to 12 45	. . . General Les		son and Recreation in		Playground.	
12 45 to 1 15	Writing. Desks.		Reading. Floor.		Mon., Arithmetic; Tu., Object Lesson; Wed., Globes; Thurs., Art of Reading. Gallery.	
1 15 to 1 45	Reading. Floor.		Arithmetic. Gallery.		Writing. Desks.	
1 45 to 2 15	Arithmetic. Gallery.		Slate Arithmetic. Desks.		Reading. Gallery.	
2 15 to 2 30	. . . Work and		Natural History, or Do		mestic Economy. . .	
2 30 to 3 0	. . . .		Work and Singing.		. . . .	

Religious Instruction from 10 to 10½ o'clock.

No. 3.—Boys' School.—Bipartite Organization

Time.	Junior Division.		Senior Division.		
H. M. H. M.	1st Class	2d Class.	Sequel.	3d Class.	4th Class.
10 0 to 10 5	. . . . . . Inspection as		to personal cleanliness.		
10 5 to 10 45	Dictation.		Home Lessons.		
10 45 to 11 15	Home Lessons and Reading.		Dictation.		
10 15 to 11 45	Writing.		Arithmetic, Algebra, Geometry, &c.		
11 45 to 11 50	. . . Rolls called and atten		dance entered in Report Book. . .		
11 50 to 11 55	. . . . . . General		Lesson read.		
11 55 to 12 30	Reading and Spelling.		Writing		
12 30 to 12 40	. . . . Recre		ation.		
12 40 to 1 10	Lesson Exercise.		Geography and Grammar alternately.		
1 10 to 1 30	Geography.		Drawing and Composition alternately.		
1 30 to 2 0	Drawing.		Reading and Explanation.		
2 0 to 2 30	Arithmetic.		Arithmetic in Desks.		

Religious Instruction from 2½ to 3 o'clock.

No. 4.—Mixed School—Attended by Boys and Girls.—Bipartite Organization.

Time. H. M. H. M.	Junior Division consists of First Class and Third Draft of Second.	Senior Division consists of First and Second Draft of Second Class, Sequel, Third, and Fourth Classes.
10 30 to 11 0	Home Lessons.	Writing
11 0 to 11 30	Writing	Home Lessons.
11 30 to 11 55	Arithmetic.	Dictation.
11 55 to 12 0	Rolls called, Report entered,	and General Lesson read.
12 0 to 12 10	Boys Arithmetic.	Girls play.
12 10 to 12 20	Boys play.	Girls sew.
12 20 to 12 50	Lesson Exercise. Girls sew.	Arithmetic.
12 50 to 1 20	Reading.	Lesson Exercise. Girls sew.
1 20 to 1 40	Drawing. Girls sew.	Grammar and Geography alternately.
1 40 to 2 0	Grammar and Geography alternately.	Drawing. Girls sew.
2 0 to 2 30	Desk Arithmetic. Girls sew 10 minutes.	Reading.

Religious Instruction from 10 to 10½ o'clock, and from 2½ to 3 o'clock.

Syllabus of Lectures on Methods of Instruction.

I.—Method in General.

a. Definition.—Literal meaning: true method is a way of transit from one to the other of related things—a unity with progression: a mental act: relations of things are its materials: it is never arbitrary: the habit of method results from education: arrangement or order is not method: its great principles are union and progression: it leads to thoughtfulness, understanding, learning, and application.

b. Importance.—In domestic affairs: agriculture: construction of a watch: discourse, private or public: poetry—a play: meditation—science: education—starting point, object to be attained, and course: in this course the teacher should assist and direct, develop facts, prevent idleness, and advance gradually.

c. Necessity for.—All is chaos without it: no convenient arrangement: no natural disposition of things: no solid progress can be made: the rambling, incoherent character of ordinary teaching.

d. Divisions.—The two great methods are Synthesis or Induction, and Analysis or Deduction: the subordinate methods are the Socratic, Didactic, Elliptical, &c.

II.—The Two Great Methods.

By these every subject may be treated.

a. Synthesis.—Literal meaning of the term: is a putting together the parts or elements of any subject, step by step: also called Induction: proceeds from the simple to the complex—the particular to the general: it is the natural method: best adapted for elementary instruction: all educationalists are agreed upon this point: its great reviver and supporter in modern times was Pestalozzi (Zurich, 1745): he first taught *sounds*, then *words*, then *language*.

ILLUSTRATIONS. — READING — letters, syllables, words, sentences, paragraphs, &c.: the difficulty of teaching reading in our language arises from the different sounds of the same letter, particularly of each vowel: this is very considerably obviated by the synthetic arrangement of our Lesson Books: examine the First Book; its structure is purely synthetic: letters taken by twos to form such words as *an*, *ox*, &c.: in the next section we have distinct lessons on ă, ĕ, ĭ, ŏ, ŭ: then a mixture of all these in the next five lessons: the next five lessons are on ă and ā, ĕ and ē, ĭ and ī, ŏ and ō, ŭ and ū, respectively: in the concluding lessons of the section we have a mixture of these several sounds: the first five lessons of the third section give the short sounds of the vowels followed by *two consonants*, as *act*, *elm*, &c.: then a mixture of these: next *a* as in *ball*: *o* in *love*: a combination or mixture of *long* and *short* sounds and *double consonants*, as in *cheese*, *shell*, &c.: *diphthongs*: *digraphs*: silent *consonants*: peculiar sounds: combinations of *three* consonants: the beauty and method of this arrangement.

WRITING affords another example of synthesis: straight lines: curves: crotchet letters: capitals: Mulhauser's system; not his invention; he reduced the number of elements and arranged them synthetically: his merit lies in this.

DRAWING, another illustration of synthesis: straight lines | — \/: curves ◟◝ ⌒ ◡ ( ): combinations of these with straight lines: the circle: the ellipse: combinations, &c.

GEOMETRY — definitions, postulates, axioms, and propositions.

CHEMISTRY — the formation of water by detonating by means of the electric spark, the proper mixture of oxygen and hydrogen.

MUSIC affords another illustration of synthesis: Hullah's system of teaching music is an admirable example of pure synthesis.

b. Analysis. — Literal meaning of the term: the separation of a compound into its component parts: also called Deduction: proceeds from the complex to the simple — the general to the particular: the opposite of synthesis: Jacotot its great supporter in modern times.

ILLUSTRATIONS: — LANGUAGE — sentences, clauses, words, and letters: CHEMISTRY — the decomposition of water by means of the galvanic battery: GEOMETRY — the deducibles: bread.

c. Application. — Analysis has been compared to the efforts of a traveller proceeding from the mouth of a river to its source, and synthesis to the efforts of the same traveller in retracing his steps to the mouth: both methods used in the discovery of truth: hence, they may be mutually employed: exclusive use of either unsuccessful: the analytic more used in the discovery of truth, the synthetic in conveying instruction: he who would teach synthetically must first analyze: the method to be used depends on the subject, and the pupils, and the teacher: every teacher should be an expert analyst: analysis cannot be used in teaching signs to children: they get their knowledge synthetically: they do not analyze: hence, synthesis must prevail in every subject: consistent facts only should be stated: avoid analysis till the mind is considerably developed: it is not to be used in teaching the junior classes: "Easy Lessons on Reasoning" — the first eight chapters analytical, and the remaining ones synthetical.

III. — SUBORDINATE METHODS.

a. Socratic consists of a series of questions logically or methodically arranged: also called Catechetical or Interrogative: either analytic or synthetic: teaching may be catechetical without being Socratic: *this form* prevails in ordinary schools: the remedy: directions for questioning: —

1. The question, both in matter and language, should be within the comprehension of the pupils.
2. It should be precise, so as to admit of a definite answer.
3. It should be such as not to admit of a simple "yes" or "no" for the answer.
4. It should not require a very long answer.
5. The questions should be methodical — a progressive order or chain of questions: simple to complex, or *vice versa*.
6. The questions should be interspersed with explanatory remarks from the teacher.

The uses of this method are two: — First, for examination: second, for conveying instruction: "*Instruct* the pupils by questioning knowledge into them, and *examine* by questioning it out of them:" the catechetical consists of three stages: preliminary questions, questions of instruction, and questions of examination: a good plan to let pupils question one another.

Cautions: — simultaneous answers: defective answers: wrong answers: correct them indirectly: random answers: good answers — approbation: answers in a pupil's own language: to arouse the listless pupil: thinking time: suggestive questions: book or author: "Is he right?"

b. Elliptic Method. — What is it: used during the progress of the lesson, that is, in teaching, and in examination: particularly applicable in examining upon an anecdote: its advantages — does not interrupt the continuity of the lesson, is more concise than the catechetical, and relieves it: directions for forming ellipses: —

1. A good ellipsis is equivalent to a good question.
2. The elliptic method should be associated with the catechetical.
3. The ellipsis should be adapted to the capabilities of the pupils.
4. It should be adapted to their attainments.
5. It should not admit of an ambiguous answer.
6. It should not end with "*what*," "*how*," &c.

c. Dogmatic. — What is it: neither analytic nor synthetic: becomes analytic when accompanied by explanation.

d. Didactic.

e. Explanatory.

f. Picturing out, &c.

PART III.

ELEMENTARY INSTRUCTION IN SCOTLAND.

PAPERS XI.–XIV.

XI. ELEMENTARY EDUCATION IN SCOTLAND.

HISTORICAL SKETCH.

THE parochial schools of Scotland have been the pride of her own people and the admiration of enlightened men in all countries. The foundations of the system were laid in 1494. In that year it was enacted by the Scotch Parliament, that all barons and substantial freeholders throughout the realm should send their children to school from the age of six to nine years, and then to other seminaries to be instructed in the laws; that the country might be possessed of persons properly qualified to discharge the duties of sheriffs, and to fill other civil offices. Those who neglected to comply with the provisions of this statute were subjected to a penalty of £20. In 1560, John Knox and his compeers hold the following memorable language, in the "First Book of Discipline," presented to the nobility.

"Seeing that God has determined that his kirk here on earth shall be taught, not by angels, but by men; and seeing that men are born ignorant of God and of godliness; and seeing, also, that he ceaseth to illuminate men miraculously, of necessity it is, that your honors be most careful for the virtuous education and godly up-bringing of the youth of this realm. For as they must succeed to us, so we ought to be careful that they have knowledge, and erudition to profit and comfort that which ought to be most dear to us, to wit, the kirk and spouse of our Lord Jesus Christ. Of necessity, therefore, we judge it, that every several kirk have one schoolmaster appointed; such an one, at least, as is able to teach grammar and the Latin tongue, if the town be of any reputation. And further, we think it expedient, that in every notable town, there should be erected a *college*, in which the arts at least of rhetoric and logic, together with the tongues, be read by sufficient masters, for whom honest stipends must be appointed; as also that provision be made for those that are poor, and not able by themselves or their friends, to be sustained at letters.

The rich and potent may not be permitted to suffer their children to spend their youth in a vain idleness, as heretofore they have done; but they must be exhorted, and, by the censure of the kirk, compelled to dedicate their sons by good exercises to the profit of the kirk, and commonwealth; and this they must do, because they are able. The children of the poor must be supported and sustained on the charge of the kirk, trial being taken whether the spirit of docility be in them found, or not. If they be found apt to learning and letters, then may they not be permitted to reject learning, but must be charged to continue their study, so that the commonwealth may have some comfort by them; and for this purpose, must discreet, grave, and learned men be appointed to visit schools, for the trial of their exercise, profit, and continuance; to wit, the ministers and elders, with the best learned men in every town. A certain time must be appointed to reading and learning the catechism, and a certain time to grammar and to the Latin tongue, and a certain time to the arts of philosophy and the other tongues, and a certain time to that study in which they intend chiefly to travel for the profit of the commonwealth; which time being expired, the children should either proceed to further knowledge, or else they must be set to some handicraft, or to some other profitable exercise."

In 1615, an act of the Privy Council of Scotland empowered the bishops, along with the majority of the landlords or heritors, to establish a school in every parish in their respective dioceses, and to assess the lands for that purpose. This act of the privy council was confirmed by an act of the Scotch Parliament, in 1633; and under its authority, schools were established in the lower and the more cultivated districts of the country. But the system was still far from being complete; and the means of obtaining elementary instruction continued so very deficient, that it became necessary to make a more complete and certain provision for the establishment of schools. This was done by the famous act of 1696, the preamble of which states, that "Our Sovereign Lord, considering how prejudicial the want of schools in many places has been, and how beneficial the establishing and settling thereof will be to this church and kingdom, therefore, his Majesty, with advice and consent, &c." The act went on to order, that a school be established, and a schoolmaster appointed in every parish; and it further ordered that the landlords should be obliged to build a school-house, and a dwelling-house for the use of the master; and that they should pay him a salary, exclusive of the fees of his scholars; which should not fall short of 5*l.* 11*s.* 1*d.* a year, nor exceed 11*l.* 2*s.* 2*d.* The power of nominating and appointing the schoolmaster was vested in the landlords and the minister of the parish; and they were also invested with the power of fixing the fees to be paid him by the scholars. The general supervision of the schools was vested in the presbyteries in which they are respectively situated; who have also the power of censuring, suspending, and dismissing the masters, without their sentence being subject to the review of any other tribunal.

It has been usually expected that a Scotch parish schoolmaster, besides being a person of unexceptionable character, should be able to instruct his pupils in the reading of English, in the arts of writing and arithmetic, the more common and useful branches of practical mathematics, and that he should be possessed of such classical attainments as might qualify him for teaching Latin and the rudiments of Greek.

It would be no easy matter to exaggerate the beneficial effects of the elementary instruction obtained at parish schools, on the habits and industry of the people of Scotland. It has given to that part of the empire an importance to which it has no claim, either from fertility of soil or amount of population. The universal diffusion of schools, and the consequent education of the people, have opened to all classes paths to wealth, honor and distinction. Persons of the humblest origin have raised themselves to the highest eminence in every walk of ambition, and a spirit of forethought and energy, has been widely disseminated.

At the period when the act of 1696 was passed, Scotland, which had suffered greatly from misgovernment and religious persecutions under the reigns of Charles II. and his brother, James II., was in the most unprosperous condition. There is a passage in one of the discourses of the celebrated Scotch patriot, Fletcher of Saltoun, written in 1698, only two years after the act for the establishment of parochial schools had been passed, that sets the wretched state of the country in the most striking point of view.

"There are, at this day in Scotland, besides a great many families very meanly provided for by the church boxes, with others who, by living upon bad food, fall into various diseases, two hundred thousand people begging from door to door. These are not only no way advantageous, but a very grievous burden to so poor a country. And although the number of them be, perhaps, double to what it was formerly, by reason of this present great distress, yet in all times there has been about a hundred thousand of these vagabonds, who have lived without any regard or subjection, either to the laws of the land, or even those of God and nature. No magistrate could ever discover which way one in a hundred of these wretches died, or that ever they were baptized. Many murders have been discovered amongst them; and they are a most unspeakable oppression to poor tenants, who, if they do not give bread, or some kind of provision, to perhaps forty such villains in a day, are sure to be insulted by them. In years of plenty many thousands of them meet together in the mountains, where they feast and riot for many days; and at country weddings, markets, burials, and other the like public occasions, they are to be seen, both men and women, perpetually drunk, cursing, blaspheming, and fighting together. These are such outrageous disorders, that it were better for the nation they were sold for the gallies or the West Indies, than that they should continue any longer to be a burden and a curse upon us."

No country ever rose so rapidly from so frightful an abyss. In the autumn circuits or assizes for the year 1757, no one person was found guilty, in any part of the country, of a capital crime. And now, notwithstanding the increase of population, and a vast influx of paupers from Ireland, there are very few beggars in the country; nor has any assessment been imposed for the support of the poor, except in some of the large towns, and in the counties adjoining England; and even there it is so light as scarcely to be felt. This is a great and signal change. We can not, indeed, go quite so far as those who ascribe it entirely to the establishment of the parochial system of education. It is, no doubt, most true, that this system has had great influence in bringing about the change; but much must also be ascribed to the establishment of a regular and greatly improved system of government; to the abolition of hereditary jurisdictions, by the act of 1748; and to the introduction of what may, in its application to the vast majority of cases, be truly said to be a system of speedy, cheap and impartial justice. Certainly, however, it was the diffusion of education that enabled the people to avail themselves of these advantages; and which has, in consequence, led to a far more rapid improvement than has taken place in any other European country.

The General Assembly of the Church of Scotland has ever taken an active interest in the parochial schools. Immediately after the passage of the act of 1696, the Presbyteries were instructed to carry it into effect, and *Synods*, to make particular inquiry that it was done. In 1704, the Assembly undertook to supply schools to such part of the highlands and islands as could not be benefited by the act of 1696. In 1705, ministers were ordered to see that no parents neglected the teaching of their children to read. In 1706, it was recommended to such as settled schoolmasters, "to prefer men who had passed their course at colleges and universities, and have taken their degrees, to such as have not." In 1707, Synods and Presbyteries were directed to send into the General Assembly returns of the means and condition of the parochial schools.

The internal dissensions of Scotland and other causes, however, withdrew the public attention from the schools; and the advance of society in other respects, and the want of a corresponding advance in the wages of teachers, and the internal improvement of the schools, all combined to sink the condition of parochial education. In 1794, the General Assembly became roused to the subject. Visitation of the schools was enjoined on the clergy; and they were particularly instructed to inquire into the qualifications of the teachers. In 1802, the Assembly issued the following declaration, &c.:

"That parochial schoolmasters, by instilling into youth the principles of religion and morality, and solid and practical instruction, contribute to the improvement, order, and success of people of all ranks; and are therefore well entitled to public encouragement: That from the decrease in the value of money, their emoluments have descended below the gains of a day laborer: That it has been found impossible to procure persons properly qualified to fill parochial schools: That the whole order is sinking into a state of depression hurtful to their usefulness: That it is desirable that some means be devised to hold forth inducements to men of good principles and talents to undertake the office of parochial schoolmasters: And that such men would prove instrumental in counteracting the operations of those who may now, and afterward, attempt to poison the minds of the rising generation with principles inimical to religion, order, and the constitution in church and state."

In consequence of this declaration by the Church of Scotland, and of the complaints which were sent up from all parts of the country, Parliament, in the course of the next session, passed the famous act of 1803, which ordains as follows:

"That, in terms of the act of 1696, a school be established, and a schoolmaster appointed in every parish, the salary of the schoolmaster not to be under three hundred marks, (16*l.* 13*s.* 4*d.*.) nor above four hundred, (22*l.* 4*s.* 5*d.*:) That in large parishes, where one parochial school can not be of any effectual benefit, it shall be competent for the heritors and minister to raise a salary of six hundred marks, (33*l.* 6*s.* 8*d.*,) and to divide the same among two or more schoolmasters, as circumstances may require: That in every parish the heritors shall provide a school-house, and a dwelling-house for the schoolmaster, together with a piece of ground for a garden, the dwelling-house to consist of not more than two apartments, and the piece of ground to contain not less than one-fourth of a Scots acre; except in parishes where the salary has been raised to six hundred marks, in which the heritors shall be exempted from providing school-houses, dwelling-houses, and gardens: That the foregoing sums shall continue to be the salaries of parochial schoolmasters till the end of twenty-five years, when they shall be raised to the average value of not less than one chalder and a half of oatmeal, and not more than two chalders; except in parishes where the salaries are divided among two or more schoolmasters, in which case the whole sum so divided shall be raised to the value of three chalders; and so *toties quoties* at the end of every twenty-five years, unless altered by parliament: That none of the provisions of this act shall apply to parishes, which consist of a royal burgh, or part of a royal burgh: That the power of electing schoolmasters continue with the heritors and minister, a majority of whom shall also determine what branches of education are most necessary and important for the parish, and shall from time to time fix the school-fees as they shall deem expedient: That the presbyteries of the church shall judge whether candidates for schools possess the necessary qualifications, shall continue to superintend parochial schools, and shall be the sole judges in all charges against schoolmasters, without appeal or review."

In the year 1828, as the statute had provided, a small addition was made to the emoluments of the parochial schoolmasters, the *maximum* salary having been increased to 34*l.* 4*s.* 4*d.*, and the *minimum* to 25*l.* 13*s.* 3*d.*

The deplorable scenes of outrage and murder, which occurred in the streets of Edinburgh on the 1st of January, 1812, made the city clergy anxious to devise some means for diminishing the mass of crime and misery which was then brought to light. The scheme first proposed, and carried into execution, was to establish sabbath schools in all the parishes within the royalty, to which they gave the name of the Parochial Institutions for Religious Education. It was soon found, however, that the usefulness of these institutions was greatly limited, in consequence of a very great number of the children, for whose benefit they were intended, being unable to read. It was therefore proposed that, in connection with the sabbath schools, a day school should be established, which was accordingly opened on the 29th of April, 1813. This day school took the name of the Edinburgh Sessional School, from the circumstance of its being superintended by a minister or an elder from each kirk-session* in the city. The object of this school is to give instruction to the children of the poor in reading, writing, and arithmetic. Five gratis scholars may be recommended by each kirk-session; but the charge to all the others is sixpence per month. For many years the average attendance has been about 500; so that the school-fees, together with occasional donations, and a small share of the collections made annually at the church doors for the parochial institutions, have hitherto been sufficient to meet the ordinary expenses of the school. At first, no particular regulations were laid down for conducting the Sessional School; but after some years, the system of Dr. Bell was partially introduced. In the year 1819, circumstances led Mr. John Wood, Sheriff-deputy of the county of Peebles, to take an interest in the institution; and that benevolent individual began by degrees to give so much of his time and attention to it, that it soon became almost identified with his name. Under his superintendence, a large and commodious school-house was erected, and the system of teaching entirely re-modeled. In the latter department of his meritorious labors, Mr. Wood did not adopt the particular views of any one writer on education, but collected from all what he thought useful, and arranged it into a method of his own. So judicious is this plan of tuition, that it has not only been crowned with complete success in the Sessional

* A *kirk-session* is the lowest ecclesiastical court in Scotland, and consists of the clergymen of each congregation, with a small number of lay elders: it generally meets on Sunday, after public worship. The next court, in point of judicial authority, is the *presbytery*, which consists of all the clergymen within a certain district, with a lay elder from each congregation: this court meets once a month. All the presbyteries within given bounds, form a still higher court, called a *synod*, which meets twice in the year. The *General Assembly* is the supreme judicial and legislative court of the Church of Scotland; it consists of clerical and lay representatives from the several presbyteries, of a lay elder from each royal burgh, and of a Commissioner to represent his Majesty, and holds its sittings at Edinburgh, once a year, for about a fortnight.

School, but has been introduced, either partially, or entirely, into many other public and private seminaries, and has, in fact, given a new impulse to the work of elementary instruction throughout Scotland.

In 1837 the Sessional School was, with the approbation of Mr. Wood, constituted the Normal School of the General Assembly, and persons intending to offer themselves as teachers in schools aided by the Education Committee, were furnished with opportunities of conducting classes daily, and of being instructed with pupils of the same standing with themselves. Previous to this movement, in 1835, the Educational Society of Glasgow had been formed, among other purposes, "for the training of teachers for juvenile schools." In 1842, both of these institutions were placed under the direction of the Educational Committee of the Church of Scotland, and the Committee of Council on Education, in that year, made a grant of $50,000 toward providing a new building for the Normal School at Edinburgh, and completing a building already commenced for the Normal School at Glasgow. The two buildings cost about $130,000. In the same year the General Assembly appointed a superintendent to visit the schools aided by the education committee, and voted to aid in the erection of not less than five hundred new schools in connection with destitute parishes.

In 1841, William Watson, Sheriff-substitute of Aberdeenshire, commenced a system of Industrial Schools in Aberdeen, which embraced within its comprehensive grasp, all classes of idle, vagrant children, and in its beneficent operation, cleansed in two years a large town and county of juvenile criminals and beggars. Out of this experiment has grown the system of Ragged and Industrial Schools, which are now found in many of the large towns of England, Scotland and Ireland.

The permanent support of public, and in some cases, free schools, is provided for in certain localities by the income of funds left by will or donation for this purpose. It has been estimated that the annual income of these funds amounts to near $100,000.

There are a number of local societies, such as that for "Propagating Christian Knowledge," founded in 1701, the Gaelic School Society, that of Inverness, Ayrshire, &c., instituted for the purpose of supplying destitute parishes with schools, and of aiding those already established. The sums annually appropriated by the societies, amount to about $75,000.

The Church of Scotland and the Free Church of Scotland, together, appropriate, out of permanent funds and contributions collected in the churches for this purpose, the sum of $50,000 in aid of schools in destitute parishes, and in educating teachers for the parochial schools generally.

In 1836, the sum of $50,000 was voted by Parliament in aid of private subscriptions for the erection of school-houses, and the establishment of Model Schools.

Notwithstanding all these efforts, the extension of the system of parochial schools has not kept up with the growth of the population, especially in the manufacturing towns, and the quality of the education given has not met the demands of educated and wealthy families.

One of the most interesting facts in the history of parochial schools in Scotland, wherever they were adequately maintained, was the attendance in them of children from families widely separated in outward circumstances—the rich and the poor, the laborer with his hands and the laborer with his head. The presence of the children of the better educated and wealthier classes gave importance to the school in the estimation of the poor, and raised the whole tone and standard of manners and intellectual culture within the school and village. It created, too, a bond of union in society, which is thus beautifully noticed by Lord Brougham, (then Henry Brougham,) in some remarks at a public dinner in Edinburgh, in 1825.

"A public school, like the Old High School of Edinburgh, is invaluable, and for what is it so? It is because men of the highest and lowest rank in society send their children to be educated together. The oldest friend I have in the world, your worthy Vice President, and myself, were at the High School of Edinburgh together, and in the same class along with others, who still possess our friendship, and some of them in a rank of life still higher than his. One of them was a nobleman, who is now in the House of Peers; and some of them were sons of shopkeepers in the lowest parts of the Cowgate of Edinburgh—shops of the most inferior description—and one or two of them were the sons of menial servants in the town. There they were, sitting side by side, giving and taking places from each other, without the slightest impression on the part of my noble friends of any superiority on their parts to the other boys, or any ideas of inferiority on the part of the other boys to them; and this is my reason for preferring the Old High School of Edinburgh to other, and what may be termed more patrician schools, however well regulated or conducted." * *

Another distinguished pupil of this school remarks: "Several circumstances distinguished the High School beyond any other which I attended: for instance, variety of ranks; for I used to sit between a youth of a ducal family and the son of a poor cobler." This fact will distinguish good public schools of a superior grade, provided they are cheap, every where. The High School, like the parochial schools of Scotland, generally is not a free school, but the quarterly charge for tuition is small as compared with the actual cost of instruction in private institutions of the same grade. The fees payable in advance are £1. 1*s.* per quarter. The course of instruction embraces all the branches of the liberal education suitable to boys, from eight to sixteen years of age.

In connection with this mention of the High School of Edinburgh, we will introduce a few historical facts, which point back to a very early period for the origin of the system of parochial schools in Scotland. The funds out of which the edifice now occupied by the high school was built, and which was completed in 1829, at an expense of £34,199, were derived, in part, from endowments belonging to the Abbey of Holyrood, founded by David I., in 1236, with which this school was connected as early as 1500. The school came into the management of the magistrates of Edinburgh in 1566. Prior to that, a grammar school had existed in the Cannongate, under the charge of the friars of the same monastery, "past the memorie of man," as is stated in a memorial to the privy council, in 1580. In the year 1173, Perth and Stirling had their school, of which the monks of Dumfernline were directors. Authentic records introduce us to similar institutions in the towns of Aberdeen and Ayr. The schools in the county of Roxburgh were under the care of the monks of Kelso as early as 1241; those of St. Andrew, in 1233; and those of Montrose, in 1329.

The success of the school system of Scotland is to be attributed to their being erected on a permanent and conspicuous foundation, and to that particular constitution which made the situation of the teacher desirable to young men of education, for its competent salary, permanence, and social consideration. Of the three modes of providing for popular instruction,—that in which the scholars pay every thing, and the public nothing; that in which the public pay every thing by a tax on property, or by avails of permanent funds, and the scholars nothing; and that in which the burden is shared by both,—the latter was adopted in the original plan of the Scotch schools. The existence of the school was not left to chance or charity, but was permanently fixed by law on every parish. The school edifice and the residence of the teacher were to be provided for by public assessment, as much as the church, or the public road, or bridge. The salary of the teachers was so far fixed by law, that it could not sink below the means of a respectable maintenance according to the standard of living in a majority of the country parishes.

Dr. Chalmers, in his valuable "*Considerations on the System of Parochial Schools in Scotland*," thus notices some of the peculiarities of the system:

"The universality of the habit of education in our Lowland parishes, is certainly a very striking fact; nor do we think that the mere lowness of the price forms the whole explanation of it. There is more than may appear at first sight, in the very circumstance of a marked and separate edifice, standing visibly out to the eye of the people, with its familiar and oft-repeated designation. There is also much in the constant residence of a teacher, moving through the people of his locality, and of recognized office and distinction amongst them. And perhaps there is most of all in the tie which binds the locality itself to the parochial seminary, that has long stood as the place of repair, for the successive young belonging to the parish; for it is thus that one family borrows its practice from another—and the example spreads from house to house, till it embraces the whole of the assigned neighborhood—and the act of sending their children to the school, passes at length into one of the tacit, but well-understood proprieties of the vicinage—and new families just fall, as if by infection, into the habit of the old ones—so as, in fact, to give a kind of firm, mechanical certainty to the operation of a habit, from which it were violence and singularity to depart, and in virtue of which, education has acquired a universality in Scotland, which is unknown in the other countries of the world."

The best minds of Scotland are at this time directed to a re-construction of the system of parochial schools, or to such an extension of its benefits, as will reach at once, the wants of the large towns, and of the sparsely populated parishes. Among the plans set forth, we have seen nothing more complete than the following, which is signed by some of the most distinguished names in Scotland.

"The subscribers of this document, believing that the state of Scotland and the general feeling of its inhabitants justify and demand the legislative establishment of a comprehensive plan of national education, have determined that an effort shall be made to unite the friends of this great cause on principles at once so general and so definite as to form a basis for practical legislation; and with this view, they adopt the following resolutions, and recommend them to the consideration of the country:—

1. That while it might be difficult to describe, with a near approach to statistical precision, the exact condition of Scotland at this moment in regard to education, there can be no doubt that, as a people, we have greatly sunk from our former elevated position among educated nations, and that a large proportion of our youth are left without education, to grow up in an ignorance miserable to themselves and dangerous to society; that this state of matters is the more melancholy, as this educational destitution is found chiefly among the masses of our crowded cities, in our manufacturing and mining districts, and in the Highlands and Islands of Scotland, where the people are not likely spontaneously to provide instruction for themselves; that the quality of education, even where it does exist, is often as defective as its quantity; and that this is a state of things requiring an immediate remedy.

2. That the subscribers hold it to be of vital and primary importance that sound religious instruction be communicated to all the youth of the land by teachers duly qualified; and they express this conviction in the full belief that there will never be any enlargement of education in Scotland, on a popular and national basis, which will not carry with it an extended distribution of religious instruction; while, from the strong religious views entertained by the great mass of the people of this country, and the interest which they take in the matter of education, the subscribers can see in the increase of knowledge only an enlargement of the desire and of the capacity to communicate a full religious education to the generation whose parents have participated in this advantage.

3. That the parish schools of Scotland are quite inadequate to the educational wants of the country, and are defective and objectionable in consequence of the smallness of the class invested with the patronage, the limited portion of the community from which the teachers are selected, the general inadequacy of their remuneration, and the system of management applicable to the schools, inferring as it does the exclusive control of church courts; that a general system of national education, on a sound and popular basis, and capable of communicating instruction to all classes of the community, is urgently called for; and that provision should be made to include in any such scheme, not only all the parish schools, but also all existing schools, wherever they are required by the necessities of the population, whose supporters may be desirous to avail themselves of its advantages.

4. That the teachers appointed under the system contemplated by the subscribers should not be required by law to subscribe any religious test; that Normal Schools for the training of teachers should be established; that, under a general arrangement for the examination of the qualifications of schoolmasters, the possession of a license of certificate of qualification should be necessary to entitle a teacher to become a candidate for any school under the national system; and that provision should be made for the adequate remuneration of all teachers who may be so appointed.

5. That the duty and responsibility of communicating religious instruction to children have, in the opinion of the subscribers, been committed by God to their parents, and through them to such teachers as they may choose to intrust with that duty; that in the numerous schools throughout Scotland, which have been founded and supported by private contribution, the religious element has always held a prominent place; and that, were the power of selecting the masters, fixing the branches to be taught, and managing the schools, at present vested by law in the Heritors of Scotland and the Presbyteries of the Established Church, to be transferred to the heads of families under a national system of education, the subscribers would regard such an arrangement as affording not only a basis of union for the great mass of the people of this country, but a far better security than any that at present exists both for a good secular and a good Christian education.

6. That in regard to a legislative measure, the subscribers are of opinion, with the late lamented Dr. Chalmers, that 'there is no other method of extrication,' from the difficulties with which the question of education in connection with religion is encompassed in this country, than the plan suggested by him as the only practicable one,—namely, 'That in any public measure for helping on the education of the people, government [should] abstain from introducing the element of religion at all into their part of the scheme, and this, not because

they held the matter to be insignificant—the contrary might be strongly expressed in the preamble of their act—but on the ground that, in the present divided state of the Christian world, they would take no cognizance of, just because they would attempt no control over, the religion of applicants for aid—leaving this matter entire to the parties who had to do with the erection and management of the schools which they had been called upon to assist. A grant by the State upon this footing might be regarded as being appropriately and exclusively the expression of their value for a good secular education.'

7. That in order to secure the confidence of the people of Scotland generally in a national system of education, as well as to secure its efficiency, the following should be its main features:—1st, That Local Boards should be established, the members to be appointed by popular election, on the principle of giving the franchise to all male heads of families being householders; and with these Boards should lie the selection of masters, the general management of the schools, and the right, without undue interference with the master, to direct the branches of education to be taught. 2d, That there should be a general superintending authority, so constituted as to secure the public confidence, and to be responsible to the country through Parliament, which, without superseding the Local Boards, should see that their duties are not neglected—prevent abuses from being perpetrated through carelessness or design—check extravagant expenditure—protect the interests of all parties—collect and preserve the general statistics of education—and diffuse throughout the country, by communication with the local boards, such knowledge on the subject of education, and such enlightened views, as their authoritative position, and their command of aid from the highest intellects in the country, may enable them to communicate.

Were such a system adopted, the subscribers are of opinion that it would be quite unnecessary either for the legislature or any central authority to dictate or control the education to be imparted in the National Schools, or to prescribe any subject to be taught, or book to be used; and should a measure founded on these suggestions become law, not only would the subscribers feel it to be their duty, but they confidently believe the ministers and religious communities in the various localities would see it to be theirs, to use all their influence in promoting such arrangements as, in the working of the plan, would effectually secure a sound religious education to the children attending the schools."

In September, 1847, on the invitation of an educational association of Glasgow, a large meeting of teachers from various parts of Scotland was convened in the High School of Edinburgh, and "the Educational Institute of Scotland" was formed. The following is the preamble of the constitution:

"As the office of a public teacher is one of great responsibility, and of much importance to the welfare of the community; as it requires for its right discharge, a considerable amount of professional acquirements and skill; and as there is no organized body in Scotland, whose duty it is to ascertain and certify the qualifications of those intending to enter upon this office, and whose attestation shall be a sufficient recommendation to the individual, and guarantee to his employers; it is expedient that the teachers of Scotland, agreeably to the practice of other liberal professions, should unite for the purpose of supplying this defect in the educational arrangements of the country, and thereby of increasing their efficiency, improving their condition, and raising the standard of education in general."

Among the modes of advancing the objects of the Institute, are specified "the dissemination of a knowledge of the theory and practice of education by means of public lectures, and the institution of libraries."

Since the foregoing account of the parochial school system was written, the author has availed himself of a brief visit to that country to gather additional information respecting the means and state of education generally in Scotland. The population, in 1851, was 2,870,784, of which number, one-sixth, or about 480,000 children between the ages of four and sixteen years, should be at school a portion of the year. From the best data he could consult, there were not much more than half that number at school in the year 1852; and of those who attended school, less than one half were to be found in the parochial schools. The following is a brief summary of the different classes of schools:

I. *Parochial Schools.*—The law, since 1696, provides for one school in each of the 1,049 parishes, which is not incorporated as a Royal Burgh, by authorizing the heritors or proprietors of land to the value of £100, with the minister, to elect, and, in default of such election for four months, the county commissioners to elect a schoolmaster. The person thus elected, after obtaining from the presbytery within which the parish is situated, a certificate of his being qualified, and signing the confession of faith and formula of the Church of Scotland, is entitled to an annual salary of not less than £25, a commodious house for a school, a dwelling house of at least two apartments and a kitchen, an inclosed garden of at least one acre, or its equivalent in money, and such school fees from the parents as shall be fixed by the heritors and minister. The teacher must comply with the regulations of the presbytery, which is represented practically by the minister of the parish. The parochial school is not strictly a primary school, but in many parishes embraces instruction which belongs to the academy or grammar school, the teacher being not unfrequently a graduate of one of the universities, and many of the scholars being fitted there for the university. Neither is it a free school. The sum (£30,000) realized from school fees, in 1851, exceeded the amount raised by tax on the heritors, exclusive of the accommodation of the school-house, and the master's dwelling and garden. The whole number attending these schools in 1852 was about 75,000.

II. *Royal Burgh Schools.*—These exist in parishes included within the limits of towns incorporated by royal charter, and which are exempt from the operation of the parochial system. They are generally grammar schools, and are established by the municipal council, and supported partly by endowment or municipal grant, but principally by school fees. The whole number of Burgh Schools does not exceed 90, with about 5,500 pupils.

III. *Sessional Schools.*—These are confined to the populous parishes, and are established and supported by the Kirk session, in addition to the parochial school. In 1851, there were 104 Sessional schools, with 11,892 scholars.

IV. *Assembly Schools.*—Since 1824, the General Assembly has maintained, out of a system of church collections, schools in destitute districts, principally in the Highlands and Islands. In 1851, there were 118 schools in these districts, and 44 in other parts of Scotland, maintained by the Assembly, besides 14 female schools, with an attendance, in all, of over 14,000 pupils. Besides these schools, the Assembly maintains two normal schools, one at Edinburgh, and one at Glasgow, erected at an expense of over £25,000, ($125,000) in which 137 teachers were in training.

V. *Society Schools.*—To aid certain localities, not reached by the parochial system, societies have been formed. The earliest of these, was the "*Society for Propagating Christian Knowledge,*" commenced in 1701, and having now a permanent fund of over £100,000, the annual income of which supports or aids about 230 schools. The *Gaelic School Society* in Edinburgh, and an auxilliary society in Glasgow, maintain about 80 schools for poor children of Highland parentage.

VI. *Adventure or Private Schools.*—In all large towns, schools are established by private teachers at their own risks, and dependent on the fees or tuition of the scholars. They originate in the real or alleged demand of additional accommodations to those provided by law, or by various religious communions, or for a better or at least a different kind of instruction.

VII. *Orphan Houses and other Endowed Schools.* — Besides the richly endowed hospitals and asylums for orphan children in Edinburgh and other cities of Scotland, there are other large endowments for the permanent support of ordinary elementary and grammar schools. These endowments yield an income of over £50,000, and support over 100 independent schools,* besides augmenting† the salaries of a still larger number of teachers.

VIII. *Schools in connection with the Free Church.*—The disruption of the Church of Scotland, and the separate organization of the Free Church, has led to prodigious efforts on the part of the latter to establish a system of schools in connection with the churches in its communion. The system embraces a college, with special reference to theological education, two normal schools for the training of teachers, a grammar school in every large town, an elementary school in connection with every church, and subordinate schools and evening classes in large congregations, and missionary schools in destitute localities. The expense is borne by a general education fund, made up of annual collections, and applicable to building purposes, and a schoolmasters' sustentation fund, in aid of teachers' salaries. The results of this movement are not fully developed—but it has absorbed into the connection of the Free Church many adventure or private schools, and thus placed them

---

* Among these may be mentioned Milne's Free School of Fochabers The founder of this school was Alexander Milne, who was born in Fochabers, but amassed an estate of £100,000 in New Orleans, which he bequeathed by will to found a Free School in his native place, for the benefit of the parishes of Bellie and Ordifish.

† James Dick, born at Forres. at his death, bequeathed an estate of over £118,788, the income of which is applied to the augmentation of the salaries of parochial schoolmasters in the counties of Aberdeen, Banff, and Moray.

under better supervision, and on a more certain foundation; and, at the same time, while it has multiplied schools in destitute districts, it has weakened the efficiency of the parochial and assembly schools by establishing competing schools in the same neighborhood. In 1851, the schools in connection with the Free Church and aided by its fund were as follows:—

424 Congregational schools—schools connected with particular congregations, and receiving aid from the Schoolmasters' Sustentation fund of the Church.
174 Side or district schools.
13 Municipal schools—planted in destitute localities.
5 Grammar schools.
2 Normal schools.

618 Schools, with 689 teachers, and 67,956 pupils, toward which the Educational Committee of the Church contributed £14,000, or about $85,000, in the year 1851. The sum contributed in school fees and local subscriptions to these schools exceeds £15,000, or $70,000.

To the pupils attending the above schools, the committee add 15,000 children attending evening schools, making 73,387 scholars under the general supervision and influence of the Free Church in 1851.

IX. *Schools in connection with the Scotch Episcopal Church, the United Presbyterian Churches, and the Roman Catholic Church.*—The disruption of the Free from the Established Church of Scotland, has led to efforts on the part of the different religious communions to establish separate denominational schools, and has awakened public attention to the religious tests and other features of the parochial system which are inconsistent with the claims of different denominations to an equality of civil privileges. The statistics of these denominational schools in 1852 were as follows:—

United Presbyterian Church	has	54	schools,	with	5,009	scholars.
Scotch Episcopal	"	"	68	"	"	5,900	"
Roman Catholic	"	"	40	"	"	5,000	"
Other denominations have		15	"	"	1,000	"	

In addition to the educational bequests mentioned in the Note on the foregoing page, the following may be cited:—

George Heriot, celebrated by Sir Walter Scott as the "*Jingling Geordie*" of James VI., was borne in 1563. He succeeded to his father's business as a goldsmith, in one of the booths then and for long afterwards attached to St. Giles' Church.

In 1597, he was appointed goldsmith to Ann of Denmark, the Queen Consort, and in 1601, jeweler to the King. The Queen was very fond of jewelry for her own use, profuse in presents of it to others, and very changeful in her taste for particular articles. In all these respects she was naturally followed by the court circles of the time.

On the removal of the court to London, Heriot, who accompanied it, found a greatly enlarged field for his business, as well as more wealthy customers. He was also a money lender, as it was then usual for men in his business to be, and before his death had amassed a considerable fortune.

Soon after his death his money, with the exception of some legacies, was invested, as he had previously wished, in the purchase of land in the immediate vicinity of the city of Edinburgh. The subsequent value of the property, as the site mainly of the new town of Edinburgh, countenanced a greatly exaggerated estimate of the original bequest, which was somewhat less than 24,000*l.*, though the annual income is now not less than 16,500*l.*

Nothing was at first contemplated, or till 1846 thought of, beyond the hospital, which bears the name of "*Heriot's*," and which was the first of the kind in Scotland. The model in the founder's mind was the Bluecoat School in London.

Instead of extending the hospital itself, as had been contemplated, an Act of Parliament was obtained to build and maintain out-schools on the Heriot foundation. These were not to be of the hospital kind, but ordinary day-schools, for the class of children that usually attend the Sessional and other schools, provided in large towns for the children of the laboring classes. The children are neither lodged, fed, nor clothed, but receive their education *gratis on condition of regularity of attendance.*

The sites have been selected in the most densely-peopled quarters of the town. Twelve have now been erected; eight for boys and girls, and four for infants.

ANDREW BELL, whose name is well known as opposed to that of Lancaster in the controversy regarding the merit of originating the monitorial system, left his fortune, with the exception of special legacies, in two large bequests, for the purpose of carrying out those educational views which he had gradually been led to consider as of the utmost importance to the whole human race.

One deed, dated May, 1830, conveyed in trust to the then provost of St. Andrew's, the two ministers of the town church, to be followed by their successors, and to Professor Alexander, to be followed by the Sheriff Depute of Fife, and his successors in office, 120,000*l.*, to be employed in the erection and maintenance of schools on the Madras, or monitorial system. Of this sum 60,000*l.* was allotted to St. Andrew's, 10,000*l.* to Edinburgh, 10,000*l.* to Glasgow, 10,000*l.* to Leith, 10,000*l.* to Aberdeen, 10,000*l.* to Inverness, and 10,000*l.* to a Naval school in London. As an equivalent to 10,000*l.*, the estate of Egmor, valued at 400*l.* a year, was left to Cupar of Fife for a similar purpose.

Another deed conveyed the residue of his estate, with special and general directions, to other trustees, of whom Lord Leven and Mr. Cook, W. S., are now the acting parties. This yielded at the time about 25,000*l.*, which has been considerably increased by accumulations from interest.

XII. SUBJECTS AND METHODS OF EARLY EDUCATION.*

BY JAMES CURRIE, A. M.

Principal of the Church of Scotland Training College, Edinburgh.

I. INTRODUCTION.—GENERAL CHARACTER OF THE INSTRUCTION.

1. PHYSICAL exercise for the healthy growth and relaxation of the body; exercises of observation, conception, and imagination, for the mind; and moral and religious lessons for the cultivation of the heart, are the principal engagements of infancy, and, therefore, of the infant school. Under physical exercise we include the right regulation of the physical circumstances in which the child receives his instruction, which, though he is outwardly passive under them, very greatly influence the tone of his mind and feelings; physical exercises, strictly so called, requiring positive bodily exertion, such as he is subjected to in the school-room; the recreation of the play-ground, where, in full apparent freedom, he is yet under superintendence; and, lastly, singing, which in one aspect of it is one of the keenest of all the physical incitements to the general work of the school. Exercises of observation and conception are given by means of things or objects such as the eye can see, the hand handle, and the ear hear; their appearance to the eye in color, form, and size; to the touch in weight, hardness, and other qualities; to the ear in sound. As a distinct exercise of observation by this last sense, is to be mentioned the combination of musical sounds by singing. Exercises of imagination are found in the elementary geographical lesson, in which the pupil is required to group natural things, such as he has already observed, variously as to place; and in reading or relating stories of real or imaginary life. Moral and religious instruction comprises doctrines or points for belief in morality and religion; feelings to be cherished, and actions to be practiced. This kind of instruction may for the most part be best given in the form of incidental reflections throughout the daily work, and exercises of devotion.

2. The instruction of the infant school is carried on through the medium of familiar conversation between the teacher and his pupils.

---

* From "*Principles and Practice of Early and Infant School Education.*" Edinburgh Thomas Constable & Co.

They can not read when they begin their course; yet they have powers which are eager for activity. The most advanced of them, though they may be able to read very easy narrative, have not that facility that enables them to extract information from what they read; and, even if by the teacher's help they can turn this to account, they ought to know, and they are able to know, much more than this source can supply them with. It is most unnatural to make their reading-power the measure of their intellectual activity. It is by conversation upon actual objects and feelings that the parent first calls forth the glimmering intelligence of the child; so it is by conversation, or, to call it by its technical name, oral instruction, that the teacher is to continue the process which the parent has begun. By this method alone is it possible to give the child a stimulus to attention; for it interposes nothing between the child and the living voice of his instructor to prevent the full play of that mutual sympathy which is the very breath of the school life. By this method alone is it possible to give an impulse to his observation, imagination, curiosity; for it submits interesting things to his inspection, while it humors his volatility by turning aside to notice any thing that attracts his own notice by the way. And by this method alone is it possible to engage the child in full activity without restraining his freedom; the teacher presents to him things of which he already knows something, and, speaking to him as a friend and companion rather than as a preceptor, easily draws from him the knowledge he is so willing to show.

3. There is another aspect of this oral instruction not less important; it is our great means for giving the child the use of his mother-tongue. When the time comes for the parent to initiate the child in this, she does not make "set" lessons on language; she speaks to him of things and feelings in which he will be interested, knowing that in learning of these he is learning to speak.* The teacher must proceed in the same way. Language is nothing apart from ideas; words must be taught to the infant in connection with things. This aspect of oral instruction is frequently forgotten in the infant school; otherwise, it would not be thrust into the subordinate place it is often found to occupy. In oral instruction, whatever subjects it deals with, the teacher should remember that he is training the child to language. He must engage each one, therefore, in conversation; he must vary the subjects of conversation, as each subject has a vocabulary particular to itself; he must watch attentively to secure a gradual increase of power over words, content at first, perhaps, with their utterance of single words, but looking, by and by, for phrases, and then easy sen-

* See Girard, chap. i.

tences. Nor must he be wearied with repetitions, as the children are just beginning their exercises in language, and require long and varied practice to learn its endless variety of forms. Whilst oral instruction is the rule in the infant school, it is pre-eminently the want of the youngest infants. The teacher may observe in the elder pupils some diminution of interest in the oral lessons; this is one of the symptoms that the time has come for advancing them from the infant school. They have now got a practical command over speech which serves them for all ordinary purposes; and they not only require, but feel a desire for, the new field of exercise which book-instruction gives. But the younger children have no such command of language; and what they want most is such a knowledge of the names of common things and actions as shall enable them to characterize these when they see them, and to hold intercourse with their fellows regarding them. Hence their acquisition of language goes on with great rapidity. The younger the children, therefore, the more should they be occupied by oral instruction.

4. What are we to say of book-learning, which in point of fact occupies a place in all infant schools? The power to read with intelligence is the greatest benefit which school-education bestows upon us; for this enables us to educate ourselves in after-life. Not unnaturally, therefore, the reading-lesson occupies the principal place in the common school. It does not follow from this, however, that it should hold, as it is commonly made to hold, the principal place in the infant school; for the proper study of it requires certain powers which the child in the first period of his education does not possess. It is self-evident that reading is an effort for the child, whilst conversation is not. Even to read mechanically is so. It is impossible for him to fix his eye upon a page, and to thread his way from word to word, and from line to line, in their close succession, without feeling a strain upon the nerves of sight, and through them upon the brain, which has only to be prolonged to do him serious injury. To read with intelligence is a double or complex effort. It includes all the effort necessary for mechanical reading, and in addition the effort which is necessary to keep the mind moving at the same rate as the eye. The mechanical motion tends from the first to outstrip the mental; and the effort to keep them together is the most painful to which the infant can be subjected. The brain is under a twofold strain; that from without through the nerves of sight, and that from within proceeding from the reflex action of the mind upon it. Well has it been said that "it is not so much the actual process of learning to read as the consequences of being able to read during early years

that are to be guarded against." From physical considerations, then —which dictate the fundamental law in infant education—we conclude that is imprudent to have the child's attention fixed for any considerable portion of a day on a book.*

5. Systematic reading from books should be delayed till the child becomes physically capable of a little conscious effort, which it does about four and a half or five years of age; that is to say, it may be carried on during the last year and a half or two years of his infant-school attendance. There would be no harm in delaying it even till the very end of this period; his progress would be all the more rapid when he did begin. But on this point the teacher may defer to the desires of parents, provided he do not urge forward the child too much with the reading-task, by keeping him at his book over an immoderate proportion of his daily time. During the first half of his infant-school attendance, the child should be prepared for learning to read rather than engaged in reading. His oral instruction will put him in possession of a large number of words with their applications; without which it is altogether a solecism to engage him with written language. It can also make him acquainted with the forms and sounds of all the most familiar words of the language, and with the elements of words, in connection with the *things* which it speaks to him about, not only without tasking him, but by way of amusement.

With these limitations we may consent to reckon the reading-lesson as one of the occupations of the infant school.

6. The following table presents at one view the different parts of the school-work :†—

PHYSICAL, ...	1. Healthy condition of the school-room. 2. Physical exercises in school. 3. Recreation in play-ground. 4. Singing.

* The limits to the use of books in infancy are nowhere better defined than in the work on *Home Education*," above referred to, chap. iv , which should be carefully read by the student. "Not a syllable of book learning," says the author, "need have been acquired, and scarcely a task learned, and yet the mind of a child in its fifth year, may be not merely in a state of the happiest moral activity, but may be intellectually alive, and actually possessed too of various information concerning the visible universe; and he may have made acquaintance with whatever presents itself under a pleasurable aspect, (and assuredly nothing but what is agreeable should be presented to the infant mind.") Speaking of the labor of the child in reading with intelligence, he says, "There is a particular jar [between the motion of the eye and that of the mind,] a want of synchronous movement, and a sense of distress, and a strain which quickly exhaust the power of attention; or if persisted in, impair the brain. . . . It is certain that the ruddy vigor of high health will almost always be found in inverse proportion to the hours in the day, during which a child has a book before his eyes."

† On the general character of early instruction, Marcel has an excellent chapter in his work on "*Language*." See book iv. chap. i.

INTELLECTUAL,
1. Objects.
2. Number.
3. Color and form.
4. Sound.
5. Geography.
6. Reading and reciting to pupils.
7. Reading and spelling.

MORAL AND RELIGIOUS,
1. Doctrines and points for belief.
2. Duties.
3. Incidental instruction.
4. Devotions.

II. PHYSICAL CIRCUMSTANCES OF INSTRUCTION.

7. It is the first and constant duty of the infant-school teacher to attend to the regulation of physical influences. He has to deal with a large number of children, of tender age, of different temperaments and degrees of health, keenly susceptible of external influence on their bodily frames, and liable to suffer from even slight irregularities. A disregard of the plainest laws of health in the school-room must, in the end, affect the health of the children; in the meantime it prevents them deriving any benefit from the work in which they are engaged. For his own sake, too, the teacher must be mindful of these laws. If he is depressed in spirits, not to say enfeebled in health, the whole school suffers. One day's work in a close room may not affect him much; but no constitution can resist the effect of a continuance of this over several years. It is in the fact that such influences operate almost imperceptibly that his danger lies. Let the sanitary state of his school-room, then, be his first thought when he enters it in the morning; and let his thoughts recur to this at the end of every lesson.

8. First in order of importance is ventilation. The school must have a steady supply of fresh air throughout the day. The symptoms which indicate neglect of this are very plain. Perhaps the teacher may often be conscious of a dimness of eyesight, a giddiness of head, a general languor and drowsiness which nothing can shake off and for which he can not well account; it is probable they are largely owing to his working in impure air. Many continue even to bear headaches, sickness, or sore throat, without ever suspecting that these are owing to the same cause. If such be the effect on the teacher, is it to be supposed that the children will escape? Their countenances and the tones of their voice are some index to the state of the school. And if the teacher will scrutinize these, as he should accustom himself to do, he will be kept from error in this matter. It is not enough that the air be fresh in the morning; or that the windows be opened and closed fitfully throughout the day, just as acci-

dent may direct his attention to the subject, or that there be one stereotyped degree of ventilation throughout the year; this is a matter that requires attention from hour to hour, and from day to day, according to wind and weather. An atmosphere which is fresh in the morning very soon becomes vitiated unless it is changed, and the teacher may not be conscious of its condition; he can not do better than go outside occasionally for the sake of comparison.

9. Another important feature is the keeping up of a proper degree of temperature in the school-room. Every school should have a fire; and the teacher should regulate it throughout the day. Where there is neither fire nor stove, we need hardly wonder that the windows should be kept close to obtain warmth. Both extremes of temperature must be avoided. If the temperature be kept habitually too high, the children will become nervously sensitive of cold. At the same time the air may be fresh and yet injuriously cold. Particularly are drafts to be avoided. As many schools are constructed, it is hardly possible to avoid these. A class should not stand immediately under an open window or behind a door.

10. The management of light is not so much attended to as it ought to be in schools. A dull, dingy room, in which the eye has to strain itself to discern objects, must depress the elasticity of children. On the other hand, a body of bright light, streaming into the faces of a class, can not but produce restlessness and inattention. If the windows are not well placed for the distribution of light, the teacher may, perhaps, modify their effects by regulating the state of the blinds. An infant school should be a light, cheerful place.* A stone-color is most suitable for the walls.

11. Children in the infant school are not capable of much tension, either mental or bodily. A great deal of inattention is often attributed to willful trifling, which would be more justly traced to the teacher's disregard of the physical capacity of the children.

The hours of school attendance should not be long; never exceeding four daily; distributed thus, two hours in the forenoon, and two in the afternoon, with an hour's interval; or better, into three sittings of an hour and twenty minutes each with two intervals of three quarters each, if the circumstances of the school admit of it. Whatever children can do in school, they will accomplish within these hours; to prolong their attendance to five or six hours, instead of aiding their progress, will only injure their health. Parents are often found to

* The management of light and ventilation is referred to in some of the inspector's reports, in the "*Minutes of Council*," *e. g.*, Rev. M. Mitchell's, 1853-54, and 1855-56, and Rev. Mr Bellair's, 1855-56.

desire this longer attendance; but the teacher must be guided neither by their ignorance nor their selfishness, but by his own consciousness of what is right in this matter; for it is he alone that would have to bear the responsibility in the event of any child being injured.

12. Every morning and afternoon should be occupied by various lessons. A lesson should not average in duration more than a quarter of an hour, and on no account exceed twenty minutes. It is hard enough to sustain the attention even for this period, and no child will be able to retain more than we can tell him within it. The teacher should subdivide his lesson rather than trespass beyond this limit. Lessons of different kinds, *i. e.*, occupying different senses, should follow each other; this is a great relief. It is absurd to speak of these frequent changes as causing loss of time.

13. Not more than three-fourths of each morning and afternoon period should be devoted to instruction which involves mental occupation. It is necessary to have short intervals between the lessons for physical relaxation; which is given either by a general change of position in the classes throughout the school, accompanied with marching, or by special bodily movements. Further, it may sometimes be necessary during the lesson to recall the wandering thoughts of one or of all by such movements for a few seconds; the teacher may easily read in the countenances of the children when such a stimulus will be beneficial. Too much either of sitting or of standing is objectionable; they must alternate. Variety in every species of activity is the rule of the infant school.

14. There is an endless choice in the selection of physical exercises; body, legs, arms, and fingers, may all be called into requisition. Bending of the body, a sudden passing from a sitting to a standing posture and *vice versa*, easy gymnastic movements of the arms, beating time with the feet, action amongst the different fingers, and imitation of the trades, are the most common. The secret of success in these is alertness in calling for them and in varying them rapidly and decidedly. They should be performed by the children, partly at word of command, but chiefly in silence, by imitation, with eyes fixed on the example of the teacher.* Free and confident motion is indispensable in the teacher whilst giving them; they will fail unless the children see and feel the influence of this. Smartness in giving these exercises is not the least of the accomplishments of the infant-school

* "And pupil teachers, if any, be present." It may be observed that these exercises are better done when *all* the assistants in the room take part in them. The children seem to expect that all present should join with them. This is the effect of sympathy. For the various physical exercises that may be given, either in school or in play-ground, see "*Exercises for the Improvement of the Senses*," (L. U. K.,) Part III.

teacher; it turns into an aid to discipline that disinclination to remain still which would otherwise disturb him. The only limitation to them is that they should not be ungraceful in themselves, or unduly noisy, or tend to produce any kind of discomfort in the class-room. Those are particularly suitable which from the rhythm of their motion admit of being accompanied by singing; of which marching is the most prominent.

15. We shall do no more than simply notice here the exercises of the play-ground, as the provisions for these will require us to speak of them more minutely afterwards. The proportion of play to work must in the case of infants be very large. The usual daily hour of interval is not enough for the purposes of training; but circumstances often make it impracticable to give more. As already indicated, the work should be twice broken by recreation; a third opportunity may be had before the children enter school in the morning. They should return home immediately, however, after the last school hour. As the play-hour serves both to give recreation to the children and to afford room for the exhibition of their dispositions in actions toward each other, it should be given under superintendence.* Such a watchfulness would serve no good purpose with advanced pupils, but the reverse; young children, however, do not feel it to be any restraint on them.

16. Finally, singing is a physical exercise of wonderful power in relieving the more serious work of the school. All must observe its calming influence after exertion, and its cheering preparative influence on exertion yet to be undergone. It is like the ventilation of the mind; giving an outlet for the oppressed and pent-up feelings of the child, the hearty utterance of which is at all times refreshing. The younger children are, the more and the more frequent the necessity for the relaxation thus afforded; there can be no successful management of the infant school without it. We shall afterwards have to notice its value as a branch of instruction; what we insist on at present is its value as an instrument in a skillful hand for keeping alive the tone and activity of the school.

III. INTELLECTUAL INSTRUCTION.

1. *The Object-Lesson.*

17. We are not to confound, as is very often done, the object-lesson of the infant school with the lesson on "common things," as that phrase is now generally understood. The latter, strictly speak-

---

* Hence the name of "uncovered school-room," which Mr. Stow has applied to the play-ground.

ing, is not designed for the infant school at all; the purpose of it is to give a certain amount of practical information about the things and processes of every-day life to children sufficiently advanced to turn it to account. The object-lesson of the infant school has quite a different purpose. Its predominant aspect is the mental exercise it gives; it is meant to awaken the intelligence, and to cultivate its different phases of observation, conception, and taste, without which little satisfactory progress can be made in their future education. It is a disciplining, not a utilitarian, process; the information it gives is a means, not an end.

18. The range of this department of instruction is exceedingly comprehensive. It draws its materials from all the branches of knowledge dealing with things which can interest the child or exercise his mind. Thus, it is Natural History for children; for it directs their attention to animals of all classes, domestic and others, their qualities, habits, and uses—to trees, and plants, and flowers—to the metals, and other minerals, which, from their properties, are in constant use. It is Physical Science for children; for it leads them to observe the phenomena of the heavens, sun, moon, and stars, the seasons, with the light and heat which mark the changes of the weather, and the properties of the bodies which form the mass of matter around us. It is Domestic Economy for children; for it exhibits to them the things and processes daily used in their homes, and the way to use them rightly. It is Industrial and Social Economy for children; for it describes the various trades, processes in different walks of art, and the arrangements as to the division of labor which society has sanctioned for carrying these on in harmony and mutual dependence. It is Physiology for children; for it tells them of their own bodies, and the uses of the various members for physical and mental ends, with the way to use them best and to avoid their abuse. It is the "science of common things" for children; for it disregards nothing which can come under their notice in their intercourse with their fellows or their superiors. And, finally, as we shall afterwards see more distinctly, it is Geography for children; since it has favorite subjects of illustration in mountain and river, forest, plain, and desert, the different climates of the earth, with their productions and the habits of their peoples, the populous city, and the scattered wigwams of the savage.

19. All the things fit to be treated of in the object-lesson may be said to be "familiar things;" at the same time, the phrase must not be too narrowly interpreted. We can not consent to confine our instruction to things which the child has the opportunity of actually seeing. By familiar things we are to understand all those things on

which he can exercise his mind in the way which is familiar to it. For example, amongst animals, the lion, the camel, the elephant, and the reindeer afford scope for reasoning of as familiar a kind as the horse, the sheep, or the dog. In the vegetable world, similar remarks may be made on the tea-plant, the sugar-cane, and the cotton-plant, relatively to the potato, the turnip, and flax—upon rice and maize relatively to barley and wheat—on the palm-tree and the cedar relatively to the fir and the oak. All the child's observation of things at home, of the materials for food, clothing, building, or industry, prepares him for observing the corresponding things in other lands, and is in turn greatly enlightened by this extended observation. Of course, things around him claim his first regard; that is not, however, because the reasoning about them is easier, but because the observation of them is more palpable and definite, and it is observation that is to be first exercised. As soon as he can reason at all, his imagination must be sent abroad. There is no force in the argument sometimes employed that his attention should be confined solely or chiefly to things about him on the ground that he may not be long at school, or that his future occupation may throw him into the midst of these. The mental exercise of the infant school must be held to be independent of such considerations of time, place, or professional prospects.

20. The features common to all infant-school teaching will be noticed further on; so that, with regard to the method of the object-lesson, it need be only here stated that, as it has in view the cultivation of the conception and the higher faculty of relation, so both of these faculties must be exercised in their proper time and degree. The former can not be furnished and stimulated, unless the object be actually subjected to the observation of the class, and that not to one sense only, but to all that are available. It is not enough, for instance, that in a lesson on "glass," the teacher should simply hold it up before the class, and on the strength of his own observation proceed to state its properties. It is *their* sight, and touch, and hearing, that are to be exercised; so that he should first show it, then put it into the hands of the children to feel it, and then ring it on the table. This is often neglected, just because it seems needless; thus it may seem enough if the teacher squeeze a sponge to show that it is soft and elastic, or if he handle lead to show that it is heavy. But this is only an exercise of sight to the class; tactual as well as ocular inspection by some, if not by all, must be allowed. How far the reasoning of a child may be carried, and in what way it is to be exercised, has been indicated already.

21. One great use of the object-lesson is to cultivate the conceptive faculty in connection with language; for which purpose it should, from first to last, present much of the descriptive part of our vocabulary, dealing first with those terms that denote qualities broadly recognizable, before descending to the finer shades. The describing and the naming the qualities of things is thus quite a legitimate resource in these lessons; still, as bodies possess the same qualities frequently in common, there is great danger of the object-lesson falling into a barren monotony of plan. To remedy this, the teacher will observe, (1.) that the universal qualities of bodies, or those which are nearly so, such as *useful*, *opaque*, *inanimate*, need be very seldom mentioned; (2.) that when qualities are given, there should be a *real* exercise of observation given with the name (§ 20;) and, (3.) that the mentioning of these qualities should not, in the general case, constitute the whole of the lesson, but that other facts should be communicated, which are interesting to be known, and which exercise the imagination, the sense of beauty, and the moral feelings. This will prevent the verbal aspect of the lesson from obtaining too great predominance over the real.

22. A very common, though little noticed, practical error in the giving of object-lessons, is the neglect to distinguish the different stages in the advancement of the children to whom they are given. An infant of four years is a very different being, intellectually, from one of six or seven; and can only to a very small extent follow a lesson addressed to him. Even in dealing with things we shall not secure the child's attention, unless we select things which interest him, and unless we address him in a suitable way. Perhaps we may distinguish three stages of the object-lesson. In the first, the pupil is required to distinguish objects by their names, to notice their parts, their color, and, a little later, their simpler properties, such as form and size; in the second, the lesson should deal chiefly with qualities and uses of things; and in the third, with a more formal statement of the various relations in which things stand to each other, resemblance, causality, &c. These three stages may correspond approximately to the first year of attendance at the school, the second year, and the third year or part of year.

23. The following list exhibits a variety of subjects suitable for the first stage :—

1.—*Natural History.*

Sheep.	Bear.	Bee.	A Tree.
Cat.	Wolf.	Ant.	Rose.
Dog.	Fox.	Spider.	Lily.
Horse.	Hen.	Butterfly.	Daisy.

Cow.
Donkey.
Goat.
Rabbit.
Hare.
Pig.
Deer.
Mouse.
Lion.
Elephant.
Camel.

Goose.
Duck.
Swan.
Crow.
Sparrow.
Swallow.
Robin.
Pigeon.
Parrot.
Pheasant.
Common Fly.

Herring.
Haddock.
Crab.
Whale.
Worm.
Adder.
Snake.
Mussel.
Whelk.
Oyster.
Snail.

Dandelion.
Potato.
Turnip.
Carrot.
Cabbage.
Grass.
Leaves.
Apple.
Pear.
Cherry.
Berries.

2.—*Domestic Economy.*

Different kinds of Houses.
" parts of a House.
" kinds of Roofs.
Things used in Kitchen.
" " Parlor.
" " Bedroom.
Things for sitting on.
" lying on.
" eating with.
" drinking with.
Breakfast-Table.
Dinner-Table
Tea-Table.

Articles for Breakfast and Tea.
" Dinner.
Things for washing with.
Parts of our Clothes.
Vessels for holding things.
A Fire.
Utensils for Fire.
Making of Tea.
" Coffee.
Porridge.
Bread.
Candle.
A Bed.

3.—*Physiology.*

The Body.
Arms.
Hands.
Fingers.
Legs.
Feet.
Toes.
Head.
Face.

The Eyes.
Mouth.
Nose.
Ears.
Throat.
Skin.
Bones.
Blood.
Voice.

Hearing.
Seeing.
Feeling.
Smelling.
Tasting.
Running.
Leaping.
Walking.
Hopping.

Swimming.
Standing.
Breathing.
Sleeping.
Dreaming.
Singing.
Dancing.
Drinking.
Eating

4.—*Industrial and Social Economy.*

Things for writing with.
" sewing with.
The Cabinetmaker's Shop.
Baker's "
Grocer's "
Butcher's "
Shoemaker's "
Tailor's "
Painter's "
Fruiterer's "
Smith's "
The Farm.
Garden.
Ship.
Sailor.
Letter-Carrier.
Soldier.

The Railway.
What their parents do in a day.
" brothers "
" sisters "
" themselves "
Materials for Clothing.
Leather.
Materials for Building.
" Furniture.
Making Stockings.
The School.
Work of the School.
The Family Circle.
One's Relations.
Things of Stone.
" Iron.
" Tin.

5.—*Common Things.*

Cart.
Table.

Clock.
Watch.

Gas-light.
Drawers.

Nails.
Thread.

Chair.	Picture.	Slate.	Rope.
Stool.	Window.	Ink.	Pen.
Coach.	Book.	Pins.	Quill.
Railway Carriage.	Scales.	Needles.	Shilling.
A Letter.	Bottle.	Scissors.	Egg.
Money.	Blackboard.	Thimble.	Penknife.

6.—*Physical Appearances.*

Aspects of Sky.	Aspects of Water.	Aspects of Winter.
" Sun.	" Vapor.	" Thunder and Lightning.
" Moon.	" Ice.	" Rainbow.
" Stars.	" Heat.	" Day.
" Rain.	" Cold.	" Night.
" Snow.	" Spring.	" a Storm.
" Clouds.	" Summer.	" a Calm.
" Wind.	" Autumn.	

Supposing an object-lesson to be given daily, the list of subjects now presented, making allowance for the geography object-lessons which are not here included, is large enough for a year's work; and it may readily be increased.

24. For the second stage or year, many of the foregoing subjects might be repeated, and information given on a larger scale; whilst a further selection of common objects should be made to exemplify the qualities of bodies and put the pupils in possession of descriptive terms. The following list is sufficient to exemplify all the more familiar qualities; it may be enlarged or varied at the teacher's discretion:—

Cork.	Salt.	Paste.	Silk.
Leather.	Whalebone.	Slate.	Barley.
India-Rubber.	Sand.	Coal.	Rice.
Sponge.	Bread.	Soap.	Pepper.
Glass.	Lead.	Horse-hair.	Ginger.
Iron.	Copper.	Feathers.	Rose.
Wood.	Gold.	Clay.	Hawthorn.
Water.	Tin.	Oil.	Tea.
Paper.	Mercury.	Vinegar.	Coffee.
Common Sugar.	Honey.	Chalk.	Milk.
Loaf-Sugar.	Gum Arabic.	Earthenware.	Balloon.
Wool.	Starch.	Putty.	Air-bubble.
Sealing-Wax.	Glue.	Wire.	Bladder.

After some practice in the observation of qualities inherent in particular objects, the idea of the quality in the abstract will gradually form itself, and the ground may be gone over again in reverse order. Thus a quality may be selected, *e. g.*, heavy, hard, smooth, brittle, elastic, tough, liquid, viscid, fibrous, pliable, fusible, porous, inflammable, or the like, and various objects which have the quality brought together, and the uses to which they are put in virtue of the quality slightly noticed.

25. In the third stage, the pupil is required to trace relations more,

particularly of resemblance and of connection by way of cause and effect. Such relations have not been altogether unnoticed in the middle series of lessons, but the teacher has greater latitude now. Most of the subjects of the second year are quite serviceable still; for there are many points connected with the form and utility of these which the pupil has not yet been able to comprehend. Bearing in mind that it is more in the tracing of incidental connections that the sense of relation is cultivated at this period than by the antithetic statements of the explicit comparison, the following list presents subjects in the latter exercise for which the pupils may be deemed quite competent:—

Dog and Cat.
Dog and Wolf.
Dog and Fox.
Newfoundland Dog and Shepherd's Dog.
Cat and Tiger.
Rabbit and Hare.
Bee and Wasp.
Snail and Whelk.
Duck and Goose.
Swallow and Sparrow.
Coverings of Birds.
Wool and Hair.
Nails and Claws.
Needle and Pin.
Pen and Pencil.
Steel-pen and Quill.
Knife and Penknife.
Cart and Wheelbarrow.
Shilling and Penny.
Cotton and Wool.
Clock and Watch.
Grate and Stove.
Snow, Hail, and Ice.
Hand and Foot.
The Teeth.
Hoof of Horse and of Camel.
Whale and Fish.
Thumb and Forefinger.
Bird and Quadruped.
Animal and Plant.
Plant and Mineral.
Tree and Shrub.
Common Shrubs.
" Flowers.
" Wild Flowers.
" Trees.
" Shells.
" Esculents.
Different states of Weather.
" kinds of Clouds.
" " Fuel.
" " Bread.
" " Soap.
" " Sugar.
" " Coal.
" " Glass.
" " Nails.
" " Stockings.
" " Lamps and Lights.
" " Gloves.
" " Locks and Keys.

26. The following are examples in outline of the different kinds of lessons suitable for the younger infants—the successive points for illustration being indicated in italics:—

I. *The Sheep.*

Subject of lesson familiarly introduced—animal you often see passing you on streets, a great many going together, what can it be? The *sheep*. Where going to? the *market*, to be *killed*—*poor* sheep—*flock* explained—the *shepherd* in charge—the *dogs*.

Where did they come from? the *fields*—in the *country*—where the *grass* grows—the *green* grass—which the sheep *eat*. Did you ever see them in the field? What doing? *walking about*—*lying down*, sometimes at the *wall*, sometimes *under bush*—*eating*.

Were you ever near one? how *afraid* it is—how *big* is it? bigger than the *cat?* its color *white*, sometimes *black*. How it feels when you *touch* or *handle* it—*soft* all over, from the *wool* on its *back*. How many legs? What they are like, and its little feet? *marks* left by a flock on the street or road. Its *face*, *ears*, &c., sometimes *horns;* and with the horns they sometimes *box*—(if the season be spring, the *lambs* should be noticed.)

The sheep is very *gentle* and *timid*, and *hurts* no one—little children sometimes *throw stones* at it, which is very *wrong*—they should be *kind* to it.

II. A Bed.

Willie—was sleeping a short time ago; what made him do so? he was *tired.* Should we let him *sleep long?*

The *use* of sleep—how *every one*, their fathers and mothers, brothers, sisters, &c., need it. *What* makes us sleep? the *time* for it?

What we sleep in? a *bed*—put off our clothes, for we are to sleep *till morning*—what is in the bed? *blankets* for warmth, *sheets* to be *nice and clean*—*coverlet*, perhaps white or blue—the *mattress* thick and soft below.

We should be *thankful* to have comfortable beds to go to at night—some *have not*—*God gives* us this and all good things—what should we *do when we* go to bed? *Ask God* to take care of us through the night—and when we rise.

III. The Mouth.

Refer to previous lessons (perhaps) on face, eyes, nose, &c. What more to be seen on the face—look at your neighbors' faces—*mouth.*

Open your mouths, shut them, point to them—different things the mouth is for—*eating* when we are *hungry*, *drinking* when *thirsty*, *singing* when *merry*, *yawning* when *sleepy*, *speaking* when we have *any thing to say*, &c.

Many things in mouth—*tongue*, which is soft—move them—little children sometimes *put out their* tongues, which is *naughty*—the *teeth* for *chewing*, *e.g.*, bread, flesh, &c.—many of them *small* and *white*, and sometimes they *come out*—and for *shutting* the mouth we have *lips.*

We should take care what we *put into* our mouths—little children sometimes *hurt themselves* by putting strange things into their mouths—they should *ask* their mothers or their teacher first.

IV. The Baker's Shop.

What do children bring to school with them? their books, playthings, but also their "*piece*" (lunch)—what they bring it for? to eat—*when* do we eat? different things we eat, bread, flesh, &c.

I have a piece of (wheaten) bread in my hand—its *color? hard* or soft? Where it comes from? the *baker's shop*—What does the *baker do?* does he give it *for nothing? what does he give it for*—you often buy for yourselves and your parents.

What have *you seen* in a baker's shop? *different* things named, with their color, and form, and degree of hardness.

How should we do without the baker, who makes so many nice things?

Yesterday I saw some *crumbs* on floor, and a small piece of bread—notice how *easily broken* it is, and how *very careful* we should be with it not to waste it.

Conclude with the anecdote of the dog that went to the baker's shop every day, with the halfpenny, and brought back the roll; or with the verses on "The Crust of Bread."

V. The Cart.

Tell me all the things you met in coming to school this morning—things named till they come to *cart*—the *man* that drove it, and the *horse* or *donkey* that pulled it.

Its parts—*wheels* and *spokes*—then the *shafts* for the horse to go in—the cart itself, its *bottom*, and *sides*, and *back*. Draw or show model of cart or its parts.

What did you see *in* the cart? *coals*—get a *number of different* things named that they may have seen in carts—have *you ever* been carried in a cart? And when the cart is heavily laden it has *two horses*, and the other pulls by a *chain*.

What could we do without the cart? Little children sometimes get into their way in the street or road; which is wrong, for they may be hurt. So when we see a cart coming, we must quickly get out of its way.

VI. Rain.

What kind of day is this, children? day described, *sunny*, *clear*, *warm*, perhaps. Is it *always* so? What *other* kind of days have we? they are named till *rain* is mentioned. What was the *last* rainy day?

Where does the rain *come from?* what does it do? *wets* every thing, streets, houses, &c.

You can not *play* on rainy days—perhaps you wish there were none—but they *are needed* to make things grow, *trees* and *grass* and *flowers*, &c.—did you ever notice how fresh and green all things look *after a shower?*

If you go out on rainy day what happens to you? your clothes are wet and spoiled, perhaps—children sometimes go *out in* rain, which they should not do.

Who sends us both rain and sunshine? Verses on the Rain.

27. The following are outlines of more advanced lessons, such as might be given at the second stage; the first on a very familiar animal, in which the information is given on a larger scale than it would be to the youngest classes, the second on an object, with a special view to illustrate the qualities of it, and the third on a quality.

I. The Elephant.

The *general* size of the animal should be first noticed; its *hight* and *bulk* make it the largest of quadrupeds; compare it in hight *with a man*, and in bulk with the *largest animal* known among us, the horse.

What kind of *legs* it must have, *thick* and *strong*, like *pillars;* what it has got for *toes.* Infer whether it has *joints* in its legs or not; *necessary* to enable it to kneel for service of man. Its *head* big and heavy, with *hanging* ears; infer the character of its *neck.* With a short neck, could it drink *off the ground?* The substitute in the shape of a *trunk;* describe this; illustrate its power by an anecdote—*Mouth* and *teeth* and *tusks*—*skin* compared with that of the horse in color and covering. Show the picture of the animal.

How *it lives*—perhaps some one may infer from its structure that it is *not flesh-eating*—eats *leaves* and *twigs of trees* in his tamed state; *rice* also is given.

Countries it lives in, and is intended for.

How it *is used* after being tamed—being strong, it can *do much work*—*carries* loads, *pulls* or *pushes* carriages, &c.—used for *riding* on—easy to *tame*, *gentle*, and *knows well* what is required of it.

NOTE.—The *inferential* or *comparative* aspect may be extended or diminished to suit the class addressed. The order here followed is, (1.) structure; (2.) habits; (3.) uses. This is not always the best order to follow. Thus, in a lesson on the "camel" the habits or mode of life had better precede the structure. The rule is to begin with whatever the children know best about the subject. In the lesson before us, all that they know about it may be its general size and appearance, with the presence of the trunk or tusks.

II. The Sponge.

Notice the various uses of the sponge for *domestic purposes*

Then its qualities *by inspection.* Its *color*, light yellow; *soft* to the touch; *light* in weight; easily squeezed by the hand, *i. e.*, *compressible;* springs back again after being squeezed, *i. e.*, *elastic;* full of little canals, *i. e. porous;* sucks in water, *i. e.*, *absorbent;* when torn, seen to consist of a *fibrous* substance.

[The different qualities here indicated must be clearly wrought out by the teacher, and verified by the class, before the terms are given. According to the advancement of the class, *other articles* may be named exhibiting any of the same qualities.]

How it is useful *for washing*—because of its *sucking in* the water, and throwing it out again *under pressure*, the fibers resuming their place again from their *elasticity*, and ready to suck in as before.

Tell the interesting story of "where and how it grows," and "how it is got."

III. The term "Porous."

The term is supposed to have been illustrated before in connection with some familiar substance—sponge, for instance, as above.

Mention *any thing porous? Sponge. How do we know* it is porous? what like is it? Full of holes or apertures. Can we always *see* the holes? No; they may be *very small.* How do we know it is porous, then? Any *other thing* that is porous? *Bread;* illustrate how it so. *Wood* is porous; illustrate this by wood that has been lying in water. *Loaf sugar* is porous; illustrate this by the appearance it presents when dropped into tea. On the strength of these illustrations, an easy definition of "porous" may be given: porous means "full of pores, or little pipes." Then they may be told of the porousness *of the skin.* [The microscope would be of great use in such a lesson.]

28. There is considerable danger that the teacher may confound the character of the "early" and "middle" object-lesson in his practice, and therefore a number of examples have been given of these, particularly of the "early," for analysis. There is less danger of erring in this way with the "higher" object-lesson, so that one outline may suffice:—

THE COMMON HEN		THE COMMON DUCK
	lives	
on the ground about our houses,		about ponds, in which it swims,
	has a body,	
short and nearly round,		long and flat, for resting on water,

	a neck,	
thick and upright,		longer and curving, to stretch under water,
	a bill,	
short and sharp, to peck in ground,		broad and flat, to grope in the mud,
	feet,	
with separate claws, fitted for walking and for scraping in the ground,		with a web, and placed far behind for swimming, so that it does not walk well,
	feathers,	
short, and not fitted for water, either for a pond or for rain.		longer, and constructed so as to be light, and to throw off the water.

29. As soon as the children can read print or script hand, this ability should be turned to account in the object-lesson. The heads of topics, or the names of qualities, should be written down to make them acquainted with the forms of the words as well as to aid the impressing of the lesson; and the blackboard should present at the conclusion of each lesson the outline of what has been said. The previous paragraph exhibits what might be the appearance of the notes on the board at the end of the lesson there sketched. The necessity of *sketching* on the blackboard for illustration, as it is felt in other lessons as well as in the object-lesson, will be adverted to heareafter.

30. The moral aspect of the object-lesson is not to be overlooked. There is abundant room, incidentally, for profitable reflection. This may take different forms. Thus, in lessons on objects drawn from the region of nature, as from animal life from the phenomena of the world, the beauty in form or in adaptation which we constantly meet with can not but impress us with the wisdom, power, and goodness of the Creator, and with a sense of the homage which is therefore due to Him. From various animals we learn useful practical lessons regarding personal or social habits; as order and diligence from the ant, perseverence from the spider, &c.; also, we have suggested to us our duty towards them. And from certain kinds of lessons such duties may be easily inferred as that of using temperately and thankfully our gifts, of kindness to others less favored than ourselves, of economy, &c. Some of these are exemplified in the outlines given in § 26. No general rules can be laid down either for the mode or the extent of such reflections; beyond these, that where occasion presents itself we are bound to avail ourselves of it, and that the reflections should be short and naturally suggested by the lesson.*

* Mayo's "*Object-Lessons*" may profitably be consulted by the teacher for materials; also "*Information on Common Objects*," published by the Home and Colonial School Society

2. *Number.*

31. Number is a property of things which the child observes very early, so that he may be exercised upon it as soon as he enters the infant school. He may be subjected to a mental training of very considerable extent in connection with number; regarding which the following remarks may be made :—

(1.) As the child comes by his first notions of number through the medium of objects, so his whole training must be based on the observation of these. He does not use numbers for their own sake, but for the sake of the things to be numbered; he counts by sight, and is not able to abstract number from the things. He knows what five balls or five horses are, but he can not reason about the number five. If it be understood that it is with number as a property of bodies that the infant has to deal, and not with the science of number, it will be very clear that he must not be occupied with rules or technical operations. This preliminary course of training is termed "on number," to distinguish it from the formal study of arithmetic. The teacher will find no aid for it in the ordinary text-books or arithmetic; he must give it orally himself.

32.—(2.) The child's observation of number will carry him over a wider range of numerical operation than might be thought possible at first view. It will enable him to work practically in all the fundamental operations. The outline of the course may be conveniently indicated by the following heads :—(*a.*) Practical Numeration; (*b.*) The Adding of Numbers; (*c.*) The Substracting of Numbers; (*d.*) Multiplying of Numbers; (*e.*) Dividing of Numbers; (*f.*) Combined Operations; (*g.*) Parts or Fractions of Numbers; (*h.*) Tables of Applied Number or Standard Measures. The details to be given under each of these heads should be studied with a view, not only to the nature of the operations, but to their order.

All we ask is that the teacher shall bear in mind that it is with infants he is dealing; that, therefore, he shall not expect them to comprehend or perform any thing that is complex; and that he shall speak to them in familiar untechnical language.

Mann's "*Handbook of General Knowledge;*" "*The Observing Eye;*" "*Book of Birds, Fishes, Trees,*" &c., published by Society for Promoting Christian Knowledge; "*Exercises for the Improvement of the Senses.*" See also the list of books given in the note on § 87, some of which are available for giving materials for object-lessons. The chief practical works on infant-school training may be mentioned here once for all; they are Wilderspin's "*Infant System,*" Young's "*Infant-School Teacher's Manual,*" (Dublin;) Chambers's "*Infant Education;*" Stow's "*Training System,*" chap. xiv., and the Home and Colonial School Society's "*Infant-School Manual,*" "*Model Lessons,*" "*Religious Instruction,*" and other publications. These last have the advantage of exhibiting minutely the gradation of infant-school work.

33.—(3.) This training in number, well conducted, is very valuable in the way of preparing for future study. The great obstacle to a useful study of arithmetic in school is the abstract way in which it is often taught, owing to which the pupil never thinks of finding illustrations of what he is taught in the things that meet him in daily life. From the habit of close association between number and things which it gives him, this preliminary training will give him a great advantage in his lessons in the upper school, even if its spirit be not there carried out as it ought to be.

34. PRACTICAL NUMERATION.—(1.) *Significance of the numbers up to ten.* Each number must be taken separately, and a lesson be given on its power. Thus for the lesson on "one," write down on the board one line | one dot . one cross + one round O &c., and have them simultaneously repeated, *one* line, *one* dot, &c.; lay off on the lines of the ball-frame *one* ball; point to various things in the school, and have them similarly named, with stress on the number. Make the class mark down *one* line, *one* dot, &c., on their slates. In the lesson on "two," show how it is formed by putting another *one* to the *one* already had; proceed quite as in the former lesson; extend and vary the questioning thus:—a boy has two *eyes*, two *hands*, &c.; a cart has two *wheels*, &c., the class supplying the words in *italics;* and conversely, how many legs has a bird? how many scales has a balance? &c. Proceed similarly with the remaining numbers in separate lessons, always keeping in view to show how each number arises out of its predecessor by the addition of another of the same kind; and for this purpose introducing each lesson by a reference to the former.

(2.) *Reckoning with the numbers up to ten*—not only from one, but from other starting points—not only forwards but backwards—not only by odds but by evens—not only in regular order but following the number of balls the teacher may lay off—the children sometimes raising a number of fingers, or marking on the slate a number of dots or lines, corresponding to the number of balls laid off.

(3.) *The symbols up to ten, in the first instance, must be learned gradually.* To verify the child's knowledge of these he may be required to lay off balls, or mark down dots, corresponding to the symbol which the teacher writes on the board in silence, and conversely to write down the symbol for the number of balls laid off by the teacher.

(4.) *In passing beyond ten,* the eleventh ball should be laid off on the line below that which has the ten, the twenty-first on the third line, and so on; so that it may be seen how eleven is ten and one;

twelve, ten and two; twenty, two tens; fifty-five, five tens and five, &c. Each number will not require a distinct lesson.

35. The Adding of Numbers.—(1.) *Adding the numbers under ten to each of them in succession; the receiving number being, in the first instance, kept constant throughout the ten additions.* Thus the first lesson would be on "adding *to* one;" 1 and 1 are 2, 2 and 1 are 3, 3 and 1 are 4, &c., the children counting in each case and then repeating the formulæ just set down. Then take the lesson backwards, and after that in any order, only keeping the receiving number the same; then apply the lesson by means of practical questions, thus: John had 1 penny, and his mother gave him 2 pennies more; how much had he? There was 1 tree standing at the water-side, and 4 more near it; how many trees in all? Do not be content with a mere number as the answers to these questions, *e. g.*, 3 to the first, and 5 to the second. Insist on the full answer, 3d., 5 trees, or, "he would have 3d," "there were 5 trees;" and the class should often simultaneously add, "for 1 penny and 2 pennies are 3 pennies, 1 tree and 4 trees are 5 trees. Devote a similar lesson to 2 as a constant receiving number; 1 and 2 are 3, 2 and 2 are 4, 3 and 2 are 5, &c., and so on up to 10, taking care, when the sum goes beyond 10, not to put more than 10 balls or 10 marks on the slate in one line, but carrying the excess to the line below. Encourage the pupils to put questions to one another, particularly of the practical sort.

(2.) *Adding the numbers under ten, in their order, to each of them in succession; the added number being now kept constant throughout the ten additions.* Thus, the first lesson would be the "adding *of* one;" 1 and 1 are 2, 1 and 2 are 3, 1 and 3 are 4, &c. For second lesson, 2 and 1 are 3, 2 and 2 are 4, 2 and 3 are 5, &c.; and so on up to 10. The exercises should be conducted precisely as the former ones. It may be well to observe at this point that already a series of not less than twenty lessons in addition alone is provided, excluding revisals. The teacher who thinks that this minute subdivision is unnecessary and that the children can get over more ground in one lesson, and who accordingly does not keep to one number for one lesson, understands neither the infant mind, nor the object with which the course is given. He destroys the gradation in it, fuses its whole materials into one mass, and in this way deprives it of any training power. This remark applies to the whole of infant-school instruction.

(3.) *Exercises of a converse kind to the two foregoing:*—whereas in those the two constituent numbers were given and the sum required, let any number now be given and its two constituents be sought, thus: what two numbers make up 4? 6? 8? All the pairs that make up any one should be obtained; thus, for 4, 1 and 3, 2 and 2, 3 and 1.

(4.) *Adding may be extended, so as to include three small numbers, and by degrees more.*

(5.) *The adding of tens, first with themselves alone*—10 and 10 are 2 tens or 20; 10 and 10 and 10 are 3 tens or 30, &c., which is just the adding of lines of balls instead of single balls; *and then with other numbers*—as 10 and 7 are 17, 20 and 5 are 25, 31 and 3 are 34. Each new number will not now need a separate lesson, for the process between 30 and 40 is just the same as between 20 and 30, and may be learned at one and the same time. Thus, let the teacher set off 20 on the two highest lines of the ball frame, and 30 on three lines lower down, say on the sixth and seventh lines; let him add to the 20 one ball on the third line, and to the 30 one ball on the eighth, then 2, then 3, &c.; it will easily be seen how 30 and 4 are 34, or how 32 and 4 are 36, just as 20 and 4 are 24, or 22 and 4 are 26, the 2 tens in the one case and the 3 in the other remaining quite unaffected by the process.

36. The Subtracting of Numbers.—If it be understood that all the operations in number are to be conducted in the same spirit as those of addition, it will be sufficient to give the outlines only of the following ones:—

(1.) *Exercises in subtracting the numbers under ten from each other in succession, the minuend being in the first instance constant.* Thus 9 from 10, 8 from 10, 7 from 10, &c.; 8 from 9, 7 from 9, &c. Subtracting should be based on addition; 9 from 10 is 1, *for* 9 and 1 are 10; 8 from 10 is 2, *for* 8 and 2 are 10, &c.; verified at each step by use of the balls, &c.

(2.) *Exercises in which the subtrahend is constant*—as 1 from 2 is 1, 1 from 3 is 2, &c., 2 from 3 is 1, 2 from 4 is 2, &c.

(3.) *Exercises in which minuend and remainder are given*—as, what must be taken from 8 to leave three? &c.; also in which subtrahend and remainder are given, as, from what must 6 be taken to leave 4? &c.

(4.) *Exercises in double subtraction*—as, take 2 from 8 and other 2, 3 from 10 and then 4, &c.

(5.) *Exercises combining addition and subtraction*—as, add 4 to 6 and then take away 2, &c.

(6.) *Exercises with the tens*—as, 10 from 17, 10 from 30, 90 from 100, 30 from 35, 5 from 35, 6 from 8, and, with it, 6 from 48, &c.

(7.) *Applied exercises to be constantly given throughout the whole series.*

(8.) *Addition and subtraction may now be conjoined with numeration;* as, count up to 100 by twos, by threes, by fours, by fives, &c.; count back from 100 by tens, by fives, by fours, by threes, and by twos; or count back from 90 by threes, (90 being a multiple of three,) from 80 by fours, (80 being a multiple of four,) &c.* But the symbols for these larger numbers must be taught very slowly.

37. The Multiplying of Numbers.—The "multiplying" of arithmetic is an artificial process derived from addition. Children have some difficulty in understanding its use, and always tend in their reckoning to fall back on the *natural* process of addition. To obviate the difficulty, the artificial process must be taught through the natural.

(1.) *Exercises in multiplying the numbers under ten by each other in succession, the multiplicand in the first instance remaining the same.* Thus:—

2 times	1 are	2			2 times	2 are	4
3	1	3			3	2	6
&c.	&c.				&c.	&c.	

The proper way to put these exercises is this:—

1 and 1 are	2, then	2 times	1 are	2
1 and 1 and 1	3,	3	1	3
1 and 1 and 1 and 1	4,	4	1	4
&c.			&c.	
2 and 2 are	4, then	2 times	2 are	4
2 and 2 and 2	6,	3	2	6
2 and 2 and 2 and 2	8,	4	2	8
&c.			&c.	

(2.) *Exercises in which the multiplier is constant.* Thus:—

2 times	1 are	2	3 times	1 are	3
2	2	4	3	2	6
2	3	6	3	3	9
&c.			&c.		

This step is more difficult than the former; any operation is not seen to rise out of the preceding one so evidently. In each of the two steps now given one number only should be taken as the subject of lesson, either as multiplicand or multiplier, and the table of results connected with it thoroughly learnt.

(3.) *Exercises in multiplying tens and in multiplying by tens.*

(4.) *Exercises in decomposing numbers into their factors.* First give one factor; as, what must 4 be multiplied by to give 12? then

---

* We have used the technical terms in the exposition for convenience sake, such as minuend, subtrahend, multiple, &c.; these, and any hereafter to be used, are addressed to the teacher, however, and should not be used before the class.

require both factors, as, what two numbers multiplied by each other give 6, 8, 9? This exercise corresponds to the decomposition of numbers under the head of addition, with which it may be compared. The teacher must carry the eye of the child along with him in this process. Let him make rectangles and squares with the balls. Thus, if he wishes the factors of 12, he should present 12 to the class, (1,) in a line, (2,) in two lines, (3,) in three or four lines, thus:—

```
. . . . . . . . . . . .     (1 × 12)
          . . . . . .       (2 × 6)
          . . . . . .
            . . . .
            . . . .         (2 × 4)
            . . . .
```

It is an interesting exercise for him to make rectangles on the ball-frame, or to get the children to make them, then cause the class to count the balls in them by counting the two sides, and notice how the removal of a row or two rows affects the result; and conversely to make them construct rectangles of which he gives the number in the sides.

(5.) *Exercises in double multiplication by small numbers, and in the adding of two multiplications.*

(6.) *Exercises of application, e. g.*—5 boys get 2d. each, how much money was given to all? John passed 3 flocks of sheep in coming to school, having 6 in each, how many sheep did he see? 2 loaves at 2d., and 3 at 3d, cost how much in all? 3 of you hold up all the fingers in the right hand, how many fingers are up? 6 of you hold up all fingers except the thumbs, how many fingers are up? In each of these 6 seats there are 9 boys, how many are there in the gallery?

The field for putting these applied questions is widening, the teacher's ingenuity must task itself accordingly.

38. The Dividing of Numbers.—As multiplication is an artificial form of addition, so division is of subtraction; the same link of connection must therefore be kept up between division and subtraction.

(1.) *Exercises where the divisor is constant.* To give the class an idea of the nature of this operation, the teacher may count 10 or 12 balls in their presence, saying that he wishes to give 2 to each child and to know how many children he can give them to; or to arrange the children into rows of 2 each and know how many rows there will be. The result will be attained, in the first instance, by taking 2 and 2 successively till the number is exhausted, *i. e.*, by subtraction. The first lesson in division should be "dividing by 2;" for which purpose the balls on the frame may be arranged in successive lines below each other, 2, 4, 6, 8, 10, and 12. Then in first line (2.) there is one 2, in second line (4.) 2 twos, &c.; and the table of results is learnt, 2 in 2 once, and 2 in 4 twice, &c. For 3 the same arrangement of the balls may be adopted; but for numbers above that they must be placed in mass to get dividends large enough. There are no better illustrations of division than those which are got by arranging the children themselves in rows.

(2.) *Easy exercises with remainders.*

(3.) *Exercises in which multiplication and division are used correlatively*—as 10 in 30, 3 times, then 3 times 10 or 10 times 3 are 30.

(4.) *Exercises of application.* If 9d. be divided among 3 girls, what will each get? How many sixpences in 18d.? weeks in 21 days? &c. In one seat, where all the children held up all their fingers, there were 100 fingers up: how many children in the seat? &c.

39. Combined Operations.—Cross-questioning is of great use to the teacher; it enters largely into his art of impressing. It connects one point of the pupil's knowledge with another, and makes them all available for mutual illustration. It may be profitably resorted to in lessons on number. For this purpose combined operations may be performed almost from the beginning of the course. Thus, when the children have got a little of addition and a little of subtraction, they may be practiced on both adding and subtracting, as parts of the same question; so with multiplication and division.

The following example shows how cross-questioning may be used in connection with any number:—

On the Number 8.—What is the last below it? Count up to it? Next above it? Count four above it? Two numbers that make it up by adding? other two? Three numbers that make it up by adding? What must be added to five to make it? Take one from it? two? three? How much greater is it than four? than two? how much less than ten? than twelve? What taken from eleven will give it? How many twos in it? fours? What number divided by two will give it? by three? What does forty give divided by it?

Then the questioning may pass on to concrete numbers:—

Eight boys having apples put them into two rows, how many in each? then into four, how many in each? Each boy got an additional apple, how many had they all now? One boy ate his, how many remained? two, how many remained? only one boy of the eight kept his, how many were eaten? Other three boys came in each with apples, how many apples were there now? with two each, how many now? Four boys gave theirs to their neighbors, how many had each of these four? and how many apples were there in all? These eight apples were taken from a stall in which there were twenty, how many remained in the stall? And so on indefinitely. Such exercises may be made very amusing; and are valuable from the readiness they encourage.

40. Parts or fractions of numbers.—Elementary notions and operations in fractions are just as available in the infant school as those in whole numbers. The half of a thing is as easy of comprehension as the double of it, the third part as three times it; that two halves make a whole or three halves one-and-a-half as that two twos make four, or three threes nine; provided the illustration given in the two cases be equally simple.

(1.) *Exercises to illustrate what a fraction is.* An apple is to be divided between Willie and his sister, what must be done with it? it must be *cut.* Will it do to cut into a big piece and a small piece? No, they must get pieces of the same size. Look at me, now, while I cut it (teacher holding up the two pieces.) Are they about the same size? Yes. Then each of them is called *a half.* How many halves in the whole? Two. Could I divide an orange into two parts of same size? Yes. What would each part be? A half. Here is a bit of string, of paper, of wood, &c., which I shall divide into two bits of same size; what do you call each? A half. Then if I put two halves together, what do they make up? The whole. Take another apple, and illustrate a third in the same way. The subdivision of the halves will show how fourths or quarters arise, of the thirds how sixths and ninths arise, and of the fourths how eighths. The fifths and sevenths must be explained by cuttings for themselves. Beyond these fractions it is not necessary to go. For further illustration it would be desirable to have a rod, say a yard long, divided into halves, fourths, and eighths, and another into halves, thirds, and sixths. The solid cube divided into eight parts, and another into six parts, would also be very useful. But the balls on the frame, and counters of any sort, may also be turned to account; for six balls may be divided into two groups or three groups, to illustrate halves, and thirds, and so on.

(2.) *Nature of the exercises in fractions. In equivalence;* how many halves in one? in two? &c., how many thirds in one? in two? &c., how many fourths in one? in two? &c.—how many fourths in a half? in a half and a fourth?—how many sixths in a half? in a half and a sixth?—how many sixths in a third? &c. *In addition;* a half and a half make? a half and a half and a half make? a half and a fourth make? one third and one third make? one third and two thirds make? one fourth and one fourth make? one fourth and two fourths make? one fourth and one half make? &c. *In subtraction;* one half from one gives? from one-and-a-half gives?—one fourth from three fourth gives? from one half gives? from one gives? from one and a fourth gives? &c. *In multiplication;* what is the double of a fourth? four times a fourth? three times a third? three times a sixth? &c. *In division;* how many halves in one? in two? in one and a half?—how many fourths in one? in one and a half? in a half? &c. *In comparison;* whether is a half or a third the greater? a third or a fourth? a half or three-fourths? a fifth or a sixth? &c. *Applied questions* may be given under all these heads, especially with the pence table. What is a farthing? how many in twopence? difference between a penny and a farthing? a halfpenny and a farthing? What must you add to a halfpenny to make twopence? &c. It may be repeated here that for verification of the results the children should manipulate with the illustrative apparatus as well as the teacher.

41. The ball-frame is the principal means of illustration used in infant schools; it is proper, therefore, to give the following cautions as to the manner of using it:—(1.) It is not to be used beyond the pupil's ability to follow it with the eye. Rapid operation with 40, 60, or 80 balls does nothing to aid the observation; it can neither lead to, nor verify, any result. When the frame is used at all, it must give *bona fide* illustration. (2.) It must be used as a means, not as an end. The child is not learning the ball-frame, but operations in number through its help. Particular manipulations, therefore, need not always be repeated after they have served their purpose. It has already been indicated that the different operations, after being performed with the aid of the frame, are to be performed without it.

42. These lessons in number may be assumed to be given by way of collective-lesson. Interest, and rapid distribution of questioning, are the elements of success in such teaching. To be interesting, the questions must deal with familiar things, must be varied, and must be simply expressed; in a word, must come into contact with the child's daily experience. To be rapidly distributed, the teacher must have at command all the possible forms in which questions may be put; with which view he should, at the beginning of his career, write down all these forms, and learn them as so many formulæ. He has then only to vary the *things* mentioned in the questions, which a little practice will enable him freely to do. It is not to be expected that a lesson of this nature can succeed unless the children feel that the teacher speaks from a full mind, and is quite at ease.

43. Standard measures.—Lessons on number must make the

child familiar with the various units of measurement used in the affairs of life. These are excellent illustrations of the different operations; and, besides, he needs to know them. He must become familiar—(1.) With the units themselves; (2.) With the relation of different units of the same kind; and (3.) With the application of them to practical purposes. For the first of these ends, the units must be constantly before him; for the second, he must see them compared, and with his own hands compare them; for the third, he must see them applied, and with his own hands apply them, to the measurement of things about him. In this way, what appears so formidable a task when presented in the shape of Reduction-tables to be learnt, will become an easy, natural, and most interesting exercise of his senses and his activity. It is needless to carry him through all the tables; those in most common use will suffice: and the first place is due to—

44. *Number as applied to Value, or the Money-table.*—The child necessarily becomes familiar with this to a certain extent without any special training, and the preceding exercises have assumed such an acquaintance; but it is well that distinct practice in the use of money be given. He must complete his acquaintance with all the coins therefore, with farthing, halfpenny, penny, threepenny-piece, fourpenny-piece, sixpenny-piece, shilling, florin, half-crown, crown, half-sovereign, sovereign, and one-pound note. Their forms should be examined, their sizes, colors, weights, sounds, and the stamps upon them; their points of resemblance and of difference noted, so that he may be able to tell them at once on seeing them, to describe them, or recognize them on description. He must be exercised in adding, subtracting, &c., different sums, in every variety of language. And he should go through little processes of buying and selling in imagination, in which he shall be accustomed to give back and get back the proper amount of change. Actual counting and handling of the money is indispensable.

45. *Number as applied to size* (linear.)—In going through a parellel process with this table, the teacher should have beside him an inch measure and a three-foot rule, to show the foot and the yard. For verifying operations, he should have twelve inches, some three-inch measures, six-inch measures, and three foot-measures; slips of wood cut to the size will do. The child should be able to tell them all at sight. The field of questions on their relative size is very wide, thus: (holding up foot-measure) how many of the smallest measures (inches) in it? what part is the inch, then, of foot? How many of the next smallest (3-inch measure) in it? of the next? How may it be made up by three slips (half-foot, and two of the three-inches?) of four slips?

of five (6-inch, 3-inch, and 3 inches?) of seven? In each case the process of comparing should be gone through. When the children are familiar with the measures, things should actually be measured. What is the breadth of this book? its length? its thickness? the hight of this picture above the floor? the length of the picture? of the pointer? of some of the children selected? the depth of this cup? this jug? the length, breadth, and thickness of this cube? the dimensions of the school-room floor by admeasurement? &c. Draw a line on your slates an inch long, up-and-down? the same even along? the same slanting? two of them? six in order? the same half-an-inch long? alternating an inch and a half-inch? two inches long? alternating two inches and one inch? three inches? &c.

46. *Number as applied to weight.*— If the spirit of the previous exercises be understood, it can not be necessary to exhibit the details of those upon weight. Suffice it to say, that the children must acquire their notions of weight by weighing. For this purpose, the teacher should have beside him a pair of scales, with the different current weights, 1 lb., 2 lb., ½ lb., ¼ lb., 1 oz., 2 oz., ½ oz., ¼ oz.; and duplicates enough to show equality, 16 oz. for the lb., two ½ lb., four ¼ lb., two 1 oz., two ½ oz., four ¼ oz. For weighing, he should have sand, small shot, or some equally convenient thing; and he should also often weigh common articles. Let the questioning be varied as before.

47. *Number as applied to square measure.*—The most convenient apparatus is a diagram of the square inch, square foot, and square yard on the school wall, white lines on a black ground; the yard divided into its nine feet, and the foot into its 144 inches. Handkerchiefs or towels may easily exemplify the yard and the foot. Any rectangular object in the school, such as the slate, the board, the map, the picture, &c., are convenient for this measurement.

48. *Number as applied to capacity.*—In liquid measure, the gill, the pint, the quart, the gallon, are the measures to be shown. In dry measure, the peck, the ½ peck, and the ¼ peck will suffice.

Lastly, *Number as applied to time* gives an important series of lessons, though there can not be ocular illustration with them. Experience, however, makes them quite intelligible; the second, the minute, the hour, the day, the week, the month, the year, should all come under review.

49. The steps in this series of lessons on applied number must be taken gradually, just as the child can bear; each one being thoroughly mastered before another is taken up. They afford scope for all the fundamental operations, and particularly for fractions. The

Reduction-tables should be learned after the practical exercises in each kind of measurement; but the children, so far from finding this difficult, will be able to construct the tables along with the teacher on the board.*

3. *On Color and Form.*

50. Color and Form should have a distinct and no unimportant place assigned to them amongst the instruments of infant-school training. They are two properties of bodies the most general, and, for the child, the most distinctive; they both appeal to the sight, and are therefore very early recognizable; they occur in endless varieties, and therefore afford ample scope for the training of the observation. Lessons on Color and Form are necessary to enable the child to form correct impressions of the things about him. But they have another aspect, the latter of them particularly. Color and Form are the elements of *representation*, pictorial and linear. An acquaintance with them is needed, therefore, before we can interpret such representations; a power of much consequence, considering the wide circle of things of which we can learn only through representation. Besides, the child is at a later period to be instructed in certain departments of the art of representation, to wit, drawing and writing; for both of these the lesson on Form is a valuable preparation.

51. Color and Form have been mentioned together because they are the proper complements of each other. Their instrumentary character in training differs, however, in these two particulars: (1.) Color, as a property of bodies, is recognized before Form. From experience we see that it fixes the attention of children earlier than Form. The reason is that the recognizing of it is an exercise of simple sensation only; whereas the recognition of Form is an exercise of complex or double sensation. Color is recognized by simple sight; Form by sight combined with motion, the motion of the muscles of the eyeball. Practically, then, we speak to infants of Color, before we speak to them of Form. (2.) Though earlier available, Color is less useful as an instrument of training than Form. The tints and shades of Color are, no doubt, exceedingly numerous, and the effects producible by their combinations, are of inexhaustible variety; but the child can not and need not notice all these. It is enough if he can discriminate the leading species (hues) of Color with a very few of their most commonly occurring modifications as to tint or shade.

* There are a few little works which may be profitably consulted by the teacher on this subject; of these may be mentioned, "*Arithmetic for Young Children,*" published originally by the Society for the Diffusion of Useful Knowledge; "*First Ideas of Number for Children,*" published by Parker, London; and Tate's "*Arithmetic.*"

But the variety of Forms which he needs to discriminate are indeed endless; of the common things about him no two have precisely the same form. And from the nature of the sense to which it appeals, variety of Form is easily distinguishable to a much greater extent than variety of tint and shade in Color.

Color.

52. The design of the lessons on color may be stated as twofold. It is (1.) to enable the child to discriminate the commonly occurring colors; and (2.) to cultivate his taste, so far as to habituate his eye to those combinations of color that are known as harmonious. Any experimenting on the physical relations of colors beyond this, such as explaining the effects of their admixture, or the numerical ratios involved in their harmony, is quite beside the mark. We have not to deal with color as a science or as an art, though it is both, but simply as a property of bodies. The elements of instruction are few, but there is constant room for their application.

53. As a natural order for the lessons on color, the following might be adopted:—

First series: On *white* and *black*, with their mixture in *grey*. White and black are not, properly speaking, colors; white is the neutralization of color, black is the absence of color. They are the extremes, however, within which the colors lie, and by which they are measured; so that a knowledge of them is necessary. And they first present themselves to notice; *light* is represented by white, *darkness* by black, and by reference to light of the sun and the darkness of night the notion of white and black is given.

Second series: Red, *blue*, and *yellow*. These are the three primary colors, so called, which produce all other colors by composition in various proportions, but can not themselves be produced by any composition.

Third series: Purple, *orange*, *green*. These are the secondary colors, so called, produced from the admixture of the primary thus—red and blue giving purple, red and yellow giving orange, and blue and yellow giving green.

Fourth series : Russet, *olive*, and *citrine*. These are the tertiary colors, so called, produced by admixture of the secondary, thus—purple and orange give russet, purple and green give olive, orange and green give citrine.

Fifth series.—Those now named are all the hues of color; but each of these hues has different tints and shades, according as it is mixed with white or black, more or less. Thus red may be varied into crimson, scarlet, pink, &c.; yellow may be varied into lemon, straw, primrose, &c.; and blue may be varied into stone, sky, slate, &c.

54. For giving these lessons on color, the teacher may have them exhibited on a board either together or singly; but the best possible color-board is one made by himself and the children with the help of a box of paints and white card. If he can not get a board for the purpose, he may procure other apparatus in its stead. He may get small squares sewed with the different colors of worsted, in the manner of a sampler; or he may find the colors exemplified in the skeins themselves, in bits of merino, silk, or ribbon, in paper, wafers, glass, &c. After the children have *observed* any color, red, for instance, they should single it out of many others; then be required to name things which show it, as blood, a rose, and other flowers; the robin, and other birds; sealing-wax, a soldier's coat, binding of a book, shawl, hair, &c.; also to think at home of as many things as they can, and mention them in the next lesson. A color need not at this time be distinguished into its different shades.

55. In seeking to give to the child some perception of harmony in color, whilst he may be told that certain colors agree beside each other, and certain others do not, it is to be remembered that it is the eye that is to be trained in the first instance, and then the mind. A sense of concord in music, whether in melody or harmony, grows up in one after hearing it exemplified frequently; without this no explanation can have any meaning. So in color; the eye must have the opportunity of dwelling frequently on harmonious combinations. When it is accustomed to these, it will instantaneously be offended by a combination which is not harmonious. The presence of all the three primary colors, either pure or in combination, being required to produce harmony, it will be understood that red and green harmonize, as also yellow and purple, blue and orange, green and russet, orange and olive, &c. This principle should guide teacher and children in the combinations they make of their slips of color in designing patterns. An eye familiar with such juxta-positions will not tolerate such as yellow and orange, blue and purple, red and orange, blue and green, orange and russet, and the like.*

Form.

56. The lesson on Form deals with forms of all the kinds of dimension; with those of one dimension or lines, those of two or plane

* For information on the subject of color, see Redgrave's little "*Manual of Color*," and corresponding chart; also, "*Hay on Harmonious Coloring*."

figures, and those of three or solids. In each case the forms must be traced, as exemplified in the common things of life.

57. To commence with lines; the annexed diagram represents what may be the first series of lessons, or some of them :—

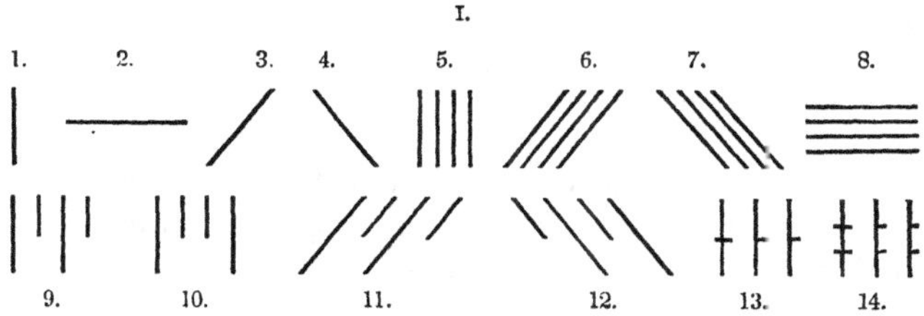

The simple straight line gives materials for a large series of lessons, as there are various ideas to be developed in connection with it, viz., straight, up-and-down, (perpendicular,) even-along, (horizontal,) sloping, equality of length, equality of thickness, equality of width between, bisection, and trisection.

58. Combinations of the straight line suggest another series of which these are examples :—

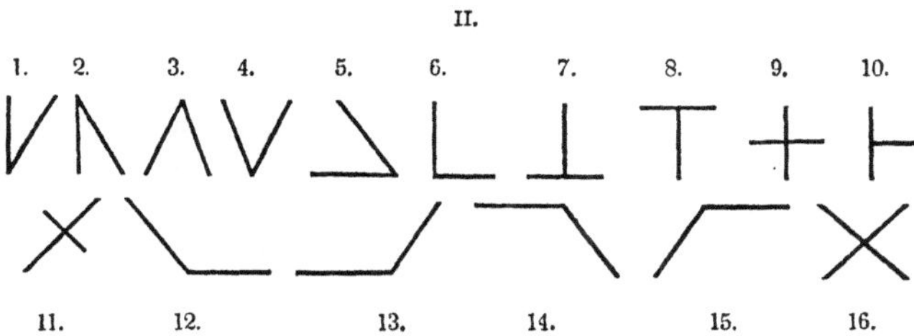

Extended by duplication thus :—

1. 2. 3. 4. 5. 6. 7. 8. 9. 10. 11. 12

59. Plane figures may be grouped according to the number of sides that constitute them; triangles of various shapes, foursided figures comprehending the square, the rectangle, the rhomb, the rhomboid, the trapezium, the polygon, including the pentagon, hexagon, and decagon.

III.

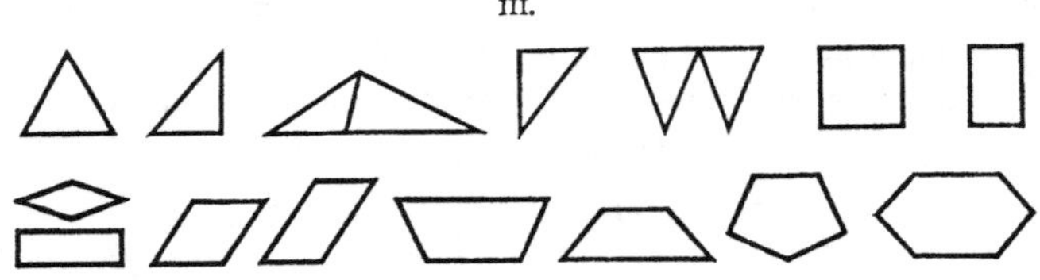

60. There is no invention exercised in the construction of these forms; but, when the children have had some practice in imitating, they should be encouraged to invent, *i. e.*, to put together the elements already learned into new patterns, combining line with line, or figure with figure, or figure with line, thus:—

IV.

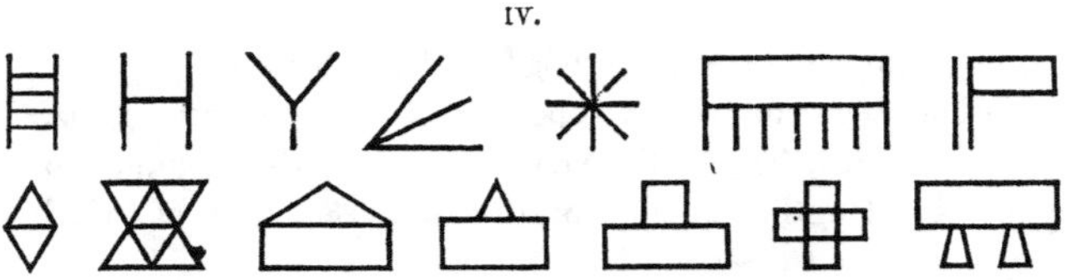

61. The curved lines are more difficult to deal with; but some practice must be given in making them also, since they occur in the letters, and in many familiar things. Thus:—

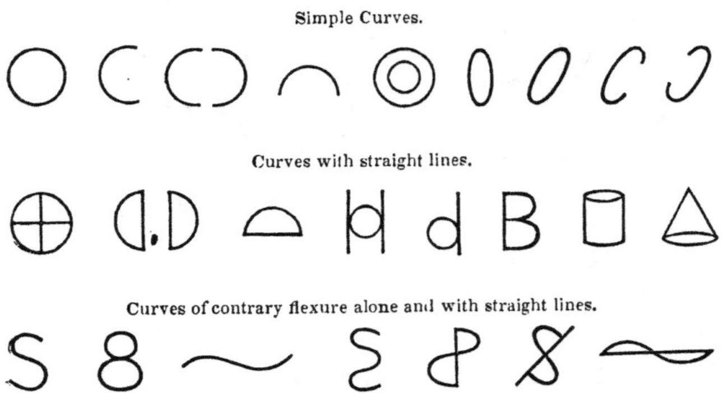

62. The mere imitation of these various forms on their slates interests the children; but the interest is greatly increased when the different forms are applied to practical purposes. This application is twofold: (1.) to commonly-occurring *forms*; (2.) to commonly-occurring *things*. Under the first fall the letters of the alphabet—both small and capital, both in print and in script. The alphabet-board is

useful here and also the letters separately on slips of mill-board; but the teacher should draw them on the blackboard, classifying them according as they are straight-line letters or curved letters, and noticing the parts they are composed of with reference to the elements already learned. A similar course should be followed with the numerals, first the common or Arabic characters, then the Roman.

63. But the application to things is more interesting still, from the appeal it makes to their curiosity and their imagination. All forms from the very simplest may be found represented in things: straight lines and figures, as in a pointer, pen, pencil, comb, book, picture, window-frame, arrow, sword, stool, table, house, castle, box, star, cross, door, &c.; curves, as in penny, sixpence, target, cup, saucer, bottle, jug, whip, walking-stick, candle-stick, extinguisher, spire, cart-wheel, spinning-wheel, knife and fork, spoon, basket, ship, pillar, chimney, flag-and-staff, clock-face, a leaf, an apple, cherry, plate, tub, bell, gun, key, drum, trumpet, a cheese, a loaf, an egg, the moon, &c., &c. The thing should be associated with the form, and some conversation held upon it, or some little story given in connection with it, whilst the outline is before the eye.

64. The apparatus for the lesson on form, so far as it has been described, is very simple; all that is indispensable is the blackboard for the teacher, and slate and pencil for the class. It will be found convenient to have the slates ruled, not over their whole surface, but partially; so as to give the children a little help without restraining their freedom of imitation. Perhaps the most convenient form of ruling is this:—

For straight lines and figures.

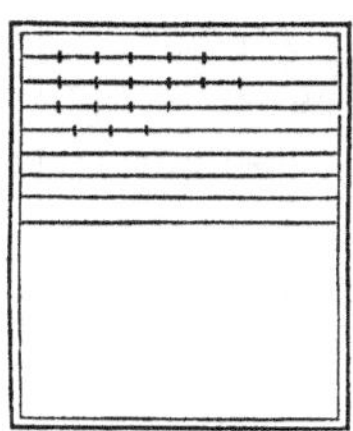

For curves.

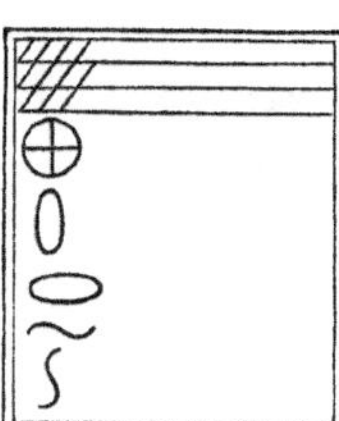

On the one side the upper half is ruled, and a few points put on some of the lines; and, on the reverse, a few lines ruled for writing, and the simplest curves are represented.

It will contribute very much to the regularity and uniformity of the lesson, that the slates should be the property of the school, each class having its own set attached to it in its own box. Though not indispensable, it is serviceable to have diagrams of form : a board, *i. e.*, on which the geometrical forms are represented, both planes and solids, with their proper shade. Very serviceable, also, is a number of slips of wood, or laths, by means of which the children can construct any of the forms, either straight lines or rectilinear figures, which the teacher draws on the board. Thus, all the examples in §§ 57–60 may be exhibited, the requisite number of children holding the laths, in vertical lines, in slanting lines, in even-along lines, in triangles, rectangles, &c., as the case may be.

65. There are two senses in which solids may be made materials for lessons on form. According to the one, the geometrical solids are exhibited and their outlines made familiar ; this is of much service, and the teacher should have a box of solids for this purpose, and a series of representations of them, shaded if possible. According to the other, by the use of solids themselves, such as cubes, parallelopipeds, cylinders, cones, pyramids, &c., the invention is taxed to construct different forms. These, in fact, are so many bricks, stones, pillars, towers, arches, &c., with which the child becomes a builder. Such engagement seems well suited for an individual child or for a family, as it must foster the taste, the imagination, and the habit of perseverence; and it may be provided in the play-ground of the infant school.

66. The lesson on Form may be given either to the whole school collectively, or to separate groups, the latter being the better way. One caution, however, should be given : it must be viewed as a lesson, and not as a mere device for occupying the children while the teacher is otherwise engaged. Doubtless, it may be made very interesting and amusing; nevertheless it is instruction proceeding upon a principle, in systematic order, and with a view to the attainment of certain results. The teacher must bestow some forethought, therefore, on its arrangement, and exercise adequate superintendence over the class engaged in it.*

67. Subjoined are examples of the lesson on Form in different stages :—

I. On the Perpendicular Line.

1. Teacher holds in his hand (suppose) a bit of string, stretched by some object attached to its other end ; children notice its appearance ; teacher then holds in

* Hints on the nature and order of the lesson or form may be found in works like the following :—Richson's "*Copies.*" (National Society ;) "*Drawing for Young Children,*" (Society for Diffusion of Useful Knowledge ;) Krüsi's "*Manual,*" or the summary of it in the Home and Colonial Society's "*Infant-School Manual.*" But any of the better kind of elementary manuals of drawing, such as Tate's or Carpenter's, will suggest many things to the teacher.

his hand a bit of string which is curled and twisted, from having been rolled round something; children notice the difference: the one even or straight, the other not.

The teacher similarly contrasts the pointer with a walking-stick or cane; also, a straight lath with a slightly-bent one.

2. Again, the teacher holds in his hand the straightened cord, (1.) perpendicularly, (2.) slantingly, and the children notice the difference; the pointer, stick, lath, &c., held (1.) perpendicularly, (2.) slantingly. This will give the further notion of ***even-up-and-down;*** which word may be used for a while instead of perpendicular.

3. Teacher asks them to watch him as he draws an even-up-and-down line on the board; they follow with the eye; he asks how it was done; examines whether it is ***straight***—whether it is ***even-up-and-down;*** places the pointer or lath along it, and they see it is. Would this do? / Why not? This? / Why not? This? | Why? Who can draw one on his own slate? All draw one; teacher looks and criticises a little.

4. Teacher asks for any common things in shape of an even-up-and-down line? A pointer held up; that is designed for —— ? a ruler, that is —— ? a flagstaff, that is for —— ? a mast of a ship, that is for —— ? some trees, which grow in the —— ?

5. They then draw on their slates a number of these even-up-and-down lines.

NOTE.—One idea is enough in one lesson. Here it is the idea of even-up-and-down. The children need not at present attend to the ***distances*** of the lines from each other, when they make a number. Another lesson similarly illustrated would be given to the slanting line to the right, another to the slanting line to the left, another to the even-long (or horizontal) line. So a distinct lesson would be given to equality in length, equality in thickness, equality in slope, and equality in width, thus:—

II. Equal Width or Distances.

1. Teacher draws | | | Count how many lines are there? what kind of lines? would this be the same? | / | Why not?—what is between every two lines? a space—how many spaces are there? If I draw another line, how many lines? spaces?

2. Teacher tells them to notice that spaces are of same width—measures them before the class. If I want all spaces to be the same, then, would this do? | | | | why not? How do you know? You don't need to measure that, you see it. Now, make three even-up-and-down lines yourselves on your slates. They draw three, and the teacher criticises a little.

3. Think of any things we could get to show even-up-and-down lines with same width between them. We could do it with fingers—three children hold one finger each together—with arms in same way—with pointers or laths—some are

called on to put these in position. Another thing yet in the school which shows them? The ball-frame. Count the wires and the spaces.

Any thing not in school which shows even-up-and-down lines at equal distances? A railing, which is made —— ? and is used for —— ? a bird's cage, which is made of —— ? and is used for —— ? grating in some windows, which is made for —— ?

4. Now make some rows of even-up-and-down lines on your slates.

III. On the Oblong or Rectangle.

1. Teacher draws it by degrees; thus, | what is this? an even-up-and-down line.  what is added here?—and here? and here?  Another way of making it—What are these? | | Two even-up-and-down lines of same length. Join them. How many lines in all? how many *kinds?* how many of each kind? Are they separate? how many corners? What is within the lines? a space? Are the lines of same length? any two of them—teacher measures them—pupils draw one for themselves, and teacher criticises a little.

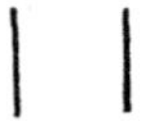

2. Name any thing you know which is drawn by four lines in this way—a slate, which is for —— ? a blackboard, which is for —— ? a map, which is for —— ? the ball-frame, which is for —— ? a book, which is for —— ? Count all the sides in these. Also a window, which is for —— ? the door, which is for —— ? a sheet of paper, which is for —— ? &c.

3. The pupils proceed to draw figures for themselves, the teacher giving them directions how to use the lines ruled on their slates, and the points indicated on them.

IV. On the Circle.

1. Teacher holds up a penny, sixpence, &c.—gets the shapes named successively—holds up a circle cut in paper—another shape more or less nearly circular—children observe difference.

2. Teacher draws on board a figure nearly circular—then a circle, the children following the chalk—teacher takes a line and measures across the center-point, and shows the children how this is always the same—draws a few such lines (or diameters) through the circle—then through the other nearly circular figure, and children observe the difference. They draw one on their slates.

3. Things named which are round—various coins—cart-wheel, used for —— ? and which well illustrates the circle; a cheese, for —— ? a chimney, for —— ? a hoop, for —— ? the sun, which —— ? &c.

4. Children then proceed to construct several on their slates.

NOTE.—Lessons on the forms of solids are the most advanced of which they are capable, and differ from the preceding lessons in this particular, that they are not fully or not at all within the child's power of drawing. But he should be taught to recognize the forms of all the solids when he sees them drawn; which he can not do till his eye is educated. With this view lessons should be given on each of the solids; as the cube, prism, pyramid, cone, &c. Subjoined is the example of a lesson.

V. On the Cylinder.

1. *To give a general notion of its form*, teacher holds it in his hand before the class—turns it on its axis vertically—the same horizontally—rolls it. It is *round*—holds its end toward the class—they recognize the circle—two ends and surface—teacher sets it on end—children name any thing corresponding in form, as a pillar—lays it down—children name something corresponding to it in outline, as a roller. Length varies; to show which it should be cut parallel to its end in one or two places.

2. *To explain its form in the drawing before the class, it being drawn on end.* Teacher places it on end—children trace its outline—its round front, how much of it seen?—the two vertical lines that bound its front—part of its base line—its top, not quite circular in appearance—all these lines actually traced—teacher draws it, or points to drawing—children trace the corresponding lines.

3. Children name a number of things cylindrical in shape, to see that it is a common form—pillar, roller or baton, tin box, a tree so far, a map or sheet of paper rolled up, a pitcher, a hat so far, &c.

4. Children intimate cylinder on their slates.

NOTE.—If the drawing before the class be shaded, this must be explained by reference to their experience. They observe things casting shadows, men, pillars, trees, &c.; thus they will understand on what side the shade should be. The drawing of a cylinder in other positions should be deferred to other lessons.

4. On Singing.

68. Singing is absolutely indispensable in the infant school. The child is naturally sensitive to sweet sounds. The mother sings to her child to soothe its sorrows and enliven its joys. The child sings to itself; almost unconsciously indeed. If it be not in possession of any melody, it will yet put sounds together; if it have learnt a melody, it will often be heard rehearsing it. Singing is a vehicle by which it expresses its feelings; producing an effect on the child which is keenly pleasurable at the moment, and which leaves him in a calm, pleased state. Every one who has seen the cordiality and unanimity with which children break out into a simple melody after some stretch of attention will understand the prominence we assign to singing. It is in infancy that the taste for singing must be founded; the period invites us to do so; if we neglect to cultivate it then, the inspiring of it will be a work of more difficulty at any future time.

69. In the infant school singing should be taught by ear and not from note. Skill in music certainly implies the power of reading from note, and an acquaintance with grammatical structure. But the study necessary to acquire this skill must be deferred till a later date. It

will equally perplex and repel the child at this stage. If we give him a taste for music by accustoming him early to its beautiful effects, he will be allured to the study in due time. At present, therefore, he learns his melodies by listening to and following his teacher's voice.

70. With regard to style of music, there are several kinds of errors made. A very common one is the exclusive, or almost exclusive, use of sacred music, perhaps even of psalmody. One of the ends—we may say the highest end—of learning to sing, is certainly to sing for devotional purposes; and the child, too, must use his gift of song in solemn worship. But whilst he must know some sacred songs, it does not suit the character of his own mind or of the music itself that he should be always engaged with this style. He must have the means of expressing the ordinary joyousness of his years; which is found in secular melody alone. Since the child sings from lightness of heart, he should be taught lively songs. The graver rhythms are unsuitable for him; and the use of the minor mode is a gross incongruity in the infant school.

71. To describe suitable melodies more minutely:—They should preserve a medium in respect of pitch, ranging between the notes D (below the first line) and E (fourth space) on the treble staff, since the voices of the children are tender, and liable to suffer from straining; the intervals between the notes should be of the simplest kind, viz., diatonic and common-chord, modulation from one key into another being, as a rule, avoided; the rhythm should be simple and well marked, such as $\frac{2}{4}$, $\frac{3}{8}$, and $\frac{6}{8}$, and then $\frac{4}{4}$ and $\frac{3}{4}$.

72. Singing in two parts or more should not be pressed on too hastily. The more advanced children may be taught to sing a second part, but it is not necessary; simple melody is attractive enough to attain all the ends of the exercise. The teacher may sing a second part at pleasure as accompaniment.

73. The difficulty in finding suitable songs lies as much in the words to be sung as in the tune itself. Verses of a purely didactic character, or which are filled with abstract sayings, are not suitable. Still worse are rhymes of a professedly utilitarian kind, arithmetical or geographical tables, and the like. Speaking generally, whatever carries the child's thoughts to the objects that he naturally finds pleasure in is suitable, so far as matter is concerned. Pieces on beautiful natural appearances, on natural objects, on animals, or stories in the ballad style, may safely be used, provided their language be simple and their sentiment correct.

74. The singing, if it is to cultivate the taste, must be done tastefully. The children may not sing artistically, but they may be ex-

pected to sing in tune without shouting, and with becoming light and shade in expression. If there be a child who seems unable to keep in tune with the rest, *i. e.*, whose ear requires more exercise in tune than the average, he should keep silence during the singing till he has attained sufficient cultivation to join in it, and not be allowed to mar the singing of the others.

For singing, in its bearing on discipline, see § 16.

5. *On Geography.*

75. Geography is one of the natural sciences, having for its subject-matter not ideas, or symbols, or formulæ, but *things*. On this account it was introduced not very long since into the course of school-studies. It was designed as a counterpoise to the too exclusively verbal and abstract character of that course. It has not, for the most part, been taught in such a way as to serve the ends of its introduction, having been greatly confined to what is really an abstract study, the study of the position of places on the map. It should be well understood that geography, viewed educationally, is a *study of things*. If this its true character be preserved, it will readily be seen that there is an aspect of it in which it is fit to be handled in the infant school. It were to be wished that there were a more familiar name to give to the study in this stage. The name "Geography" is too scientific. The lessons contemplated in it really fall under the object-lesson. They are a series of object-lessons on the earth, with its more striking external aspects, its products and occupiers; and we treat of them separately from the object-lesson in general, only because they are the germ of what in the subsequent stages of the child's progress is recognized as a distinct and important branch of study.

76. Map-geography, in the ordinary sense of the word, is no part of the work of the infant school. It is very common to begin geography by setting before the class—after telling them what the shape of the earth is, and what a map is meant to be—a map of Europe; and to give them the names of the countries, mountains, rivers, bays, islands, straits, towns, &c. But this is altogether an anticipation of the work of the upper school. In the infant school it gives a certain knowledge of the piece of paper before them called a map; but as the children can comprehend neither what a map is, nor what it is for, it gives them no *real* instruction whatever. It is to no purpose that it be made simple or even amusing by the teacher's ingenuity, and that the children become actually expert in naming the places pointed out. The work itself is not that which should be engaging their attention. They can not at this stage realize the "geography of locality or relative position."

77. The geography of the infant school should be pictorial and descriptive. Commencing with the elements of natural scenery that fall under the child's observation, and carefully noting their distance and relative direction from the school and from each other—the hill, the mountain, the brook, the river, the plain, the forest, the moor, the rich mold, the island, the sea, the cliff, the cape, the castle, the village, the city, that may be seen in prospect from the school; the productions of his own land—its animals, its trees, and flowers, and herbs, its metals; the men of his own land—their occupations, their customs, their habits, their food, their clothing; it should seek to make the child realize the corresponding features of other lands and climes by comparison with what it has observed in its own. We should ever set before his eye, when possible, specimens and pictures of foreign products and scenes, and for the rest appeal to his imagination to take off the impressions from our vivid descriptions. Such is an outline in brief of the course the instruction should follow.

78. *Examples of subjects of lessons in Home-Geography.*—Let the subject be "*rivers.*" What a variety of instructive matter is suggested by it! their source in the little springs welling forth amongst the hills from the bosom of the earth—the descent of the many small rills from the mountain side to the valley—the length, depth, and gradual increase of the main stream—the influence of the season of the year upon them—the smooth, clear, low water in summer, and the dark, swollen, angry torrent in winter—the character of the land through which they flow for fertility—the uses to which man puts rivulets and rivers—the one a source of power for industrial purposes, the other the highways of commerce and of traveling, both adding to the riches and civilization of a people. All these considerations are involved in the idea of "river;" and there are few of them that could not be illustrated by reference to the brook that may pass the school or the river that may flow through the city.

Let the subject be "*mountains.*" There may be some hill near the school which the children may have beguiled a summer's day in climbing. They are to observe its shape—whether it be broad and flat, or steep, and in part precipitous—whether it be a single hill, or one of a range—the matter of which its surface is composed, whether earth or rock in any of its forms—the covering of its surface, whether grass, or heather, or shrubs—the animals that may be browsing on its slopes—the streams which may leap down its sides—the climate varying with the hight till they reach the cool of the summit—the cornfields at its base, extending more or less up the slope—then the woods, and, lastly, the grass—the toilsomeness of the ascent, and the time required for it—and, perhaps, the metals or minerals dug out from it.

Let the subject be one of the phenomena of "climate."—On a "*winter's day*" let them observe the thick flakes of the falling snow, whitening the face of nature, or the hardening influence of the clear frost covering our lakes, ponds, and roads with ice—the rapid motion and the thick covering necessary for comfort—the fires we need in our houses—the care we need to take of our animals—the unproductiveness and barrenness of nature at the time—the short day, and the long night. On a "*summer's day*," again, the mild air—the clear, blue sky—the moderate motion and the lighter clothing—the face of nature beaming with animal life, and clothed with the rich vegetable green—the treasures in the fields—the long day and the short night.

In these lessons on geography, scientific order is of little consequence. The true point of commencement is with what the children see and know. Thus, if we give a lesson on "rivers," we just take them in imagination to the river side, and exercise their senses on what is before them. The river is (suppose) broad, deep in the middle, shelving, clear or brown, smooth or broken in surface; its banks are pebbly, or rocky, or grassy, and so on. For the next lesson, we take them to a spot further up where different phenomena are seen, and then further up still to its source; next take them down the river till they come to the point at which it falls into the sea, or into some other river. Proceed in the same spirit, and by similar subdivisions, with mountains, matters of climate, &c., constructing the lessons entirely after the manner of the object-lesson, as exemplified in §§ 26–28.

79. It is when these and a series of such minute pictures of "home" are conceived, that the child's imagination can take wings to other lands. He can expand the idea of the river at home till it reaches the Rhine, or the Nile, or the Mississippi, or the Amazon, and the circumstances of the one till they pass into those of the others; the mountain at home till he shall see the Alps, with their fertile valleys and lower slopes, and their woods above, reaching upwards to the everlasting snow; or till he shall conceive Etna with its teeming sides and magnificent prospects and the smoke rising from its volcano top. From the "winter's day" at home he may realize the dreary desolation of the Arctic zone, with its freezing temperature, its wilderness of ice, its stunted vegetation, its dearth of animal life, its short cheerless days, and its humble fur or skin-clad dwellers; and the "summer's day" at home may lead him to fancy himself beneath the scorching blue sky of the tropics, with the want of rain, the rapid and

abundant growth of plants and animals, the overpowering heat of day and the dews of night, the jungle or the desert.

80. In this series of lessons the names of countries are sparingly dealt with, a few typical ones alone being given: typical, *i. e.*, of the different climates, but without map in the meantime. And it will be observed that the lessons are not expressly given on particular countries, as Egypt, or Arabia, or Lapland. A country is too vague an idea for a child at this time; he must have some definite object on which to rest his conceptions. Hence, the series is given on natural features, of which he can see certain examples around him, and these are stated as being in particular climates or countries. He associates the country with the object, not the object with the country. And the same holds in the series as now to be continued.

81. To have the means of describing the different regions of the earth more particularly, the teacher should proceed with a series of object-lessons on their productions. Thus, the lion, elephant, camel, tiger, wolf, bear, hyena, kangaroo, buffalo, reindeer, dog, sloth, serpent, whale, shark, eagle, vulture, ostrich, &c., are for geographical purposes so many types. So in the vegetable world are the palm, the olive, the bread-fruit, the vine, the cotton-plant, the tea-plant, the coffee-plant, the sugar-cane, rice, maize, cinnamon, cedar, mahogany, and the like. So with respect to man and his habits would be a series on the articles of food, clothing, and building. In the course of these lessons some of the principal countries—*not every country*—would have been noticed so frequently, that the children must have accumulated a number of ideas regarding each.

82. During this course of instruction, the only maps used are pictures—pictures of objects such as have been alluded to under the object-lesson, and pictures of scenes typical of countries. It is much to be wished that this latter kind of pictures were greatly more numerous and accessible for schools than they are. Thus the map of Arabia for the infant school should be a desert scene, exhibiting the general features of the desert and the sky, the caravan in whole, the camel as an animal, and the Arab himself in his usual costume. On the same principle should we have Egypt represented by its river and its pyramids; India by its rice-fields, its jungles with their fierce inhabitants, its mountain-passes with their elephant trains; China by its tea-plantations; Australia by its bush with the native and the kangaroo; the South Sea Islands by an assembly of natives on land or in their canoes; South America by its forests and its pampas; North America by its cotton-fields and its sugar-fields; the Indian territory by its prairies and buffaloes; the Esquimaux by his sledge

and dogs; Turkey by its mosque and worshipers; Spain by its wild mountain-pass and picturesque traveler; Switzerland by its jagged peaks and chamois-hunter; Italy and Greece by their ruins; Lapland by its reindeer and sledge; and, to come to our own country, Britain by its several scenes of the river crowded with shipping, of the busy factory, of pastoral and agricultural life, and of the hills of the north and west, with the sheep and the deer and the birds that occupy them.

83. The geography of the infant school is thus a series of object-lessons connected by a geographical link. It but prepares materials for the formal study of geography. It may be thought that the use of the map would facilitate the instruction; but it is quite immaterial whether the map be in the school at all or not. It is the business of the next stage of progress to "*localize*" all that has been learnt; which it does by going regularly over the map, and fixing down in position the countries which as yet are only names to the children. The utmost use of the map that should be made in the infant school is to go over with the elder infants, if time permit at the end of their course, on a physical map of the world distinctly outlined so as to show the features of districts, the general outline of what they have already learnt—showing the position of the different countries with whose names they are familiar, collecting all their knowledge regarding each, and explaining how the directions of north, south, east, and west, which they have already learned from observation of the sun's course, and which they have been taught to apply to the whole district about them over which their eye can reach, are exhibited on the map.*

6. *On Reading to the Children.*

84. Reading to the children is an important resource of the infant-school teacher. Considering the universality of this practice in infant family training, it is singular that it should have been so much neglected in school. The benefit of it seems clear and indisputable, in the one case as in the other. It is not for the sake of any instruction conveyed by it that we recommend this practice; the child receives his instruction otherwise. But two advantages flow from it, which are very apparent. The first is the stimulus which it gives the children to learn to read for themselves; and this is peculiar to reading *to* them as distinct from addressing them in words of our own. Let the teacher avowedly read before them; let him manage it so as to

* For giving descriptive lessons on geography, the best helps are familiar accounts of places or of travels. See also, "*First Ideas of Geography*," (Parker;) and "*Near Home*" and "*Far Off*," (Hatchard.)

interest them in what he reads; let him cluster pleasant associations around the book; let him show them how *he* knows the stories only by reading, and how they must learn to read for themselves to know the stories recorded in books; let him, in a word, be thus constantly showing them, directly and indirectly, what a pleasant thing it is to be able to read, and there is certainly present to their minds a stimulus to exertion, a motive of a noble sort or the germ of one, the love of knowledge for its own sake. The second advantage is the culture it imparts to them—culture of the imagination and of the heart, for it is to these the reading should appeal. Direct address, or the relating of stories, may attain the same end; but, even if all teachers had the power of vivid description and picturesque narrative, which they have not, their resources are greatly extended by the use of the book. It presents them with an indefinite range of beautiful ideas, clothed in a fair and ample drapery of words. These have a permanent existence withal, and may be read again and again, affording to the child renewed pleasure at every repetition. Reading to the children, moreover, supposing it conducted in a way to interest them, accustoms them to close and self-sustaining attention.

85. The greatest obstacle to the practice of reading is one of a practical kind; the difficulty of procuring suitable books to read from. To set forth all the characteristics of a child's book would be to recapitulate much of what has been said in the former part of this treatise; but the teacher may be aided in his judgment by bearing the following cautions in mind: (1.) The subject of it must be a story, of which the interest centers distinctly on a person, or on some object actually or virtually personified. Science and history, therefore, however much simplified and garnished, are from their very nature unsuitable; the one being too abstract, the other too complex. (2.) The book must appeal to the imagination, and not merely to the reason or understanding. A cold didactic style, however clear, has no attractions for children. (3.) In speaking to the feelings the book must not assume too great a degree of self-consciousness in the children. Some otherwise suitable books are spoilt by a perpetual moralizing in set terms, and calling for reflections of a nature quite beyond the children to make; forgetting that the morality should be inwoven into the entire web of the narrative, and that they imbibe the impression of it in silently identifying themselves with a personage whose sentiments and actions are moral. (4.) In teaching morality the book must be careful to base it on a sure foundation. A false morality is a dangerous, yet very common, fault in a child's book. Virtue is very frequently associated with personal and temporal advantage, as when "getting

on in the world" is made the basis for inculcating truthfulness and honesty; and vice is frequently condemned on the ground of personal and temporal disadvantage alone. If virtue and vice be grounded on no deeper basis, the child's morality must in course of time be rudely shocked, and perhaps overthrown. Sometimes virtue and vice are founded on extreme cases of reward and punishment. Thus the boy who robs nests has often assigned to him the fate of falling from a tree into a river and being drowned; or the lying child goes on in a wicked course, till perhaps he comes to the gallows, or, like Ananias, is struck dead. Such consequences either rarely or never occur; and if no other penalties of vice are mentioned, the child will conclude from its never seeing these particular ones occur that there are none at all. (5.) The book should portray virtue for imitation rather than vice for avoidance. It is not prudent to anatomize vicious characters before the young, to trace their steps through their various schemes, to show up their designs; even for the purpose of denouncing them. As has been well remarked, "the infectious nature of vices is not destroyed by the reproach which may be attached to them." There is no use of giving children an experience of evil they had better be without. Let their innocence be preserved as long as it may; the knowledge of good and evil will come soon enough. Not the dark side of human nature, then, but the bright should be held up as the picture on which they should dwell. (6.) The subject of the book may either be level to their experience, or it may be remote from it; but the story should not be improbable. Robinson Crusoe and the Fairy Tales are equally admissible. "Once upon a time there was a troop of boys, notorious for all kinds of juvenile wickedness, engaged in a bird's nesting expedition. One, better than the rest, and associated with them then only by accident, was shocked at their profanity and cruelty. They lost their way in a wood and were benighted, and had to sleep under a tree. Presently noises were heard from the howling of the wild beasts. The good boy withdrew from his comrades; who were attacked and destroyed by the beasts. He escaped." This outline, taken from a book professing to be a child's book, shows, with other faults, the absurd improbabilities often set before children. (7.) The sentiment and style of the book should be unaffected. The flattering prettinesses sometimes addressed to the young with the view of getting them to listen, regarding either their personal appearance, or their actions and dispositions, can only breed conceit and affectation in return. And, in point of style, there is an *excess* of expression, a studied affectation and overdoing of childish words, which by no means add to the beauty or simplicity of the narrative.

86. Books for children fall under two classes; those whose subject-matter is real, and those in which it is fictitious. For the former kind many incidents in biography, and many biographical incidents in history, ought to be available. But much less is available than would at first sight appear; which is fully explained if we recollect that a large proportion of these incidents are connected with crime and punishment, and that it is not so much the quiet and unobtrusive virtues they record, as the more noisy and popular. Besides, biography and history are seldom or never written for children. On the whole, the teacher may make more use of these by studying the incidents himself and relating them to the class, simplified in style and somewhat idealized. There remain to be noticed those books which embody fictitious narrative. The utilitarian spirit has almost entirely banished from the present generation the old nursery tales; Cinderella, Aladdin, Sinbad, and the fairies are in disgrace. These and similar tales must and will be brought back again, being fitted for children in all time. They are much superior in respect of healthy influence to the generality of the books which for the present have superseded them. They are not professedly moral tales; they are tales of imagination and amusement; but neither are they immoral; of none of them can worse be said than that they leave morality where they found it. Whilst many of them, especially the fairy tales, have certainly a distinct moral influence, separating good from evil by a wide and impassable gulf, instead of mingling them up together as is now so commonly done. From these tales the teacher may make a selection suitable for his purpose. Stories about animals, and dialogues on familiar processes and things, are very attractive to children, and easily accessible. The fables of Æsop and such like have at all times been favorites with children, and have the advantage of having somewhat escaped the general ostracism of our day. Perhaps the fable is improved for the purposes of reading when neatly done into verse. Next might be named extracts from the works of writers like Miss Edgeworth, Mrs. Barbauld, Mrs. Lee, Maria Hack, Peter Parley, and others; till we come to tales like Sandford and Merton, and Robinson Crusoe. Extracts might also be made from some other established fictions—of course to be somewhat prepared by the teacher. And there is a large variety of children's papers in current publication, where he may find something to serve his purpose. But he should carefully peruse beforehand whatever he reads, to see that its sentiment be correct; even "religious tales," so called, should not be exempted from careful scrutiny with this view, as it is seldom they handle religious truth without distorting it or dislocating its parts.

87. Reading to children, with the view of stimulating the imagination, must be carefully regulated in amount. It is not prudent to let this faculty be dormant; but it is worse to over-excite it. Two or three weekly readings of about twenty minutes each are amply sufficient. But the teacher should watch the effect of his reading on the individual temperaments of the children. Some are more liable to be excited than others; who should accordingly be less frequently present at the reading.*

7. *On Reading and Spelling.*

88. Learning to read is unquestionably a *task* for the child. It should, therefore, not be seriously undertaken until he is fit to encounter a task; it must be carried on with a very careful regard to his strength; and it should be the object of his instructor to make him feel it to be a task as little as possible.

89. The proper view to take of the child learning to read is that he is learning to recognize in written forms the words with which he is already familiar *in speech*. We only surround him with difficulties if we regard his reading-book at this period as the means of extending his vocabulary. He acquires words in the conversational lessons, the natural vehicle for his acquiring them; his reading, let it be repeated, should be nothing more than the recognition of what is already familiar to him. If this be allowed, four things will follow. *First*, he should not begin to read from books till he has considerable acquaintance with spoken language; an acquaintance not only with all the fundamental words denoting relation, some of which occur in every sentence we utter, but with the names of all the familiar things about him, and with the most common qualities of things.

* On this whole subject, see "*North British Review*," August, 1854; "*Necker*," vol. ii., book iv., chap. viii., and "*Home Education*," chap. x. A few books suitable for reading from to children may be mentioned:—

"*Evenings at Home.*"
Edgeworth's "*Early Lessons.*"
"*Winter Evenings, or Tales of Travelers*," by Maria Hack.
Mrs. Lees' "*Anecdotes of Animals.*"
——— "*Familiar Natural History.*"
"*My own Treasury*," by Mark Merriwell.
"*Peter Parley's Tales.*"
Bingley's "*Tales about Animals.*"
"*Lessons from the Animal World*," (Society for Promoting Christian Knowledge.)
"*Life of a Bird*," do.
"*The Nursery Tales.*"
Gammer Grethel's "*German Fairy Tales.*".
"*Granny's Wonderful Chair*," by Frances Browne.
Æsop's "*Fables.*"
"*Woodland Rambles, or Conversations on Trees.*"
"*The Mine*," by Rev. I. Taylor.
"*Arabian Nights.*"

This list may be largely increased by any teacher who will spend an hour in a bookseller's shop.

Secondly, the reading-lesson should consist of words which have a sense for him, and not only so, but of sentences which express complete thoughts; otherwise there is nothing for him to recognize. Lessons consisting of columns of single words, and much more of columns of syllables or parts of words, are not suitable. He should have in all his lessons the stimulus and pleasure which arise from the recognition by the eye of what is already known to his mind. *Thirdly*, the subjects of his reading-lessons should be things with which he is familiar from his observations. He will recognize most readily what he best understands and sympathizes with. *Fourthly*, his reading must be systematically interwoven with his speech. He should be engaged in a conversational lesson on the subject he has been reading about, which shall embody the words he has read. This will give a practical aspect to all he reads, and secure from the beginning the habit of reading with the understanding.*

90. For the purposes of the reading-lesson we may reckon two periods in infant-school attendance. The one is the preparatory period, that in which the child is being prepared for reading, rather than actually reading; the other is that in which reading from books is a systematic lesson. We may consider the middle of the fifth year as the boundary between the two; so that the first shall extend over a year at least. During this period the child is unfit to be subjected to tasks. He may be engaged with the first formal steps of reading, as we shall see; but the real preparation for his subsequent reading is the frequent conversational lesson, which develops his general intelligence and gives him some power over spoken language.

91. His preparatory lessons in reading should leave him in possession of all the fundamental words in written language, and of a number of the names of familiar things and qualities. The method of giving these lessons is still matter of opinion. The old way, and perhaps still after all the common way, is to teach the sounds of words apparently by associating these with the series of letter-names in the words; but this is to teach spelling rather than reading. It is evident that there is no natural association between the names of the letters composing a word, and the sound of the word. More recently it has been sought to gain the end by decomposing words according to the powers or sounds (and not the names) of the letters. This method is certainly capable of doing good service when properly used; but it has suffered somewhat from injudicious application. The

* The reader will find the argument for carrying the child's understanding along with what he reads, and the manner of doing so, fully stated in Pilans' "*First Letter on the Principles of Elementary Teaching*," see "*Contributions to Cause of Education*," pp. 8, &c.

attempt to apply it universally to English words leads to an elaborateness and intricacy of system quite unsuitable for a class of infants; who do not learn reading, or any thing else, by rules. Finally, it has been proposed to teach the child to read without the aid of either the common or the phonic spelling; the words being simply viewed as pictures, with which the eye is to make itself familiar, *in whole*, as it does with other pictures.

92. Our first aim in teaching the child reading must be to make his path interesting; our second, to make it clear. To attain the first, we must awaken his curiosity, intelligence, and activity about the things of which he reads; to attain the second, we must give him whatever aid is to be derived from a rational classification of letters or of principles of sound. There is certainly a danger of trusting too exclusively to the second, from the very fact that it requires us more or less to construct a *system* of procedure for ourselves; it should be remembered, however, that whilst the aid derived from this source may seem to make the child's path clear, it does not necessarily make it interesting. That is secured only when we attain our first aim; which must therefore be viewed as the higher of the two. But good teaching will keep both in view, and will strive to make them act harmoniously in support of each other. With these preliminary remarks, the order and method of the early lesson may now be suggested:—

93.—(1.) *The Alphabet.*—The names of the letters must be learned, not so much for any direct use they are of in learning to read, but just because they are the names of things that require frequently to be spoken about. And they may be acquired at the very beginning of the course, in a short time, and not only without causing the child any trouble, but with positive interest to him. By far the best way is by the use of letter-cards and slates. Whatever order the letters are taken in, let the card first be shown to the class, the form of the letter carefully traced and described, a drawing of it made on the blackboard, and from that by the children themselves on their own slates, and the name frequently repeated in course of the process: when they have all been gone over in this way, with the necessary revisals, let the teacher question them on the cards at random, adding an easy or perhaps amusing description of the forms, and let the children question each other with them in various ways as their ingenuity may suggest. Both the capitals and small letters may be learnt in this way.* Thus the lessons on the Alphabet are rather form-lessons than reading-lessons.

* What Locke says of reading is interesting. He recommends that children be amused into a knowledge of letters and words; suggesting the use of an ivory ball with twenty-six sides,

94.—(2.) *Words of two Letters.*—These words should be learnt at once, having the sounds attached to their forms without any analysis into their separate letters. They are almost all irregular in sound, and do not admit of phonic analysis, even if it were desirable. The most convenient way of teaching them is to have them printed on separate cards like the letters, and a similar process gone through with them. The ingenuity of the children may be agreeably and profitably exercised in arranging them into sentences. For this purpose there should be a board or frame conveniently constructed, so as to admit of a row of sentences being placed on it. To these words of two letters many words should be added which consist of only two sounds, though of three letters, *e. g.*, *are*, *you*, *the*, &c.; and some of the most common of three sounds, *and*, *but*, *with*, *not*, and such like. If this apparatus can not be had, lesson-sheets are the best substitute; but an interest attaches to the use of such an apparatus which even lesson-sheets can not attain.

95.—(3.) When they come to read from the lesson-sheets, the class should be taught to perceive analogies of sound in words; that is to say, they should be exercised in phonic analysis. Thus the words *at*, *an*, *ox*, *all*, *in*, *it*, &c., are the roots of so many classes of words:—

at	an	all	ox	in	it
b-at	c-an	b-all	b-ox	f-in	b-it
c-at	f-an	c-all	f-ox	p-in	f-it
f-at	m-an	f-all		s-in	h-it
h-at	p-an	h-all			p-it
m-at	r-an	t-all			s-it
r-at	v-an	w-all			
s-at					

Whenever, therefore, a number of words from any such class occurs in a reading exercise—*e. g.*, *bat*, *cat*, *fat*—they should be compared, so that the *common* element *at* may be recognized, and also the *different* elements, to wit, the sounds attached to the letters *b*, *c*, and *f*. The number of classes of words thus formed may be largely increased

---

and a letter on each, for the child to play with; or four dice, one for vowels, the rest for consonants to throw words with. "I know a person," says he, "who, by pasting on the six vowels on the six sides of a die, and the eighteen consonants on the sides of other three dice, has made this a play for his children, that he shall win who, at one cast, throws most words on these four dice; whereby his eldest son [yet a child] has played himself into spelling, with great eagerness, and without once having been chid for it, or forced to it."—"*Locke*," sects. 148-155. Compare these lines in Cowper's "*Conversation:*"—

> "As alphabets in ivory employ,
> Hour after hour, the yet unlettered boy,
> Sorting and puzzling, with a deal of glee,
> Those seeds of science called his A, B, C,
> So language," &c.

The idea of cheating the child into knowledge, however, is not quite sound, as going to confound work with play. In the infant school we must accustom the child to the idea of *work* but this work may quite well be made agreeable.

by taking as roots certain syllables which are not words, but from each of which a number of words arise by the prefixing of a consonant; *e. g.*,

-ot	-ug	-og	ill	-ad
c-ot	h-ug	b-og	b-ill	b-ad
h-ot	m-ug	d-og	h-ill	l-ad
l-ot	d-ug	h-og	m-ill	h-ad
n-ot	r-ug	f-og	t-ill	s-ad
p-ot	j-ug	l-og	k-ill	m-ad
r-ot		fr-og		
sh-ot				

and some others. These words, it must be understood, do not occur to the class, as they are here given, tabularly. The reading-lessons are constructed so as to present them in course, and they are selected from these for the purpose of analysis. Classes of which *can*, *cat*, *car*, *cap*, are types, having the common element first and the differing one at the end of the word, should also be examined. No great number of reading-lessons is required to put the children in possession of all the sounds of the letters, both consonants and vowels. When this is done, they have the key to reading in their hands; and they should be required systematically to use it henceforward.

96. No reading-book should be put into the hands of the class during these early lessons. This is a point of some importance; a class who are obliged to look individually at their books are thereby precluded from that mutual sympathy and common activity which is necessary to their success in any exercise. Lesson-sheets are an intermediate resource between the letter and word cards just described and the use of the reading-book. The cards and lesson-sheets, and the blackboard and their own slates, should be the sole materials for the instruction in reading of a class under four and a half years of age.

97. The teaching should be continued in the same spirit when the child takes the reading-book in hand. (1.) The phonic analysis should accompany each lesson, so that he may have every facility which the ear can afford to reading. And the teacher may observe that, whilst it would certainly be better to have the lessons arranged in the reading-book for this analysis, he is not altogether dependent on whether they are so or not. By using his blackboard he may give analogies of sound from every lesson. Irregular words can not be thus analyzed; their sounds should be at once told. (2.) The subject of every reading-lesson must be carried home to the child's understanding, so that it may be thoroughly lodged amongst the things which have an interest for him. And not only *at the time* should

teacher and pupils talk over the subject; it will be found very conducive to the end in view to recommend it to their attention over the evening so that they may collect any points of information at home about it which they can, and to recur to the subject on the morrow or soon after. (3.) If the moral aids to the reading-lesson be wanting, it will avail little to have those of an intellectual or mechanical sort. It is they alone that can supply motives to the child for exertion. Patience, kindliness of temper, good humor, keep the child pleased with itself, and with its teacher; which is essential to success. It is not indispensable that the child should be pushed on rapidly; but it is indispensable that he should like the work he is engaged in. Success in teaching the elements of reading seems often a very arbitrary thing; it is the moral qualities of the teacher which will be found to explain the results.

98. Reading includes not only the power of recognizing words, but of uttering their sounds correctly; and to this aspect of it great attention should be paid in the infant school. Children pick up the sounds of words by imitation, so that they are liable to error from two causes; either from having wrong models for imitation, or from their own imperfect imitation of their models. Under the first head are to be reckoned provincialisms of all sorts, but also deliberate mispronunciations encouraged in them by their parents under the notion of accommodating their speech to the wants of the children in point of simplicity. Under the second head we may set the confounding of similar or allied sounds by the vocal organs, or the imperfect formation of difficult sounds; the confounding of the liquids *l* and *r*, *s* and *th*, *t* and *k*, *ghr* and *r*, &c. Such impurities of articulation occur in every infant school; the pupil who exhibits them should be taken apart, and be made to observe the true sounds with the ear and the manner of their formation by the vocal organs with the eye, till he can utter them.

99. Another fault to be guarded against is indistinctness, arising either from a general feebleness of articulation, or from the suppression or slurring of some part of the sound of a word. This occurs most readily with the liquids, especially when two of these, or a liquid and a dental, follow each other in successive syllables. To correct this fault, if it have been already incurred, the pupil should be accustomed to full and strong utterance of all the parts of the word, even overdoing it for a time; reading sentences with a slight pause after each word, and words with a slight pause after each syllable. The most certain preventive of this fault in an infant school is the habit of distinct and forcible articulation in the teacher, in speaking as well

as reading. The value of this habit as a qualification in an infant-school teacher is for the most part not sufficiently estimated.

100. These are the faults to which infants are most liable in their reading. But the teacher must cultivate, so far as there is opportunity, all the recognized qualities of good reading; *e. g.*, proper time, which consists not only in stopping at the pauses, but in giving proper lengths to the vowel-sounds, as, *feel*, *sweet*, *good*, *dream*, *broad;* proper tone and pitch, which varies with each voice, but which is equally free from monotonous drawl or sing-song on the one hand, and from an irregular scream on the other.

101. The practice of simultaneous reading, moderately indulged in, may be attended with some good effects. *First*, in respect of time, it tends to correct both the extremes of quick and of slow reading by requiring conformity to one standard. *Secondly*, it tends to highten distinctness of utterance from the very effort needed to observe a measured time. One is always struck by the degree to which distinctness characterizes simultaneous utterance. *Thirdly*, it tends to modify any peculiarities of tone in individual readers; after a little practice, a harmony of intonation is almost always established. Too much, however, must not be expected from simultaneous reading; it tends to correct faults rather than to impart any positive excellence.

Spelling.

102. According to the common way reading is acquired through spelling. This relation should be reversed; spelling should be learned through reading. There should be no formal lesson on spelling given during the preparatory lessons on reading; and yet it would be a mistake to suppose that the child is not learning to spell during these, for spelling is a habit of the eye. The forms of words must be familiar to the eye before there can be any spelling. This then is the contribution which the early lessons in reading make to the child's progress in spelling—and it is a great one—that they stamp the images of the words on his mind, so that his eye recognizes them when it sees them, and, consequently, any deviation from their form.

103. The elder infants may be practiced in spelling; but not alone upon any prepared amount, nor in any one lesson in particular. It may be introduced as effectively in the object or form-lesson as in the reading-lesson. The exercise is designed to test their intimacy with the forms of the words that have come before them during their preparatory lessons in reading. It holds with spelling, as with reading, that the subject should be words forming a sense. Besides the names of things, sentences should be spelt through, by single words or by a

number of words together. Much is attained if the children can spell monosyllabic words with some facility when they leave the infant school.

104. As spelling is learnt, not for the purposes of spoken language, but for those of written, so spelling and writing must be conjoined as soon as practicable. The elder infants, who have previously had practice in writing on their slates the letters of the alphabet, and also the simplest kinds of words, may profitably be engaged in this rudimentary dictation-exercise, which serves the double end of teaching them both writing and spelling.

Grammar.

105. Grammar is sometimes taught in the infant school, but with little propriety. The teacher is often tempted to introduce the elements of this subject by seeing that the children seem to understand his familiar oral illustrations of noun, verb, and other parts of speech. But this understanding is not real; it can be turned to no practical account. Nothing whatever is gained by such an anticipation of future studies. The work has all to be done over again; and it occupies time which may be more profitably occupied with subjects of whose propriety there can be no dispute. Therefore it should be altogether deferred.

IV. RELIGIOUS INSTRUCTION.

106. "Our Father who art in heaven" should be the key-note of all the religious instruction conveyed in the infant school. In these words "is comprised all religious truth, as the plant is in the seed." God is our father; for He is the creator of ourselves and of all we see around us. He is our father; and, as a father, He provides lovingly and carefully for all His children. He is our father; and, when He sees His children in danger, He rescues us from it, having even sent into our world his Son, who is our elder brother, to save us from our greatest danger—the death of sin. He is our father; and so we have "the bright hope of eternal life, for why should a father give life to his children in order afterwards to slay them?"* He is *our* father, loving not one only, but all the members of His great family; who ought, therefore, to love one another. He is our father; and so should we give to Him all the love and reverence and obedience which are due to a father. He is our father *in heaven*, all-wise therefore, holy, and good; and so should we try to be like Him, and humbly seek to know and do His will. He is our father in heaven; and,

* These quotations are from the work of Girard, already referred to for the manner in which it exhibits the whole course and spirit of religious instruction.

if we be dutiful children, He will take us to dwell with Himself in light forever and ever. "Our Father in heaven!" words worthy, from their inexhaustible depth of meaning, and fullness of obligation, to preface the model prayer which our Divine Teacher, the Son of our Father in heaven, hath given us!

107. This idea of "God our Father in heaven" must be made the center of the whole circle of doctrines we teach to children. The circle is wide; but in traversing it we must ever keep the center in our eye, as the sun which gives light and life to the whole. There is no difficulty in reaching the infant mind with doctrines like the following; which, so far from being received by it as strange, seem to it quite natural, from that "sense of God" which pervades its being: God the creator of the world and of man—God the preserver of all—His attributes of power, wisdom, eternity, unchangeableness, omniscience, omnipresence, holiness, truth, goodness—His Son, our Redeemer, Teacher, Example—the love, reverence, and obedience we owe Him—our sinfulness, and our duty to follow holiness—the Scriptures, His Word, which we should read—prayer—the reward of the good—the shortness of life—death—life in heaven with himself. This outline comprehends the substance of our religion; and is an amply sufficient basis on which to rear instruction in its practical duties.

108. Every thing depends on the *manner* in which we convey this instruction. In this we must have respect to the laws which regulate the whole instruction of the infant school. An abstract style of teaching is unsuitable, however clear our proofs or simple our phraseology. The "Catechism" is the exponent of this style of teaching, and can never, therefore, be the vehicle of effectual instruction by itself. Its forms of expression are mere words to the child.* We must use the conversational form of instruction, which allows us to present to the child whatever subjects and phases of subjects are fit for him. And these oral lessons must convey their teaching by means of "examples" or "illustrations." The doctrines of Scripture must be learned from the narrative of Scripture; and thus the two will be interwoven as they should be, each throwing light on the other. The complexion presented by the religious instruction of the infant school to a person viewing it as a whole is that of a series of stories, which, in the first instance, engage the imagination and feelings of the child from their

* The teacher is often obliged, in deference to the wishes of parents, to use a catechism. There are one or two simple catechisms constructed for children. In teaching the catechism, there are but two alternatives, either to hear the children simply repeat it, or to connect the illustrative method of instruction with it. The mere explaining of its words and sequence conveys no ideas to the child.

own interest; but each of which suggests a doctrinal lesson, and the whole series of which is so arranged as to leave the child in possession of a connected scheme of the doctrines of the Bible. If this manner of teaching by story be followed, there is little danger of the instruction falling into the great error which most besets it, that of becoming too theological; which it does either when it tries to explain abstruser doctrines, which are as difficult for men to comprehend as for children, or when it uses technical theological terms instead of the language of every-day life. In stating the doctrines as they successively flow from the daily lesson, by far the best way is to express them in selected texts from Scripture, clear, short, and emphatic; which the children should commit to memory and often be made to repeat. It is well to have a series of these on the school-walls; but they are for the most part not sufficiently, often they are never, used.

109. The following scheme will exemplify the nature of the lessons; and the teacher may expand it indefinitely. It will be seen that the channels of instruction are various; being most commonly incidents from Old or New Testament history, sometimes the parables of our Lord, and sometimes mere descriptions addressed to the imagination. The same truth may be enforced by many lessons, for the sake of impressiveness, either in the same aspect or in different aspects:—

Truth to be Learned.	Channel of Instruction.	Texts.
God our Father....	Comparison with earthly Parent. Parable of Prodigal Son.	"Our Father who art in heaven." Ps. ciii. 13.
God the Creator....	of the world. " heavens. " man and beast. (Descriptive Lessons.)	Gen. i. 1. Ps. xxxiii. 6.
God the Preserver..	Incidents in the life of Noah, Abraham, David, Daniel, Elijah, Peter, Christ.	Ps. xxxvi. 6. Ps. cxlv. 20.
God's Power	Creation. Flood. Red Sea. Miracles in life of Daniel, Peter, Christ.	Ps. clxvii. 5. Luke i. 37. Matt. viii. 27.
Omniscience.......	Incidents in life of Abraham, Moses, Elijah, Peter, Pharaoh, Herod.	Acts i. 24. 1 John iii. 3-20.
Omnipresence......	Jacob. Daniel. Christ.	Prov. xv. 13. Gen. xxviii. 16.
Holiness	Our first parents. Flood. Sodom. Abraham, Moses, &c.	Ps. cxlv. 1 John i. v.
God our Redeemer in Christ. Christ our example, teacher, elder brother, intercessor, Saviour	Under this head may be introduced the chief incidents in the life of Christ, both parables and miracles.	Corresponding Texts.

TRUTH TO BE LEARNED.	CHANNEL OF INSTRUCTION.	TEXTS.
Our own sinfulness. Holiness alone from the Lord........	Moses. Israelites. David. Peter.	Do.
Death............	Any of the prominent characters in Scripture.	Do.
Resurrection	Christ's; Lazarus'.	
Future State of Life or Death........	Parable of Lazarus. Transfiguration. Our Lord's parable of sheep and goats.	

By filling up this outline a little, a series of lessons for a year might easily be constructed. And this would suffice for the purposes of doctrinal instruction in the infant school; it would be better to revise in the second year than to extend the course. In this case, a higher style of treatment would be necessary; which might be varied by sometimes basing the instruction on Scripture emblems. These are not less excellent a field of instruction for the younger infants than for the elder, who can bring the knowledge of Scripture incidents already acquired to bear on their illustration.

110. The same method must be followed substantially in teaching moral and religious duty. The only difference is that in addition to the incidents of Scripture the teacher will find a large store of anecdotes in secular narrative serviceable as the ground-work of his instruction. He should be acquainted with many of these; indeed, he should be a reader of biography for the purpose. With each lesson a text of Scripture should be committed to memory. In this way should be enforced the whole range of virtues appropriate to children: obedience to parents, to teachers, respect to old age, truthfulness, honesty, justice, a forgiving spirit, kindness, kindness to animals, avoiding story-telling and nicknames, charity to the poor, patience, meekness, diligence, faithfulness to trust, redeeming the time, order, punctuality, economy, cleanliness, &c., &c. Many stories may be found for each of these, in addition to those which the teacher's imagination may construct from observing the children's conduct toward each other; so that this practical religious instruction is always going on, and yet is ever fresh.

111. Apart from the formal religious lesson, much instruction may be given incidentally, suggested either by what is observed in the course of the secular lessons, or by circumstances which occur in the daily intercourse of the school. Such instruction is very valuable; it is the test of the sincerity of the formal instruction—that which shows to the children that the teacher's mind habitually turns to the solemn truths he teaches in the religious lesson, and which exhibits the proper

use to make of these truths—that which alone gives a religious character to the whole work. It is that which inclines the child to try every thing by the light of God's law, and to take a Christian view of all His works. At the same time little can be said of it except that it should be given; the time and manner of giving it can be reduced to no rule. But the teacher who keeps in view the high moral ends of his teaching will never lack opportunities at which, without any abruptness or forcing, to drop the word in season into the willing ear of the child.

112. Whilst it will hold as a rule that in seeking to reach the mind with religious instruction, the same principles of teaching must be followed which are approved of in the secular lesson, it will always contribute to effectiveness of impression that the whole treatment should give indications of greater seriousness of manner than the ordinary school-work demands. A powerful influence will be exercised on the young mind if it is wont to see sacred subjects handled in a way which betokens the reverent recognition by teacher and pupils of a Power before whom both must bow. Any expedients in class-management, therefore, which interfere or seem to interfere with this, may well be dispensed with, even though experience recommends them for adoption in the secular lesson. The object of this is to set bounds about the religious lesson, that it may be indeed felt by all to be, what it is, a religious thing.

113. Specimens of the different kinds of lessons are subjoined by way of appendix. With reference to these, it may be observed that the subject-matter of the religious instruction is the same for the younger as for the elder infants. Their less advanced condition must be provided for in the manner of giving the instruction. The story, the object that forms the emblem, the features of the scene, in a word, whatever appeals to the observation must be dwelt upon, and the abstract instruction diminished in relative amount; the lesson itself should also be shorter, and the language more familiar.

Examples 1.

Christ's Power—Scripture Narrative—Matt. viii. 23–27.

Introduction.—Jesus' habit of going about preaching—traveled like other men—how travelers go? he would go mostly on foot, for he was poor—he lived much about the Sea of Galilee—often crossed it—how would he do so? where would he get the boat?

Scene described.—Describe the scene here—he and his disciples (name some) embarking—a little ship with a sail—the hills round the lake—how the gusts of wind sometimes come down—the storm raised—the large waves breaking over the vessel—what would they feel? why? and what would become of them?

Jesus.—What did they do at last? How they found Jesus—strange—was he in any danger? why not? what they thought he would do to them—they had seen him do strange things before. Ought they to have been afraid then? They should have trusted Him. What he told them.

The miracle.—What he did—his *word*—the wind ceased and the big waves fell, and there was a calm—danger removed. They had often seen a change, but none like this—what was strange here—what would they think? And other sailors who might be there who did not know him? Suppose the same case now.

Lessons.—What they said—what Jesus showed—could any man show such power? Jesus was God—and how good he was to his disciples, even though they were wrong—they would like to have such a friend.

Personal application.—Where is Jesus now? Powerful still, and good still, though we can not see him. Let us be his friends, and love him, and ask him to do us good; he sees us and hears us, and he will do it.

2.

114. God's goodness—Scripture Emblem—"The Lord is my Shepherd."

The emblem illustrated variously in its natural use.—What the shepherd does:—

Watches his sheep on the hill-sides, and in the fields—keeps away danger, either from men or wild animals.

Feeds them—seeks out the best pastures—the green pastures—beside the quiet streams—not amongst the rocks—or brings them food into the fields, when there is not grass for them.

What the shepherd does.—Leads them carefully from one place to another—how he gathers them from the hills or the field—watches them along the road, that none stray—and carries the young ones when they are tired.

Sometimes he is himself in danger—among the hills when he loses his way, or when snow comes—but he faces this danger for his sheep—for he is kind, and patient, and watchful.

The spiritual truth.—Who is the Shepherd spoken of here? Who can be the sheep? Christ says, "I am the good shepherd, and know my sheep, and am known of mine—the good shepherd giveth his life for the sheep." The kind of people that are his sheep? Those who love and obey him—how safe they must be with such a shepherd!

Personal application.—We need guidance in the world—for, like sheep, we are weak—let us love and follow Christ, that we may be his sheep, and that he may care for us.

Note.—Lessons on emblems very often fail from too great refinement in tracing the analogy; the truth is then apt to be lost sight of in verbal distinctions. We may illustrate the emblem in its natural use variously, as has been done above under three heads; but we are not to seek for as many corresponding heads in enforcing the fact symbolized in the emblem.*

* The teacher may derive assistance in giving lessons on emblems from Stow's little work on "*Bible Emblems.*"

19

3.

115. Christ's love for children—Scripture precept—"Suffer little children," &c.

Scene described.—Describe the scene of Jesus preaching to the people—he often did so—one time he was preaching, and there was a crowd around him—men and women, and *children* too. And the people were pleased with his mild and loving words—they brought their children to hear him—why? What they must have thought of Christ. He had always blessed people and done good to them.

The children received.—Disciples were there, as they always were—stopped the people—thought their Master had no time. He *had* very much to do, but he did not turn away the little children. He saw what they were doing, and prevented them.

Jesus' words.—His words—"*Suffer*"—suppose you ask me to let you go out, then I allow you, or *suffer* you—suppose you are writing on your book, and I tell you not to do it, then I "*forbid*" you. What Christ said, then, was that his disciples were to let the mothers bring their children to him, and not to stop them.

Lessons.—Christ cares for children as well as for men—he was once a little child himself. If he loves them what should they do to him? What he wishes them to be? Kind and obedient, &c., as he was—and if they are so he will bless them. He has many children in heaven with himself.

4.

116. One of a series of lessons on the Lord's Prayer—"Thy kingdom come."

Introduction.—The terms *King*, *Kingdom*, and *Subjects*, illustrated correlatively.

God's kingdom.—*Kingdom* amongst men is a particular part of the earth, as England, France, &c. Kingdom of God not like this—ranges over the whole earth, and has men of every nation and clime—the Briton, the Frenchman, the African from the sandy deserts, the Laplander from his icy plains and hills, &c. (Draw out this picture somewhat.)

Its laws.—*Kingdom* amongst men governed by certain laws—sometimes good and sometimes bad. Christ Kingdom has laws too—tell me some of them. Here is one, "Thou shalt love the Lord thy God," &c.—here is another, "Live at peace with all men,"—and another, "Do justly, love mercy," &c.—and another, "If thy brother offend thee, forgive him," &c. These are good laws—we must try to keep them—how happy men would be if all kept them!

Its prospects.—*Kingdom* of God not yet spread over whole world—name (descriptively) some people who are yet without it—once it only included one people (the Jews,) in a little country—now it has spread over much of the world—it will spread every where—Christ's promise.

How it is to be spread.—How the *Kingdom* of God is to be spread—by men preaching to the nations who are not in it—missionaries—what we can do—support them with our money when we have any—many missionaries in different lands, and needing to be supported—something else we can all do—pray God to help the missionaries, and to make the heathen willing to listen to them—nothing can be done without this.

Lessons.—Repeat prayer for spread of the Gospel, § 119. When Christ was on earth, he taught us to pray—and one of the things he told us was, to pray thus: "Thy kingdom come"—what we should pray for frequently.*

5.

117. Moral lesson—on Truth.

Introduction.—Children, you have all seen the cherry-tree growing—on the house-wall, with its long branches like arms, tacked to the wall to keep them up—sometimes on the school-wall.

The cherry-tree.—A story of a cherry-tree. One was growing on the wall of school, and it had much fruit on it—perhaps a basketful of cherries. It belonged to the teacher, and though not in the play-ground, the children could reach some of the branches, and the cherries on them—would it be right in the children to touch them? why not? We should take nothing that is not our own. Well, they did not touch them.

The crime.—Two little boys came to school—once they passed the tree and stood to look at it—and, as they looked, they wished for a cherry—one asked the other to pull one, but he would not—then he told him to touch it, and see how nice and big it was, which he did—when he had it in his hand, the other pushed his arm, and the cherry came off—the little boy was much afraid, and cried—the bigger one picked it up and divided it, and told him to say nothing about it.

The discovery.—By-and-bye the teacher missed the cherry, and asked some of the children, but they could not tell him of it—he asked the bigger of the two boys, who hesitated, and at length blamed his companion—the little boy was going to be punished, but, when the teacher asked him, he told the whole truth.

The indirect lie.—Which of the two do you think should have been punished? why? The little boy actually broke it off, but he could not help it—he did not know what was coming—dishonesty of big boy, and then, when the master asked, he told a lie. It was a lie, even though he himself did not pull it. This shows us that we may tell a lie, when our words may state truly what took place. Children sometimes tell lies in this way.

Practical lessons.—What would the rest of the children think of the boy who told the lie? Would they love him? trust him? Would God be pleased? what does he wish us to do? He will bless the child who speaks truth. Let us always tell the truth, then, even though it may lead us into punishment. Our hearts will tell us we have done right, and all that know us will think well of us.

Point to, and have repeated, the Scripture maxim on truth. Repeat the prayer against lying, § 119.†

118. Exercises of devotion are the practical recognition of all we

* For helps in giving religious instruction to infant classes, the teacher may with advantage consult the little works "*Peep of Day*," "*Line upon Line*," Draper's "*Stories from the Old and New Testaments*," "*Religious Instruction for Children*," by Miss Mayo; and works like Kitto's "*Daily Readings*," which supply materials for descriptive lessons.

† Since writing this lesson, I find that the incident related in this story happened in one of Mr. Wilderspin's schools. The reader may see it given at length in his "*Infant School System*," chap. x.; where he should turn to see the precise use to which the incident was put when it occurred.

learn regarding religion. Of course no infant school is opened or closed for the day without them; but perhaps more fruit might be reaped from them than is often attempted. They include two parts, sacred song and prayer. For the former, the children should learn a few hymns, or verses of hymns, suited to their capacity, after due explanation of their contents. To all, particular tunes should be attached; and, after they have been learnt, they should never be sung simply as singing exercises; a feeling of solemnity must attach to them. For the latter, it is common to use the Lord's Prayer, both in the morning and the afternoon, having it repeated simultaneously by the children in a becoming posture and manner. This is very proper; but it is desirable that other forms of prayer should be lodged in the children's minds; short, simple, and expressing each a single want. They should be called on to repeat these during the day's work, as occasion may suit, that they may both acquire the spirit of prayer, and become familiar with its proper elements. The following are offered as specimens for the elder infants; and the teacher may construct others for himself:—

119. Morning prayer.—O God, thou hast been very good to me through the night. I have laid me down and slept, for Thou hast kept me. Keep me through this day. May I ever think "Thou, God, seest me." May I do what is right. May I obey my parents and teachers. May I be kind to my companions and to all. O God, help me to be good, as Jesus was. Amen.

Evening prayer.—O God, Thou has kept me safely through this day; and I thank thee. O God, who lovest little children, Thou hast given me what I need: food to nourish me, a house to shelter me, and friends to love me. Help me to think of Thee more, and to do what Thou desirest me. Watch over me in my sleep, O God, for Jesus' sake. Amen.

A prayer for friends.—O my God, all good things come from Thee. Thou hast made me, and Thou keepest me by day and by night. Thou hast given me father and mother, and sister and brother, and friends, to love me and watch over me. O God, do Thou bless them. Give me a good heart that I may love them and be kind to them. And do Thou help us all to do Thy will, as Jesus did. Amen.

For a sick child.—O our heavenly Father, be kind to our sick companion. Thou hast done this: Thou knowest what is good for us all. Thy will be done. Be Thou, O God, near him, and give him rest. May he feel Thee beside him, and be at peace. Comfort his friends who are watching him. Restore him to us, if it please Thee, O God, for Jesus' sake. Amen.

For the spread of the gospel.—O God, Thou hast given us thy Holy Word to tell us what is right, and we thank Thee. Thou hast sent Jesus, thy Son, to bless us. Thou hast told us of heaven where we shall dwell with Thee, if we are good. Thou hast told us to put away sin: O God help us! May all the children in the world soon hear of Thee, and of thy Son, and of heaven; so that they may put away sin. And then we shall all serve Thee together, for Thou art our Father in Heaven, who lovest us all. O God, hear us! O God, save us! O God, let all the world soon know Thee and thy Son! for Jesus' sake. Amen.

AGAINST LYING.—O God, Thou hatest lying lips. I have sometimes said that which was not true; make me sorry for it, and do Thou forgive me. Help me to tell the truth at all times, to my parents, my teachers, and my companions; for this is pleasing to Thee, O God. When I am tempted to tell a lie, may I remember that Thou art near me, and hearest what I say. Grant this, O God, for Jesus' sake. Amen.

It is well that the children should learn some prayers like these to say by themselves. In addition to this, they may often repeat after the teacher short ejaculatory prayers, in keeping with the subject of the lesson, consisting of a single sentence; without formally learning them. This will give them the habit of prayer, and the benefits which result from a prayerful frame of mind.

XIII. METHODS OF INSTRUCTION.—GENERAL PRINCIPLES.*

BY THOMAS MORRISON.

METHOD.

1. In strict propriety of language, the term method has reference to the particular mode in which the subject matter of education is developed and presented to the mind. It is merely the outward form, while instruction is the substance. It is the shell, while the instruction communicated is the kernel. But the kernel determines the form of the shell, not the shell that of the kernel. So it is in method—it must be determined by the object we aim at; it will take its complexion from the views we entertain in regard to what constitutes education. If we consider education as consisting in the communication of a certain number of facts, in loading the memory without cultivating the imagination or the reason, we need pay but little attention to the method by which we accomplish the desired result, provided we do reach it. But if, on the other hand, we regard education as the development of an inward life, as the evolving into active and harmonious exercise the various principles of our nature; and if we believe that these principles exhibit themselves in a determinate order and according to fixed general laws; then the method by which we can secure this development becomes of great importance. So long as we hold low and inadequate, or, it may be, entirely erroneous views in regard to the end of education, so long will we pay little attention to the methods we pursue; but, in proportion to the comprehensiveness and soundness of our notions regarding education, will be the care and anxiety exhibited to follow what reason and experience have proved to be the best methods of conducting the education of the young. And this question of method is not one of secondary importance, which the teacher may neglect or not according to his pleasure. He can only neglect it at his peril; for, properly put, the question resolves itself into this—how

---

* "*Manual of School Management, for the use of Teachers, Students, and Pupil-Teachers.*" Glasgow: Hawthorn, p. 356. Contents.—I. Introduction. II. Teacher. III. School-house. IV. Registration. V. Classification. VI. Organization. VII. Discipline. VIII. Method. IX. Alphabet. X. Reading. XI. Examination. XII. Spelling. XIII. Writing. XIV Arithmetic. XV. Grammar. XVI. Geography. XVII. History. XVIII. Form and Coloı XIX. Singing. XX. Oral Lessons. XXI. Religious Knowledge.

can I best communicate instruction to a child so as best to secure the development of all those powers which the Creator has bestowed upon him ? How can I best train him to discharge his duties here, and to be prepared for the life to come? In all questions of method, accordingly, the first point to be settled is what is the end of education, and when this has been determined, there arises the second point demanding a solution—how can this end be most effectually secured? Method solves the second problem; but its solution depends upon our having a thorough understanding of the first. There are two methods by which a subject may be developed and presented to the mind—the Synthetic and the Analytic.

2. We do not propose to balance these two methods against each other, and to determine which of them ought to be employed in any given instance, for the judicious teacher will employ either according as he finds it suitable to the subject of instruction, to the proficiency of his pupils, and to the accomplishment of the end he has in view. Synthesis commences with principles and rises from these by regularly connected steps to the conclusion aimed at; it ascends from the particular to the general. It is the logical method of developing truth. We have admirable specimens of this method in the propositions of Euclid, where the reasoning, based on a few axioms or universally admitted truths, proceeds in regular logical sequence, until the conclusion sought is arrived at. Analysis, on the other hand, commences with the general and proceeds to the particular. The following illustration, taken from the writings of Dugald Stewart, may serve to give not only the probable historical origin but also the application of these two terms:—

"Suppose a knot of a very artificial construction to be put into my hands as an exercise for my ingenuity, and that I was required to investigate a rule, which others, as well as myself, might be able to follow in practice, for making knots of the same sort. If I were to proceed in this attempt according to the spirit of a geometrical Synthesis, I should have to try, one after another, all the various experiments which my fancy could devise, till I had, at last, hit upon the particular knot I was anxious to tie. Such a process, however, would evidently be so completely tentative, and its final success would after all, be so extremely doubtful, that common sense could not fail to suggest immediately the idea of tracing the knot through all the various complications of its progress, by cautiously undoing or unknitting each successive turn of the thread in a retrograde order, from the last to the first. After gaining this first step, were all the former complications restored again, by an inverse repetition of the same operations which I had performed in undoing them, an infallible rule would be obtained for solving the problem originally proposed; and at the same time, some address or dexterity, in the practice of the general method, probably gained, which would encourage me to undertake, upon future occasions, still more arduous tasks of a similar description."

Such then is the meaning of the two terms. Now although the Synthetic method be admirably adapted for presenting truth in a systematic form, it is questionable if it be in all cases, especially with the young, the best method of communicating truth. Children long for realities, for things, but by this method they are kept for a long period on the outskirts of the subject; the way has to be cleared; definitions have to be settled; and first principles laid down, on which to rear the intended structure. But all this preparatory work, essential in a scientific treatise on any given subject, is wearisome to children; they are unable to appreciate what is not near and tangible. Now analysis possesses this advantage that it takes things as they really exist, presents them in their every-day dress to the minds of children, and thus not only interests them by the exhibition of what is familiar to them, but exercises their ingenuity in leading them to discover their properties. If Synthesis be the logical method of developing truth, Analysis may be called the natural. Its work must precede that of synthesis. In childhood, and on to a considerably advanced state of boyhood, we know that the perceptive faculties are principally exercised, and that the logical do not manifest themselves until a later period. The exercise of the perceptive faculties, indeed, prepares the way for the due exercise of the logical. It is on the facts collected, and the observations made in childhood and boyhood, that the man reasons and compares. It would follow from this that with children we should most frequently employ the analytic method. We may give an illustration of these remarks by referring to two very opposite methods of teaching Geography. According to the synthetic method, a book of definition is put into the hands of the children. These definitions are carefully committed to memory, little care being taken to see that they are practically understood. When these definitions have been lodged in the memory, the child is gradually led on step by step, and ends exactly where he ought to have begun—with things around him. Now this method would be admirable, if our object were to give the child a strictly systematic view of the subject; indeed, by no other method could we accomplish this. But while we are thus laying down our definitions, and our first principles, there is danger of disgusting the child altogether. He can not see the far off object we have in view, and hence he wearies of our dry prelections, and ceases to take any particular interest in what has no immediate concern with him. But by the analytic method, we begin at home. The small hill, seen from the school window, with the stream running down its side, is made the basis of a lesson on the mountain and river systems. The child is at once interested. He knows the hill; he has forded the stream; he has played on the slopes of the one; and cast his tiny line into the other. The teacher, who commences in this method, will find that he has touched a sympathetic chord in the breasts of his scholars, and he will be enabled to lead them almost at will. Definitions can be wrought in as the lessons proceed, and after a time, when analysis has cleared the way, synthesis will step in and arrange into a beauteous whole the *disjecta membra*, which have hitherto floated on the surface of the mind. We shall have frequent occasion in the remaining chapters of this work to refer to the application of these two methods; and in the meantime we shall content ourselves with remarking that he who would adequately fulfill the duty of an instructor, would require to study carefully the human mind, and to mark and observe its mode of working, that he may thereby be enabled to suit his instruction to the circumstances of his scholars, and to wield at will either of the methods we have briefly described. "In nothing is the really able and skillful master more easily discriminated from the sciolist, and mere adherent to a method or system, than by his ability to interchange these forms at will, and, when one mode of presenting the illustration or statement of a new truth or fact to the mind, does not succeed in riveting attention and in securing its clear and vivid apprehension, to have recourse instantly and with perfect naturalness and ease to another and more suitable expedient. This is the true test of a skillful teacher; and, in the hands of such a man, the conduct of the processes of intellectual instruction will include the chief formal peculiarities of every rational method that has been propounded. Nothing can give this mastery of methods, but a complete and philosophical examination and a thoroughly intelligent appreciation of all, and to this lofty exercise it is most desirable that the aspiring teacher should immediately and strenuously address himself."*

3. While the analytic and synthetic methods are, strictly speaking, the only two methods that can be used in presenting truth to the mind, the practical application of them may and often does vary according to circumstances. Thus we may teach individually, simul-

* Report by John Gibson, Esq.—"*Minutes of the Committee of Council on Education,*" 1848-49-50, vol. II., page 614.

taneously, or mutually by making the pupils instruct each other. It is to be observed, however, that these various plans have reference, not to the method by which truth is developed, but to the particular way of handling, if we may so term it, the pupils. Whether the teaching be individual, simultaneous, or mutual, it must proceed on one or other of the methods we have described in the preceding paragraph. In individual teaching, each pupil is brought immediately and directly in contact with the mind of the master, and may thus be expected to receive a more powerful and lasting impression than when he is addressed as one of many. It is not meant that, in individual teaching, each scholar is examined alone. The scholars, whether the instruction be individual or simultaneous, are arranged in classes. What we mean by individual teaching is that each child in any one class is singled out and made to perform his share of the work. Thus, is the lesson a reading one, each pupil in the class reads a certain portion; and so in regard to any particular lesson. This being premised, we say that it is only by individual teaching that the master can come into direct and immediate contact with each scholar, and that he can effectually secure that the prescribed task has been performed, or the necessary explanations received and understood. When we remember that education owes its chief value to the direct influence which a thoroughly equipped and well-furnished mind brings to bear on the young; that it is this collision of a fully developed and matured understanding with the crude embryo notions of the young, which kindles their intellectual life, and molds their plastic spirits; we can not fail to perceive that any plan which brings the master-mind of the school most closely in contact with the minds of the scholars is a plan which ought not to be neglected. Hence the teacher, who considers the high end of education, will constantly endeavor to be in living contact with the intellectual life of his scholars. He will endeavor always to have a connecting wire between himself and them, along which the pulsations of his own mind may travel, and beget similar pulsations in them. But not only is individual teaching thus valuable and important, it is the only safe mode of ascertaining that a prescribed task has been performed. Children, like others, are easily overlooked in a crowd; and when care is not taken to see that each child does most regularly and punctually do his duty, we throw temptations in his way which are sometimes too strong for his honesty. And in regard to explanations, of some rule suppose in arithmetic, the only mode of testing the extent to which the explanation has been clearly and thoroughly understood, is to single out successive individuals in the class and cause them to repeat what has been explained. In every case, in which any explanation of a general principle has been given, the teacher should satisfy himself of the reception of the information by questioning individuals. We shall have occasion, as we go on, to show more fully the application of these remarks. In the meantime we may repeat that in teaching, the more each child is individualized, the more closely the master deals with him alone, the greater likelihood will there be of his instruction taking effect, and springing up in the full luxuriance of a rich and fruitful harvest.

4. The term *simultaneous*, as employed in education, is sometimes used to denote that the children are taught in classes, and not one by one. We employ it here, in opposition to the term *individual*, to signify that the questions are addressed to the whole class indiscriminately, and that the whole class are invited and expected to answer. The advantages of such a plan, if skillfully and judiciously used, are, that it enables the master to accomplish a larger amount of work, and to develop more powerfully the sympathy of numbers, than is possible in individual teaching. But the dangers of such a plan in the hands of an unskillful or lazy teacher are manifold and obvious. An unskillful teacher is apt to deceive himself, and to do incalculable injury to many of his pupils, by failing to perceive that the answers to his questions, or the filling up of his ellipses, proceeds only from a few pupils, and that too generally from those who were acquainted with the subject, while those who were ignorant of it, and who, on that very account, ought to be the objects of his special care, remain ignorant still. The lazy teacher has recourse to the method to save himself from trouble, and to conceal from himself and others the general inefficiency of his teaching. Where the teaching is purely simultaneous there can be but little of that direct contact of mind with mind, which gives to education its highest value. The master is working, to a large extent, in the dark. He can not tell the peculiar idiosyncrasy of each child; he can not guage his mental caliber; and is thus deprived of his greatest lever as an educationist. In its own place simultaneous instruction is useful, but if used alone, it is utterly pernicious. Its proper sphere is when the master is elucidating general principles; when he is discussing some law or principle, suppose, in Geography; when he is explaining some rule in Arithmetic, or giving some general lesson in Science. For such purposes, simultaneous instruction is admirably adapted. So long as the master is engaged with the general, he may teach, not only successfully, but perhaps most successfully, on the simultaneous method, but the moment he leaves the general and comes to the particular, he must refrain from the simul-

taneous, and adopt the individual method. Thus, for example, in giving to a class an explanation of the rule of simple subtraction, the master may convey the general principle to his pupils simultaneously; indeed we believe that he will find this the true and safe method. But he will commit a sad mistake if he adhere to the simultaneous method when he comes to apply the rule to particular examples. As soon as he thus begins with particulars, he must individualize his scholars, in order to ascertain that each pupil has thoroughly grasped and mastered the explanation for himself. This illustration will tend to show the place and power of simultaneous instruction. One great end of education should be to educe the individuality of each child; this end ought never to be lost sight of, and it is because we dread the effect which simultaneous teaching would have on this end, that we would caution the young teacher to be sparing in the employment of it, but rather constantly to aim at the establishment of a living and life transfusing sympathy between himself and each of his pupils, by bringing himself daily and habitually in contact with their mental life.

5. Mutual Instruction has not produced the results which, at first, it seemed to promise. Nor is this to be wondered at, when we reflect that the fundamental idea of pure mutual teaching was false. The object aimed at by it was noble; and the founders of it were actuated by the most philanthropic motives. Children were growing up ignorant and untrained; and it was a truly laudable and praiseworthy enterprise to attempt to train them by the assistance of the more advanced scholars. And, moreover, at a time when money was profusely lavished on all schemes, except on education, the plan had the seeming advantage of educating many at a small expense. But, as we have said, the plan was based on a wrong principle. The true end of education was lost sight of, and the blind were set to lead the blind. Children, whose notions on all things were crude and ill-formed, were intrusted with the work of educating other children, whose mental attainments were almost on a level with those of their instructors The mutual or monitorial system has, in consequence of this fundamental error, proved a failure. It has been superseded by the Pupil-Teacher System, which possesses this advantage over that which it has supplanted, that the agents it employs are more advanced in years, and it is to be expected in intelligence also; that they serve a regular apprenticeship, and pursue a systematic course of training. But even with these advantages, we would fain hope that the pupil-teacher system is but the prelude to something still better, and that the time is not far distant when, instead of raw lads being sent to operate upon

the young, every school will have its regularly trained master and its quota of trained assistants proportioned to the number of scholars in attendance. We had occasion in a previous chapter to point out the proper sphere of pupil-teachers in the school. We merely refer to the subject again, with the view of impressing on teachers the absolute necessity of intrusting to pupil-teachers only such kind of work as we have shown them to be capable of performing.

6. In questioning a class of children, there are certain points to which the young teacher would do well to attend. We have already stated the extent to which the simultaneous and individual methods of examination may be respectively employed; and we have shown that the latter is the safer and more effective of the two. But in individual examination, it is not necessary that the teacher commence with the pupil at the top of the class, and go regularly through. Such a plan, if the class is large, would have the effect of leaving the large majority of the scholars comparatively idle during those portions of the examination which did not immediately concern themselves. The consequence would be that those who were not being directly examined would be apt to become careless and inattentive, and thus distract the master's attention. In order to obviate these disadvantages, the master should first state the question to the whole class; and, after allowing sufficient time for reflection, he should then single out some scholar indiscriminately to give the answer. In this way, the attention of all is kept up, and the examination proceeds quietly and unostentatiously, it may be, but very effectively. Each child is liable to be called upon to answer any or every question, and he is thus kept from being indifferent. The time spent in conducting an examination in the mode we have described is not greater than in the ordinary way. But even were it greater, the plan, if adopted, will amply repay any loss of time, for what seems to be lost in time is compensated for by the entireness and thoroughness of the work. A judicious master will, by a single glance of the eye, know whom to select to give the answer, and his power over the whole class will be as great as over each unit of the class. Such a method of questioning combined with occasional simultaneous questions, will prevent the spirits of the children from flagging, and will sustain the interest unbroken to the close of the examination. Every question should be stated clearly, succinctly, and with strict avoidance of all ambiguity in the expression of it. Any thing approaching to technical terms should be seduously guarded against, until it is known that the terms are clearly understood by the children. General abstract terms are useful, only when their meaning is clearly perceived by the mind.

When once their true signification has been thoroughly grasped, such terms are of the highest utility, inasmuch as they save much needless repetition. But they are only of value when understood. The teacher, before making use of such terms, will accordingly see to it that the scholars have formed a clear conception of their meaning. Thus, for example, to one who can interpret them, the terms employed in natural history possess a deep significance, and a few such will often convey to a naturalist a more accurate notion of the thing signified than whole pages of verbose description. But the ability to repeat these terms is not co-extensive with the ability to interpret them; and it is quite within the bounds of possibility that children may be taught to repeat all the classifications of a Cuvier, without having the slightest understanding of their meaning. In putting questions, accordingly, and in accepting answers, the teacher should take particular care to use or to receive no word, the meaning of which is not understood. The question should be graduated to suit the capacity of the scholar. There should be no excuse either for no answer or for a wrong one. Every child should be expected to answer; and if in any case his inability to answer arises from his not understanding the question put, the teacher should at once throw it into a different form, or, if it be too complex, he should resolve it into its constituent parts. Every expedient should be had recourse to in order to secure an answer from each child, and not merely to secure an answer, but the correct one. Such a plan develops the confidence of the child in his own powers, and when we have taught a boy that he can do a thing, we have put him on the way of actually doing it. The child should be required to give a complete answer to every question. The mere substance of the answer should not be accepted —the matter of it is very important, but, in some respects, the form of it is equally so. The answer should contain a completely developed proposition; for, in such a case, the teacher can turn the examination on any lesson into one of the best, because a practical, means of teaching correct speaking. Dry grammatical rules will never by themselves teach the correct method of speaking or writing the English language. It is the reduction of these rules to practice that is useful, and every lesson should form an exercise in the correct use of language. The pupil should also be encouraged to give the answer in his own terms, and it will frequently be found that these terms, although perhaps not strictly pure, are yet remarkably expressive. A double benefit results from such a plan; an opportunity is furnished of giving the correct expression for the thing signified, and at the same time the master learns whether the pupil has acquired the knowledge of the thing itself, or whether his knowledge is confined to the mere name. In some respects, the mere knowledge of the name is utterly valueless, compared with the idea which the name represents, and it is of the utmost consequence to distinguish accurately how far the child's knowledge really extends; and this can be best done by allowing him to give utterance to his views in his own words. But, as we have remarked, for all terms which are merely provincial, the teacher ought to substitute the word which is the real sign of the idea. Questions should be so framed as not to contain the answer, and, in putting them, the voice should be so modulated as not to suggest it. If these things are not attended to, the question serves no good purpose—it is a waste of time. In history, a question of the following kind is of no value whatever—"Was not Elizabeth of England contemporary with Mary Queen of Scots?" There can be no doubt as to the answer, and the question is useless. Neither should questions, requiring for answer the monosyllables yes or no, be introduced, except as leading questions, when they furnish the basis of a continued examination. The great end of this kind of examination is to stimulate thought, not to call forth mere smartness; and hence the examination should be conducted calmly, with great deliberation, and with a due regard to the ability of the particular pupil. Young teachers are very apt to confound rapid questioning and answers with sure and effective teaching, and to imagine that the largest amount of work is performed, where there is most excitement and physical movements. We would take it upon us to caution all young teachers against being misled by this too current belief, for, in many instances, the very reverse would be nearer the truth. Some minds may be so formed as *to think* with great rapidity, but the vast majority are not so constituted; and, as the true teacher must rest satisfied with nothing short of the evolution of thought, he must learn carefully to discriminate between the semblance and the reality of actual thinking.

7. Much of the information communicated by the teacher to the children will be given in oral lessons. Almost all the branches of education should be taught, to a large extent, orally, and this holds especially true of lessons on science, natural history, and such like subjects. Text-books on such branches are comparatively of little service, and those at present in use are so miserably adapted to their purpose that they frequently do more mischief than good. But however excellent the text-book may be, the master's own mind must, after all, be the chief storehouse whence the information of the pupils is derived. Now in conducting these oral lessons, when the object is

not to examine the pupils on the amount of knowledge which they possess, but to consolidate and extend that knowledge, it is evident that direct questioning will not, by itself, be sufficient. Direct questioning, whether conducted individually or simultaneously, forms an admirable method of taking stock of the pupil's acquirements, but it is not equally well adapted to lead the pupil on to new regions of thought, and new fields of observation. For it will be observed, that in oral instruction the teacher assumes that the child is ignorant of the facts which he is about to state, and of the conclusions which he intends to deduce from these facts. No doubt, a question may be of such a suggestive nature, as to lead the pupil to divine almost intuitively the answer, and may in this way become the means of leading him on from one point to another, until an entirely new subject has been brought before him. But, in general, it will be found that such suggestions can be far more effectively given by introducing to the pupil's notice a certain portion of the statement, and, when he has thus obtained the requisite hint, by allowing him to complete the idea. This prevents the lesson from degenerating into a mere lecture, which, as an educational power, is utterly valueless where children are concerned. The teacher is introducing his pupils into a new untried field. He will do them little good if he walk rapidly through, discoursing eloquently it may be, on its wonders and beauties; but he may arouse their attention, secure their interest, and thus set them a thinking, if he moves slowly forward, giving a hint here, and a hint there, but allowing the pupils to discover for themselves the objects of interest which lie in their path. Here, we believe, lies the great value of *Ellipses* in education, and, if properly conducted, their power is undoubtedly great. But the young teacher would require to guard sedulously against the abuse of them. When by their assistance he has led his pupils one decided step onward, he must pause and ascertain by direct question to what extent the point arrived at has been understood. For it is quite possible that a great fund of information may have been communicated, and that the children may have filled in the ellipses properly, but this is no valid proof that the lesson as a whole has been received, and thoroughly mastered by the children. To ascertain this, they must be subjected to a rigorous cross-examination, which, however, need only embrace the leading points in the lesson, for if these are clearly understood, it is an almost infallible sign that the whole bearings of the subject have been comprehended. Ellipses are thus mainly valuable in communicating information, but the working in of that information into the very texture of the mind must be accomplished by questioning, or, as in the case of arithmetic, by requiring the pupil actually to reduce to practice the information he has received. Questions and Ellipses are thus not the opposites but the complements of each other. Each has its own place in education, and each may be made to subserve the most important ends. But it is only when the two go hand in hand that good will result; if either (and especially if ellipses, being by nature the weaker power,) is allowed to usurp an undue influence, the instruction will, to the extent of that usurpation, be unsatisfactory. And we may remark, in conclusion, as was remarked in a former paragraph, that he will most efficiently fulfill the high ends of his office, who can employ these methods at will, and who can have recourse to either when he finds it most suitable to reach and to arrest the minds of his pupils.

EXAMINATION.

8. The information which children derive, even from the most carefully prepared series of school books, ought to bear, in every rightly conducted school, a very small proportion to that which they obtain from the well-stored mind of the master. Not only is this the case, even the information contained in the books will not take its full effect on their minds, unless it has been thoroughly wrought in by close and rigid examination. In order, therefore, to secure that the lessons are understood, the master must, from the youngest class to the highest, institute a searching analysis of what has been read. In the younger classes, this examination will be mainly confined to questions which exercise the observing faculties and the simplest ideas of relation; but as the pupils advance in years and in understanding, the analysis will embrace questions tending to cultivate the reasoning powers and imagination; and at a still later period those of abstraction and generalization. We do not mean that the teacher should frame his questions with the special view of cultivating these faculties in their due order; we believe this to be impossible; for in every lesson there will necessarily be questions which appeal more or less to all these various faculties. The teacher, however, who is acquainted with the order in which these faculties develop themselves, will, from this knowledge, derive many valuable rules to guide him in examining a class on any given lesson. Thus, for example, with a class of very young children, in whose lesson the names of the sun and moon occurred, he would never once dream of attempting to explain the way in which these bodies are related to each other; or, should the seasons be mentioned, he would confine himself to a few general questions on the characteristics of each, without entering on an explanation of the causes which produce them. In questioning a class

upon the subject matter of a lesson, the teacher should employ every opportunity of deepening, extending, and consolidating the knowledge of the subject which the children may have acquired from the reading-book or from other sources. In order to illustrate our meaning, we shall give one or two examples of lessons suited to different stages of advancement, with brief notes of examination on each.

9. Examples for examination.

Junior Classes.

Example 1.—The rat sat on a mat. The fat cat ran to the rat. The rat ran in-to the box? Can the cat go in-to the box? No, the fat cat can not go in-to the box.

On the assumption that the children are familiar with the forms of the words, and can read the lesson with tolerable fluency, we would proceed to question them on its meaning. And here we would remark that, even at this early stage, it is desirable to lead the children to analyze the sentences. We need say nothing to them of the term analysis—it will be learned in time enough.

Examination.

What two animals does your lesson speak about? Have you ever seen a rat? A cat? Which is larger? Which is stronger? Where was the rat sitting? What was it doing on the mat? What was sitting on the mat? What is a mat? Where do you see it? What is its use? If a little boy got his shoes dirted what should he do before going into the house? The mat is used for—*wiping the shoes.* The rat sat on—*a mat.* Was that its own place? Where should it have been? As it was sitting on the mat who saw it? What kind of cat was it? And what did the fat cat do? The fat cat ran—*to the rat.* (Describe the running—show how the cat would sit and watch, and then bound forward. This will amuse and interest the children, and keep them fresh for the remainder of the examination.) Do you think the rat would wait on the mat? What would it do? It would—*run away,* run away to—*its hole.* Where did it run? What is a box? What made of? How would it get into the box? What must have been in the box? You see then the rat ran into—*the box* through—*a hole.* Did the cat go into the box? Why not? The hole would not let in—*the cat,* but it let in—*the rat.* Would the cat go away from the box? What would it do? It would—*watch* beside the—*box,* to see if the rat—*would come out,* &c.

Many other questions might be put—anecdotes told, and such interest thrown into the lesson that the children would be sorry when it was over. We have thrown in a few ellipses in the foregoing examination—the words in *italics* being supposed to be filled in by the children.

Example **2.—Look at the Lion.** He is a fierce, cruel beast. He is very strong and very terrible. He has strong limbs; a long, flowing, shaggy mane; and a long tail. His roar is very fearful, and very terrible; it is like thunder. The lion is often named the king of beasts. The lion is sly; he is a beast of the cat kind, and all beasts of the cat kind are sly and cunning. He creeps behind a bush, or a tree, then crouches down and springs suddenly on his prey, &c.

Such a lesson as this should be accompanied if possible with a drawing of the animal described; for words, however clear and explicit, will convey to the minds of children but a faint idea of the form and shape of an animal which they have never seen. The first sentence presupposes that the children have a picture before them. In lessons of this kind, the two main points to be attended to are—that the children know the meaning of the terms used, and then their application in the particular passage. We shall endeavor to indicate these points in the following sketch.

Examination.

What have you been reading about? Well here is a picture of the lion. Have any of you ever seen one? What kind of beast is he? He is—*fierce and cruel.* What is the meaning of fierce? of cruel? (If no answer is given, take some illustration to assist them in bringing out the meaning. In all probability, they have a very good conception of the meaning, but want words to express it. Contrast is often useful in assisting them in this respect; thus, Would you call the sheep a fierce and cruel beast? What would you call it?—*mild and gentle.* Now is the lion like the sheep? He is not—*mild and gentle.*) If I were going to describe a boy to you, so that you would know him when you saw him—would I say that he was fierce and cruel? I would tell you what he—*was like.* I might tell you what kind of clothes he—*had on,* &c., but I would not say that he was—*fierce and cruel.* Now then what would you use these words for? (to tell his disposition, or his character.) When I say that the lion is fierce and cruel, what then do I describe? (his character.) (In this way the right application of these terms is acquired, and the best possible foundation laid for the correct use of language.) Does your lesson say any thing else about the character of the lion? (Such a question will at once show if your meaning in the preceding examination has been understood. If the children answer, that he is sly and cunning, you may rest assured that they have followed you.) Yes, he is—*sly.* Like what other animals? What is a mark of all animals of the cat kind? They are—*sly and cunning.* How do you know that he is sly and cunning? Why is he said to creep? Have you ever seen an animal of the same kind do the same thing? What animal? When? When he gets behind a tree what does he do?

(Show this by an appropriate action.) How long will he crouch? and when some animal comes up, what does the lion do? How does he spring? Why suddenly? What on? &c.

In the same manner the terms employed to describe the form, the parts, and the roar of the lion may be gone over; and if this be done with life, with appropriate action, and with apt illustrations, the children will follow the course of the examination with intense interest. We have seen two hundred little children so excited by a lesson of this sort, graphically given, that they would scarcely have been surprised had they seen the lion spring on its prey, so real had the master made the picture.

Under this same division we shall give a short poetical extract, and make one or two observations on the mode in which it should be treated.

Example 3.

Hark the mower's whistling blade,
How steadily he mows;
The grass is heaped, the daisies fade,
All scattered as he goes.

So Time, as with a stern delight
'Mid human havoc towers,
And sweeps resistless in his might
Kingdoms as grass and flowers.

The flowers of life may bloom and fade,
But He, in whom I trust,
Though cold, and in my grave-clothes laid,
Can raise me from the dust.

There are in this passage three distinct parts—the natural picture, drawn from a very common incident—the analogy between this picture and time—and the contrast between the fading flowers, and the wreck of kingdoms and the Immortal who looks on; and these three must be gone over in their order. Notice first the picture—What is a mower? what does he do? why is his blade called a *whistling blade?* Note the second line. What is meant by mowing *steadily?* Show the effect—the grass is heaped—can not resist—it falls before the blade. Note also the particular term "daisies,"—it makes the picture more graphic. The poet does not content himself with the somewhat general term *grass*, but he singles out the "daisies," why? They are beautiful—objects of interest to children, and this one word vivifies the whole picture—although beautiful, they must fall before the whistling blade. Similar instances of the use of particular terms may be noticed, *e. g.* our Saviour's allusions to the "lilies," the "ravens," &c. Milton's description of Satan,—"Sat like a cormorant." Notice secondly the analogy. What is compared to the mower? Why is Time so compared? What does the mower do? and what Time? (*mows*, *sweeps*.) What sound does the blade give? What clause in the second part corresponds to *whistling* (as with a stern delight.) The blade seems to—*whistle*, so Time seems to feel—*a stern delight.* The blade mows among—*grass and daisies*, so Time towers among—*human havoc.* Note the exact application of *human*, that it means—*havoc produced among men*, and not—*havoc caused by men.* How does the mower move? (steadily,) how does Time? (resistless in his might.) Bring out also the effects produced by each, and show how Time has swept kingdoms, by instancing some. Notice thirdly the contrast. I—any one, who saw and observed the things mentioned in the two previous stanzas—will not thus perish—I may be cold, and laid in grave-clothes, but still He, in whom I trust, can raise me. Compare Job, xix. 25, 26. John, xi. 25, 26. With a class somewhat advanced compare also such a passage as the following:—

> 'Tis night, and the landscape is lovely no more;
> I mourn, but, ye woodlands, I mourn not for you;
> For morn is approaching, your charms to restore,
> Perfumed with fresh fragrance, and glittering with dew;
> Nor yet for the ravage of winter I mourn,
> Kind nature the embryo blossom will save,
> But when shall spring visit the mouldering urn!
> O, when shall it dawn on the night of the grave!

Compare also the whole of the eighth paraphrase.

Senior Classes.

10. In examining the senior classes, the same *kind* of questions should be put as in examining the junior; the main difference in the questions should be one of *degree.* Both in prose and in poetical extracts the terms employed must be carefully explained, correct definitions given, the figurative use of words pointed out, and the aim and scope of the whole passage laid bare by a skillful analysis of all its parts. The information contained in the passage should be largely supplemented by suggestions and ellipses on the part of the master, and, as far as possible, each lesson should be complete in itself. Whatever be the particular aspect of a subject which the lesson treats of, that aspect should be a whole. If the lesson, for example, regards a leaf, the form, structure, and use of leaves should be brought out, and their relation to the trees on which they grow. In this way, each part of any given subject will fall into its proper place, and the mind will acquire the important habit of grouping things together by natural principles of association, and of calling

them up when necessary. The derivation and formation of words, the changes which they have undergone both in form and meaning, and their composition, should be noticed and illustrated. In poetical extracts, the figures and the imagery employed should be dwelt upon, the use and application of them should be shown by examples, and care taken to foster the habit of a rigid adherence to the correct use of language. In advanced classes, the reasoning of the author should be examined; the premises on which he builds noticed, and the conclusions drawn from these premises tested. In this way, fallacies in argument may be detected, and the best possible foundation laid for a thorough study of logic; and all this without having recourse to the mystical jargon with which professed treatises on logic too frequently perplex the young student. It need scarcely be remarked that no false sentiment should pass unchallenged, come from whatever source it may; the morbid sentimentalism which disfigures too much of our literature should be sternly exposed, and every effort made to enlist the sympathies and the affections of the young on the side of what is true and honest and of good report. We can not give full illustrations of all these remarks; we shall content ourselves with one or two meager outlines.

Example 1.—The mariner's compass is a wonderful though a simple instrument. It consists of nothing more than a needle and a card; and yet it enables the mariner to traverse the pathless sea with perfect confidence. The needle, being converted into a magnet, or loadstone, which is easily done--and being balanced on a point above the center of the card—always points to the north: and the sailor has therefore only to examine the card, on which the cardinal points, east, west, north, and south, are marked, to know in what direction he is steering.*

In conducting an examination on such a passage as this, (which we have selected on account of its succinctness,) it would be well to have either a real compass, or a representation of it. If, however, the teacher has neither, he can easily have recourse to the blackboard, which will enable him to give the pupils a tolerably correct idea of the instrument. The leading points to be brought out are the two parts of the instrument, the relation in which they stand to each other, and the use which the sailor makes of it. It consists of a needle and a card—an ordinary needle would not suit—why?—it must point to the north, which a common needle does not do. Hence what must be done to the needle? How is this done? (the lesson does not state this, the teacher must, therefore, bring it out by illustration and suggestion.) We have now the needle prepared. What else does the lesson say is necessary? What kind of card? What is written on it? But will it do to lay the needle on the card? Why

* M'Culloch's "*Series*," p. 43.

not? What must be done? Thus we train out the two parts, and their relation to each other. Then what does the sailor do? How does he know his direction? (This can be illustrated on the blackboard.) More particularly—what is the mariner's compass said to be? why is it called a *compass?* Why the *mariner's compass?* What is a mariner? What other name is given to him in the passage? He is called a mariner because—*he is engaged on the sea*, and a sailor because—*he sails on the sea.* How do you know that the compass is a *simple instrument?* that it is a *wonderful instrument?* Why is the sea called *pathless?* What do you mean by a *path?* (In this way the exact meaning of the word is brought out, and the children can, in future, apply it correctly.) The derivation of some of the words might also be pointed out, but of this more anon.

Example 2.—It has been already mentioned, that water exposed to the air is gradually converted into a state of vapor, which, on account of its specific levity, ascends into the atmosphere. This vapor presents itself in various forms. When the air holds it in solution, it is invisible, just as salt dissolved in water is invisible; but when the vapor condenses, the watery particles become visible either in the form of clouds and mists suspended in the atmosphere, or in that of rain, dew, snow, and hail, falling to the ground.*

Substance of lesson (to be given by the pupils in answer to questions by the teacher.)

1. Water exposed to the air is gradually converted into vapor
2. On account of its lightness the vapor ascends into the atmosphere, where
3. It assumes different forms, which are visible or invisible.

(*a*) Invisible when the air holds it in solution.
(*b*) Visible when it is condensed so as to form clouds, rain, dew, &c.

The above may be obtained from the pupils in something like the following manner:—What follows on water being exposed to the air? Is this vapor the same weight, lighter, or heavier, than the air? What is the consequence? What forms does it then assume? When is it invisible? What is meant by the air holding it in solution? Can you give an illustration of that meaning? Because the clouds and mists are easily moved about by the currents of the air, what are they said to be? When does the vapor assume the form of clouds and mists? When does it assume the form of rain, snow, hail and dew? Such an examination as the above will enable the teacher to form an idea as to how much of the lesson is understood by the pupils; and if time permit, the facts of a previous lesson on evaporation may be revised and used in explanation of the statements made in this lesson. This will train the pupils to use the information they possess, and to realize the truth, "knowledge is power." The analysis may be thus continued. How is water converted into vapor? How

* M'Culloch's "*Course of Reading*," p. 249.

does the air convert the water into vapor? What is the name given to this process? On what does the amount of evaporation depend? &c.

Example 3.—While a plant differs from an animal in exhibiting no signs of perception or voluntary motion, and in possessing no stomach to serve as a receptacle for its food, there exists between them a close analogy both of parts and functions. The stem and branches act as a frame-work or skeleton for the support and protection of the parts necessary to the life of the individual. The root serves the purpose of a stomach by imbibing nutritious juices from the soil, and thus supplying the plant with materials for its growth. The sap or circulating fluid, composed of water, holding in solution saline, extractive, mucilaginous, saccharine, and other soluble substances, corresponds in its office to the blood of animals; and in its passage through the leaves, which may be termed the lungs of a plant, it is fully exposed to the agency of light and air, and experiences a change by which it is more completely adapted to the wants of the vegetable economy.*

Subject of lesson. Analogy between a plant and an animal. Before noticing the analogy, it is necessary to dispose of the points of difference.

AN ANIMAL *has*	A PLANT *has not*
Perception,	Perception,
Voluntary Motion,	Voluntary Motion,
A Receptacle for food.	A Receptacle for food.

What is meant by perception? If I prick you with a pin what do you feel? What sensation have you? Now, do you think a plant feels pain like you? It has neither the sensation nor the perception of *pain.* What is meant by motion? What by voluntary motion? Did you ever see a plant moving? (Some may answer yes, which will furnish an opportunity of bringing out clearly the meaning of the term *voluntary motion.*) In the same way notice the difference in respect of stomach. An animal then differs from a plant, in that the former has—*perception, voluntary motion,* and a *receptacle for its food;* while the latter—*has not.*

2. Analogy both of parts and functions.

1st.—Of parts.

(*a*) An animal has a frame-work or skeleton; a plant has also a frame-work in the stem and branches.

(*b*) An animal has lungs; a plant has also lungs in the shape of leaves.

2d.—Of Functions.

(*a*) In both, the frame-work supports and protects the parts necessary to the life of the individual.

(*b*) In the plant, the root serves the same purpose as the stomach in the animal.

(*c*) The sap of the plant corresponds in its office to the blood of animals.

(*d*) As the blood of animals is exposed to the action of the air in its passage through the lungs, so the sap of plants in its passage through the leaves.

(*e*) The sap thus exposed is more completely adapted to the wants of the vegetable, as the blood is to the wants of the animal economy.

Each of these parts must be clearly elucidated, in order that the

* M'Culloch's "*Course of Reading*," p. 126.

children may have a thorough understanding of the lesson. We need not, however, enter into details, as we have already indicated the mode of procedure.

Example 4.

The sky is changed !—and such a change ! Oh night,
The storm, and darkness, ye are wondrous strong,
Yet lovely in your strength, as is the light
Of a dark eye in woman ! Far along,
From peak to peak, the rattling crags among,
Leaps the live thunder ! Not from one lone cloud,
But every mountain now hath found a tongue,
And Jura answers, through her misty shroud,
Back to the joyous Alps, who call to her aloud !

And this is in the night :—Most glorious night !
Thou wert not sent for slumber ! let me be
A sharer in thy fierce and far delight,—
A portion of the tempest and of thee !
How the lit lake shines, a phosphoric sea,
And the big rain comes dancing to the earth !
And now again 'tis black—and now, the glee
Of the loud hills shakes with its mountain mirth,
As if they did rejoice o'er a young earthquake's birth.

If the previous stanzas have been read, the force of the exclamation at the beginning of the passage will be at once apparent. It may be noticed that such contrasts are frequent in Byron's poetry. Some of his finest passages depend upon the effect produced by the introduction of opposites. Thus in his description of "Waterloo," he passes from the brilliant scenes of a ball-room to the bloody field of battle. In "The siege of Corinth," he draws a beautiful picture of the sea sleeping calmly in the moonlight, and immediately thereafter introduces us to a scene so awfully horrible as to make the blood run cold. Various questions may be put on the passage—we can only give a specimen of a few. What two figures of speech are employed in the first stanza? (apostrophe and personification.) Where is the apostrophe? Give other examples of the same figure. Point out the particular words which indicate the personification, (leaps, answers, joyous, &c.) What two qualities does the poet associate with the night, and storm and darkness? Are these qualities necessarily connected? Taking the common ideas regarding these qualities, do we generally conjoin them? What illustration does the poet use to enforce his meaning? Point out the terms in the illustration which corresponds to the terms in the thing illustrated. Show the propriety of the epithet *live* as applied to thunder. What idea does the sound of the words "the rattling crags among, leaps the live thunder" seem intended to convey? Give other instances where the sound is made to echo the sense, as in Milton's famous line "On their hinges grate harsh thunder," &c. What are the mountains represented as doing? What particular mountains are singled out? Notice the effect produced by thus as it were localizing the description. "Every mountain" is a somewhat vague term, but by introducing "Jura" and the "Alps," the poet gives his description a local habitation, and the mind realizes it far more easily than if he had employed only general terms. Notice the graphic position in which the poet, in imagination, puts these mountains; the Alps, as if in sympathy with his own spirit, rejoicing in the storm, and calling aloud to Jura, which re-echoes the shout. Why is Jura said to be covered with a shroud? &c. The second stanza should be gone over in the same manner.

Example 5.

I dare do all that may become a man;
Who dares do more is none.

A passage so full of meaning as this is, should be thoroughly impressed by illustrations and examples, on the mind of youth. It teaches, in few but significant words, what constitutes real manliness, regarding which boys are apt to entertain such erroneous ideas. The teacher should first point out the full force of the expression "that may become a man," by showing clearly man's position, duty and destiny, as revealed in the word of God. A catalogue of those things which become a man is given in Philippians iv. 8. The teacher should refer to this passage, and show that he only who dares do such things in spite of scorn, mockery or obloquy, deserves the name of man; and he who dares not do these things is no man.

Example 6.

That which in *mean* men we entitle—patience,
Is pale cold cowardice in *noble* breasts.

The nature of the morality taught in this passage will depend on the meaning we attach to the words—*mean* and *noble*. The teacher should point out the ambiguity which lurks under them. By referring to the context, it will be seen that the words really signify—*low born* and *high born*. In this sense it will be easy to show that the statement is erroneous; that patience is becoming the *noble* as well as the *mean;* that one rule of conduct is applicable, in God's sight, to both. If the words are employed, which, according to present usage, they may be, to denominate respectively the class, who, from want of spirit, tamely submit to any injury, and the class who, like Paul before the Roman governor, stand upon their undoubted rights, then the lesson taught is good, and may be impressed strongly on children.

11. An acquaintance with the sources from which our language is derived is valuable on many accounts; indeed no one can be said to have received a thorough English education who is ignorant of the history and the development of our language. Frequently it happens that a knowledge of the root of a word supplies the key to its meaning, although it can not be denied that as frequently the literal meaning conveys but an imperfect idea of its present application. Thus the literal meaning of *import* would not impart any thing like a full picture of the signification of the word. And not only is this the case, it is also to be remembered that words have, in the course of centuries, entirely changed their meaning, and are now used in senses very different from what they were originally, *e. g.*, the words *villain*, *pagan*. Again, in many words the meaning, as determined by the root, still remains; but an additional meaning has been analogically superadded, *e. g.*, in the words *apprehend*, *apprehension*, *sentence*. Now in all these cases the mere knowledge of the root will not serve any high end in education, and we would be inclined to condemn, as a piece of what is popularly termed clap-trap, those exhibitions, still too common, in which children repeat with great volubility all the derivatives of the more common roots, without having the faintest idea of their true signification. Derivation is generally taught synthetically; a list of roots, prefixes and affixes, is placed before the child, and he is compelled to commit to memory the whole, with the representative words to the bargain. This is reversing the natural order. Derivation ought to be taught analytically. The child should not be troubled, at least until considerably advanced, with any ugly, unmeaning string of roots. And yet derivation should and may be taught from an early period, and in the following manner. In the ordinary reading books, when a compound word, such as *tea-pot*, occurs, the attention of the pupils should be turned to it, and it should be pointed out that the word consists of two separate significant words. They might be asked to give other words formed in the same way, such as *wind-mill*, *house-top*, *&c.* In a similar manner secondary words should be dealt with. Such words as *runner*, *courser*, *tanner*, *&c.*, would furnish opportunities of analysis, and it could be easily shown that the termination *er* produced a change on the original word, and that the change of signification was well nigh uniform. So also with such words as *wisdom*, *kingdom*. Adjectives and adverbs should be treated in a similar way, and it would be no difficult thing to show by such words as *kingly*, *manly*, *royally*, *manfully*, that the termination *ly* changed nouns into adjectives, and adjectives into adverbs. We need not multiply examples, the principle

is evident, and the only one which accords with the true idea of education. In regard to the roots or stems of words, the same method should be adopted. In such words as *missionary, permission, demission, proceed, recede, succeed, &c.*, the children would at once perceive a common element. The meaning of this common part should then be given, and when this has been done, it should be shown that in all the words this meaning may be traced. After exercises of the sort we have described have familiarized the pupils with the leading roots, a list of prefixes, stems, and affixes, arranged systematically, should be put into their hands, and may be committed to memory, although in reality this is of very little consequence. It is of the utmost importance, however, in going over this list, and in forming words from it, to notice clearly the literal meaning, and also the present application of the word. To make sure that the children thoroughly understand the correct use of the term, they should be made to construct short sentences in which it occurs. Thus, when the meaning of *import* has been explained, a sentence should be asked for, such as, *England imports cotton from America.* We need only remark further that in the advanced classes, the history of words should be traced; the changes in meaning which they have undergone should be used as illustrative of corresponding changes in the sentiments, the habits or the religion of the people. On this aspect of the subject we may refer the reader to the admirable little work on "*The Study of Words*," by Dean Trench.

THE TRIPARTITE SYSTEM OF ORGANIZATION.

PROF. MOSELEY, one of her Majesty's Inspectors of Schools, gives the following account of the Tripartite System of School Organization, which is a modification of the plan first tried by Mr. Oliphant, in the Sessional School at Edinburgh.

The first, and essential element of it, is the separate room for oral instruction, the devotion of the labors of the head-master chiefly to this object, (relieved occasionally by the second-master or pupil-teacher, with whom he exchanges duties,) and the throwing of the children in three great divisions successively into that room, for an hour twice a day, for the purpose of that instruction. Every other element of the plan admits of modification, but not that. If that feature of it be sacrificed, then the most important results which I contemplate from it, will, in a great measure, I conceive, be lost. It is no longer the plan which I recommend, or one from which I anticipate any very decided advantage.

Whilst in all that requires the independent exercise of judgment and discretion in the business of instruction—in all that involves the sanctions of religion, and considerations of moral responsibility, and thus needs to be presented to the mind of a child with the gravity and the authority which can only be brought to it by the mind of an adult teacher; and in all that concerns the development of the judgment and intelligence of the child—the direct interference of the master in its education is necessary to any useful result, as well in reference to the youngest child in the school as to the oldest; I am not prepared to deny that there are certain elements in the business of a school, which, being essentially mechanical in their nature, may, under due supervision and with proper limitations, be conducted on the principle of mutual instruction. Reading, for instance, may, I conceive, as to its mechanical elements, and with a view to that individual instruction and mechanical practice which it requires, be taught by the aid of monitors—as young even as some of those to whom the whole business of instruction is intrusted in our existing schools—provided that each reading lesson so given is checked by a subsequent examination of the master; and that the subdivisions of children placed at any time under the instruction of a single monitor, do not exceed eight, or at the most ten, in number.

I will suppose the subjects of instruction in elementary schools to admit of the following division:—

1. Those which are properly the subjects of oral instruction.
2. Reading.
3. Writing, slate arithmetic, drawing, committing to memory—being silent occupations.

For these three subjects, I suppose separate localities to be assigned. A gallery and a separate room for oral instruction. Parallel desks arranged in groups for writing, &c. An open area or floor for the subdivisions receiving instruction in reading.

Corresponding to these three distinct branches of instruction, I propose that the children be formed into three equal divisions, and that, when the morning devotions and the Bible lesson have terminated, each division passes to one of these localities, and receives instruction in those elements of knowledge which are proper to that locality.

Calling the divisions, for instance, I., II., and III.; division I., will take its place in the gallery for oral instruction; division II., at the desks for writing, &c.; and division III., (in subdivisions of from 6 to 10,) upon the floor of the school-room, for instruction in reading, (or in the room set apart for that purpose, with a gallery, &c., if it be proposed to adopt the simultaneous method of teaching reading.) Now it will be observed, that there are three hours in the morning, and, in summer, three hours in the afternoon devoted to school business. I suppose the above distribution of the school to remain during the first of these hours. At the expiration of that hour, a change takes place: that division which was in the gallery receiving oral instruction, passes to the desks, for practice in writing, &c.; that which was at the desks, to the floor of the school-room for reading; and that which was reading, to the gallery, for examination by the head-master in that reading lesson in which the whole division has been receiving the instruction of the monitors. This arrangement continues during the second hour; a similar change takes place at the commencement of the third; and so each division passes in its turn (in the course of the morning,) under the personal examination and oral instruction of the master; each is occupied during an hour in writing, slate arithmetic, &c.; and an hour is devoted by each to mechanical instruction in reading.

If the localities appropriated to, 1. Oral Instruction; 2. Slate Arithmetic; 3. Reading, be represented respectively by the letters A, B, C, and the three equal divisions of the school by the symbols I., II., III., the following time-table will represent compendiously the arrangements which I have described in detail:—

Hours.	I.	II.	III.
9 to 10	A	B	C
10 to 11	B	C	A
11 to 12	C	A	B

It will be observed, that the first or lowest division of the school is occupied during the first hour in reading; that it is then placed under oral instruction, which oral instruction, conducted by the head-master, is supposed to be founded (where that is practicable,) upon the reading lesson which the children have just been practicing, and which always commences with an examination as to the extent to which they have acquired the power to read it mechanically. For the results of this examination, the monitors who have been employed in teaching it are supposed to be held, in some degree, responsible. The teaching of that lesson to each child in his subdivision, being understood to be assigned to the monitor as his task; the due performance of which is afterwards to be inquired into in every case by the master.

In carrying out this plan, I propose that the boys and girls should, in the morning, be taught together; I claim, however, the services both of the master and the mistress then, as well as in the afternoon. For schools whose average attendance of boys and girls does not exceed 100 this will be enough. For every additional 25 children, there should be a pupil-teacher; and if the number exceed 200, one of these at least should be replaced by an assistant-master.

The station of the mistress is to be the reading-room; that of the pupil-teacher the desks, where writing and slate-arithmetic are taught; and that of the master the gallery, where oral instruction is given.

I propose, then, in respect to the hours of morning instruction, that the teaching of reading shall be intrusted to the mistress.

That for the purpose of this instruction, each of the three divisions of the school shall, during the hour when it occupies the reading-room, be formed into two sections, one being composed of as many of those children who are most backward in their reading as the mistress can herself adequately instruct in a single class; the other section being broken up into subsections, each composed of not more than eight children, and each placed in charge of a monitor.

The whole of the children of each of the great divisions is, when in the reading-room, to be occupied in reading the same lesson; and the time-table of the schools to provide that, when the hour allotted to it in the reading-room is expired, it shall be transferred to the gallery for oral instruction by the head-master, such oral instruction always commencing with an examination upon the reading lesson which has preceded—first, as to the ability of the children read the lesson accurately; secondly, as to their intelligence of the subject-matter of it. If the reading lessons be properly selected, they will frequently serve as the foundation of that oral instruction of the master which is to follow this examination. In those schools to which no infant school is annexed, some of the children will probably be so young, and so imperfectly instructed in reading, as to render it expedient that they should remain in the reading-room during the period assigned for instruction of the lowest division in writing, and during one of the two periods allotted every day to the oral instruction of that division. This is a modification of the plan in respect to which the master will exercise his discretion.

The writing, practice of arithmetic, drawing, &c., will be placed under the supervision of the pupil-teacher or assistant-master, who will nevertheless relieve the head-master, changing places with him from time to time, and taking up his task of oral instruction; but not at any other times, or in respect to any other subjects, than such as are prescribed in the school routine, and have received the sanction of the School Committee. It is not, however, to be supposed that the master to whom the duty of oral instruction is assigned is constantly to be occupied in *talking*. His duties include examination and the hearing of lessons; and from time to time he will pause, and require the children to write down their recollections of the lesson he has been giving.

In the afternoon I propose that the girls should be taught to sew by the mistress, in the room appropriated in the morning to reading; and that the boys be formed into three divisions, as in the morning, and similarly occupied; the two divisions employed in oral instruction and writing occupying one of the remaining rooms, and the other being appropriated to reading, under the supervision of the assistant-master or pupil-teacher. The number of children composing each division being greatly less in the afternoon than in the morning, I anticipate that the supervision of that division which is occupied in writing, under the care of an elder child, or monitor, will not interfere materially with the important task of oral instruction, with which he is more particularly charged, more especially as that task is not supposed to be incessantly plied, but alternated with periods when the children under oral instruction may be writing out exercises on their slates, or working examples in arithmetic, the principles of which branch of science I suppose to be taught as an important department of oral instruction. The duties of the master will be relieved by those of the assistant-master or pupil-teacher in the afternoon as in the morning, and under the same circumstances.

It is a characteristic feature of this arrangement, and that which I have principally in view in recommending it, that it brings each individual child, from the least to the greatest, every day, during one-third of its school-hours, under the personal instruction of the master; that it places the master under the most favorable circumstances which I can devise for conveying that instruction to him; that it compels him to take up the study of the child from the moment when it first enters the school, and that it entirely takes away from the duties of the master that voluntary and irresponsible character which they are made to assume, by a system which provides for the carrying out of the entire business of instruction without his intervention; that it emancipates the children from the monotonous control of the monitors, and from the noise of the reading-room, during two-thirds of the day; that when the children are under monitorial instruction, it places them in groups, under the charge of each monitor, less in number by one-half than the classes usually assigned to the charge of a monitor, all day long, by the existing system; that for the *great* business of the elementary school, *Reading*, its most tedious and difficult task, it provides, moreover, the services of an adult teacher (the mistress,) who is supposed to employ assistance of monitors only in respect to those children whom she is unable to teach herself; that each reading lesson so given it followed by an examination, as to the success with which it has been given, by the master; that whilst the services of the mistress are rendered available in respect to that branch which, however important, does not (under the circumstances,) suppose in the teacher that higher degree of attainment and general ability for the management of a school, which are so rarely found united in a mistress—it secures, nevertheless, to the girls (to whom it is at least as necessary as the boys) the highest order of instruction which the school will supply; that in respect to existing schools, it provides for this, without dispensing with the services of the mistress, or altering the present arrangements as to her salary; that, in respect to new schools, it enables the master to employ the services of his wife in the business of the school, under circumstances (with reference especially to that higher standard of education at which we aim,) in which they would not otherwise be available; that it economizes the labors of the pupil-teacher, making, by the union of the two schools, one such teacher sufficient where two would, if the schools were separated, be necessary.

Lastly, that, providing for those technical branches of instruction which are not only valuable in themselves, but necessary to secure that public opinion of the parents favorable to the school, on which its success must after all depend, it provides further for that oral instruction of a more general kind, which aims at results less tangible, indeed, but the highest contemplated in education, and the most valuable; that extends the benefits of this form of instruction from the highest to the meanest and lowest child, and that it brings to it the master spirit of the school, and all the sanctions with which the authority of the highest office can surround it; that in respect to his own individual part in the labor of teaching, it does not leave the master to the influence of no other motive than his own sense of duty, or that desire for excellence which it is so difficult to preserve in a remote and unobserved school, subject as it is to the antagonism of those prejudices which, lingering in the public mind, too frequently interdict all sympathy in his labors; but that it contemplates a system of instruction in which his labors shall constitute an integral part, and prescribes the subjects which he shall teach himself, and the times when he shall teach them.

XIV. LESSON ON COLOR.

BY D. R. HAY.

There are three distinct kinds of color in nature, viz., yellow, red, and blue. The first is most allied to light, and is a color having no characteristic tone; the second is characterized by warmth of tone; and the third by coolness of tone. Yellow, red, and blue, are called the primary colors, because out of their various modes of combination all other colors, either in nature or art, are produced. The three colors which arise from the binary union of these primary colors are orange, purple, and green, orange being composed of yellow and red—purple, of red and blue—and green of blue and yellow; they are therefore called secondary colors. All other colors in nature and art arise from the union of the whole three primary colors, under an infinite variety of modifications, in respect to the relative proportions in which they are combined.

White and black represent light and darkness, and are not therefore considered as colors. When yellow, red, and blue, of corresponding intensities, are united together in equal quantities, a neutral gray, similar to the union of white and black, is the result; because it is the nature of these colors when in triple union, to neutralize each other.

These simple facts would clearly exhibit themselves in a diagram constructed like the accompanying one (but without the dotting and straight lining by which color is there represented,) by coloring the space within the two curved lines D A F and D O F with pure yellow—the space with the similar lines D B E and D P E with pure red—and the space within the similar lines E C F and E N E with pure blue.

The colors thus put together must be of equal intensity, and quite transparent. Gamboge yellow, crimson lake, and Prussian blue, are quite suitable for ordinary purposes of this kind. Each color should be thoroughly dry before the other is put on, and then applied quickly in order to prevent the washing up of those first laid on. By this means the space D A F L remains yellow, D B E G red, and E C F M blue, while the space D G L is orange color, E G M purple, F L M green, and the center space G L M gray, all arranged in harmonious order, both as to that of succession and union.

The primary and secondary colors follow each other in the order of a primary and secondary alternately, as in the rainbow. The yellow, which being neutral as to tone unites with the warm-toned red on the one side in the production of orange, and on the other side with the cool-toned blue in the production of green, while the red and blue neutralize their respective warmth and coolness in the production of the secondary purple. The manner in which the most powerful harmonies of color occur within this circle is as follows:—on the line A E we find opposed to the neutral-toned primary color yellow, the secondary color purple, in which the warm-toned primary color red, and the cool-toned primary color blue, have mutually neutralized each other, and thereby constituting purple, the true harmonic accompaniment to yellow. On the line B F, we find opposed to the warm-toned primary color red, the secondary color green, in which the cool-toned primary color blue is united with the neutral-toned primary color yellow, thus constituting green, the true harmonic accompaniment to red. On the line D C, we find opposed to the cool-toned primary color blue, the secondary color orange, in which the warm-toned primary color red is united with the neutral-toned primary color yellow thus constituting orange color, the true harmonic accompaniment to blue.

DIAGRAM OF OOLORS.

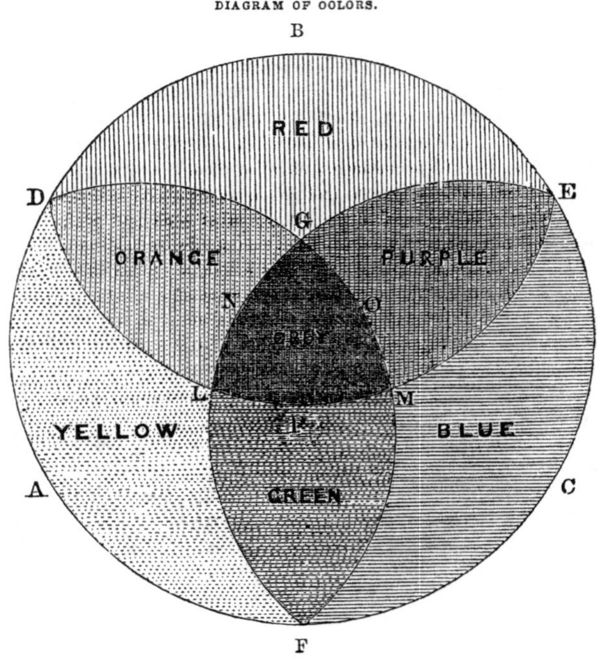

The primary colors may be represented as follows:—

The contrast between each of these three pairs of harmonizing colors, is relieved by the neutral gray which occurs in the space G L M.

These varieties of tone in the three primary colors thus produce that harmony to which the eye responds with so much delight when dwelling upon the beauties of nature; and a proper knowledge of this species of harmony would enable us to render truly beautiful many of the most simple products of our labor.

PART IV.

ELEMENTARY INSTRUCTION IN ENGLAND.

PAPERS XV.–XVIII.

XV. ELEMENTARY EDUCATION IN ENGLAND.

HISTORICAL SKETCH.

We propose to introduce an account of several of the best training schools of England, the most efficient and hopeful agency now at work in the educational field, with a brief sketch of the history of public schools in that country, drawn from various sources.*

I. The earliest mention of a school in England, dates back to the permanent introduction of Christianity; and for many centuries afterwards, schools even of the most elementary character, were only found in connection with monasteries and cathedrals. Even these were mostly swept away by the Danish invasion, so that King Alfred, about the year 880, was obliged to invite learned prelates from abroad,—John of Saxony from Corbie, Asser of St. Davids, and Grimbald the provost of St. Omer, in Normandy, to establish schools for his own subjects, and especially such as were destined for the service of church and state. To the support of these schools, and particularly the one connected with the monastery of Ethelingey, he set apart one-ninth of his revenue. To the centuries immediately following, we may trace the foundation of many existing educational establishments, by eminent prelates—to the "song scole" where poor boys were trained to chant, and the "lecture scole" where clerks were taught to read in the service of the church. Sampson, Abbot of St. Edmunds, himself a poor boy, founded a school at Bury St. Edmunds for forty boys, in 1198. Langfranc and Anselm, archbishops of Canterbury, had both exercised the profession of teacher in the schools of their monasteries, and both established schools. Joffrid, Abbot of Croyland, procured teachers from Orleans where he was educated, and established them at Cotenham in 1110, which is thought to be the origin of the university at Cambridge. William of Wykeham, Bishop of Winchester, to relieve poor scholars in their clerical education, and for the support and exaltation of the Christian faith, and the improvement of the liberal arts, founded a college in 1382 at Oxford, and in 1387 at Winchester, as a nursery of the former. In schools thus established, the dignitaries of the church, while they trained up poor youth for the service of the altar, and made the clergy respected by

* Companion to the British Almanac for 1847. Sir James Kay Shuttleworth's Public Education from 1846 to 1852. Low's Charities of London.

their learning, in reality introduced a new power into society, to soften and control the influence of birth and wealth. Few of the laity could read, and the law which existed in England till within the last twenty years, by which the severity of the statutes against felony was modified by what was called "benefit of clergy," shows how gradually the ability to read was extended beyond the religious orders. In early times, clergymen claimed the privilege of being exempt in certain cases from criminal punishment by secular judges. They appeared in clerical habits, and claimed the *privilegium clericale*. At length the ability to read was of itself considered sufficient to establish the privilege, and all offenders who claimed their "clergy" had to read a passage from the Psalms, which came to be humorously called "the neck verse." This was no merely theoretical privilege, for the ability to read, absurd as it may appear, saved an offender in the first instance from the full penalty of his crime. There is a curious case recorded in the Paston Letters, as happening in 1464. Thomas Gurney employed his man to slay "my Lord of Norwich's cousin." They were both tried and convicted of the crime. Thomas Gurney pleaded his clergy, and was admitted to mercy as "clerk convict;" the less guilty servant, being unable to read, was hanged. But the rank of Thomas Gurney gave no assurance that he possessed any knowledge of letters. Some amongst the highest in rank affected to despise knowledge, especially when the invention of printing had rendered the ability to read more common than in the days of precious manuscripts. Even as late as the first year of Edward VI. it was not only assumed that a peer of the realm might be convicted of felony, but that he might lack the ability to read, so as to claim benefit of clergy; for it is enacted that any Lord of the Parliament claiming the benefit of this act (1st of Edward VI. cap. 12,) "*though he can not read*, without any burning in the hand, loss of inheritance, or corruption of his blood, shall be judged, deemed, taken, and used, for the first time only, to all intents, constructions, and purposes, as a clerk convict." That the nobility were unfitted, through ignorance, for the discharge of high offices in the State at the time of the reformation, is shown by a remarkable passage in Latimer's "Sermon of the Plough," preached in 1548: "Why are not the noblemen and young gentlemen of England so brought up in knowledge of God, and in learning, that they may be able to execute offices in the common weal? * * * If the nobility be well trained in godly learning, the people would follow the same train: for truly such as the noblemen be, such will the people be. * * * Therefore for the love of God appoint teachers and schoolmasters, you that have charge of youth, and give the teachers stipends worthy their pains." Honest old Latimer thus demanded that "the young gentlemen" of England should be educated; that the hundreds should be well brought up in learning and the knowledge of God," so that "they would not, when they came to age, so much give themselves to other vanities."

II. The suppression of the monasteries by Henry VIII., and the diversion of the funds left by charitable persons for the education and support of the poor, was followed by the destruction of a large portion of the schools of the kingdom, for which a partial atonement was made by the endowment out of these funds of a class of schools, now known as grammar schools. That all the lands and buildings of the Catholic church were not thus appropriated, is evident from the following extract from a sermon preached by Thomas Lever, a master of St. John's College, Cambridge, before king Edward VI., in 1550: "Your majesty hath given and received by act of Parliament, colleges, chantries, and guilds, for many good considerations; and, especially, as appears in the same act, for erecting of grammar schools, to the education of youth in virtue and godliness, to the further augmenting of the universities, and better provision of the poor and needy. But now, many grammar schools, and much charitable provision for the poor, be taken, sold, and made away, to the great slander of you and your laws, to the utter discomfort of the poor, to the grievous offense of the people, to the most miserable drowning of youth in ignorance, and sore decay of the universities." The same plain speaker accuses the rapacious courtiers with having applied the funds for the maintenance of learning to their own profit: "Yea, and in the country many grammar schools, which be founded of a godly intent, to bring up poor men's sons in learning and virtue, now be taken away by reason of a greedy covetousness of you, that were put in trust by God and the king to erect and make grammar schools in many places, and had neither commandment nor permission to take away the schoolmasters' livings in any place." And yet, according to Strype, the ecclesiastical historian who quotes these passages, the creatures of the crown did not altogether succeed in their career of rapacity; for the "good king was so honest and just" as to apply the spoils of the religious houses and chantry lands, "in a considerable manner," to "pious ends." Twenty-one grammar schools are enumerated as thus founded by Edward VI.; and several of these are still amongst the most flourishing institutions of the country. The example continued to be followed during a century and a half; and many free grammar schools were established for the instruction of poor children in the learned languages. * * * From these often humble and unpretending edifices has issued a series of names illustrious in the annals of their country—a succession of men, often of obscure parentage and stinted means, who have justified the wisdom of the founders of grammar schools in providing education for those who would otherwise have been without it, and thus securing to the State the services of the best of her children.

According to the digests of the reports made by the commissioners for inquiry into charities, presented to Parliament in 1842, the annual income of the grammar schools of England and Wales, amounted to 152,047*l.*; but some schools were exempted from the inquiry.

About the time of the revolution the commercial classes, who had grown into wealth and consequent importance, began naturally to think that schools in which nothing was taught but Latin and Greek were not altogether fitted for those who were destined to the life of traffic. Uneducated men who had pushed their way to fortune and honor generously resolved to do something for their own class; and thus we came to see in every town, not a free grammar school, but a free school, over whose gates was generally set up the effigy of a boy in blue or green, with an inscription betokening that by the last will of alderman A. B. this school had been founded for twenty poor boys, to be clothed, and taught reading, writing, and arithmetic. With a comparatively small population these free schools, were admirable beginnings of the education of the poorer classes. While the grammar schools were making divines and lawyers and physicians out of the sons of the professional classes and the wealthier tradesmen, the free schools were making clever handicraftsmen and thriving burgesses out of the sons of the mechanics and the laborers; and many a man who had been a charity-boy in his native town, when he had risen to competence, pointed with an honest pride to the institution which had made him what he was, and he drew his purse-strings to perpetuate for others the benefits which he had himself enjoyed.

The annual income of the schools we have described, distinguished in the digests of the commissioners as "Schools not Classical," is returned as 141,385*l.* With the addition of 19,112*l.* for general educational purposes, the total income of *endowed charities for education* in England and Wales is 312,545*l.*

Comparing all the returns, we may say in round numbers that the income of the endowed schools is 300,000*l.*; the number of schools 4,000; and the number of scholars 150,000.

The 300,000*l.* thus derived from the rent of land, rent charges, funded securities, &c., during three centuries, has been the foundation upon which has been built up much of the sterling worth of the English character. One hundred and fifty thousand children have been receiving, for a long series of years,—some the most liberal education, some the commoner rudiments of worldly knowledge, all of them religious instruction.

They have kept alive the liberal studies which have nourished a race of divines, lawyers, physicians, statesmen, that may challenge comparison with those of any nation. They have opened the gates of the higher employments to industry and talent unsupported by rank and riches. They have mitigated the inequalities of society. They have ploughed up the subsoil of poverty to make the surface earth stronger and richer. What the grammar schools have done for the higher and middle classes, the free schools have done for the lower in a different measure. They were the prizes for the poor boy who had no ambition, perhaps no talent, for the struggles of the scholar; they taught him what, amongst the wholly untaught, would give him a distinction and a preference in his worldly race,—and he was unenvied by the less fortunate, because they knew that there was no absolute bar to their children and their kindred running the same course.

III. With the beginning of the present century a new era in popular education in England commenced by the formation of voluntary associations to extend the blessings of knowledge, human and divine, to the great mass of the people. Prior to this, there had been individuals in advance of their age, who had advocated universal education.

Sir Thomas More, in his "Utopia," professedly written to describe "the best state of a public weal," says, "Though there be not many in every city which be exempt and discharged of all other labors, and appointed only to learning—that is to say, such in whom, even from their very childhood, they have perceived a singular towardness, a fine wit, and a mind apt to good learning—yet *all in their childhood be instructed in learning*. And *the better part of the people*, both men and women, *throughout all their whole life, do bestow in learning those spare hours* which we said they have *vacant from bodily labors*." This is the condition to which the people of England are surely tending—the condition of *elementary instruction for all children*—the habit of *self-culture for all adults*.

In his celebrated "Wealth of Nations," first published in 1766, Adam Smith, advocating the instruction of almost "the whole body of the people" in "the most essential parts of education," says, "The public can facilitate this acquisition by establishing in every parish or district a little school, where children may be taught for a reward so moderate, that even a common laborer may afford it; the master being partly, but not wholly, paid by the public; because if he were wholly, or even principally paid by it, he would soon learn to neglect his business. In Scotland, the establishment of such parish schools has taught almost the whole common people to read, and a very great proportion of them to write and account. In England, the establishment of charity schools has had an effect of the same kind, though not so universally, because the establishment is not so universal." This seed was altogether sown upon barren ground. The establishment of parochial schools, which would have taught the children of the laboring classes habits of foresight and independence, could not be thought of whilst the easier system was at hand to keep them in the condition of degraded pauperism.

The state of education in England at the commencement of the present century, is described in few words by Malthus, in his celebrated "Essay on Population," published in 1803: "We have lavished immense sums on the poor, which we have every reason to think have constantly tended to aggravate their misery. But in their education, and in the circulation of those important political truths that most nearly concern them, which are perhaps the only means in our power of really raising their condition, and of making them happier men and more peaceable subjects, we have been miserably deficient. It is surely a great national disgrace, that the education of the lower classes of the people in England should be left merely to a few Sunday schools, supported by a subscription from individuals, who can give to the course of instruction in them any kind of bias which they please. And even the improvement of Sunday schools (for, objectionable as they are in some points of view, and imperfect in all, I can not but consider them as an improvement) is of very late date."

At the time when Malthus wrote this, SUNDAY SCHOOLS had not been in efficient existence more than twenty years. The indefatigable founder of these valuable institutions, Mr. Raikes of Gloucester, wrote in his newspaper, in 1783, "Some of the clergy in different parts of this country, bent upon attempting a reform among the children of the lower class, *are establishing* Sunday schools for rendering the Lord's Day subservient to the ends of instruction, which has hitherto been prostituted to bad purposes." From the hour when Mr. Stock, the benevolent rector of St. John's, Gloucester, met Mr. Raikes at his own door, where they talked of the necessity of doing something to ameliorate the deplorable state of the poor children around them, the system of Sunday schools has gone on most surely and rapidly developing. In 1785, "the Society for the Support and Encouragement of Sunday schools;" and in 1803, the "Sunday School Union," were established. We can overrate the positive benefits which have been arrived from the extension, and unjust to depreciate the importance of these schools as part of a great system of national progress. There were in 1852, 2,000,000 scholars in 20,000 schools.

In the absence alike of any old parochial system of education, and of endowments for popular instruction worthy of mention, it is not surprising, however, that, thus sustained, the Sunday school, during the last half century, should have become a great institution in the manufacturing districts, where the old parochial system of religious ministration was equally defective. The feelings of employers, parents, and teachers, all united in the erection and support of the Sunday school; not in most instances, without a high regard for its secular as well as religious uses, *which is now however gradually giving way to a desire to make its duties more purely spiritual.* The first step usually taken in furtherance of this desire, is to teach writing and arithmetic on two or three evenings of the week, instead of a part of the Sunday. The next step, seeing that the great majority of the children, especially in poor neighborhoods, are still occupied on the Sundays chiefly in learning the mere art of reading though the Scriptures and Scripture extracts are the text-books, is to endeavor by the establishment of public day schools within the same walls, or in the same neighborhoods, gradually to get the young prepared for a higher task on the Sunday,—that of possessing themselves more fully of the truths unfolded in the words which they have elsewhere learned to decipher. The first step has generally been taken; the second, but partially; and yet with effects upon the Sunday school itself which will challenge the deepest feelings of gratitude, in observing the labors of the best Sunday schools of the manufacturing towns.

In 1807, Mr. Whitbread came forward in the House of Commons, to propose a plan for the "exaltation of the character of the laborer" by the establishment of parochial schools. On this occasion Mr. Whitbread, said, "I can not help noticing to the house that this is a period particularly favorable for the institution of a national system of education, because within a few years there has been discovered a plan for the instruction of youth which is now brought to a state of great perfection, happily combining rules by which the object of learning must be infallibly attained with expedition and cheapness, and holding out the fairest prospect of utility to mankind." This plan was the MONITORIAL SYSTEM, propounded nearly at the same time by Dr. Bell and Mr. Lancaster. Mr. Whitbread's proposal for parochial schools was honored by no very favorable reception by the legislature of that day. It proposed as limited an amount of education as might have mitigated the jealousies even of those whose confidence in the stability of our institutions was founded upon the possibility of keeping the people in ignorance. It proposed that the poor children of each parish should receive two years' education, between the age of seven and fourteen. The advantages of education even of this limited kind were weighed in the money-balance and the moral-balance of the opinions of that day; and some said that it was monstrous to think of taxing the occupiers of lands and houses in order that all the children of the country should be taught to read and write; and some that it tended to give an education to the lower classes above their condition. Mr. Windham, came forward with the often repeated assertion, that "if the teachers of the good and the propagators of bad principles were to be candidates for the control of mankind, the latter would be likely to be too successful." Mr. Whitbread's bill was of course laid on the shelf.

The origin of the monitorial system is attributed to Andrew Bell and Joseph Lancaster—by the friends of each, the latter founding the British and Foreign School Society in 1805, and the latter, the National Society in 1811—the origin of which is thus described by Sampson Low in his "Charities of London."

Whilst superintendent of the Military Orphan Asylum at Madras, in 1791, Dr. Bell one day observed a boy belonging to a Malabar school writing in the sand; thinking that method of writing very convenient, both as regards cheapness and facility, he introduced it in the school of the asylum, and as the usher refused to teach by that method, he employed one of the cleverest boys to teach the rest. The experiment of teaching by a boy was so remarkably successful, that he extended it to the other branches of instruction, and soon organized the whole school under boy teachers, who were themselves instructed by the doctor. On his return to England, he published a report of the Madras Orphan Asylum, in which he particularly pointed out the new mode of school organization, as far more efficient than the old.

The publication took place in 1797, and in the following year Dr. Bell introduced the system into the school of St. Botolph's, Aldgate, London.

He afterwards introduced it at Kendal, and made attempts with small success to obtain its adoption in Edinburgh. Settling down soon after as rector of Swanage in Dorchester, he was secluded from the world for seven years; yet he retained his strong opinion of the value of the new system of education, and had the school at Swanage conducted on that system.

In the meanwhile Joseph Lancaster, son of a Chelsea pensioner, in the Borough-road London, opened a school in his father's house, in the year 1798, at the early age of eighteen. He had been usher in schools, and being of an original, enterprising, and ardent character, he had himself made improvements in tuition. Dr. Bell's pamphlet having fallen in his way, he adopted the Madras system with eagerness, making various alterations in its details. In the year 1802, he had brought his school into a very perfect state of organization, and found himself as well able to teach 250 boys with the aid of the senior boys as teachers, as before to teach 80. His enthusiasm and benevolence led him to conceive the practicability of bringing all the children of the poor under education by the new system, which was not only so attractive as to make learning a pleasure to the children, but was so cheap as exceedingly to facilitate the establishment and support of schools for great numbers of the poor. He published pamphlets recommending the plan, and in one of them ascribes the chief merit of the system to Dr. Bell, whom he afterwards visited at Swanage. His own school he made free, and obtained subscriptions from friends of education for its support. The Duke of Bedford, having been invited to visit it, became a warm and liberal patron of the system. Lancaster pushed his plan with the ceaseless energy of an enthusiast; nothing daunted or discouraged him; he asked subscriptions for new schools from every quarter; and at length he was admitted to an interview with the king (at Weymouth in 1806.) Being charmed with what he heard of his large designs, the admirable order and efficiency of his schools, and also with the simplicity and overflowing benevolence of the man, his majesty subscribed £100 a year, the queen £50, and the princess £25 each, to the extension of the "Lancasterian system." The king also declared himself to be the patron of the society which was soon afterwards formed to promote education on this system. Such was the origin of the "British and Foreign School Society."*

Dr. Bell's method thus publicly brought forward and advocated, in process of time was adopted in the Lambeth schools, by the Archbishop of Canterbury: and in the Royal Military School, by the Duke of York's authority; numerous schools forthwith springing into existence upon

* Originally designated "The Royal Lancasterian Institution for promoting the Education of the Children of the Poor." In 1808, Lancaster resigning his affairs into the hands of trustees, it assumed more of the character of a public institution. Mr. Lancaster died in 1838, supported, in his latter days, solely by an annuity purchased for him by a few old and attached friends. Dr. Bell died in 1832, leaving the princely sum of £120,000 for the encouragement of literature and the advancement of education.

what is known to this day as *the Madras system;* the distinctive features between these and such as were founded by Lancaster's party, consisting in the extent to which the religious instruction should be mixed with the secular; the former, as a clergyman of the established church, advocating the inculcation of the truths of Christianity as held in the church articles and formularies; the latter, representing the dissenting interests, admitted the reception of the Bible as the foundation of all instruction, but *without any note or comment.* This still remains the essential difference between the two societies and the schools conducted on their principles. In 1808, Dr. Bell endeavored to induce the government to take up his plans, and to establish "A National Board" of education, with schools placed under the management of the parochial clergy. In this he failed, but friends of the established church rallied round him, and, through their efforts and under the patronage of the bishop and clergy, the National Society was eventually formed in 1811.

The earliest voluntary agency of popular education was "the Society for Promoting Christian Knowledge" founded in 1698, to aid in the establishment of charity schools, and the publication and circulation at a low price of religious books. By 1750, the society had aided in the establishment of sixteen hundred Church Charity Schools. From 1733, when the society began to report its annual issues of publication, to 1840, it had distributed upwards of 94,000,000 millions of books and tracts. The annual returns for publication is about £55,000, and its income from dividends, contributions and legacies, about £33,000.

The Religious Tract Society was instituted in 1799, for circulating religious works of its own, in the British dominion and foreign countries, under the direction of a committee of churchmen and protestant dissenters. Its total distribution to March, 1849, was nearly 500,000,000 of copies of its publication. Its gross income is £60,000 per annum, of which £12,000 was derived from annual subscription.

The first school established in Great Britain, exclusively for *adults,* was at Bala, a village in Merionethshire, in 1811, by Rev. T. Charles, minister of the place. This was so successful as to induce their establishment in other places. In 1812, William Smith, aided by Stephen Prout, commenced a similar school in Bristol, which led to the establishment of the "Bristol Institution for instructing the adults to read the Holy Scriptures." In 1813 the object was extending to teaching writing. In 1816, a similar society was founded in London. These schools were introduced into over thirty towns in the course of a few years.

The first *evening school* was established in Bristol in 1806, by the "Benevolent Evenings School Society" to afford gratuitous instruction to the sons of the laboring poor, who from the nature of their circumstances are obliged to work hard during the day for their subsistence. Instruction was confined to reading, writing, and arithmetic. Up to 1849, 13,002 persons had been enrolled as members of the schools.

Both adults and evening schools accomplished much good, and prepared the way for the gradual extension of the system of Mechanic

Institutes, into which they have been merged. Through their instructions, upwards of 30,000 of the poor of England, 180,000 of Wales, 30,000 of Ireland, and a large number in the Highlands of Scotland, making an aggregate of over 250,000 adult persons were taught to read.

In 1815 the first infant school* was established by James Buchanan at New Lanark, under the auspices of Robert Owen; and in 1819 at London, under the patronage of Mr. Brougham and Lord Lansdowne, and others; and through the labors of one of the first teachers, Mr. Wilderspin, its methods were widely disseminated throughout the kingdom. These methods were greatly improved and more wisely applied in the model schools of the Home and Colonial Infant School Society, founded in 1836. The objects of the society are, 1. To qualify masters and ministers, by appropriate instruction and practice. 2. To visit and examine schools when required. 3. To circulate information, and prepare books and fixtures appropriate to these schools.

The history of the *Mechanics' Institution* through all its phases of development, from the earliest young men's mutual improvement society established in London, in 1690, with encouragement of Defoe, Dr. Kidder, and others, under the name of "Society for the Reformation of Manners"—the Society for the Suppression of Vice—"the Reformation Society of Paisley" in 1787; the Sunday Society in 1789, the Cast Iron Philosophers in 1791, the first Artisans' Library in 1795, and the Birmingham Brotherly Society in 1796, all among the working classes of Birmingham;—the popular scientific lectures of Dr. John Anderson, to tradesmen and mechanics in Glasgow, in 1793—the establishment of the Anderson's University at that place in 1796, and the incorporation into it of a gratuitous course of elementary philosophical lectures by Dr. Birbeck in 1799, for the benefit of mechanics,—the Edinburgh School of Arts in 1821, the Glasgow Mechanics' Institute, the Liverpool Mechanics' and Apprentices' Library, and the London Mechanic Institution in 1823—which from this date, through the labors of Dr. Birbeck, Mr. Brougham and others, spread rapidly all over the kingdom until there are now over 700 societies scattered through every considerable village, especially every manufacturing district in the kingdom, numbering in 1849, 120,000 members, 408 reading-rooms, and 815,000 volumes—constitute one of the most interesting chapters in the educational or social history of Great Britain. They have created a demand for a system of national education, which found its first expression in Parliament in 1833, in a grant of £20,000, on motion of Lord Althorpe.

In 1825, as one of the direct results of the extended and growing in-

* The founder of infant schools was J. F. Oberlin, Pastor of Waldbach in the Ban de la Roche, in the north-eastern section of France, who in his educational reform in his parish appointed females, (paid at his own expense,) to gather the poor children between the ages of 2 and 6 years, and instruct and interest them by pictures, maps, and conversation, and to teach tnem to read, knit, and sew. In Germany there is now a class of schools called Kribben—or Cradle—and Garden Schools where literally infant children, whose mothers are obliged to go out to work by day, are received and properly cared for and instructed during their absence.

terest in mechanic institutions and popular libraries, the "Society for the Diffusion of Useful Knowledge" was formed, which commenced immediately a series of cheap and useful publications in a great variety of subjects, and thus lead the way to a new era in English literature—the preparation of books adapted in subject and mode of treatment, as well as in price, to the circumstances of the great mass of the people. In 1831, this society commenced a quarterly journal of education, which was discontinued in 1836, at the close of the tenth volume. In 1836, two volumes of essays on education, several of them delivered as lectures before the American Institute of Instruction, was published by this society. These twelve volumes, and the four volumes* published by the Central Society of Education, composed of several of the most active and liberal-minded members of the former society, contributed a large mass of valuable information as to the organization, administration, and instruction of public schools in different countries, and prepared the way, in 1839, for the appointment of the Committee of Privy Council on Education. Before noticing briefly the action of Parliament, and the measures of this government committee, we will conclude our sketch of the voluntary agencies in behalf of popular education.

Among the most important agencies now at work in Great Britain, are the Industrial, Ragged† and Reform Schools, designed for pauper, neglected, and criminal children.

Ragged schools in London had their origin in the operations of the London City Mission—the first school being founded in 1837, in Westminster, by Mr. Walker, an agent of that society. Its success led to the establishment of similar schools in the most debased and debasing streets of the metropolis, and gathered in mendicant and ragged children, already sunk in ignorance and vice, and unfit to mix with the scholars of an ordinary school. In 1844, the Ragged School Union was formed to encourage and assist those who teach in this class of schools, and to suggest plans for their extension and more efficient management. In 1852, the union embraced 60 schools with 13,000 children, and had an income from subscription and contributions of about $14,000, in addition to the sums contributed in each locality for its own schools.

The most systematic and successful enterprise of this class was instituted and carried out by William Watson, Sheriff-substitute of Aberdeenshire in Scotland, who organized, in 1841, a system of industrial schools which embraced in its operations all classes of idle vagrant chil-

---

* The fourth volume entitled the Educator, consisted of the prize essay written by John Lalor, "On the necessity and means of elevating the social condition of the Educator," and other essays by James Sampson, Rev. E. Higginson, and others.

† The first Ragged School was instituted by John Pounds, a poor cripple in Portsmouth, who, while pursuing his vocation as a shoemaker in a vicious neighborhood near the dock-yards in that town, gathered into a school in his shop, such outcasts as he could by kind word, and needful food, until before his death in 1839, he had instructed over five hundred children who would otherwise have grown up in ignorance, and led lives of vice and crime. He died leaving—

For epitaph, a life well spent,
And mankind, for a monument.

dren, and cleared a large town and county of juvenile criminals and beggars—thereby establishing an enviable reputation as a wise political economist, an efficient magistrate, and a practical benefactor of his country and race. His plan, which was developed gradually, embraced, first, gratuitous education. This succeeded only partially. He next, held out, three substantial meals a day, and four hours of useful but self-imposed occupation. This was a stronger inducement; but all the vagrant children did not come. Then, under the police act, all street begging was prohibited, and all found begging were sent to the industrial school for food, instruction, and work. And to reform those who still gained their bread by thieving, a child's asylum was founded, to which these young criminals were sent to school, or be taught useful knowledge and a trade, instead of to a prison. By these various agencies, street vagrancy and juvenile crimes has been annihilated. Some of the features of this system have been tried in all of the large towns in the kingdom, and with great success; and the success has been greater or less, as the plan adopted embraced more or less of the Aberdeen system. The whole number of ragged schools in the kingdom in 1852, was about 180, with about 20,000 pupils; of these about 4,000 attend industrial classes.

The first reform school was instituted by the Philanthropic Society, in 1788, for criminal and vagrant children in London, which was removed in 1848-9, to Redhill, near Reigate, and farm labor substituted for industrial training in shops. More than 3,000 boys have been admitted, of which number over two-thirds were reclaimed from criminal and vicious habits, and permanently improved. Similar schools have been from time to time formed by other societies with the same object in view, for particular sections of the country; the most successful of which, are the Refuge for the Destitute at Hoxton, and the Warwick County Asylum at Stratton.

The system of discipline and instruction adopted in these professedly reform schools, has been introduced into county gaols, and houses of correction, and with good results, especially into the County House of Correction at Preston, of which Rev. John Clay has been chaplain for many years. The success of these schools and methods of instruction, and the enormous increase of juvenile delinquencies in the large towns of England, induced Parliament in 1836, to make provision for the establishment of a governmental institution for young criminals at Parkhurst, in the Isle of Wight, which was opened in 1839. Although the system of discipline adopted, partook too much of that of a prison, and the industrial training was confined almost exclusively to shop labor, in which large numbers were employed together on the silent system, and the reformatory results were not, in consequence, so satisfactory as in institutions conducted on the Family and Farm School plan at Mettray, in France, and other places on the continent, still enough has been done, to awaken a desire and determination to extend and improve all existing means, not only of reforming, but of preventing the growth of juvenile destitution and crime. Committees of Parliament, and conferences of those interested, have taken the subject into serious consideration, and there is now reasonable ground to believe that efficient steps will be taken to improve the physical condition and homes of the poor generally, to establish infant and elementary schools in the "infested districts" of large towns, to infuse the industrial and religious element into elementary schools for all classes, and above all to infuse the law of kindness, and restore the affections and relations of the family among those in whom, by the accident of birth, these affections and relations have been extinguished or perverted.

Schools of the same general character under the name of Schools of Industry, not only for vagrant children, and in connection with prisons for juvenile offenders, but for children of the poor and laboring classes generally, had been previously established. One of the earliest was instituted by Mr. Joseph Allen, in Linfield, and another at Ealing Grove, by Lady Byron, in which the regular occupation of the pupils in shop, garden, and farm labor, is found to be both economical, and highly conducive to their intellectual and moral culture.

In 1840, the Poor Law Commissioners, reported the extraordinary fact that there were 64,570 children in the workhouses of England, under 16 years of age, and 58,835 between the ages of 2 and 16. These children were chiefly orphans, illigitimate, or deserted, or the childern of persons physically or mentally incapable to discharge the duties of guardianship. From the wretched system of providing for the education and industrial habits of this class of children, it was ascertained by inquiries conducted by Mr. Hickson, into the previous history of the inmates of gaols, that both crime and pauperism recruited their ranks to a large extent from the workhouses. Mr. Hickson urged the immediate establishment of District Industrial Schools for workhouse children, and of wholly separating them from the contaminating influence of adult pauperism. The experiment was commenced at Norwood, in 1836, by Mr. Aubin, with over 1,000 children of all ages under fifteen, and was continued and perfected by him, under the superintendence of Dr. Kay, the assistant Poor Law Commissioner for the Metropolitan District. The success of the enterprise was such as to induce Parliament in 1846, to provide for the formation of school districts or Parochial Unions, within which all the pauper children should be collected into district schools, to be trained to industrious habits, and instructed in such useful knowledge as is suitable to their condition. To carry out this plan, the sum of £30,000 ($150,000) was voted in 1847, for the salaries of schoolmasters in these schools, and the government has since erected a Normal School,* at Twickenham, twelve miles out of London, for the special purpose of training teachers for workhouse and reform schools, at an expense of over £41,000 ($200,000.) The good influence of these improved schools is already felt, and that influence will be increased as soon as better

* For a description of Kneller-Hall Training School, see page 791, *et. seq.*

trained teachers are introduced into all the workhouse, district, and reform schools of the kingdom. There are now over five hundred workhouse, and district schools under the charge of the Poor Law Commissioners in which there are nearly one thousand teachers employed.

The beneficial results of introducing drawing into the evening classes, and day schools of the Mechanic Institutions and the acknowledged dependence of English manufactures in ornamental work on the taste and invention of neighboring countries in consequence of the special education provided by the government of these countries, for all who obtain employment in the various branches of artistic manufacture—induced the government to establish, in 1837, Schools of Design—a central school at Somerset House in London, and provincial schools in several of the principal manufacturing towns; and an annual grant of about $30,000 was made towards their support. The government in 1852, extended its plan so as to aid in giving elementary instruction in the arts of drawing and modeling, in any class or grade of educational institutions, which will conform to the regulations of the Board of Trade, by whom the parliamentary grant is expended.

In 1847, the "Lancashire Public School Association," was formed at Manchester, and promulgated a plan for establishing schools for the county upon the basis of local representation and taxation, and non-interference with religious instruction. The objects of the association were set forth in public addresses, pamphlets, and newspapers, until the local agitation expanded into a national movement. A conference was held at Manchester on the 30th October, 1851, at which over 2,000 persons, many of them delegates from different parts of the kingdom, were present when it was agreed to convert the Lancashire Society into a "National Public School Association, to promote the establishment, by law, in England and Wales, of a system of free schools, which, supported by local rates,* and managed by local committees, especially elected for that purpose by the rate-payers, shall impart *secular* instruction only; leaving to parents, guardians, and religious teachers, the inculcation of doctrinal religion, to afford opportunities for which, it is proposed that the schools shall be closed at stated times in each week." Both the county and national association have been instrumental in bringing before the public mind of England the right and duty of taxation, by the people themselves, for the support of a system of public education, and of subjecting schools established under authority of law, and aided by parliamentary grant, or local taxation, to the management of such officers as the people may elect, whether of the clergy or laity.

---

* At this meeting a letter was read from Edward Lombe, Esq., the owner of an estate of 15,000 acres in the neighborhood of Norwich, transmitting a draft for £500 ($2,500) "in aid of the objects of the association—the protestant right of private-judgment in matters of religion, and the old Saxon right of local representation—

The holiest cause of pen or sword,
That mortal ever lost or gained."

The principles asserted by the association will be embodied in the report of a select committee of the House of Commons appointed to consider a bill to promote education in Manchester and Salford. The bill on which the committee was raised, was not introduced by the association, but as a substitute for it, by parties which are in favor of extending and improving the plan of governmental aid and inspection to schools in connection with religious communions now in operation.

IV. The first movement in parliament toward a system of national education, was made in 1807, by Mr. Whitbread who introduced a bill into the House of Commons to establish a school in each parish for poor children, between the ages of seven and fourteen. The bill met with no favor.

On the 21st of May, 1816, Mr. (now Lord) Brougham, a member of Winchelsea moved for the appointment of a select committee of the House of Commons "to inquire into the state of education of the lower orders of the metropolis," and to consider what may be fit to be done with respect to the children of paupers who shall be found begging in the streets, or whose parents have not sent such children to any of the schools provided for the education of the poor. Mr. Brougham had already taken an active interest in the educational movements of the day. So early as 1808, he had assisted in extending the institution of Mr. Lancaster, and in organizing the British and Foreign School Society, and had contributed two very able articles to the Edinburgh Review in 1810, and 1812, on the education of the poor, and in vindication of the methods of Lancaster, and the plan on which that society was proceeding in establishing schools without any religious test. He entered on the business of the committee with so much zeal and industry as to be able to submit a report on the 19th of June, which was followed by four additional reports—by which a flood of light was thrown on the educational destitution of the metropolis, on the inefficient manner in which many public schools were conducted, and the misapplications of funds destined to education. In 1818, the committee was revived with more extensive powers, which enabled it to inquire into the education of "the lower orders" through the whole of England and Scotland, and by construction, into educational charities generally, including the universities and great public schools. This committee addressed circulars to every parish in England, Scotland, and Wales, by which materials were collected for a statistical exhibit, filling three folio volumes, of the state of education in the whole kingdom. The labors of this committee were closed by presenting a plan for national education, countenanced and supported by the State, in which an attempt was made to accomodate the new system to the existing order of things, so as to improve and confirm schools already established, and harmonize the administration of schools composed of children of all denominations with a conceded deference to the authority of the church of England. The bills embodying this plan were introduced in 1820, and were lost between the conflicting jealousies, selfishness, and hatred of ecclesiastical authorities.

and professing religious communions—and the whole subject was postponed for nearly fifteen years before its consideration was again resumed in the English parliament.

Mr. Brougham was more immediately successful in his attempts to induce parliament to turn its attention to the abuses of educational charities. The reports of the committee appointed in 1816 and 1818, had brought to light a great body of curious and interesting information respecting the state and conduct of many schools founded by charitable persons in and near the metropolis. At the close of the session in 1818, he brought in a bill for the appointment of a commission to inquire into charities in England for the education of the poor. The disclosures of the committees on education had excited a public jealousy, which no device of persons interested in maintaining venerable abuses, could lull or elude; and although the field of inquiry was at first narrowed down to a particular class of endowments, a commission was appointed, which has been continued, enlarged, and renewed, until their reports fill thirty folio volumes, and cover 28,840 charities; and the work is not yet done. The total value of these charities reported on, is estimated at £75,000,000, and the annual income at £1,209,395. By the publicity already given to the management of these charities, the income has been increased, and it is calculated that by the improved system of administration, this income can, be raised to £4,000,000—or $20,000,000, a large portion of which, can by act of parliament, without any violence to the will, but in the spirit of the original devises, be appropriated to promote the education of the people.

The year 1833 was signalized by an Education Inquiry, undertaken on motion of Lord Kerry, into the existing means of education for the poorer classes; and an annual grant* of £20,000, voted by the House of Commons on motion of Lord Althorpe, for the building of school-houses in England and Wales, under the direction of the Lords of the treasury. This sum was applied by the treasury in aid of private subscriptions for the erection of schools for the education of poor children, in connection with the National Society, and the British and Foreign School Society.

In 1834, a select committee was appointed by the Commons "to make inquiries into the present state of education in England and Wales, and into the application and effects of the grant made in the last session for the erection of school-houses, and to consider the expediency of further grants in aid of education." This committee reported the minutes of evidence taken before them, respecting schools in connection with the two great societies, and the school system of Prussia, Ireland, Scotland, France, together with the views of distinguished educationists, such as Lord Brougham, Dr. Julius, Prof. Pillans, and others.

In 1835 Lord Brougham brought the subject of national education before the House of Lords, by moving a series of resolutions, which

* A similar grant of £10,000 was voted for the same purpose in Scotland. A grant of £4,328 had been previously made (in 1831) to the Commissioners of National Education in Ireland, which has been gradually increased to the sum of £125,000, in 1851.

contemplated among other things the encouragement of infant schools, the establishment of seminaries, where good teachers might be trained, and the appointment of a board of commissioners, to establish and superintend the teachers' seminaries, and the just application of the funds voted by parliament for the promotion of education, and for the protection of all charitable trusts for the same purpose. The resolutions were read and ably advocated by the mover, but no action was had respecting them. During this year the sum of £10,000 was voted by parliament toward the erection of normal, or model schools.

In 1836, Lord Brougham brought two bills before the House of Lords, and renewed the same in 1837, embodying the principles set forth in his resolutions of 1835, and providing in addition for a local school committee, to be appointed by the town council in corporate towns, and the voters of the agricultural districts, as well as the imposition of a tax on property by the rate payers. These bills were fully explained and the reasons for their adoption eloquently urged, both in 1837, and in 1838, but without success.

This defeat of his favorite measure, was followed soon after by a published letter to the Duke of Bedford, in which Lord Brougham urges on the friends of an independent system of national education, to unite in support of the measures which the government would soon propose—by which aid would be extended to schools supported by religious denominations, as the only practicable scheme which there was any chance of carrying.

" For the first time we have had the attention of parliament fully directed to the subject of education ; attracted, no doubt, by other motives than the mere zeal for popular improvement, led by sectarian animosity, whetted by factious rage, yet still pointed, for whatever reason, to this great question, which, as it never before had obtained any share of parliamentary favor, so, I presume to think, never henceforth can, with its prodigious intrinsic merits, cease to occupy the Legislature, for its own sake, until it is finally and satisfactorily disposed of by some great national measure becoming the law of the land. It is thus that the wisdom of an overruling Providence, bringing general good out of partial evil, orders so as some superficial irritation, some flying ache, shall excite our attention to the deep-seated mischief that is preying upon our vitals, lead us to probe its hidden source, and enable us to apply the needful remedy, long after the superficial feeling that first gave us the warning shall have been passed away and been forgotten. The ignorance of the people, the origin of all the worst ills that prey upon our social system, has become at length the object of Legislative regard ; and I defy the constituted authorities of this free country to delay much longer in applying the appropriate cure, by eradicating a disease, as easily cured as it is fatal if neglected.

In 1839, Lord John Russell, communicated to the Privy Council, the desire of the Queen, that he and four other members of the council, viz., the Lord Privy Seal, the Chancellor of the Exchequer, the Secretary, of State for the Home Department, and the Master of the Mint, should form a Board, or Committee for the consideration of all matters affecting the education of the people.

The Committee of Council on Education were fortunate in their selection of Dr. James Phillip Kay, (now Sir James Kay Shuttleworth) as Secretary. Dr. Kay had early interested himself in improving the condition of the manufacturing population, and in 1832 published an elaborate essay on the "Moral and Physical condition of the working classes employed in the cotton manufacture of Manchester." He was soon after made one of the Assistant Commissioners of the Poor Law Board. While acting in this capacity in the Norfolk or Suffolk district, in 1836, he submitted to that board a report on the evils of the system of apprenticeship education under the old Poor Law, and, in 1838, "a plan for the proper training of pauper children, and on district schools," which was made the basis for a reorganization and improved management of schools for this class of children. In 1839, having been removed to the superintendence of the Metropolitan district, he was specially charged with the improvement of schools in workhouses, and in maturing the school of industry at Norwood, into an example of what district schools for pauper children might become. To accomplish this, Dr. Kay made himself personally acquainted with the best methods of school management and teaching, as practiced in the schools of Scotland, Belgium, Holland, and France, and entered on the difficult task of training up a class of teachers moved by Christian charity to the work of rescuing by an appropriate physical, industrial, intellectual and religious education, the outcast and orphan children, from the mischief wrought by vicious parentage and cruel neglect. This was the origin of the training school at Battersea,* which was sustained until its success was beyond question, mainly, by the personal efforts and large pecuniary sacrifices of its projectors. While maturing the plan of this institution, Dr. Kay was appointed Secretary of the Committee of Council on Education; and to his industry, enthusiasm in the work, and great administrative talents, may be attributed the large measure of success which has attended the efforts of that committee to extend and improve the means of elementary education, and especially the system of governmental inspection, and training of teachers in 1843, he assumed the name of Shuttleworth, in consequence of receiving a legacy from a person of that name, and in 1849, on retiring from the office with shattered health, he was knighted by the Queen for his services to the cause of popular education—the first and only instance of honorary distinction conferred for this grade of public service.

Under his able administration the measures of the Committee of Council have been framed, and under his instructions and correspondence, these measures have become almost a system of national education.

---

* A full description of the Battersea Training School will be found on page 201, *et. seq.*

What—and how extensive—these measures of Government for the advancement of education really are, is not, we believe, generally known; we have therefore collected the following particulars in respect to them from the volume of Minutes for the years 1848-9-50, which is now before us. They appear to be framed with a due regard to the rights of conscience and the diversities of religious opinion; and, with a wise and statesmanlike precaution on the part of the Government, to avail itself of local sympathies, and to stimulate voluntary contributions.

1. Aid is offered by these minutes towards the erection of school buildings; and since the year 1839 Government has contributed under this head an aggregate sum of £470,854, towards the erection of 3782 school-houses, drawing out, thereby, voluntary contributions to, probably, four times that amount, and affording space for the instruction of 709,000 more children than could before be taught. These grants have been distributed as follows:—

	Amount of Grant.	Number of Schools aided.	Number of Children for whom Accommodation is Provided.
England.........	£399,368	3255	622,823
Scotland	41,563	302	47,814
Wales	27,418	198	33,198
The Islands......	2,505	27	5,165

Eighty-two per cent. of the whole amount granted under this head has been paid to Church-of-England schools.

2. Aid is offered toward the erection of normal schools for the training of teachers or for the improvement of the buildings of such schools; and the total amount thus granted in aid of eighteen normal schools, is £66,450; of which £35,950 is to the Church of England; £12,000 to the British and Foreign School Society and the Wesleyan body; and the rest to the Scotch Church.

3. Aid is offered towards the *maintenance* of such students in these normal schools, as shall appear, on examination, to possess the qualities and attainments likely to make them good teachers, in sums varying from £20 to £30 annually for each student. The total sums so contributed to thirteen training schools were, in the year 1847, £1705; in 1848, £2138; in 1849, £2373.

4. Annual grants are paid in augmentation of the salaries of such teachers of elementary schools as, upon examination, have been judged worthy to receive certificates of merit, such certificates being of three different classes, and the augmentations varying from £15 to £30. The number of teachers so certificated is 681, and the total amount payable annually in augmentation of their salaries £6133.

5. Stipends are allowed to apprentices to the office of teacher, increasing during the five years of their apprenticeship from £10 to £18. The number of schools in which such apprentices have been appointed being 1361, and the number of apprentices, 3581.

6. Provision is made for the instruction of these apprentices by annual payments to the teachers to whom they are apprenticed, being at the rate of £5 annually for one, and £4 for every additional apprentice, their competency to instruct them being tested by annual examinations. The sums payable under the three last heads are stated in the following table:—

Denomination of School.	Number of Schools.	Number of Certificated Teachers.	Number of Apprentices.			Amount conditionally awarded for year ending 31 Oct. 1850.
			Boys.	Girls.	Total.	
						£ s. d.
National, or Church of England Schools..	973	482	1,638	910	2,593	49,472 10 0
British, Wesleyan, and other Protestant Schools, not connected with the Church of England,	181	69	434	159	593	10,356 10 0
Rom. Cath. Schools..	32	10	46	33	79	1,323 10 0
Schools in Scotland, connected with the established Church,	82	39	161	28	189	3,492 0 0
Schools in Scotland, not connected with the Estab. Church.	93	81	100	27	127	3,467 0 0
Total	1,361	681	2,424	1,157	3,581	68,111 10 0

7. They offer supplies of books, apparatus, and school fittings, at reduced rates, the reduction being effected by the purchase of large quantities at wholesale prices; and by grants to the extent of one-third of these reduced prices. The total reduction thus effected averages sixty-two per cent. on the retail price: and, the total amount of the grants so made by the Government being £6664, it is probable that the retail price of the books, maps, &c., so distributed, is not less than £17,500.

8. They provide for the annual inspection of normal schools, and of all elementary schools in which apprentices are appointed, or which are taught by certificated teachers. Also for the annual examination of apprentices and of candidates for the office of apprentice, and of teachers who are candidates for certificates of merit.

For this purpose they maintain a staff of twenty-one inspectors of schools, —of whom eleven are inspectors of church schools; two of British and Foreign, and Dissenters' schools; and two of Scotch schools; one of Roman Catholic, and five of Workhouse schools. The cost of this inspection, in 1849, for salaries and travelling expenses, was £16,826. The schools at present liable to inspection are 12 normal schools, 4296 elementary schools, and about 700 workhouse schools.

The general result of this action of the Government on the education of the country, *in respect to quantity*, may be gathered from the fact, that in the ten years from 1837 to 1847, the number of children under education in Church schools had increased from 558,180 to 955,865, being an increase of eight elevenths.

It was not, however, so much in respect to the *quantity* of the education of the country, as in regard to its *quality*, that an alteration was needed: and it is in this respect that most has been done. The two questions of quality and quantity have, however, a relation to one another, for a good school is almost always a full one. This relation of the number of the scholars to the quality of the school is strikingly illustrated in the returns made from schools in which certificated teachers and apprentices have been appointed, and which are, therefore, regularly inspected. These schools may be reasonably supposed to have improved from year to year: and it appears that the numbers of children who attend them have, in like manner, steadily advanced. In the first year after these measures came into operation, 1847-8, the total number had thus increased 74·5 per cent.; in the second year, 16·66 per cent. No third year's apprenticeships are yet completed.

The whole question of the quality of the instruction, after all that regulations can do, will be found to be involved in the character of the teacher; for such as is the teacher, such invariably is the school. The first step towards the formation of a more efficient body of teachers was taken by Sir J. P. Kay Shuttleworth and Mr. E. Carleton Tuffnell, when, in the year 1840, they founded a school at Battersea for training Masters for the schools of pauper children,—maintaining it at their private cost, aided by some of their friends. That no personal exertions might be wanting to its success, Sir J. P. Kay Shuttleworth went to reside in it; adding to his duties as Secretary to the Committee of Council on Education the cares and difficulties of a position, in which, surrounded by youths but recently the inmates of workhouses, he sought to lay the foundation of a new and improved state of education throughout the country. This honorable example of private benevolence has been followed by various public bodies. The National Society soon afterwards established St. Mark's College, Chelsea,—an institution for the training of a superior class of Church schoolmasters,—and Whiteland's House School, for the training of mistresses: And within four years of that time there had sprung up no less than seventeen diocesan schools for the training of teachers of Church schools. These are now increased to twenty, of which Chester, York, Durham, Cheltenham, and Caermarthen are the principal. The Battersea school having been transferred to the National Society in 1844, there are now twenty-three or twenty-four training schools in the country for the education of Church schoolmasters.

The existence of these training schools, the people of England and the Church of England owe to the Committee of Council. Their importance is not to be measured by the amount of good they have been able up to this time to do, or are now doing. They are poorly supported; the number of students who attend them is small, not exceeding in the whole from four to five hundred, and the education pursued in them at present appears to be but imperfectly adapted to the formation of the character of the teacher. But our conception of that character is as yet very imperfect in England: and in all that concerns the formation and development of it, we have no experience to guide us. Each of the training schools admits of development; and the State would do well to lend its aid to this end with a more liberal hand (we should say a less sparing hand) than it has hitherto attempted;—respecting, as far as is consistent with guarantees for the proper application of its aid, the independence of each, and allowing them to manifest themselves under that distinctive character towards which they may severally tend. Each, taken with its individuality, might thus become a depositary of local educational sympathies and a centre of local action. And looking to the progress which the whole question of education is making, and to the fact that, whenever the country is properly supplied with parish schools, not less than 2000 students will, probably, require to be kept within the walls of these training schools to supply the vacancies for teachers which will annually arise in Church schools alone, there can be no doubt of the importance of this part of the system.

Far more important, however, than any aid which the Government has yet given to the establishment and maintenance of training schools, is that which it has rendered in providing that candidates shall be properly educated and prepared for admission to them. Nothing has so interfered with the success of such institutions as the impossibility of finding a sufficient number of qualified candidates. The office of the national schoolmaster is but little in repute; and but few persons have, hitherto, been accustomed to seek it, except such as, for the want of sufficient ability, or energy, or industry, have been unsuccessful in other callings, or who labor under infirm health or bodily deformities. These were considered indeed good enough for the purpose; until that inveterate prejudice was got rid of, that education is a privilege of men's social condition, and to be graduated according to it. It is a legitimate deduction from this principle, that a teacher of the lowest standard in attainments and skill is competent to the instruction of children of the lowest class. The converse proposition is to rule the future of education. The education of those children who are the most degraded, intellectually and morally, being the most difficult task,—is to have the highest qualities of the teacher brought to bear upon it.

The three or four thousand pupil teachers, having been selected as the most promising children in the schools in which they have been brought up, and having been apprenticed to the work of the school for five years, and educated under the careful superintendence of the clergy and the inspectors of schools, will when they have completed their apprenticeship, present themselves for admission to the training schools. So selected and so trained from an early age, they cannot fail, after two or three years' residence in them, to form a body of teachers such as have never before entered the field of elementary education in England. The *worst* training of the normal schools cannot mar this result; and we have reason to hope for the *best*. This, then, is the bright future of education. If the apprenticeship of new pupil teachers is continued at the same rate as heretofore, from 1000 to 1500 will annually complete their apprenticeship; and nearly as many will complete annually their training in the normal schools; so that nearly that number of teachers will every year be prepared to enter on the charge of elementary schools.

The following are the conditions annexed to grants:—

1. In respect to grants for the *building* of schools, it is stipulated that the site shall be legally conveyed to trustees, to be used for ever for the purposes of a school.

2. That the buildings should be substantial and well adapted to the uses of a school.

3. That the State, by its inspector, shall have access to the school, to examine and report whether the instruction of the children is duly cared for.

4. To these conditions there have been added, since the year 1848, certain others, well known as 'the Management Clauses;' having for their object to secure to the laity, in all practicable cases, what appears to be a due share in the management of the schools.

5. To grants for the augmentation of teachers' salaries, and for the stipends of pupil teachers, it is made a condition that certain examinations shall be passed, the subjects of examination being specified beforehand. These subjects include, with secular instruction, a detailed course of elementary religious instruction, to be conducted in Church schools in strict accordance with the formularies of the Church of England.

6. To grants for apparatus and books, no other conditions are annexed than that the Committee of Council shall be certified on the report of one of its inspectors, that the assistance is needed; that the books and apparatus sought are proper to the use of the school; and that the teachers are competent to make the proper use of them.

These measures of the Committee of Council appear excellently calculated to promote the interests of education. But the best measures depend for their success upon their execution; and these have been so administered as to secure the cordial acceptance of the various parties locally interested in schools.

These measures were not adopted without encountering the most violent and determined opposition. Even the appointment of the Committee of Council, was denounced in the House of Lords by the Archbishop of Canterbury, who carried an address to the crown, praying for its revocation by a majority of 111 votes; and in the House of Commons, Lord Stanley, the author of the system of national education in Ireland, missed carrying a similar motion in the first instance by five, and on a second occasion by only two votes. Even the continuance in office of Lord Melbourne's administration was periled by his declaration in favor of these measures. By degrees the jealousies and opposition of the different religious communions has been conciliated, and a system of elementary education, under the local direction and support of religious bodies, and the general supervision and pecuniary aid (mainly in the qualification and encouragement of teachers,) of the Committee of Council, has grown up to the proportions represented in the following table:

Denomination of Schools.	Number of Schools.	Number of Pupils.	Total Income.
Church of England Schools...	17,015	955,865	£817,081
British and Foreign do ...	1,500	225,000	161,250
Wesleyan do ...	397	38,623	27,347
Congregational do ...	89	6,839	4,901
Roman Catholic do ...	585	34,750	16,000
Ragged do ...	270	20,000	20,000
Totals..................	19,856	1,281,077	£1,046,579

The following are the educational statistics of England and Wales, gathered from the census of 1851:

Public day schools,..		15,473
Number of persons on the school books,..................	Males,	791,548
	Females,	616,021
	Total,	1,407,569
Attending at the schools on the 31st March, 1851,..........	Males,	635,107
	Females,	480,130
Private day schools, 31st March, 1851,.........................		29,425
Number on the school books,............................	Males,	347,694
	Females,	353,210
Attending on March 31st, 1851, ...	Males,	317,390
	Females,	322,349

Proportion of scholars on the books to the (1 scholar in 8½ persons) population, 11.76 per cent.

Number of scholars in attendance to school on books, 83⅓ per cent.

The progress of elementary education is exhibited in the following table:

	Day scholars.	Population.	Proportion of Day scholars to Population.
In 1818........	674,883	11,398,167	1 to 17
1833........	1,276,947	14,417,110	1 to 11½
1851........	2,108,473	17,922,768	1 to 8½

Increase of population from 1818 to 1851, 57 per cent.

Increase of day scholars from 1818 to 1851, 212 per cent.

In view of these facts Lord John Russell, and Sir James Kay Shuttleworth, the former in a speech in the House of Commons, and the latter in a volume just published, (1853,) advocate an extension of the measures now in operation, in preference to a system of National Education, based on municipal management and taxation. Sir James thus speaks of the policy of parental contribution in connection with public grants and private subscription.

A weekly payment from the parents of scholars is that form of taxation, the justice of which is most apparent, to the humbler classes. Every one who has even an elementary knowledge of finance is aware, that no tax can be largely productive from which the great mass of the people are exempt.

The moral advantage of a tax on the poor in the form of school pence is, that it appeals to the sense of paternal duty. It enforces a lesson of domestic piety. It establishes the parental authority, and vindicates personal freedom. The child is neither wholly educated by religious charity, nor by the State. He owes to his parents that honor and obedience, which are the sources of domestic tranquillity, and to which the promise of long life is attached. Let no one rudely interfere with the bonds of filial reverence and affection. Especially is it the interest of the State to make these the primal elements of social order. Nor can the paternal charities of a wise commonwealth be substituted for the personal ties of parental love and esteem, without undermining society at its base.

The parent should not be led to regard the school as the privilege of the citizen, so much as another scene of household duty. Those communities are neither most prosperous, nor most happy, in which the political or social relations of the family are more prominent than the domestic. That which happily distinguishes the Saxon and Teutonic races is, the prevalence of the idea of "*home.*" To make the households of the poor, scenes of Christian peace, is the first object of the school. Why then should we substitute its external relations for its internal—the idea of the citizen, for that of the parent—the sense of political or social rights, for those of domestic duties—the claim of public privilege, for the personal law of conscience?

Parliament has not been entirely neglectful of the education, as well as the health of children employed in factories. The first act in their behalf was passed in 1802. This proving insufficient, other provisions were adopted from time to time, after very minute inquiries into the condition of this class of children, and protracted contests in parliament, until by the law as it now stands, every child (between the ages of 8 and 13 years) employed in a factory, must attend school *three hours* every day, between the hours of eight o'clock in the morning, and six o'clock in the afternoon. The person, whether parent or employer, who receives any direct benefit from the wages of a child, must take care that the child attend; and to show that this attendance is regular, the employer must obtain from the schoolmaster, on Monday of every week, a certificate in a form prescribed by the statute, showing the number of hours the child was at school on each day of the week previous. This certificate must be preserved for six months, and produced to an inspector on demand. The law imposes a fine for every case of neglect on the part of the employer. Inspectors are appointed by the Home Office, to visit factories and schools, with full powers to examine any person upon oath on the premises, employ surgeons to examine into the condition and arrangements for health, to cause defective machinery to be repaired, to set up a school for factory children, where none exist, and to report annually, and when required to the Home office.

NOTE.

RESOLUTIONS submitted to the consideration of the House of Lords, on the 24th of July, 1854, by Lord Brougham.

1. That the increase in the means of education for the people, which had begun a few years before the year 1818, when the first returns were made, and had proceeded steadily till the year 1833, when the next returns were made, has been continued since, although less rapidly as regards the number of schools and teachers, but with considerable improvement both in the constitution of the additional seminaries, and in the quality of the instruction given:

2. That the returns of 1818 give as the number of day schools of all kinds 19,230, attended by 674,883 scholars; of Sunday schools 5,463, and Sunday school scholars 425,533; the returns of 1833, 38,971 day schools and 1,276,947 scholars, and 16,828 Sunday schools and 1,548,890 scholars; the returns of 1851, 46,042 day schools and 2,144,378 scholars, 23,514 Sunday schools and 2,407,642 scholars:

3. That the population having increased during these two periods from 11,642,683 to 14,386,415 and 17,927,609, the proportion of the day scholars to the population in 1818 was 1 in 17.25, of Sunday scholars 1 in 24.40; in 1833, of day scholars 1 in 11.27, of Sunday scholars 1 in 9.28; in 1851, of day scholars 1 in 8.36, of Sunday scholars 1 in 7.45; showing a more rapid increase, but more especially of Sunday scholars, in the first period than in the second, while the population has increased more rapidly during the second period; its increase being at the rate of 180,000 a year during the first period, and 197,000 a year during the second:

4. That there is reason to believe that the returns of 1818 are less than the truth, that those of 1833 have considerably greater omissions, and that those of 1851 approach much nearer the truth; from whence it may reasonably be inferred that the increase during the first fifteen years was greater than the returns show, that the increase during the last eighteen years was less than the returns show, and that the increase proceeded during the last period at a rate more diminished than the returns show:

5. That before the year 1833 the increase was owing to the active exertions and liberal contributions of the different classes of the community, especially of the upper and middle classes, whether of the Established Church or of the Dissenters, the clergy of both church and sects bearing a large share in those pious and useful labors:

6. That in 1833 the plan was adopted which had been recommended by the education committee of the House of Commons in 1818, of assisting by grants of money in the planting of schools, but so as to furnish only the supplies which were required in the first instance, and to distribute those sums through the two school societies, the National and the British and Foreign:

7. That the grants of money have since been largely increased, and that in 1839 a committee of the Privy Council being formed to superintend their distribution, for increasing the number of schools, it has further applied them, for the improvement of the instruction given, to the employment of inspectors and the training of teachers:

8. That of the poorer and working classes, assumed to be four-fifths of the population, the number of children between the ages of three and fifteen are 3,600,000, and at the least require day schools for one-half, as the number which may be expected to attend school, regard being had to the employment of a certain proportion in such labor as children can undergo; and that consequently schools for one-eighth of the working classes of the poor are the least that can be considered as required for the education of those classes:

9. That the means of education provided are still deficient; because, of the 2,144,378 day scholars now taught at the schools of all kinds, not more than about 1,550,000 are taught at public day schools, the remaining 500,000 being taught at private schools, and being, as well as about 50,000 of those taught at endowed public schools, children of persons in the upper and middling classes, so that little more than 1,500,000 of the day scholars are the children of the poor, or of persons in the working classes; and thus there are only schools for such children in the proportion of 1 in 9.6 of the number of the classes to which they belong, instead of 1 in 8, leaving a deficiency of 300,000, which must increase by 20,000 yearly, according to the annual increase of the population:

10. That this deficiency is considerably greater in the large towns than in the other parts of the country, inasmuch as it amounts to 130,000 in the aggregate of the towns which have above 50,000 inhabitants, and is only 170,000 in the rest of the country; the schools in the great towns being only for 1 in 11.03 of the working classes, and in the rest of the country for 1 in 9.2 of these classes, deducting 50,000 taught at endowed schools:

11. That the deficiency in the number of teachers is still greater than in the number of scholars, inasmuch as eight of the largest towns appear to have public day schools with 208 scholars on an average, the average of all England and Wales being 94 to a school, that there are assistant and pupil teachers in many of these schools, and paid masters in others, but that there is the greatest advantage in increasing the number of teachers, this being one of the chief benefits of Sunday schools, while the plan formerly adopted in the new schools of instructing by monitors among the scholars themselves, is now properly allowed to fall into disuse:

12. That the education given at the greater number of the schools now established for the poorer classes of people is of a kind by no means sufficient for their instruction, being for the most part confined to reading, writing, and a little arithmetic; whereas, at no greater expense, and in the same time, the children might easily be instructed in the elements of the more useful branches of knowledge, and thereby trained to sober, industrious habits:

13. That the number of infant schools is still exceedingly deficient, and especially in those great towns where they are most wanted for improving the morals of the people and preventing the commission of crimes:

14. That while it is expedient to do nothing which may relax the efforts of private beneficence in forming and supporting schools, or which may discourage the poorer classes of the people from contributing to the cost of educating their children, it is incumbent upon Parliament to aid in providing the effectual means of instruction where these can not otherwise be obtained for the people:

15. That it is incumbent upon Parliament to encourage in like manner the establishment of infant schools, especially in larger towns:

16. That it is expedient to confer upon the town councils of incorporated cities and boroughs the power of levying a rate for the establishment and support of schools under the authority of and in co-operation with the education committee of the Privy Council; care being taken as heretofore that the aid afforded shall only be given in cases of necessity, and so as to help and encourage, not displace, individual exertion:

17. That the permission to begin and to continue the levying of the rate shall in every case depend upon the schools founded or aided by such rate being open to the children of all parents *upon religious instruction being given, and the Scriptures being read in them*, but not used as a school-book, and upon allowing no compulsion either as to the attendance of religious instruction or at divine service in the case of children whose parents object thereto and produce certificates for attending other places of worship:

18. That the indifference which has been found of the parents in many places to obtain education for their children, and a reluctance to forego the advantages of their labor, by withdrawing them from school, is mainly owing to the ignorance of their parents, and this can best be removed by the encouragement of a taste for reading, by the establishment of mechanics' institutions, apprentices' libraries, and reading-rooms, and by the abolition of all taxes upon knowledge:

19. That in towns there have been established upward of 1,200 of such institutions and reading-rooms, with above 100,000 members, but that by far the greater number of these members are persons in the upper and middle classes, a very small proportion only belonging to the working classes; but it has been found in some parts of the country, particularly in Cumberland, that when the whole management of the affairs of the institutions is left in the hands of the working-men themselves, a very great proportion of the attending members belong to that class, and both by frequenting the rooms and taking out the books to read, show their desire of profiting by the institution:

20. That in every quarter, but more especially where there are no reading-rooms in the country districts, the great obstacle of diffusing useful knowledge among the people has been the newspaper stamp, which prevents papers containing local and other intelligence from being added to such works of instruction and entertainment as might at a low price be circulated among the working classes, and especially among the country people, along with that intelligence:

21. That the funds given by charitable and public spirited individuals and bodies corporate, for promoting education, are of a very large amount, probably, when the property is improved and the abuses in its management are corrected, not less than half a million a year; and that it is expedient to give to the Board, formed under the Charitable Trusts Act of 1853, such additional powers as may better enable them, with the assent of trustee and special visitors (if any,) to apply portions of the funds now lying useless to the education and improvement of the people.

The operations of the Committee of Council for 1858, are set forth in the following extracts :—

Fifty-four inspectors, including 20 assistant inspectors, were employed in visiting schools, and in holding examinations, during the past year. They visited during that period 9,384 daily schools, or departments of such schools, under separate teachers. They found present in them 821,744 scholars; 5,495 certificated teachers; and 13,281 apprenticed teachers. They also visited 38 separate training colleges, occupied by 2,709 students in preparation for the office of schoolmaster or schoolmistress. In December last, these students, and 2,087 other candidates were simultaneously examined for the end of the first, second, or third years of their training, or for admission, or for certificates, as acting teachers. The inspectors also visited 539 schools for pauper children, containing 47,527 inmates, and 118 Reformatory, Ragged, or Industrial Schools, containing 7,793 inmates. These numbers came under actual review, and were the subject of separate reports, within the period to which our present statement refers.

The following statement exhibits the expenditure from the Education Grant, classified according to Object of the Grant—both in 1858, and also from 1839 to December, 1858.

OBJECT OF GRANTS.	For the Year ended 31 December, 1858.			From 1839, to 31 December, 1858.		
	£	s.	d.	£	s.	d.
In building, &c., Elementary Schools,	140,826	8	8	913,449	11	3½
In building, &c., Normal or Training Colleges,	10,388	10	6	169,295	6	5
In providing Books, Maps, and Diagrams,	5,403	15	4	30,991	3	9½
In providing Scientific Apparatus,	313	16	7	3,930	1	9
In augmenting Salaries of Certificated Schoolmasters,	74,041	3	8	349,841	11	7
In paying Salaries of Assistant Teachers,	5,904	5	10	23,770	17	1
In paying Stipends of Pupil-teachers,	221,719	5	9	1,236,793	4	3
In Capitation Grants,	49,522	13	7	125,047	13	11
In Annual Grants to Training Colleges,	73,731	17	7	328,365	15	4½
Reformatory and Industrial Schools,	27,025	15	1	57,441	17	1
Pensions,	589	8	4	2,384	15	0
Inspection,	39,276	5	0	314,577	11	10½
Administration, (*Office in London*,)	17,211	11	8	83,868	3	5½
Poundage on Post Office Orders,	1,954	17	3	9,632	4	6
Agency for Grants of Books, Maps, and Diagrams,	963	13	11	5,677	17	5
Total,	668,873	8	9	3,655,067	14	9½.

In the following Table the expenditure is presented according to denomination of the Receipts.

OBJECT OF GRANTS.	For the Year ended 31 December, 1858.			From 1839, to 31 December, 1858.		
	£	s.	d.	£	s.	d.
On Schools connected with—						
Church of England,	428,770	13	9¾	2,385,427	16	3¼
British and Foreign School Society,	54,293	9	1½	324,985	[illegible]	0¼
On Wesleyan Schools,	42,751	17	7½	173,570	5	3½
On Roman Catholic Schools (Great Britain,)	36,258	7	8½	129,890	16	0
On Parochial Union Schools (for inspection,)	5,666	18	9	117,870	4	7
SCOTLAND, On Schools connected with—						
Established Church,	46,774	14	5	232,961	0	8
Free Church,	31,609	0	0	185,877	16	7¾
Episcopal Church,	5,536	15	7¾	18,903	7	0¾
Other Schools,	....			212	6	9½
Administration (as in Table above,)	17,211	11	8	83,868	3	5½
Total,	668,873	8	9	3,655,067	14	9½

From 1839 to December 31st, 1858, 3,427 school-houses have been built, and 1,639 houses have been enlarged and improved at an expense of £2,-958,132 (near $15,000,000)—toward which the Committee have appropriated £913,450 out of Parliamentary Grants, and individuals or societies have raised by subscription £2,039,683.

There are 36 Training Colleges under inspection. The premises, which generally include from two to five acres of land, have cost 378,350*l.*, in which amount is included 118,514*l.* from the Parliamentary grant. The number of students at the end of the year 1858, was 2,709.

During the year 1858, we paid from the Parliamentary grant the sum of 49,077*l.* in exhibitions for the maintenance of individual students, the sum of 21,012*l.* 17*s.* 7*d.* to the Treasurers of the colleges, in proportion to the merits of the examination passed by the inmates at the end of each year of their training; and 1,392*l.* in aid of the salaries of special lecturers; making a total of 71,481*l.* 17*s.* 7*d.*

The great cost of these institutions, and the important place which they hold in the present system, has occupied our careful attention. The best of the pupil-teachers proceed to them for professional training; remain in them, with public exhibitions, for two years as Queen's scholars; quit them to become certificated schoolmasters and schoolmistresses, and, in that character, prepare other apprentices to run the same course.

The present number of pupil-teachers is now (May, 1859,) approaching 15,000, and this number is calculated to yield 2,619 who annually complete their period of service (five years,) and 2,280 candidates for Queen's scholarships.

Pensions are allowed to teachers under certain conditions. Pensioners must have served for fifteen years in school, and their schools must have been, during seven of those years, under inspection. Age or infirmity is a condition of every pension (30*l.* per annum being the maximum for an elementary teacher,) and the pension may be withdrawn on proof of misconduct, or of sufficient means of livelihood from other sources.

The following sums were granted for Education, Science and Art, in 1859.

Public Education in Great Britain,	£836,920
Science and Art Department,	93,394
Public Education, Ireland,	249,468
Commissioners of Education, Ireland, Office Expenses,	655
University of London,	3,650
Universities, &c., in Scotland,	7,650
Queen's University in Ireland,	2,297
Queen's Colleges, Ireland,	4,800
Royal Irish Academy,	500
Belfast Theological Professors, &c.,	2,500
British Museum (Establishment,)	77,425
British Museum (Buildings,)	22,270
British Museum (Purchases,)	3,000
National Gallery (including purchases of Pictures,)	15,985
Scientific Works and Experiments,	6,439
Royal Geographical Society,	500
Royal Society,	1,000
Total,	1,328,453

Among the resplendent names of modern English literature, Thomas Babbington Macauley and Thomas Carlyle stand preeminent, and in their writings, both Mr. Macauley and Mr. Carlyle appear the earnest advocates of popular education.

In his place in the House of Commons, in 1847, Mr. Macauley came forward to defend the minutes of the Committee of Council on Education, to which, as Member of the Privy Council, he had given his assent.

I hold that it is the right and duty of the State to provide for the education of the common people. I conceive the arguments by which this position may be proved are perfectly simple, perfectly obvious, and the most cogent possible. * * * All are agreed that it is the sacred duty of every government to take effectual measures for securing the persons and property of the community; and that the government which neglects that duty is unfit for its situation. This being once admitted, I ask, can it be denied that the education of the common people is the most effectual means of protecting persons and property? On that subject I can not refer to higher authority, or use more strong terms, than have been employed by Adam Smith; and I take his authority the more readily, because he is not very friendly to State interference; and almost on the same page as that I refer to, he declares that the State ought not to meddle with the education of the higher orders; but he distinctly says that there is a difference, particularly in a highly civilized and commercial community, between the education of the higher classes and the education of the poor. The education of the poor he pronounces to be a matter in which government is most deeply concerned; and he compares ignorance, spread through the lower classes, neglected by the State, to a leprosy, or some other fearful disease, and says that where this duty is neglected, the State is in danger of falling into the terrible disorder. He had scarcely written this than the axiom was fearfully illustrated in the riots of 1780. I do not know if from all history I could select a stronger instance of my position, when I say that ignorance makes the persons and property of the community unsafe, and that the government is bound to take measures to prevent that ignorance. On that occasion, what was the state of things? Without any shadow of a grievance, at the summons of a madman, 100,000 men rising in insurrection—a week of anarchy—Parliament beseiged—your predecessor, sir, trembling in the Chair—the Lords pulled out of their coaches—the Bishops flying over the tiles—not a sight, I trust, that would be pleasurable even to those who are now so unfavorable to the church of England—thirty-six fires blazing at once in London—the house of the Chief Justice sacked—the children of the Prime Minister taken out of their beds in their night clothes, and laid on the table of the horse guards—and all this the effect of nothing but the gross, brutish ignorance of the population, who had been left brutes in the midst of Christianity, savages in the midst of civilization. Nor is this the only occasion when similar results have followed from the same cause. To this cause are attributable all the outrages of the Bristol and Nottingham riots, and all the misdeeds of General Rock and Captain Swing; incendiary fires in some district, and in others riots against machinery, tending more than anything else to degrade men to the level of the inferior animals. Could it have been supposed that all this could have taken place in a community were even the common laborer to have his mind opened by education, and be taught to find his pleasure in the exercise of his intellect, taught to revere his Maker, taught to regard his fellow-creatures with kindness, and taught likewise to feel respect for legitimate authority, taught how to pursue redress of real wrongs by constitutional methods? * * * Take away education, and what are your means? Military force, prisons, solitary cells, penal colonies, gibbets—all the other apparatus of penal laws. If, then, there be an end to which government is bound to attain—if there are two ways only of attaining it—if one of those ways is by elevating the moral and intellectual character of the people, and if the other way is by inflicting pain, who can doubt which way every government ought to take? It seems to me that no proposition can be more strange than this—that the State ought to have power to punish and is bound to punish its subjects for not knowing their duty, but at the same time is to take no step to let them know what their duty is

I say, therefore, that the education of the people ought to be the first concern of a State, not only because it is an efficient means of promoting and obtaining that which all allow to be the main end of government, but because it is the most efficient, the most humane, the most civilized, and in all respects the best means of attaining that end. This is my deliberate conviction; and in this opinion I am fortified by thinking that it is also the opinion of all the great legislators, of all the great statesmen, of all the great political philosophers of all ages and of all nations, even including those whose general opinion is, and has ever been, to restrict the functions of government. Sir, it is the opinion of all the greatest champions of civil and religious liberty in the old world and in the new; and of none—I hesitate not to say it—more emphatically than of those whose names are held in the highest estimation by the Protestant Nonconformists of England. Assuredly if there be any class of men whom the Protestant Nonconformists of England respect more highly than another—if any whose memory they hold in deeper veneration—it is that class of men, of high spirit and unconquerable principles, who in the days of Archbishop Laud preferred leaving their native country, and living in the savage solitudes of a wilderness, rather than to live in a land of prosperity and plenty, where they could not enjoy the privilege of worshipping their Maker freely according to the dictates of their conscience. Those men, illustrious for ever in history, were the founders of the commonwealth of Massachusetts; but though their love of freedom of conscience was illimitable and indestructible, they could see nothing servile or degrading in the principle that the State should take upon itself the charge of the education of the people. In the year 1642 they passed their first legislative enactment on this subject, in the preamble of which they distinctly pledged themselves to this principle, that education was a matter of the deepest possible importance and the greatest possible interest to all nations and to all communities, and that as such it was, in an eminent degree, deserving of the peculiar attention of the State. I have peculiar satisfaction in referring to the case of America, because those who are the most enthusiastic advocates of the voluntary principle in matters of religion, turn fondly to that land as affording the best illustration that can be any where found of the successful operation of that principle. And yet what do we find to be the principle of America and of all the greatest men that she has produced upon the question? "Educate the people," was the first admonition addressed by Penn to the commonwealth he founded—"educate the people" was the last legacy of Washington to the republic of the United States—"educate the people" was the unceasing exhortation of Jefferson. Yes, of Jefferson himself; and I quote his authority with peculiar favor; for of all the eminent public men that the world ever saw, he was the one whose greatest delight it was to pare down the functions of governments to the lowest possible point, and to leave the freest possible scope for the exercise of individual exertion. Such was the disposition—such, indeed, might be said to be the mission of Jefferson; and yet the latter portion of his life was devoted with ceaseless energy to the effort to procure the blessing of a State education for Virginia. And against the concurrent testimony of all these great authorities, what have you, who take the opposite side, to show? * * * Institutions for the education of the people are on every ground the very description of institutions which the government, as the guardians of the people's bests interests, are bound to interfere with. This point has been powerfully put by Mr. David Hume. * * * After laying down very emphatically the general principle of non-interference and free competition, Mr. Hume goes on to make the admission that there undoubtedly may be and are some very useful and necessary matters which do not give that degree of advantage to any man that they can be safely left to individuals. Such matters, he says, must be effected by money, or by distinctions, or by both. Now, sir, if there ever was a case to which that description faithfully and accurately applies, I maintain that it is to the calling of the schoolmaster in England. That his calling is a necessary and an useful one, is clear; and yet it is equally clear that he does not obtain, and can not obtain, adequate remuneration without an interference on the part of government. Here, then, we have the precise case, if we are to adopt the illustration of Hume, in which the government ought to interfere. Reasoning *à priori*, the principle of free competition is not sufficient of itself, and can not supply a good education. Let us look at the facts. What is the existing state in England? There has, for years, been nothing except the principle of non-interference. If, therefore, the principle of free competition were in reality a principle of the same potency in education as we all admit it to be in matters of trade, we ought to see education as prosperous under this system of free competition as trade itself is. If we could by possibility have had the principle of free competition fairly tried in any country, it would be in our own. It has been tried for a long time with perfect liberty in the richest country under the heavens, and where the people are not unfriendly to it. If the principle of free competition could show itself sufficient, it ought to be here; our schools ought to be the models of common schools; the people who have been educated in them ought to show the most perfect intelligence; every school ought to have its excellent little library, and its mechanical apparatus; and, instead of there being such a thing as a grown person being unable to read or to write, such an individual ought to be one at whom the people would stare, and who should be noted in the newspapers; while the schoolmaster ought to be as well acquainted with his important duties as the cutler with knives, or the engineer with machinery; moreover, he ought to be amply remunerated, and the highest respect of the public ought to be extended to him. Now, is this the truth? Look at the charges of the judges, at the resolutions of the grand juries, and at the reports made to every public department that has any thing to do with education. Take the reports of the inspectors of prisons. In Hertford House of Correction, out of 700 prisoners, about half were unable to read, and only eight could read and write well. In Maidstone jail, out of 8,000 prisoners, 1,300 were unable to read, and only fifty were able to read and write well. In Coldbath-fields, out of 8,000, it is not said that one could read and write well. If we turn from the reports of the inspectors of prisons to the registers of marriages, we find that there were nearly 130,000 couples married in the year 1844, and of those more than 40,000 of the bridegrooms and more than 60,000 of the brides could not sign their names, but made their marks. Therefore one third of the men and one half of the women, who are supposed to be in the prime of life, and who are destined to be the parents of the next generation, can not sign their names. What does this imply? The most grievous want of education. * * * And it is said, that if we only wait with patience, the principle of free competition will do all that is necessary for education. We have been waiting with patience since the Heptarchy. How much longer are we to wait? Are we to wait till 2,847, or till 3,847? Will you wait till patience is exhausted? Can you say that the experiment which has been tried with so little effect has been tried under unfavorable circumstances? has it been tried on a small scale, or for a short period? You can say none of these things. * * * It was at the end of the 17th century that Fletcher of Saltoun, a brave and able man, who fought and suffered for liberty, was so overwhelmed with the spectacle of misery his country presented, that he actually published a pamphlet, in which he proposed the institution of personal slavery in Scotland as the only way to compel the common people to work. Within two months after the appearance of the pamphlet of Fletcher, the Parliament of Scotland passed in 1696, an act for the settlement of schools. Has the whole world given us such an instance of improvement as that which took place at the beginning of the 18th century? In a short time, in spite of the inclemency of the air and the sterility of the soil, Scotland became a country which had no reason to envy any part of the world, however richly gifted by nature; and remember that Scotchmen did this, and that wherever a Scotchman went—and there were few places he did not go to—he carried with him signs of the moral and intellectual cultivation he had received. If he had a shop, he had the best trade in the street; if he enlisted in the army, he soon became a non-commissioned officer. Not that the Scotchman changed; there was no change in the man, for a hundred years before, Scotchmen of the lower classes were spoken of in London as you speak of the Esquimaux; but such was the difference when this system of State education had been in force for only one generation; the language of contempt was at an end, and that of envy succeeded. Then the complaint was, that wherever the Scotchman came he got more than his share; that when he mixed with Englishmen and Irishmen, he rose as regularly to the top as oil rises on water. * * * Under this system of State education, whatever were its defects, Scotland rose and prospered to such a degree that I do not believe a single person, even of those who now most loudly proclaim their abhorrence of State education, would venture to say that Scotland would have become the free, civilized country it is, if the education of her people had been left to free competition without any interference on the part of the State. Then how does this argument stand? I doubt whether it be possible to find, if there be any meaning in the science of induction as applied to politics, any instance of an experiment tried so fully and so fairly, tried with all the conditions which Lord Bacon has laid down in his *Novum Organon*, and of which the result was so evident. Observe, you take these two countries so closely resembling each other in many particulars—in one of these two countries, by far the richer of the two, and better able to get on with free competition, you have free competition; and what is the result? The Congregational Union tell you that it is a result, indeed, to make us ashamed, and every enlightened foreigner that comes amongst us, sad. In the other country, little favored by nature, you find a system of State education—not a perfect one, but still an efficient one—and the result is an evident and rapid improvement in the moral and intellectual character of the people, and a consequent improvement in security and in prosperity such as was hardly ever seen before in the world. If this had been the case in surgery or in chemistry, and such experiments and results had been laid before you, would it be possible for you not to see which was the wrong course and which the right? These arguments have most fully convinced me of a truth which I shall not shrink from proclaiming in the face of any clamor that may be raised against it—that it is the duty of the State to educate the common people.

Mr. Carlyle has uttered many indignant rebukes of the niggardly policy of the English government in respect to the education of the people.

Who would suppose that education were a thing which had to be advocated on the ground of local expediency, or indeed on any ground? As if it stood not on the basis of everlasting duty, as a prime necessity of man. It is a thing that should need no advocating; much as it does actually need. To impart the gift of thinking to those who can not think, and yet who could in that case think; this, one would imagine, was the first function a government had to set about discharging. Were it not a cruel thing to see, in any province of an empire, the inhabitants living all mutilated in their limbs, each strong man with his right arm lamed? How much crueller to find the strong soul, with his eyes still sealed, its eyes extinct, so that it sees not! Light has come into the world, but to this poor peasant, it has come in vain. For six thousand years, the sons of Adam, in sleepless effort, have been devising, doing, discovering, in mysterious, infinite indissoluble communion, warring, a little band of brothers, against the great black empire of necessity and night; they have accomplished such a conquest and conquests; and to this man it is all as if it had not been. The four and twenty letters of the alphabet are still Runic enigmas to him. He passes by on the other side; and that great spiritual kingdom, the toil-worn conquest of his own brothers, all that his brothers have conquered, is a thing non-extant for him; an invisible empire; he knows it not; suspects it not. And is it not his withal; the conquest of his own brothers, the lawfully acquired possession of all men? Baleful enchantment lies over him from generation to generation; he knows not that such an empire is his, that such an empire is at all? O, what are bills of rights, emancipations of black slaves into black apprentices, lawsuits in chancery for some short usufruct of a bit of land? The grand "seed-field of time" is this man's, and you give it him not. Time's seed-field, which includes the earth and all her seed-fields and pearl-oceans, nay her sowers too and pearl-divers, all that was wise and heroic and victorious here below; of which the earth's centuries are but furrows, for it stretches forth from the beginning onward even unto this day!

"My inheritance, how lordly, wide and fair;
Time is my fair seed-field, to time I'm heir!"

Heavier wrong is not done under the sun. It lasts from year to year, from century to century; the blinded sire slaves himself out, and leaves a blinded son; and men, made in the image of God, continue as two legged beasts of labor; and in the largest empire of the world, it is a debate whether a small fraction of the revenue of one day (30,000*l.* is but that) shall, after thirteen centuries, be laid out on it, or not laid out on it.

NORMAL SCHOOL

OF THE

BRITISH AND FOREIGN SCHOOL SOCIETY, BOROUGH ROAD, LONDON.

The following account of the Borough Road Normal School of the British and Foreign School Society is compiled from a report of Joseph Fletcher, Esq., one of her Majesty's Inspectors of Schools, to the Committee of Council on Education, submitted April 7, 1847, and from documents published in the Annual Reports of the Society.

The Normal establishment of the British and Foreign School Society is situated in Borough Road, at the corner of Great Union Street, London, and consists of two Normal Schools, one for male, and the other for female teachers, and two large model schools, one for boys and the other for girls, in which one thousand pupils are daily under instruction, on the monitorial system. These latter schools, while incidentally benefiting the neighborhood in which they are situated, are mainly sustained for the purpose of exhibiting in actual practice the most improved methods of instruction, and as a means of training in the art of teaching, and in the management of children the various classes of persons who enter the institution for this purpose. This was the leading object of the school, the nucleus of the present establishment, originally organized by Joseph Lancaster, near the present site, in 1798. At first it was attempted to raise a number of monitors into pupil teachers, and in 1805 the sum of $400 was raised, by donations, expressly as a capital "for training school masters" by boarding youths of the right character, at the institution. This was the germ of all subsequent normal schools for training elementary teachers in England. The attempt to erect a plain building to accomodate the young men and lads, whom Mr. Lancaster undertook to qualify for schoolmasters, led to a series of embarrassments, from which he was relieved in 1808 by the generous subscription of Joseph Fox, and others, who organized, for this purpose, (including the King and Royal Family,) an association called the "Royal Lancasterian Institution for promoting the Education of the Poor," which was afterwards changed to the "British and Foreign School Society," as more descriptive of its widening aim and influence. Regarding the instruction of the people as a national object, it has always maintained that it ought to be treated nationally, as belonging to towns rather than to churches, to districts rather than to congregations. So early as 1808 the cardinal object of the society is thus set forth in one of its rules.

> The institution shall maintain a school on an extensive scale to educate children. It shall support and train up young persons of both sexes for supplying properly. instructed teachers to the inhabitants of such places in the British dominions, at home and abroad, as shall be desirous of establishing schools on the British system. It shall instruct all persons, whether natives or foreigners, who may be sent from time to time for the purpose of being qualified as teachers in this or any other country.

Every year, from the enactment of this rule, persons were admitted to the school for a longer or a shorter period of time, to observe, learn, and practice the methods of classification and instruction pursued therein. In 1818, forty-four teachers were trained, and subsequently recommended to schools; in 1828, the number had increased to eighty-seven; in 1838, it amounted to one hundred and eighty-three, and in 1846, it was over two hundred.

The committee of the society were painfully conscious that many teachers who resorted to the school, were but poorly prepared in energy of character, tact, and christian spirit, to make good teachers; or if qualified in these respects, would stay long enough in training to acquire the requisite attainment and practical skill. "For such persons a period of *two years*, rather than *three months*, is required; and until this can be afforded, the quality of the instruction imparted in country schools, must of necessity be very unsatisfactory. In the absence of better provision, however, these considerations only enhance the importance of that which has been already affected; and afford additional reasons for sustaining and enlarging, as far as may be practicable, the facilities which are now afforded by your training department for the preparation of teachers."

In 1839, the Committee of Council on Education was formed, and in the course of the year, they proffered to both the National Society, and the British and Foreign School Society, a grant of £5000 towards the erection of two Normal Schools. This society therefore resolved to improve an opportunity which presented itself for the purchase of land adjoining to their premises in the Borough Road; and having obtained from the Corporation of the City of London an extension of the ground lease, which was cheerfully accorded on the most liberal terms, they determined to erect, thereupon, buildings capable of accommodating at least sixty resident candidates, together with libraries and lecture-rooms sufficiently extensive for the instruction of a much larger number, so that fifty or sixty more may, if it should be found desirable, lodge and board in the neighborhood, and attend as out-door pupils.

The new normal schools were completed in 1842, at an expense of £21,433 7s. 9d. defrayed by £5000 from Government, £1000 from the Corporation of London, £14,716 10s. 10d. from the friends of the institution generally, £276 15s. an offering from British School teachers who had been trained in it, and the remaining £440 1s. 11d., from the sale of old materials. The new buildings were opened on the 29th of June in the same year, when Lord John Russell presided at an examination of the model schools, and a report was read, which concluded by saying that, "To state in detail the precise course of instruction to be pursued in this new building, would as yet be premature. It may at present be sufficient to state, that it is intended that the course of instruction shall be very considerably enlarged, that additional teachers shall be engaged, that the time now devoted by candidates to preparatory training, shall be extended to the utmost practicable limit, that facilities shall be afforded for the attendance and instruction of the teachers of country schools, during a portion of their vacations, and that, as heretofore, every improvement in education which may be introduced either at home or abroad, shall receive immediate attention, be fairly subjected to the test of experiment, and if found really valuable, at once adopted."

This great establishment is divided into two entirely distinct portions, forming respectively the male and female departments; the former occupying the eastern, and the latter the western portion of the buildings, between which there is no direct means of communication whatever, except by a private door, opened once a-day, to permit the young women to take their seats in the back part of the theatre, during the daily conversational lecture of the principal of the normal school on the art of teaching and governing in a school. Each department, again, has its respective normal and model school; and each of the normal schools is divided into two classes, forming respectively the senior and junior divisions of the young persons und ertraining. The whole is under the constant general supervision of the Committees, meeting on the premises, and of the Secretary, resident in them; but the whole of their active management devolves upon the officers hereinafter named.

The following are considered as the general and primary QUALIFICATIONS REQUIRED IN ALL CANDIDATES, whether male or female:—

1. *Religious Principle.*—Whilst the Committee would disclaim anything approaching to a sectarian spirit, they consider it indispensable that persons to whom the moral and religious instruction of youth is confided should exemplify in their lives the Christian character, and be conscientiously concerned to train up their youthful charge "in the nurture and admonition of the Lord." In requiring the most explicit testimonials on this important point, the Committee feel that they are only fulfilling the wishes of their constituents; an opinion which is confirmed by the fact, that in almost all the applications they receive for teachers, it is expressly stipulated that they must be persons of decided piety, and that no others will be accepted.

2. *Activity and Energy.*—These are essential.

An indolent or inactive person can never make an efficient schoolmaster or schoolmistress. The arrangements of a school on the British system, when well conducted, considerably diminish the amount of labor required from the teacher; but it is a system which peculiarly demands liveliness and activity both of body and mind.

3. *A competent share of Talent and Information.*—The Committee have no desire to change in any respect the great principle on which they first set out—that of imparting to the laboring classes elementary instruction in reading, writing, and arithmetic; but the present state of society requires that a teacher should possess the ability to give instruction in higher branches of knowledge. Indeed, if teachers are to exercise any valuable influence over their pupils, they must themselves be intelligent; they must be able to inform and interest children generally, and to draw out and strengthen their feeble powers.

In addition to these qualifications, the Committee esteem it desirable that the candidate should possess kindness, and great firmness of mind, combined with good temper; in short, those dispositions of heart which gain so much on the affections of the young. The age of the applicant should not be less than twenty, nor more than thirty; and all candidates receive the following "general notices:"—

1. Candidates received into the Institution *on the reduced terms*, are understood to pledge themselves to act (as far as practicable) on the great leading principles adopted by the Society.

2. Candidates who do not subject the Society to any cost on their behalf, are considered at liberty to engage themselves as teachers of schools connected with other educational bodies, or attached to particular denominations of Christians.

3. All persons, on completing the term for which they are accepted, must withdraw from the Institution; and (if candidates for schools under the Society) must reside with their friends until suitable openings occur.

Normal School for Young Men.

The officers of the male department are, for the

Normal School—A Principal—Vice-Principal and Teacher of Drawing and Music.

Model School.—A Superintendent and Assistant.

Household.—A Curator and Housekeeper.

The *domestic* arrangements (subject to the oversight of a sub-Committee) are placed under the care of the housekeeper and the curator.

The duty of the housekeeper is to direct and control all matters relating to the board and lodging of the young men. She is required to provide the requisite food, to engage the domestic servants, and to secure at all times order, cleanliness, and punctuality in those portions of the establishment which fall under her supervision. All accounts of disbursements are transmitted to the accountant for examination monthly.

The duty of curator embraces all matters connected with the daily and hourly supervision of the students, and the maintenance of order, cleanliness, and harmony throughout the establishment. He is—

1. To keep a record of all persons entering or leaving the establishment, or attending any of the classes.

2. To see that all the rooms used by the students, or their teachers, are always clean, and well ventilated.

3. To preside with the housekeeper at all meals; to conduct family reading morning and evening; and to be responsible for the adherence of every student to all the regulations laid down for his guidance while in the institution.

He is further to give *a daily written report* to the secretary, whose private apartments, though distinct from the general establishment are within the building, and through whom, in case of irregularity, appeal can at once be made to the Committee.

The *dietary* provided for the students is plain, but varied, substantial, and abundant.

A medical practitioner, residing in the immediate neighborhood, is called in (free of cost to the student) on the first appearance of indisposition.

There are dormitories in the male department for only 45 students; 27 in separate rooms, and 18 in nine larger rooms, with two beds in each. The remainder of the 66 pupils in this department, on the day of my general examination, were occupying apartments in the neighborhood, in houses of respectability, in which it is proposed that hereafter they shall be hired for them by the officers of the Institution. All, however, board in the house. The principal and vice-principal of the normal school and the superintendent of the model school are respectively charged with the proper occupation of the students' time, according to the Tables hereafter given; and at all intervening periods their employments are under the general superintendence of the curator, who marks lists to check their employment of the time assigned to private study, whether individually or under mutual monitors, and has charge of the manners and conduct of the young men generally, enlisting the aid of the two senior students for the time being. The young men perform no household services, beyond cleaning their own shoes and brushing their own clothes; for the time of their stay is too short to justify the sacrifice of any portion of it to industrial occupations. Indeed, most of them have already had a complete course of industrial education in the trades and occupations from which they have respectively come.

Rules to which every Student is expected rigidly to conform.

I. Relating to Sleeping Apartments:—1. To rise every morning at 6 o'clock when the bell rings.

2. Before leaving the room to uncover the bed-clothes, and to see that all books, articles of dress, &c., are placed in the drawers. For every article found in the room a fine will be enforced.

3. On no occasion whatever, without special permission, to have a candle, match, or other light in the room. (As the violation of this rule will endanger the safety of the building, any offender will be specially reported to the Committee, and probably directed to leave the institution.)

4. Every student is to confine himself to his own bed-room, and to have no communication with any other, conversation not being allowed after retiring for the night.

5. All washing and cleaning the person to be performed in the respective rooms; the troughs on the landing never to be used for that purpose.

6. The bed-rooms to be finally vacated for the day at five minutes to nine, and under no pretence whatever is any student to visit them again until bed-time. At no period will he be allowed to go up stairs in shoes worn during the day.

II. Relating to the Classes:—1. To be present in the school of design at half-past 6 o'clock in the morning to answer to the roll, and then to proceed to the classes.

2. To be present at the additional roll-calls at the undermentioned times, viz., five minutes to nine, five minutes to two, and half-past nine in the evening.

3. To attend all the classes during the day at the precise time. From twelve to one to be invariably devoted to exercise in the open air. If no letters or parcels have to be delivered, the time to be occupied in walking out.

4. From half-past eight to half-past nine in the evening to be devoted to the preparations of the studies. The students who have finished will be required to maintain order and silence, that no interruption may be occasioned to those who are studying.

III. Relating to Meals:—1. To be ready for breakfast punctually at a quarter past eight; dinner at a quarter past one; tea at a quarter past five; and supper at half-past eight; at which hours the bell will ring.

2. On entering the dining-room for any meal, every student to remain standing in his place until the housekeeper and curator have entered and taken their seats; and on the housekeeper rising to leave the room (which sign indicates the conclusion of the meal), every student will be expected to rise, and the one nearest to the door to open it.

3. During meals no reading will be allowed; silence must be observed, and the strictest propriety of behavior maintained, rudeness, selfish eagerness to be assisted before others, or indecorum of any kind, will be noticed, and expose the parties to merited rebuke.

IV. Relating to other Periods of Time:—1. No singing, loud talking, or unnecessary noise in the passages, or in any part of the building, will be tolerated. No throwing of ink, or other careless or filthy habit, will on any account be suffered. Parties offending will be specially reported to the Committee.

2. No book, paper, article of dress or of other use, will be allowed, under any pretext, to lie about any of the rooms or passages; a place being appointed for everything, everything must be in its place. For every offence a fine will be enforced, and the article detained until it is paid.

3. No student is to be absent from the premises without the permission of the curator, or (if in

class hours) of the teacher of the class from which he wishes to be absent; and he is **never to be** out later than half-past nine.

4. On Sunday he will be expected to attend twice at his accustomed place of worship, and to spend the remainder of the day in quietness and propriety.

5. Never to enter the depository except on business.

In order to carry the above regulations into effect the curator is strictly charged by the Committee to impound all articles left about, and on no account to return them to the owners without payment of the fine; and, further, never to allow any violation of these rules to pass without severe rebuke.

As, however, many offences may be committed where the guilty party cannot be discovered, the two senior students (for the time being) will be held responsible for all such misdemeanors. If injury be done to any part of the rooms, or unnecessary dirt brought in, it will be their duty to find out and report on the offender; in which case he will be required to remove or repair it.

All fines to be spent in books for the library.

The following is the official outline of the Normal School of Young Men :—

I. Persons eligible.—Subject to the general qualifications already enumerated, *five* classes of persons are eligible for admission.

Class A.—Young men desirous of becoming teachers, who wish to be introduced to a school by the Committee, and are prepared to remain in the institution twelve months.

Class B.—Young men desirous of becoming teachers, who wish to be introduced to a school by the Committee, but are unable to remain longer than six months.

Class C.—Youths and other persons who desire to adopt the profession of a teacher, but wish subsequently to be at their own disposal. These are considered as private teachers, and are required to pay the fees attached to each class.

Class D.—Teachers elected to schools, or already conducting them, but desirous of attending, for some limited period, any of the classes, with a view to farther improvement.

Class E.—Missionaries or other persons proceeding abroad, with a view to the promotion of education in foreign parts.

II. Times of Admission.—Class A.—January and July.

Class B.—January, April, July, and October.

Classes C, D, and E.—Monthly, by special correspondence with the Secretary.

Classes A and B are expected to board in the establishment. Reduced charge, 6s. a week; the whole sum to be paid in advance.

Class C cannot be admitted to board or lodge. They must also pay in advance the fee required on entering each class.

Classes D and E may be admitted to board by special arrangement.

III. Mode of Application.—The first step to be taken by the candidate is to *write a letter to the Secretary*, stating briefly his *age*, *state of health*, and *present employment;* also *whether he is married or single*, and, if married, *what family* he has.

Secondly, he should mention, generally, the amount of his attainments, and state the length of time he could devote to the work of preparation.

Thirdly, whether he has had any practice in communicating instruction to children, either in day or Sunday schools; whether he has ever been engaged in benevolent efforts for the improvement of the poor; and whether he has been in the habit of attending any means of general or religious instruction beyond the ordinances of public worship.

This letter, which should be as brief as circumstances will admit, should be accompanied by *explicit testimonials* from the clergyman or minister of the church or congregation with which the candidate may be connected, and from one or more persons to whom he may be known, as to his possession of the qualifications already mentioned as indispensable.

On receipt of these communications, the Secretary will bring the application before the Committee at their first meeting, and afterwards communicate further with the candidate.

The sub-Committee appointed to investigate the testimonials of candidates meets at the house of the Institution, in the Borough Road, on the first Monday in every month, at 10 o'clock in the forenoon

If the candidate reside in or near London, he should attend the Committee at this time, *but not unless he has had on some previous day a personal interview with the Secretary.*

Supposing the Committee to be satisfied with the letter and testimonials, the candidate will be informed when he is to present himself for preliminary examination, on the following points :—

1. *As to his Health.*—It will be required that persons admitted into the Institution shall be in good health, and free from any serious physical defect; and that they shall either have had the small-pox or have been vaccinated.

2. *As to the Amount of his Knowledge.*—He must read fluently and without unpleasant tones; he must write a fair hand, spell correctly, be well acquainted with the first four rules of arithmetic, and have some general acquaintance with geography and history.

If the result of this examination be on the whole satisfactory, the candidate (having paid the amount required) receives a certificate, on delivery of which to the Curator he is presented with a copy of the rules of the establishment, and either received into the house or introduced to the classes he wishes to attend. If the result be unsatisfactory, a written report to that effect is made to the Secretary, who will then communicate with the Committee, and with the candidate or his friends.

By these preliminary inquiries and investigations, it is hoped that in the majority of cases subsequent disappointment may be prevented; but as it is impossible to decide, *prior to actual experiment*, whether any person has or has not that peculiar tact in the management and *control* of children, and those powers of arrangement, as applied to numbers, without which no teacher can successfully carry out the combinations of a British school,—every candidate is required to hold himself ready to withdraw from the Institution should he be found thoroughly deficient in the art of managing, interesting, and controlling children.

The Committee do not in any case *pledge themselves* to furnish candidates with situations; but as hitherto they have been in the habit of receiving applications for teachers from the numerous friends of education in different parts of the country, they have reason to hope that it will generally be in their power to recommend the candidates they may train to parties thus applying.

IV.—Vacations.—Midsummer.—Four weeks from the Friday preceding Midsummer day.

Christmas.—One week from the Friday preceding Christmas-day.

Easter.—From the Thursday preceding Good Friday to the Wednesday in the ensuing week.

At the Midsummer vacation every student is required to leave the Institution, and to provide himself with board and lodging during that period.

V.—Table of Classes.—Class I.—*Grammar and English Composition*:—Students of Six Months.—A course of English Grammar, including the chief roots (especially the Anglo-Saxon,) and derivatives of the language. *Composition.*—Forms of letters, notes, &c. Abstracts of remarks and lectures will be looked over, with a view to the correction of errors in orthography or composition.

Students of Twelve Months.—An extended course in the construction of the English language. So much of comparative grammar as may be understood by those assumed to know only one language. *Composition.*—A systematic course. Essays on some branches of teaching.

Class II.—*Elocution: Readings in Prose and Poetry*:—In this class the pieces read are selected from the Third Lesson Book, and are accompanied by systematic interrogation from the notes. The pupils are also required to interrogate one another.

Class III.—*Arithmetic and Mathematics*:—This class includes—

1. *Arithmetic.*—Principles from De Morgan.
2. *Geometry.*—Books ii. iii. iv. v. vi. of Euclid's Elements.
3. Elements of algebra and trigonometry.

Class IV.—*Model Lessons in Natural Philosophy, Natural History, Botany, and Chemistry*:—The object of these lessons (which, with the aid of suitable books of reference, are *prepared* by the pupils before breakfast) is twofold; *first*, to render them sufficiently acquainted with the various subjects treated in the Fourth Lesson Book, to enable them to teach that book intelligently; and, *secondly*, to exhibit to the tutor the extent of their knowledge, and the degree of ability possessed for imparting the same to children. The instruction given in natural philosophy is of a popular kind, suited to the acquirements of students, some of whom may be acquainted only with the elementary parts of pure mathematics.

Class V.—*Art of Teaching.*—This class, at which all the teachers in training (both male and female) are required to attend, is held in the lecture-room of the institution.

The time is occupied in criticism on the gallery lesson of the day, in a conversational lecture on some topic connected with the principles or practice of teaching, and in the examination of written notes.

The course consists of 60 lectures, and is completed in 12 weeks.

Class VI.—*Practical Simultaneous Lessons.*—This class (at which all attend) is conducted in the gallery class-rooms, where the teachers in turn are required to give collective lessons; after which, the criticisms of the teachers who have been spectators are required to be given in the lecture-room. The tutor then comments on various defects and merits in the lessons.

Class VII.—*Bible Lesson*—This class is conducted in the model school, each teacher being required to instruct and question a draft of 10 or 12 children, on a given subject, under the inspection of the tutor and the superintendent of the school.

Class VIII.—*School of Design.*—This class is separated into two divisions, upper and lower. In the upper, drawing is taught, in the following order:—

1. Maps and charts.
2. Machinery
3. Architecture
4. Figures and landscapes

(2–4) with and without models.

In the lower division, writing is taught, and then simple geometrical figures, and outlines of maps.

Class IX.—*Geography and History.—Geography.*—Geography of the chief countries of the globe, including their main natural features, towns, manufactures, government, population, and social condition. Connexion between the political and physical geography of countries. Leading features of mathematical geography.

History.—General history, ancient and modern.

Class X.—*Arithmetic (Lower Class).*

Arithmetic.—Written and mental.

Geometry.—A course of practical geometry. The first book of Euclid's Elements.

Mensuration.—An elementary course.

Class XI.—*Elements of Physics.*—This class is simply intended to furnish the required information for the ordinary teaching of the Fourth Lesson Book.

Class XII.—*Vocal Music.*—This class is maintained by a separate voluntary subscription, and attendance is optional on the part of the students. The methods and books both of Mr. Hickson and Hullah are adopted.

*** The books required for each class, which are few and inexpensive, must be purchased by the student.

VI.—*Examinations.—Weekly Examinations.*—Every candidate will undergo a strict examination as to the amount of work performed during each week: he is required to record in a journal his labors and progress; and it is then ascertained, by a series of questions, whether that which he supposes himself to have acquired be thoroughly understood and digested. He is also examined as to the mode in which he would communicate to others the knowledge he has gained.

Half-Yearly Examinations:—

Examiners.—Professor————————————Coll.
Professor———————————Coll.

Certificates of proficiency will be granted at the discretion of the examiners.

Any schoolmaster who has been instructed by the Society, or who may be engaged in conducting any school in connexion with it, may (by previous notice to the Secretary) offer himself for examination, in order to obtain a certificate of proficiency.

The lower class examination will embrace—

Reading; writing; arithmetic (written and mental;) grammar; geography; English history; knowledge of the Scriptures; elements of geometry, drawing, and music; and the art of teaching.

The higher class (in addition) practical geometry; mensuration; the elements of algebra and trigonometry; natural philosophy; an extended course of mathematical and physical geography; construction of maps; and drawing, as applied to mechanics and architecture.

As the object of the Society is to prepare teachers, and not merely to improve students, the books used as text-books are, as far as practicable, those used in the schools, and the examinations will be conducted with special reference to the ultimate object in view, viz. effective teaching.

The male department is, in effect, subdivided into distinct sections, placed respectively under the principal of the normal school, making the preliminary examinations, conducting the studies of the senior class, and giving three-fifths of the lectures to the whole in "pedagogy," or the art of teaching and governing in a school; under the vice-principal of the normal school, conducting the studies of the junior class as well as those of the morning classes of the female students, and likewise conveying the other two-fifths of the instruction in "pedagogy;" and under the superintendent of the model school, who has the entire disposal of that section, and the arrangement of the students' exercises in it. The junior class consists, in the main, of those whose stay in the institution has not exceeded three months; the senior class, of those whose stay has exceeded that term.

Amongst those admitted as students, very great variety obtains in respect to attainments and capacity. Hence classification, at first, is almost impracticable. This, added to the difficulty occasioned by the entrance of new students at every period of the quarter, creates no little embarrassment in the management of the junior class, especially when the numbers are so large. Almost every one, on his entrance, is totally ignorant of some one or more of the branches of study pursued; hence it becomes necessary to adopt, to a great extent, the tedious and distracting plan of individual instruction. Very few of them can read *well*, that is, with intelligence and correctness of pronunication, while the monotonous tones of some, and the almost inveterate provincialisms of others, require much time and attention to correct. Besides, unhappily, many of those whose *general acquirements* are of a fair average character, have comparatively neglected orthography and reading, and consequently very much of their time during their stay in the class is necessarily devoted to these elementary studies. Some again, have made apparently fair progress in arithmetic, grammar, &c., previous to admission; but though able to perform the operations in one science, and give definitions or parse sentences in the other, it is found, on examination, that their knowledge is merely by rote, and that the principles in both cases are not at all understood: they know that the thing is so and so, but they cannot tell why. Again, some who are, to some extent acquainted with principles, are quite unable to communicate their information to others, especially to children, and their efforts rather resemble awkward attempts at lecturing than intelligent teaching. All the time that can be spared from learning and practising the art of teaching has to be employed by this junior class in a vigorous effort to repair the deficiencies of their own elementary education. For this purpose they form a very interesting school of primary instruction under the Vice-Principal.

The following is the course of study of the junior class during the quarter ended 31st March, 1847, as described by its tutor, Mr. Saunders:—

Grammar.—The parts of Speech, and the Exercises upon them in Allen and Cornwell's Grammar, using also the Latin Roots there given; and the first part of Cornwell's Young Composer.

Geography.—General principles, Mathematical and Physical—Varieties of the Human Race —General features and divisions of Europe—Physical Geography of England—Text-book: Cornwell's Geography.

Natural History.—The great divisions of the Animal Kingdom—Radiata in detail—Text-book: Mrs. Lee's Introduction to Natural History, and Cuvier.

Writing.—Improvement of the style in four hands.

Arithmetic.—Principles and practice from Notation to Compound Proportion inclusive—and Square and Cube Roots.—Text-books: Crossley's Calculator and Thompson's Arithmetic.

Arithmetic (Mental)—All the Rules in Crossley's Intellectual Calculator.

Linear Drawing.—Geometrical Figures in Dyce's Designs, and in Francœur's Linear Drawing.

History.—Roman and Saxon England in Outline—Norman period with the Feudal System and the Crusades in detail—Text-books: Pinnock's Goldsmith, revised by Dr. Taylor, and Macintosh's History of England.

Natural Philosophy.—General Divisions—Properties of Matter and Laws of Motion—Text-books: Peschell's Physics and Moseley's Illustrations.

Mensuration and Geometry.—Plane Figures—Text-books: Pasley's Practical Geometry, and Elliot's Geometry and Mensuration.

Elocution.—A series of 24 lessons in prose and poetry—Text-books: the Society's Lesson Books, and Allen's English Poetry.

Scripture—Geography and History of Canaan from the call of Abraham to the present time—Text-book: Horne's Introduction to the Study of the Scriptures.

Various other works are used as sources of illustration, and the students are referred to them for further information, in their future hours of leisure.

The junior class is assembled on five evenings in the week, for two hours and a half, from 6 to half-past 8 o'clock, and on the morning of Saturday for four hours, from 9 to 1 P.M. The evening of *Monday* is occupied by devoting one hour to English Grammar, one hour to Geography, and half an hour to the elements of Physics. The lessons having been previously prepared during the period allotted to study in the morning, one of the students is selected by the tutor to examine the class in the lesson on grammar appointed for the evening. His questions are addressed to the members of the class individually, and on the failure of any one to reply to the question proposed, it is put to another, and another. This is required to be done with as much rapidity and precision as possible, and should every one in the class fail to reply satisfactorily, the interrogator must then explain the subject to them, and examine them again. "The exercises on the different rules of grammar, as corrected by themselves, are read from their exercise books, every exercise being written before a lesson is considered as past, and a record of it is then made in their journals. During the whole of this time the tutor is with them, occasionally asking questions on the lesson under consideration, pointing out to the class the errors of the questioner and their own. At the close of each lesson the students are required to mention anything which to them may seem objectionable in the manner in which the questions are put, or in errors of pronunciation, or any other which they may have observed; and yet further to show how they would have proceeded under the same circumstances. This plan of friendly but searching criticism is carried on with every lesson superintended by one of the students. The geographical lesson is given by one of the students, previously appointed, much in the same manner as the simultaneous or gallery lessons are given in the model school—that is, he furnishes them with information on the particular country or countries beyond what they may already possess; having ascertained the latter by questions at the commencement of the lesson. About half an hour is occupied in this manner, and then another half hour by another of the students in interrogation on the same subject; thus it is speedily ascertained if the information has been received by them, and also whether their notions are clear and distinct. In physics the same course is pursued, and, when requisite and practicable, experiments are introduced, drawings and diagrams used, and objects exhibited."

The evening of *Tuesday* is occupied for the first hour in writing in copy-books, each copy being submitted to the tutor; the errors are pointed out, and a line written by him with special reference to those errors; the student is thus furnished with a copy precisely adapted to his wants. The next hour is devoted to drawing. In this, as in writing, the measure of success depends mainly on individual practice, and therefore the teaching is individual rather than simultaneous. Very few have practiced even drawing from copies before they came to the institution. Those who have, possess the facility of hand and eye which the preliminary exercises in this class are chiefly designed to convey. But the greater number require very careful introduction to the first notions and habits of representing forms on a plane surface, or even of drawing straight lines, and measuring them into relative lengths, without which they are quite unprepared to use the models which are introduced in the senior drawing classes. They make these first sketches in charcoal, so as to admit of correction, chiefly from simple geometrical figures in the published books of the Government School of Design, or from enlarged copies of those contained in Francœur's "Linear Drawing," prepared for the schools of France, organized on the Lancasterian system. This hour is the only one in the week devoted to drawing by those who are under the instruction of Mr. Saunders; but it suffices to give a habit of using the eye and the crayon. Mental Arithmetic occupies the next half hour; and as mental calculations depend so much on the ability to combine numbers rapidly and to detect their relations, much of the time devoted to them is occupied by tables and analyses of numbers, forming a firm basis on which to build up rapid and correct calculations.

On *Wednesday* evening the first hour and the last half hour are occupied in the same manner as on Monday, but the hour from 7 to 8 is devoted to the History of England; the lesson being treated precisely in the same manner as the geography.

On *Thursday* evening the first hour is devoted to Elocution. The members of the class standing in a circle in the School of Design, the tutor reads about a page in the style and spirit which he wishes should characterize their reading. The students then read in turn: at the close of the reading of each, observations on the excellences or defects of the reader are elicited from his companions; the teacher makes his own remarks on these observations and on the reading itself; and the pupil who sits next in rotation resumes the text. The next hour is devoted to Practical Geometry, for their exercises in which the students occupy seats at the desks in the School of Design, and each is furnished with a slate, compasses, triangle, and ruler. The problem to be executed is then distinctly enunciated by the tutor; the first step in its performance is explained and exhibited on a large black board, each copying it on his slate by means of instruments; the second step is then explained and illustrated in like manner. When completed, the question occurs, 'What have you done?' And if the answer does not agree with the conditions of the problem, the discrepancy is pointed out and corrected. If the performance is correct and the reply satisfactory, the figure described is obliterated from the board and the slates, and the problem has to be executed again without any direction whatever. If this can be done, the next is proceeded with, and so on. As most of the students on entering are altogether ignorant of geometry, no very great amount of progress can be made: but a good foundation may be laid for future improvement. The text-book used is one well adapted to the age of the students, combined with their want of early practice. It is Pasley's "Complete Course of Practical Geometry and Plan Drawing." It is employed to illustrate their practice in drawing from copies of geometrical figures, and simple problems in mensuration are pertinently introduced. The remaining half hour of Thursday evening is devoted to written arithmetic, or, in the conventional phrase of the schools, to "slate arithmetic." It is applied to the development of principles, or the application of them to practice, as may be required. In either case the students themselves are called upon to explain to their fellows the lesson received from the tutor, and to exhibit illustrations of it on the black board.

The first hour of *Friday*, as of Tuesday, evening, is devoted to Writing. The second hour to Elocution or Reading, in like manner as the first hour of the preceding evening: and the concluding half hour is employed in a lesson in Physics, as on Monday and Wednesday.

On *Saturday* morning the first hour is devoted to Modern History and Geography; the second to examinations in Arithmetic, especially in principles; the third to examinations in Grammar and Etymology, particularly Greek and Latin roots; and the fourth to Scripture Geography and History; all of them conducted in the same manner as the lessons already described.

"It should be observed that one of the lessons for each evening is given by the tutor as a model for imitation by the students, all the subjects being taken by him in turn, and attention particularly directed to the points of failure on the part of the students, and the errors into which they are most likely to fall. It might perhaps be supposed that, from remarks being freely made on each other's performances, some exhibitions of ill-feeling might be produced, but I believe myself fully justified in saying that no one instance of the kind has occurred. One advantage gained by these friendly criticisms is, that in very many instances the fault which passes unnoticed when committed by the student himself is apparent to him in another; and hence his correction is applied to his companion and himself at the same time.

"The number of exercises which they are required to write gives them much practice in orthography; but besides this, an hour of one morning in each week is devoted exclusively to writing from dictation; the exercises being examined afterwards by two students appointed to that office by the tutor, who also afterwards examines them again himself. In addition to this, each one in the class is required to write a letter once a week to the tutor, the writer being allowed to select his own subject: this exercise is of great service, as displaying the mental peculiarities of the writer, and affording a medium of private and confidential communication. In the examination of these letters attention is devoted to the most minute points, such as the mode of address, manner of folding, &c.

The members of this junior class also attend, with those of the senior class, the course of 60 lectures on teaching, &c., delivered by the Principal and Vice-Principal of the normal school; making rough notes while the lecture is being given, and writing out afterwards a fair abstract of it in a book furnished to them for that purpose; these abstracts also are examined and corrected by the tutor. During four hours and a half (from 9 till 12, and from 2 till half-past 3) of every day, the students are engaged in teaching classes of boys in the model school "under the close observation of the tutors, one of whom is always present, for the purpose of noticing and pointing out to them their defects, and the mode of supplying them; thus the lessons learned in the normal school are carried into practice in the model school, and the application of theory to practice conducted under strict supervision." Such is the course contemplated; but there appeared to me to be great room for improvement in the practical employment of this valuable portion of time; improvement connected with an economy of opportunities in other departments of the training in this institution, in describing which it will be convenient again to revert to the labors of the model school.

During the past year an additional Bible class to the one mentioned in the Time Table has been established at the request of the students, the time of meeting being from 9 to 10 on the Sunday morning, and though their being present is perfectly voluntary, almost every one of them has been regular and constant in attendance; and the anxiety of many who have left the institution to have copies of the notes of the subjects taken up in the class, since their removal, affords an evidence of the value they set on the instruction communicated.

At the close of the first three months of their stay, the members of this class are put through another general examination by the Vice-Principal, in the presence of the Committee; and from among them the numbers in the upper class are then filled up, so as to leave behind only the few who are yet unprepared to proceed with the rest to any profitable result.

Upper Class in Normal School.

"The upper class," states the Principal of the normal school, "consists of students of not less than three months' standing. Their attention has been directed to the following subjects:—the English Language, Mathematics, Natural Philosophy, and Natural History. These studies have been pursued with me from 6 till half-past 8 during three evenings in the week.* The course, as to method, has been uniform, the instruction having been given in the form of conversational lectures, based, as far as possible, upon the lesson-books of the Society as text-books. As much information has been thus afforded as the students have been supposed to be able to master by study in the early morning of the following day, either privately or in class; and the consciousness that the next time the subject should be taken up it would be commenced by a searching interrogation as to what is known of the last given lesson, has acted as a sufficient stimulus to persevering industry.

"*The English Language.*—This has been treated under three distinct heads. First, that which is ordinarily called *Grammar*, viz., the distinctions in the nature of words, the inflectional changes they undergo, their relations to each other, and the influence they exert in consequence of those relations. In short, syntax and etymology, exclusive of derivation. The aim has been never to give any term, definition, or rule, except as the representative of an idea,—to supply the notion before the words that express it. The *general* principles of language have been given, too, as far as they could be understood by those not having the power of comparison from the want of acquaintance with two languages. Thus the universal fact has been taught, that languages have a tendency to get rid of their inflectional forms, and to express their relations by particles and position; and hence has the reason been shown why the rules of position are so much more important in a language in its recent than in its earlier condition. English and Anglo-Saxon have, perhaps, been instanced.

"The second direct study of English has been the *Formation and Derivation of Words.* These have been taught from lists of Anglo-Saxon, Latin, and Greek primitives found in the grammar. Etymologies have been explained, too, incidentally in connexion with the reading, and the various scientific terms from time to time occurring. In this study extreme accuracy has been insisted on, as it has been felt that persons not unfre-

* Two whole evenings in each week are devoted to Drawing and Music, under the teacher of those branches.

quently render themselves ridiculous, by dabbling in a foreign language with which they have not a correct acquaintance as far as it goes.

"*Composition* is the third means that has been employed for teaching the English language. It has been felt to be important that a teacher should be able to express his thoughts in suitable language and in a proper order. In the exercises, importance has been attached to neatness of writing and unaffectedness of style. Considerable advantages have attended this employment. It has been so pursued as to form a new study of English, showing the structure of the language and not of the words, logical and not grammatical relations. Truer, because more extensive views of the nature of their mother-tongue have thus been obtained, than could have been secured had the same time been devoted to the mere study of grammar. I regret to say that in a few instances, too (especially in the teachers selected by local committees), it has not been without its advantages even in regard to orthography.

"We have not yet found time for a systematic course on *English Literature*. It has not, however, been entirely neglected, but has been taken up incidentally in connexion with the composition. For as the exercises found in the text-book are for the most part selections from our best classic authors, fitting opportunities have been afforded, as each came under observation, for giving a slight biographical notice, the characteristics of his style, his principal works, and the recommendation of those deemed most valuable.

"*Geography.*—A good deal of attention has been given to geography. It is attempted to make this an *inductive study;* certain conditions are given, from which certain consequences are to be inferred. Thus the students are expected to discover that the currents of the rivers of Eastern Europe are slow, and of Western Europe rapid; after having been told that the former have their rise at a slight elevation and have a lengthened course, and the latter originate in the high land of Central Europe, at no great distance from the sea. Political and social geography are thus shown to be in a great degree dependent on physical geography; the reason is seen why one nation is agricultural and another commercial; why a certain manufacture should be carried on in a particular locality in preference to every other; and why an alteration in the mode of manufacture should involve a change in its seat. Thus that Holland is agricultural and England manufacturing; that our cotton manufacture is carried on in South Lancashire and the edges of the neighboring counties, and not in Lincolnshire; that our manufactures generally are travelling north and west; and that iron, which was once largely manufactured in Kent and Sussex, is now only smelted on the great coalfields, are not merely so many facts, but highly interesting facts; interesting, because regarded as effects, the causes of which are perceived, and have probably been discovered, by the student himself.

"The *Etymology* of geogrophical names forms an important feature in this branch of knowledge. The name of a place often tells its condition or history; and the explanation of the same by calling into exercise the power of association, increases the probability of its being remembered. Thus the name *Buenos Ayres,* still shows the *salubrity* of the *air* of that town; *Sierra,* the Spanish name for a range of hills, the *saw-like* appearance which it presents; New *York* tells us that it was once a colony of England, and those who know that it was first called New *Amsterdam,* know, too, that it was founded by the *Dutch; Virginia,* shows that it was colonized in the reign of our *virgin* queen, Elizabeth; *Carolina,* during that of Charles (*Carolus*). The term *fell,* applied to mountains in the north of England, the south of Scotland, and in the islands of the north and west, shows that these parts of the country were occupied by some tribe or tribes of Scandinavian origin; while *ben* or *pen* found in the most mountainous regions, confirms the facts of history, that these high grounds were unconquered by the northern invaders, and continued in the possession of the original Celtic inhabitants. In thus finding out the cause of the fact, and the cause of the name, the reason has been exercised and the study rendered highly philosophical; and a science which has often been thought to consist only of lists of hard unmeaning words, has been made attractive in a more than usual degree.

"*History.*—This study has been almost exclusively confined to the few great prominent events which have distinguished the history of any country. These have been a good deal amplified—traced to their causes, and pursued to their consequences. Shortness of time necessitates such a method. But irrespective of this, it is considered the best for a first course; for, as these salient events are only the visible development of principles, an acquaintance with these affords a key, as it were, to most of the subordinate intermediate occurrences. The events of English history receive by far the most attention, as do also those nearer our own times, compared with the more remote. In considering the events of other countries, constant reference is made to what was going on at the same time in England. It is thus frequently seen, that the same principle is developing itself at different places at the same time: *e. g.* the struggle between ecclesiastical and kingly power in France and Germany, at the time of our Henry II. and his Archbishop Becket.

"*Mathematics.*—A full and systematic explanation of the *principles of Arithmetic* has formed a part of this study, and has been productive of great advantage to the teachers. Some who have entered the institution as good mathematicians, have been found to be unable to give a reason for the mode of performing the elementary parts of arithmetic. An acquaintance with rules by no means includes a knowledge of principles; but he who understands principles can make rules for himself. A strong interest has been excited, as the principles involved in the most ordinary operations have been evolved, and the effect of this has shown itself remarkably in the different manner of teaching a class of boys in the model school before and after such explanation; dulness on the part of the teacher has been succeeded by spirit, and lassitude on that of the boys by the most lively attention.

"*Demonstrative Geometry* has been pursued, but for the most part by each student independently, such being, in my opinion, the only way in which the advantages attendant on its pursuit are to be realized in the highest degree. The acquirements have, consequently, been very various, from only a few propositions to several books, according to ability and previous attainments. In all cases, however, though not equally, the great object has been secured—*mental drilling.*

"Only the elements of *Algebra* and *Trigonometry* have been taught, and these not systematically. The first has been introduced in connexion with the explanation of the principles of arithmetic, the algebraic formulæ being given as the representatives of *general* truths. Trigonometry has been required for the explanation of certain facts of natural philosophy, especially those of astronomy, and has been then introduced.

"*Natural Philosophy.*—It has been attempted to teach this branch of knowledge so as to combine the popular with the scientific. It has been made *popular* by drawing the illustrations from those phenomena which are every day before our eyes; and, fortunately, the great truths of physics are almost always capable of such illustration. But the *merely* popular has been avoided, by directing attention, not only to results, but to the methods by which such results have been obtained. There are some truths, of course, only to be demonstrated by the higher mathematics. These are quite beyond our reach, and are either entirely omitted or explained by the nearest analogical approximation. But in numerons instances, perhaps most, the principle of a method admits of illustration by means of very elementary mathematical knowledge. Thus the students learn, not only that the sun and planets are at such a distance, but the manner in which such results are obtained is given, and shown to involve only the same principles as are employed in the simplest land surveying.

"*Natural History.*—Up to the present time only zoology has been considered. Subsequent to the lectures on this subject, visits have been made, with great advantage, to the Regent's Park Zoological Gardens and the rooms of the British Museum containing the specimens of natural history.

"In the case of the few students who remain with us more than six months, the afternoons of Monday, Wednesday, and Friday, from 2 to half-past 3, are devoted to the further study of mathematics, original composition, and Latin. As regards the latter subject, the progress made is small indeed. It amounts to little more than removing some of the initiatory difficulties attendant on the study of a new language, and showing the student how he may hereafter pursue it with the best prospect of success. Yet slight as is the amount of knowledge obtained, it has not been without its value as affording a glimpse into the nature of language in general, which is not to be obtained by the individual who has no acquaintance with any but his own."

Drawing and Music.—Two whole evenings in every week, those of Monday and Wednesday, are devoted by the senior class to drawing; and three-quarters of an hour is given at the close of every day to singing The course adopted in the scheme of drawing lessons is, in the first instance, to convey to the students, in a series of familiar explanations, such principles of perspective as may be sufficient to enable them to delineate correctly simple lines in various positions. This is done on the black board with chalk; and when the class has evinced a degree of proficiency in such exercises, our next step is to introduce solid forms, involving a further acquaintance with principles which are then progressively laid down. As soon as practicable, the mere outlines on board are superseded by the use of paper, which is continued to the end of the course. The models in use in the classes are the series published under the sanction of the Committee of Council on Education; and we have also, as time and the skill of the student would permit, introduced many simple objects for exercise, such as articles of furniture.

The time devoted to vocal music is necessarily limited; and the lessons are given at the close of the day, to prevent interference with any of the more important studies. The elementary lessons are based on Wilhem's system, as improved by Mr. Hullah; but one lesson in each week is devoted to the practice of simple school-pieces, published in "The Singing Master" of Mr. W. E. Hickson, which is found to be of considerable use in creating an air of cheerfulness, and relieving the more serious exercises.

Art of Teaching and Governing in a School.

The *theory* of teaching and governing, is given in a series of lectures on pedagogy, which are delivered every day in the theatre of the institution, the course running through three months. Of these lectures the students are required to make abstracts. Among these, is a series on mental philosophy; it being deemed of importance, that those who have to influence mind, through the agency of mind, should know something of its operations. Through these lectures the *science of education* is generally understood.

But education is an *art* as well as a science, and as in every other art, perfection is to be obtained only by practice. This practice is se ured by the attendance of *all the students in the model school* for four hours and a half during each day. They pass, step by step, through all the parts of the school, commencing with the lowest draft of boys, and ending with the charge of the whole. During this time, they are always under observation; and when any one manifests a want of skill in teaching or government, he is requested to leave the draft, his error is privately pointed out to him, and such directions are given as are considered proper to obviate it. Should the error be of a kind likely to characterize more than the individual, it is noted down and made the subject of observation to all the students when together in the theatre.

The second method of improving the practice is, to assemble all the students in one of the gallery class-rooms, and then to require one of them, who has been previously appointed and furnished with a subject, to give a collective lesson to about a hundred boys. Every one is then engaged in noting down what he considers the defects or merits of the lesson, embracing points of grammar, manner, knowledge, government, &c. At the conclusion of the lesson, all the teachers adjourn to the theatre of the institution, and in turns give their opinions of the lesson. When all have finished, observations are made by myself, first on the criticisms of the observers and then on the general points of excellence or defect which have characterized the lesson.

The third mode of improving the practice is by means of lessons given by the students in turn to all the rest. The chief difference between this method and the last is, that errors are checked as they arise. There is no noting down deficiencies; but as soon as one is observed, the teacher is stopped, the defect pointed out, and he is at once required to rectify it. Before boys, this method would be obviously improper, as the moral influence of the teachers would be destroyed by it. But, among themselves, it is found to work very amicably. Indeed, it has been gratifying to me to witness the good temper with which the criticisms have been all but universally given and received. On the entrance of some students, the observations have been rather intended to show the acuteness of the speaker than to benefit the teacher who has given the lesson. But this has soon righted itself, and almost always without the necessity of intervention on my part.

The following is a list of the Conversational Readings to the whole of the students on the art of teaching and governing in a school, which form the quarter's course; five being delivered on five several days in each of twelve weeks, three by the Principal, and two by the Vice-principal. The first 36 form the course given by the Principal, and the remaining 24, that by the Vice-principal. At the commencement of each quarter these courses are begun again.

1. On the objects which a teacher should have in view in adopting his profession.
2. On the circumstances which make a teacher happy in a school.
3. On some of the essential moral qualifications of a teacher
4. On the essential intellectual qualifications of a teacher.
5. On the establishment of authority.
6. On gaining ascendency over the minds of children.
7. On combination and arrangement.
8. On routines of instruction and formation of plans.
9. On the monitorial system—its use and abuse.
10. On the selection of monitors.
11. On the training of monitors.
12. On the collective or simultaneous system.
13. On the art of teaching the elements of reading to very young children.
14. Illustrations of the mode of using the First Lesson Book.
15. On various methods of teaching spelling.
16. On the mode of using the Second Lesson Book.
17. On object-lessons for young children.

18. On the interrogative system, with illustrations.
19. On analytical teaching generally, with illustrations from the Third Lesson Book.
20. On synthetical teaching; illustrations from the Third Lesson Book.
21. On the art of reading with animation and expression.
22. On Scripture questioning, generally; on Scripture geography, and methods of teaching it.
23. On teaching writing.
24. On the use and nature of numbers.
25. On teaching arithmetic.
26. On the mode of using the Fourth Lesson Book.
27. On teaching geography.
28. On teaching grammar.
29. On teaching drawing.
30. On teaching vocal music.
31. On the philosophy of the human mind as applicable to education.
32. On attention and memory.
33. On association.
34. On conception.
35. On imagination.
36. On the principal writers on education.
37. On rewards and punishments.
38. On emulation.
39. On common errors relating to punishments, and on corporeal punishments.
40. On moral and religious influence generally.
41. On the promotion of a love of truth, honesty, benevolence, and other virtues, among children.
42. On cleanliness and neatness, kindness to animals, and gentleness.
43. On promoting obedience to parents, respectful demeanor to elders, and general submission to authority.
44. On the private studies of a teacher.
45. On the course to be pursued in organizing a new school.
46. On keeping the various registers of attendance and progress.
47. On the ventilation of school-rooms and dwellings.
48. On school furniture generally.
49. On some of the circumstances which affect the condition of the laboring classes.
50. On the elements of political economy.
51. On machinery and its results.
52. On cottage economy and savings' banks.
53. On the duties of the teacher to the parents of the children, and to the Committee.
54. On the formation of museums and collections of apparatus, and the management of school libraries.
55. On keeping up a connexion with old scholars.
56. On the *order* in which a teacher should attempt to accomplish the various objects he has in view.
57. On school examinations generally.
58. On raising and filling a school, and on the circumstances which make a school popular.
59. On the various ways in which a teacher may co-operate with other benevolent efforts, such as temperance societies and Sabbath schools.
60. Brief summary of the teacher's duties *in* school, *out of* school, and in relation to the children, their parents, the Committee, and to society at large.

The 4½ hours devoted to daily practice by the students in the monitorial labors of the model school, with an occasional gallery lesson, has already been described; and several times a week the Principal casts a careful glance around their drafts, and makes notes of the defects observable in them, to form the subject of observations in the conversational lecture of the evening. If the students were staying, as they ought to stay, for two years, instead of six months, this amount of time spent in the model school would be in excess; and the actual amount of valuable time devoted to its labors, is a sacrifice which challenges a vigilant superintendence and an amount of ambulatory instruction which shall turn it to the best account. The practice in gallery teaching is necessarily unfrequent, where there are only three classes placed under it every morning; but over this, also, the same eye is extended at like intervals: and every afternoon, at half-past three o'clock, occurs the gallery lesson, by a student teacher, in the presence of the Principal or the Vice-principal and the whole body of the students, expressly to form the subject of mutual criticism, and of a final critique by Mr. Cornwell, on adjourning to the theatre at 4. In the theatre, after taking the criticisms of the students on the lesson just delivered, which seem generally to be limited to the superficial defects of grammar, pronunciation, or want of order in the gallery, the Principal or Vice-principal makes a far more searching exposure of its essential defects, which are carefully analyzed; and concludes by throwing in the remarks required by his miscellaneous notes on the class and gallery teaching of the day. He then proceeds with the conversational lecture for the day, into each of which the student's limited period of residence compels him to throw a large amount of instruction, so tersely expressed, and yet so condensed, as to require all the earnestness of the young men at once to seize and assimilate it. No one, however, can be present at one of these conversational lectures without being struck by the weightiness of the matter which it contains, and the aphoristic vigor with which it is endeavored, not merely to lay it before, but to engrave it into the minds of the hearers.

The tenor of the course may be gathered from the results contemplated in the following set of queries, drawn up by the Principal, and contained in the Society's "Manual:"

Questions to test a School.

The following questions have been drawn up for the use alike of Committees and teachers. They indicate the points to which a teacher should direct his attention, and the course a Committee should take in order to ascertain the condition of a school. The questions are supposed to be put to the teacher:

Reading:

Do you *define* and *limit* the portion to be read? Is the portion assigned of such *moderate length* as to allow of its being read three or four times?

Do your monitors question readily on the lessons that have been read?

Have you the *specimens*, *models*, or *diagrams*, that are necessary to illustrate such lesson?

Do you rest satisfied if one boy is reading in the draft, or do you see that *every child is attentive* while one is reading? Do you also forbid the monitors approaching the boy who is reading, and require him always to stand where he has a view of the whole draft?

Do you pay attention to the *style* of reading, particularly with the elder boys?

Do you correct a bad style by having very *familiar* sentences read?

By requiring the boys to *tell* you something, to write it down, and then to read it from *their own writing?*

Do you teach the *meanings* of words in connexion with the reading, as found *in sentences*, rather than with the *spelling* in which the arrangements must be arbitrary?

Do you point out on the map all the places occurring in the lesson read?

Do the boys exhibit seriousness of manner while reading the Bible?

Spelling:

Do you sometimes teach and test spelling by the *dictation* of sentences to be written?

Do the elder boys sometimes *copy* pieces of poetry and the exercises in grammar, with a view to improvement in spelling?

Do you have the more difficult words that occur in your collective lessons spelt?

Interrogation:

Do you or your monitors, question on every *subject* taught?

Do you occasionally require *mutual* questioning on the part of the elder boys?

Does your questioning include the *three* different stages? 1. During reading, the explanation of such words or allusions as are necessary to *understanding* the lesson? 2. After the books are closed, with a view to *impressing* the *facts* of the lesson on the memory? 3. The explanation of the *etymologies* of words and the imparting such *incidental* information as is naturally associated with it?

Do you avoid indefinite questions, and such as by admitting of only "Yes!" or "No!" encourage guessing?

Writing:

Are the books kept clean, free from blots, and without the corners being turned down? *

Do you furnish the boys with good copies, avoiding those which have improper contractions?

Have you a black board on which you write in chalk a copy for the lower boys who are unable to write?

Arithmetic:

Do you teach arithmetic by the black board? Have you one in each draft?

Do you in teaching arithmetic commence with and constantly refer to *sensible objects?*

Are the numbers in your *lower* classes always those of *little value?*

Do you invariably insist on every number being *read* to ascertain whether its value is understood?

Do your monitors *question* at every step in the process of a sum? *e. g.* Why do you carry only one when you borrow ten?

Are the *terms* and *marks* explained? *e. g. What do £. s. d. mean?* Why is the rule called compound subtraction? What are these "marks" used for?

---

* The books may be kept smooth by tying them up between two pieces of board.

Do you connect the book knowledge of the more advanced boys with the objects around them? *e. g.* What is the quantity of timber in the trunk of a tree whose height and girth, both at the root and part where it branches off, have been measured by themselves? The number of gallons the school water-butt will hold? The contents of a field, whose shape and sides they have ascertained?

Grammar:

Do you *explain* every definition, rule, &c., *before* allowing the boys to commit them to memory?

Do you make your boys understand that language determines grammar, and not grammar language? That the rules of grammar are only the recognized usages of language?

In explaining the etymologies of words are you extremely careful to give the right *quantities* and *terminations* of the roots?

Geography:

Do you teach the *physical* features of any district first?

Do you make the boys acqoainted with their own *neighborhood* and *country* before attending to more distant parts?

Have you a map of the neighborhood in the school?

In commencing geography do you require the boys to make a map of the play-ground, or some well-known part? Do you explain latitude and longitude by a reference to this map?

Do you require the boys occasionally to point towards the place under consideration? *e. g.* When Dublin has been pointed out on the map, do you say, *Now point to Dublin itself?*

Drawing:

Do you commence with *chalk* drawing on the black board?

Are your monitors so proficient as to be able to *sketch off* any object illustrative of their lesson?

Collective Teaching:

Do you abstain from teaching collectively those subjects which depend for their improvement on the amount of *individual practice*, as reading, spelling, &c.?

Do you test the *efficiency* of your collective teaching by *individual questions?*

Do you sometimes require the elder boys to make a written *abstract* of their lesson? Is this looked over with a view to the spelling among other things?

Do you make use of *ellipses?* the *number* varying inversely as the age of the child?

Are your collective lessons to the *whole* school especially devoted to subjects connected with *manners*, *morals* and *religion?* Do those to the *younger* boys relate to the various familiar objects, utensils, and operations about them? Are those to the elder boys given *systematically? i. e.* Is each lesson part of a system of knowledge?

Is your collective teaching especially characterized by *simplicity* both of language and illustration, and by *animation?* *

In using numbers do you make them intelligible by referring them to *known standards? e. g.* If you were stating that some trees are near 300 feet high, would you say that they were twice, three or four times, as the case may be, as high as some well-known object?

Monitors:

Do you devote an *hour a day* specially to the training of your monitors?

Is it your prime object in this training to give your monitors the *art of teaching*, and do you make the impartation of knowledge subservient to this?

Do you train every monitor in the *very lessons* he has to teach?

Is the mass of your school employed in some *quiet* exercise, as writing, while you are engaged with the monitors?

Have you a good general monitor to whom you can intrust the mass of the school during your training of the monitors?

Do you require the same monitor to teach the *same lesson* that he may be thoroughly competent to that lesson?

Have you a *double set* of monitors, that while one set is teaching the other is learning?

Do you from time to time, add to your monitor's class, to act as *auxiliaries*, in the absence of the regular monitors, such boys as you deem likely to be suited to the office?

Do you associate with the office of monitor as many *pleasing* circumstances as you can?

Do you pay them? Have they as such the use of the school library? Do you treat them with marked consideration? Do you occasionally accompany them in little excursions, to places in your neighborhood distinguished in history, or for beautiful scenery, or to museums, gardens, &c.?

Do you impress on your monitors that they should correct no mistake till they have ascertained that none of the boys in their draft can? Do you exemplify this in your own teaching?

Discipline:

Is order the *habit* of your school?

Have you perfect *quietness* during writing?

Do you *drill* your boys occasionally, with a view to securing habits of prompt obedience?

Do you have the movements to and from the desks made in an orderly way? Do you generally have the tables *repeated* or sung simultaneously at this time? Do you sometimes have the movements made with perfect quietness, as a means of discipline? Are all the exercises conducted as *quietly* as is consistent with the full development of the powers of the children?

Do you have all those subjects which depend for their improvement upon *practice*, such as reading, spelling, &c., taught *individually?*

Is every exercise conducted *under observation*, that the boys may feel that any inattention or disorder is certain of detection?

---

* Many of the points suggested here are as important in connexion with other kinds of teaching as in collective; but as the evils of neglecting them would be increased in proportion to the number taught, it has been teemed advisable to throw them under this head.

Have all the children at all times someting to do, and a motive for doing it?
Do you abstain from giving a second command till the ***first*** has been obeyed?
Do you abstain from ***calling out***, except on puite necessary occasions?
In stopping or directing the whole school, do you give your commands so loud as to be heard by all, and no ***louder?***
Are you ***strict***, without being ***severe?***

If you find the general discipline becoming at all lax, do you have those exercises which are most faulty, gone through as you wish them, ***after*** the regular ***school hours?***

Habits of the School:

Is your room ***clean?***
Do you have it well ***swept***, and ***dusted*** every day?
Do you see all the school ***furniture*** put in its proper place, before you leave the school-room?
Is your room well ***ventilated?***
Do the boys exhibit ***subdued and gentle manners*** in their intercourse with each other?
Are the boys generally ***clean*** in their ***persons*** and ***dress?***
Do you carefully prevent ***idling*** about the school, or in or near the gates, &c., or in the play-ground?
Are your boys orderly and ***respectful*** to their superiors?
Do you discourage ***tale-telling***, except in reference to very serious faults?
Do you keep your drafts of about a ***uniform size***, not less than nine, nor more than twelve?
Do you take care that boys of the same class are of about the same ***attainments***, and in a collective lesson of the same ***mental capacity?***
Have you the ***form*** of the drafts distinctly ***marked*** on the floor, by cutting into it, painting it, or letting a wire into it?

Examinations:

Have you ***stated periods*** of ***examination***, in order to the removal of the competent to higher classes?
Do the children ***know*** these ***periods***, that they may work with a view to them?
Are the intervals between these periods of such ***moderate length in a child's estimation***, as to influence his exertions?
Have the parents any means of knowing when their children are advanced?
Have you an evening examination, at least once a year, for the parents and friends of the children?

General:

Do you require every ***error*** to be ***corrected*** by the boy ***making it***, after it has been corrected by another?
Is every matter ***explained before*** it is committed to memory?
Do you keep up your connexion with the ***old scholars***, by occasional meetings, or in any other way? Are they allowed the use of the school library?
Do your children ***love*** you? Have you a strong ***sympathy*** for children, and pleasure in their company?
Is your teaching ***intellectual?*** Do the children really ***understand*** what they are learning? Do you make every subject taught a means of ***intellectual development?***
Do your children come to school ***regularly*** and in time?
Do you give time and attention to subjects according to their ***relative importance?*** e. g. Reading above every thing, the history and circumstances of your own town or locality in preference to more distant parts?
Do you rather aim at giving the boys a ***good*** acquaintance with a ***few*** subjects, than a very superficial acquaintance with many?
Are your exercises generally characterized by ***little repeating*** and ***much questioning?***
Do you keep a ***register*** of the ***attendances*** of the children, and of their school ***payments?***
Do you rest satisfied if you obtain an ***answer*** to a question ***from one***, or do you repeat and remodel the question till the matter is ***understood by all?*** Do you impress this maxim upon your monitors, ***that all teaching is for the whole class?***

Model School.

The "Boys' School" connected with this establishment probably stands unrivalled in England, as a model of order and discipline, and of the collective instruction of a large number of children on the monitorial system. It is composed of 760 boys, from the age of six to twelve or thirteen years. The register is always full, and the attendance is regular and punctual, (averaging daily 700,) although the children are gathered from one of the poorest neighborhoods of the city. The school is not free, (except when there are more than two from the same family,) and yet being *good*, there is no difficulty in collecting in advance the fee of 2*d*. per week. On account of the large number of classes into which the school is divided the normal pupils enjoy unrivalled opportunities, both of observation and practice of the method of instruction pursued, which are not exclusively monitorial, but a mixed system of the monitorial and simultaneous, in which, however, the monitorial is the ground-work of the whole.

Female Department of the Normal School.

The mode of obtaining admission, conditions, organization and instruction of this department are substantially the same as those in the male department. The immediate class instruction and practice are conducted under female teachers, while the pupils of this department attend daily in the theatre, or lecture hall on the lectures on the art of teaching given to the young men. In addition to, or modification of the course pursued by the young men, the female Normal pupils are instructed in the art of teaching needlework; in the best method of training girls to household duties; and especially in those methods of communicating religious knowledge, which, under the blessing of God, are most likely not only to make the young acquainted with, and interested in Holy Scripture, but to bring them practically under the influence of its sacred truths.

Mr. Fletcher, in his Report describes a peculiar practice of the Model Girls' School:—

Nor must I omit from express notice the perfect system of industrial instruction in needlework, and the economy of clothing, through which the whole school is passed. The outline of it given in the Society's "Manual of the System of Teaching in the Model Girls' School," is no paper theory, but a simple description of a well-ordered and vigorous set of classes, embracing the whole school, for an hour and a half every morning. "When at needlework the children are seated at desks, arranged in classes, according to their proficiency. The first or lowest class is seated further from the platform, and the others, in numerical order, in front of it. The number of classes depends on the different kinds of work taught in the school, each kind occupying a separate class. The number in general use is 11. From the higher classes the best workers are selected for monitors; two are appointed for each class. One instructs for one week, whilst the other is at work under the direction of her monitor; consequently each superintends the class and works alternately; and each monitor continues at the same desk until she is appointed monitor to a higher class. Every girl continues to sit at the same desk while she remains in the class. There are also two platform monitors, who alternately superintend and work one week. But all the monitors of classes, and the girls under their care, are under the superintendence of the general monitor. Every Friday morning the girls are allowed to bring their own work.

The children in the higher classes are provided with lap-bags, made of brown holland. These are marked 1, 2, 3, &c., for as many as the desk contains. The number of the desk is also marked upon them; thus $\frac{5}{8}$ signifies that the bag belongs to the fifth girl in the eighth desk. Before the children take their seats, the bags are placed by the platform monitor on the class monitor's desks, and by them given to their girls. The class work and all garments in hand, are collected by the class monitors, and placed on the ends of the desks ready for the platform monitor to deliver to the mistress. The monitor of each desk is furnished with a pair of scissors, thread-paper, needle-case, and a bag large enough to contain all the implements that belong to her desk. They are also supplied with a few thimbles and needles, for which they are responsible to the platform monitor. The children in the lower classes use colored cotton for the class work, as it renders the stitches more conspicuous, and consequently facilitates general inspection. It also excites an interest, as the promise of a choice of some pretty color is a strong inducement to a child to perform her work neatly.

At the time assigned for closing the labor of the morning reading drafts, viz., at a quarter past 10 o'clock, the general monitor rings the bell as a signal for the business of the drafts to cease; and, after a pause, the command is given for the girls to turn to the right or to the left, as the order may be. The order is then given, and the whole of the children walk in a line along the passage round the school, and each girl, as she comes to the end of it, steps in behind the desk to which she belongs, and goes to her proper place at the desk. Each monitor does the same, taking her place at the head of the desk. Each child being now opposite to her own slate, a command is given to take their seats, which they do instantly.

A signal is now given for the monitors to distribute the bags, after which they return to their seats, and another signal is given for each girl to tie her own bag to the desk before her. A signal is again given for the monitors to examine their girls' hands to see if they are clean, and that each is provided with a needle and thimble. The platform monitor now supplies the class monitors with any additional work they may require for their girls, which the class monitors give out; also a needleful of cotton to each child, and then return to their seats. A command is now given for the whole school to show work, that is, to hold it up in their left hand to see that each is furnished with work. The bell is then rung, each child holds down her work and immediately begins; and the monitors pass down the desks to instruct them. When a child wants work she holds up her left hand as an intimation to her monitor, who steps forward and supplies her. If a monitor wants a fresh supply she makes a like signal to the platform monitor. When a girl wants thread she holds up her right hand, and her monitor supplies her. If a monitor wants a fresh supply she makes a like signal to the platform monitor. At half past 11 o'clock the mistress examines the work of each child; those who merit rewards have a ticket, and those who have been careless and inattentive forfeit one, or are confined after school.

At a quarter before 12 the bell rings for the girls to show work, and the monitors to pass down the desks and collect the needles and thimbles An order is then given for the children to put the class work into the bags, and the monitors to collect all articles in hand, and deliver them to the platform monitor, who takes them to the platform. The monitors then take their seats. The order is now given to untie bags, when each child unties her own; a second order is given to take them off; and a third, to fold them up. Each child folds her own neatly, with the number in view, places it on the desk before her, and puts her hands behind her. The bell then rings for the monitors to collect bags, which they do, placing them one on the other in order; they then put them neatly into the bag belonging to their desk; also their scissors, thread-papers, needles and thimbles. The monitors are then ordered to the platform with their bags, where they deliver them to the platform monitor. They then return to their seats, and the report of the good and inattentive girls is read *aloud* by the monitor-general; the good receive tickets, and the negligent must either forfeit tickets or stay in after school hours. As soon as the reports are taken, all the children are exercised out of their seats, to stand each opposite to her own slate, with her hands behind her. A signal is given for the girls to turn, when they are dismissed in order, one class following the other in a line along the sides of the school."

For the details of the instruction in each class, I must refer you to the "Manual." The first class is for hemming, in two divisions, one composed of those who have not learned to fix a hem, and who are taught on waste paper, as being less expensive than linen or cotton, and answering the purpose just as well; and a second, in which they practice hemming on small pieces of calico. The second class, also in two divisions, is for sewing and felling, and running and felling; first division learning to fix their work in paper, and the second to execute it. The third class is for drawing threads and stitching; the fourth for gathering and fixing gathers; the fifth, for button-holes; the sixth, for making buttons and sewing them on; the seventh, for herring-bone stitching; the eighth, for darning; the ninth, for making tucks, and whipping; and the tenth, for marking. The eleventh is the finishing class. There is at present no knitting or netting class; and fancy work is expressly excluded and discouraged.

"As it is highly desirable that the children, as soon as they have learned to work, should be employed in something useful, this class comprises the girls who have passed through the preceding, and are here engaged in making and completing garments. The children in this class are taught economy in purchasing, cutting out, and repairing various articles of wearing apparel; they are made acquainted with the waste occasioned by the want of proper consideration and exactness in domestic arrangements, and the miseries frequently produced by mismanagement and inattention. In order to impress upon their minds this useful branch of female instruction, they are interrogated, in various ways, on the common concerns of life. When the teacher proposes a question, she waits until each child in the class has had an opportunity of returning an answer, according to the knowledge she possesses. She then comments upon each of these answers in a way that will enable the *children* to decide which is the most suitable course. To assist the teachers in these exercises, they are furnished with a few examples of questions and answers, which they may carry out to a much greater extent." These also will be found in the "Manual," together with engraved patterns for cutting out the commonest garments. The highest industrial section of the school forms in fact a class for collective teaching of the most practical and improving kind, including as many ideas on household management generally as can be conveyed. Specimens of needlework, made up in portfolios for the use of teachers, and arranged in the order of the above classes, are sold at the Society's Depository; and the beautiful patterns of every variety of garment, made up in tissue paper by the finishing class against the time of the annual meeting, are quite little works of art.

The propriety and industry exhibited throughout these industrial classes is as perfect as their system; and a student teacher in each class has the advantage of co-operating in, and doing as much as she can of, the work of superintending each successive class, from the lowest upwards; the sewing classes, in this respect, presenting no peculiarity distinguishing them from those devoted to other exercises. The discipline and moral tone of this school present throughout a standard well worthy of its exemplar character. It has a library of above 250 carefully selected volumes, besides a small library of reference for its monitors. Great advantage, too, must arise from a certain small proportion of the children being retained in connexion with the institution until a riper age, and even then not giving up their intercourse with it. In fact, the whole department is a family as much as a school; and no higher praise can possibly be bestowed upon it.

Art of Teaching and Governing a School.

Three hours and a half each day are devoted by the female students to practice in monitorial or gallery teaching in the Girls' Model School; and in alternate weeks another hour and a half is given daily, by each of the two classes, to the practical labors of the needlework drafts. At the close of the afternoon's gallery lesson, they all adjourn to the theatre, on the back seats of which they take their places to hear the criticism on the gallery lesson which has been given by one of the young men, followed by the lecture on "pedagogy" for the day, in the course already described.

A like criticism of the afternoon's gallery teaching, and of the draft teaching for the day, in the model girls' school, is taken on the opening of the evening classes. It is conducted with some spirit, and the concluding remarks of the normal school teacher, Miss Drew, are exceedingly acute and judicious. A weekly conversational lecture occupies two hours of every Saturday morning, and is given by the experienced superintendent, Mrs. Mac Rae, to the whole of the female student teachers, seated at their needlework in the gallery. The following are the heads of her course :—

1. On the various motives for entering on the profession of a teacher.
2. On some of the essential moral qualifications of a teacher.
3. On the selection of monitors.
4. On organizing a new school.
5. On training monitors.
6. On teaching the elements of reading, with illustrations of the method of using the First Lesson Book.
7. On the various methods of teaching spelling, with illustrations.
8. On training suitable monitors to assist in teaching needlework.
9. On teaching arithmetic.
10. On domestic economy and orderly habits.
11. On school furniture, and the order of a school-room.
12. On the cleanliness of a school-room, and ventilation.
13. On the duties of monitors.
14. On the various offices in the school.
15. On improving an old school.
16. On the judicious treatment of the monitors.
17. On the duties of a teacher to the committee, and to the parents of the children.
18. On a week's occupation in the model school, and the advantages of cultivating a spirit of inquiry.

These lessons of the superintendent, *applying* all which the students are learning in the normal school, to the circumstances into which they are about to be introduced, are highly interesting, vividly instructive, and imbued with a truly Christian spirit. Drawing from the experiences of a quick and refined perception, they embody indeed practical lessons of adherence, to unfailing truth and untiring patience, from which others than teachers might profit. The following is the Examination Paper on the Art of Teaching and Governing in a School, answered by Ann Inglefield, 25th March, 1837 :—

1. How will a teacher best establish her authority in a school ?—By firmness, joined with kindness of manner and impartiality in all her conduct; giving her commands clearly and definitely; expecting prompt and cheerful obedience ; let the children see that principle governs her conduct: this, with good information and a pleasing manner of communicating, are not likely to fail of success in establishing the authority of a teacher in her school.

2. What will especially demand your vigilance in giving a collective lesson ?—That the attention of the children be kept alive by the interesting information and manner of the teacher; that the supervision be constant, and the order preserved.

3. How will you endeavor to have good monitors ?—By efficient training and interesting them in the work, imparting to them superior information, and reposing confidence in them when found worthy.

4. State some of the uses of the monitorial system, and of the defects which may be indulged under it ?—A greater number of children can be instructed at one time than by one individual.

The monitors acquire the art of communicating the information they gain; they must be examples to their drafts; and by these means they are likely to prove, as they grow up, more useful members of society.

The defect would arise from the mistress indulging self-ease and neglecting her monitors, or leaving too much of the school duties to them.

5. How will you endeavor to get good reading in a school ?—By attending to the punctuation, emphasis, rising and falling inflection, aspirates and non-aspirates, and tones of the voice.

6. What will demand especial attention in the arithmetic classes ?—That the children perfectly understand the rules and their uses.

7. How will you convey to children the first notions of geography ?—By illustration, as describing the earth by an orange.

8. What powers of the mind should an object lesson be directed to cultivate ?—Observation, attention, reflection.

It is difficult to imagine a combination of advantages greater than that enjoyed by the student teachers in the female department of this institution, including, as it does, the animated and faithful instruction of the principal teacher of the normal school and the vice-principal of the companion department, the lectures on teaching and governing in a school, delivered to the students in both departments by the principal and vice-principal of the normal school for young men, an admirable model school, and the faithful counsels conveyed by the superintendent in her daily management and weekly addresses. The effect of this combination is indeed very marked, if the superior activity and orderliness of mind shown by the senior over the junior section, during my presence in the school, afford any fair measure of its amount. Considering however, that the female students, though as much instructed as the male students, and possessed of superior manners, are yet not generally equal to them in physical resources, and in the enthusiastic energy which brings a considerable proportion of the latter into the field of instruction, it is not less to be regretted in their case than in the male department, that the young teachers have not the advantages of a longer stay to strengthen their acquirements, their capacities of teaching, and, I might even add, their general character, before they enter upon the arduous duties of their very responsible situations. The time of their stay is far too short to accomplish all that is desirable in these respects; although the means provided are, I sincerely believe, sufficient, with God's blessing, to render them able, modest, and Christian teachers. Among the circumstances incidentally conducive to this result, I would recall especial attention to the fair proportion of *pupil* teachers to be found in the model school, at the head of the monitor's class, giving a moral firmness, as well as intellectual strength, to its organization, eminently beneficial to the *student* teachers, at the same time that they enjoy the further advantage of the head teachers of the normal and model schools themselves daily superintending, correcting, and teaching in the classes.

It is a leading object in the management of this institution to train up a race of teachers who shall not only elevate the office by the respectability of their attainments, but adorn it by the fervor of their poetry. Each candidate is presented, on admission, with a copy of the following hints, accompanying the regulations to which he will be expected to attend :

I. *Let your mind frequently and seriously revert to the* OBJECTS *which are to be obtained by your residence in the Society's House.*—You have at once to acquire and to communicate, to learn and to teach, to govern and to submit to government ; and you have to do this, not in relation to one mind only, but to many minds,—of different quality, under varying circumstances, —as an exemplar, and as subordinate to others. You have MUCH to do. Therefore—

II. *Redeem your Time.*—Do not think it sufficient to attend regularly and diligently to *appointed* studies, but improve the intervals of time which will necessarily elapse between these stated employments. Secure the minutes, for minutes compose hours. Ten minutes, diligently improved every day, will amount to an hour in the course of a week; and an hour thus redeemed *every day*, will be equal in value to no small portion of a year.

III. *Cultivate Habits of Order.*—Avoid negligence in personal appearance. Be always neat and clean in your apparel. Let those pursuits which are most important in reference to your expected engagements receive the greatest share of your attention ; and never suffer these to be interrupted or superseded by others of a more general nature. Do not allow levity and trifling to usurp the place of rational cheerfulness. "Avoid the very appearance of evil." Attend to all established regulations. He who wilfully breaks rules which are calculated to promote the welfare of the community to which he belongs, is the common enemy of all.

IV. *Cherish a kind and friendly disposition towards your Associates.*—Let this be shown by a general spirit of courtesy,—a willingness to assist where help may be needed, and especially by the communication to others of any knowledge you may exclusively possess. Manifest a decided disapprobation of unbecoming conduct wherever you observe it ; and, jealous for the honor of the body to which you belong, endeavor to stimulate every pupil to diligence and zeal in the pursuit of those great objects for the attainment of which all are alike receiving the countenance and aid of the Society.

V. *Exercise a constant Spirit of "Watchfulness unto Prayer.*—Remembering that you are responsible to God for the right improvement of the advantages you enjoy, the talents you possess, and the time placed at your disposal; seek daily for "the wisdom which cometh from above," and "the grace which bringeth salvation." Be yourself a diligent and devotional student of that book you are emphatically to teach; and never forget that "all Scripture is given by inspiration of God, and is profitable for doctrine, for reproof, for correction, for instruction in righteousness; that the man of God may be perfect, thoroughly furnished unto good works." (2 Tim. iii. 16, 17.)

Periodical examinations of the student teachers take place in the presence of the Committee, and upon the results of these examinations its members appear to base their assertion, that by the efforts of the Society, restricted as those efforts may ever have been by external obstacles and internal want of resources, "more elevated views of the teacher's office and duty have been promulgated; a greater moral power has been given to popular instruction; and, as a necessary consequence, the school-master has been in some measure raised in public estimation, though not by any means so much as the importance of the office deserves. Letters from all parts of the country have borne testimony to the patience, diligence, and piety of many of the laborers whom the Society have sent forth. The best evidence, however, of the general satisfaction which has been given, is to be found in the increasing applications for teachers, which pour in from all quarters; a demand largely exceeding the ability of the Committee to supply."

If by any means its resources could be so augmented, and its duties so shared with supplemental institutions, that it could retain its student teachers on terms consistent with their interests and those of the schools to be supplied, for quadruple the time of their present stay,—for two years instead of six months,—such an arrangement alone would ultimately be productive of incalculable advantage to that great branch of the popular education of England which comes under its influence.

The teachers trained in the institution, resident in and near the metropolis, enjoy the advantage of periodical meetings in the theatre of the institution for professional discussions; as likewise of attendance at a course of lectures provided by the Society each winter since 1837, for their gratification and instruction. During the summer vacation a number of male teachers of British schools, from various parts of the country, known to the Committee through their inspectors, as persons who would really profit by such an opportunity for supplemental study, are invited to a rapid course of instruction in the art of teaching and governing in a school, and to take up their residence in the Society's house during its continuance. This opportunity of revising and improving upon their actual methods is of great value; and those who have enjoyed the advantages of it are warm in acknowledging them. Indeed, the British school teachers throughout the kingdom generally, maintain relations with the parent Society, because it is the centre of all applications for new teachers, and, therefore, the principal source of promotion.

XVII. PLAN OF ORGANIZATION AND INSTRUCTION

IN THE MODEL SCHOOLS OF THE BRITISH AND FOREIGN SCHOOL SOCIETY.*

I. FITTINGS AND ORGANIZATION.

Section 1.—*School Fittings.*

1. THE *form of room* best adapted to the working of the British System is that of a parallelogram, its proportion varying according to the extent of its area. At the lower end of the room a raised platform should be erected, from which the master can overlook the operations of the whole school when necessary, and conduct the changes.

The ground space should be divided into three parts; that nearest the platform being left clear for draft work; the next portion fitted with writing desks; and the upper part having a gallery or galleries for collective lessons.

The windows should be in the roof, or elevated at least six feet from the ground. A strip of blackboard should be fixed on the walls three feet from the ground, and should run up each side of the school-room as far as the commencement of the gallery division.

The desks and gallery should be so arranged that, when the pupils are seated, each one may face the platform. Behind the platform a class-room may be erected, fitted with a gallery capable of seating one section of the school, for the purpose of model and trial lessons. This gallery may also be fitted with broad desks, so as to be useful for drawing classes.

2. If a school be purely monitorial, it is necessary that the whole of the instruction should go on in one large room, so fitted up as to allow the master to exercise constant oversight over all its details. When, however, responsible and efficient assistants are engaged, it will be found much better to make such a subdivision of the school into separate compartments as shall isolate each class and its teacher from the rest, and thus preserve them from interruption. In order to secure this advantage without interfering with the master's powers of exercising general superintendence, the best plan will be to divide the several classes from one another during the hours of teaching by means of curtains, so suspended that they can be readily removed or shifted whenever the teacher requires to have an uninterrupted view of the whole.

3. As the work of a school is all performed by the children either when standing in semicircular drafts, or sitting in desks for writing, or arranged in a gallery for simultaneous instruction, the most natural and obvious arrangement for a school is that of a triple division, the first portion being an open area, the second fitted with writing-desks, and the third with a gallery. The Model Schools of the society have recently been reorganized on this principle.

The open space nearest to the platform is intended for classes when standing;

* From the "*Hand-Book of the British and Foreign School Society.*" London, 1856.

it should be measured off accurately into equal portions, and the lines indicating the forms of the draft stations should be carefully marked. This may be done either by grooves in the floor, or by iron wire let into it. A strong box should be provided for each of these drafts, which may serve both to contain the books and slates, and to furnish a seat for the teacher. Each class should also have a blackboard. For those classes which do not face the wall, and for the galleries, it will be well to mount the blackboard on a movable easel.

The forms and desks in the second or middle section of the room must be fixed firmly in the ground; the legs or supports, if of wood, should be six inches broad and two inches thick; but cast-iron legs are preferable, as they support the desk-board with equal firmness, occupy less room, and have a much neater appearance; their number, of course, will be in proportion to the length of the forms. A form twenty feet long will require five. The corners of the desks and forms should be rounded, in order that the children may not hurt themselves.

Desks and forms are occasionally so coupled together as to form one movable block. When well and firmly made, they will be found to stand almost as steadily as fixed desks. Though somewhat more expensive, this plan will be found advantageous in cases where it is desired, either for Sunday-school or other purposes, to alter the arrangement of the school-room, or economize its space. As a general rule, the room should be so constructed as to allow seven square feet of area for each child intended to be accommodated. Schools are often inconveniently and unhealthily crowded when the number of children exceeds this proportion.

4. The space or passage between a form and the next desk should be one foot six inches; the horizontal space between a desk and its form three inches; the breadth of a desk twelve inches; the breadth of a form six inches; the hight of a desk twenty-eight inches; and the hight of a form sixteen inches. Every child being seated upon his form, occupies a space of eighteen inches in length of the desk. When semicircular classes are formed on the sides of the room, the passage between the walls and the ends of the forms and desks should be eight feet.

Flat desks have been found to be on the whole more convenient than those with an inclined surface. No beading is then required, to interfere with the convenience of the writer's arm. When the desks are arranged in groups, the passage between their extremities should not be less than two feet in width. Inkstands should be sunk in the desks, and when not in use should be well covered. A long sliding strip of wood, of the same length as the desk, will often do this more effectually than separate lids.

It is not desirable that more than fifty children should be seated on a gallery at the same time. It is seldom, indeed, that even this number can be taught collectively in a thoroughly efficient manner. As a general rule, forty is a sufficiently large number to be placed under simultaneous instruction in this way.

In constructing a gallery, space may be economized by making each step seven inches high, and placing upon it a seat rising five or six inches above. The feet of the children are then placed *under* the seat in front of them. When the same plank serves both for a step and a seat, more space is required, and much dirt is occasioned.

5. It is highly desirable, even if the school be not very large, that there

should be space enough for a play-ground or yard, in which the children may assemble before they go into school, or during the hours of recreation. The soil of this yard should be of gravel to the depth of one foot. It should be enclosed by a wall of suitable hight, and have a communication from the street, without passing through the school-room. There ought to be a good supply of fresh water, either from a pump or cask, with conveniences for the children to wash their hands and faces.

It is also desirable, for the accommodation of the pupils, that one side of the yard be furnished with seats, and a part covered, in order to protect the children from inclemency of weather.

Where there is sufficient ground, it is a good plan to lay out some of it as little flower-beds with borders. In well-disciplined schools these will not be injured by trampling or neglect, and they furnish a good exercise in self-restraint for the children, besides a test of the general moral influence in favor of order and neatness existing in the school.

Apparatus for encouraging gymnastic exercises in the play-grounds of boys' schools can be obtained at a small cost, and is a very desirable appendage to a school. The simplest and most approved contrivance for this purpose is a circular swing, consisting of an upright pole about fifteen feet high, with a horizontal wheel at the top, to which five or six ropes are attached. This is an excellent method of promoting healthy muscular exertion.

Section 2.—Sections and Drafts.

6. A large school should be divided into sections, containing as nearly as possible fifty pupils each; each section should be divided into drafts, containing from ten to fifteen pupils; and the children in each section should continue there for every study until promoted to the next. A child should not be in one section for arithmetic, and in another for writing or reading, but should continue in the same section for all his studies.

But although a child should remain in the same section, and thus be under the care of the same pupil teacher, or elder monitor, until permanently promoted, he need not be in the same draft of that section for every study. If the section be divided into four drafts, he may happen to be in the first for ciphering, in the fourth for reading, or in the second for writing, and so on for the rest. It is *desirable*, however, that, as far as possible, his progress from draft to draft should be uniform, for every exercise carried on in the section.

7. As the basis of the above classification, the degree of attainment in *reading* may be regarded as fixing the section to which any child in the *lower* portion of the school belongs; and skill in arithmetic may determine position in the upper. While the children are only able to read the Daily Lesson Books, Nos. I. and II., and the sequel, the difference in their skill in reading is more marked than in arithmetic; but when they commence reading the Daily Lesson Book, No. III., the difference of their skill in the latter study is more easily ascertained than in reading.

Section 3.—Classification for Reading.

8. For the purpose of registering progress in *reading*, the school is divided into six classes. The following are the attainments and lessons of each class:—

(*a.*) The alphabet, and easy words of two and three letters. Lesson Book, No. I., p. 8 to 15, inclusive.

(*b.*) Words of one syllable. Lesson Book, No. I., p. 15 to 45, inclusive.
(*c.*) Words of two and three syllables. Lesson Book, No. II.
(*d.*) Words of three and four syllables. Sequel to Lesson Book, No. II.
(*e.*) Words of four syllables. Lesson Book, No. III., and Scripture Selections.
(*f.*) Any kind of reading. Lesson Book, No. IV., and the Bible.

9. In a *large* school each of these classes might form a section, while in very small ones a section will include several classes.

In each section *definite lessons* should be taught. In the *junior* divisions of the central schools all the lessons of the Lesson Books, Nos. I., II., and Sequel, are divided into portions for a fortnight's reading, and in each section every such portion is taught at a different draft station. Thus, all the lessons in these books are taught within the fortnight to different drafts of boys.

The reading books, Nos. III. and IV., are then divided amongst the sections of the *upper* school, so that each section has a distinct portion, which lasts three months; the whole section reading the *same lesson* at the *same time*. This is done that the superintendent of the section may put the boys together on the gallery for a general analysis of the lesson, after it has been read and explained in drafts.

10. The plan of reading is so arranged as in most cases to allow two days for the reading and study of one lesson. In small schools so many lessons can not, of course, be proceeding at the same time; but the principle should every where be followed out of dividing the lesson books into such portions as can be taught in a given time, and having the same portion always taught in the same section. Every day should have its appointed lesson, and every lesson should be carefully read, and thoroughly analyzed and explained.

Section 4.—*Classification for Writing.*

11. For writing a different classification is followed. The sectional division (of fifty pupils each) is here retained. The children of the lowest sections are employed *on slate*, with pieces of slate-pencil inserted in pencil-holders. The position of the body and hand, the forms of letters, and the elementary principles of writing, are thus taught before the expense of writing on paper is incurred. Children should not, however, be kept from copy-books longer than is absolutely necessary; the additional trouble entailed by the use of pen, ink, and copy-book, is more than repaid by the better means of training and improvement which they afford.

12. Each section is divided according to the number of desks allotted to its use during this exercise. Thus, if five desks, accommodating ten boys each, are used for the purpose of writing, the ten best writers would sit in the front or first desk, the ten next best in the second desk, and so for the rest.

The copy-books of each section, when not in use, should either be kept in a small box, containing as many divisions as there are desks in the section, or they should be tied up between two stout boards, somewhat longer and broader than the books themselves. In this case pieces of pasteboard may be used to separate the books belonging to the different desks. In every instance the copy-books of each section should be kept entirely distinct from those of every other.

Section 5.—*Classification for Arithmetic.*

13. For arithmetic the school is divided into ten classes.

The *first* class is engaged in receiving lessons on the first ideas of number, and the elementary operations of arithmetic, illustrated by the ball-frame, marbles, peas, and other familiar objects. The use of figures, both Arabic and Roman, is also explained, and the children are further occupied, when in drafts or at writing desks, in acquiring an extended knowledge of the tables or in writing down figures *neatly*.

14. The other *nine* classes in arithmetic are formed according to progress; each *rule*, simple and compound, requiring a distinct class; and each class spending *part* of its time in recapitulating the work of the classes below. The tenth class is made up of all who have passed what are commonly called the elementary rules of arithmetic, as applied to weights and measures.

15. The number of children in each class will of course vary according to the number in the school. For example, in a school containing 200 children, and forming four sections of 50 each, the highest section would probably contain all the boys in the tenth or highest class of arithmetic, and the lowest might form the first class. The second and third sections would then be composed of children engaged in studying the four first rules of arithmetic, simple and compound.

The teacher should never fail to draw out a plan of study, providing for careful attention to each operation in its proper place, and for recapitulation. In most cases the first class, besides going through the work set down for them, would find time to go through a preliminary course of *practice* on the first rules, where the principles given would be exemplified by themselves on their own slates by very *simple and familiar* illustrations.

Section 6.—*Classification for other Studies.*

16. When the children have been carefully separated into sections for the purposes of collective teaching and moral superintendence, and again subdivided into drafts according to their skill in reading, writing, and arithmetic, but little further subdivision will be necessary for other studies. The *sectional* division will, of course, do for every subject taught collectively, that is, *to the section as a whole;* the reading drafts will serve for spelling, derivation, grammar, and geography; the arithmetic drafts for mental arithmetic and tables; and the writing subdivisions, for all exercises carried on in the desks.

17. If a child is found whose reading qualifies him for the *third* draft in the section, while his knowledge of grammar renders him fit only for the *second*, it will be easy to make him for a time an exception to the general rule, by keeping him in the second draft while grammar is being studied; or, which will generally be preferable, by putting him in the second draft for reading also, until he is sufficiently advanced for promotion in grammar.

II. AGENCY EMPLOYED.

Section 1.—*Pupil Teachers.*

1. Each section of the Borough Road School is placed under the care of a pupil teacher, who is expected to marshal his children in order, before entering the school-room, and to lead them quietly to their places. He is also considered responsible for the regular and punctual attendance of the children in his section, their general order and cleanliness, and their progress in their studies. He keeps a roll-book, in which he marks the daily attendance of his children; examines them as to their advancement at stated periods; and recommends the

most proficient for promotion, as vacancies occur in the next higher section of the school. These children are again examined by the pupil teacher of the section to which they have been advanced, and any unsuitable promotions are reported to the head master. The *elder* pupil teachers take their turn in conducting the changes of the school, and in its general superintendence.

2. An hour and a half is devoted out of the regular school hours to the instruction of the pupil teachers in those branches of knowledge necessary to qualify them to pass the annual examination by Her Majesty's Inspector. Regard is also had to the probability of their becoming candidates for Queen's scholarships; and the most promising among them receive instruction during the first half of each year, so as gradually to prepare them for that more extended examination.

The *morning* of each day, before the school commences, is considered the best time for the regular hour and a half's study, where such a course is practicable: if this can not be done, part of the time should be taken from twelve to one o'clock in the middle of the day; and the rest before going home in the evening. It is desirable not to bring them back to school after once leaving it for the day, as such a course interferes greatly with their time for *private* study—a habit of the utmost importance to them.

3. A somewhat different principle is followed in the instruction of the pupil teachers from that which rules the teaching in the school. While much is necessarily done *for* the children, by *bringing down* the lessons to the level of their mental capacity, the pupil teachers are led to do *most* for themselves. They have their text-books and home lessons on each particular subject of study, and the teacher chiefly busies himself in *testing* the amount of labor which they have brought to bear on the preparation of their lessons, and the accuracy of its results; in removing their difficulties; in calling attention to general principles; and in adding to their stock of knowledge, by supplying from his own resources what the text-books in use may not contain.

4. Besides the instruction just mentioned, the pupil teachers have a distinct course of lessons on "Method;" and another course, having for its object the supplying of information connected with the regular lessons of the school, as well as the mode of communicating it.

Twice a week also they give what are called "criticism lessons," where each pupil teacher, in turn, gives a collective lesson, or teaches a draft of children in the hearing of his fellow-teachers, and is afterward subjected to friendly criticism and correction. In addition to this, a sketch of every collective lesson given in the school by the pupil teachers is previously prepared, and submitted to the inspection and criticism of the superintendent.

5. For the purpose of familiarizing them with all the operations and lessons of the school, and enabling them to teach both the younger and elder children in it, they change their sections every six months. By this means they superintend every section of the school during the period of their apprenticeship.

6. It has been mentioned that the elder pupil teachers take their turn in superintending the school: the duties are—

(*a*) To see that the school bell is rung five minutes before each school time.

(*b*.) To preserve order while the children are taking their places, and during the whole of the school exercises.

(*c*) To report if any of the pupil teachers are not at their posts at the appointed time, or if they leave them during the school exercises.

(*d.*) To conduct the school changes as quickly as possible, and in a quiet and orderly manner.

(*e.*) To report if the furniture and apparatus in use in the sections are not put away into their proper place when done with, agreeably to the school motto—"a place for every thing, and every thing in its place."

(*f.*) To superintend the sweeping of the school-room after the children are dismissed, and to prevent disorder out of school hours, either in the school-room or play-ground.

Section 2.—Monitors.

7. Schools established on the plan of the British and Foreign School Society were formerly distinguished by their adoption of a plan, sometimes denominated the *mutual*, and sometimes the *monitorial*, system.

The collective method of instruction has long been engrafted on this system; and for some years pupil teachers, apprenticed by the government, have assisted in the central school, as in many others, in giving enlarged development to the education afforded. In other schools elder boys are retained by the committees for a year or two with a small stipend, and supply, in some measure, the places of those more regularly apprenticed.

Still the use of monitors is not abandoned. When *combined* with collective teaching by the master and pupil teachers, and with superintendence and training by the same agency, it may be made very valuable. To show this, it is only necessary to point out the insuperable difficulties with which the teacher of a large school is beset when first entering on his office, and then to see how well he may overcome the whole by a *judicious use* of monitors.

8. In the first place, to secure perfect quietness and attention in such circumstances, before any address is made to the minds of the scholars, the eyes and voice of a single person, even after long practice, are scarcely sufficient. But granting that a single teacher *may* have the whole of his scholars brought into prompt compliance with distinctly expressed orders given to the whole; yet when, in addition to the silence and attention of a minute or two, that of an hour is required, nothing but the faculty of keeping every mind among them interested in the subject on which he is addressing them, could command attention, or restrain noise.

But it is impossible for a teacher to address a large number of children of different ages, and different degrees of acquirement, so as to be intelligible to all, interesting to all, and instructive to all, at the same time. The lessons given to the oldest, including the language in which the ideas are clothed, and the ideas themselves, would exceed the comprehension of the younger children; and no sooner should he turn to address himself to these, than the others would perceive he was dwelling on matters with which they were quite familiar, and was using language too childish to merit their attention.

By a careful arrangement, however, of the school into sections and drafts, adjusted according to the relative acquirements of the scholars, and by appointing over each a pupil teacher or elder boy, assisted by monitors chosen from their own number, the master at once secures closer inspection, and makes it possible for all to be addressed at the same time on the subjects, and in the manner and language best adapted to the actual progress of each.

9. So far a manifest advantage is secured. But it may be objected that monitors, being but children, must, as teachers, be very unequal to adults; and

moreover, that while thus engaged in giving instruction to others, they must be losing ground themselves. Both objections are very natural, but admit of the most satisfactory refutation. In the first place, children, while thus acting the part of subordinate teachers, feel a sense of the responsibility and of the comparative importance assigned to them, quite sufficient to make them anxious to perform their parts well, and readily to adopt the recommendations, and follow the injunctions, given by the head-master. He can also suspend, remove, or change his monitors, as he may think proper, without doing them that personal injury, or provoking that personal resentment, which would probably result from the exercise of a like freedom toward older and less dependent assistants.

Besides which, children are, in many respects, the most efficient instructors of companions less advanced than themselves. The lessons they teach, even the very simplest, and on that account to adults the most uninteresting, having been learnt by themselves but a short time before, and thereby still retaining somewhat of the interest of novelty, are communicated to others with more zest than adults can possibly feel.

For the same reason, monitors can sympathize far more readily with the difficulties of their pupils, having but just emerged from those difficulties themselves; and in their explanations, all their ideas and expressions are not only more directly addressed to the precise perplexity which has made explanation necessary, but are those, also, of persons of the same rank and habits, and of nearly the same age with the children to whom they are addressed. *In some respects*, therefore, monitors are well fitted to be the agents in communicating instruction; and *in some cases* it is obvious that they are not merely useful, but, with the scanty funds allotted to public schools, absolutely necessary.

10. To the other objection, that monitors, while acting in that capacity, must, as scholars, be either stationary or retrograde, it may be answered, first, that they are so engaged only during a part of the school time. Accordingly, while the latter are engaged in other exercises, and superintended by the pupil teachers, the former may be collected as a class by themselves, receiving from the teacher instructions which they of the whole school are best prepared to meet, because, in respect of knowledge, they most nearly approach him. In the second place, while teaching others what they themselves best know, they are familiarizing their minds more and more with these past acquisitions; and in the discharge of the trust committed to them are learning the practice of many excellent virtues. The system hence embraces a wider field, both for the observation and the exercise of moral practice, and for the improvement of the intellectual faculties.

But the probability that monitors will derive any positive moral improvement from the discharge of their duties must, of course, very much depend on the manner in which the head-master exercises his general superintendence. If, in consequence of the Divine blessing attending his wisdom and care, these youths should acquire some practice in the virtues of fidelity to their trust, and of patience, good temper, and strict impartiality toward their inferiors, may we not indulge the hope that many of them will be enabled to continue the exercise of these valuable qualities throughout their future lives?

11. The selection and training of these agents is, therefore, a most important branch of the teacher's duties, requiring the exercise of all the skill, judgment, and information he possesses. A master should be constantly looking out for such boys as may, by means of his training, become qualified for monitors. He

should endeavor to discover what particular offices in the school they are most suited to fill, keep a memorandum of their names, and note the duties which he conceives they may be competent to discharge. He then, aided by his pupil teachers, should instruct them in all their personal and relative duties, insist on subordination to their superiors, explain to them the necessity of such subordination, and impress the importance of the charge they have undertaken. He should encourage kindness and good-will toward the boys whom they are appointed to direct, and he should show them the necessity of the strictest impartiality in the discharge of their several duties. Much time should be also devoted to their instruction, particularly in the art of questioning.

12. Two sets of monitors are needed in schools where this agency *alone* is secured, in order that one set may be engaged in teaching, while those composing the other are either at work as pupils in their respective stations, or being trained for the performance of their monitorial duties. Half an hour every day should be set apart for the latter purpose. It is recommended that this half hour should be taken at a different time each day of the week, so that the master may never have his attention drawn off from the working of the school during the same exercise more than once in each week.

13. In selecting these agents the master should have respect not only to general intelligence, but to cleanliness of person, propriety of conduct, and good moral habits. He should also endeavor, by every means in his power, to secure their attachment to himself, so that their service may be one of affection, and not of constraint or fear. When a sufficient number has been chosen, the master should proceed to train them—

First. In the maintenance of order in their drafts, and in the exercise of kindness and impartiality toward their children.

Second. In the methods of teaching the subjects in which they take a part.

14. An important inquiry, often made, is, *How* should they be trained? The following plans, amongst others, may be adopted:—

(*a.*) The master should sometimes call them together, explain their duties and responsibilities, and notice, in a kind and friendly manner, whatever may have occurred during the performance of their duties; administering, at the same time, either praise or censure, as the cases may require.

(*b.*) He should take classes before them in different subjects as a model for their imitation, directing their attention to the points which he wishes most particularly to notice.

(*c.*) He should give them short lessons or lectures on the rules for preserving order, and for the right use of the methods of explanation, interrogation, and ellipsis. It is a useful variation of this exercise to get the monitors to write short essays on these subjects, the master collecting them afterward, and pointing out errors or omissions to the assembled class.

(*d.*) He may form the monitors into a class, and having selected a lesson, require the monitor who has to teach that particular lesson to give it to the moniters just as he would teach it to his own draft. As the lesson proceeds, the master may occasionally stop the teaching, and say to the rest, "Is that what you would have said?" "How would you have brought out that fact without telling it?" &c.*

* The point the teacher should aim at is not merely that of supplying information but, having the lesson given just as he wishes it to be taught to the boys. By this repeated training

(*e.*) Let one of the monitors take a draft of children on any lesson he will *afterwards* have to teach, the rest of the monitors being provided with paper or slates, on which they should write criticisms on the manner of giving the lesson. After the lesson is over, and the draft sent away, these criticisms should be read over by those who have written them, the master taking care to have merits noticed as well as defects, and adding such observations as may appear necessary.

(*f.*) Assemble the monitors in class, and let them mutually question each other on the rules for preserving order, and on methods of teaching, or on a lesson appointed for this exercise some few days previously.

(*g.*) Let them take home the lessons they are to teach in their drafts the next day, and write the explanations and questions on them which they intend to use while teaching, before the lesson is given; and let these preparations be examined and criticised by the master in presence of the assembled monitors. This and several of the preceding methods are valuable as exercises on spelling and composition.

(*h.*) The master should frequently listen to the monitors while actually teaching in their drafts, making entries in a book kept for that purpose. These notes should be read and made the subject of comment at the next meeting of the monitors' class. Where pupil teachers are engaged in addition to monitors, one of these youths should always be present with the master at the training lessons, and may soon be made very useful in assisting to conduct them.

15. Besides these *teaching monitors*, the most careful pupil in each section should be made *section monitor;* he should be chosen and directed by the pupil teacher, and his duties would be to take care of the books, pens, and maps, belonging to his portion of the school, and to give out and collect slates, pens, and books.

16. To get these various duties performed cheerfully, *rewards* must sometimes be given. The instruments chiefly employed for this purpose are reward tickets of nominal value, which are given to deserving boys as a token of their good conduct, and withdrawn whenever it is requisite to punish. The number granted for good, or withdrawn for improper conduct, is necessarily discretional.

The general tendency of reward tickets, when judiciously distributed, is to prevent or correct faults, which would otherwise require corporal punishment or dismission. They accomplish, however, a much more important end, when they excite, as they frequently do, the coöperation of the parents. The acquired ticket is equal to a letter of approbation from the teacher to the parent, and calls forth praise; while, on the other hand, their diminution in number, or the absence of any increase, excites inquiry.

These tickets should be called in at stated periods; the name, class, amount, entered in a book; and a choice of prizes, consisting of articles combining utility with juvenile interest, should be purchased, and each one, in turn allowed to select to the amount of tickets he has gained.

17. Where rewards are given to the monitors *as such*, they should be determined by the proficiency which his draft or class makes. It is not desirable to give the *same* amount of reward to each monitor, but let the better have more

---

the monitors will be constantly improving; their positive excellence depending, however upon the standard the teacher exhibits in his own teaching, and upon the skill, and industry, and research he brings to bear in the process. He must bear in mind that on his success in this particular depends very much of the efficiency of his school.

than the average amount, and the worse less. Thus, if the average payment of the reading draft monitors be 2*d.* a week, some might receive for any one week 3*d.*, and some only 1*d.* The *standard* in reference to the READING should be, the ability to read the assigned portion off readily, to spell and explain all the words occurring in it, and to have a good knowledge of the subject, independent of the book or tabular lessons. In ARITHMETIC, they should readily work questions given under the rule, give a familiar explanation of the principles involved, and very readily read off every number operated on. In WRITING, advance must be determined not merely by excellence of the characters written, but also by the neatness and cleanliness of the book, viz., freedom from blots and mistakes, and with the corners of the book not turned down. This clean and neat writing should be much insisted on by the teacher.

18. These rewards, however, are only the direct means of encouragement. Those of a more indirect character are often, in a good teacher's hands, vastly more influential. Some of the chief of these indirect means may be mentioned—

(*a.*) The monitors should be a kind of upper class standing between the master and the scholars, and having constant communication with both. The master should consult with them on his various plans; and, as long as they continue in office, treat them with great confidence and kindness.

(*b.*) He should avail himself of opportunities to visit objects of interest, accompanied by his monitors. In London, the Zoölogical Gardens or Museum; and in the country, a beautiful view, a ruin, or any other object of local interest, might be taken, or an excursion for the purposes of natural history. He might also sometimes join in their sports with good effect.

(*c.*) The monitors, should, *as such*, have free access to the school library. The desirableness of such a library, consisting of well-selected books, is obvious; it provides a fund of amusement as well as of instruction for the children, interests their parents, and tends to keep the pupils from evil influences in the streets.

III. METHODS OF INSTRUCTION.

Section 1.—*General Principles.*

1. The first great and leading principle of all sound education is that it is a teacher's duty to pay more regard to *the formation of the character* of his scholars, than to their success in any or in all the branches of learning professedly taught. With a view to enlighten their judgment, and to bring the munder the influence of right impressions with respect to moral good and evil, it is considered to be of the utmost importance that they should, from the first, be taught to distinguish between matters of permanent and immutable obligation, and mere comparative degrees of attention and diligence. Every manifest infraction of the Divine law ought, therefore, to be treated in a very different manner from slowness in the common school exercises, or even from the petty misdemeanors of unthinking and volatile minds. On occasions of the former kind, teachers are expected to show that visible concern and sorrow which such offences will undoubtedly excite in every virtuous mind; and, if possible, to bring the offender, by earnest remonstrances, to a conviction of his sin.

2. In allowing children to enliven their school exercises by giving and taking places, there seems to be nothing inconsistent with christian morals; yet were the same practice admitted in matters of moral merit or blame, dangerous con-

sequences might ensue. This, and every similar practice, ought, therefore, to be avoided, and great care should, on the other hand, be taken that no child be tempted or encouraged to indulge in feelings of self-satisfaction on the occasion of another's fault.

3. *Deference to parental authority*, united with regard to parental assistance, is another important principle not to be lost sight of. Parents are the natural guardians of their children; and, however they may occasionally be sunk in ignorance and vice, they seldom entirely lose the sense of their responsibility, or become altogether incapable of exercising authority to some good purpose; so that, in a great majority of instances, the most beneficial results may be derived from a clear acknowledgment of their claims, and a sedulous courting of their assistance. The British system respects this natural and important principle in various ways. While it discourages all neglect of Divine worship, it leaves to the parents to direct in what manner, and at whose hands, their children shall on that day receive religious instruction. Teachers are recommended to maintain a constant communication with parents, respecting the habits and principles of the scholars; by which means they may greatly improve the influence of parental authority, and also strengthen both that authority and their own; as their pupils will thus perceive that there is a cordial coöperation between their natural guardians at home, and the authorities they are taught to respect in school. The prescribing of home-tasks presents another mode by which parental interest may be excited, and parental assistance engaged.

4. *Respect for the teacher*, and implicit obedience to his commands, are principles which should be assiduously cultivated; but it must be the respect of dutiful affection, not that proceeding from slavish submission. Higher motives will, doubtless, grow up, as the scholars become better acquainted with a good teacher's character, and more capable of appreciating qualities that command respect; but, even before they have all advanced thus far, habits of prompt obedience must be universally established. With children who are restless, volatile, and unused to restraint, mechanical motions of the body, as they are at once easily understood, and readily performed, afford the best means of inculcating these habits; and no teacher ought to rest satisfied until he has brought every child to sit, stand, speak, or be silent, on the instant of the command being given. Until this point be gained, time is daily lost, not only to the careless and disobedient, but to the whole school; and when habits of partial obedience have once been tolerated, the difficulties to be overcome are greatly increased. If, on the other hand, teachers will respect their own authority, by never giving commands which they do not expect to be immediately obeyed, nothing will be found more easy than to make obedience the general and settled habit of the school.

5. But it is not by means of respect for authority, nor by habits of obedience, alone, that British schools propose to accomplish their objects. There are, indeed, many exercises which mere authority may enforce; but, under such a course of discipline, intellectual improvement would be slow, and the results on the temper and character would be worse than doubtful. Happily, no sooner is this, the first step as it were, of the teacher's progress past, than abundant resources are presented for securing a course of occupation, at once pleasant and profitable, which it is the province of system to methodize, and regulate to the best advantage. To a healthy child, the activity of the mind is not less natural than that of the body. As by free and voluntary movements the limbs and

muscles are strengthened and invigorated, not only without pain, but with positive delight, so it is with respect to the mind. But if we would excite free and pleasant mental exertions, the mind, in its first efforts, must be invited to no more exertion than is suited to its infant capacities, and its limited knowledge. Commencing thus, its powers will be found at every step to acquire new force and elasticity, to be capable of greater and greater attempts, and of longer attention to one subject; and these advancing energies it must be the object of the teacher so to discipline and inform, that in their progressive development they may come more and more under the permanent influence of right principles, and be applied to those objects only which are innocent and useful.

6. Again, the mere acquisition of knowledge is made subservient to the development of the mental and moral powers. Education is not considered to mean the *putting in* of so much information, but the *bringing out* of mental activity; exercise being the law of mental as well as of physical growth. In the light of this principle ideas are given before words, things before the signs which express them, the concrete before the abstract, reasons as the foundation of rules. The things which are familiar to the children are made the starting-point from which the teacher guides his pupils to wider views and more enlarged acquirements, leading them along by slow and gradual steps, and making sure of one advance before attempting the next.

7. Another principle continually kept in mind is to suit subjects of study, and the manner of treating them, to the progressive development of the mental faculties. Thus the exercises and lessons of the younger pupils are intended chiefly to exercise their *perceptive* faculties, while, as they advance in age and mental power, reason, judgment, and memory are more particularly exercised. In every stage, however, the knowledge which is likely to be useful to them after leaving school is made the *instrument* of their moral and mental training.

8. Proceeding on these principles, in *reading* the scholar is taught from the first to associate meaning with the symbols he is learning; and this meaning is so explained and illustrated as to make even these first efforts interesting as well as doubly instructive. A child likes to tell what it knows about the simple objects with which it is most conversant. The words which are used to express objects are first presented to him, and he is taught by familiar questions to associate with each its appropriate meaning, and its proper sound.

9. From this time forward every lesson proceeds on the same principle; the words, phrases, and sentences brought before the scholar's eye, being such only as can add to his information, or interest his feelings and his conscience; all others are excluded as useless and repulsive. Thus not only do those exercises interest the attention which would otherwise fatigue and annoy it; but the invaluable habit of looking for a meaning in every word and sentence read becomes fixed and permanent.

Section 2.—Preparatory Section.

10. The first section of the lower school is composed of children from four years of age. As these generally enter the school unable even to read the alphabet, and with minds altogether untrained, they are put through a course of instruction more elementary than that generally given in British schools, but agreeing with it in principle. The design of this course is to fit them for entering upon the more advanced and systematic exercises of the school, not only by giving them the necessary preliminary information, but by training them to

exercise their powers of observation and reflection on the familiar objects by which they are surrounded.

11. With this view, their food, clothing, and playthings—the common earth-stones and minerals—the materials in daily use in the school-room, as well as the bricks, mortar, and wood used in its construction—the animals and vegetables which they see most frequently, and are likely for that reason to think about least—all these are laid under contribution, in order to develop the faculties with which their Creator has endowed them; to make them useful, intelligent, and kind in their intercourse with others; and to implant habits of thoughtful reverence toward Him for whose glory all things were made. The most remarkable events recorded in the Holy Scriptures are also daily brought before them in the gallery in such a manner as to educate both their conscience and their intellect, and to promote good moral habits amongst them. The important influence which may be thus exercised upon their home associations can scarcely be overrated; the innocent prattle of the school-boy may by these means frequently become the gentle instrument of correction to the ignorance and vice of the parent.

12. The *alphabet* is introduced to this section by means of collective lessons. When the children are seated in the gallery, the teacher shows some familiar object having a short name. He first puts a few questions on the object itself. The name is then written on the school slate, and analyzed into its component *letters;* the sounds of these are given, and then their names. The sound of the second and third letters put together is then asked for; and other letters are placed before them, forming other simple and well-known words, on which the children are also questioned.

When eight or ten letters are thus learned, the teacher prints them in a line on the large slate, at the dictation of the children. He then points to them at random, getting the children to name and describe each, and to compare it with others: first having the hands up of those who wish to answer, and then pointing to the one whom *he* wishes to speak.

It is a judicious plan to let several try to describe each letter, as by this means not only are their little minds set to work in attempting to express their thoughts in suitable language, but several ways of describing the same thing will also probably be brought out. A little physical exercise may then be allowed, a verse or two of a simple school piece sung, and the children be led to their reading stations.

13. The children are now employed in their drafts in picking out the letters and words just learnt in the gallery, from the Daily Lesson Book, No. I., in broad sheets; while the monitor or pupil teacher leads one and another of the pupils to the blackboard or slate provided at each draft station to print the letter or word which he names. He also questions on the information already given respecting the object exhibited at the commencement of the gallery lesson, and on the other words formed during the progress of that lesson.

14. The next change finds these children in the writing desks, with slates on the desks before them, and pencils, fixed in holders, in their hands. The teacher now prints on the blackboard one of the letters learnt, and questions on the direction and comparative length of the lines composing it; bringing out the ideas straight, curved, vertical, horizontal, oblique, or parallel. He then pursues the same course with the rest of the letters which form the subject of the lesson, the children imitating them on their slates, first from the teacher's copy,

and afterward from dictation. The alphabet is thus quickly and easily learnt, while at the same time the minds of the children are developed, and much useful information imparted respecting words and things.

15. In the same familiar and conversational style courses of lessons are given, on the first principles of language, number, and form; on objects, animals, vegetables, and colors, accompanied by practice in reading and spelling, from the Daily Lesson Book, No. I., and a familiar course of lessons on the principles of writing.

16. Lessons on the most remarkable events of Scripture alternate with those just mentioned, and the aid of Scripture prints is called in, to help the perceptions of the children, and to assist in sustaining attention. The following is a brief sketch of the manner in which such a lesson is conducted. Suppose the subject to be, The Children of Israel crossing the Red Sea.

(*a.*) The teacher hangs up the print in front of the gallery, and pointing to the various figures depicted on it, asks in turn who they are—what they are doing—and why there? thus bringing out the chief points of the story in a simple and graphic manner.

(*b.*) He reads the narrative from Exodus, chap. xiv., putting questions as to the meaning of the words and phrases as he proceeds.

(*c.*) He closes the book, and goes over the story again, mingling questions, ellipses, and simple narration, thus endeavoring to lead the children to realize all the incidents of the scene, and placing them as far as possible in the position of spectators.

(*d.*) If the lesson has been properly given, the children will be able to state the lessons to be drawn from it—namely, that the Lord will help his people in trouble; and the sin and folly of striving against God. The teacher then seeks to apply these lessons to the daily life of the children, basing a few short and simple remarks on facts which have occurred in the actual school or home experience of those before him.

Having thus briefly indicated the methods pursued with the very youngest children, we proceed to notice the subjects taught and the methods employed with the rest of the school.

Section 3.—*Collective Teaching.*

17. A collective lesson differs very materially from a lecture. In the latter the children are passive listeners, in the former they are lively actors. By means of questions and occasional ellipses, their minds are kept continually at work; and the teacher, taking those in the class whose mental powers are least developed as his standard of simplicity, acts and speaks before the gallery as a fellow-inquirer after truth, while he leads them imperceptibly on in the path he had previously marked out.

18. As the lesson proceeds, both the analytical and synthetical processes of investigation are brought into use. Suppose a common earthenware cup to be the subject of the lesson. The object is held up before the section seated in the gallery, and they are asked to name the parts—as the inside, outside, handle, rim, or bottom. Should any hesitation occur, the teacher does not *tell* them what he is seeking for, but, passing his finger round the part in question, he asks, "What is this?" The names of the several *parts* are then written on the blackboard. The *qualities* are next asked for: here the cup is passed round among the children, and they are told to look at it, feel it, or smell it, thus em-

ploying their several senses in turn. Other properties are suggested by com paring this cup with other cups; finally, those qualities which render it fit for the uses to which it is put are elicited; and the whole is successively written on the blackboard.

19. The teacher next asks the *form* of the cup? how it became so formed? of what it is made? and how it happens that a substance so *hard* could be brought to such a form? He thus brings out from the children the fact that it is made of clay, and that when the cup was made the clay was *soft*, and not hard as they now see it. Having, by this mode of investigation, arrived at the *beginning* of the process by which the cup was made, he shows a piece of soft clay, of the kind used for the cup, and gets the children to describe what they *think* was done *first*, and what *next*, in the manufacture of the object before them; always correcting their errors by describing the *actual* steps in the manufacture—exhibiting specimens of pottery illustrative of the different stages—and by means of a small model of a potter's lathe, exemplifying the process. When the lesson is given to the younger children a description of the parts and qualities occupies the greater portion of the time; but with the elder pupils these are quickly brought out, and the manufacturing processes are more particularly dwelt upon.

20. The great advantage of collective teaching is, that it brings the trained mind of the teacher into direct and immediate communication with the comparatively untrained and uninformed minds of his pupils. Hence, for the development of the powers of the mind, for influencing the affections and directing the understanding to right views of moral and spiritual truth, for checking evil habits and encouraging good ones, the collective lesson, in the hands of a well-trained, earnest-minded, and *christian* teacher, is a powerful instrument for good.

21. In order to give a collective lesson well, the teacher must not only be well acquainted with the subject he has in hand, but must have the *matter* arranged in a logical and well-considered order. No collective lesson should be given until a sketch of it has been carefully prepared by the teacher for his own private use. This sketch should show the principal ideas intended to be dwelt upon during the lesson, numbered and arranged in their logical order, precisely as they are intended to be given. Under these "heads," the *manner* of bringing out each idea should be indicated; the illustrations intended to be used written down, and some of the principal questions recorded. The sketch should thus exhibit both the *matter* and the *manner* of the lesson, and should realize to the reader, as nearly as possible, the lesson itself. At the end of the sketch the teacher should note down what objects or diagrams will be wanted, and have them ready before commencing his teaching.

22. The *dangers* of this method of instruction are, however, many; and mischief, as the result, is by no means uncommon. The two principal dangers are mentioned, that they may be guarded against.

First. Collective teaching is not unfrequently quite *ineffective*, owing to the teacher's being contented with merely talking for a certain time. It is very easy to talk prettily to boys for half an hour, even in such a way as to interest them; and yet, owing to want of attention to some of the points about to be mentioned, no permanent result may remain. The children have been pleased, but not instructed.

Secondly. It is sometimes efficient to only *a portion* of the boys. If the "gallery" contain boys of very different attainments, when the language and and general cast of teaching is fitted for the more advanced, it is too difficult for the others; and on the other hand, when descending to the capacity of the younger, the lesson appears frivolous to the older boys.

23. The following, then, are some of the chief points to be attended to:—

(*a.*) Children receiving a collective lesson at the same time should be of about the *same degree of mental standing.*

(*b.*) The teacher should be supplied with *specimens*, *models*, or *diagrams*, illustrative of his subject. He should also, from time to time, sketch out such objects, or portions of objects, as he may find, during the lesson, require more illustration than he has provided. This, of course, implies that the teacher is, to some extent, a draughtsman. There should be large maps, too, in the room or division in which these lessons are given.

(*c.*) A large *blackboard* should be placed before the gallery, for purposes of illustration, and also to receive the main headings of the lessons; so that when the teacher has finished his lesson, he may occasionally form the gallery into drafts, and by means of his pupil teachers institute a searching individual examination of all who have heard it. This use of the blackboard is particularly valuable in the training of monitors. Its advantages are numerous. It requires the teacher to be master of his subject, and methodical in his arrangement of it; and thus, by presenting the whole in the *natural association* of its various parts, tends to secure the retention of what is taught. It teaches spelling too,* and the reading of written characters.

(*d.*) Attention is best secured, particularly with the younger pupils, by the teacher's making a pause, and then leaving some of the words to be supplied by the pupils. Thus:—

Teacher.—The feet of the camel are——
Pupils.—Broad.
Teacher.—And——
Pupils.—Spongy.
Teacher.—And——
Pupils.—Spreading.
Teacher.—And therefore the camel is fit for traveling on——
Pupils.—Sands.
Teacher.—It is used in——
Pupils.—Africa.
Teacher.—And——
Pupils.—Arabia.
Teacher.—And——
Pupils.—Persia.
Teacher.—And——
Pupils.—India.
Teacher.—Many of them traveling together are called a——
Pupils.—Caravan.

The teacher must, however, take care that no ellipsis is left for the pupils to supply with words or facts they can not be expected to know. Thus, "The olive tree lives——." If he find that no pupil is acquainted with the fact wanted, he should tell it himself, rather than allow the mischievous habit of

* As the lesson proceeds, the teacher should require the pupils to spell the principal words occurring. The spelling of words as they are actually found in sentences, whether oral or written, is by far the most effective mode of teaching it.

guessing. After he has told them, he should again make the ellipsis, which would of course be supplied by the pupils.

Repeating ellipses to this extent, however, and so closely following each other, are not admissible in practice, except for the purpose of recapitulation; the better plan is to have many questions and few ellipses.

(*e.*) There should be much *individual questioning.* This is one of the ways in which the real efficiency of a lesson can be tested. The eye of the teacher should pass rapidly over the gallery, and wherever he detects inattention, a question to the individual should be put, on something that had just been taught. This recapitulatory individual questioning should follow every class of facts stated.*

(*f.*) A habit of *induction* should be cultivated. Thus, when the teacher has said that the elephant has a very large head, and two very heavy tusks, he should lead the pupils to *tell him,* though they may not before have been aware of the fact, that the neck must be short, and the cartilage and muscles very strong. So, when he has told them of the great quantity of vegetable food the animal eats, he might say "Do you think it is found, then, in hot or cold countries?" If not answered, he would say, "Where do grass, and herbs, and trees grow most abundantly?"

Pupils.—In hot countries.

Teacher.—Then, as the elephant eats so much of this kind of food, in which do you think he is found?

Pupils.—In the hot countries.

Teacher.—Why?

Pupils.—Because most of his food grows there.

(*g.*) The whole should be conducted with great *animation.* The want of this shows itself by a very slow enunciation of words, by long pauses between sentences, and by a want of ease in the carriage of the body. Not unfrequently, also, teachers are too wordy; every word that does not tend to make the thought clearer makes it more obscure.

(*h.*) *Simplicity* is indispensable. The absence of this quality shows itself sometimes in the use of language and illustrations that the pupils can not comprehend; and sometimes in assuming that their knowledge is greater than it is. The constant use of individual questioning will enable the teacher to discover when he is thus shooting over the pupils' heads.

(*i.*) The *time* of the lesson must not be prolonged, after the children are evidently wearied out. With a judicious teacher, even the younger may be interested for half an hour, and the elder for a longer time.

24. The notes on the blackboard may either be written as the lesson goes on, or (which is preferable,) the teacher may bring out all the points under one head first, and then put down the notes on the board while recapitulating *that part* of the lesson; sometimes writing from the dictation of the pupils; and then, of course, correcting their errors, both of fact and language. At the end of the lesson there should be a general recapitulation of the whole from the blackboard.

If the lesson were the elephant, the blackboard should present an appearance at its close somewhat similar to that exhibited in the specimen lesson following. The words in italics would on the blackboard be underlined; those in capitals be doubly underlined.

* If the teacher find that the pupils to any considerable extent are unable to answer these recapitulatory questions, he may assume that his teaching is bad. No lesson is well given by a teacher which is not fully received by those taught.

Specimen of Notes for a Collective Lesson.—The Elephant.

1. Description.—*Thick-skinned. Hight*, 7 to 12 feet; *weight*, 5,000 to 6,000 lbs.=40 men. *Head*, large, hollow in front. *Tusks*, 2, ivory and enamel; 5 to 6 feet; 100 to 150 lbs. *Teeth*, $\frac{2\,2}{2\,2}$ 8 molars—structure: mode of growth, renewed. *Trunk*, 6 to 8 feet long; finger, thumb, hand—*uses*, obtain food, convey to mouth, lift objects. *Neck*, short, thick muscles, and pax wax very thick.

2. Kinds.—*Asiatic*—*head* long, front somewhat concave—4 *hoofs* on hind feet—*ears* small. *African*—*head* rounder—3 *hoofs* hind legs—*ears* larger 3½ feet × 2½—*use*, carry manure—not now tamed.

3. Where found.—*Asiatic*—Hindostan, Burmah, Ceylon, and South of Asia generally. *African*—Africa, South of Senegal.

4. Habits.—*Social*, 3,000—*herbivorous*—2 or 3 cwts., browse soft roots—(sweetmeats, sugar-canes)—*gentle*—*fond of bathing*—sprinkle dust over himself (flies)—*cautious* in going over new ground or bridge—*sagacious*.

Uses.—Food (African)—ivory—carrying and drawing, man on neck—goad—war—hunting.

It is better to write on the blackboard only the words indicating the principal ideas, leaving the rest to be supplied by the children from memory during recapitulation.

Section 4.—Class Teaching—Reading.

25. When the children have been divided into sections and drafts, according to the principles already stated (*ante* § § 2 and 3,) the next business is to assign to each section and draft a *station* in the school-room, and *a definite portion* of the reading lessons. This section and these drafts will thus represent a particular stage of progress. All the reading lessons will, in this way, be divided among the successive drafts, so that a boy commencing with the lowest draft, and passing the proper time at each draft station, will have read and been questioned on every lesson contained in the books, or exhibited on the lesson boards.

26. Periodical examinations should be made of the progress of the children in this as in every other subject; each child taking his place in the class *at the commencement* of each exercise, according to the position obtained by him at these examinations, which should take place every fortnight. Promotions should be made as vacancies occur in the next higher draft or section.

27. Having determined on the portion for each section and draft, and put every section under the superintendence of a pupil teacher or elder monitor, the next object of the master is to select agents (monitors) to assist in teaching. His efforts must be zealously directed to the training of these monitors. He must secure their ability to spell, read, and explain the meaning of every word of the lesson; they must be much exercised in questioning on it, and be prepared with numerous and pertinent illustrations and applications. *No monitor should be allowed to superintend a lesson till the master has taught the whole of it minutely to him and exercised him in the mode of giving it.* This is not very difficult, because the whole number of lessons being divided among the whole number of draft monitors, only a small number of lessons are required to be given by any one monitor; and the required information, being thus defined and limited, is easily supplied. When, also, it is recollected that the monitors do not pass forward with the boys, but remain to teach the same lessons to the succeeding occupiers of the stations, it is evident that a master of ordinary diligence may make, and permanently secure, a very capable set of monitors.

28. The lessons used for the lower sections are partly on boards, and partly in books; the sections above these read entirely from books. The board or tabular lessons consist of the lessons of Daily Lesson Book, No. I., in sheets. The books consist of a set of four; the first book, called Daily Lesson Book, No. I., contains the alphabet and lessons of one syllable, in prose and rhyme; the second, or Daily Lesson Book, No. II., is a spelling book, with reading lessons not exceeding three syllables; the Sequel to Lesson Book, No. II., consists of easy reading lessons, on man, his dwellings, and wants, interspersed with poetry and interesting tales; the third, or Daily Lesson Book, No. III., consists of lessons on very varied subjects, in poetry and prose, chiefly of a moral and religious character; the fourth, or Daily Lesson Book, No. IV., has a more scientific character, including series of lessons on general history, physics, and natural history: the whole having copious notes, hints for monitors and teachers, roots of words, and tabular facts.

This course of reading is *in addition* to the daily reading of the Bible and the volume of Scripture Extracts.

29. After the course of lessons on the alphabet and easy words of two and three syllables given to the youngest section, the pupils commence at page 16 of the first lesson book. The monitor having directed the attention of his draft to the first word, tells those who know it to raise their right hands, and then points to one of them, who says, "*S-double e,—see;*" he then questions on the meaning of the word, and on the use of sight. The succeeding words are treated in the same manner. The explanation of the words relieves the mere literal lesson. As the lesson approaches its termination, the monitor leads them to define the words *dew, grass, rain,* and *land,* as shown at the foot of the page; exercises them in the application of the words *wet* and *cool;* and terminates with the *lesson*—"*Every thing has its use.*"

30. As the words in columns at the top of the page occur in the reading lesson, the monitor should not allow the reading to begin till the boys can tell these words without spelling them. In the first instance all the words would be gone through thus—*s-double e—see, t-h-e—the.* But before reading, the boys should be able to mention them at sight; as, *see, the, dew.*

31. After the pupils have *read* through the first lesson book, a more systematic course of treatment, in connection with the lessons thus read, is adopted. This consists of—

(*a.*) *Questions before reading.* The teacher announces the subject of the lesson, and by a few searching questions ascertains what the children already know about it, endeavoring at the same time to excite a curiosity to know more. By this exercise he is able to adapt his teaching to the requirements of the class, besides showing them how much they have yet to learn in connection with this lesson.

(*b.*) *Questions, explanations, and illustrations, during reading.* The children, having opened their books at the page indicated by the teacher, commence reading. Each boy is required to read so as to be heard by all in the class. Considerable attention is paid to the slow, distinct, and clear utterance of every word, to pronunciation, inflection, and emphasis, the teacher himself frequently reading as a model, and, where necessary, requiring the class to read after him simultaneously, with slow and distinct enunciation. If any correction is required after a pupil has finished reading the passage appointed to him, the rest of the boys are encouraged to raise their hands, and the teacher singles out one, or several in turn, to make the correction.

At the end of each sentence, or paragraph, the meaning of the words and phrases composing it are questioned upon, copiously illustrated, and pictured out before the class; the teacher making use, for this purpose, of the blackboard, objects, diagrams, and simple explanations. He should also require one or more of the pupils to give the sense of the passage in his own words, before proceeding to the next portion of the lesson. This second exercise is considered by far the most important part of the reading lesson.

(c.) *Analysis of the lesson after the books are closed.* In this course the lesson is gone over again sentence by sentence, and completely analyzed and illustrated. For this purpose the notes under the head "*subject*," at the foot of each page in Lesson Book, No. III., are very useful. Information immediately connected with the matter in the lesson, whether relating to natural history (in which questions of classification and habits occur,) or geographical terms requiring reference to a map, is brought out from the class or supplied by the teacher, and the lessons flowing directly from the subject are deduced.

32. The lessons of the Daily Lesson Books, Nos. III. and IV., being adapted to more advanced boys, require a full investigation of the etymology of the words. For this purpose they are provided with notes of a much more complete kind than those which precede them.

The fourth book is used both as a general reading book in the most advanced classes, and as a *text* book for the particular subjects into which it is divided.

Section 5.—Class Teaching—Interrogation.

33. The mode of conducting interrogative exercises may be best shown by a specimen; one, therefore, is given on a paragraph taken from the lesson book.

Specimen Lesson on Interrogation.—Daily Lesson Book, No. IV., pp. 76, 77.

Ruminating Animals.—Cud-chewing or ruminating animals form the *eighth* order. These, with the exception of the camel, have no cutting teeth in the upper jaw, but their place is supplied with a hard pad. In the lower jaw there are eight cutters; the tearers, in general, are absent, so that there is a vacant space between the cutters and grinders. The latter are very broad, and are kept rough and fit for grinding the vegetable food on which these animals live, by the enamel being disposed in crescent-shaped ridges.

The great peculiarity of the cud-chewers is the power which they possess of bringing back the food into the mouth, after it has been swallowed, to be further masticated. They have four stomachs, and very long intestines; vegetable food requiring to be kept in the body for a longer period than animal food.

The fore feet, having nothing whatever to do with the food, are not adapted either for feeling or seizing, but simply, like the hind feet, for giving support. They are composed of a solid horny substance, divided into two parts; hence these animals are sometimes called cloven-footed animals.

This order is divided into two families, viz., hornless and horned animals. In the first family are the camel and musk, and the second includes deer, sheep, goats, antelopes, giraffes, and oxen. These animals are more useful to man than any others; many of them draw and carry burdens, and nearly all are used for food.

Teacher.—What have you been reading about?

Pupil.—Ruminating animals.

Teacher.—Give me another name for ruminating.

Pupil.—Cud-chewing.

Teacher.—What is the root of the word?

Pupil.—Rumen, the cud.

Teacher.—What does the termination *ate* mean?

Pupil.—To do or act on in some way.

Teacher.—Ruminate, then, is to——

Pupil.—To act on the cud.

Teacher.—What *division* of animals do the cud-chewing form?

Pupil.—The eighth order.

Teacher.—Of what class?

Pupil.—Of the class Mammalia.

Teacher.—What is the class Mammalia?

Pupil.—It includes all animals that bring forth their young alive.

Teacher.—Next boy.

Second Pupil.—And that suckle their young.

Teacher.—To which of the sub-kingdoms of nature does the class Mammalia belong?

Pupil.—To the sub-kingdom Vertebrata.

Teacher.—How many orders has this class Mammalia?

Pupil.—Nine.

Teacher.—Name the first order.

Pupil.—Two-handed animals.

Teacher.—Give me an example.

Pupil.—Man is the only one.

Teacher.—Name the second.

Pupil.—Four-handed animals.

Teacher.—Give me an example.

Pupil.—The monkey.

Teacher.—Name the third order.

Pupil.—Killing animals.

Teacher.—Give me an example.

Pupil.—The lion.

Teacher.—Name the fourth order.

Pupil.—Pouched animals.

Teacher.—Give me an example.

Pupil.—The kangaroo.

Teacher.—Name the fifth order.

Pupil.—Gnawing animals.

Teacher.—Give me an example.

Pupil.—The rat.

Teacher—Name the sixth order.

Pupil.—Front teethless animals.

Teacher.—Give me an example.

Pupil.—The armadillo.

Teacher.—Name the seventh order.

Pupil.—Thick-skinned animals.

Teacher.—Give me an example.

Pupil.—The elephant.*

Teacher.—Name the eighth order.

Pupil.—Ruminating animals.

---

* These questions should be put to recapitulate the chief points of former lessons. No lesson of a *series* should be given without reference to those given before, especially the last *The effectiveness of teaching depends in a very great degree on its repetition.* Jacotot's maxim is a very wise one—"*Repetez sans cesse,*" (Keep repeating.)

Teacher.—How are they distinguished from other animals with respect to teeth?

Pupil.—They have no cutting teeth in the upper jaw.

Teacher.—Where are the cutting teeth in animals that have them?

Pupil.—In the front of the mouth.

Teacher.—Point to yours.

Teacher.—What other name is given to them besides?

Pupil.—Incisors.

Teacher.—What is there in the front of the upper jaw of ruminating animals?

Pupil.—A hard pad.

Teacher.—How do they get their food, then, without top front teeth?

(*Pupils silent, probably.*)

Teacher.—How do we get grass?

Pupil.—Cut it down.

Teacher.—How?

Pupil.—With a scythe.

Teacher.—With what does the cow lay hold of the grass when she is eating?

Pupil.—Her tongue.

Teacher.—With what does she cut it?

Pupil.—Her front teeth.

Teacher.—She does not bite it, then, but——*

Pupil.—Mow it.

Teacher.—But are all the ruminating animals without top cutting teeth?

Pupil.—No, the camel has them.

Teacher.—And another animal, a good deal like the camel, found only in South America, and used to carry burdens over the plains and mountains?

Pupil.—The lama.

Teacher.—Why should there be this difference with regard to these animals?

(*Not answered, probably.*)

Teacher.—In what sort of countries is the camel found?

Pupil.—In sandy countries.

Teacher.—Where there is rich herbage or poor?

Pupil.—Poor.

Teacher.—On what, then, does he subsist besides grass?

Pupil.—On thorny shrubs and thick twigs of trees.

Teacher.—Suppose, now, he has no teeth, but only a flat pad?

Pupil.—He would not then be able to snap them off.

Teacher.—Then why has the camel incisors in both jaws when other ruminants have not?

Pupil.—Because he could not get his food without them.

Teacher.—What do we learn of the Creator from this?

Pupil.—His power and wisdom.

Teacher.—His power and wisdom in suiting the animal to the food he has——

Pupil.—To eat.

Teacher.—And the place he is——

Pupil.—To live in.†

---

* In explanations in questioning on the reading, as well as in the gallery, it is often desirable for the teacher or monitor to pause before some of the chief words; thus leaving the boys themselves to supply them. Care must, however, be taken, not to make such ellipses as the boys can not supply.

† Here it should be observed that the teacher has told nothing, but by means of judicious questions has *led* the boys to *discover* a fact for themselves. This system of INDUCTION is of the first importance in questioning. It should be a rule, subject in practice to many exceptions, but still a general rule, that *nothing should be told the children, which by suitable questions they can discover for themselves.*

Teacher.—How many cutting teeth have most ruminants in the lower jaw?

Pupil.—Eight.

Teacher.—What kind of teeth are seldom found in them?

Pupil.—The tearers.*

Teacher.—What other names have these teeth?

Pupil.—Canine teeth; eye teeth.

Teacher.—Point to yours.

Teacher.—If the tearers are absent, then there must be between the cutters and grinders——

Pupil.—A space.

Teacher.—What sort of grinders have the ruminants?

Pupil.—Very broad.

Teacher.—And very——

Pupil.—Rough.

Teacher.—Why have they them broad and rough?

Pupil.—Because vegetable food requires more grinding down than animal.

Teacher.—But how is the tooth kept thus rough?

(*The Pupils, perhaps, do not answer.*)

Teacher.—You read in the lesson *the enamel is disposed in crescent-shaped ridges.* What is the enamel?

Pupil.—The hard, shining part of the tooth.

Teacher.—What part of our tooth is it?

Pupil.—The covering of that part which is out of the jaw-bone.

Teacher.—What do you mean by disposed?

Pupil.—Placed.

Teacher.—Name the root of the word.

Pupil.—Pono, I place.

Teacher.—What is crescent-shaped?

Pupil.—Shaped like the moon before it is a half moon.

Teacher.—Draw a crescent.†

(*One of the class draws it on the blackboard.*)

Teacher.—What is the root of the word?

Pupil.—Cresco, I grow.

Teacher.—Applied to the moon, then, when she is——

Pupil.—Growing larger.

Teacher.—As the ruminants have to grind their food so much, what would be the consequence if the tooth were just covered with enamel as ours is?

Pupil.—It would soon be worn away.

Teacher.—And if it were wholly of enamel?

Pupil.—It would wear quite smooth, and would not grind the food.

Teacher.—Now what do we use to grind corn with?

Pupil.—Millstones.

Teacher.—And do they always grind smooth?

Pupil.—No.

Teacher.—Why not?

Pupil.—Because some are of that sort of stone that has one substance in it harder than another, and when the soft wears away, the harder portions remain, making the surface rough.

---

* If the teacher should find that the leading facts, with regard to teeth, are not known by the boys, he should make them the subject of his next gallery lesson.

† The chalk and blackboard should be made use of in all branches of teaching. In any difficulty the teacher should be able to sketch off a daigram, and thus explain the matter by the sense of sight. He might also, as in this case, test the correctness of the boys' knowledge, by requiring them to draw the object.

Teacher (*exhibiting a bullock's tooth.*)* Now, here is a bullock's tooth; you see the enamel is in crescent-shaped——

Pupil.—Ridges.

Teacher.—The enamel goes down into the body of the tooth; then, as the grinding goes on, which part wears away first?

Pupil.—The ivory between the enamel.

Teacher.—And leaves the enamel——

Pupil.—Higher.

Teacher.—And keeps the tooth constantly——

Pupil.—Rough.

Teacher.—Tell me some other animals you have been reading about that have very different sorts of teeth.

Pupil.—The gnawers have the enamel only in front.

Teacher.—Why?

Pupil.—That by the ivory, which is softer, wearing away, the tooth may be constantly sharp.

Teacher.—Some other animals.

Pupil.—The back teeth of the flesh-eaters cross each other like scissors.

Teacher.—Why?

Pupil.—Because they only require to tear or cut their flesh, not to grind it.

Teacher.—But what sort of motion must the jaw of the ruminant have in order to grind his food?

Pupil.—A sideways motion.

Teacher.—Have you seen this motion?

Pupil. Yes.

Teacher.—When?

Pupil.—When a cow was lying on the grass.

Teacher.—But can not all animals move their jaw the same way?

Pupil.—No; the flesh-eaters can only move it up and down.

Teacher.—Like——

Pupil.—A pair of scissors.†

Teacher.—What other motion of the jaw do you remember?

Pupil.—The gnawers can not move it at all sideways, but thrust it forward and backward a little.

Teacher.—Like what?

Pupil.—A saw.

Teacher.—But what is it that these ruminants can do that especially distinguishes them from other animals?

Pupil.—They can chew the cud.

Teacher.—What is this power said to be to them, as it belongs only to them?

Pupil.—A peculiarity.

Teacher.—Give me the root of that word.

Pupil.—Peculium, one's own property.

Teacher.—What do you mean by chewing the cud?

Pupil.—Bringing back the food to the mouth to be chewed over again.

Teacher.—Another word for chewed.

Pupil.—Masticated.

---

* Whenever it is practicable, the object under consideration should be exhibited; and it is particularly desirable that a collection of objects should be made in every school that would tend to illustrate the reading lessons. Such a collection, properly labeled to match the pages of the reading lessons, would secure accuracy of perception, and be a great saving of time. These would make the best object lessons.

† At this point it would be necessary for the teacher to put many of these questions over again, to ascertain that there has been a perfect comprehension of the subject.

Teacher.—As these animals can do what others can not, they must have something which others have not. What is that?

Pupil.—They have four stomachs.

Teacher.—What is the use of these four stomachs?

(*Pupils do not answer.*)

Teacher.—After the food has been a little chewed, it is passed into the first stomach, sometimes called the paunch, where it is a little softened; from that it goes into the second, where it is formed into balls; the animal, when it pleases, brings it into the mouth again, where it is further chewed; the animal then swallows it a second time, not into the first stomach, but in the third, where it is a little digested; and it then passes into the fourth stomach, where the digestion is completed.

(*Teacher repeats questions. What is the first stomach called?*)

Teacher.—Which stomach is the largest?

(*Pupils silent.*)

Teacher.—The first. But when is it of no use?

Pupil.—Before the animal eats grass.

Teacher.—Well, this stomach does not become large till that time. What helps these animals in the digestion of their food, besides these stomachs?

Pupil.—They have very long intestines.

Teacher.—Why do they need such long intestines?

Pupil.—Because vegetable food requires to be kept longer in the body than animal food.

Teacher.—Then what sort of animals have short intestines?

Pupil.—Those which live on flesh.

Teacher.—The term for these?

Pupil.—Carnivorous.

Teacher.—Name some animals.

Pupil.—The lion, the eagle.

Teacher.—Of what use are the fore feet to ruminating animals?

Pupil.—To support them.

Teacher.—Are the fore feet of any other use to *other* animals?

Pupil.—Yes.

Teacher.—What?

Pupil.—In some they are used to catch and hold the prey.

Teacher.—Give me an example.

Pupil.—The lion, and all the cat kind.

Teacher.—What other uses?

Pupil.—Some use them for holding by.

Teacher.—As the——

Pupil.—Monkeys.

Teacher.—Any other use?

Pupil.—Some use them to burrow with.

Teacher.—As the——

Pupil.—Rabbit.

Teacher.—What are the feet of ruminants composed of?

Pupil.—Of a hard, horny substance.

Teacher.—Hollow?

Pupil. No, solid.

Teacher.—Into how many parts is the foot divided?

Pupil.—Two.

Teacher.—What are these animals called in consequence?

Pupil.—Cloven-footed.

Teacher.—What do you mean by cloven?

Pupil.—Cut, slit, cleft.

Teacher.—How many families are in this order?

Pupil.—Two.

Teacher.—What are they?

Pupil.—Hornless and horned.

Teacher.—What do you mean by hornless?

Pupil.—Without horns.

Teacher.—Give me some other words ending in less.

Pupil.—Lifeless, leafless, heartless, &c.

Teacher.—And these mean——

Pupil.—Without life, without leaf, without heart.

Teacher.—Name some animals belonging to the hornless family.

Pupil.—The camel, the musk.

Teacher.—Point them out.*

Teacher.—Some belonging to the horned family.

Pupil.—Deer, sheep, goats, antelopes, giraffes, and oxen.

Teacher.—Point them out.

Teacher.—What is said of these animals with regard to man?

Pupil.—That they are more useful to him than any others.

Teacher.—Of what use are they?

Pupil.—For food.

Teacher.—What part of them?

Pupil.—The flesh, the milk.

Teacher.—Give some examples of those whose flesh is eaten.

Pupil.—The cow, sheep, deer.

Teacher.—Name some whose milk man uses.

Pupil.—The cow, reindeer, goat.

Teacher.—Of what other use are they?

Pupil.—As beasts of burden.

Teacher.—Give me an example.

Pupil.—The camel.

Teacher.—Name another use.

Pupil.—Beasts of draught.

Teacher.—Give examples.

Pupil.—Ox, reindeer, *horse.*†

Teacher.—Is horse right?

Second Pupil.—No.

Teacher.—Why not?

Pupil.—Horses do not chew the cud.

Teacher.—How might you know from the form of the horse that he is not a ruminating animal?

Pupil.—By his hoof.

Teacher.—How does it differ from that of the ruminants?

Pupil.—It is undivided, while that of the ruminants is cloven.

Teacher.—Well, of what other use are ruminants?

Pupil.—Their covering makes our clothing.

Teacher.—Give me an example.

Pupil.—The sheep, the goat, the camel.

Teacher.—Name any other use.

---

* Some plate containing representations of the principal kinds of animals should be presented to the boys for this purpose.

† This error is introduced to show how it should be corrected: not merely by stating that it is an error, or even telling what is right, but by showing in what the wrongness consists. Further questions might be asked as to why he thought the horse was a ruminant; when the boy would probably say, "It eats grass." The error having been then traced back, a false association might be easily removed by showing that though all ruminants eat grass, all animals that eat grass are not ruminants.

Pupil.—Their skins are made into leather, their fat into candles, their horns into knife-handles.

Teacher.—Seeing these animals are so useful to man, where may we expect to find them?

Pupil.—Wherever man is.

Teacher.—Tell me the ruminants of hot countries.

Pupil.—The antelope, the giraffe, the lama.

Teacher.—Of the temperate regions.

Pupil.—The ox, the sheep, the deer, the goat.

Teacher.—Of very cold countries.

Pupil.—The reindeer.

Teacher.—What does so wide a scattering of these useful animals teach us about our Creator?

Pupil.—That he cares and provides for man.

34. By means of questions, a test is constantly applied as to the degree in which any subject is understood, and facilities are afforded for explanation of difficulties, as well as for the imparting of information *connected with*, though not actually forming a part of it. Interrogation is, therefore, made use of in *every branch* of teaching. In connection with reading, it is, however, especially important. The good teacher will find it necessary generally to bestow *more time* on the explaining of a lesson by questions, and in imparting such incidental information as may be naturally associated with it, than in the mere mechanical exercise of reading.

35. The questions employed, whether in class or during a gallery lesson, are of two kinds—explanatory questions, and questions of examination. The first are used during the progress of the lesson; the second, for the most part, at the end of it. The teacher makes use of *explanatory questions* in order to lead the children, by short and easy steps, to work out the subject of the lesson for themselves. By their aid he stimulates the minds of his pupils to continued active and healthy exertion, and makes them co-laborers with himself in the work of education, instead of being listless *hearers* only; and while he supplies them with facts, where really necessary, he carries them forward through a rigid and carefully built up course of induction to the gaol which he has throughout the lesson kept clearly in his own view.

Sometimes questions of examination are employed *at the commencement* of a lesson, in order to ascertain what knowledge the children already possess on the subject of it, so that the teacher may come down to their level, and adapt his instruction to their actual wants. They are used *at the end*, when he wishes to ascertain how far they have really understood what has been going on, and how much of it is laid up in their memory, so as to be available for future use.

36. The following rules should be observed in the use of interrogation:—

(*a.*) The questions and answers, when put together, should present the subject as a connected whole; hence questions should follow each other in logical order.

(*b.*) Simple language should be used, such as will convey the meaning of the question clearly to the pupil's mind; hence every question should be definite.

(*c.*) It is not wise to tell a *part* of the answer, such as the first word, or any other part of it.

(*d.*) Questions which require or admit a simple *yes* or *no* as an answer should be avoided.

(*e.*) The minds of *all* the class should be kept at work; the answers should not be taken from a *few* only.

(*f.*) Wrong answers should be frequently noticed; they point out *where* the teacher's attention is wanted. The class should be questioned into the right answer, not told it.

(*g.*) Care should be taken to ascertain whether the answer given to a question shows a clear and distinct idea; if not, further explanations should be given, and more questions put. A few ideas clearly and distinctly worked into the minds of the children are better than many misty and indistinct ones.

(*h.*) The *language* of the answers ought to be good; inaccuracies should be pointed out, and answers which are only *partly* correct rectified.

37. The method of ellipsis is also used both during the progress of a lesson, and for the purpose of recapitulation. When employed while the lesson is proceeding, it is useful as a relief to the questioning, and as a means of testing the attention and comprehension of the pupils; when used at the close, it furnishes a convenient method of summing up the substance of the information imparted.

The principal rules observed in using the ellipsis are these:—

(*a.*) Ellipses should be *mixed with* questions.

(*b.*) Questions should never end in ellipses.

(*c.*) If an ellipsis be filled up incorrectly, the children should not be told, but be led by questions, illustrations, and other ellipses, to the truth.

(*d.*) Ellipses for younger children should be shorter than those for elder ones.

(*e.*) Ellipses should be such as the children can be expected to supply.

Section 6.—Class Teaching—Spelling.

38. Spelling is taught chiefly *in connection with reading;* all the difficult words occuring in the first book being spelt previous to the reading of the lesson.

In the *second lesson book* there is a list of words *connected with* the lesson, though not always occurring in it, which are treated in the same way.

In the *third* and *fourth* books all the difficult words occurring in a lesson should be spelt *after* the lesson has been read, in the course of interrogation. The meanings should also be required, and the etymologies of such words given as tend to make the explanation clearer. This spelling and explaining of words found in sentences is much more effective than learning columns by rote that have no relation but that of juxtaposition.

39. Another mode of teaching spelling is by *dictation.* This is of two kinds. Either the teacher of a class spells a word, and the boys write it after him; or, as in the advanced classes, the teacher reads a few sentences from some book, without spelling any of the words, and the boys take them down. These sentences are then looked over, and the errors marked, which the boy is required to correct. This last is found to be a valuable exercise; but the value depends, in a great degree, on the boy actually *writing the words correctly that he had before written wrong.* The master or teacher must not be satisfied with merely pointing out the error. The first kind of dictation is practiced every school-time in the lowest classes; the second only occasionally, in the higher classes.

40. A third mode of teaching this exercise is by the tabular lessons, or spelling columns of Lesson Book, No. II., when each boy in his turn spells a word, the monitor conducting the exercises generally in the same way as with the Reading Lessons.

The abstracts of gallery lessons, which the elder boys are frequently required to write at the close of the lesson, is another mode of testing and improving their spelling.

41. In addition to these methods, all, except the youngest children make spelling a part of their home lessons. Two or three times a week those in the middle classes are expected to bring ten or a dozen words written down on paper or slate, and syllabically divided; while the elder children bring either a written account of some object or animal previously specified, or the abstract of the last collective lesson which they have attended. Attempts at composition by the more advanced children further test and improve their spelling, whether the exercises are entirely original, or taken from the more systematic series found in Dr. Cornwell's "*Young Composer.*"

Section 7.—Class Teaching—Writing.

42. The children, when writing, are seated and arranged according to their sectional division, and they are subdivided into desks according to their proficiency in the art, (*ante* § 4.) The forms of the letters, the mode of sitting, the manner of holding the pen, and the *principles* of writing, are learnt in the lower sections, the pupils practicing on slates.

43. The *straight stroke* is first introduced, and its uniform thickness, slope, and varying lengths pointed out; then the upper and lower ties; and then the place of the dot over the *i*. Such words as *tin* or *pit* are then written on the blackboard for practice.

After these *the curve* is explained, and the letters *o, c, e, a, d,* g, formed; these are each taken up in turn, and their correct formation shown. Words formed by these letters, and the elements given in the preceding lesson serve as exercises at this stage.

The remaining portions of large text letters are treated in the same way. Then the capitals are given, classified according to their similarity of form, with instructions as to their hight and breadth; and then numerous exercises are written on the blackboard to be imitated by the children.

44. During the whole of this preliminary course, and indeed whenever the children are occupied in writing, the proper mode of holding the pencil or pen is particularly insisted upon, as well as the right position of the body, fingers, and book. A diagram, showing a hand with the pen and fingers in their proper position, is placed on the wall of the writing division, as a model to which attention is frequently directed. The teacher also instructs his pupils by holding a pen in his hand in front of the section, and then calling attention to *the manner* in which he holds it, whenever such a course appears necessary.

45. When the children have gone through this course, and have learnt to write freely and correctly on slate, they are allowed to write in copy-books. The same mode of classification is employed as in slate writing. A monitor is appointed to give out copy-books, pens, and copy-slips, where these are used. (It is better, however, to use books which have copies engraved in them, as this saves much time and prevents confusion.) When the books and pens are distributed, the writing commences at the word "Begin!" The teacher then moves from desk to desk to preserve order in the section, pointing out errors, or getting the children to discover them by comparing their own writing with the copy. Sometimes he takes a boy's copy-book to the front of the section, imitates on the blackboard the malformations of letters or words which he finds in

it, and then questions as to where the errors are. He then places by their side the correct forms, and shows their superiority. By this method he keeps up a knowledge of the principles and elements learnt in the lower sections.

46. At the close of the writing lesson the general superintendent of order commands, "Writers"—"Finish lines!"—"Clean pens!"—"Lay down pens!"—"Hands down!"—"Collect pens!" The monitor collects the pens of the section, and takes them to the place where they are to be kept until the next writing lesson. (It is recommended that each boy keep a small pen-wiper in his pocket on which to clean his pen.) The writing is then inspected by the teacher, the superintendent commands, "Shut books!"—"Collect books!" and the books are collected by the monitor, tied between small wooden boards, and taken to the place assigned for their reception.

The maxims recommended to masters in this department are, 1. Regard *quality* rather than *quantity;* and, 2. Aim rather at making a knowledge of writing *general*, than at producing *excellence* in a *few* of the senior pupils.

Section 8.—Class Teaching—Arithmetic.

47. Arithmetic is taught to the *younger* children both in the gallery and at the draft stations; as children advance in the practice of the art, it is, however, found impossible to secure a sufficient number at the same stage of progress to form a gallery; it is therefore taught to those more advanced sections at the draft stations alone. The great *object* sought to be attained in teaching this branch is, the cultivation of the mental faculties, by the impartation of such a knowledge of the powers and properties of numbers, and of the principles and rules of arithmetical science, as shall, when combined with facility in its operations, enable the pupils to solve any questions which may occur in after-life with intelligence, correctness, and dispatch.

48. It is impossible, in a manual like the present, to describe in detail all the methods employed to impart a thorough knowledge of so important and extensive a subject. All that can be done is to indicate the general principles on which the instruction is founded.

The first ideas of number are given in the gallery. The ball-frame is placed before the pupils, and they are taught to count the balls on the first wire; then their fingers, buttons, panes of glass in the school-room window, or the seats on the gallery. They are also taught to add, to multiply, to subtract, and to divide small numbers. Thus, sensible objects are made the medium of communicating their first ideas of number.

49. As the children become familiar with these operations, the number is increased; they are taught to count and work questions mentally with the balls on *two* wires; then on *three*, and so on, until they are familiar with the whole frame. The same exercises are also gone through with beans, buttons, and similar objects, so as to prepare the way for the *abstract idea* that the *result* of an arithmetical operation is not affected by the articles which are the subjects of calculation; thus, six cows and five cows make eleven cows, and six buttons and five make eleven buttons: hence, $6+5=11$.

50. As the instruction proceeds, it becomes more definite and methodical, though continued for some time longer without the use of figures. Addition is first explained, and simple exercises worked, either on the ball-frame, with beans, or by means of strokes drawn on the school slate. Then multiplication

is taken up, and its connection with addition shown. Subtraction and division are treated in the same way; and toward the close of the course, Arabic and Roman numerals are explained, the principle of the local values of figures brought out, and easy examples worked in both systems.

51. While this course is gone through in the gallery, the children are exercised in their drafts on very simple questions in the tables, and in mental arithmetic; correctness and dispatch being always required.

The children are also employed at their writing desks during this course in *copying* and learning the names of the Arabic and Roman numbers; not so much for use at this stage, as for exercises on form, and to facilitate future progress.

52. In prosecuting the study of *written arithmetic* in the middle and upper sections, every rule is preceded by a lesson upon the principle on which it is founded. Instead of giving rules first and examples afterward, the rule is deduced from examples. While questions involving abstract numbers are by no means excluded, the majority of the exercises are given on subjects occurring in the every-day life of the children. A great number of examples of this kind are found in Crossley's "*Intellectual Calculator*," a copy of which is placed in the hands of every teacher of a draft: each child, also, in this part of the school, should have a copy for home and individual practice. The number of children in the school—of bricks in any wall which the boys may have seen building—the population of the town, the county, or the country—all furnish abundant questions for practice. Lessons on the principles of arithmetic are also given at stated periods from De Morgan.

53. In order to promote a business-like dispatch in obtaining the answer to a question, the teacher sometimes writes a sum on the blackboard, and pointing to it, says, "The quickest." Each boy copies the figures as rapidly as he can, solves the question, and exhibits the result to the teacher, who, with a glance, compares it with the key, and says, "First," "Second," or "Third," according to the order in which they correctly exhibit. This method will always be a favorite one with quick boys, and is in several respects really advantageous. It is pursued in every class after the first.

Particular attention is paid to *numeration* throughout these sections, some portion of time in every week being specially devoted to it; and the questions and answers, in all cases, whether read by the teachers or pupils, are given according to their *local* value; thus, 9824 would be given as nine thousand, eight hundred, and twenty, and four; not nine, eight, two, four.

54. The ordinary method of class instruction is as follows:—The boys being arranged, the monitor distinctly announces the question: if complicated, he repeats it once or twice; then pausing to allow time for its being understood, he says, "Begin;" and each boy eagerly strives to work it out and present his slate first for approval. If right, and first, the monitor says, "First;" to the next boy, "Second;" and the draft is instantly, as it were, sifted, the slow or inefficient being at the bottom. Copying is not practicable.

As soon as all have completed the operation, the teacher interrogates, thus—"What have you done?" "How?" "Why?" "Any other way?" &c.; and their knowledge of the principles on which the rule is founded is thoroughly examined. This examination is a very productive exercise, and should seldom be omitted; for as it rarely happens in long solutions that the pupils obtain their results the same way, the replies to these questions often elicit much valuable remark respecting the principles upon which their particular calculations are founded.

It is to the variety of methods used in obtaining the results, coupled with the pupil's subsequent reasoning on the correctness of the principles which he has selected, that we look for proof of the reality of his attainments.

55. Rules in the central school are introduced rather as suggestions, when the difficulties of the question are thoroughly understood, and have baffled the pupil's ingenuity; he is then gradually led on by a succession of questions, till the whole truth breaks upon his mind with a clearness and beauty which form the best incitement to renewed investigation. Arithmetic, thus taught, becomes a fine mental discipline, and strengthens the intellectual powers, instead of resting only on the memory.

56. There are two points of obvious importance, which respect the mere working out of the question, viz., correctness and dispatch. The attainment of the latter is, generally, a matter of great difficulty; yet without it the experienced arithmetician is often plainly deficient in buying and selling, and in transacting affairs where ready calculation is required. To supply this defect, not only are contracted methods on slate encouraged, such as bringing any number of tons, hundred-weights, quarters, and pounds, into pounds in one line—working by aliquot parts and approximations—or calculating part of a question abstractedly, and part on the slate; but a great variety of questions are given specially for pure mental solution.

57. Great attention is paid to a ready knowledge of ARITHMETICAL TABLES, since without this, arithmetic is almost useless in its practical application. In all, except the lowest section, portions of the tables are daily given to be learnt at home, for examination when the children return to school. This desirable but difficult object will also be promoted by having them said or sung during the various evolutions of the school, especially when going from and into the desks. As this occupies some portion of each school time, they will be easily learnt. This repetition does not, however, supersede the necessity of *rapid irregular* questioning upon them; as boys are frequently able to repeat a table from beginning to end without being competent to apply any part of it when required. The repetition of tables during changes should not, however, be *always* allowed; it is useful as a matter of discipline to require boys occasionally to walk with perfect quietness; while at other times school pieces may be sung.

The tables of money, weights, and measures, are first introduced in the gallery. Here the actual objects about which the tables are formed are as far as possible exhibited. Long, square, and cubic measures, are shown in their connection with length, breadth, and thickness; and the pupils are required to measure the school-room gallery and other things by which they are surrounded, and then to announce the results in different denominations. In like manner, when treating of measures of capacity, a pint or quart are shown, and made the subject of various calculations.

58. MENTAL ARITHMETIC is taught in every section of the school, and in every draft, and proceeds from the simplest questions, involving no more than a knowledge of the tables, to very complex and difficult operations. The work of each draft is so arranged, both in tables and mental arithmetic, as to form an introduction to the written arithmetic of the next draft.

As the children proceed, they are exercised in forming numbers by the addition of other numbers, as 12=(4+5+3)=(7+3+2)=(6+5+1;) 16=(2+3+4+5+2)=(4+5+6+1,) &c. Also in finding the fractors of numbers, as 18=(2×9)=(3×6;) 36=(4×9)=(6×6)=(9×4)=(12×3)=(18×2;) in discovering the common multiples and common divisors of small numbers; and in the combination of different rules—such as taking a number from the sum of three others, multiplying the remainder by a given number, and dividing the product by another. In this way, they are exercised mentally on the various properties of number, and the principles applicable to it, before they are introduced to the more difficult and extended processes of written arithmetic.

59. Before entering on the study of division, the children are put through an elementary course of fractions. The formation of fractions, their notation, and the alterations in value caused by changing the numerator, the denominator, or both, is drawn from the pupils; the *principles* on which reduction, addition, subtraction, multiplication, and division of fractions depend, are explained; the rules are deduced; and the pupils are then required to show the reason for every operation which they perform. The questions brought forward at this stage are of the simplest kind, the object being rather to give *ideas* and *principles* than to produce dexterity. The subject is more fully taken up afterwards in the "*Calculator.*"

60. Various objects are operated upon in teaching this preliminary course. A line drawn with chalk on the blackboard affords perhaps the readiest illustration. Suppose the pupils were asked, "What is the difference between $\frac{1}{3}$ and $\frac{1}{4}$?" and could not answer, the teacher would draw a line thus, divided into quarters:—

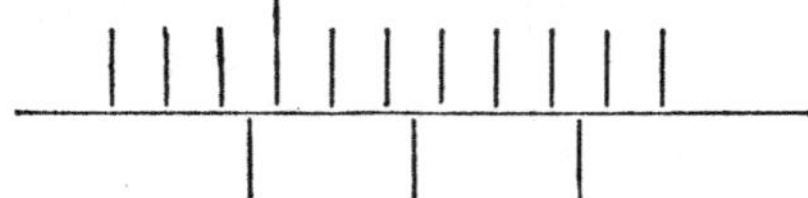

He would then say,

How many parts is the line divided into?

Pupil.—Four.

Teacher.—What then is each part called?

Pupil.—A fourth.

Teacher.—Or——

Pupil.—Quarter.

The teacher would then divide each quarter into three equal parts, and would say to some boy, "Count how many parts."

Pupil.—Twelve.

Teacher.—What then is each part called?

Pupil.—One-twelfth.

Teacher.—As there are twelve-twelfths in the whole line, how many are there in the third of the line?

Pupil.—Four.

The teacher, after marking off four of the parts, says, "What have I marked off?"

Pupil.—Four-twelfths.

Teacher.—Which are equal to——

Pupil.—One-third?

Teacher.—Now show me one-quarter of the whole line—now one-third of the whole—now show me the difference between one-quarter and one-third—well, what part of the whole line is that?

Pupil.—One-twelfth.

Teacher.—Why?

Pupil.—Because there are twelve such parts in the whole line.

Teacher.—And when any thing is divided into twelve equal parts, each of them is called a——

Pupil.—Twelfth.

Teacher.—Then what is the difference between one-third and one-fourth?

Pupil.—One-twelfth.

The *term* fractions should not be used in this stage of advancement.

61. In like manner simple proportion is preceded by a course of mental arithmetic, explaining the properties of ratios and proportion, especially exhibiting that on which the common "Rule of Three" is founded. Questions are then given, the answers to which can be obtained, or the road to them shortened, by dividing or multiplying one or more of the terms, and the principles on which these operations are founded are shown. By this method the children are prepared for the study of proportion in their books, and their intelligent comprehension of the questions found there is facilitated.

62. In all these drafts much scope is allowed to the pupil teachers beyond the line of questioning just referred to. They are at liberty to vary the questions to any extent, so long as the attention of the boys is kept up. Such questions as these constantly occur: "What is the value of a dozen articles at 3*d.*—at $4\frac{1}{2}$*d.*—at $9\frac{3}{4}$*d.*—or at 1*s.* $5\frac{1}{2}$*d.*?" or, "What is the value of any number of dozens or grosses?" or, "What is the square of 4,—or 1,—or 6,—or 9?" &c.

In the more advanced drafts the questions become much more difficult, and include the following range: "What is the square of 27, of 53, of 225?" &c. "What does 7 cwt. 3 qrs. of any article come to, at 1*d.* per lb., or at $9\frac{1}{4}$*d.* per lb.?" "What will 37, or 75, or 139, or 3185, or any other number of articles amount to, at $2\frac{1}{2}$*d.* each, or at $5\frac{1}{4}$*d.*, or at $8\frac{1}{2}$*d.*, or 3*s.*, or 7*s.* 6*d.*?" &c., &c. "In 35 yds. 3 qrs. of cloth, how many English, French, or Flemish ells?" "Reduce 4*s.* $8\frac{3}{4}$*d.* to the fraction of a pound sterling; or $9\frac{1}{4}$*d.* to the fraction of a crown; or 3 qrs. 15 lb. to the fraction of a cwt. or ton." "Multiply $\frac{2}{3}$ of $\frac{5}{6}$ by $\frac{1}{2}$ of $\frac{1}{2}$ of $1\frac{1}{2}$." "Add $\frac{5}{8}$ of a shilling to £$\frac{3}{5}$." "Reduce 12*s.* $6\frac{1}{2}$*d.* to the decimal of a shilling or pound sterling." "What is the interest of £251 10*s.* 6*d.*, at 5 or 6 per cent., for a number of years and months?" To these might be added a large proportion of the questions usually found in most books of arithmetic.

Section 9.—Class Teaching.—Grammar and Composition.

63. English composition, mental or written, precedes and accompanies the study of English grammar throughout the whole school.

In the lower sections mental composition is taught so as to enable the children to express their thoughts correctly, and at the same time to form an introduction to the study of grammar.

64. The youngest pupils are taught composition in the gallery. In the first lesson they are asked to mention the *names* of some of the objects which they see around them, and to spell them, as *desk*, *slate*, *book*, or *wall*. These names are written in a vertical column on the school slate. The pupils are then required to put a word before each noun, expressing its color, or some other quality belonging to it, as *grey* slate, *wooden* desk, *new* book, *white* wall. The words grey, wooden, or new, are then successively spelt, and the teacher writes them before the words which they severally describe. The children in the gallery are then asked, if they can express the meaning of the phrases, such as

grey slate in another way. The sentences, "the slate is grey," or "the wall is white," are thus brought out, and written down. Other names are then given and treated in the same manner. This is generally found to be enough for one lesson.

65. In the same way, at succeeding lessons, the names of objects are mentioned, qualities are added, and actions which they can perform are specified; the sentences being constructed, and the words spelt, by the children, and then written down by the teacher before the gallery. Then follow questions as to *how* and *when* these actions may be done, and the differences in the *kinds* of actions. As the pupils advance, the effect produced in a sentence by taking a word from it, or adding one to it, is elicited from them by interrogation. Thus the various modifications of which a *thought* is capable, and the distinctive offices of the various words in a sentence, are impressed upon the children's minds, and wrought out in their practice, before a single technicality of grammar is placed before them. Hence when they commence the study of grammar they are prepared to understand that the distinctions existing among the words of a sentence are not arbitrary, but have their origin in the nature of language itself.

66. At this stage of progress the regular study of grammar is commenced, and it is considered an advantage that, in the earlier steps of this study, the knowledge previously obtained is again brought under the notice of the pupils, though in a different form. The teacher commences by saying, in as clear a manner as possible, that every word in the language, like every pupil in the school, belongs to some class. Stopping some seconds to ascertain that this simple fact was well understood, he might remark that the only difference is, that there are eight classes of pupils in the school, but nine classes of words. This would be followed by saying,

Teacher.—Tell me the names of any things you see.

Pupil.—Desk, slate, inkstand, box, pen.

Teacher.—Tell me the names of some things you saw in coming to school.

Pupil.—Horse, cart, house, boy.

Several being mentioned, the question would be put, "What have you told me about these things?" *Ans.*—"Their names." Now the teacher would observe, "All these names which you have mentioned belong to one class; the name of that class is *Nouns;* all names belong to it, for the word Noun means Name. A noun, then, is the name of any person, animal, place, or thing." Here it should be observed, that neither the term nor the definition is given till the thing itself is understood. Throughout this and every other study the necessity for the term should be felt before it is supplied.

67. After the pupils have furnished a number of nouns for themselves, the teacher should write out the sentences under the nouns as found in the grammar. He should then require each pupil in his turn to point out the nouns occurring in the sentences, which he should then underline. Thus, after having written out the first sentence, "The father sent John into the garden," he would say to the first pupil, "Point out a noun."

Pupil replies.—Father.

Teacher.—Why is father a noun?

Second Pupil.—Because it is the name of a person.

Teacher.—And a noun is——

Third Pupil.—The name of any person, animal, place, or thing.

The teacher would then underline the word "Father," and say to the next pupil, "Another noun."

Fourth Pupil.—Boy.
Teacher.—Why is boy a noun?
Fifth Pupil.—Because it is the name of a person.

The word "Boy" would then be underlined.

Teacher.—A noun is——
Sixth Pupil.—The name of any person or thing.
Teacher.—Give me another noun.
Seventh Pupil.—Garden.
Teacher.—Why is garden a noun?
Eighth Pupil.—Because it is the name of a thing.
Teacher.—A noun then is——
Ninth Pupil.—The name of any person or thing.

The word "Garden" would then be underlined. All the sentences in that exercise should in succession be written on the blackboard by the teacher, and treated in the same way.

68. The teacher would next ask the pupils again to name some nouns, and singling out one named that would best answer his purpose, "boy," for instance, he would write it down on the blackboard.

Teacher.—But are all boys alike?
Pupils.—No.
Teacher.—Some are——
First Pupil.—Strong.
Second Pupil.—Tall.
Third Pupil.—Good.
Fourth Pupil.—Bad.
Teacher.—Well, what do all these words, *strong*, *tall*, *good*, *bad*, tell us?
Pupil.—Something about the boy.
Teacher.—Yes, but what?
Pupil.—What sort of a boy he is.

(The teacher might then hold up his book and say, "Tell me any thing you can about this book.")

First Pupil.—It is a small book.
Second Pupil.—It is clean.
Third Pupil.—It is useful.
Fourth Pupil.—It is printed.
Teacher.—These words, *small*, *clean*, *useful*, *printed*, tell us——
Pupil.—What sort of a book it is.
Teacher.—Well, all such words as these are called Adjectives. An adjective, then, is a word that shows the quality of noun.

The teacher would then turn to the exercise on adjectives in Cornwell's "*Grammar for Beginners*," and write out the sentences under it, and, as in the nouns, require the boys (1) to point out the adjectives, (2) to give the reason for their being so called, and (3) to repeat the definition. The adjective in the exercise would be underlined by the teacher. One of the adjectives, *strong*, for instance, would be written before the noun *boy* on the blackboard.

69. He would now hold up some object, and say, "What is this?"

Pupil.—A slate.
Teacher.—What word did you use before slate?
Pupil.—A.

Teacher.—What is this?
Pupil.—An eye.
Teacher.—What did you use before eye?
Pupil.—An.
Teacher.—What gives us heat and light?
Pupil.—The sun.
Teacher.—What word did you use before sun?
Pupil.—The.
Teacher.—If I were telling you about some boy who was strong, I should say he is——
Pupil.—A strong boy.

The teacher would here put *a* before *strong boy* on the blackboard.

Teacher.—Well, the words *an*, *a*, and *the*, are called articles. An article, then, is a word put before a noun, to show the extent of its signification.

Sentences from exercises on "the article" in the grammar would then be written on the board, and this part of speech would be pointed out, explained, and defined in the same way as the noun and the adjective.

The exercise would then proceed thus:—

Teacher.—Tell me any thing you can do.
Pupil.—Run, walk, talk, eat, drink, learn.
Teacher.—What do all these words mean?
Pupil.—Doing something.
Teacher.—Well, what have you seen a strong boy do?
Pupil.—Jump, leap, wrestle.
(Teacher writes *jumped* after *strong boy* on the blackboard.)
Teacher.—Now all words that mean doing something are called verbs.
(Here the usual definition is repeated.)

Exercises upon the verb would then follow.

70. Again taking up some object, the teacher would say, "What is this?"

Pupil.—A book.
Teacher.—And this?
Pupil.—A box.
Teacher.—Where is the book now with regard to the box?
First Pupil.—On it.
Second Pupil.—In it.
Third Pupil.—Near it.
Fourth Pupil.—Over it.
Teacher.—What do these words, *on*, *in*, *by*, *over*, show?
Pupil.—Where the book is with regard to the box.
Teacher.—(Pointing to the words on the blackboard,) "A strong boy jumped, where?
Pupil.—Over the ditch.
Teacher.—Which word shows the place of the boy with regard to the ditch?
Pupil.—Over.
Teacher.—Other words that would show the same.
Pupil.—Into the ditch, across.
Teacher.—All words that show the place of one thing to another are prepositions.

The exercise on prepositions from the grammar would then follow, and the exercise proceed.

Teacher.—But when different persons are doing the same thing, do they do it all alike? Do all write alike?
Pupil.—No.

Teacher.—Some write——

First Pupil.—Well.

Second Pupil.—Badly.

Third Pupil.—Carefully.

Fourth Pupil.—Slowly.

Teacher.—What do all these words show.

Pupil.—How the writing is done.

Teacher.—How might a boy jump?

Pupil.—Timidly, courageously, fearlessly.

(Teacher writes *fearlessly* in the sentence.)

Teacher.—Words that show how a thing is done, or when and where it is done, are called ADVERBS.

The exercise from the grammar follows as before.

71. The other parts of speech would be taken in the same way; till at last the teacher would have a sentence combining them all, as, perhaps, A *strong boy jumped fearlessly over the ditch: but indeed he almost fell in.* The advantage of making up a sentence in this way is, that it serves as a model sentence to the pupils, by which they can try others at a future time.

In this mode it will be observed that (1.) The pupils, by the judicious questions of the teacher, themselves supply a great number of the kind of word under consideration. (2.) The *name* is given by the teacher. (3.) The definition is read. (4.) The pupils select all words of the kind required from others in a sentence. (5.) Give an explanation. (6.) Repeat the definition.

72. As soon as the pupils have acquired the power of readily distinguishing the parts of speech, the teacher must return and take particulars of each; such as the number and gender of nouns, and kinds of verbs.

In Syntax, the rules should be educed by the pupils themselves, from observing the usage of the language. Thus, with a class commencing the first rule, the teacher would not dogmatically say, "A verb must agree with its nominative in number and person;" but would proceed somewhat in this way:—

Teacher.—What do you do every day before you come to school?

Pupil.—I eat my breakfast.

Teacher.—And what does he do?

Pupil.—He eats his.

Teacher.—Then we say he——

Pupil.—Eats.

Teacher.—But I——

Pupil.—Eat.

Teacher.—What, then, are *he* and *I* in the sentences?

Pupil.—Nominatives.

Teacher.—What difference is there in them?

Pupil.—*I* is the first person, and *he* the third.

Teacher.—Then nominatives of different persons——

Pupil.—Have not the same part of the verb.

Teacher.—But if I were telling some one the same about you all, what should I say?

Pupil.—They eat their breakfast.

Teacher.—What person is *they?*

Pupil.—The third person.

Teacher.—Is this like the third person singular?

Pupil.—No.

Teacher.—What is the difference?

Pupil.—He eats; but they eat.

Teacher.—Then nominatives of different numbers——

Pupil.—Have different parts of the verb.

Teacher.—Well, then, the general rule is this—A verb agrees with its nominative in number and person.

73. The above is given as a sketch of the general mode of instruction with regard to this part of the subject. In practice, the teacher will often find that he has to put many more questions before the pupils will be able to draw the rule or inference. But if in some cases it is more difficult to teach the children to *think*, than "to learn," it must be borne in mind that the first is always incomparably more valuable than the second; that in fact this individual discernment of principles, and the mental vigor which is the consequence of it, are among the chief ends of intellectual education.

74. In teaching the derivation of words, free and extended use should be made of the blackboard. For example, if the teacher were explaining words derived from Anglo-Saxon roots, he would put down such roots under each other, forming one column, and the derivations to the right hand, forming another. Then, taking Dr. Cornwell's "*Grammar*," he might say, "Bugan" means "to bend." When this was written down, he would add:—

Teacher.—Tell me any words made from it?

(*Pupils silent, perhaps.*)

Teacher.—When one man bends to another, what do we say he does?

Pupil.—Makes a bow.

Teacher.—An instrument we bend in order to shoot with, is called——

Pupil.—A bow.

Teacher.—That part of a tree which bends off from the trunk?

Pupil.—A bough.

Teacher.—That part of a coast which forms a bend by the running in of the ocean?

Pupil.—A bay.

Second Pupil.—A small bay.

Third Pupil.—A bight.

Teacher.—The bend of the arm is called——

Pupil.—The elbow.

Teacher.—The other part of elbow is derived from the word *elne*, meaning an arm. These words would be written down as they were mentioned; and then another root written under *bugan*, and derivatives discovered by the pupils from it in the same way.

The board would present this appearance at the close:—

Bugan ... to bend ... bow, bough, bay, bight, el-bow (elne, an arm.)

Ceapian ... to buy ... chop (chop and change,) chaffer, cheap, chapman, Cheapside, Chepstow (stow, a place.)

The pupils should, in all cases, find out the derivatives for themselves if possible. If any difficulty is experienced, the teacher should refer to the prefixes or affixes, which will generally remove it. Thus, if the derivatives from *traho*, I draw, *tractus*, drawn, were sought, the teacher might ask the question, "What prefix means '*together?*'"

Pupil.—Con.

Teacher.—Then to draw together is——

Pupil.—To con-tract.

Teacher.—What stands for "*separation?*"

Pupil.—Dis.

Teacher.—Then to draw aside is——
Pupil.—To dis-tract.
Teacher.—What prefix means "*out?*"
Pupil.—Ex.
Teacher.—Then to draw out is——
Pupil.—To extract.*

75. Lessons, and exercises on composition, from Cornwell's "*Young Composer*," accompany the study of grammar throughout the school, the exercises being *oral* in the gallery, and *written* in the desks. Grammar is taught only at the draft stations; while derivation and composition are studied in the gallery and at the desks, as well as in connection with the reading at the draft stations.

76. Besides lessons on composition, the elder children frequently have exercises given them to be written at home in the evening, and brought next morning for examination and criticism. Sometimes they are required to write all they know about an animal, as a cow, a dog, or a lion. At other times a familiar object is chosen, as a knife, or a kettle; while occasionally they are expected to answer questions in writing on some one of their school studies, or to bring an abstract of a recent collective lesson. In examining these papers notice is taken, not only of the composition, but of the spelling, punctuation, place of capitals, and the correctness and fullness of the information contained in them. This is found to be one of the most valuable exercises carried on in the school.

Section 10.—*Class Teaching—Geography.*

77. GEOGRAPHY is taught to all the children, both in the lower and upper schools, in two distinct courses, proceeding parallel with each other.

The first relates to physical geography; the second to the study of maps.

In teaching physical geography, an explanation and definition of the different forms and appearances of land and water is first given. The idea of a plain is brought out by directing the attention of the children to *some level* piece of ground in the neighborhood, from which other tracts, of larger extent and different appearances, are described to them. Then follow the ideas of a *swelling* of the ground, a hillock, hill, mount, mountain, which are treated in like manner. Starting from a plain again, the teacher gives to the gallery the ideas of hole, hollow, vale, valley, defile, and then draws out the definitions. In a similar way other definitions are taught, closing with a general recapitulation, at the end of which the pupils are expected to have obtained a tolerably correct notion of the general appearance of the globe.

78. As the course proceeds, the children are made acquainted, by means of simple and inductive gallery lessons, with the form of the earth, of which they are required to give proofs. To this is added latitude and longitude; the motions of the earth, and their causes; the great continents and seas, their general forms and relative proportions; mountains, and table lands, rivers, springs, lakes, plains, deserts, and volcanoes, each of which forms a separate lesson. Then follow lessons on the distribution of man, animals, and vegetables, over

* A teacher who is not acquainted with Latin, should be extremely careful, in teaching the derivatives from that language, to get the *quantities* of the vowels, and the *termination* of the roots, correctly. By neglecting this, he may make himself ridiculous. He should indeed abstain from teaching any part of this branch, till he has himself studiously prepared and thoroughly mastered it.

the earth's surface; the consideration of the earth as a part of the solar system; and the method of measuring a degree on the surface of the globe. The whole is closed by lessons on eclipses, tides, winds, currents, climate, meteors, and the geological structure of the earth's crust.

79. At the time when this course of instruction commences, another on Map Geography is also begun; one lesson every week being given in the first, and two in the second.

The study of *maps* is commenced by a lesson on the measurement of space, in which the children are taught to realize the idea of an inch, foot, yard, or mile, by reference to a foot rule; to the length and breadth of the school premises; and to the distance from the school to their homes and other well-known places. Lessons are then given on the following subjects preparatory to the study of maps:—the cardinal and semi-cardinal points, by reference to the place of the sun at midday; plan of the school-room and its boundaries; relative positions of known objects; the school-room on different scales; plan of the neighborhood; plan of London.

80. The idea of latitude is introduced by drawing a line on the school-room floor from east to west; the teacher then asks, "On which side of this line are you sitting?"

Pupil.—The *north.*

Teacher.—On which side is that wall?

Pupil.—The *south.*

Other places in like manner are referred to on the same line, and the terms north and south latitude are given. The line from which latitude is really reckoned is then explained, and the fact disclosed that *we* are living in a northern latitude. Longitude is unfolded in a similar manner, by drawing a line from the north to the south side of the school-room.

81. The first map introduced is that of the county in which the school is situated, when the knowledge already gained is brought to bear on the study of it. Next follows a map of the surrounding counties, then a chart of the river Thames, and then a map of England. When this part of the course has been fairly mastered, the children are taken to the map of the British Isles, to the study of which they devote about two months. The Eastern and Western hemispheres; the scenes of Sacred History; Europe, Asia, America, Africa, and Oceania, succeed. In these, the parts most intimately connected with England, such as Australia, Hindostan, the West Indies, and the United States of America, receive special attention. With those pupils who remain in school a sufficient time to proceed beyond this point, a course of lessons on the map of the ancient world is adopted, embracing the main facts of Ancient History.

82. In taking up the study of a map with a section of the school, the physical features should be taught first:—the great mountain ranges, plains, rivers, and lakes; then the political divisions; then the towns. The dependencies of the political and social geography of a country on its physical features should be constantly pointed out: as, for example, why our manufactures are traveling westward? why Liverpool has risen so rapidly to first-rate importance as a port? why the capital of England is just where it is? In studying any particular country, however, before entering on details, its position with regard to the neighboring states should be thoroughly understood by the pupils. Thus, if the country were Palestine, it should be first shown on a map of the world, and

then on a map of Asia, the pupils pointing out the countries around it, and naming them. The teacher would then proceed with the physical features, in the order before mentioned; its divisions; and then its towns.

83. These particulars will be best taught by means of *large school-room maps*, the children being seated in the gallery and the teacher pointing to each place, as it is found in Dr. Cornwell's "*School Geography*," during the lesson. Skeleton maps, too, entirely without names, may be used with advantage in the drafts, provided the teacher is well acquainted with the map before him. The boys should also be occasionally furnished with slates, or with chalk and a blackboard, and be required to draw various portions of the world. Their acquaintance with a country may sometimes be tested, by requiring them to fill up these bare outlines, without seeing a map. Thus, the teacher might say, "Put down on the board Mount Lebanon, the Jordan, or Jerusalem."

84. When a lesson has been gone through by the teacher on the skeleton map, mutual interrogation sometimes ensues; each boy in turn, beginning at the last, puts a question, and rises or falls in proportion to his skill in questioning, and the extent of his knowledge. The scope of the questions they are allowed to put is very extensive: they may propose questions on points of general history, or biography, which have not been mentioned by the teacher, but the knowledge of which they have attained by reading or conversation.

If we suppose the map to be Palestine, and Tyre to be the spot under consideration, some such questions as these would probably be put:—

Teacher.—Where is it?
Pupil.—On an island.
Teacher.—Describe the situation of the island.
Pupil.—It is at the eastern extremity of the Levant, opposite the northern part of the Holy Land, from which it is separated by a narrow strait.
Teacher.—What occasioned its erection on an island?
Pupil.—Its being attacked by Nebuchadnezzar.
Teacher.—For what was it remarkable?
Pupil.—For commercial prosperity.
Teacher.—In what class of powers should we place it?
Pupil.—Naval.
Teacher.—Was the second Tyre ever taken?
Pupil.—Yes.
Teacher.—By whom?
Pupil.—By Alexander the Great.
Teacher.—Cite a passage of scripture relating to that event.
Pupil.—Isaiah xxiii.
Teacher.—What is Tyre now?
Pupil.—A place resorted to by fishermen to dry their nets.
Teacher.—The prophecy respecting this?
Pupil.—Ezekiel xxvi. 14.
Teacher.—To what power does it now belong?
Pupil.—To Turkey.
Teacher.—What nation in modern times did it most resemble, and in what particulars?

To such questions as these a more irregular but not less searching course of mutual interrogation ensues, as—

Teacher.—What city in Africa was founded by a colony from Tyre?
Pupil.—Carthage.

Teacher.—How did Alexander's army approach the walls of Carthage?

Pupil.—By a mole.

Teacher.—What city did he advance against, after taking Tyre?

Pupil.—Jerusalem.

Teacher.—How long did Nebuchadnezzar besiege old Tyre?

Pupil.—Nearly fourteen years.

Teacher.—How long did new Tyre detain Alexander.

Pupil.—Seven months.

Teacher.—Mention the year in which Tyre was destroyed by Nebuchadnezzar, and also that in which it was taken by Alexander?

Pupil.—572 and 332, before the Christian era.

Teacher.—Why is it called the daughter of Sidon by Isaiah?

Pupil.—Because it was built by the Sidonians.

Teacher.—Mention the prophecy which foretold its destruction by Nebuchadnezzar.

Pupil.—Ezekiel xxvi. 26, and following verses.

Teacher.—What chapter describes the sources of the wealth of Tyre?

Pupil.—Ezekiel xxvii.

Teacher.—What prophecy was fulfilled after Alexander quitted Tyre?

Pupil.—That it should be forgotten seventy years, (Isaiah, xxiii. 15.)

Teacher.—Where is the prophecy of Alexander's success at Tyre to be found?

Pupil.—In Isaiah xxiii. 11, 12.

These, and many other questions might be put and answered in much less time than this account is written. If the question be not prompt, or the answer ready, another boy quickly proceeds, or the teacher again takes the subject up. In this way all the information any one may possess will be elicited and communicated to the rest.

85. A very large amount of the knowledge gained in geography is acquired incidentally, in connection with the reading classes. Every place occurring in a Reading Lesson, whether in the Bible or the Lesson Books, should be pointed out on a map, and information relating to it should be imparted. Thus, if the children are reading that Alfred concealed himself in the island of Athelney, the teacher should put questions to bring out the following facts; or, if unknown, he should state them. (1.) Athelney is in the west of England. (2.) In the county of Somerset. (3.) It is an island formed by the rivers Tone and Parret. (4.) It received its name Athelney (meaning Nobles' Island,) because Alfred and his nobles here concealed themselves. In reading the 27th chapter of Acts, the ancient geography of the most important places eastward of Italy, on the northern and eastern shores of the Mediterranean, should in like manner be taught, in order to render the chapter intelligible.

86. When this course of map geography has been so arranged as to give a tolerable notion of the various countries of the world, and of such particulars respecting them as are most necessary to be known during the far too limited period of school education, it is felt that there are some portions which require to be more minutely studied. With this view *blank maps* of England, the British Isles, Palestine, and Europe, Australia, and the United States, have been prepared, and one of them is studied at each draft station during some one or other of the exercises in each week. This plan enables the teachers of the various sections to revise and fix the knowledge already obtained by the children during the collective lessons, as well as to extend their acquaintance with the particular parts of geography most likely to be useful to them.

Section 11.—Class Teaching—Miscellaneous Lessons.

87. Enough, it is hoped, has been said to show *the methods* employed in the education of children at the central school. It will therefore be sufficient merely to specify the remaining subjects, and to point out what is communicated in connection with each.

88. *Courses of collective lessons* are arranged and given on English History; the Philosophy of Health; Natural History; Objects and Manufactures; the Philosophy of Common Things; and Political Economy. • Reading lessons are also found on most of these subjects in the Daily Lesson Book, No. IV., and are studied in the middle and upper part of the school.

All that can be attempted in these branches is to give the pupil sound general views concerning them; to impart a desire for the acquisition of further knowledge; to exhibit the method of carrying on the study of each or all to the best advantage; and to make them instruments for developing a spirit of intelligent, humble inquiry concerning the works of God and the laws of their being.

89. In *English History*, the leading events of different periods with their causes and consequences—the gradual development of the constitution of our country—its trade, commerce, and literature, and the condition of its people at the various epochs of their history, are dwelt upon.

90. In lessons on the *Philosophy of Health*, the composition of the atmosphere, and the part it bears in the formation of the blood—the effects of bad air—insufficient or improper food and drink—the benefits arising from cleanliness in the skin, clothes, and dwellings—and the consequences arising from bad water, and want of drainage, as illustrated by reference to the structure of the skin, lungs, and blood of the human frame, form the substance of the instruction given.

91. In *Natural History*, the adaptation of the parts and constitution of animals and vegetables to their habits, places of abode, and food, are taught in connection with the best known and most remarkable specimens in each kingdom; and suggestions are given as to the way in which these exhibit the wisdom and goodness of their great Creator. This part of the course is followed by another on classification; and the whole is concluded by bringing to the notice of the children the leading facts in animal and vegetable physiology.

92. The *manufacture* of the articles in daily use by the children is brought forward in connection with the objects themselves. The lessons on the *philosophy of common things* explain the construction of a child's syringe; the common pump; fire engine; thermometer and barometer; the telescope and microscope; the steam-engine and its varied applications; the diving bell; balloons, and mariner's compass, and the principles on which their construction depends.

93. The laws which regulate supply and demand, as illustrated by the varying prices of labor, and of the articles of food and clothing in daily use among the children; the nature and value of money, and its use in the operations of trade and commerce; the relations which labor and capital bear to each other; the ways in which rapid, safe, and cheap communication between the different parts of the same country, and the various nations of the earth, serve to increase and cheapen the necessaries and comforts of life; how war not only destroys life and capital, but also does much to prevent the reproduction of wealth: these, and such other lessons as may appear necessary to show the

conditions of a nation's prosperity, together with the duties men have to sustain to each other and to the state, as masters, servants, or citizens, are explained and exemplified in the lessons on political economy.

Section 12.—*Class Teaching—Drawing.*

94. In the central school this exercise consists of the following course:—

(*a.*) Lineal drawing on slate or blackboard. The influence of lineal drawing in assisting to produce a good handwriting has long been noticed. Both tend to develop the faculty of form. This exercise is therefore given to the whole school, and consists, in the first place of outlines of geometrical forms, accompanied by questions as to the length of lines and the size of figures, and the division of lines into halves and quarters. The text-book in this part of the course is Pickton's "*Lineal Drawing.*" Afterwards, outlines of simple objects of furniture, flowers, and ornaments of various kinds are drawn. The teacher is furnished with a pair of compasses and a graduated ruler, and thus corrects the attempts of the pupils, when necessary, with perfect accuracy. Here, two objects are aimed at, (1.) the training of the eye; (2.) the training of the hand.

(*b.*) Botanical, animal, map, and general drawing, from copies and specimens.

(*c.*) Model and object drawing, in which Butler Williams's course of model drawing is accompanied and followed by the delineation of objects, with illustrations of the main principles of perspective.

(*d.*) Design drawing, in which the children are put through a preliminary course of practice in combining straight and curved lines into pleasing figures. They are afterwards taught to draw from plaster casts, and then encouraged to originate designs which may be useful for the purposes of ornament and manufacture.

(*e.*) Geometrical drawing with instruments, intended to teach the pupils the construction of such problems as are most required among carpenters, masons, and handicraftsmen in general.

(*f.*) Architectural and plan drawing, including the various parts of a common building, such as staircases, closets, &c., as well as the different styles and orders of architecture.

Lineal drawing is practiced first with slate and pencil, then on blackboard with chalk, and afterwards on paper, in pencil and crayon.

Section 13.—*Class Teaching—Vocal Music.*

95. The exercises on this subject consist of two divisions:—

(*a.*) Singing by ear. Simple school and marching pieces are taught to the whole school. These are set to cheerful and instructive words, and serve to convey much useful information, as well as to recommend moral precepts in a pleasing manner. The practice of these simple pieces forms an agreeable change from the more difficult exercises of the school, and enlivens the changes from one study to another.

(*b.*) Singing from notes. Those children who show an aptitude for the study of vocal music are formed into three classes, and spend about three half-hours every week in the study and practice of this art.

96. The *first* class is introduced to the subject by the teacher producing a sound with his own voice, and exemplifying the differences in length, pitch, and loudness; the children imitating at every step. After a few sounds have been

thus taught, and the method of representing them with their pitch and length by *notes* on a *staff*, the pupils are trained to produce any sound named by the teacher. He then practices them, by pointing to the different lines and spaces on the staff at random, and requiring the class to produce the sound thus indicated. The great object at this stage is to give the children an idea of *music* as distinct from the signs employed to represent it.

The next step consists of a selection from the sheet exercises contained in Hullah's system of vocal music, relieved by the occasional practice of easy school pieces, previously written out on the large music board.

97. The *second* class is introduced to the use of music books; two pupils singing from one copy. The music in use consists of selections from Crampton's school pieces, Curwen, Hickson, and the least difficult portions of Hullah's Part Music.

The *third* class is composed of the pupil teachers and a few of the most advanced among the children. The publications of Hullah and Novello are those chiefly in use.

The whole course is accompanied by the frequent use of *sol-fa-ing*, and as much of the theory of music as is necessary to render it intelligible and useful.

IV. SCRIPTURAL INSTRUCTION.

1. More importance is attached to scripture teaching in the daily occupation of the central school than to any other branch of instruction. It is believed that direct religious instruction and training must form the basis of every true system of education, and that the Scriptures should be made the *text-book* of that instruction and training. With this view a scripture collective lesson is given daily to the younger children, until they are able to read the book of scripture selections published by the Society. After this stage two scripture lessons are given in the gallery every week; and three-quarters of an hour on each of the other three days are employed in scripture reading.

2. The subjects of the gallery lessons from scripture are—its narratives; its parables and miracles; its doctrinal portions; the attributes of God; moral duties; and scriptural emblems and illustrations.

Bible geography, history, and biography, the government and public worship of the Jews, Jewish sects and customs, are taken up in the reading classes.

The general principle on which this division proceeds, is, that whenever it is the *chief* object to train the affections, and develop the moral nature, the collective lesson is the most effective instrument; while scripture reading in drafts (each child having an open copy of the Word of God in his hand,) is most useful when matters of detail are concerned, or individual searching of the Bible is required.

3. The same general principles should guide the teacher in giving the scripture lesson as have been already stated under the head "Collective Teaching;" a calm and quiet tone of voice, and a reverent manner, should be always preserved; and the teacher should not make statements, or draw conclusions, on his own authority, but continually refer to the Word of God.

The sketches of these lessons, however, differ materially from those on secular subjects. Two are given below, one on a narrative lesson, and one on an emblem lesson, as specimens of the two distinctive methods of preparing them.

Sketch of a Scripture Narrative Lesson.—The Prodigal Son.—LUKE XV. 11—24.

I. EXPLANATION.

v. 11. *He*—Jesus.

v. 12. *Portion of goods*—that part of his father's property which fell to his share. Explain eastern custom of dividing patrimony.

His living—his property; all that belonged to him.

v. 13. *Wasted his substance*—spent all he had.

Riotous living—feasting, gambling, &c.

v. 14. *Mighty famine*—great scarcity of food.

v. 15. *Feed swine*—disgraceful service; why?

v. 16. *Would fain*—wished very much.

v. 17. *Came to himself*—began to think in a proper manner about his evil ways. When was he out of his mind?

v. 18. *Heaven*—God, who is in heaven.

Before—against.

v. 19. *Worthy*—why not?

v. 20. *Had Compassion*—was sorry for him.

v. 23. *Fatted calf*—always one ready; why?

v. 24. *Dead—Lost.* The father looked upon his son as entirely lost; as much so as if he was dead.

II. DESCRIPTION.

(*a.*) What persons are mentioned?—what is said about *one* of them?—impatient of control, wishes to leave home, sells his goods, leaves home, perhaps with several servants, and with much show and pomp—look at him as he goes along the road—tell me what you see—goes a great distance from home, why?—lives in splendor—bad companions.

(*b.*) When do we hear of him next?—what is he doing?—how came he there?—spent his money, bad companions will not help him—no food—tries to get work—has not learnt how to get his living—takes care of swine—how did he feel there?—what did he wish to do?—why?—what does he say?—where does he go?

(*c.*) Let us look at him as he returns—compare with his setting out from home, hungry, barefooted, ragged, humble—which was best state?—comes near home, sees some one at door, who is it?—feels afraid that his father will turn him away—hesitates—shall he go back—father sees him—what does he do?—(*Here bring out the scene at meeting.*)

III. APPLICATION.

1. Who meant by father?—by son?—by his wishing to leave home?—what meant by his going away?—spending his substance?—in a far country?—feeding swine?—returning?—father very kind to his returning son—God is kind to repenting sinners who seek his pardon.

2. What can *we* learn from this? We are sinners, what should we do? When these points are brought out, the teacher concludes with a *few* words of application to the children' own circumstances.

4. The above is a sketch of a lesson given some time ago to a section of the school; it was intended to direct the attention of the pupil teacher to the *points* to be noticed, and to the *manner* of noticing them, as well as to the *order* in which they should be taken up. The children being seated in the gallery, and a few exercises gone through, for the purpose of fixing their attention, the master took up the Bible, announced the chapter and verse, and, after a few questions, began to read at the 11th verse. As the reading proceeded, the meaning of certain words was asked, and several questions were put for the purpose of exciting thought and preventing inattention. When the reading was

finished, the teacher closed the book, and commenced *the "Description;"* the object in this part of the lesson being to *vivify* the narrative, by means of graphic description, questions, and ellipses; so that the children might realize in their minds, *as a connected whole*, the various circumstances spoken of, and so the way be prepared for the lesson to be deduced. The "Application" was then *drawn from* the children, and the lesson was applied to their own case, and impressed upon their minds by two or three words of serious remark on the marvelous love of God to sinful man. It should be observed that the *sketch* lay on a table beside the teacher, but was only once referred to for a moment or two during the course of the lesson.

Sketch of a Scripture Emblem Lesson.

" *The beginning of strife is as when one letteth out water; therefore leave off contention before it be meddled with.*"—PROVERBS xvii. 14.

I. THE FIGURE.

(*a.*) Who has seen a piece of water in motion? What is its name? *The Thames.** Tell us what you saw on it. *Boats, ships, packets.* What moves them along? *Steam, wind, oars.* Yes; but some were moved along——*By the water.* The water, then, moves——*with great force.* Who could stop it? Still less able to do so near the sea. Where does this river rise? How do you think it appears there? *Narrow, shallow, has little power.* There you might easily control it or turn it aside.

(*b.*) There is a noted river in North America, which falls down a precipice with great force, what is it called? *Niagara.* For some time it flows on peacefully and quietly, then it begins to move more quickly; why? It goes on moving quicker and quicker; at length it comes to a precipice; what happens to it then? *It tumbles down with very great force and noise.* Suppose any one tried to stop or turn it? *He would be carried away, and dashed to pieces.* Yes, it carries down boats, ships, any thing that comes in its way (*tell anecdote of persons carried away by it.*)

(*c.*) Allude to the tragedy of Holmfirth; repeat the circumstance. Before the water burst out, the reservoirs could easily have been made to keep it in; but they were neglected. In the dead of the night the water burst out; it rushes on, carries away houses, men, women, and children, trees, every thing in its way. Destroys much property, and many lives; but all this might have been easily hindered by keeping the water in its basin.

(*d.*) What country is it that the sea is kept from overflowing by means of dykes or banks? *Holland.* Sometimes these dykes give way; sea rushes over the land, destroys people, crops, houses, every thing in its way. Once a little boy was walking beside one of these dykes, saw the sea oozing through a little hole in it, put his finger in, and stopped it, until help arrived. What would have happened had not the hole been stopped? But all this was very easily prevented by stopping the sea out at first.

II. THE MEANING.

Repeat the verse. What is likened to water "let out?" Explain strife. Quarreling; trying who shall be master. Speak of nations striving; England and France; thousands killed, money wasted, misery and death brought on both nations. Imagine one of the battles; thousands of soldiers on each side, with swords, bayonets, cannons; they rush at each other; then hundreds lie dead on the field; hundreds groaning with wounds. Mothers are left without husbands, children without fathers, sisters without brothers, what misery and death are

* Words in Italics signify answers given by the pupils.

caused! How could this have been prevented? *By a few kind words at first; by not beginning to quarrel.* Bring out consequences of individuals quarreling. Hatred for life, fighting, frequently murder; easily prevented by a little kindness at the beginning.

III. APPLICATION.

What can we learn from all this? What does the verse say? "*Therefore leave off,*" *&c.* Apply to children's own conduct toward each other. Boys playing, disagree, call names, perhaps fight, injure and sometimes kill each other. Show how much better to avoid beginning to quarrel. No good, but great harm arises from quarreling. Now, children, let me have a few more verses on this subject. Those children who know any raise their hands. (*Teacher, pointing to one*) You give us one, if you please. "*Hatred stirreth up strife, but love covereth all sins.*" What, then, is the cause of strife? *Hatred.* If, then, we do not wish to quarrel, what is to be done? *Keep from hating one another;—love one another.* It is an honor for a man to cease from strife. Those, then, who keep from quarreling are—— *The best, the most honorable. Where there is no talebearer the strife ceaseth.* We should, therefore——*Not tell tales*, or *speak evil one of another.*

Give another passage. "*An angry man stirreth up strife.*" We should therefore avoid——*Being angry.* Now let us have, in a few words, what we have learnt in this lesson. *Strife or quarreling is easily stopped in the beginning.* But leads to much misery if—— *We go on with it.* And because——What leads to quarreling? *Hating one another; speaking evil, and telling idle tales; anger.* Therefore we should love each other; keep from evil speaking, and from——*Anger.* Name one who set us an example in these things. *Jesus Christ.* Mention an instance. *When he was reviled, he reviled not again.* Another. *When he was beaten and spit upon, he answered not a word.* Again. *He prayed for his enemies on the cross.* Yes; and he tells us to——*Love one another, even as I have loved you.*

These scripture collective lessons should never be given by the pupil teacher or monitors, intended as they are to enlighten the judgment and draw out the affections of the children. No one should attempt to give them who does not himself in some degree feel the power of the truths they teach.

5. The following may be taken as a specimen of *an interrogative* lesson.

LOWER CLASS.

'*Seek ye the Lord while he may be found, call ye upon him while he is near.*"

Teacher.—Who are to seek?

Pupil.—All men.

Teacher.—Whom are we to seek?

Pupil.—The Lord.

Teacher.—When are we to seek the Lord?

Pupil.—While he may be found.

Teacher.—Whom are we to call upon?

Pupil.—Upon Him.

Teacher.—While who is near?

Pupil.—He.

Teacher.—Who is meant by He?

Pupil.—The Lord.

Teacher.—What is meant by seek?

Pupil.—Inquire after.

Teacher.—How are we to call on the Lord?

Pupil.—In faith.

Teacher.—What name is given to the act of calling on the Lord?

Pupil.—Prayer.

The advantages derived even from this first step are considerable. The children are habituated to search for sense in all they read; they are taught to analyze each sentence; and they gain much scriptural information. Nor is the facility which they acquire of expressing their ideas a matter of small importance. To give a correct or clear definition, clear conceptions of the subject are essential, and clear conceptions can not be obtained without attention and reflection.

HIGHER CLASS.

"*If thine enemy hunger, feed him; if he thirst, give him drink: for in so doing thou shalt heap coals of fire on his head.*"

Teacher.—What are we to do if our enemy hunger?

Pupil.—Feed him.

Teacher.—What are we to do if our enemy thirst?

Pupil.—Give him drink.

Teacher.—What shall we do by giving food and drink to an enemy?

Pupil.—Heap coals of fire on his head.

The teacher, in addition to such questions as these, would ask, "What is meant by 'enemy?'* 'hunger?' 'coals of fire?'"

6. When the teacher has ascertained that the facts or history of the passage, and the words occurring in it, are understood, the questioning should be still further carried out, to develop the general bearing: to explain the etymology of the principal words; to adduce collateral passages; and especially to enforce the application. Thus,

Teacher.—Why are we to feed our enemy?

Pupil.—Because the scriptures command it.

Teacher.—Give me another passage which proves it.

Pupil.—Be not overcome of evil.

Teacher.—Give me another.

Pupil.—Love your enemies; bless them that curse you; do good to them that hate you.

Teacher.—What is meant by heaping coals of fire on the head of an enemy?

Pupil.—Melting or softening him by kindness.

Teacher.—Give me some proof that this is the meaning.

Pupil.—Because, if taken in the other sense, it is doing him an injury, which is contrary to the scriptures.

Teacher.—Prove this by some passage of scripture?

Pupil.—In the parallel passage, (Prov. xxv.) it is added, that "For this the Lord shall reward thee." Another replies, "Over come evil with good." And another adds, "If thou meet thine enemy's ox, or his ass, going astray, thou shalt surely bring it back to him again."

Teacher.—Show how kindness to an enemy has this melting or softening tendency.

---

* The teacher should endeavor to let the scriptures be their own interpreter. To remove any misconception, he should lead the class to other passages in which the word or phrase occurs. Suppose that the draft is not able to give a suitable answer to the question "What is an enemy?" The master or teacher should say, "Give me another passage in which the word enemy occurs." They would probably cite the one in the parable, "The enemy that sowed them is the devil." And he would ask again, "What did the enemy there?" *P.* "He sowed tares among the wheat." *T.* "Did he get any wheat by sowing the tares there?" *P.* No!" *T.* "For what purpose did he sow them?" *P.* "To injure the man." *T.* "What name then is given to one who tries to injure another?" *P.* "An enemy." The object is frequently obtained by simply referring to the etymology of the word. Thus the teacher would say, "*Enemy* is derived from *amicus*, a friend, and *in*, not. An enemy, then, is one who is——" *P.* "Not a friend."

Pupil.—A soft answer turneth away wrath; or another, using his own words, might reply, "David spared Saul in the cave, when Saul was seeking his life: and when David called after him, and he knew what kindness David had shown him, he said, Is this thy voice, my son David? and Saul lifted up his voice and wept." And another might make such a remark as this, which would be accepted: "When we do wrong to any one else, and they do good to us in return, we are ashamed of having hurt them."

Teacher.—To whom, then, is this command addressed?

Pupil.—To all.

Teacher.—Do all men obey it?

Pupil.—No.

Teacher.—Why do they not?

Pupil.—Because the heart of man is evil.

Teacher.—What, then, is one mark of an evil mind?

Pupil.—An unforgiving spirit.

Teacher.—What of a spiritual?

Pupil.—A spirit of love.

Teacher.—To which of these does kindness to an enemy belong?

Pupil.—To the spiritual mind.

Teacher.—Whom should we try to resemble?

Pupil.—Christ.

Teacher.—Who are spoken of in the scriptures as enemies to God?

Pupil.—All men.

Teacher.—How has God treated us?

Pupil.—Loved us while we were enemies.

Teacher.—What may we learn from this?

Pupil.—That if God so loved us, we ought also to love one another.

Teacher.—To what extent are we to love one another?

Pupil.—As ourselves.

Teacher.—What is the first lesson we may learn from this subject?

Pupil.—That if our enemy be in our power, we are to repay his hatred with love.

Teacher.—What other lesson?

Pupil.—That our efforts must be directed to remove this hatred, and that we should pray to God to change his heart.

Teacher.—What other lesson?

Pupil.—That of the goods of which God has made us stewards, we are to be ready to dispense when the distribution will be productive of good.

It would not be convenient or judicious to carry out questions to this extent upon every sentence read, but it is hoped that no regularly initiated teacher will either find difficulty or feel a disinclination to make its style and spirit his daily practice in the higher classes.

In addition to this mode of interrogation, it is also useful to allow the boys to question each other occasionally, beginning at the last boy, and allowing the questioner to take precedence of all not able to answer his question.

V. NEEDLE-WORK.

1. As the arrangements, discipline, and methods of teaching employed in the girls' school are identical with those pursued in that for boys, it would be a mere waste of paper to recapitulate statements or directions already sufficiently clear and minute.

Certain variations in the time table, necessary in order to make room for the acquisition of an art so indispensably necessary to girls as that of needle-work, will have to be made; but these will suggest themselves to every intelligent teacher, and will be modified by the peculiar circumstances of each school.

It is therefore only necessary to add, for the guidance of female teachers, that the following classification in methods of teaching needle-work has for many years been adopted at the Girls' Model School, and has been found to work very advantageously.

2. When the scholars are employed at needle-work, they are seated at desks, and arranged in classes, according to their proficiency. The first, or lowest class, is seated farthest from the platform, and the others in numerical order before. The number of classes depends on the different kinds of work taught in the school, as each kind constitutes a class. The number in general use is eleven.

3. From the higher classes the best workers are selected for monitors; two are appointed for each class; one instructs for one week, whilst the other is at work under the direction of her monitor; consequently each superintends the class, and works alternately; and each monitor continues at the same desk, until she is appointed monitor to a higher class. Every girl continues to sit at the same desk while she remains in the section. There are also two monitors, who alternately superintend and work one week. But all the monitors of classes, and the girls under their care, are under the superintendence of a pupil teacher appointed for the purpose. Every Friday the girls are allowed to bring their own work.

4. The children in the higher classes are provided with lap-bags, made of brown holland; these are marked 1, 2, 3, &c., for as many as the desk contains. The number of the desk is also marked upon them; thus, $\frac{5}{8}$ signifies that the bag belongs to the fifth girl in the eighth desk.

5. Before the children take their seats, the bags are placed by the platform monitor on the class monitors' desks, and by them given to their girls. The class-work, and all garments in hand, are collected by the class monitors, and placed on the ends of the desks, ready for the platform monitor to deliver to the mistress. The monitor of each desk is furnished with a pair of scissors, thread-paper, needle-case, and a bag large enough to contain all the implements that belong to her desk. They are also supplied with a few thimbles and needles, for which they are responsible to the platform monitor. The children use colored cotton for the class-work, as it renders the stitches more conspicuous, and consequently facilitates general inspection; it also excites an interest, as the promise of a choice of some pretty color is a strong inducement to a child to perform her work neatly.

6. A quarter of an hour before the time devoted to needle-work, the business of the school is stopped by a given signal, and the girls are sent to their seats by an exercise suited to the arrangement of the school-room. Each monitor then takes her position at the desk, and at a given sign distributes the work to her class.

7. A signal is now given for the monitors to distribute the bags, after which they return to their seats, and another signal is given for each girl to tie her own bag; a signal is again given, for the monitors to examine their girls' hands, to see if they are clean, and that each is provided with a needle and thimble. The platform monitor now supplies the class monitors with any additional work they may require for their girls, which the class monitors give out, also a needleful of cotton to each girl, and then return to their seats. A command is now

given for the whole school to show work; that is, to hold it up in their left hand, to see that each is furnished with work. The bell is then rung, each child holds down her work, and immediately begins; and the monitors pass down the desks to instruct them. When a child wants work, she holds up her left hand, as an intimation to her monitor, who steps forward and supplies her. If a monitor wants a fresh supply, she makes a like signal to the platform monitor. When a girl wants thread, she holds up her right hand, and her monitor supplies her. While the children are at their work the teacher should pass through the classes to examine it, and at the close of the time allotted to this exercise reward those who merit it, and detain any girls who have been inattentive to do a certain portion of work after.

8. The bell rings for the girls to show work, and the monitors to pass down the desks, and collect the needles and thimbles. An order is then given for the children to put the class-work into the bags; and the monitors to collect all articles in hand, and deliver them to the platform monitor who takes them to the platform. The monitors then take their seats. The order is now given to untie bags, when each child unties her own; a second order is given, to take them off; and a third, to fold them up. Each child folds her own neatly, with the number in view, places it on the desk before her, and puts her hands behind her. The bell then rings for the monitors to collect bags, which they do, placing them one on the other, in order; they then put them neatly into the bag belonging to their desk; also their scissors, thread-papers, needles, and thimbles. The monitors are then ordered to the platform, with their bags, where they deliver them to the platform monitor; they then return to their seats, and the report of the good and inattentive girls is read *aloud.* When this exercise is concluded the children are exercised out of their seats, and either resume their studies or are dismissed, according to the time the needle-work is conducted.

NORMAL SCHOOLS; and other Institutions, Agencies and Means, designed for the Professional Education of Teachers. By Henry Barnard, Superintendent of Common Schools in Connecticut. Hartford, 1851.

The above work was first published in 1847, to aid the establishment of a Normal School in Rhode Island, and afterwards circulated largely in Connecticut for the same object. It was enlarged in 1850, and published as one of a series of Essays which the author as the Superintendent of Common Schools, was authorized by the Legislature to prepare for general circulation in Connecticut, to enable the people to appreciate the importance of the State Normal School, which had been established on a temporary basis in 1849. The documents embraced in this treatise are of permanent value.

In addition to an account of the organization and course of instruction in the best Normal Schools in Europe and in this country, it embraces elaborate papers on the nature and advantages of Institutions for the professional training of teachers, by Gallaudet, Carter, Stowe Emerson, Everett, Humphrey, Mann, and others.

LEGAL PROVISION RESPECTING THE EDUCATION AND EMPLOYMENT OF CHILDREN IN FACTORIES AND MANUFACTURING ESTABLISHMENTS; with an Appendix on the Influence of Education. on the Quality and pecuniary value of labor, and its connection with Insanity and Crime. By Henry Barnard, L L. D. F. C. Brownell, Hartford. 84 pages.

This pamphlet of 84 pages, was prepared by the author in 1842, to fortify some recommendations contained in his Report as Secretary of the Board of Commissioners of Common Schools, for more thorough legislation to protect the health, morals, and souls of children from the cupidity of employers, and of parents, and at the same time to show how the productive power of the State could be augmented, and the waste of property, health and happiness, might be prevented by such an education as could and should be given in Common or Public Schools. The statistics and legislation on these subjects are of permanent and universal interest.

PRACTICAL ILLUSTRATIONS OF THE PRINCIPLES OF SCHOOL ARCHITECTURE. Third edition. By Henry Barnard. Hartford; F. C. Brownell. 1856.

This work is an abridgment by the author, of his large treatise on School Architecture, made originally for a Committee of the American Association for the Advancement of Education, and adopted as the first of the series of Essays prepared for general circulation in the state of Connecticut. An edition of 5000 copies was printed for circulation in Great Britain, at the expense of Vere Foter, Esq., of London.

CONNECTICUT COMMON SCHOOL JOURNAL; Vol. I, to Vol. VIII.

The Conn. Common School Journal was edited and published by Mr. Barnard, as Secretary of the Board of Commissioners of Common Schools, from Aug. 1838 to Aug. 1842; and as Superintendent of Common Schools in Conn., from 1850 to 1855. On the 1st of Jan. 1855, its publication was assumed by the State Teachers' Association.

Reports and Documents relating to the Common School System of Connecticut. Hartford: Case, Tiffany & Co.

This Volume is made up of different numbers of the Connecticut Common School Journal, which contain separate documents of permanent value. It makes a large quarto volume of 400 pages, in double columns, and small type. Price $1.00.

I.—DOCUMENTS CONNECTED WITH THE COMMON SCHOOLS OF CONNECTICUT FROM MAY, 1838, TO MAY, 1842.

Reports of the Board of Commissioners of Common Schools, for 1839, 1840, 1841, 1842
Barnard's Report—Legislative Document, 1838.
" Address of the Board of Commissioners of C. S. to the People, 1838.
" First Annual Report to the Board of C. C. S., 1839; Second do. for 1840; Third do. for 1841; Fourth do. for 1842.
" Report on Education in other States and Countries, 1840.
" " Public Schools in Boston, Providence, Lowell, Worcester, &c., 1841.
" Address on School-houses in 1839.
" Report on Public Schools of Hartford, 1841.
" Remarks on the History and Condition of the School Laws of Connecticut, 1841.
" Report on the Legal Provision respecting the Education and Employment of Children in Factories in various States and Countries.
" Letter to a Committee of the Legislature on the Expenses of the Board of Commissioners, 1841.
Reports of School Visitors in most of the Towns in Connecticut, for 1840 to 1842.
Summary of the Legislation of the State respecting Schools from 1647 to 1839.
Act to provide for the better Supervision of Common Schools, passed 1838.
Act giving additional powers to School Districts and School Societies, 1839.
Revised Common School Act, 1841.
Report and Act for repealing the Board of Commissioners, 1842.

II.—DOCUMENTS OR ARTICLES RESPECTING THE SCHOOL SYSTEM OF OTHER STATES AND COUNTRIES.

Condition of Public Education in Scotland, Ireland, England, and Wales, from various sources.
" " " Holland, by Prof. Bache, Cousin, and Cuvier.
" " " Prussia, by Prof. Bache, Cousin, Wyse, and Prof. Stowe.
" " " Duchy of Baden, and Nassau, by Prof. James.
" " " Austria, by Prof. Turnbull and Bache.
" " " Tuscany, from Qu. Review.
" " " Switzerland, from Journal of Education, and Prof. Bache
" " " Bavaria and Hanover, by Hawkins.
" " " Saxony, by Prof. Bache.
" " " Russia, by Prof. Stowe.
" " " France, by Mrs. Austin and Prof. Bache.
" " " Belgium, from Foreign Qu. Review.

III.—NORMAL SCHOOLS, OR TEACHERS' SEMINARIES.

History of Teachers' Seminaries.
Essays on, by Rev. T. H. Gallaudet.
Address respecting, by Prof. Stowe.
Account of in Prussia, by Dr. Julius.
" " France, by Guizot.
" " Holland, by Cousin.
" " Europe, by Prof. Bache.
" " Massachusetts, by Mr. Mann.
" " New York, by Mr. Dix.
Normal Seminary, Glasgow.
Teachers' Departments, New York.
State Normal School at Lexington, Mass.
Borough Road School, London.
Primary Normal School, at Haarlem, (Holland.)
Seminary for Teachers, at Weissenfels, Prussia.
" " Potsdam, "
Primary Normal School at Stettin.
" " " Brühl and Neuweid
Normal School at Versailles, France.
" " Kussnacht, Switzerland
" " Beuggen, "
" " Hofwyl, "

IV.—ACCOUNT OF PARTICULAR SCHOOLS.

Infant Schools.
Model Infant School, Glasgow.
" " " London.
Quaker Street Infant, "
Infant School in Lombardy.
" " Rotterdam.

Evening Schools.—Schools of Industry, &c.
Evening School in London.
School of Industry at Norwood.
" " Ealing.
" " Lindfield.
" " Gowers Walk.
" " Guernsey.
" " Warwick.
" for Juvenile Offenders, Rotterdam.

Public Schools of Various Grades.
Primary School at the Hague.
Intermediate School at Leyden.
Borough Road School, London.
Sessional School, Edinburgh.
High School, Edinburgh.
School for the Poor, Amsterdam.
Primary School, Berlin.
Dorothean High School, "
Burgher School, "
Higher Burgher School, Potsdam.
Lovell's Lancasterian School, New Haven

Schools of Agriculture, &c., &c.
City Trade School, Berlin.
Commercial School, Leghorn.
Agricultural School at Templemoyle.
Institute of Agriculture, Wurtemburg.
School of Arts, Edinburgh.
Polytechnic Institute, Vienna.
Technical School, Zurich
Institute of the Arts, Berlin.
Mechanic Institutions, London.
" " Manchester
Factory Schools.
Adult Schools. Sunday Schools.

TRIBUTE TO GALLAUDET.—A Discourse in Commemoration of the Life, Character, and Services of the Rev. Thomas H. Gallaudet L L. D., delivered before the citizens of Hartford, January 7th, 1852, with an Appendix. By Henry Barnard, L L. D. Philadelphia: H. Cowperthwait & Co.

The above Discourse was delivered before the citizens of Hartford, and published at their request. The Appendix contains several productions of Mr. Gallaudet, of permanent value, with a History of Institutions for Deaf-mutes, in different countries, and particularly of the American Asylum at Hartford, by the author of the Discourse.

CONTENTS.

PESTALOZZI AND HIS EDUCATIONAL SYSTEM.

PESTALOZZI AND PESTALOZZIANISM:—Memoir, and Educational Principles, Methods, and Influence of John Henry Pestalozzi, and Biographical Sketches of several of his Assistants and Disciples; together with Selections from his Publications. In Two Parts. By HENRY BARNARD, LL.D. New York: F. C. BROWNELL, No. 12, Appleton's Building.

PRICE.—*Part I, in paper covers,* $1 25; *Part II, in paper covers,* $1.25; *Parts I and II, in paper covers,* $2.00; *do., in half calf,* $2.50.

PART I.

PART II.

EDUCATIONAL BIOGRAPHY; or Memoirs of Teachers, Educators, and Promoters and Benefactors of Education, Literature, and Science. By Henry Barnard, LL.D. PART I. *Teachers and Educators.* Vol. I., United States. NEW YORK: F. C. Brownell, 413 Broadway. HARTFORD: F. B. Perkins. *Illustrated Edition:* PRICE, $3.50, in half Turkish Morocco, or English Calf.

CONTENTS OF VOLUME I.

We are glad to see that Dr. Barnard has consented to let his publishers bring together into one volume, the memoirs of eminent American Teachers and Educators which have appeared in the first series of the *American Journal of Education.* Richly bound, and illustrated with over twenty Portraits, from engravings on steel or copper by our best artists, it is the most creditable tribute which has yet been paid in English Literature to the scholastic profession. It forms a splendid and appropriate gift-book to Teachers, and Promoters of Educational Improvement.—*Connecticut Common School Journal, for February,* 1859.

This elegant and useful contribution to educational literature will, we trust, receive a cordial welcome from teachers. Nothing ever issued from the press could be a more appropriate ornament for the teacher's library or center-table.—*Massachusetts Teacher, for February,* 1859.

GERMAN UNIVERSITIES.

THE GERMAN UNIVERSITIES. Being the fourth volume of the *History of Education.* By KARL VON RAUMER. Re-published from the "*American Journal of Education,*" edited by HENRY BARNARD. LL.D. New York: F. C. BROWNELL, No. 346, Broadway. 250 pages. Price $1.50.

CONTENTS.

PAPERS

For The Teacher.

Number Two—1860.

CONTENTS.

OBJECT TEACHING AND ORAL LESSONS ON SOCIAL SCIENCE AND COMMON THINGS, WITH VARIOUS ILLUSTRATIONS OF THE PRINCIPLES AND PRACTICE OF PRIMARY EDUCATION, AS ADOPTED IN THE MODEL AND TRAINING SCHOOLS OF GREAT BRITAIN.

Published and for sale by

F. C. BROWNELL, 25 HOWARD STREET, NEW YORK.

GEORGE SHERWOOD, LAKE STREET, CHICAGO.

PRICE, $1.50 bound in cloth.

PAPERS

For The Teacher.

Number Four.

CONTENTS.

EDUCATIONAL APHORISMS AND SUGGESTIONS, ANCIENT AND MODERN.

Published and for sale by

F. C. BROWNELL, 25 HOWARD STREET, NEW YORK.

GEORGE SHERWOOD, 124 LAKE STREET, CHICAGO.

PRICE, $1.50 bound in cloth.

THE AMERICAN JOURNAL OF EDUCATION.

EDITED BY HENRY BARNARD, LL. D.

FIRST SERIES. FIVE VOLUMES.

THE FIRST SERIES of Barnard's American Journal of Education consists of five volumes, each volume having an average of 800 pages, embellished with at least four portraits from engravings on steel, of eminent teachers, educators, and promoters of education, and with a large number of wood-cuts, illustrative of recent improvements in the structure, furniture, and arrangements of buildings designed for educational uses.

The series, uniformly and neatly bound, with an index to each volume, and a general index to the whole, will be delivered to the order of subscribers, and forwarded by express, or otherwise, as may be directed, at the expense of the subscriber, on the following

TERMS: For the entire series, in seventeen parts or numbers, - - -	$10,50.
" " " in five volumes, bound in paper covers, -	11,25.
" " " " " bound in cloth, - - -	12,50.
" " " " " bound in leather, - -	15,00.

THE FIRST SERIES will be found to contain important contributions to,—

1. A HISTORY OF EDUCATION, ancient and modern.
2. ORGANIZATION, ADMINISTRATION, AND SUPPORT OF PUBLIC INSTRUCTION.
3. ELEMENTARY INSTRUCTION IN THE PRINCIPAL COUNTRIES OF EUROPE.
4. NATIONAL EDUCATION IN THE UNITED STATES; or contributions to the history and improvement of common or public schools, and other institutions, means and agencies of popular education in the several states.
5. SCHOOL ARCHITECTURE: or the principles of construction, ventilation, warming, acoustics, seating, &c., applied to school rooms, lecture halls, and class rooms, with illustrations.
6. NORMAL SCHOOLS, and other institutions, means, and agencies for the professional training and improvement of teachers.
7. SYSTEM OF PUBLIC EDUCATION FOR LARGE CITIES AND VILLAGES; with an account of the schools and other means of popular education and recreation in the principal cities of Europe and in this country.
8. SYSTEM OF POPULAR EDUCATION FOR SPARSEDLY POPULATED DISTRICTS.
9. SCHOOLS OF AGRICULTURE, and other means of advancing agricultural improvement.
10. SCHOOLS OF SCIENCE, applied to the mechanic arts, civil engineering, &c.
11. SCHOOLS OF TRADE, NAVIGATION, COMMERCE, &C.
12. FEMALE EDUCATION; with an account of the best seminaries for females in this country and in Europe.
13. INSTITUTIONS FOR ORPHANS.
14. SCHOOLS OF INDUSTRY; or institutions for truant, idle, or neglected children, before they have been convicted of crime.
15. REFORM SCHOOLS: or institutions for young criminals.
16. HOUSES OF REFUGE, for adult criminals.
17. SECONDARY EDUCATION; including 1. institutions preparatory to college, and 2. institutions preparatory to special schools of agriculture, engineering, trade, navigation, &c.
18. COLLEGES AND UNIVERSITIES.
19. SCHOOLS OF THEOLOGY, LAW, AND MEDICINE.
20. MILITARY AND NAVAL SCHOOLS.
21. SUPPLEMENTARY EDUCATION; including adult schools, evening schools, courses of popular lectures debating classes, mechanic institutes, &c.
22. LIBRARIES; with hints for the purchase, arrangement, catalogueing, drawing and preservation of books, especially in libraries designed for popular use.
23. INSTITUTIONS FOR THE DEAF AND DUMB, BLIND, AND IDIOTS.
24. SOCIETIES FOR THE ENCOURAGEMENT OF SCIENCE, THE ARTS, AND EDUCATION.
25. PUBLIC MUSEUMS AND GALLERIES.
26. PUBLIC GARDENS, and other sources of popular recreation.
27. EDUCATIONAL TRACTS; or a series of short essays on topics of immediate practical importance to teachers and school officers.
28. EDUCATIONAL BIOGRAPHY; or the lives of distinguished educators and teachers.
29. EDUCATIONAL BENEFACTORS; or an account of the founders and benefactors of educational and scientific institutions.
30. SELF-EDUCATION; or hints for self formation, with examples of the pursuit of knowledge under difficulties.
31. HOME EDUCATION; with illustrations drawn from the Family Training of different countries.
32. A CATALOGUE of the best publications on the organization, instruction, and discipline of schools, of every grade, and on the principles of education, in the English, French, and German languages.
33. EDUCATIONAL NOMENCLATURE AND INDEX; or an explanation of words and terms used in describing the systems and institutions of education in different countries, with reference to the books where the subjects are discussed and treated of.

BARNARD'S AMERICAN JOURNAL OF EDUCATION.

THE following circular is addressed in answer to numerous inquiries on one or more of the points briefly treated of.

REGULAR SUBSCRIBERS. The terms to regular subscribers are $4 for the year, or for two volumes, or for four consecutive numbers. To non-subscribers the charge is $1.50 per number, and $3 for a single volume.

SPECIMEN NUMBERS. To persons applying for specimen numbers of *Barnard's American Journal of Education*, with a view of becoming subscribers, a copy of the last number issued will be mailed, on receipt of seventy-five cents, half the price at which single numbers are sold, and twelve cents in stamps for prepayment of postage, at the office of publication.

POSTAGE. The law applicable to postage on this quarterly periodical is as follows: "For each periodical, not exceeding three ounces in weight, to any part of the United States, one cent; for every additional ounce or fraction of an ounce, one cent. If paid quarterly or yearly in advance, at the office where the same is either mailed or delivered, then half the above rates are charged." The weight of each number of this Journal is from thirteen to seventeen ounces; making full postage from eleven to fifteen cents per number, or from forty-four to sixty cents a year; and postage paid in advance, at either end of the route, six to eight cents per number, or from twenty-two to thirty cents a year.

MAILING. The numbers of the Journal—done up in single wrapper of stout post-office paper, and, when addressed beyond New England and New York, tied up with strong twine—are mailed to the post-office address of each subscriber who has paid up his subscription for the year, on or before the day of publication of each number, viz., the 15th of March, June, September, and December. If a number does not reach its destination in due time, the fault is not with this office.

EXCHANGES. The publisher looks for the usual courtesy of a notice of the reception, and a specification at least of the *subjects of the several articles*, from those journals which have solicited an exchange, and an omission of this courtesy is supposed to indicate that no further exchange is desired.

THE FIRST SERIES. A general index (*sixty-four pages, nonpareil, double columns*,) of the topics treated of in the first five volumes of the Journal, will be sent, free of expense, to the address of any person making application for the same.

BOUND VOLUMES. Volumes I. II. III. IV. V. VI. VII. VIII. and succeeding volumes when completed, will be furnished, neatly and uniformly bound in cloth with an Index to each volume, and a General Index to each five volumes, at $3.00 for single volume, and $2.50, for two or more volumes.

MEMOIR OF PESTALOZZI, RAUMER'S GERMAN UNIVERSITIES, AND PAPERS FOR THE TEACHER. Subscribers and purchasers of complete sets of the *American Journal of Education* are advised, that nearly all of the contents of these separate works have been, or will be, embraced as articles in the Journal; and that, unless they wish to have them in a compact and convenient form, they need not purchase them.

FREDERIC B. PERKINS,

Publisher of Barnard's American Journal of Education.

Hartford, Conn., 1860.

Holbrook School Apparatus Company.

OFFICES, { 25 Howard St., New York, ... } F. C. BROWNELL, Sec'y.
{ 122 and 124 Lake St., Chicago, Ill. } GEO. SHERWOOD, Pres.

PRICE LIST, January, 1860.

No.		
No. 1.	Orrery	$10.00
" 2.	Brass Orrery	12.50
" 3.	Best Brass Orrery	15.00
" 4.	Tellurian	....
" 5.	Geared Tellurian	8.00
" 6.	Brass Geared Tellurian	10.00
" 7.	Brass " " nicer	12.50
" 8.	Brass " " best	15.00
" 9.	Celestial Sphere	8.00
" 10.	Celestial Sphere, with sections	
" 11.	Gyroscope, two rings	5 00
" 12.	Gyroscope, three rings	8.00
" 13.	Gyroscope, " " best	10.00
" 14.	Barnard's Expla'tion of Gyroscope	.25
" 14a.	Snell's Explanation of "	.25
" 15.	Pyrometer .... $4.00 and	5.00
" 16.	Terrestrial Globe, (5-inch,)	1.50
" 16a.	" Toy Globe, (3-inch,)	1.00
" 17.	Terrestrial Globe, (8-inch,)	5.50
" 18.	Do., Brass Mounted, in Meridian	8.00
" 18a.	Do., with Horizon and Quadrant	10.00
" 19.	Hemisphere Globe, (3-inch,)	1.00
" 20.	Hemisphere Globe, (5-inch,)	1.50
" 21.	Dissected Cone	1.50
" 22.	Do., with colored sections	2.00
" 23.	Geometrical Forms, large	2.50
" 23a.	Shepherd's Decimal Blocks	2.50
" 23b.	Geometrical Forms	1.00
" 24.	Arithmetical Solids	1.00
" 25.	Geom. Forms and Arith. Solids	1.50
" 25a.	Geometrical Forms and Arithmetical Solids, in wood box	2.00
" 26.	Numeral Frame, 100 balls	.63
" 27.	Numeral Frame, 144 "	.75
" 28.	Cube Root Blocks	.50
" 29.	Double Cube Root Blocks	.75
" 30.	Sixty-Four Inch Cubes, $2.00 to	3.00
" 31.	Magnets .... .25, .50, .75, and	1.00
" 32.	Pointing Rods .... .25 and	.50
" 33.	" " extra long	.75
" 34.	Blackboard Rubbers, No. 3	.50
" "	Do., smaller, No. 2	.40
" "	Do., smaller, No. 1	.30
" 35.	Alphabet Blocks	.75
" 36	Alphabet Blocks, Cubes	1.00
No. 37.	Glass Ink Wells, per doz.	$ .75
" "	Do. with iron covers, per doz.	1.50
" 38.	Glass Ink Wells, in metal case, per doz.	2.50
" 39.	Glass Pump	2.50
" "	Glass Forcing Pump	3.50
" 40.	Glass Syphons ...... .25, .50, and	.75
" 41.	Primary Drawing Slate, No. 1	.25
" "	" " " No. 2	.30
" 41a.	Boston Primary Slate, No. 1	.25
" "	" " " No. 2	.25
" 41b.	Noiseless N. Y. Drawing Slate	.20
" 41c.	Noiseless Boston " "	.26
" 42.	High School Slate, No. 1	.30
" "	" " " No. 2	.35
" 43.	Double " " No. 1	.60
" "	Double " " No. 2	.70
" 44.		
" 45.	Primary Drawing Book	.10
" 46.	Teacher's Letter to Parents, per hundred	2.00
" 47.	Universal School Register, .. .25, .50, .75, and	1.00
" 47a.	Class Register ...... .25, .38, and	.50
" 48.	First Lessons in Astronomy	.20
" 49.	Teacher's Guide to Illustration	.50
" 50.	Letter Table, on Stand	15.00
" 51.	Figure Table, large	4.00
" 52.	Letter Table	2.25
" 53.	" " smaller	1.75
" 54.	" " "	1.50
" 55.	" " "	1.00
" 56.	" " "	.75
" 57.	Figure Table	.75
" 58.	" "	.50
" 59.		
" 60.	Primary School Set	5.00
" "	" " " in wood box	5.50
" 61.	Common School Set	20.00
" 62.	Common School Set	30.00
" 63.	Common School Set	25.00
" 64.	Common School Set	34.00
" 65.	High School Set	45.00
" 66.	High School Set	50.00
" 67.	High School Set	60.00

READ WHAT EDUCATORS SAY.

THE undersigned have found the success of our efforts in behalf of education much retarded by the very general deficiency in schools of proper Furniture, Apparatus, Maps and Charts, and of the various aids and incentives to study.

One of the principal causes of this want has been that teachers and those interested in schools, neither knew what articles were made, suitable for school uses, nor where to procure them.

We are confident that School Officers and Teachers would receive important aid from an establishment which should,

1. Collect specimens of everything that is made or published for schools, whether American or Foreign, and supply all such articles wanted;
2. Make such new articles as the ingenuity and experience of practical teachers prove desirable, and keep samples of every new thing for inspection, thus keeping up with the age in all improvements;
3. Supply information as to building and furnishing school houses;
4. Provide a Catalogue of articles, so that persons from a distance can order; and send out occasional bulletins with advices of new articles.

The Teachers' Home,

Conducted at New York, by F. C. BROWNELL, and at Chicago, by GEORGE SHERWOOD, takes this department of labor, proposing to carry out such a plan; and we cordially welcome it as an educational power, and commend it, and its conductors, to the confidence and general patronage of Teachers and School Officers in the several states, believing that their generous sympathy and co-operation in this enterprise, will promote the true interests of education.

APRIL 20, 1859.

NEWTON BATEMAN,
State Superintendent of Public Instruction of Illinois.

J. W. BULKLEY,
Superintendent of Public Schools of Brooklyn, N. Y.

DAVID N. CAMP,
Superintendent of Common Schools of Connecticut.

LYMAN C. DRAPER,
Superintendent of Public Instruction of Wisconsin.

MARK H. DUNNELL,
Superintendent of Common Schools of Maine.

HENRY C. HICKOK,
Superintendent of Common Schools of Pennsylvania.

JOHN D. MATTHEWS,
Superintendent of Public Instruction of Kentucky.

IRA MAYHEW,
Eight years Superintendent of Education in Michigan.

JOHN D. PHILBRICK,
Superintendent of Public Schools of Boston.

WM. H. WELLS,
Superintendent of Public Schools of Chicago, Illinois.

J. S. ADAMS,
Secretary of Vermont Board of Education.

J. M. GREGORY,
Superintendent of Public Instruction of Michigan.

THOMAS H. BURROWES,
Superintendent of Schools in Pennsylvania.

HENRY BARNARD,
Chancellor of the University of Wisconsin.

GEO. N. BIGELOW,
Principal of Framingham State Normal School, Mass.

D. H. COCHRAN,
Principal of N. Y. State Normal School.

MARSHALL CONANT,
Principal of State Normal School, Bridgewater, Mass.

ALPHEUS CROSBY,
Principal of State Normal School, Salem, Mass.

RICHARD EDWARDS,
Principal of St. Louis Normal School, Missouri.

C. E. HOVEY,
Principal of Illinois State Normal School.

WM F. PHELPS,
Principal of New Jersey State Normal School.

ANSON SMYTH,
State School Commissioner of Ohio.

J. P. WICKERSHAM,
Principal of Lancaster Co. Normal School, Penn.

C. H. WILEY,
Superintendent of Common Schools, N. Carolina.

SAMUEL L. RUGG,
Superintendent of Public Instruction of Indiana.

D. FRANKLIN WELLS,
Principal of Normal Dept., Iowa State University.

A WELL FURNISHED SCHOOL-ROOM.

It may be serviceable to Committees and teachers to find a list of the articles required to furnish a school-room *well*. Accordingly such a list is given, classified for different grades of schools, and with prices for each article.

REQUISITES FOR A PRIMARY SCHOOL.

Pupils from 4 to 9 years of age.

1. Primary Chairs, with an iron basket to hold the books, . . $1 25
2. Primary Double Desk and Chairs for all but the youngest, for two pupils, ... $4 50 to 5 25
3. Ventilating Stove, admitting fresh air, costs, . 18 00 or 25 00
4. Blackboard. May be made on the wall, and covered with Holbrook's Liquid Slate which costs, per quart, ... 1 50
5. Blackboard Crayons, per gross, ... 38 to 50
6. Blackboard Rubbers, each, ... 30, 40 to 50
7. Pointers, each, ... 25 to 50
8. Letter Cards of Capitals and small letters to set up in a grooved stick, forming words, per box, ... 2 00
9. Alphabet Tables, having movable letters, . . 1 50 to 2 25
10. Primary School Tablets, or charts for punctuation, spelling, reading, geometrical drawing, &c., set of 10, ... 5 00
11. Numeral Frame, small size, to hold in the hand, at . . 75
    Or a large sized one mounted on stand, with the upper frame grooved for spelling cards, ... 10 00
12. Primary Drawing Slate, with copies on the frame—one for each pupil, ... 25
13. Holbrook's Primary Drawing Book, to accompany the slate, 10
14. Geographical Cards, showing a *map* and a *picture* of the same divisions of land and water, set of six, ... 3 00
15. Primary School Set of Holbrook's Apparatus, . . { 5 00
    Containing . . . . . packed in wood box, { 5 50
    a. Terrestrial Globe, 5 inch, ... 1 50
    b. Hemisphere Globe, 3 inch, ... 1 00
    c. Box of Geometrical Solids, ... 1 50
    d. Numeral Frame, ... 63
    e. Magnet, ... 25
    f. Guide to Illustration, to explain their uses, ... 38
    Separate articles at above prices, Total, . . 5 25
16. A Map of the State, colored in Towns and Counties,
17. School Mottoes for moral culture, book of 20, ... 50
    Two Mottoes on a card, cost, ... 20
18. A set of Weights and Measures, ... 2 00 or 3 00
19. A Thermometer, ... 67 to 1 00
20. A Clock, ... 1 50 2 50 or 3 00

All these articles may be procured at the Teachers' Home.

Address F. C. Brownell, New York, or George Sherwood, Chicago, Ill.

REQUISITES FOR A GRAMMAR SCHOOL.

Pupils from 9 to 14 years of age.

1. SEATS AND DESKS; for two pupils, cheap style. . . .		$3 75
Best style, " "	6 00 to	6 50
2. VENTILATING STOVE, Thermometer Clock, Blackboard, Crayons, Rubbers, Pointers and Mottoes, as described for the Primary School.		
3. HOLBROOK'S COMMON SCHOOL APPARATUS, a set packed for		33 00
Comprising,		
a. Numeral Frame, . . , ...	75	
b. Geometrical Solids, ...	1 50	
c. Magnet, ...	25	
d. Hemisphere Globe, 5 inch, ...	1 50	
e. Terrestrial Globe, 8 inch, . . (5 50, 8 00 or	10 00	
f. Tellurian or Seasons Machine, ...	8 00	
g. Orrery, ...	10 00	
h. Cube Root Blocks, ...	50	
i. Guide to Illustration, explaining their uses, . .	50	
Articles furnished separately, at above prices. Total,	33 00	
4. OUTLINE MAPS, Mitchell's set of ten maps, price, . .		12 00
Fowle's, " of eight maps, " . .		7 00
Pelton's, " of six " " . .		25 00
Mitchell's set in price, size, system and correctness, are better adapted to the wants and means of most schools than any other set published.		
5. MARINERS' COMPASS, ...	25 to	75
6. ELOCUTIONARY CHART, ...	2 50 or	3 00
7. CHART OF AMERICAN HISTORY, ...	2 50 or	6 00
8. CHIROGRAPHIC CHART, ...	1 00 or	4 00
9. GRAMMATICAL CHART, ...		2 50
10. PHYSIOLOGICAL CHARTS, a set of 8 or 10, . . .	6 00 or	10 00
11. GEOLOGICAL SPECIMENS or Cabinet, ...	3 00 or	5 00
12. A SLATE GLOBE, 9 inch, or 12 inch, ...	6 50 or	12 00
13. A GLASS SYPHON, ...	25 to	75
14. A GLASS PUMP, ...		2 50
15. A MICROSCOPE, ...	2 50 or	4 00
16. A MAGIC LANTERN, small, ...	3 50 or	5 00
17. MAP OF THE WORLD, on Mercator's Projection, . .	3 00 or	10 00
18. MUSICAL SCALE INDICATOR, ...		8 00
A Blackboard should be made on the wall entirely around the room. HOLBROOK'S LIQUID SLATE applied to a common hard finished wall, gives the best and cheapest known surface for Blackboard use. Price per quart, -		1 50

All these articles can be procured at the Teachers' Home, by addressing F. C. Brownell, New York, or George Sherwood, Chicago, Ill.

REQUISITES FOR A HIGH SCHOOL.

Pupils from 14 to 20 years of age.

To enumerate *all* the articles desirable for schools of this grade, would require a catalogue of itself. A few of the more important and necessary ones will be given, which should be found in every High School or Academy.

1.	SEATS AND DESKS, single, ...	$4 50 or 6 50
	" " double, for two pupils, . .	6 50 or 8 50
2.	VENTILATING STOVE, or other healthy mode of heating, Thermometer, Clock, Blackboard, Crayons, Rubbers, Pointers, Mottoes, &c., which are needed in all schools, as described for a Primary School.	
	The BLACKBOARD should be made on the wall and entirely round the room. LIQUID SLATE applied to a hard finished wall makes the best blackboard surface known. Price per quart, ...	1 50
3.	AN ORRERY, representing the Solar System, . .	10 00 to 15 00
4.	A TELLURIAN, or Season Machine, . . .	8 00 to 15 00
5.	HOLBROOK'S CELESTIAL SPHERE, ...	8 00
6.	A PAIR OF 12 IN. GLOBES, ...	24 00 or 28 00
7.	WHITALL'S ASTRONOMICAL PLANISPHERE, for each pupil in Astromony, mailed for	2 00 or 2 50
8.	A Slate Globe, 12 to 18 inches, ...	12 00 to 30 00
9.	ASTRONOMICAL CHARTS, set of 16, ...	15 00 to 20 00
10.	ELOCUTIONARY CHART, ...	2 50 or 3 00
11.	HALL'S GEOLOGICAL CHART, the largest, best and only good one in America, ...	9 00
12.	PHYSICAL MAPS of the world, ...	10 00
13.	" " of North America, ...	9 00
14.	" " of Geographical Elements, ...	9 00
	Also Physical Maps of South America, Europe and Africa as wanted, each, ...	9 00
15.	REDFIELD'S CHART of the Animal Kingdom, or Zoology, .	10 00
	The same uncolored, ...	7 00
16.	A GLASS PUMP, ...	2 50 or 3 50
17.	A GLASS SYPHON, ...	50 or 75
18.	A MICROSCOPE, ...	10 00 to 25 00
19.	A MAGIC LANTERN and sliders, ...	25 00 to 50 00
20.	A TELESCOPE, ...	20 00 to 40 00
21.	AN AIR PUMP, and accompaniments, ...	25 00 to 100 00
22.	AN ELECTRICAL MACHINE, and accompaniments, .	25 00 to 100 00
23.	A GYROSCOPE, ...	8 00 to 10 00
24.	APPARATUS, Illustrating Mechanics, . . .	20 00 to 50 00
25.	A MAP STAND, ...	10 00
26.	A GEOLOGICAL CABINET, ...	3 00 to 20 00

Pupils will collect a cabinet of Minerals, Shells, Curiosities, &c., if a case is provided.

27. A good LIBRARY OF REFERENCE, as well as a general Library should be in every Grammar or High School.

School Libraries are furnished at the Teachers' Home, at a liberal discount. Catalogues of Books for School Libraries, sent on application to F. C. Brownell, New York, or George Sherwood, Chicago, Ill.

HOLBROOK'S APPARATUS ARRANGED IN SETS.

No. 60. PRIMARY SCHOOL SET, containing, PRICE

Globe, No. 16, ...	$1.50	Hemisphere Globe, No. 19, .	$1.00
Geometrical Solids, No. 25, .	1.50	Numeral Frame, No. 27, . .	.63
Magnet, No. 31, ...	.25	Guide, No. 49, ...	.38

Packed in paper box for $5.00 ; in wood box, ... $5 50

No. 61. COMMON SCHOOL SET, containing,

Tellurian, No. 5, ...	$8.00	Globe, No. 18, ...	$8.00
Geometrical Solids, No. 25, .	1.50	Hemisphere Globe, No. 19, .	1.00
Cube Root, No. 28, . . .	.50	Numeral Frame, No. 27, . .	.63
Guide, No. 49, ...	.38	Magnet, No. 31, ...	.25

Packed in wood box with lock, for 20 00

No. 62. Same as No. 61, with Orrery, No. 1, added, . . . 30 00

63. COMMON SCHOOL SET, containing,

Orrery, No. 1, ...	$10.00	Tellurian, No. 5, ...	$8.00
Globe, No. 16, ...	1.50	Hemisphere Globe, No. 20, .	1.50
Geometrical Solids, No. 25a, .	2.00	Numeral Frame, No. 26, . .	.75
Cube Root, No. 28, . . .	.50	Magnet, No. 31, ...	.50
Guide, No. 49, ...	.50		
		Total, ...	25.25

Packed in wood box, with lock for 25 00

No. 64. Same as No. 63, with Globe, No. 18a, in place of No. 16, 34 00

65. HIGH SCHOOL SET, comprising,

Orrery, No. 2, ...	$12.50	Tellurian, No. 6, ...	$10.00
Celestial Sphere, No. 9, . .	8.00	Globe, No. 18a, ...	10.00
Geometrical Solids, No. 25, .	1.50	Hemisphere Globe, No. 20, .	1.50
Cube Root, No. 28, ...	.50	Magnet, No. 31, ...	.50
Guide, No. 49, ...	.50		
		Total, ...	45.00

Packed in wood box, for safe transportation, ... 45 00

No. 66. Same as No. 65, with Gyroscope, No. 11, added, . 50 00

67. HIGH SCHOOL SET, comprising,

Orrery, No. 2, ...	$12.50	Tellurian, No. 7, ...	$12.50
Celestial Sphere, No. 9, . .	8.00	Globe No. 18a, ...	10.00
Geometrical Forms, No. 23, .	2.50	Hemisphere Globe, No. 20, .	1.50
Dissected Cone, No. 21, . .	1.50	Sixty-four-inch Cubes, No. 30,	2.00
Gyroscope, No. 12, . . .	8.00	Magnet, No. 31, ...	1.00
Guide to Illustration No. 49, .	.50		
		Total, ...	$60.00

Packed in wood boxes, for safe transportation, ... 60 00

Any article may be added to or omitted from these Sets, by making the proper difference in price.

www.ingramcontent.com/pod-product-compliance
Lightning Source LLC
LaVergne TN
LVHW020930110826
845150LV00004B/819